050

# Theoretical Anthropology

# DAVID BIDNEY

# *Theoretical Anthropology*

**COLUMBIA UNIVERSITY PRESS**

*New York, 1953*

*The research for this volume and its publication were made possible by funds granted by the Wenner-Gren Foundation for Anthropological Research, Inc. The Foundation is not, however, the author or publisher of this publication; it is not to be understoood as approving, by virtue of its grant, any of the statements made or views expressed therein.*

# *Preface*

THIS WORK is the product of a decade of research in the interdisciplinary field of cultural anthropology and social philosophy. Originally begun in 1942 as a research project sponsored by the Viking Fund of New York City (now known as the Wenner-Gren Foundation for Anthropological Research), the study was continued and prepared for publication at Indiana University. Some of the chapters in this book were originally published elsewhere, but the papers on which they are based have for the most part been thoroughly revised and integrated with the rest of the book.

The title of this volume, "Theoretical Anthropology," was carefully chosen to indicate the scope of this study. First, it is intended as a contribution toward a historical, critical, and constructive study of the theoretical, metaanthropological postulates and assumptions underlying the development of modern cultural anthropology. Secondly, the title was selected deliberately to draw attention to the historical fact that anthropology, like the other sciences, has its body of theory, as well as its capital of empirically established facts, and that theoretical anthropology merits the serious consideration of social scientists as a distinct branch of anthropology.

Hitherto there has been a tendency for anthropologists, especially in the United States, to lay major emphasis upon field work and the gathering of ethnographic data, leaving it up to the ethnographer to introduce concepts and hypotheses pragmatically as the data seemed to require. Theory was not valued for its own sake, but rather as a means to practical research. In justification, the perpetual youth of anthropology was alleged as the reason for stressing fact-gathering to the exclusion of theoretical, or "philosophical," speculation. In his presidential address to the Anthropological Section of the British Association for the Advancement of Science in 1911, W. H. R. Rivers stated: "About America it is less easy to speak, because it is unusual in that country to deal to any great extent with general theoretical problems. The anthropologists of America are so fully engaged in the attempt to record what is left of the ancient cultures of their own country that they devote little attention to those general questions to which we, with no ancient culture at our doors, devote so much attention." Rivers' comment held true until comparatively recent times. Within the past twenty-five years, however, North American anthropologists have shown an ever-increasing concern about theoretical problems of anthropology and their bearing upon the humanities and other social sciences.

In the forefront of this intellectual approach has been A. L. Kroeber, to whom I have the privilege of dedicating this work. He, more than any other contemporary anthropologist, represents a broad humane perspective, which comprehends the culture history and philosophy of the humanities, on the one hand, and the empirical, statistical research of the field-ethnographer and area specialist, on the other. I owe to Kroeber especially a debt of gratitude for his moral support and sympathetic understanding, notwithstanding my challenging criticism of his own earlier position. As the pages of this book indicate, his writings have provided me with the stimulus and perspective which determined in large measure the orientation of my thought.

To Cornelius Osgood I am indebted for having stimulated my interest in problems of ethnological theory while I was instructor in the philosophy of science in the Graduate School of Yale University during 1940–42.

I wish to express my thanks and appreciation to the Graduate School of Indiana University, and to my colleagues in the Department of Anthropology and the Department of Philosophy, C. F. Voegelin and N. P. Stallknecht, for their generous cooperation in allowing me time to complete the arduous task of preparing the manuscript for publication. I am also indebted to the Graduate School of Indiana University, for special research facilities and for a grant to aid in the typing of parts of the manuscript and the preparation of the bibliography.

The chapter on "The Concept of Myth" is based in part upon research conducted in 1950 under the auspices of a Guggenheim Fellowship in anthropology.

Finally, I should like to acknowledge with gratitude my obligation to the Founder and Board of Trustees of the Wenner-Gren Foundation for Anthropological Research, who have sponsored and supported my research over a period of years and have made the publication of this volume possible. In addition, I have had the good fortune to be closely associated with Dr. Paul Fejos, the Director of Research of the Wenner-Gren Foundation, whose vision and faith have kept this research project alive. At a critical time, when many educators and anthropologists could see little value in basic theoretical and interdisciplinary research, he was as a rock of strength and held firm against all adverse criticism. For his faith and courageous support I am profoundly grateful.

It has been a pleasure to be associated with Mr. Henry H. Wiggins and Miss Ida M. Lynn, of the Columbia University Press. In her capacity of Assistant Editor, Miss Lynn has been most helpful in making and suggesting editorial revisions.

DAVID BIDNEY

*Bloomington, Indiana*
*February, 1953*

# Permissions and Acknowledgments

I wish to express my indebtedness and obligation to the authors and publishers of the works cited in this volume. All works cited are listed in the bibliography at the end of the text. I am especially indebted to the following authors and publishers for written permission to utilize previously published material:

The *American Anthropologist* for permission to reprint some of my articles.

Appleton-Century-Crofts, Inc., for permission to quote from *Social Psychology*, by Kimball Young, copyright 1947.

The Conference on Science, Philosophy and Religion in Their Relation to the Democratic Way of Life, Inc., New York, for permission to reprint papers originally prepared as contributions to symposia.

Farrar, Straus & Young, Inc., for permission to quote from *The Science of Culture*, copyright 1949, by Leslie A. White.

Harcourt, Brace and Company, Inc., for permission to quote from *Anthropology*, by A. L. Kroeber, copyright 1923, 1948, and from *Language*, by Edward Sapir, copyright 1921.

Alfred A. Knopf, Inc., for generously allowing quotation without specific permission from *Man and His Works*, by Melville J. Herskovits, copyright 1947, 1948.

The Macmillan Company of New York for permission to quote from *Race, Language, and Culture*, by Franz Boaz, copyright 1940, and also from *The Web of Government*, by R. M. MacIver, copyright 1947.

Rinehart & Company, Inc., for permission to quote from *The History of Ethnological Theory*, by Robert H. Lowie, copyright 1937.

Charles Scribner's Sons for permission to quote from *Aristotle Selections*, edited by W. D. Ross, copyright 1927.

Peter Smith, publishers, for permission to quote from *Culture and*

*Ethnology,* by Robert H. Lowie, reprinted 1929 by permission of Horace Liveright.

Yale University Press for permission to republish my chapter from *Ideological Differences and World Order,* edited by F. S. C. Northrop, copyright 1949.

# Contents

# Contents

# Theoretical Anthropology

# 1

# *The Problem of Man and the Human World*

MAN has always been a problem to himself. Throughout the ages he has sought to understand himself and to lead a harmonious existence in a society of men. The history of human civilization may, from one point of view, be understood as the history of man's ideas of himself and of the practical consequences to which these ideas have led him.

## 1. THE PSYCHOLOGICAL CONDITIONS OF THE PROBLEM OF MAN

Psychologically, man is a problem to himself because he alone has the ability to reflect upon himself and his experiences. Man is a self-reflecting animal in that he alone has the ability to objectify himself, to stand apart from himself, as it were, and to consider the kind of being he is and what it is that he wants to do and to become. Other animals may be conscious of their affects and the objects they perceive; man alone is capable of reflection, of self-consciousness, of thinking of himself as an object.

Man is also a rational animal in the sense that he can conceive concepts or meanings having universal significance. It is this ability to formulate concepts or symbols which renders him a semantic animal and enables him to engage in logical or rational processes of thought. While sharing with the rest of the animal kingdom the ability to perceive signs which have an immediate, pragmatic value with reference to a given situation, only man has the ability to conceive universal symbols or meanings and thereby to create a language by which to communicate the cumulative results of his experience and reflection. It is this symbolic function which has enabled man to create language and culture and has opened up for him a "new dimension of reality" not available to the rest of the animal kingdom. According to Sapir's definition, "language is a purely human and non-instinctive method of communicating ideas, emotions, and desires by means of a system of voluntarily produced symbols." [1]

This view of the significance of symbolic language implies that there is an irreducible distinction in kind between the mental functions of man, on the one hand, and that of the animal kingdom, on the other. It presupposes, as Cassirer has suggested, a theory of evolution by mutation or emergence of new kinds and species, which may be contrasted with the Darwinian theory of gradual evolution, according to which there is only a difference of degree between man and the rest of the animal world. There is, in short, an irreducible gulf between the actual or potential human power of conceiving and symbolizing and the mental functions of man's nearest animal relatives. This explains why all attempts to reconstruct the origin of language have proved so futile and barren and why linguists have reached the conclusion "that the data with which they are concerned yield little or no evidence about the origin of human speech." [2] From a purely functional perspective, however, we may assume that human language originated from man's desire to communicate his experiences and thoughts to other human beings and that human speech is both a cause and an effect of social communication. Being a cunning animal, man used his historically acquired power of speech to deceive as well as to inform others, but it seems scarcely reasonable to assume, as Sturtevant does,[3] that "language must have been invented for the purpose of lying."

Man's uniqueness is also manifested by the fact that he is an imaginative animal, having the ability to imagine supersensuous entities suggested to him by his sense experience. Other animals may imagine previous sense experience, as in dreams, but the human imagination alone creates a new realm of possibility and make-believe. Thus, man lives not only in the common-sense world of experience but also in the peculiarly human world of his own fertile, creative imagination. For primitive man this imaginary, supersensuous world is a magic world of perpetual miracles, where anything can happen and practically nothing is impossible. This primitive imagination is the source of poetry, myth, religion, and art. As human thought matures and imagination is guided by rational reflection, the irrational extrapolations of the imagination are curbed and the realm of the possible is brought into

[1] Sapir, *Language*, p. 7.
[2] Sturtevant, *An Introduction to Linguistic Science*, p. 40.
[3] *Ibid.*, p. 48.

closer contact with the sphere of the practical and the actual. The rational imagination then becomes the source of scientific and cultural invention, enabling man to envisage possibilities of achievement which formerly could be entertained only as delusions of wishful thinking. But even rational thought never wholly subjugates the irrational imagination, which through artistic creativity and mythological rationalization affords an avenue of escape from the gross and painful realities of our daily experience into the realm of ideal possibilities and comforting delusions.

As a rational animal, man is motivated by the quest for intelligibility, for meaning in his life and the world in which he exists. Because of his capacity for reflection and symbolic conceptualization man also seeks to understand the significance of his conduct, as well as his origin and destiny. Even primitive man has his myths, in which he gives expression to his creative imagination by speculating upon the origin of his society and culture and attempts to provide some answer to the great enigmas of birth and death. These reflections constitute a primitive ethnology, and hence it may be said that the study of man is among the oldest of human enterprises. Man is conscious of himself as a historical creature having a beginning and an end and cannot refrain from speculating upon his origin and destiny. Even if his conduct and institutions are not always in accord with the dictates of reason, he nevertheless seeks to cover up his irrationality by finding a plausible reason for doing what he desires to do or finds himself doing. Rationalization is thus the tribute which emotion pays to reason in order to conceal the latter's deficiencies. Myth, religion, art, philosophy, and science are the historic expressions of man's quest for an intelligible world, for a world of meaning and value.

## 2. THE FACTUAL AND THE NORMATIVE PROBLEMS OF MAN

In reflecting upon himself man has been confronted with two basic problems: First, What is man? Secondly, What ought he to be or become?

The first problem is factual and is primarily one of self-knowledge. Has man a universal nature; is he endowed from birth with certain potentialities and tendencies to act which prescribe his range of activity and define the pattern of his development regardless of particular historical and cultural conditions? According to traditional psychology the answer was in the affirmative. In modern psychology, however, the concept of human nature has tended to disappear, owing to the reaction against the theory of instincts and the emphasis of behavioristic psychologists upon the factor of conditioning. Besides, preoccupation with the problem of human nature has been traditionally the concern of the philosophers, and modern scientific psychology would deal only with empirically verifiable data.

The reaction against the concept of human nature has been strengthened also by the tendency of sociologists and anthropologists to regard human nature as a function of society or of culture, as a historical product whose actual determinate character depends upon the society or the culture of which it is a product or effect. The historical materialism of Karl Marx represents but one extreme version of this general tendency of contemporary social science. In modern anthropology, for example, cultural determinism has been the most characteristic thesis, and anthropologists have been wont to stress the primary role of culture in conditioning man as a member of society and to minimize the underlying factors of man's precultural or metacultural nature. Universal human nature, it has been argued, has no explanatory value in helping us to understand the diversity of human cultures; only historical cultural experience can explain culture.

As against this majority trend, the Freudian psychoanalysts have been the stanch advocates of a concept of human nature. Similarly, clinical psychologists, such as Arnold Gesell, have stressed the concept of growth and maturation with reference to the universal phases of child development.

Of particular interest in this connection is the work of Géza Róheim. In his latest study [4] he has taken up the problem of a universal human nature and has sought to establish the validity of this concept by reference to comparative psychoanalytic studies of various primitive cultures. While Róheim considers himself essentially a Freudian, he has, nevertheless, modified Freud's original thesis to the extent of denying the validity of the primal horde theory as presupposing the Lamarckian theory of the inheritance of acquired characteristics and Haeckel's law of ontogenesis as a recapitulation of phylogenesis. Instead of the primal horde theory and the assumption of an innate, unconscious racial memory, Róheim postulates that the unity of mankind is based upon certain universal biological facts, namely, the prolonged infancy

---

[4] Róheim, *Psychoanalysis and Anthropology: Culture, Personality and the Unconscious.*

of man and the generally juvenile character of *homo sapiens* as compared with other animals.[5] Compared to the growth rate of our body,
he points out, our sexuality is relatively premature and hence defense
mechanisms are evolved to protect the ego against premature libido.
As against the implicit Platonism of Freud and Jung, presupposed in
the notion of the innateness of the content of the unconscious and the
actual universality of its symbolism, Róheim, avowedly following
Bastian, postulates "a potentially universal symbolism." Thus, as against
the uncritical notion that psychological phenomena have to be actually
universal, he argues that a symbol may be potentially universal in the
sense that it may be verbalized by some in a universal biologically
conditioned situation, and may be subsequently accepted by others
as a valid medium for expressing what was in their own unconscious.[6]
Thus, a snake as a symbol of the penis, is an example of a potentially
universal symbol which is articulated by some individuals in a wide
variety of cultures and is then accepted by others, who in turn utilize
this symbol in their dreams as a means of expressing their psychological
conflicts. What is universal, for Róheim, is the human situation which
leads the individual to introject the conflict between his juvenile
wishes for the love and protection of his mother and the requirements
of his mature self, his superego, which prohibits his juvenile incestuous
desires. Thus, the Oedipus complex is not an inherited latent content
of the unconscious, but a certain disposition to react emotionally to
a universal human experience. Under the influence of Gesell, Róheim
is inclined to look upon the Oedipus complex as a stage in the development of the individual closely related to other forms of magical or
prelogical thinking. Human nature may be said to condition certain
tendencies to formulate potentially universal symbols and to become
involved in emotional conflict under the stress of family relations. The
cultural symbols and institutions which are so conditioned by human
nature may in turn affect the personality of the individual, but it must
not be forgotten that behind culture lies the human nature which originated the process. The human unconscious, notwithstanding cultural
diversity and cultural conditioning, involves mechanisms of reaction
and symbols of expression which are potentially universal and hence
transcultural.

According to Róheim, there are certain patterns of behavior as expressed through the symbolism of the unconscious which are potentially

[5] *Ibid.*, p. 489.                          [6] *Ibid.*, pp. 22, 443.

universal and hence independent of particular cultural contexts. The unconscious is said to be ontogenetically acquired in the lifetime of the individual; it is not inherited phylogenetically as a racially acquired characteristic. Thus, psychoanalysis and cultural anthropology are not considered to be in conflict, since there is no logical necessity for interpreting the Oedipus complex narrowly as referring to aggression toward the biological father; what is significant in the Oedipus complex is the emotional conflict brought about by the juvenile characteristics of human nature. It is the inherent conflict within human nature itself between the id, the superego, and the ego-ideal which is universal, notwithstanding the diverse forms of cultural expression in which this latent conflict appears.

Theoretically, it is essential to distinguish between the empirical, psychobiological postulates of psychoanalysis as revised by Róheim and his particular interpretation of the concept of culture. It is one thing to draw attention to the psychobiological conditions of the cultural process; it is quite another matter to reduce culture to psychology. He states explicitly: "Culture is but the extension of delayed infancy in which the memory images or symbols of past generations are united with parent and child. Therefore, when we talk of phenomena explained in terms of culture what we are really talking about is psychology. . . . Psychoanalytic thinking is *reductionist* but not *monistic*." [7]

Modern cultural anthropologists are unanimous in their insistence upon the relative autonomy of cultural facts and in their opposition to the reduction of culture to psychology. Some culturologists have even gone to the extreme of regarding culture as "superpsychic," but all have agreed that culture is a historical process which does involve something more than psychological phenomena. Róheim, however, still tends to confuse cultural and psychological phenomena by reducing all cultural phenomena to various modes of symbolizing latent psychological processes.

Culture may be said to determine the mode of man's social existence, while nature prescribes the ontological conditions and limitations of his power of existence. The scientist concerned with the study of nature therefore views man as an intrinsic part of the order of nature subject to its universal laws. But the humanist points out that the scientific perspective, with its quest for determining factors beyond human con-

[7] Róheim, *Psychoanalysis and Anthropology: Culture, Personality and the Unconscious*, pp. 439, 450.

trol, is not sufficient, since man is not only a part of the order of nature but also a being who, through his self-reflective intellect and creative imagination, is able to transcend the cosmic order of nature by setting up for himself norms of conduct which do not apply to the rest of nature. How this is possible has never been explained, and in this sense man continues to be his own greatest mystery. Man's dilemma lies in the fact that he is trying to do the apparently impossible, namely, to be a part of nature and yet to be in a measure independent of it, to be an active participant in the drama of nature and yet a spectator at the same time.

While there is still need for further clarification as regards the biologically inherited nature of man and the universal potentialities which underlie all human efforts, contemporary anthropologists agree that culture is an essential factor in determining the final form in which human nature expresses itself. Man has a secondary or acquired "nature"—his personality—which he acquires through life in a given community. This cultural character or personality presupposes the primary or given nature of man as its necessary condition. Thus, man's nature is to be viewed *sub specie aeternitatis* as a part of the order of nature and *sub specie temporis* as a historical product of cultural experience. The two approaches are complementary, and both are essential for a proper understanding of man in society.

### 3. THE PROBLEM OF HUMAN FREEDOM

The dual nature of man, his determinate, psychobiological structure and functions, on the one hand, and his indeterminate, historically acquired cultural personality, on the other, presupposes a certain measure of human freedom, or self-determination. Man is a cultural problem to himself because he is capable of choosing between alternatives and to envisage new forms of expression which he may realize. Any given culture or mode of life thus represents an original choice on the part of its adherents taken collectively, since other "designs for living" are equally compatible with human nature. In what follows I propose to distinguish three levels or types of freedom, namely, psychobiological, cultural, and moral, or normative, freedom.

Man's natural freedom is, as Hobbes, Spinoza, Locke, and Rousseau understood, identical with his psychobiological power of action. By nature man is free insofar as he can and does act so as to satisfy his basic needs and desires. In this sense, as Rousseau proclaimed, man is born free. By nature, therefore, man may be said to be potentially free to do all the things which he has the innate power to do in relation to his geographical and social environment. Man's natural, biological freedom is thus relatively absolute or absolute in its kind, inasmuch as it is limited only by human potentialities in relation to the geographical and biological environment. From this it follows that man's natural, potential freedom varies with the conditions of his environment, for example, his freedom in the tropics or in the desert is not identical with his freedom at the polar regions or in temperate zones. Furthermore, individuals tend to differ in their biological freedom in accordance with their psychophysical powers, the strong and healthy man being freer to act than is the weak or sick man.

It should be noted in this connection that man's biological freedom is historically acquired both phylogenetically and ontogenetically. Prehistoric man probably lacked some of the psychobiological powers which historical man acquired in the process of evolution. Similarly, from an ontogenetic point of view each individual is subject to growth and development in time and passes through various stages in the course of his life span. Thus, the infant is not as free to act as is the mature adult, and the aged man is excelled by the man in his prime.

Furthermore, each individual human being develops his powers of action through sociocultural conditioning, and to this extent his natural freedom is culturally mediated. Thus, the individual learns to walk and talk as a member of society, but would probably not do so if raised in a feral society. Since various societies condition their members in diverse ways, it follows that members of diverse cultures will differ also in their actual, effective psychobiological powers; for example, an individual raised in a forest culture will develop muscular abilities which the urban dweller will lack. It is because man's biological freedom is also culturally and historically conditioned that man is ontogenetically the most adaptable and freest of animals, since the pattern of his activities is not limited to the same extent by his innate endowment as is the case with the rest of the animal kingdom.

As Malinowski, in particular, has pointed out, culture enlarges the scope of human freedom through the invention of artifacts which enable man to increase the range of his activities as well as his efficiency and to control the forces of nature by adapting them to the satisfaction of human needs and desires. Thus, through art, man is now able to do much which he could scarcely imagine himself doing in previous ages; for example, the airplane has made it possible for him to fly, and radio and television have enabled him to communicate at a speed and distance hitherto beyond his wildest fantasies. Through the development of inventions and the division of labor, society has made it possible for the individual to achieve a degree of freedom from toil and freedom for aesthetic activities which the unaided individual could not possibly achieve by himself. Thus, a circular process is set up in which man's psychobiological freedom promotes cultural achievement, and culture in turn promotes the growth of human freedom.

Culture, however, not only enlarges the scope of human biological freedom but limits it as well. Every culture is a prescriptive system which prescribes the sphere and mode in which instinctive and acquired human potentialities are to be exercised. All cultural freedom is bought at the price of cultural authority and restraint. Cultural freedom is essentially a restricted freedom imposed by a given society upon its members in the interests of social survival and well-being. Every society prescribes limits to the individual's freedom and regulates his conduct through established institutions, for example, the universality of marriage regulations. Every individual in a state of culture thus acquires a limited number of rights and liberties as well as duties or obligations toward his fellowmen. Societies differ, however, in the range of restrictions imposed upon the individual and in the degree of autonomy which is permitted. In all cultures, whether primitive or civilized, there is necessarily some degree of tension between the spheres of natural and cultural liberty, since every culture system tends to prohibit some forms of activity which the average individual would fain gratify at one time or another. This constitutes, as Freud has observed, the inescapable burden of civilization and provides a perennial source of aggression and conflict within society.

Finally, there is normative or ideal moral freedom which may be defined as action in accordance with a rational ideal of the good for man in society. Moral, or normative, freedom presupposes some knowledge of the nature of man and of the kind of conduct which conforms to the ideal requirements of his nature. Man is said to be free only when his actions conform to the categorical imperatives of this rational ideal which prescribes what man ought to do and the kind of existence he should prefer. Normative freedom is far narrower than natural or biological freedom, since the former involves the exercise of human power with reference to a determinate ideal and to the consequences of

one's actions for one's self as well as for others. The moral ideal itself
is something conceived by reason, and though suggested by the data
of experience and culture it is not derived entirely from them. It is
an ideal of individual perfection and of social justice which only cultural man can conceive, and yet it transcends any given actual form of
culture. The moral ideal may be described as postcultural, or metacultural, since it serves as a norm for the regulation and transformation of culture and does not derive its authority or validity from any
given historical culture. It was the intellectual intuition of such a rational, moral ideal which led philosophers to construct utopias and to
postulate a "law of nature" by which to evaluate social and cultural
conventions and the positive laws of given states. The "law of nature,"
it is interesting to note, was conceived by Aristotle as a moral postulate
for the evaluation of human conduct in the context of the political state,
and it only later acquired the modern scientific connotation of some
positive uniformity in the sequence of natural phenomena.

In comparison with precultural psychobiological freedom and cultural freedom, ideal or normative freedom is postcultural, or metacultural, and serves as a norm for evaluating the cultural process itself.
In the phenomenon of the human conscience we have evidence of the
individual's ability to evaluate critically given historical customs and
institutions and to construct new forms of cultural expression more in
conformity with the practical ideals of reason. That is why social philosophers concerned with the problem of human freedom and cultural
progress have acknowledged the desirability of permitting some scope
for the exercise of freedom of conscience even when the latter involves
deviation from the accepted social norms. All freedom of thought is in
the last analysis justified by the fact that only by the exercise of such
freedom is cultural progress possible.

The requirements of natural, cultural, and normative, or ideal, freedom are not necessarily in harmony with one another and do, in fact,
tend frequently to conflict. There is, and must be, a certain basic interrelation between the three levels of freedom, since the higher freedom
cannot exist independently of the lower. Cultural freedom is dependent
upon natural, biological freedom, and normative freedom is approximated only through some form of cultural freedom.

Theoretically one can conceive of three stages in the evolutionary
development of freedom from the biological through the cultural to
the normative, although it must be kept in mind that historically no

such clear line of demarcation occurs. Since biological freedom is precultural, philosophers at one time imagined a "state of nature" which preceded the civic or cultural state, thereby confusing a logical postulate with historical fact. The assumption of a state of nature did, however, have the practical consequence of pointing up the role of the political state and of organized society in civilizing man and in regulating his freedom. Natural freedom, it was seen, without cultural regulation, inevitably leads to intolerable anarchy. Similarly, cultural freedom is never quite satisfactory, since no cultural system gratifies completely the psychobiological desires and needs of the individual. In fact, the more complex a culture becomes and the larger the society to which it pertains, the less opportunity there is for the individual to participate actively and fully in the life of the community, so that social culture tends to impoverish rather than to enrich the life of the individual. It is this that Rousseau had in mind when he complained that man is born free, but is everywhere in chains. That is why the appeal of going "back to nature" and to some more primitive form of life awakens such a sympathetic response in modern man, who would shake off the burden and tension of his complex civilization. Those who are not prepared to take the road back to some mythical state of nature seek rather to reform their society and culture in accordance with some ideal order which, it is expected, would provide greater scope for the development of human potentialities. Hence, appeal is made to an ideal moral freedom which is both positive and negative—positive in that it validates man's desire for greater freedom of expression in realizing his idea of the good and negative in that it proclaims the right to freedom from given cultural abuses and compulsions.

The history of philosophical utopias from Plato's *Republic* to Lenin's *State and Revolution* is significant as demonstrating Western man's constant efforts to imagine a form of society free from the abuses and tyrannies which have hitherto prevailed. All utopias, whether religious or secular, are the result of a wish to exemplify a bit of heaven on earth, and some of their modern adherents prophesy that the realization of their particular utopia in the near future is inevitable, either because of the dialectic of history or divine Providence. But whatever the particular philosophy of history which is used to validate a given utopian vision, utopias are significant as cultural constructs which transcend the given historical cultures of their inventors.

All forms of cultural idealism demonstrate that man is not only a product of cultural conditioning and cultural determinism—as modern anthropologists are wont to stress—but is also the originator or author of his culture systems, the self-determined creator and efficient cause of his cultural conditions and patterns. Underlying all cultural freedom and cultural determinism is the intellectual and imaginative creativity of man which enables him to construct ideal norms and "laws of nature" in the light of which he attempts to regulate his life in society. There would be no cultural determinism unless certain men were determined of themselves originally to initiate cultural processes and institutions by which to govern themselves. Before culture became an entity, a superorganic reality to be studied objectively by the anthropologist or culturologist, it had to be conceived and willed into existence by ordinary men concerned with fulfilling their needs and desires. In brief, behind all cultural freedom and cultural determinism one must postulate a metacultural, normative freedom without which human nature and culture as we know them would be inconceivable.

### 4. MALINOWSKI ON FREEDOM THROUGH CULTURE

The most comprehensive analysis of the concept of freedom in contemporary anthropological literature is to be found in Bronislaw Malinowski's *Freedom and Civilization*. His central thesis is that freedom cannot be discussed outside the context of culture.[8] All freedom is, for him, ultimately cultural freedom and in this sense is said to be one and indivisible. Furthermore, freedom is essentially social and hence a definition of freedom in terms of one individual is said to be "not viable." "The concept of freedom," he writes, "can only be defined with reference to human beings organized and endowed with cultural motives, implements and values, which *ipso facto* implies the existence of law, an economic system and political organization—in short, a cultural system. . . . In all this we find that freedom is a gift of culture."[9] "Right through our analysis," he continues, "there runs the thesis that freedom is the successful unimpeded course of the cultural process, bringing full satisfaction of all needs."[10] Cultural freedom is then analyzed into two basic types, namely, freedom of security and freedom of prosperity. Freedom of security is said to comprise all the protective mechanisms which culture provides for the survival of the

[8] Róheim, *Psychoanalysis and Anthropology: Culture, Personality and the Unconscious*, p. 52.
[9] *Ibid.*, pp. 25, 29.        [10] *Ibid.*, p. 39.

human species, while freedom of prosperity refers to the increment of freedom brought about through man's power of exploiting his environmental resources.

We find, nevertheless, that Malinowski does distinguish between biological freedom and cultural freedom. Thus, he writes: "It is important to register the concept of biological freedom, which might be called the pre-cultural definition of freedom, because it contains the minimum definition of the concept and it applies to man as well as animals." [11] Culture is, then, said to increase man's biological freedom by increasing his control of environmental circumstances.

Furthermore, Malinowski assumes without proof that cultural freedom will bring full satisfaction of all needs. If this were so, then, indeed, there would be no need to go beyond given historical culture systems for the full attainment of human freedom. As a matter of fact, however, no human culture system does or can bring full satisfaction of all needs and desires. It may be argued that eventually human freedom must be expressed in some cultural context, but this does not require us to say that all freedom is a gift of culture. Malinowski, it would appear, does not distinguish between ideal, or normative, freedom which may ultimately be approximated in some cultural institutions, and actual, or positive, cultural freedom which is realized through given institutions. Ideal, or normative, freedom is a prescriptive ideal which transcends all given cultures and indicates the way to future cultural progress. Normative freedom provides a measure for cultural freedom, but is not itself ever fully realized in any given culture. Malinowski, it seems, employs the concept of freedom within civilization as an ideal objective for mankind to pursue and at the same time speaks as if freedom were actually realized in the course of the cultural process. It may be granted that given cultures do provide "an initial installment in freedom," but ideal freedom in the sense of the unimpeded satisfaction of all needs is not a function of any given cultural process, and it is misleading, therefore, to speak of freedom as a gift of culture.

Malinowski himself came to realize toward the end of his study that "from the very beginnings of civilization, freedom has been the prerequisite for all constructive work in the maintenance and development of culture. It can also, therefore, be stated that culture is the gift of freedom at the beginning of humanity and throughout its develop-

[11] *Ibid.,* p. 103.

ment." [12] He reversed himself completely and postulated that human freedom is the condition of cultural development, whereas formerly he had insisted upon the opposite thesis. He did not, however, realize the full import of this admission and continued to speak in his "Epilogue" of the increment of freedom brought about by culture and of how "freedom is generated in the partial or total submission of individuals or groups to authority." [13] He saw no incompatibility between his thesis that freedom is a function of social culture and his individualistic doctrine that a liberal culture must leave some room "for the still voices of consciences." [14]

In sum, it would appear that Malinowski's *Freedom and Civilization,* while full of valuable insights, is not a coherent work. Written during the Second World War, it demonstrates his passionate concern for the preservation and development of democratic values and his unqualified militant opposition to all forms of totalitarian tyranny. As a cultural anthropologist he maintains the position that all human freedom is a function of culture and is to be understood only by reference to some cultural context. Culture is then said to be the primary source for the increment of man's original animal freedom. On this basis, it followed that there could be no freedom apart from some given cultural authority and that individualistic "free-floating" freedom was but a delusion. Logically, this argument would lead Malinowski right back to the position of Boas with which he professed to disagree, namely, that the person who is completely in harmony with his culture feels and is free.[15] He realized, however, that on this latter assumption even totalitarian culture could be interpreted as an exemplification of freedom and therefore rejected the implication as involving "the subjective fallacy." [16] All freedom, he argued, ultimately is realized under cultural conditions, but we must distinguish between "intrinsic constraints," which cannot be eliminated from purposeful human action and "arbitrary constraints" which are imposed by the abuse of power.[17] As a democrat and a liberal, Malinowski could not help but affirm his faith in individual liberty and in a transcultural ideal of freedom which would embrace all the peoples of the world.

### 5. SELF-CONSCIOUSNESS AND CULTURAL INDETERMINISM

Cultural anthropologists are inclined to demonstrate the role of culture in determining the course of human conduct and in restricting

---

[12] Róheim, *Psychoanalysis and Anthropology: Culture, Personality and the Unconscious,* p. 320.

[13] *Ibid.,* p. 321.  [14] *Ibid.,* p. 326.  [15] *Ibid.,* p. 62.

[16] *Ibid.,* p. 84.  [17] *Ibid.,* p. 321.

human freedom. What is usually overlooked is the fact, demonstrated in everyday experience, of man's self-consciousness, which enables him, individually and collectively, to reverse himself and to attempt to reform his ways in accordance with rational requirements. Since culture is the gift of human freedom, man is able to determine, within limits, the direction which the cultural process should take in the light of his experience and aspirations. That is why precise prediction of future trends is so unreliable, since being self-conscious of the trend of a given cultural process in the past, a society is able to alter its direction, either by modifying the given cultural practices or by setting up new institutions and regulations. Nothing demonstrates man's primordial freedom in the creation or invention of cultural processes and patterns more than his ability to choose between cultural alternatives once he has become conscious of them and is prepared to make the necessary effort to achieve one rather than the other. To be conscious of the pragmatic consequences of a given course of action in increasing or diminishing cultural freedom is to evaluate it and to determine the desirability of continuing it in the future.

In the last analysis, reversal or modification of cultural trends is possible because human freedom involves a circular concept of cultural causality—rather than a linear one—acccording to which man is the efficient cause of the cultural process and culture in turn affects man. It is this inherent circularity of the cultural process which makes all long-range prediction so contingent. A scientific study of the cultural conditions of a given society will throw much light upon its past and present history, but it does not provide an infallible indication of future tendencies. In human affairs, it would appear, there is, and can be, no precise science of the cultural future, since prediction is always contingent upon human decision and critical evaluation. In other words, human self-conscious freedom makes for some measure of cultural indeterminism. It is significant that none of the secular prophets of modern history who have spoken in the name of science have been generally successful in predicting the course of social events.

Paradoxical as it may appear, cultural determinism and cultural indeterminism are not incompatible in practice, since the concepts refer to complementary factors in the life of man and society. Cultural indeterminism is postulated because culture is not a closed system, but rather an open one, subject to the directive agency of human intelligence. On the other hand, some degree of cultural determinism characterizes human life, and the cultural anthropologist may study comparatively the significant correlations between culture, personality, and society. A knowledge of the universal processes underlying cultural change and cultural integration is essential for an understanding of human history and for the practical regulation of human affairs. But culture is not merely something to be contemplated as if it were an entity independent of man and human efforts; it is by its very essence a process dependent for its very existence upon human effort and intelligence. That is why cultural anthropology is not a natural science in the same sense that physics is, but rather primarily a historical and normative science preparing the way for the arts of the educator and reformer.

## 6. THE NATURAL WORLD AND THE CULTURAL WORLD

Corresponding to the distinctions drawn between human nature and cultural personality, natural freedom, and cultural freedom, a distinction must also be made between the concept of the natural world and that of the cultural world. The natural world is the geographical world of phenomena which we perceive about us. It is that to which man must adjust and with which he must reckon in order to survive. But supervening upon this given or discovered natural world there is the cultural world, the human world of symbolic constructs and cultural inventions which man himself has fashioned.

Man may be conceived as living in a five-dimensional world. First, there is the world of nature, that which offers resistance to human efforts and whose powers and laws he must obey. Secondly, there is the conceptual or symbolic world, by which he interprets and envisages the natural world. Thirdly, there is the world of cultural reality, the man-made world of artifacts and socifacts which is the creation of society. Fourthly, there is the ideal world of conceptual possibilities and values which transcend both the actual world of nature and the actual world of culture, the ideal world of utopias and the intelligible world of ideal forms. Fifthly, there is the private world, which the ego inhabits and which it does not share with others.

Thus, in one sense, man may be said to discover the world in which he lives, and in another sense he may be thought of as constructing and creating or fashioning his world. The philosophical realist has drawn attention to the fact that nature exists independently of man; that it is "given" to him and confronts him as a datum of experience. The philosophical idealist, following Kant, claims that the mind of man gives order to nature and attributes to nature an order which is a function or product of the mind's own categorical structure. Both are right, it would appear, in what they affirm, but they tend to go to extremes in denying the truth of the opposite position. The realists tend to adopt a naïve empiricism and to deny the factor of human creativity and inventiveness in formulating theoretical constructs by which to understand and to explain the order of natural phenomena. The idealists, on the other hand, tend to deny the existential "thing-in-itself" and do not give due weight to the postulate of an order of nature which man must discover and obey in order to survive. A sound and adequate view of the relation of man and nature must take into consideration both the subjective element of the mind's creativity and the objective factor of the independence of nature.

From a historical humanistic perspective it may be shown that man's ideologies and cosmologies testify to his range of vision and to his inventiveness as an architect and fashioner of worlds. The world in which man lives is a human world in the sense that cultural man is its measure and creator; for man, the world of nature is as he thinks and imagines it to be. While nature may be presumed to remain constant, our human cultural views undergo continuous transformation, for example, the Greek philosophers did not envisage the Copernican world of the Renaissance and the Newtonian world of the eighteenth century differs radically from the modern view of Einstein. The origin of new theories is beyond prediction, since one cannot foretell the direction of human discovery and inventiveness. Nevertheless, these changing intellectual views are not arbitrary, since man's ideas of himself and his world are suggested by the phenomena of nature and have to conform practically to the actual dynamic forces with which he is confronted. Besides, there are certain logical requirements which a theory must satisfy, such as intelligibility and coherency with reference to the data of experience, which limit the number and character of scientific theories.

In contemporary philosophy of science, Max Planck has put forward the thesis that natural science requires the postulation of a metaphysical reality behind the phenomenal reality known by the senses. He writes:

We call the ultimate reality the real world in the absolute metaphysical sense of the word real. This is to be construed as expressing the fact that the real world—in other words, objective nature—stands behind everything explorable. In contrast to it, the scientific world picture gained by experience—the phenomenological world—remains always a mere approximation, a more or less well divined model. As there is a material object behind every sensation, so there is a metaphysical reality behind everything that human experience shows to be real. . . . Near as the desired goal may seem, there always remains a gaping chasm, unbridgeable from the point of view of exact science, between the real world of phenomenology and the real world of metaphysics. . . . The fact that although we feel inevitably compelled to postulate the existence of a real world, in the absolute sense, we can never fully comprehend its nature, constitutes the irrational element which exact science can never shake off.[18]

According to Planck, the scientific method of investigation does not put us immediately or directly in contact with ultimate reality, with the "irrevocably real," as the positivists maintain; ultimate reality is rather an ideal, a postulate of the scientific mind which exact science gradually approximates through a process of verification and self-correction, but which can never be completely known or verified. That is why exact science is, in the last analysis, probable or hypothetical knowledge subject to constant revision. The scientific world picture of a given period is said to be an improvement upon the practical world picture of common sense somewhat as the world picture of the adult is an improvement upon that of the child. Nevertheless, science, by gradually enlarging its perspective, does provide our only means of gaining insight into the nature and laws of ontological or metaphysical reality. Our knowledge of this metacultural reality is culturally or symbolically mediated; but these symbolic constructs are, nevertheless, the means of transcending themselves, of indicating a reality beyond themselves of which they are the true symbols.

Similarly, Albert Einstein and Max Born are conscious of the role of ultimate assumptions or fundamental beliefs in the construction of scientific theory and of the need for constant revision of these mental constructs in the light of new evidence. At present, the traditional postulate of all natural science, namely, that objective reality is governed by determinate laws, is under question, and Einstein, for one, still retains his faith "in the perfect rule of law in a world of something objectively existing which I try to catch in a wildly speculative way," while Born believes that quantum theory requires the postulation of a world of chance.[19]

[18] Planck, "The Meaning and Limits of Exact Science," *Science*, 1949, pp. 319–27; reprinted in his *Scientific Autobiography and Other Papers*.
[19] Born, *Natural Philosophy of Cause and Chance*, pp. 122–23.

The history of scientific thought demonstrates clearly the absolutistic fallacy involved in asserting that the scientific world view of any given period is final and authoritative for all time. Viewed in historical perspective, the accepted scientific views of one age are seen to be the outmoded mythology of another. In recent times the rate of scientific research and speculation has become so accelerated that often "scientific" theories—that is, theories put forth by scientists—succeeded one another with bewildering rapidity, so that cautious scientists have come to regard their speculations as largely pragmatic hypotheses subject to constant revision. Hence, there is a tendency on the part of contemporary philosophers of science to put the major emphasis upon the so-called method of science rather than upon positive scientific knowledge. As against the authoritarian notion that science is to be venerated as an absolute oracle, Stephen Leacock speaks for the skeptical layman when he states: "When the scientist steps out from recording phenomena and offers a general statement of the nature of what is called 'reality,' the ultimate nature of space, of time and the beginnings of things, of life, of a universe, then he stands exactly where you and I do, and the three of us stand where Plato did—and long before him Rodin's primitive thinker." [20]

Leacock undoubtedly protests too much in arguing that the metaphysical speculations of the modern scientist are no better or more significant than those of a primitive philosopher. He overlooks the all-important point that scientific theories are subject to constant critical revision in the light of new facts and that this self-corrective process tends to be cumulative and progressive. The geocentric theory of the Middle Ages has been superseded by the heliocentric theory of the modern world, but it is highly improbable that the latter theory will in turn become outmoded. Nevertheless, Leacock's critical essay does focus attention upon the tendency of some scientists to engage in uncritical and wildly speculative theorizing of a philosophical nature in fields which are outside the range of their competence. We must learn to distinguish between philosophical theories put forward by scientists and scientific theories which have been empirically verified. In accepting uncritically every dogmatic utterance expressed by scientists one succeeds only in undermining the authority of science.

As William James noted, from a pragmatic point of view our world philosophies and ideologies may be evaluated in terms of their moral

[20] Leacock, *Last Leaves*, p. 38.

and practical consequences for human life. Other intellectual requirements being equally satisfied, a theory of nature and man which restricts human thought and provides little validation of human endeavor
is to be set aside in favor of one that enlarges and validates human efforts. So far as the cultural life of man is concerned, the principle of
*cogito ergo sum* and of *ago ergo sum* contains a basic truth, since in
acting upon the belief that he can direct his historical destiny in some
measure, man tends to verify this belief in practice. In general, a
humanistic evaluation of man's role in nature which views him as
participating in nature's evolutionary advance, rather than as an automaton, subject to blind mechanical forces, stimulates human creative
effort and thereby produces the factual, cultural evidence which validates this vision.

# 2

# *The Concept of Culture and Some Cultural Fallacies*[1]

ONE of the most encouraging features of contemporary social science is the increasing recognition of the importance of theoretical analysis. Social scientists, it is held, must endeavor to emancipate themselves from the "armchair taboo" and from the blind worship of barren experimentalism. The isolation of theoretical from practical research, it is realized, leads either to empty, unverified speculation or to incoherent aggregates of data. Especially in the sphere of cultural anthropology dissatisfaction is being expressed with texts which do not pay sufficient attention to theoretical problems. In addition to knowing what the facts are, the modern student wants to know how the facts can be ascertained and what they mean.[2]

## 1. THE DEVELOPMENT OF THE CONCEPT OF CULTURE IN MODERN ETHNOLOGY

The one concept which is predominant in contemporary social thought is that of culture. Cultural anthropologists and sociologists are in general agreement that human culture is acquired by man as a member of society and that it is communicated largely through the symbolism of language. There is sharp disagreement, however, as to the definition and scope of culture and the function to be attributed to it.

From a philosophical point of view, the most significant feature of current definitions of culture is the fact that they presuppose either

[1] Based in part on my papers "On the Concept of Culture and Some Cultural Fallacies," *American Anthropologist*, XLVI (1944), 30–44, and also "On the Philosophy of Culture in the Social Sciences," *Journal of Philosophy*, XXXIX (1942), 449–57.

[2] See Klein, "Psychology's Progress and the Armchair Taboo," *Psychological Review*, XLIX (1942), 226–34; Blumer, "The Problem of the Concept in Social Psychology," *American Journal of Sociology*, XLV (1939–40), 707–19; Ford, review of Hoebel's *Man in the Primitive World, American Anthropologist*, LII (1950), 245–46.

a realistic or an idealistic approach. The realists as a group tend to conceive culture as an attribute of human social behavior and usually define culture in terms of acquired habits, customs, and institutions. Culture so conceived is inseparable from the life of human beings in society; it is a mode of social living and has no existence independent of the actual groups to which it is attributed. Examples of realistic definitions of culture are to be found in the writings of Tylor, Boas, Malinowski, and many other authors who have been influenced by them.[3] Realists, however, differ among themselves as to whether culture is to be defined entirely in social terms to the neglect of the individual or whether individual variations are to be considered essential to any given culture. Boas, Sapir, and more recently Lynd have stressed the role of the individual in the cultural process, but on the whole the tendency in the past has been to identify culture with "all standardized social procedures," and to refer to the individual indirectly as one who is affected by the habits and customs of the group.

On the other hand, idealists tend to conceive culture as an aggregate of ideas in the minds of individuals, as a "stream of ideas," "conventional understandings," and "communicable intelligence."[4] Osgood's definition is the most articulate formulation of this type. According to the latter, "Culture consists of all ideas of the manufacture, behavior, and ideas of the aggregate of human beings which have been directly observed or communicated to one's mind and of which one is conscious."

Other cultural anthropologists are inclined to define culture in terms of "patterns" of behavior and "designs" for living. Culture is thought to be a conceptual "construct" and therefore is said to be an abstraction from the actual, noncultural behavior which exemplifies it.[5] Linton, Kluckhohn, and Gillin have in the past expressed themselves to this effect. This position may be described as "conceptual idealism" in order to differentiate it from the "subjective idealism" of those who identify culture with communicated ideas. Both positions

[3] Tylor, *Primitive Culture*, Vol. I; Boas, *The Mind of Primitive Man* and "Anthropology," in *Encyclopaedia of the Social Sciences;* Malinowski, "Culture" in *Encyclopaedia of the Social Sciences*, "Anthropology," in *Encyclopaedia Britannica*, and *A Scientific Theory of Culture and Other Essays;* Dixon, *The Building of Cultures;* Wissler, *An Introduction to Social Anthropology;* and Lynd, *Knowledge for What?*

[4] Osgood, "Culture: Its Empirical and Non-empirical Character," *Southwestern Journal of Anthropology*, VII (1951), 202–14; Marett, *Man in the Making;* Redfield, *The Folk Culture of Yucatan;* Osgood, *Ingalik Material Culture;* Ogburn and Nimkoff, *Sociology;* Schmidt, *The Culture Historical Method of Ethnology.*

[5] See ch. v.

are idealistic, inasmuch as they define culture as something conceived, or perceived, by minds.

The idealistic view of culture approximates in some respects the normative idea of culture presupposed by educationists, for whom culture connotes the cultivation of the mind or "spirit" together with the products of this mental culture. For the educationists culture has thus come to refer to the whole tradition of intellectual ideals, to the intellectual and artistic achievements of mankind. As Werner Jaeger has observed,

Culture, having once meant the process of education, came to mean the state of being educated, and then the content of education, and finally, the whole intellectual and spiritual world revealed by education into which any individual according to his nationality or social position is born.[6]

Some modern anthropologists, it would appear, have discarded the normative, or ideal, features of educational culture, but have retained this essentially subjective, individualistic, idealistic approach. They are inclined to stress the role of language as all-important in the communication of cultural traditions and hence to regard culture as consisting primarily of ideas communicated to the mind, thereby implicitly committing themselves to a form of Berkeleyan subjective idealism.

Among anthropologists culture is also conceived objectively and impersonally as "the social heritage," as the sum of the historical achievements of human social life which has been transmitted in the form of a tradition or inheritance. Man is said to be born into a cumulative artificial environment to which he is trained to adapt himself, in addition to the natural geographic environment, which he shares with other animals. The social heritage is, however, conceived differently by realists and idealists. The former, putting the emphasis upon heritage, hold that the cultural heritage consists of the body of material artifacts, as well as of nonmaterial ideas, institutions, customs, and ideals. This position is exemplified in the work of Boas, Lowie, Malinowski, and Dixon. On the other hand, the idealists, implicitly following in the tradition of Plato and Hegel, maintain that the social heritage is a "superorganic" stream of ideas and that any particular culture is an abstraction from the historical complex of ideational traditions. This position, exemplified in the work of Kroeber, Sorokin, and Spengler, may be termed "objective idealism," since its advocates regard culture as a heritage of ideas that have a transcendent reality

[6] Jaeger, *Paideia; the Ideals of Greek Culture*, p. 300.

of their own independent of the individuals or societies which happen to bear them. A similar transcendental concept of culture is put
forth by historical materialists, such as Leslie A. White, but the latter
regard technology and the material conditions of social life as the primary, or determining, factors in the evolution of culture.[7]

Objective, metaphysical cultural idealism and materialism are the
antitheses of the humanistic position according to which man is the
efficient cause and final cause of his sociocultural heritage. That is, for
the objective impersonal idealist and materialist culture is a transcendental, metaphysical entity which has made man what he is and to
which he must conform as to his historical destiny; whereas for the
personal idealist culture consists of the norms and ideals of behavior
which man himself has created and which have no existence apart from
the human mind. On either idealistic basis "material culture" is a
contradiction in terms, since the "real" cultural entities are the conceptual norms and patterns, not the particular artifacts which exemplify them.[8]

One major source of confusion in contemporary ethnological theory
is the tendency on the part of many anthropologists to combine the
dynamic, humanistic conception of culture with the impersonal, transcendental notion involved in the idea of the social heritage. The issue
is whether culture is to be understood as essentially a mode of living
in which each individual participates actively or whether it is a reified,
objective achievement which man acquires from his ancestors more
or less passively. Contemporary culture theory seems to be divided on
this issue, some writers defining culture in terms of physical and mental
acquired capabilities and customs, while others enumerate the various
kinds of material and nonmaterial culture products which comprise the
entity called culture. The confusion is increased by the fact that many
writers first present a dynamic, anthropocentric definition of culture
and then proceed to specify the contents of culture in terms of impersonal cultural products. Thus, even Sapir informs us that a culture is
"what society does and thinks" and then, in another paper, states that
culture "embodies any socially inherited element in the life of man,
material and spiritual." [9]

[7] White, *The Science of Culture,* esp. ch. xiii; also White, "Ethnological Theory,"
in *Philosophy for the Future,* ed. by Sellars and others, pp. 357–84.

[8] Rouse, *Prehistory in Haiti,* pp. 15–17.

[9] Sapir, "Language, Race and Culture," in *The Making of Modern Man,* ed. by
V. F. Calverton, pp. 142–54; also "Culture, Genuine and Spurious," reprinted in
*Selected Writings of Edward Sapir,* ed. by D. G. Mandelbaum.

The identification of culture with the social heritage is, to my mind, not only a misnomer but also a serious error, since it implies that the essential feature of culture is the fact of communication and transmission, whereas I maintain that the essential feature is the combination of invention and acquisition through habituation and conditioning. It is not at all essential for a cultural trait to be communicated, even though it usually is. This point may be illustrated by comparing the anthropologist who acquires ideas about a native culture with the natives themselves. The visiting anthropologist obtains information about a native culture, but the culture itself would not be attributed to him because he himself is not "acculturated," that is, because he does not practice or profess the ideals of the native culture in his daily life. Similarly, artifacts gathered by anthropologists and placed in museums are not our culture-objects, because they are not made or actively utilized by us, even though we have acquired or "inherited" them from their original owners. Besides, it is a commonplace of daily experience that man is not content to live by the practices or customs of his ancestors, but, driven by a sense of wonder and a feeling of boredom, as well as by intermittent desires to improve the material and social conditions of his life, he is led to introduce new ways of living and new articles of manufacture. In brief, human culture is historical because it involves change as well as continuity, creation, and discovery of novelties together with the assimilation of traditions. To define culture as a social heritage is to ignore the equally significant element of historical novelty and discontinuity.

It follows, further, that if human culture consists primarily of acquired forms of behavior, sentiment, and thought, then no inventions or culture-objects *per se* are constituent of culture. Artifacts, "socifacts," and "mentifacts" are, so to speak, "cultural capital," the surplus which results from cultural life, but in themselves and apart from their relation to the adherents of a given culture they are not primary or constituent elements of culture.[10] All cultural products are abstractions when separated from the cultural process manifested in the life of a society. In and by themselves these products are but symbolic manifestations of cultural life. It is the use or function of an artifact, its contribution to cultural life in a given social context, which is significant—not the artifact in and by itself. According to the functionalists, the nature or essence of an artifact is relative to its function in, or

[10] Eubank, *The Concepts of Sociology*, p. 357.

significance for, a given culture, and one must not therefore speak of an object as being the same when its cultural function has been changed, even though its perceptible form remains identical. This explains why in general the functionalists are more concerned with giving a description of the interdependence of cultural institutions than with tracing the history of a custom or the diffusion of material trait-complexes. I am inclined to agree, therefore, with those who maintain that the term "material culture" is a misnomer in that we thereby divorce the object of knowledge from the knowledge and art of the manufacture and use of the artifact. I would suggest that we substitute the terms "technical" and "nontechnical" culture instead of the usual tripartite classification of material, social, and intellectual culture.

Furthermore, all culture includes individual and social poles which are distinguishable, but not actually separable. Thus, as so many writers have insisted, all culture is social in origin; it is acquired by man, as Tylor observed, "as a member of society." We acquire our culture as a social heritage from the experience and example of others; and in this sense, as Marett has suggested, culture is "communicable intelligence." But this, as Sapir and Lynd have insisted, should not mislead us into overlooking the role of the individual in modifying or adding to his cultural heritage. Individuals not only fail to conform to ideal social patterns but also initiate many changes which later become universally accepted. A survey of anthropological and sociological literature will convince one of the justice of Sapir's criticism that

culture as it is ordinarily constructed by the anthropologist is a more or less mechanical sum of the more striking or picturesque generalized patterns of behavior which he has either abstracted for himself out of the sum total of his observations or has had abstracted for him by his informants in verbal communication. . . . Cultures, as ordinarily dealt with, are merely abstracted configurations of idea and action patterns, which have endlessly different meanings for the various individuals in the group.[11]

Culture, Sapir argued, is not something merely given; it is rather something to be gradually discovered. If we view persons-in-culture realistically, we shall take account of the particular psychological motivations of individuals, the variety of their endowments, and the degree of influence which the social institutions and ideals have upon their

[11] Sapir, "The Emergence of the Concept of Personality in a Study of Cultures," *Journal of Social Psychology*, V, 408–15.

conduct, as well as the reciprocal influence which the individuals exercise upon their cultural environment.

Thus, cultural behavior may be socially acquired by man "as a member of society" without necessarily being social or common to all the members of the society. Society is a necessary, but not a sufficient, condition of cultural activity. Certainly if the seventeenth-century philosophers erred in conceiving a cultureless individual living in "a state of nature," modern thinkers seem to be going to the opposite extreme in socializing culture. The category of the social and that of the cultural are not identical, as is commonly supposed, since there may be social phenomena which are not cultural facts, such as the size of a given population, and cultural phenomena which are not social, such as the creation of a poem by an individual.[12] If one keeps in mind the inherent polarity of the individual and the community, practical interindividual behavior and common cultural patterns, he will avoid the extremes of completely socializing culture, after the manner of Durkheim and Sumner, or of completely individualizing it, as some psychologists are inclined to do. It is the business of anthropologists and sociologists to determine whether a given cultural practice or achievement was derived from personal experience and individual initiative or whether it was the product of common education or habituation. Some of the contradiction and disparity between contemporary ethnological theory and practice results in large measure from the inner contradiction involved in conceiving culture in terms of social habits or patterns which neglect individual differences and then proceeding to note individual peculiarities, cultural alternatives, and autobiographic experiences.

In the process of the history of ethnological thought, human culture, in both its physical and its mental aspects, has come to mean the process, as well as the state, of being cultured, together with the achievements or products of man's self-cultivation. In general, it appears, the realists have stressed the notion that culture is the state of being cultured and refers to that modification of behavior and thought, taken individually and collectively, which is the result of the process of self-cultivation. The idealists, in turn, have maintained that culture is either primarily mental, or intellectual, cultivation, or else that culture consists of the stream, or tradition, of ideas, the social

[12] Allport, "The Group Fallacy in Relation to Social Science," *American Journal of Sociology*, XXIX (1923–24), 688–703; Ostwald, quoted in White, *The Science of Culture*, p. 116; Taylor, *A Study of Archeology*, pp. 105–9.

heritage of the past.[13] It is obvious that neither party is wrong in what it affirms, but only in what it denies; an adequate conception of culture requires the union of both the realistic and the idealistic theses.

A culture consists of the acquired or cultivated behavior and thought of individuals within a society, as well as of the intellectual, artistic, and social ideals and institutions which the members of the society profess and to which they strive to conform. In other words, a culture must be understood in its practical and theoretical aspects. Normative, impersonal, ideational culture has no existence unless it it practiced and influences men's behavior and thinking in social life. Practical, real, or actual culture—the actual behavior and thought of men in society—is not intelligible apart from the social ideals which men have created or discovered for themselves and endeavor to realize in their daily lives. It is the task of the empirical social scientist to determine to what extent there is agreement between theory and practice in any given culture and whether the culture is "genuine" or "spurious" in Sapir's sense of the terms, that is, to what extent it allows for maximum participation on the part of its adherents.[14] Although contemporary anthropologists and sociologists, such as Sapir, Linton, Kluckhohn, and Lynd, have noted the disparity which often exists between "ideal" and "behavioral" patterns of culture, for them the distinction is between culture patterns, or conceptual constructs, not between ideal and actual behavior.[15] Similarly, the term "habit," so often employed with reference to culture, is ambiguous, since it is used to refer to actual behavior, as well as to "patterns" of behavior and thought.

It should be noted in this connection that the terms "theory" and "practice" have a double meaning. On the one hand, "practice" refers to the actual behavior and beliefs of the members of a society, whether they are conscious of them or not, as contrasted with their professed ideals and beliefs. As Sapir has observed, there is often an unconscious patterning of behavior which serves to differentiate the members of a given society from those of other societies.[16] On the other hand, the

13 Blumenthal, "A New Definition of Culture," *American Anthropologist*, XLII (1940), 571–86.

14 Sapir, "Culture, Genuine and Spurious," *American Journal of Sociology*, XXIX (1924), 401–29.

15 Sapir, "The Emergence of the Concept of Personality in a Study of Cultures," *Journal of Social Psychology*, V, 408–15; Linton, *The Study of Man*, pp. 100–101; Kluckhohn, "Patterning As Exemplified in Navaho Culture," in *Language, Culture and Personality*, ed. by Leslie Spier and others; Lynd, *Knowledge for What?* pp. 19–40.

16 Sapir, "The Unconscious Patterning of Behavior in Society," in his *Selected Writings of Edward Sapir*, pp. 544–59.

terms "theory" and "practice" may also be used in a more limited sense to refer to thought and action, respectively. In either instance, the dichotomy of theory and practice is not an epistemic distinction among ideas only and refers to cultural phenomena of different orders. Theory and practice may be said to be the irreducible constitutent categories of culture; they are not merely different kinds of ideas. The basic epistemological question concerning any given culture concerns the degree of correspondence between the theoretical and the practical elements within it. The degree of cultural integration is also evaluated to some extent by the conformity and harmony of these two factors.

Man, it appears, is a cultural animal because he is a rational, as well as rationalizing, animal. Man lives in accordance with his ideals of what he thinks and feels he ought to be and acts as he thinks he is. But sooner or later he discovers that some of the social ideals communicated to him by his society are not to his liking or do not lead to satisfactory results. Thus, institutions and practices originally intended as means for the amelioration of human existence become sanctified as ends-in-themselves and lose their connection with the functions for which they were originally intended. But instead of changing ideals to conform to changes of practice, societies frequently continue to profess allegiance to the old ideals.[17] Or else they change their theories without a corresponding change of practice. In either case, there results a disparity between professed sociocultural theory and the actual practices of individuals and societies.

It should be noted, furthermore, that cultures differ in the emphasis which is placed on theoretical speculation as contrasted with action or overt behavior. One culture may make an ideal of practicality, whereas another may idealize the life of theoretical and ecstatic contemplation. This is, perhaps, best exemplified by the traditional ideals of Western and Oriental cultures and the corresponding attitudes toward time and economic activities. Primitive cultures as a whole are largely concerned with practice, and comparatively little with theoretical speculation. Among literate cultures, Matthew Arnold has contrasted the spirit of Hebraism and Hellenism which to him represent the ideals of moral conduct and disinterested speculation, respectively.

From this standpoint we can appreciate the significance of the conflict between the realistic and the idealistic positions outlined at the beginning of this chapter. The realistis, we have seen, define culture in terms of acquired habits, customs, folkways, and mores and tend

[17] Myrdal, *An American Dilemma.*

to ignore the ideal, or normative, aspects of culture. On this basis, social ideals are logically nothing but a sort of statistical average of actual practices. The realists tend to confuse the actual aspects of culture with ideal culture by assuming that the covert, or professed, ideals are carried out in practice, whereas often this is not the case. This I should call *the positivistic fallacy.* The positivists, in general, fail to recognize that rational, or conceptual, ideals have an objective reality of their own as ideas and that they are to be distinguished from the practices, or customs, which they condition or to which they lead. Thus, John Dewey [18] states that "customs in any case constitute moral standards. For they are active demands for certain ways of acting." Customs and folkways are not ideal standards; they may serve as the stimulus for setting up or erecting conceptual standards. The validity of a given norm or ideal standard is distinct from the actual practice to which it leads. The ideal of what ought to be is not identical with what is the custom, or practice. On the other hand, normative idealists tend to define culture in terms of social ideals and to exclude the actual practices as not properly constitutive of culture. This may be called *the normativistic fallacy.* In brief, it is as fallacious to assume that an account of what occurs or is practiced is a sufficient description of a culture as it is to assume that the ideals professed by members of a society are actually adhered to in practice. Every culture has its ideal and practical aspects, and it is an indispensable function of the social scientist to show their interrelation and the measure of their integration in any given society. The degree of cultural lag between the ideals and the practices of a given society is an important indication of the extent of its cultural integration.

Cultural idealists who conceive of culture as essentially a logical construct or abstraction still fail to explain how it is possible for abstract, logical entities, what the philosophers call an *ens rationis,* to "interact" with concrete, actual entities, such as individuals and societies. It would seem but common sense to insist that only cultural man or society is capable of acting or interacting in the efficient sense of that term. To attribute power of activity to cultural ideas and constructs is to commit *the metaphysical fallacy of misplaced concreteness.* Only by viewing culture in both its theoretical and its practical aspects do we eliminate the necessity of trying to explain how it is possible for an abstract, logical construct to "interact" with an individual or so-

[18] *Human Nature and Conduct,* ch. v.

ciety, or of assuming that pragmatically such logical constructs must be treated "as if" they had a substantial existence and power of their own.

## 2. TYPES OF CULTURAL CAUSALITY

It is important in this connection to bear in mind the various kinds of causality and their application to the concept of culture. If we, following Aristotle, distinguish between the material, formal, efficient, and final causes or conditions of natural phenomena, then it becomes obvious that we may not speak of culture in general as being a cause of behavior without specifying which kind of cause we mean. Cultural products, such as artifacts, mentifacts, or socifacts, are the material, formal, and final causes of cultural development; they are not the efficient causes or active agents. That is, cultural achievements and products do influence individual and social life by providing the material means, as well as the formal or patterned stimuli, for the acquisition of a specific form of behavior, feeling, or thought, and to this extent the study of abstract cultural objects and ideas is of pragmatic value to the anthropologist. Similarly, cultural ideals are final causes of cultural processes; they provide the ends, or goals, which men strive to attain or realize. Communicated ideals can influence people to act, but it is the individuals or societies themselves who act or are motivated to act—not the ideas or cultural ideals. That is, only individuals and societies are the efficient or active causes of cultural processes. As Lynd has argued,[19] we must not separate and oppose man and culture, since it is the cultured man, or the man-in-culture, who acts and elaborates his culture. Social scientists who speak of an entity called "culture" which somehow interacts with societies, makes progress, and eventually decays, tend to confuse efficient causality with formal, material, and final conditions of cultural activity of persons in society. Culture considered in both its realistic and its idealistic aspects requires a union of all four modes of causality. The position of the Marxian historical materialists who stress the role of material technology as the primary factor in determining the evolution of cultural forms is as one-sided and simplistic as is that of the historical idealists who attribute to ideas the primary, active causal role. The proponents of both positions tend, in theory at least, to underestimate the function of man as a self-determining, active agent who is affected by cultural products and patterns,

[19] Lynd, *Knowledge for What?*

but is, nevertheless, the primary efficient agent of the cultural process itself.

### 3. THE CONCEPT OF THE SUPERORGANIC

It is generally agreed among anthropologists that culture is a super-organic phenomenon, but it is important to bear in mind that the concept of the superorganic may be, and has been, interpreted in at least three distinct senses.

According to Herbert Spencer, who originated the term, "super-organic evolution" is a process which supervenes upon organic evolution. Thus, he writes: "If there has been Evolution, that form of it here distinguished as super-organic must have come by insensible steps out of the organic. But we may conveniently mark it off as including all those processes and products which imply the co-ordinated actions of many individuals." [20] For Spencer, then, there are various groups of superorganic phenomena, such as the social organization of bees and wasps, bird communities, and gregarious animals. Human superorganic evolution is only a more complicated form of superorganic evolution in general, and the latter is not, therefore, peculiar to man. Sociology is said to deal with the superorganic phenomena which human societies exhibit in their growth, structures, functions, and products.[21] The superorganic environment of any society is said to consist of the action and reaction between a society and neighboring societies.[22] There is also "that accumulation of super-organic products which we commonly distinguish as artificial, but which, philosophically considered, are no less natural than all other products of evolution." Among these superorganic products, Spencer enumerates material appliances, language, science, customs, laws, philosophies, aesthetic objects, and art in general, including music, drama, and literature.

These various orders of super-organic products [Spencer explains], each developing within itself new genera and species while growing into a larger whole, and each acting on the other orders while reacted on by them, constitute an immensely-voluminous, immensely-complicated, and immensely-powerful set of influences. During social evolution they are ever modifying individuals and modifying society, while being modified by both. They gradually form what we may consider either as a non-vital part of the society itself, or else as a secondary environment, which eventually becomes more important than the primary environments—so much more important that

[20] Spencer, *Principles of Sociology*, I, 4.
[21] *Ibid.*, p. 7.                [22] *Ibid.*, p. 12.

there arises the possibility of carrying on a high kind of social life under inorganic and organic conditions which originally would have prevented it.[23]

The important point to note here is that for Spencer the superorganic is an attribute of intrinsically social processes and products which is applicable to animal, as well as human, societies. Human superorganic activities differ in kind from those of animals and are vastly more complicated than the latter. Spencer does not set apart the sphere of superorganic phenomena from that of organic phenomena; the superorganic phenomena are directly dependent upon the organic and vary with the latter. The social superorganic is for Spencer, not something which transcends the organic, but rather a kind of superorganism subject to its own organic laws of evolutionary development. Hence, Spencer continued to speak of society as if it were a kind of organism. The secondary environment constituted by the aggregate of superorganic products is superorganic by virtue of the fact that it is dependent upon the co-ordinated action of the members of given human societies. Its superorganicness lies in its social dependence, not in its independence of human society.

A second meaning of the term, and one which most social scientists would find acceptable, is that "superorganic" refers to the fact that cultural evolution is not limited by man's organic structure. Human culture is said to be superorganic in the psychological sense that man's capacity for invention and symbolization enables him to create and to acquire new forms of cultural life without any corresponding change in his organic structure. This conception of the superorganic not only fails to exclude, but even necessitates, an internal relation between culture and the psychological nature of man. That is, while the facts of psychology are not considered sufficient in themselves to explain all the diversity of human cultures, they are, nevertheless, indispensable for understanding some of the universal characteristics of human culture, as well as the motivations underlying special cultural phenomena. It should be noted, furthermore, that insofar as culture is said to depend upon the psychological, superorganic nature of man, cultural phenomena may be explained by reference to the individual, as well as to society. Thus, unlike Spencer's concept of the superorganic, the psychological superorganic concept refers, not primarily to the processes and products of social interaction, but rather to the fact of man's unique psychological capabilities, which enable him as an individual, as well

[23] *Ibid.*, pp. 13–14.

as collectively, to transcend in his cultural achievements his purely biological limitations. The superorganicness of culture lies in its independence of organic determinism and involves the human capacity for self-determination and self-expression.

Thirdly, as employed by A. L. Kroeber in his paper on "The Superorganic," the term is used to designate the nonorganic, or that which transcends the organic.[24] In adapting Spencer's term to his theory of culture, Kroeber adhered to the former's identification of the social and the superorganic, but restricted its application to the sphere of human "super-organic products." Furthermore, Kroeber accepted Spencer's distinction of the three levels of evolution, namely, the inorganic, the organic, and the social, but differs from the latter in regarding social, superorganic evolution as a new emergent process characteristic of human culture, or civilization, only. According to Spencer, the superorganic is but a further extension of the organic into the social sphere and connotes "all those processes and products which imply the coordinated actions of many individuals." That is why Spencer is able to speak of the superorganic activities of insects and animals besides those of man. For Kroeber, however, the superorganic refers exclusively to the social products and achievements of man which constitute the order of culture, or civilization. At that time Kroeber was particularly concerned to separate the sphere of the organic from the level of the social, and he therefore insisted upon the independence of the latter from the former. As against the doctrine of the inheritance of acquired characteristics which Spencer accepted and the theory of a racial character and psychology of different nations put forth by Le Bon and eugenicists such as Galton and Pearson, Kroeber maintained that historical, cultural phenomena were "superpsychic" and that their development and evolution were independent of psychobiological organic evolution. This was his "Copernican revolution."

As Kroeber put it,

The reason why mental heredity has nothing to do with civilization, is that civilization is not mental action but a body or stream of products of mental exercise. Mental activity, as biologists have dealt with it, being organic, any demonstration concerning it consequently proves nothing whatever as to social events. Mentality relates to the individual. The social or cultural on the other hand, is in its very essence non-individual. Civilization as such begins only where the individual ends; and whoever does not in some measure perceive this fact, though as a brute and rootless one, can find no

[24] Kroeber, "The Superorganic," *American Anthropologist*, XIX (1917), 163–213.

meaning in civilization, and history for him must be only a wearying jumble or an opportunity for the exercise of art.[25]

And again:

Two wholly disparate evolutions must be recognized: that of the substance we call organic and that of the other substance we call social. Social evolution is without antecedents in the beginnings of organic evolution. It commences late in the development of life. . . . This origin occurred in a series of organic forms more advanced in general mental faculty than the gorilla, and much less developed than the first known race that is unanimously accepted as having been human, the man of Neandertal and Le Moustier. . . . A new factor had arisen which was to work out its own independent consequences . . . a factor that had passed beyond natural selection, that was no longer wholly dependent on any agency of organic evolution, and that, however rocked and swayed by the oscillations of heredity that underlay it, nevertheless floated unimmersibly upon it. . . . The dawn of the social thus is not a link in any chain, not a step in a path, but a leap to another plane.[26]

Here we have the first statement, so far as I know, of the doctrine of emergent evolution as applied to the history of human civilization. As against Spencer and other sociologists, Kroeber maintains the complete disparity of biological and cultural evolution. He conceives of culture as being "superpsychic" because he differentiates "mental action" from the "body or stream of products of mental exercise," identifying culture with the latter.[27] Culture is the superorganic, superpsychic product of social mental processes; it is not the actual social processes. Thus, Kroeber writes:

All civilization in a sense exists only in the mind. Gunpowder, textile arts, machinery, laws, telephones are not themselves transmitted from man to man nor from generation to generation, at least not permanently. It is the perception, the knowledge and understanding of them, their ideas in the Platonic sense, that are passed along. Everything social can have existence only through mentality. Of course, civilization is not mental action itself; it is carried by men, without being in them.[28]

Kroeber, it appears, is here committed to a theory of Platonic idealism with reference to culture, since culture is said to consist of the objective ideas which subsist independent of the minds which happen to conceive them. Culture, or civilization, is conceived paradoxically both as

[25] *Ibid.*, pp. 192–93.
[26] *Ibid.*, pp. 208 ff.
[27] "The Possibility of a Social Psychology," *American Journal of Sociology*, XXIII (1917–18), 633–50.
[28] "The Superorganic," *American Anthropologist*, XIX (1917), 186.

a social product of the human mind and also as a body or stream of ideas independent of the psychobiological nature of man. In seeking to avoid an organic, psychobiological determinism of culture, he was led to accept a theory of objective idealism which was no less deterministic, since it completely separated man from the products of his social activity.

Logically, Spencer's thesis of the identity of the social with the superorganic is not compatible with Kroeber's identification of the superorganic with the superpsychic. Spencer, it will be recalled, originally identified the sphere of the social with that of the superorganic, because for him the superorganic was an attribute, or derivative, of social processes; superorganic phenomena were directly dependent upon organic nature and varied with the structure and functions of the latter. For Kroeber, superorganic phenomena are independent of the organic and psychological levels; culture does not comprise "mental action" of individuals interacting with one another, but only "the body or stream of products of mental exercise," the stream of ideas which subsist independent of individual minds. On this premise, culture appears as an entity *sui generis,* of which man is the vehicle or carrier, but not the originator and source of its being. As Kroeber puts it,

Civilization, though carried by men and existing through them, is an entity in itself, and of another order from it. The entity civilization has intrinsically nothing to do with individual men nor with the aggregates of men on whom it rests. It springs from the organic but is independent of it.[29]

Culture, of course, is borne only by vitally and mentally organized beings aggregated into societies. But these individuals and societies are merely the prerequisite condition of culture, not its being.[30]

These explicit statements make it appear that for Kroeber culture, or civilization, is an entity independent in its being from both individuals and societies. Hence, culture, as an independent level of reality, may be said to be not only superorganic and superpsychic but also "supersocial," since its evolution and history do not depend directly upon society. Logically, on this premise, one must differentiate the level of the social from that of the cultural, since the cultural constitutes a "higher" level than the social. In practice, however, Kroeber, as did the other anthropologists of his generation, continued to identify

[29] Kroeber, "Eighteen Professions," *American Anthropologist,* XVII (1915), 283–88.
[30] "The Possibility of a Social Psychology," *American Journal of Sociology,* XXIII (1917–18), 633–50.

the cultural superorganic with the social, while insisting upon the distinction between culture and society. In his paper "So-Called Social Science," written many years later, we find him designating four main levels of phenomena, namely, "the inorganic, organic, psychic and socio-cultural," [31] thereby still identifying the sphere of the social with that of the cultural.

He admits, however, that "society carries culture; and it is composed of persons with individual psyches. Within the uppermost level, culture can therefore be construed as the top, society as the bottom stratum." Later, in his revised *Anthropology* and especially in his volume of collected essays, *The Nature of Culture*, Kroeber finally recognized the logical necessity of differentiating explicitly between the categories of the social and the cultural.

### 4. THE CONCEPT OF LEVELS OF REALITY AND THE THEORY OF EVOLUTION

The issue involved may be indicated by special reference to the concept of levels of phenomena in nature. Spencer's three levels, namely, the inorganic, the organic, and the social, or superorganic, are, like Comte's levels, both empirical and hierarchical. The levels of phenomena are based on properties which are empirically observable, and the levels are hierarchical in the sense that they may be arranged in a logical sequence of higher and lower forms of organization and function which is independent of the theoretical problem of sequence in the historical process.

The earliest systematic classification of organisms on an empirical functional basis is that of Aristotle. According to Aristotle,

The facts about soul are akin to the state of affairs about figures; the prior is always present potentially in its successor, both in the case of figures and in that of living things; e.g., the triangle in the quadrilateral, the nutritive power in the perceptive. Therefore we must ask, species by species, what is the soul of each, e.g., what is the soul of the plant and what that of man or of the beast. We must, however, examine into the reason why the faculties are thus related by succession. The perceptive faculty is not found without the nutritive; but the nutritive is separated from the perceptive in plants. Again apart from the faculty of touch none of the other senses is found, but touch is found without the others; for many of the animals have neither sight nor hearing nor smell. Of creatures that have perception, too, some have the power of locomotion and others have not. What comes last and is possessed

[31] "So-Called Social Science," *Journal of Social Philosophy*, I (1935–36), 317–40.

by fewest is reasoning and thought; for among mortals those that possess reasoning possess also all the others, but those that possess each of these do not all possess reasoning; some do not possess even imagination, and others live by this alone. The theoretical reason is matter for another inquiry.[32]

Aristotle, therefore, classified organisms empirically as vegetative, animal, and rational, the higher organism containing the potentialities of the lower in addition to powers and functions of its own.

It should be noted, furthermore, that Aristotle also formulated an epistemological theory of the classification of the sciences. Here, however, his principle of classification was ontological theory, rather than empirical observation. The sciences were arranged in hierarchical order according to their degree of abstraction, the more conceptual the subject matter and the less reference to sense data, the higher the degree of perfection and scientific validity attributed to it. Thus, physics, or the study of the contingent material objects of nature, was lowest in the hierarchy of the sciences, mathematics was the next, and metaphysics and theology comprised the highest form of science, since the latter were concerned with pure forms conceived by reason alone. "Scientific knowledge," Aristotle maintained, "is not possible through the act of perception." [33] This epistemic classification of the modes of knowledge, which was first systematically formulated in Plato's *Republic*, continued to serve as the basis of scholastic thought in the Middle Ages and later, until it was challenged in the sixteenth and seventeenth centuries by Francis Bacon and Descartes. In modern Catholic philosophy this Aristotelian scheme is still recognized.[34]

We must distinguish accordingly between two distinct problems, namely, the epistemological and methodological problem of the classification of the sciences, and the ontological problem of the levels of natural phenomena. Aristotle employed an empirical classification of animals in his zoology and psychology and was the first to suggest a *scala naturae* of the animal kingdom, but classified the sciences on an ontological basis in accordance with the principle of the primacy of form over matter. Thus, whereas levels of organic life were determined empirically, the sciences were rated higher or lower in the scale in accordance with the abstractness of their objects rather than by their verifiability. In this way it came about that metaphysical speculation as to the hierarchical order of the cosmos rather than empirical investi-

[32] Aristotle, *De anima*, 415a, in *Aristotle Selections*, ed. by W. D. Ross, pp. 206–7.
[33] *Posterior Analytics*, 87b.
[34] Maritain, *The Degrees of Knowledge.*

gation of natural phenomena became the primary object of interest in subsequent philosophical thought.

As a result of these philosophical and theological speculations, there were formulated three distinct principles, namely, the principle of levels, the principle of continuity, and the principle of plenitude. The principle of levels was an assertion that all things in nature were to be graded in a scale according to their degree of perfection of being and power. In practice this led to a synthesis of empirical observation as to the qualitative differences among natural phenomena and purely speculative interpolations as to the possible higher levels of metaphysical reality. Thus, the number and types of levels of being varied with the basic types of philosophical systems. Secondly, the principle of continuity meant, in Kant's formulation, "a continuous transition from every species to every other species by a gradual increase of diversity." This principle precludes "leaps" between the various species to be found in nature.[35] Thirdly, the principle of plenitude postulates a maximum of diversity in the phenomena of nature. When the principle of levels was combined with that of continuity, one arrived at the notion of a "hierarchical continuum," that is, levels of phenomena arranged so that they constitute a series differing in degree, but not in kind. If the principle of plenitude were added to the concept of a hierarchical continuum, one arrived at the postulate of an "infinite hierarchical continuum" such that one could suppose an infinite number of links between the lowest and the highest orders of reality. This was "the great chain of being" at its maximum.

It should be noted, however, that the principle of plenitude and that of continuity were not necessarily coimplicated. If the principle of plenitude were combined with the principle of levels and the principle of continuity were excluded, then logically one could arrive at the notion of a world of maximum diversity whose phenomena could be arranged in an infinite series without intermediate links between the various forms. Thus, while all three principles may be logically harmonized with one another, they need not be, and as a matter of historical fact have not always been, so combined. One could stress, as the Romanticists did, the principle of maximum diversity (plenitude) at the expense of the principle of continuity; or else, one may ignore the principle of levels and end up with an infinite continuum lacking in discrete levels. I feel compelled to disagree, therefore, with Love-

[35] Lovejoy, *The Great Chain of Being,* pp. 240–41.

joy's conclusion in *The Great Chain of Being* [36] to the effect that "the principles of plenitude and continuity—though the latter was supposed to be implied by the former—were also at variance with one another." Lovejoy distinguishes only the two principles of plenitude and continuity but does not differentiate the hierarchical principle of levels from that of continuity. That is why he sees an inner contradiction between the postulate of continuity and that of maximum plenitude and concludes that "the history of the idea of the Chain of Being—insofar as that idea presupposed such a complete rational intelligibility of the world—is the history of a failure." [37] My conclusion is that the metaphysics of the classical philosophers is not incoherent and does not suffer from an inner contradiction in its basic principles.

It should be noted, furthermore, that the principle of levels and the principle of plenitude are compatible with either a static metaphysics, in which time is secondary, or with a dynamic cosmology, in which time and temporal process are paramount. Thus, the levels of reality and the plenitude of being as viewed by the Neo-Platonists, such as Plotinus, was a purely logical scheme in which the lower levels were conceived through and as emanating from the higher and ultimately from "the One," which is highest. Similarly, in the cosmology of medieval thought, as developed by St. Augustine, Maimonides, and St. Thomas, the cosmos is conceived as created by God *ex nihilo* so as to manifest plenitude and hierarchical levels of being. The concept of "angels" was found compatible with the principle of plenitude, since they represented a level of pure, though finite, intelligence, above that of man, but below that of God. [38] Perhaps the outstanding example of the metaphysics of the plenitude of being in its static form is that of Spinoza, who combines in his philosophy. elements of Neo-Platonism, Aristotelian scholastic philosophy, and speculations derived from the new cosmology of the Renaissance. Spinoza's attempt to conceive all things through God or nature (*natura naturans*) may be interpreted as a "Copernican revolution" whereby all the levels of natural phenomena are conceived from the perspective of the supreme being rather than from the finite anthropocentric perspective of man. [39]

Similarly, the great chain of being was conceived as the product of a temporal process. [40] The ground for this approach was prepared by

---

[36] Page 332.          [37] *Ibid.*, p. 329.          [38] *Ibid.*, p. 80.
[39] Bidney, *The Psychology and Ethics of Spinoza.*
[40] Lovejoy, *The Great Chain of Being*, ch. ix.

critical rationalists, such as Voltaire, who questioned the widespread belief that nature was actually organized according to the principles of continuity and plenitude. As against this belief, it was argued that some species were now extinct and that others were in process of extinction. A clear distinction was drawn between actual empirical continuity in nature and merely speculative imaginary notions of natural and supernatural forms of being. In fact, the skeptics indicated, there do seem to be leaps in nature and the assumption of a continuous scale of being is nothing but a product of "presumptuous imagination."

From a metaphysical perspective, the Hebrew-Christian conception of a creator who made the world in time and who intervenes in human affairs led logically to the idea of a linear theory of time according to which there was room for actual historical novelty. A distinction was drawn between the ideally possible and the actually existent forms of nature, and the idea was advanced that not all that was possible or conceivable by the divine intelligence necessarily existed at one time. The principles of continuity and plenitude were understood by eighteenth-century writers, such as Leibnitz and Kant, as regulative ideal possibilities, whose verification was assured in the course of time because of divine providence and omnipotence, but which were not actually realized in nature at any given time. According to Leibnitz, nature is always increasing in perfection and there is a creative advance of nature in time.

It should be noted that the temporalization of the chain of being according to the principles of levels, continuity, and plenitude was quite compatible with the idea of fixed species. All that the doctrine of continuous creation in time implied was that nature was not a finished, perfect product once created by God, but rather an essentially unfinished, imperfect product which is forever being augmented and changed so as to allow for a maximum of kinds and degrees of being.

Of the two principles, continuity and plenitude, the former proved the more significant for the development of the modern theory of evolution. On the whole, the principle of plenitude tended to stimulate speculative cosmological thought as to the infinity of the forms of being and the existence of other worlds, thereby also promoting mythological fancies concerning the actual existence of creatures for which there was no empirical evidence—for example, mermaids. Metaphysically, the principle of plenitude led to the concept of a "block universe" wherein time was of secondary importance, since it was assumed that all possible forms of being were actually in existence as a consequence of divine omnipotence—for example, in the philosophy of Spinoza. By contrast, the principle of continuity, as formulated by Leibnitz, was subject to empirical verification and led to the quest for "missing links" between the known species of nature. Between the modes, or species, of being there was no impassable gulf, but only differences of degree from the lowest to the highest forms. In the biology of the eighteenth century, acceptance of the principle of continuity led Buffon to formulate the idea of "intermediate species, belonging half in one class and half in the other." [41]

Once the Aristotelian theory of the fixity of species was abandoned, the way was prepared for the concept of the evolution of forms of being in accordance with the principle of a hierarchical continuum. Thus, John Locke, in his *Essay concerning the Human Understanding*, denied that man has any knowledge of "real essences" and concluded that our conceptions of species are merely "nominal essences," which do not correspond to any fixed natural boundaries in natural species.[42] Logically, also, the principle of continuity *per se* implies that there are intermediate species which participate in two forms of being, so that there can be no precise, clear-cut distinction or division into species— a point Buffon made in his *Histoire naturelle*. It was not however, until the principle of the hierarchical continuum was combined with the hypothesis of a temporal natural process that the evolutionary principle of the transformation of species was formulated. Leibnitz, in particular, made explicit suggestions as to the possible transformation of the species of animals. The philosopher Schelling also conceived the chain of being as subject to a universal evolutionary process of becoming.

This faith in the continuity of natural forms was also a stimulus to the development of a science of physical anthropology. As Lovejoy has observed,[43]

But the program of discovering the hitherto unobserved links in the chain played a part of especial importance in the beginnings of the science of anthropology. The close similarity in skeletal structure between the apes and man had early been made familiar; yet careful zoologists recognized apparent solutions of continuity, anatomical as well as psychological, in this region of the series. Leibnitz and Locke had asserted a greater degree of continuity than could yet be actually exhibited at this important point. It therefore be-

[41] Lovejoy, *The Great Chain of Being*, p. 230.
[42] *Ibid.*, pp. 228–29.  [43] *Ibid.*, pp. 233–34.

came the task of science at least to increase the *rapprochement* of man and ape.

Hence, there was a growing interest in the characteristics of the "savage races," to determine whether they were identical anatomically with the civilized races or, perhaps, constituted a lower, intermediate stage of life between man and the apes. Rousseau and Monboddo went so far as to assert that man and the higher apes were of the same species.

It follows from the foregoing analysis that the postulate of levels of reality is independent of a theory of evolution which may be introduced to explain the order of their emergence in time. According to classical metaphysics, the lower form was understood as derived from or produced by the higher, since it was assumed that the efficient cause could not be less perfect than its effects. The modern theory of evolution is in this respect the exact antithesis of the classical theory, and postulates that the higher level is to be derived from the lower. Insofar as the principle of the levels of natural phenomena is based on empirical evidence its validity is independent of any ontological theories concerning the actual process by which this order of levels has been brought about.

The theory of evolution may itself be interpreted ontologically in various ways. Thus, if one stresses the principle of continuity and denies that there are any leaps or discontinuities in nature, then one is led logically to deny disparate kinds of being. One is then led to postulate a "qualitative continuum," such that all members share essential qualities in common, while differing only in degree of complexity from one another. Ultimately, this may lead to the concept of a single prototype, or "Urbild"—a hypothesis advanced by J. B. Robinet, Goethe, and Herder.[44] In other terms, if one adheres exclusively to the principle of continuity one is inevitably led to a monistic type of metaphysics which envisages all phenomena as modes or modifications of a single kind of substance. Thus, the process of evolution may be understood in terms of either a materialistic or an idealistic metaphysics. The materialist reduces all mental phenomena to functions of matter; all so-called higher levels or phenomena are merely "epiphenomena," having no independent functions of their own. Similarly, the idealist reduces the physical phenomena of nature to objectifications of mind. On this basis, the principle of hierarchical levels of phenomena is

[44] *Ibid.*, pp. 278–80.

explained away as an appearance incompatible with the principle of continuity.

On the other hand, if one were to begin with the postulate of discrete levels of reality which are independent of and have nothing in common with one another, then one could conceive a theory of emergent evolution according to which new levels of phenomena supervene upon one another without being affected by the lower level from which they emerged. According to this approach, the origin of a phenomenon and its actual form and value are independent of one another. Thus, William James argued in his *Varieties of Religious Experience* as against the "medical materialists" that the validity of religious experience is independent of the state of one's physical health. Similarly, one may speculate, as Alexander does in his *Space, Time and Deity*, on the emergent categories of reality, such as life, mind and deity, without bothering how the levels of reality may be interrelated empirically. Obviously, a theory of emergent evolution on a cosmic scale has much in common with the classical metaphysical scales of being which were also conceived as a series of hierarchical forms of being subsisting independently of one another.

Finally, one may interpret the theory of evolution, as I should be inclined to do, as involving a metaphysical pluralism which would allow for disparate forms of being, while adhering to the principle of continuity. This would mean accepting the postulate of actual empirical levels of phenomena, together with the necessary intrinsic relations of higher and lower phenomena.

There is a relation of polarity between the higher and the lower levels of phenomena, such that while each level is dependent upon the other, it also enjoys a measure of independence or autonomy. The concept of evolution thus involves a synthesis of opposites, the principles of continuity and discontinuity, dependence and independence, common elements and qualitative novelty. Evolution involves a hierarchical continuum; it is a process involving new forms of being supervening upon the "material" provided by the lower levels. There is, so to speak, discontinuity-in-continuity. If the history of the principles of levels, continuity, and plenitude may be said to have taught us anything, it is that any one principle taken in abstraction from the others ultimately leads to a denial of those others. Thus, if one take the principle of continuity alone, one would soon become involved in the paradoxes of Zeno as to the infinity of stages between any discrete phenomena, so that it becomes difficult to conceive any genuine qualitative disparateness. The principle of continuity, apart from the postulate of levels and diversity, soon leads to the reduction of all qualitative differences to a single kind of reality, whether it be materialistic, idealistic, or hylozoistic. This may be termed "the fallacy of reductionism." Similarly, if one were to take the principle of plenitude alone, one would be led to assume a multitude of discrete entities unrelated to one another. This may be termed "the nominalistic fallacy," since this approach implies that universals are but names and that there is no ontological basis for relations among things. Finally, if one consider the principle of levels alone, one assumes a series of discrete forms of being unrelated to one another. This may be termed "the fallacy of formalism," since forms of being are not related to the actual processes of nature. The theory of emergent evolution which I propose synthesizes all three principles by limiting the role of each in relation to the others.

Evolution is possible because there is continuity in the development of natural forms combined with the emergence of novelties, or qualitative variations. There is neither absolute continuity nor absolute discontinuity, but a hierarchical continuum of limited possibilities evolving in the process of time. Evolution is not a completely intelligible process, for we do not explain by reference to it why and how it is possible for new variations to emerge; all we can say is that they are "spontaneous" and "chance variations," which is but another way of saying that we do not know how they originate. All the scientist can do is to trace the known conditions and interrelations of the various kinds of phenomena without presuming to have explained thereby the entire course of nature. Our human rationality is in the last resort grounded in the given irrationality of nature as we find it. An empirical approach to nature requires that we seek to understand the phenomena of nature as given in all their complexity and interrelatedness and that we do not explain away any of the data of experience in order to obtain a simple coherent theory. For the penalty of ignoring the data and postulates of experience, such as the effective relations between all levels of phenomena, is that human thought becomes the victim of its own abstractions and ends by denying the dynamic possibilities of nature and life which it was originally called upon to explain and guide.

## 5. THE METHODOLOGICAL AUTONOMY OF LEVELS OF PHENOMENA

What is significant in the theory of the classification of the sciences in modern times, as exemplified by Comte and Spencer, is that the attempt was deliberately made to break away from the old ontological classification of the sciences, inherited from Plato and Aristotle, and to provide instead a purely empirical classification. According to Comte, the inorganic, physical sciences deal with the most simple and universal phenomena. Next, the biological sciences, which presuppose the phenomena of the physical sciences, are more particular and complex. Finally come the social sciences, which presuppose the data of the organic sciences. Similarly, Spencer distinguished three levels of phenomena, namely, the inorganic, the organic, and the superorganic or social. For Spencer superorganic phenomena were but extensions of organic phenomena into the social sphere, and hence the former were not intelligible apart from a knowledge of the kinds of organisms involved in any particular type of superorganic process.

Methodologically, the principle of the hierarchical, empirical classification of the sciences requires that we distinguish "the necessary condition" from "the sufficient cause." The lower level of phenomena is the necessary condition for the actualization of the higher level, but the higher level is not thereby "explained" by or deduced from the lower. For practical purposes the phenomena of a higher level may be studied provisionally "as though" they were independent of the lower level until a synoptic view of the interrelations between the levels can be achieved. The higher level is not reduced to the lower because of any demonstration of the common elements it shares with the latter.

The fact remains that the higher level manifests empirical functions and powers, that is, dimensions of reality, not to be found in the lower levels. In the course of scientific development the principle of continuity leads to the discovery of intermediate disciplines, such as biochemistry, which combine the techniques and data of two disciplines. The interdependence of the levels of natural phenomena implies that no level is in fact completely intelligible apart from reference to the levels below it. Physical and chemical phenomena are most closely related, but biological and biochemical processes now seem to be inseparably connected also. Similarly, it is to be expected that with the development of psychosomatic medicine we shall learn more about the interdependence of psychological, cultural, and biological phenomena.

At each level we may begin with the postulation of certain data which cannot be deduced from the lower levels. As a methodological device, or fiction, it may be pragmatically useful to study the phenomena of a given science "as if" they were independent of other levels. This is particularly easy for physicists, chemists, and biologists, who deal with disparate objects which may be segregated for special treatment. The problem becomes more difficult in the case of psychologists who wish to study psychological phenomena to the exclusion of biological processes, since the two sets of data obviously pertain to the same object. Similarly, sociologists and anthropologists, who are interested in social behavior and its products, cannot investigate their data except by reference to actual human organisms. That is, psychological, sociological, and cultural phenomena do not exist independently, and hence may not be said to constitute distinct ontological levels or to be conceived through themselves alone. Methodologically it is possible to abstract the latter phenomena and to treat them temporarily "as if" they were independent of the organisms upon which they depend.

In his paper "Sociology and Psychology," [45] published originally in 1916, Rivers argued for an independent science of sociology which, though ultimately related to the data of psychology, may provisionally be pursued independently. While he grants that the final aim of the study of society is the explanation of social behavior in terms of psychology,[46] he asserts that as a matter of method the two disciplines must be kept apart, since there is the danger of mistaking the assumptions of one science for genuine explanations. "It is just because it is at present so difficult to distinguish between cause and effect that each science should at present be followed so far as possible as though it were an independent discipline." [47] In his earlier lectures, *Kinship and Social Organization*, Rivers had demonstrated also by reference to his ethnological research that the social facts of relationship in primitive societies were to be explained by antecedent social conditions, not, as Kroeber at that time maintained, by linguistics and psychology.[48]

Rivers was in effect making two distinct points, although neither he nor his contemporaries clearly differentiated them. First, he was arguing for the methodological provisional independence of a science of sociology from social psychology, while granting that social phenomena are actually epistemic abstractions from the total psychosocial situation. Sociology was to be treated "as though" it were an independent

[45] Rivers, "Sociology and Psychology," in *Psychology and Ethnology.*
[46] *Ibid.*, p. 5.  [47] *Ibid.*, p. 6.
[48] *Kinship and Social Organization*, p. 92; Kroeber, "Classificatory Systems of Relationship," *Journal Royal Anthropological Institute*, XXXIX (1909), 77–84; also Kroeber, "The Morals of Uncivilized People," *American Anthropologist*, XII (1910), 437–47.

discipline, because of the uncertainty of the conclusions and results of the psychology then available, but this purely pragmatic separation did not preclude future close connections. Secondly, in his lectures on *Kinship and Social Organization* he maintained the more radical thesis that the general character, as well as the details of systems, of relationship and classification in primitive societies has been strictly determined by social conditions and that psychological "interpolations" do not serve to explain the nature and variety of these social phenomena. As he put it: "These psychological elements are, however, only concomitants of social processes with which it is possible to deal apart from their psychological aspect." [49] In this respect Rivers adhered to the earlier position of Morgan and McLennan that the nature of the classificatory systems to be found in primitive societies had been determined by antecedent social conditions, as against Kroeber's argument in his earlier paper that the mode of using terms of relationship depends entirely on linguistic and psychological factors. In his insistence upon the autonomy of social phenomena and their independence of psychological phenomena, Rivers went beyond the purely pragmatic argument he advanced later. The thesis of the provisional methodological separation of sociology from social psychology was justified on empirical grounds as a means of ensuring scientific accuracy in explanation. The thesis of the factual independence of sociology from psychology went beyond the empirical evidence; it converted a provisional *de facto* separation into a *de jure* ontological independence.

In other words, Rivers did not distinguish clearly between the empirical and the methodological problems of the classification of the sciences, on the one hand, and the metaphysical, problem of the relation and number of the various levels of reality, on the other. The proposition that psychological elements were only the concomitants of social processes which could be understood apart from their psychological aspects was a logical generalization which went beyond the empirical facts available to Rivers. It implied an ontological separation of levels of phenomena which was equivalent to a declaration of independence.

When we turn again to Kroeber's paper on "The Superorganic," we can discern a similar ontological argument with reference to the concept of culture, but expressed far more distinctly. According to Kroeber the level of "social" phenomena involves a "leap to another

[49] *Kinship and Social Organization*, p. 92.

plane," to a new emergent level of reality which has nothing in common with the inorganic and organic levels. Historically Kroeber may be thought of as having accepted Rivers's earlier criticism of his attempt to explain kinship terms by reference to psychological motivations and linguistic usages and, in agreement with the latter, to have accepted also a rigid determinism of social phenomena. Apparently they differed to the extent that Rivers still adhered to Spencer's position that the sphere of the social comprises the actual behavior, the processes, as well as the products, of social interaction, while Kroeber identified the sphere of social phenomena with the mental, cultural products of social interaction.

Thus, Kroeber came to regard the abstract mental products of society, which he called culture, or civilization, as a reality *sui generis*, subject to autonomous historical processes of development which were independent of psychological experience and actual social behavior. He thereby converted an epistemic, or methodological, abstraction into a distinct ontological entity, which he understood as an independent emergent level of reality, no longer subject to natural selection and the laws of organic evolution, but subject instead to an equally rigid historical determinism of its own. This I venture to call the *culturalistic fallacy*. The culturalistic fallacy may be said to be committed when one defines culture as an ideational abstraction and then proceeds to convert or reify this *ens rationis* into an independent ontological entity subject to its own laws of development and conceived through itself alone. No fallacy is committed simply in abstracting cultural products or achievements from the context of social behavior in which they originate; this is legitimate and often pragmatically useful. The culturistic fallacy is committed only when this logical abstraction comes to be regarded as if it actually were a reality *sui generis*, a superpsychic, supersocial entity independent of man, individually and collectively. The culturalistic fallacy is the result of "elevating" a pure form or abstraction to the level of a substantial natural force which is self-explanatory and ontologically self-sufficient—a procedure which is reminiscent of the Platonic doctrine of transcendental Forms of Ideas, which were also supposed to subsist independently of individual minds and particular natural phenomena.

The culturalistic fallacy may be best understood as the opposite of the "naturalistic fallacy," which consists of the attempt to "reduce" cultural phenomena to the level of the organic and the psychological.

Thus, the Lamarckian doctrine of the inheritance of acquired characteristics exemplified by Freud's theory of the primal horde and the Oedipus complex, the notion of determinate, innate national characters of Le Bon, as well as that of a racial unconscious mind, as in Jung's theory of myth, are examples or products of the naturalistic fallacy, since such characteristics may be better accounted for in terms of historically acquired cultural properties which may vary with time and circumstances. In seeking to avoid the naturalistic fallacy of organic determinism of cultural characteristics, Kroeber and those of his generation who shared his theory of the autonomy of culture went to the opposite extreme and committed the culturalistic fallacy by hypostatizing culture into a historical superpsychic reality independent alike of individual initiative and of collective human efforts.

Kroeber's paper on "The Superorganic" has since become a classic in American anthropological literature, and his term "superorganic," rather than Spencer's term, has achieved recognition among American scholars, although British anthropologists, such as Radcliffe-Brown, still adhere to the Spencerian usage.[50] It should be noted, however, in fairness to Kroeber, that the essentials of his concept of culture were shared by other American anthropologists of his generation who were students of Boas, as he was. What I find original with Kroeber at this stage is that he was the first to formulate a theory of the emergent evolution of cultural phenomena and a deterministic philosophy of culture history which Boas and most of his other students did not share. It is significant that among Boas's students, Sapir, Goldenweiser, Swanton, and others openly criticized Kroeber's concept of the cultural superorganic when his paper was originally published.[51] Their common criticism was to the effect that there was no chasm between the social and the psychic, between social culture and the individual, and that it was self-contradictory to exclude man himself from the study of culture history. This professed criticism did not, however, prevent them from continuing to refer to culture as a reality *sui generis* and to cultural method as constituting a closed system intelligible through itself alone. Among contemporary anthropologists, Lévi-Strauss, White, and Hoebel may be cited as "culturologists" who still adhere to Kroe-

[50] Radcliffe-Brown, "Evolution, Social or Cultural?" *American Anthropologist,* XLIX (1947), 78–83; also Bidney, "The Problem of Social and Cultural Evolution: a Reply to Radcliffe-Brown," *American Anthropologist,* XLIX (1947), 524–27.
[51] See especially *American Anthropologist,* Vol. XIX (1917), for criticisms of Kroeber's paper.

ber's original concept of the cultural superorganic, although in the revised edition of his *Anthropology* (1948) Kroeber himself, no longer adheres to the sharp antithesis between the organic and the superorganic which he formerly professed. Hoebel wrongly interprets the opposition to Kroeber's classic view of the superorganic "as a legacy of behaviorism in psychology." [52]

[52] Hoebel, *Man in the Primitive World*, p. 428.

# 3

# *Ethnology and Psychology*

THE FACT that all Kroeber's American contemporaries shared a common historical approach to cultural phenomena must, in the last analysis, be attributed to the common influence of Franz Boas, who literally dominated the field.

## 1. BOAS AND THE PSYCHOHISTORICAL APPROACH

Boas had undoubtedly stressed the importance of history in relation to culture and was steadfastly opposed to all forms of biological determinism, such as racism, as involving a confusion of biology and culture history. In *The Mind of Primitive Man* he set forth his conviction that there is no fundamental difference between the mind of primitive man and that of civilized man and that whatever differences exist between the achievements of different races could be accounted for on historical grounds rather than in terms of innate biological differences. He was, in fact, opposed to all forms of absolute determinism, whether biological, geographical, or historical, and wished to allow scope for the complexity of causal factors, as well as for the "laws of chance," in culture history. According to Boas, "The whole problem of the development of culture is therefore reduced to the study of psychological and social conditions which are common to mankind as a whole, and to the effects of historical happenings and of natural and cultural environment." [1]

Boas was strongly opposed to the unilinear theory of cultural evolution because it tended to presuppose a priori psychological determinism which he thought was not substantiated by empirical studies of actual primitive societies. "There is no reason," he argued, "that would compel us to believe that technical inventions, social organization, art and religion develop in precisely the same way or are organically and indissolubly connected." [2] It seemed obvious to him that "innumerable accidental causes intervene which cannot be predicted and which

[1] *The Mind of Primitive Man*, p. 33.  [2] *Ibid.*, p. 155.

can not be reconstructed as determining the course of the past." [3] He was, therefore, equally opposed to a culturological, historical determinism, such as Kroeber's, which excluded the psychological motivations and reactions of the individual, as well as any form of biological and geographical determinism.

## 2. LOWIE ON "CULTURE AND ETHNOLOGY"

Among the former students of Boas, Lowie tends to approximate most closely the former's basic position. It is, therefore, of special interest to examine some of his early writings with a view to indicating the common cultural approach of this period and the reasons which led him and Kroeber, among others, to stress the self-explanatory nature of cultural phenomena.

In his public lectures on *Culture and Ethnology* Lowie maintained that while a certain type of organic basis was an absolute prerequisite of human culture there had been no essential change in the human organism during the historic period and that therefore the universal organic nature of man cannot serve to explain the diversity of historic human cultures. Nevertheless, he concedes that while there is no proportional relation between race and culture, a relatively minute change of hereditary ability might produce enormous cultural differences. "This," he remarks, "is only a special form of the Darwinian doctrine of the survival value of small variations, applied not to the question of the struggle for existence, but to the creation of new cultural values." [4] This would seem to suggest that there is no absolute divorce between the organic and the cultural levels of phenomena, since slight organic variations do give rise to such enormous cultural disparities.

Nevertheless, in discussing the relation of psychology to culture Lowie maintains that cultural facts may not be explained by psychological principles. As he puts it,

It is clear that cultural phenomena contain elements that cannot be reduced to psychological principles. The reason for the insufficiency is already embodied in Tylor's definition of culture as embracing "capabilities and habits *acquired* by man as a member of society." The science of psychology, even in its most modern ramifications of abnormal psychology and the study of individual variations, does not grapple with *acquired* mental traits nor with the influence of *society* on individual thought, feeling and will. It deals on principle exclusively with innate traits of the *individual*.[5]

[3] *Ibid.*, p. 176.      [4] Lowie, *Culture and Ethnology*, p. 42.
[5] *Ibid.*, p. 16.

In other words, according to Lowie culture is a historically acquired, socially determined phenomenon, whereas psychology is limited, by his definition, to the study of the innate traits of the individual; culture is a product of social interaction, while psychological phenomena are innate, organic, essentially individual characteristics. Hence, there can be nothing in common between cultural and psychological phenomena. Culture is therefore said to be "a thing *sui generis* that demands for its investigation a distinct science." [6] The similarity to Kroeber's position is obvious and suggests a common source of influence in Spencer, Boas, Rivers, and Durkheim. Lowie, however, is careful to point out that he is opposed to the tendency to completely separate psychology and ethnology.[7] Psychology can provide us with a knowledge of the concomitants, or some of the conditions for the emergence, of specific cultural phenomena, since cultural facts must not contravene psychological principles.[8] Nevertheless, "The 'capabilities and habits acquired by man as a member of society' constitute a distinct aspect of reality that must be the field of a distinct science autonomous with reference to psychology." [9]

The motivation behind Lowie's argument is his fear that if he grants that psychology is qualified to explain cultural phenomena, then the latter would be "reduced" to psychological phenomena. It is this fear of reducing cultural phenomena to the lower level of the psychological which led him, as it led Kroeber and Rivers, to postulate the autonomy of the higher level. The alternatives, as they were commonly envisaged at the time, seemed to be either "reduction" or "autonomy." The doctrine of evolution, as well as empirical observation of natural phenomena, suggested the notion of distinct levels of phenomena which were qualitatively different and irreducible. Hence, it was argued, the fallacy to be avoided at all costs was reductionism. Each basic science was thought to deal with an autonomous level of reality and to be understood through itself alone. Thus, instead of the continuity of natural phenomena which the Darwinian theory of evolution suggested, sociologists and anthropologists emphasized the discontinuity of cultural phenomena. This was clearly formulated by Kroeber, as we have seen, into a theory of the emergence of a new level or plane of reality, at least so far as social or cultural achievements were concerned.

---

[6] Lowie, *Culture and Ethnology*, p. 17.     [7] *Ibid.*
[8] *Ibid.*, p. 25.     [9] *Ibid.*, p. 26.

Thus, Lowie concludes:

Psychology, racial differences, geographical environment, have all proved inadequate for the interpretation of cultural phenomena. The inference is obvious. Culture is a thing *sui generis* which can be explained only in terms of itself. This is not mysticism but sound scientific method. The biologist, whatever metaphysical speculations he may indulge in as to the ultimate origin of life, does not depart in his workaday mood from the principle that every cell is derived from some other cell. So the ethnologist will do well to postulate the principle, *omnis cultura ex cultura.* This means that he will account for a given cultural fact by merging it in a group of cultural facts or by demonstrating some other cultural fact out of which it has developed. The cultural phenomena to be explained may either have an antecedent within the culture of the tribe where it is found or it may have been imported from without. Both groups of determinants must be considered.[10]

Culture thus appears as a closed system. We may not be able to explain all cultural phenomena or at least not beyond a certain point; but inasmuch as we can explain them at all, explanation must remain on the cultural plane.[11]

Here Lowie has presented us with a clear analysis of the logical presuppositions underlying the theory of the autonomy of cultural phenomena. It is significant that in a footnote reference is made to Rivers's lectures on *Kinship and Social Organization* [12] in support of his thesis that social or cultural phenomena are to be explained in terms of antecedent cultural conditions. I find in Lowie's work the first explicit expression of the postulate *omnis cultura ex cultura,* together with the corollary that culture is to be understood as "a closed system." The basic thesis is, however, shared by Rivers and Kroeber.

Lowie did not accept the strict cultural and historical determinism postulated by Rivers and Kroeber. Like Boas, he, too, made allowance for purely contingent, unpredictable events and factors in culture history. We find him stating:

That a particular innovation occurred at a given time and place is, of course, no less the result of definite causes than any other phenomenon of the universe. But often it seems to have been caused by an accidental complex of conditions rather than in accordance with some fixed principle. . . . A given culture is, in a measure, at least, a unique phenomenon. In so far as this is true it must defy generalized treatment, and the explanation of a cultural phenomenon will consist in referring it back to the particular circumstances that preceded it. In other words, the explanation will consist in a recital of its past history; or, to put it negatively, it cannot involve the

[10] *Ibid.,* p. 66.     [11] *Ibid.,* p. 95.     [12] Page 92.

assumption of an organic law of cultural evolution that would necessarily produce the observed effect.[13]

Lowie, it appears, appreciated the point that the theory of strict cultural determinism involved the assumption of an "organic law" of cultural evolution, and he would, therefore, have none of it. Instead, he insisted, as did Boas, upon the historical uniqueness of given cultures owing to the accidental complex of conditions which happened to prevail at a given time and place. So far as he could see, there was no a priori necessity for given cultural innovations. It is, however, difficult to reconcile Lowie's thesis that culture constitutes a "closed system" and that culture is a thing *sui generis* with his "open" theory of culture history and the uniqueness of each culture.

He was doubtless convinced, as Rivers had shown with reference to kinship terminology and social organization, that there may be a "functional relation" between cultural phenomena which renders intelligible some degree of parallelism of cultural development in different parts of the world. He was, therefore, concerned to find some way of reconciling "the principle that a cultural phenomenon is explicable only by a unique combination of antecedent circumstances with the principle that like phenomena are the product of like antecedents." [14] His thesis is that "in either case we have past history as the determinant." That is, for unique cultural phenomena or for a unique culture as a whole we must seek some unique historical antecedents, and for similar or recurrent culture complexes we require general historical antecedents. These general "historical" antecedents may, however, differ in degrees of generality and hence in the number and kinds of phenomena which are explained by them. As an example of this kind of explanatory principle Lowie cites "the tendency of age-mates to flock together," which has given rise to corresponding social organizations throughout the world.[15] Other examples are "the rationalistic explanation of what reason never gave rise to" [16] and "cultural inertia, or survival."

Upon closer examination it turns out that these causal, or determining, principles of explanation are really psychological, not "historical" and cultural, although they are expressed in a cultural context. There is nothing historical about the tendency of age-mates to flock together; it is a purely psychological tendency, based upon mutual recognition

[13] Lowie, *Culture and Ethnology*, pp. 82–83.      [14] *Ibid.*, p. 90.
[15] *Ibid.*, p. 92.                                   [16] *Ibid.*, p. 94.

of similar interests, which provides the stimulus for the formation of a
specific type of social organization. Similarly, the rationalistic explanation of nonrational customs and rituals is a psychological fact of
human nature, although the particular form which the rationalization
may take depends upon the given cultural and social context. In like
manner cultural survival, or inertia, is a psychological postulate and
refers to man's irrational preference for indigenous culture traits and
traditional customs. Finally, when Lowie refers to the principle of
selection as a tendency whereby "the preexisting cultural pattern synthesizes the new element with its own preconceptions," [17] it becomes
obvious that he is attributing to abstract culture patterns a psychological ability to synthesize cultural traits.

Apparently, therefore, in his general type of explanation Lowie did
introduce purely psychological principles as causes and determining
factors of general cultural tendencies. By not distinguishing clearly
between psychological postulates and tendencies, on the one hand, and
the historical, cultural context in which these psychological factors
manifested themselves, on the other, he continued to speak and think
as if culture, or culture history, were a "closed system" in which the
explanation of cultural phenomena always remained on the cultural
plane. It seems fair to say that Lowie tended to "reduce" social psychology to the level of culture history, since he limited psychology, by a
priori definition, to innate and individual phenomena. Any tendencies
such as the flocking together of age-mates, rationalization, inertia, and
selection were interpreted by him as general "historical," or antecedent,
cultural principles, although no modern psychologist would exclude
them from the sphere of psychology.

In his study *Primitive Religion* Lowie returned to the problem of the
relation of history and psychology. We now find him writing:

Sometimes the historical and the psychological point of view are contrasted
as if they were necessarily antithetical. Nothing is further from the truth. The
psychological facts of religion are the most fundamental that a history of
religion can deal with; without them, indeed, such a history would be well-
nigh meaningless. On the other hand, it is equally true that an insight into
the psychology of religious phenomena is impossible without reference to the
conditions that preceded and accompanied them.[18]

He now recognizes the "interdependence of psychological and historical factors on higher levels of civilization." [19] Religious phenomena

[17] *Ibid.*          [18] Lowie, *Primitive Religion,* p. 185.          [19] *Ibid.,* p. 188.

may not be deduced from inborn instincts and cannot be understood apart from objective cultural and historical conditions. "The path to psychology," he concludes, "lies through history." [20] One cannot understand the psychological reactions of an individual or group, so far as religion is concerned, apart from a knowledge of the historical and cultural conditions which underlie them. Lowie, it appears, eventually modified the sharp antithesis between culture history and psychology which he, in common with others, had maintained in his *Culture and Ethnology*. Religious phenomena are seen to be neither purely psychological nor purely cultural, but a complex of psychological and historicocultural factors. Lowie did not, however, resolve the problem of the relation of ethnology and psychology.

What was required, but was lacking at the time, was a concept such as "ethnopsychology" to indicate the synthesis of psychological and cultural factors. The difficulty under which Lowie labored was one which he shared with his contemporaries and immediate predecessors. Thus, William James, in his *Varieties of Religious Experience*, goes to the opposite extreme in reducing the varieties of religious phenomena to those of psychology, since he, for his part, had not yet recognized the distinctness of the cultural factor in psychological experience. According to James, "religion . . . shall mean for us the feelings, acts and experiences of individual men in their solitude, so far as they apprehend themselves to stand in relation to whatever they may consider the divine." [21] James, it seems, tended to abstract the psychological individual from his sociocultural environment, as if psychological phenomena could be understood apart from cultural ones. He maintained explicitly that the origin of a religious phenomenon and its present value, or significance, were independent of one another and therefore felt justified in excluding all data of culture history as irrelevant to an understanding of the psychology of religious experience. In this respect James anticipated the functionalistic, pragmatic attitude of the functionalists in ethnology, who also tended to ignore the historical background of cultural phenomena. Lowie's approach in his *Primitive Religion* is the antithesis of that of James in that the former gives primary consideration to the historicocultural factors as determinants of religious experience, while granting that psychological experiences and motivations are involved. The two disparate approaches

[20] Lowie, *Primitive Religion*, p. 204.
[21] *Varieties of Religious Experience*, pp. 31–32.

may be harmonized logically in terms of an ethnopsychology which would investigate the interrelation of cultural and psychological factors in any given culture.

The reason why Lowie failed to recognize the role of psychology in his *Culture and Ethnology* was his conviction that culture constituted a closed system. As against this thesis, one can argue that if culture originated in time and is not eternal, then it cannot be a closed system analogous to a circle. Human culture, like human history in general, has a beginning, and ultimately we must turn to man, to human nature as the active, efficient cause of cultural phenomena and the limiting condition for the emergence of a specifically human form of culture. The notion of a closed culture system, far from being self-intelligible, is in the long run unintelligible. For the short run, it is undoubtedly pragmatically useful, and indeed necessary, to explain given cultural phenomena through their proximate social, cultural, and historical conditions. But if we are to avoid the culturalistic fallacy, we must not be misled or tempted to convert this epistemic and methodological abstraction into an ontological principle which maintains the actual autonomy of cultural phenomena. Lowie recognized the close connection between the organic and the cultural factors in discussing the relation of culture and race, but this momentary insight apparently did not prevent him from adhering to the theory that cultural phenomena constitute a closed, self-intelligible system.

Furthermore, Lowie, in common with Kroeber and Rivers, tended to contrast the categories of the psychological and the individual, on the one hand, and the sociocultural, on the other, as if they were mutually exclusive. There is no logical basis, however, for identifying the social and the cultural to the exclusion of the individual. The individual is not merely the passive carrier of social culture; he is also an active agent in originating and modifying his culture. Similarly, we must not contrast the cultural and the psychological, since concrete subjective culture involves a synthesis of psychological and cultural factors. No single cultural phenomenon is intelligible in itself, since it always involves the union of a natural phenomenon with some historically acquired or initiated modification brought about through the agency of man. The original source of the culturalistic fallacy is the attempt to identify culture exclusively with the "social products of mental exercise." This is an arbitrary procedure, since one deliberately abstracts the products of social behavior from the actual, social, psychological behavior which produced them and then reifies this social abstraction into an entity *sui generis* independent of man. It is a completely circular argument, first to abstract cultural ideas from their concrete cultural context and then to define culture as a logical construct or abstraction. Concrete human culture comprises, as Spencer and Rivers imply, the actual social behavior of man as well as the products of this behavior. In other words, culture has a subjective, as well as an objective, aspect, and there is no rational basis for maintaining that only the objective aspect, the cultural achievements or products, is culture, but not the subjective aspect, which includes all the historically acquired, actual forms of behavior and experience. On the other hand, it is nothing short of intellectual bias to identify culture with the ideational products of society to the exclusion of the concrete, actual modes of conduct and the socifacts and artifacts which are its direct products.

### 3. CLARK WISSLER ON "CULTURE AS HUMAN BEHAVIOR"

In his paper "Psychological and Historical Interpretations for Culture"[22] Clark Wissler, who was Lowie's chief at the American Museum of Natural History, provided a clear analysis of the relation of psychology and ethnology as it was understood at that time, which probably influenced Lowie's views. Psychology is said to deal with the innate, original nature of man, and cultural phenomena were defined as "the acquired activity complexes of human groups." Wissler was particularly concerned to fight the tendency to reduce culture to psychology by explaining cultural phenomena in terms of psychological principles. Psychology, he argued, will not tell us why any particular association of ideas is made by a particular individual and will not explain the origin of particular inventions, such as the bow, or of exogamy. That is, psychology deals with the universal and innate in human nature and may not therefore be employed to explain the particular and unique in human historical experience. Culture phenomena may be understood and explained only in terms of social history and are not to be deduced from universal psychological principles. The notion, therefore, of a psychology of religion, law, or sex restrictions is, according to Wissler, "worse than meaningless for they at once assert what is contradictory to psychology itself." The science of culture and that of psychology represent two distinct types of phenomena and require entirely disparate approaches. According to Wissler,

[22] *Science*, XLIII (1916), 193–201.

The point we are coming to is that the anthropological conception of culture is entirely consistent with the psychological view, for it asserts that neither mental bias nor biological attributes are of the least avail in explaining the origin of specific culture traits and that it is only when we know history of a case that we can give anything like an adequate account of its origin. It is thus clear that when we are dealing with phenomena that belong to original nature we are quite right in using psychological and biological methods but the moment we step over into cultural phenomena we must recognize its historical nature. This is why anthropologists object to much that passes for the psychology of religion, art etc. in which many of the results obtained by use of the historical method are put on a level with those obtained by other methods and then interpreted as facts of evolutionary or other non-learned activities.[23]

The alternatives originally envisaged by Wissler were, then, either some theory of innate ideas or psychic unity of mankind, such as Bastian and the classical evolutionists maintained, or else a complete separation of historicocultural phenomena from those of psychology. As against psychological determinism of culture, he accepted the thesis of historical contingency and "psychic accidents" in order to explain cultural invention and its development at a given time and place. Wissler was prepared to grant that underlying cultural phenomena were innate psychological "instincts" which motivated the origination of cultural phenomena, but these universal instincts failed to account for the diversity of cultural phenomena and their particular, unique forms of expression. Only history could explain what was unique in cultural phenomena. Psychology could render the best service to anthropology by clarifying the innate as distinct from the acquired elements in human behavior and providing a distinct empirical criterion for distinguishing psychological from cultural phenomena.

In *Man and Culture* Wissler went far toward demonstrating the close interrelation of psychology and ethnology and modified the sharp antithesis he had previously set up between the spheres and methods of these disciplines. In his chapter entitled "Culture as Human Behavior" he quotes from Lowie's *Culture and Ethnology* to the effect that "culture is a phenomenon in itself to be explained in terms of itself" and then adds this significant comment:

One can readily see the insufficiency of such an attitude, but we should not overlook the fact that the majority of anthropologists are hard-headed empiricists, who regard it as their job to record and describe the phenomena of culture and not be troubled with origins, processes and least of all, with

[23] *Ibid.*

laws. To suggest to them that the ideal objective of anthropology is a rational control of cultural processes is to invite derision. They regard theirs as a pure science, and leave to others the problems of the hour.[24]

Apparently, therefore, Wissler had come to recognize the "insufficiency" of completely separating cultural and psychological phenomena, and he was no longer prepared, as he had been a few years earlier, to insist upon the complete methodological autonomy of culture. In his *History of Ethnological Theory* [25] Lowie fails to take into consideration Wissler's modified views and continues to criticize him for a position he originally expressed in a paper of 1914. Wissler apparently anticipated Lowie's criticism by criticizing Lowie in advance.

According to Wissler's new view, the antithesis of the psychologically innate and the culturally learned breaks down when we consider the fact that man's "equipment for culture" is itself innate. In order to explain the origin of culture as a distinctively human phenomenon we must postulate innate psychological mechanisms which constitute man's primary equipment for culture. Man cannot respond to natural stimuli or acquire specific cultural traditions except within the limits of his innate equipment, though we still do not understand what these limits are.

Wissler now distinguishes between the universal cultural patterns and the particular, historical content with which these universal patterns are associated. The universal human cultural pattern is said to comprise speech, material traits (shelter, dress, tools, and so forth), art, mythology and scientific knowledge, religious practices, family and social systems, property, government, and war.[26] Within the limits of the culture pattern there is, however, room for infinite variations and expansions, and it is these historically acquired variations in content which distinguish one culture from another.[27] The origin of the culture pattern is explained by reference to man's innate equipment for culture, by his instincts and drives, which impel him to engage in cultural processes and to participate in the culture into which he is born. As Wissler puts it,

Man builds cultures because he cannot help it; there is a *drive* in his protoplasm that carries him forward even against his will. So it follows that, if at any time the continuity of culture were broken, the human group would begin to construct anew according to the old pattern.[28]

[24] Wissler, *Man and Culture*, p. 252.          [25] Page 263.
[26] *Ibid.*, p. 74.          [27] *Ibid.*, p. 79.          [28] *Ibid.*, p. 265.

There is cultural continuity because man is by nature equipped for and impelled to culture building and cannot help inventing culture forms according to predetermined patterns; cultural continuity is not // an accident of history, but a direct consequence of the psychobiological nature of man. Culture is not an "objective construct" whose existence is independent of man; it depends, rather, upon man's innate equipment and biological inheritance. As against the superorganic view of culture, Wissler maintains:

So any view that shuts its eyes to the biological basis for culture and especially to the reflective response, must be inadequate, for then we must conceive of culture as an extra-biological phenomenon that happened to get hitched on to the genus Homo instead of something else. And such, in fact, is the historical explanation theory when carried beyond its depth.[29]

An adequate theory of culture must explain the origin of culture and its intrinsic relations to the psychobiological nature of man. To insist upon the self-sufficiency and autonomy of culture, as if culture were a closed system requiring only historical explanations in terms of other cultural phenomena, is not to explain culture, but to leave its origin a mystery or an accident of time. The view of the superorganicists that culture is independent of the psychic nature of man and that man is but the carrier, or vehicle, of culture leaves unexplained the relation of man to culture. On the latter assumption, it would appear, as Wissler suggests, that the relation of man to culture is accidental, since culture is thought of as an "extra-biological phenomenon that happened to get hitched on to the genus Homo instead of something else." The notion that culture is a reality *sui generis,* a new emergent level of reality independent of man, makes man a contingent appendage to culture, since theoretically, on this assumption, any other animal would have done just as well. The significance of insisting upon the biological basis for culture patterns lies in the fact that it establishes the inherent, necessary relation between man and the universal pattern of human culture. While the innate original nature of man is not the only or a sufficient explanation of cultural phenomena, it does serve to explain the factors which determine the general pattern of culture, as distinguished, for example, from the pattern of behavior of the social insects. This view still leaves scope for the greatest variety in the contents of human cultures and allows one to take into consideration the conditioned re-

---

[29] *Ibid.,* p. 278.

sponses and the environmental influences, as well as other fortuitous causes which historical research may reveal.

As compared with Bastian, Wissler maintains that there are universal patterns of culture and universal psychological mechanisms or drives, but no universal innate *Elementargedanken*, or elementary ideas. They agree that there is a psychological determinism of culture, but differ in their interpretation of the psychological factor. The universal culture patterns are innate, or inborn, in the sense that they are a direct conse-quence of man's biological equipment. Thus, the antithesis between the innate psychological factors, on the one hand, and the acquired historical cultural phenomena, on the other, which Wissler, in common with Lowie and Kroeber, had previously upheld, is now seen to be invalid, since the potentiality for inventing culture patterns is not historically acquired, although the culture facts, the contents of cultures, are his-torically acquired, being "habits of response taken on by the individual himself together with those imposed by the tribe." [30] One may say, therefore, that psychology does determine culture directly, but only so far as the universal human pattern is concerned.

This does not imply a reduction of culture to psychology, since the specific content of culture is historically determined and may not be deduced from psychological principles. Put in Kantian terms, one may say that there is, according to Wissler, a universal cultural a priori as regards the universal forms of culture, but not as regards their contents. The human mind provides the form, pattern, or types of culture, but not the "stuff," or material content. Put in terms of logic, it may be said that Wissler recognized that there are cultural universals, as well as cultural particulars. Hence, the argument, which Wissler himself previously adduced, that culture deals with historical particulars, whereas psychology deals with the universals of human nature, is no longer tenable. Since there are cultural universals, one may, indeed must, introduce the necessary psychological principles to account for them. The notion of the "unity of the human mind," far from being ir-relevant to cultural explanations, is intrinsically relevant to the ex-planation of universal patterns, but not to particular cultural traits.

In introducing the notion of universal cultural patterns, Wissler im-plicitly introduced logical "realism" into the study of cultural phe-nomena and undermined the position of logical "nominalism" and the preoccupation with cultural historical particulars which he, in com-

[30] *Ibid.*

mon with others, had previously maintained. Both psychology and ethnology, he realized, deal with universal phenomena which may be causally interconnected, and the complete disparity which was supposed between the objects and the methods of these disciplines is no longer justified.

Furthermore, according to Wissler the psychobiological determinism of culture does not mean that culture is the direct product of unconscious, irrational, instinctive responses and acts. Following Boas, he maintains that there have been no significant changes in man's innate equipment or behavior since the dawn of the Paleolithic period and is therefore prepared to attribute rational reflective thought to early man. Man's rationality, which distinguishes man from the animals, consists primarily in his ability to reflect upon his own actions and feelings and to generalize upon his experiences. The initial step in the cultural process was the response of man's innate thinking mechanism. Wissler therefore dissents from the view that language and other traits of culture were well formed and their modes of social functioning established before any kind of reflective thinking was brought to bear upon these acts.[31] His main thesis is that "culture is an accumulative structure developed out of the reflective thinking of man." [32]

Wissler's thesis as to the innate, biological basis of culture led him to deny the prevalent view that culture was essentially a product of society and social intercourse and to maintain instead the individual basis of cultural phenomena. Since man is by nature a "culture builder," there is no foundation for the belief of the seventeenth- and eighteenth-century philosophers in a precultural "state of nature" followed by a politically instituted cultural state.[33] The nineteenth-century sociologists and anthropologists, such as Comte, Durkheim, Spencer, and Tylor, still continued to assume the essentially social origin of culture and therefore differentiated the sphere of the social, or cultural, from that of individual organic and psychic phenomena. According to Wissler's thesis, however, culture is grounded in the innate structure and functions of the human organism and its continuity depends, therefore, not upon society, but upon the individual acting in relation to other individuals. Cultural phenomena are said to be the unique achievements of human responses, especially of reflective thought, but this is not held to imply the independence of culture or its historical autonomy. Culture is developed in a social context, but is primarily the product of

[31] *Ibid.*, p. 276.      [32] *Ibid.*, p. 274.      [33] *Ibid.*, pp. 270–71.

individual effort and initiative. Otherwise, to begin with the logical priority of society and culture is to ignore the necessary biological basis of the cultural process. Seen from this perspective the later functionalism of Malinowski may be understood as an extreme expression of the view that culture is the product of the organic nature of man and that it originates as a response to human needs and desires. Malinowski, however, continued to refer to culture as a "reality *sui generis*," thereby failing to realize the incompatibility between the organic and the superorganic views of culture.[34]

## 4. THE ORGANIC VERSUS THE SUPERORGANIC THEORY OF CULTURE

In their attempt to counteract the reduction of cultural to psychological and organic phenomena, Boas and the members of what Goldenweiser has called "the American school of Historical Ethnology" put forward the postulate of the uniformity of human nature in historical times. Since, it was argued, human nature remains constant, one cannot deduce historical, contingent cultural phenomena from it. Human nature is one, but cultures are many. Hence, the earliest attempts were made to separate the sphere of psychology from that of culture. Psychology was said to deal with the non-temporal laws of human nature, while culture dealt with historical particular phenomena. The postulate of the identity of human nature and the psychic uniformity of man was also employed to demonstrate that the underlying psychological processes in primitive and civilized man were identical, notwithstanding the obvious disparity of cultural expressions. Cultural evolution, it was maintained, does not require a corresponding evolution in human mentality. The presence of universal patterns of culture was taken as evidence of psychic uniformity and the constancy of human nature.

Thus, the concept of the irreducibility of cultural phenomena had a twofold significance: it meant, first, that ethnology had a method of its own, namely, historical analysis as distinct from psychological or biological analysis; secondly, that the independence of cultural from organic phenomena was an argument against the theory of the evolutionists, which assumed natural laws of cultural development together with parallelism of stages of development for humanity as a whole. The first approach was methodological and epistemological, since it insisted upon the logical irreducibility of cultural phenomena and the epistemic fact that the latter could not be deduced from universal

[34] Malinowski, "Culture," in *Encyclopaedia of Social Sciences*, III, 621–45.

psychological or organic phenomena. The second approach was primarily ontological or metaphysical and led to the notion of the autonomy of culture as a level of phenomena *sui generis*.

The theory of linear cultural evolution through fixed parallel stages of development was based partly on the unfounded assumption that cultural evolution was based on biological evolution. Cultural evolution was simply organic evolution carried over into the sphere of the superorganic. And since biological evolution was thought to be gradual and progressive, leading to new levels of organic life, so, it was thought, cultural evolution was also necessarily gradual and progressive. By way of justifying this faith in the hierarchical development of cultural phenomena, the evolutionists employed "the comparative method" of selecting different culture forms from diverse societies and arranging them in a scale from the simple to the complex, regardless of their actual temporal sequence. The argument was circular, since it began by assuming a hierarchical order of development and then arranged cultural institutions and patterns to fit this preconceived theory, disregarding the actual historical sequence of these cultural phenomena in the social context in which they, in fact, appeared. The cultural evolutionists, in other words, really substituted logic for history and confused logical scales for actual historical sequence. Boas, Goldenweiser, and other students of the former appealed to the facts of historical ethnology to demolish this a priori theory of cultural development and parallelism.

In addition to this antievolutionistic criticism, the Boas school came to the conclusion that cultural phenomena could not be deduced directly from the facts of biology or psychology. Cultural phenomena were to be explained in terms of other cultural phenomena, with the exception of those universal patterns which could be accounted for by the postulate of the psychic uniformity and universality of original human nature. The historical approach implied also that historic cultures were to be studied empirically and inductively rather than deductively, that theories or generalizations were to be constructed to fit the accumulation of empirical, positive facts, and that data were not to be abstracted from their historical context to fit a preconceived theory. This led to historicocultural pluralism, to the study of cultures as discrete entities, to be understood in terms of their unique histories, as compared with the evolutionistic approach, which was concerned with the study of the evolution of humanity as a whole. Historical reconstruction and speculation as to the stages of cultural development were frowned upon as reminiscent of the comparative method of the evolutionists, and historical investigation was limited to specific culture areas. Regional culture patterns and the diffusion of culture traits in given areas were to be investigated without any preconceptions of finding verification for specific cultural laws or universal tendencies. As Goldenweiser has put it:

Over and above all this, Boas's outstanding contribution was the historical point of view, in accordance with which native cultures were to be investigated in their restricted historic-geographical homes. The dominant perspectives here included the physical environment, the neighbouring cultures, and the many intricate psychological associations formed between the different aspects of culture.[35]

The basic minimum of Boas's approach comprised the postulates of the irreducibility of cultural phenomena, as well as their nondeducibility from organic or psychological phenomena. From these postulates two types of inference could be, and were, made. On the one hand, it could be maintained that culture was an autonomous superorganic reality *sui generis* subject to its own laws of development and independent of organic and psychological phenomena. This, as we have seen, was the ontological thesis of Kroeber, who accepted the determinism of the evolutionists, such as Spencer, but substituted a purely historical determinism for the biosocial determinism of the former. It should be noted, furthermore, that while Kroeber took over the deterministic approach of the cultural evolutionists, he sided with the Boas school in denying the notion of necessary, or inevitable, cultural progress or specific stages of cultural evolution. Culture was to be understood as a closed, self-intelligible system of reality, but without any specific direction. Kroeber's theory of the cultural superorganic was in the last analysis a theory of cultural evolution minus the idea of progress.[36]

The other alternative was to maintain the humanistic thesis that culture was the product of voluntary and self-conscious human effort in adjusting man to his environment and the environment to man. This alternative, on the whole, was taken by Boas himself and by most of his students, including Wissler, Lowie, Goldenweiser, Haeberlin, Sapir, and Radin, among others. On this theory, the ultimate source of culture was the creative mind of the individual, but culture patterns also ex-

[35] *History, Psychology and Culture,* p. 154.
[36] Kroeber, *Anthropology* (1923), p. 8.

ercised a deterministic influence in regulating the thought and behavior of the individual. As Goldenweiser understood so clearly, this implied that "the accidental and the deterministic appear as two inseparable ingredients of the historical process." [37] Law and order in cultural reality were not facts, but trends, or tendencies, strong enough to regulate in part the chaos of accidental fact.

The issue was never, however, clearly and sharply formulated, either in the ethnological discussions of the first quarter century or in Lowie's *History of Ethnological Theory.* While, as noted, there was some outspoken criticism of Kroeber's theory of the superorganic, his critics accepted in principle the idea of the superorganic nature of culture and continued to speak of culture as a closed historical system and as a reality *sui generis,* subject to its own laws of development. The majority of American ethnologists, as well as their European contemporaries, adopted some sort of compromise eclectic position, which combined elements of both approaches—a tendency we have illustrated by reference to Wissler, Lowie, and Malinowski. Culture was said to be an organic instrumental phenomenon, originating in the individual, as well as a superorganic autonomous historical process; it was subject to natural laws of development, and yet subject to human control; it was a social heritage, and yet affected by the reactions of the individual.

With the emergence of the new interest in the cultural approach to the study of personality and the psychoanalytical study of cultural materials the issue was brought to a head, the cultural superorganicists maintaining that ethnology was "history or nothing," while the cultural individualists maintained, with Kardiner and Linton, that the locus of culture was in the mind of the individual.[38] Even Kroeber has revised, with considerable hesitation, the extreme views which he had held for the past thirty years, and in his revised *Anthropology* (1948), as well as in his recent papers, has called for a re-examination of the relation of culture theory and psychology, with special reference to the role of the individual as the efficient cause of culture.[39] In Leslie A. White, however, the theory of the cultural superorganic has now found a militant champion, who is prepared to battle to the bitter end

[37] Goldenweiser, *History, Psychology, and Culture,* p. 31.
[38] Linton, *The Study of Man;* Kardiner, *The Individual and His Society.*
[39] Kroeber, "White's View of Culture," *American Anthropologist,* L (1948), 405–15; "The Concept of Culture in Science," *The Journal of General Education,* III (1949), 182–96.

in the name of a science of "culturology" against the "reactionaries," who are prepared to acknowledge the role of the individual and of collective man in controlling his cultural destiny.[40]

It is rather amusing to find Lowie criticizing Wissler for the view the latter put forward in a paper of 1914, while ignoring his later position in *Man and Culture*, as well as Lowie's own earlier position in *Culture and Ethnology*, which was identical with that of Wissler for the same period.[41] He writes:;

According to Wissler we saw that cultural diversity has a solely historical basis. But the subject Wissler discusses is the direction of movement in basketwork, in other words, motor processes, a concept ethnographically significant because cultures vary with regard to such processes, but obviously one transferred from psychology. Further, Wissler cites evidence to show the difficulty of an individual change from sewing in a clockwise to counterclockwise direction or vice versa, even though the initial choice of either alternative be accidental. He is thus invoking another psychological concept, habit; and habit is not without pertinence to our cultural problems.[42]

Lowie, in brief, is now criticizing Wissler for reducing psychological to cultural phenomena, just as he himself had done in his own earlier work.

Wissler himself was inclined to accept the hypothesis that "the human factor is not a constant but a variable." "It is quite possible," he admitted, "that some groups of mankind have by biological evolution come to excel others in quickness, accuracy, and the intensity of response. They may also have come to inherit more energetic drives." [43] The disparity of cultures, he holds, may be explained as a resultant of two variables, race and environment. Man is a "self-domesticated animal," and it may well be that there is some "back-kick in culture, that speeds the evolution of his native talents." [44] On the point of possible organic racial differences Lowie was also prepared to grant significant correlations between racial inheritance and cultural achievements.

In his *History of Ethnological Theory*, Lowie at times refers to culture as being in itself an abstraction apart from the persons in which it is exemplified. He now states constructively:

Once freed from the fallacy that psychology is to explain culture without residue, the ethnographer profits, first of all, by the psychologist's "case

[40] White, *The Science of Culture.*
[41] See Lowie, "Psychology and Sociology," *American Journal of Sociology,* XXI (1915), 217–29.
[42] Lowie, *History of Ethnological Theory,* p. 271.
[43] *Man and Culture,* p. 301.          [44] *Ibid.,* p. 305.

method." He must not forget that the culture he investigates is a living reality only as mirrored in its bearers; the two are as inseparable as the sides and angles of a triangle. In other words, the culture by itself is an abstraction; the reality is adequately described by exhibiting samples of personality responding to the social setting. The correct procedure is to give an adequate definition of both.[45]

Here Lowie recognizes that culture, far from being an entity *sui generis,* is, after all, but an abstraction when taken apart from the persons in which it is realized. This position prepares the way for the study of personality in culture.

Lowie came to see also that in seeking to avoid the fallacy of reducing cultural to psychological phenomena, ethnologists had gone to the opposite extreme by maintaining the complete autonomy and self-intelligibility of cultural phenomena—a point Goldenweiser had also made.[46] He states:

While the hierarchical scale of the sciences does not properly express their relations, matters are not mended by simply reversing the ladder nor do we progress by clinging to a single rung. Actually the analogy is misleading because the interrelations of the sciences are of a quite different character. Of course culture cannot be subsumed under mental processes, otherwise there would be no ethnology at all—no more than there would be a biology if organisms grew and bred merely by the laws of gravitation and of chemical affinity. When the autonomy of our subject is once granted, however, declarations of independence grow repetitious. Our position towards psychology should correspond to that assumed towards geography: we cannot explain all of our phenomena through it, but neither can we explain them fully without it.[47]

Here Lowie presents the problem of the relation of the sciences and of the levels of phenomena with which they deal. He does not explain, however, how the so-called autonomy of ethnology is to be understood and how it may be reconciled with the notion of interdependence. Those who insist so repetitiously upon the autonomy of culture, namely, the superorganicists, mean to assert an ontological principle as well as an epistemic fact. The ontological issue is whether cultural phenomena constitute a closed system and are independent of psychological processes, that is, superpsychic, or whether in the last analysis they cannot be understood or be said to exist, either wholly or in part, independently of the mind of man. Apparently Lowie finds the insistence of the super-

[45] *History of Ethnological Theory,* p. 269.
[46] *History, Psychology and Culture,* pp. 59–62.
[47] *History of Ethnological Theory,* pp. 263–64.

organicists upon the autonomy of culture rather tiresome, but he provides no clear-cut answer to the problem which they raised. To the best of my knowledge he has never repudiated the position of his earlier *Culture and Ethnology.*

Actually, the historical ethnologists, in seeking to avoid the "psychologistic fallacy," as it may be called, of reducing cultural to psychological phenomena, were led to commit the "ethnologistic fallacy" of reducing psychological to cultural phenomena in order to uphold their theory of the autonomy of culture. The assumption underlying these fallacious attempts to reduce cultural and psychological phenomena to one another is the implicit belief that cultural phenomena are simple or homogeneous. The psychologistic fallacy is committed because of failure to understand that cultural ideas and experiences derive their content from the data or objects of nature as empirically observed. The content of culture does, indeed, depend upon psychological processes and mechanisms, but cannot be deduced from the latter, for the simple reason that otherwise all epistemology, all knowledge, would have to be innate, or independent of sense experience. In other words, the psychologistic fallacy rests in the last analysis upon the assumption of an egocentric, subjective idealism which regards cultural ideas as simply direct expressions of an ego, or mind.

If, however, it be granted that our ideas refer to objects other than themselves which exist independently of our minds, then it follows that cultural knowledge is a complex phenomenon comprising a subjective, as well as objective, element. Culture is, indeed, a function of mind, but of mind acting upon, or in relation to, an objective natural environment other than itself. In other words, culture is a correlative phenomenon always involving an actual relation to some natural phenomenon as well; nature as a whole is the condition of culture, and there is no culture apart from a nature which is cultivated or conceived. Any particular social trait, such as incest or exogamy, does, indeed, involve some psychological motivation; without the sex impulse there could be neither marriage nor sexual taboos. However, the particular form and content of the cultural traits depend upon man's beliefs concerning the nature of the objects of his experience, including himself, as well as the alleged consequences of his behavior. These beliefs and attitudes are the products of epistemic reflection and historical experience of nature and therefore cannot be deduced from the universal psychological processes and mechanisms of human nature. Diverse cultural beliefs and practices will involve distinct mental processes and a knowledge of psychology will be required for a complete explanation or understanding of any cultural phenomenon whatsoever; but the actual cultural data must be taken as historically and epistemically given, since they cannot be deduced or derived from an analysis of human nature alone.

The so-called autonomy of culture is ultimately an epistemic autonomy and is based upon the fact that cultural phenomena comprise ideational elements, as well as psychological processes. Many of the attempts to write a psychology of the various categories of culture, such as the psychology of religion, art, and so forth, involve the psychologistic fallacy, since they tend to reduce the cultural, historically acquired element to that of a universal psychological process and do not take into consideration the nonpsychological epistemic data of cultural experience. The historical ethnologists, in turn, regard only the fact that cultural phenomena are historically acquired or produced and therefore neglect the psychological and epistemic processes which make this cultural experience possible. It is assumed uncritically that "history" is a distinct, self-intelligible process which somehow occurs independently of the thoughts and motivations of the persons involved. In brief, the ethnologistic fallacy tests upon the invalid assumption that history *per se* is a sufficient cause or condition of culture, while the psychologistic fallacy rests upon the equally unfounded assumption that psychology alone is the sufficient condition of cultural phenomena.

### 5. THE CONCEPT OF PSYCHOCULTURAL EVOLUTION

Our thesis is that neither psychology nor history is a sufficient cause or condition of culture, because the latter is an inherently complex phenomenon comprising both psychological and historically acquired experience of nature. Concrete, actual experience is psychocultural and involves a creative synthesis of psychological activity and cultural achievement in relation to a given environment. Culture involves three distinct elements, namely, organisms, ideas, and objects. The psychologists tend to stress organism, mind, and its ideas and to neglect the objects of nature which provide the content of culture productivity, for example, Wundt's folk psychology. The historical ethnologists consider only mind and its objective cultural products, but tend to neglect the active thought and organic motivation which provide the dynamic factors which originate and continue the cultural process. A realistic and integral approach to culture comprehends all three factors in active interrelation. Integral culture is the process and product of psychophysical exercise upon the objects of nature.

The problem still remains, however, as to the relation of historical, evolutionary culture to human nature. If culture is a direct, necessary expression of human nature, how is one to explain the evolution of culture patterns in time? In my opinion the problem remains insoluble as long as one does not admit that human nature, like culture, evolves or unfolds in time. This may be understood on the assumption that while the innate biological potentialities of man remain more or less constant the actual, effective psychophysical powers and capabilities are subject to development in time. What I am suggesting is comparable to the eighteenth-century notion of the perfectibility of human nature, which seems to have dropped out of the picture in contemporary ethnological thought. Human nature may be perfected by proper cultivation of human potentialities. This implies that actual, historical human nature varies with the state of human culture and that the two are not to be conceived as independent of each other. Human nature and human culture are polar entities which may not be understood adequately apart from each other; each taken by itself is an abstraction from the concrete actuality, which is a union of the "matter" of human nature with the "form" of culture. Human nature and culture are historically correlated phenomena which vary together in time. The point I wish to make does not raise the problem of racial differences, but only the possibility of the cultural perfectibility of human nature as an acquired, historical achievement which varies with different cultures. The potentiality for achieving some degree of perfection is a biologically inherited human characteristic, but the actual achievement is a psychocultural, historical product, acquired by the art of culture and continued through the process of education.

Our modern emphasis in anthropology is upon culture as the product of human, historical achievement, and man, the maker and originator of culture, is not considered part of the cultural process. Man is the concern of that branch of anthropology known as "physical anthropology," which takes up such problems as the evolution of man and the comparative anatomy of "races." Ethnology, on the other hand, is said to be the study of human cultures and comprises all human customs, institutions, artifacts, and the products of mental exercise. The science of culture as practiced is the study of these impersonal, superorganic, historical products of society and the "laws" of their development. Only recently have anthropologists discovered that man's personality is affected by his cultural experiences and that the study of "personality in culture" is a significant part of anthropology. Under the influence of the psychoanalytical theory, however, the study of personality has come to mean the analysis of the personality structure of the individual as affected by the Oedipus complex and the social relations which prevail in a given culture.

By contrast, education, as understood by the classical philosophers and educators from the time of Plato onward meant the cultivation of human nature with a view to activating or realizing a given ideal of man. Similarly, human culture may be understood to comprise, in part, the art of human self-cultivation or self-conditioning, with a view to the development of human capabilities in relation to a given environment. Culture, as mentioned earlier, has its subjective, as well as its objective, aspects and includes not only the objective products of social life but also the historically acquired capabilities and activities of man. Whatever is learned is cultural, including the ability to learn itself, which is mediated by cultural experience and cultural conditioning. Man's acquired capabilities, to which Tylor referred in his celebrated definition of culture, are psychocultural, not only cultural. Man's capabilities are developed in the context of a society and its culture, but they are nonetheless psychological, as well as cultural, facts. Hence, a dynamic psychology is concerned with the growth and development of human potentialities in the process of education and cultural conditioning, for example, Gesell and Ilg's work *Infant and Child in the Culture of Today.* The notion that psychology is limited to the study of innate human nature and its processes, while culture is the study of acquired human characteristics, simply is not tenable and leads to the ethnologistic fallacy of reducing psychological to cultural phenomena. By contrast, the notion of psychocultural phenomena makes it possible to entertain an evolutionary theory of human nature and human mentality as affected by historical, cultural conditioning.

According to our psychocultural thesis, one may attach significance to such apparently outmoded terms as "primitive mind" and "civilized mind." Mind or mentality so understood is a historical product of psychocultural conditioning and may therefore be changed in time. People of the same innate psychological potentialities may differ significantly in mentality because of cultural conditioning. Since different cultures produce different types of mentality, one may therefore differentiate between the primitive mind, or the mind of man under the conditions of primitive cultural thought, and the civilized mind, or the mind of man under the conditions of modern scientific civilization. One evaluates the mentality corresponding to a given culture by the characteristic functional traits of its adherents as compared with those of participants in some other culture.

Goldenweiser implies a similar psychocultural approach when he writes in his essay "Psychology and Culture":

In view of the above considerations, it is often assumed that historical explanations preclude psychology. This is erroneous. To illustrate: Modern culture differs from primitive culture; one primitive culture differs from another; a modern national culture, that of France, differs from another, that of Germany. The explanation for all this is historical. So much being granted, there is still ample room for psychological illumination. The differentia of modern and primitive culture are determined by history. This provides the background for what may be called the modern mind and the primitive mind. But types of mind may in turn be used as a basis for psychological interpretations. In other words, there is such a thing as the primitive mind, just as there is a French mind and a German mind, even though the explanation for such "minds" must be sought in history, not in biology. Granting this much, certain peculiarities in French literature may be referred to the logical rigour of the French mind, certain aspects of German science to the thoroughness (Gründlichkeit) of the German mind, certain aberrations in primitive technology to the mysticism of the primitive mind.[48]

In a footnote to a preceding paragraph Goldenweiser adds: "In all 'explanations' of culture certain psychological postulates are necessary, but they are seldom sufficient. The sufficient explanations are historical, and the latter, of course, are mere statements of what has actually occurred."[49]

Goldenweiser, it appears, conceives of "history" as the sufficient principle of explanation of cultural peculiarities, whereas he holds that in the case of cultural universals, the principle of psychic unity is sufficient. My point is that it makes no difference whether the cultural phenomena are universal patterns or peculiar to a particular society; in all instances neither psychology alone nor history alone is a sufficient cause or reason. One cannot deduce culture from psychology even if the culture patterns be universal, since the actual cultural phenomenon always has

[48] *History, Psychology, and Culture*, pp. 66–67.
[49] *Ibid.*, p. 66.

an epistemic content which is dependent upon the natural environment. Similarly, in the case of cultural peculiarities the explanation is never only historical, but is rather psychohistorical. The psychological element is not a concomitant of culture, but is an integral constituent in every instance. The term "history" as used by Goldenweiser already contains implicitly the psychological elements which he later professes to find in purely historicocultural phenomena. He thus employs the same method as do the other members of the "American school of historical ethnology," but nevertheless is prepared to grant, as against the superorganicist position, that psychological explanations are relevant to culture history. That is, while adhering to the fallacious assumption that psychological and historical phenomena are self-explanatory, he does acknowledge the close connection of cultural and psychological phenomena at all levels of generalization, and thereby he comes to the conclusion, by a process of convergence, that there are different types of cultural mentality. My thesis is that the concept of historical types of cultural mentality may be logically understood in terms of a theory which denies the complete autonomy of psychology and history and maintains instead a psychohistorical approach to the study of psychological and cultural phenomena. Instead of a pure culture history and pure psychology, proceeding independently of each other, I propose a *psychohistory* and an *ethnopsychology*, which take cognizance of both elements as essential to a holistic approach.

Furthermore, with reference to the problem of cultural evolution, the psychocultural approach enables us to postulate different stages in the evolution of the human mentality without, however, assuming any necessary laws of mental development for humanity as a whole. There is an evolution of human culture and of the human mentality which is, or may be, cumulative and progressive, because in the sphere of culture, at least, there is an inheritance of acquired psychocultural characteristics. Through the process of education and cultural conditioning an individual or group may acquire the "collective representations" or distinctive modes of thought of a given culture, thereby acquiring through historical inheritance and actual transmission the cultural mentality of one's predecessors. There is progress in thought insofar as the thought of a later period is more rational and scientific than that of an earlier time. Comte and Lévy-Bruhl were not, therefore, wrong in principle in postulating stages of mental development or in contrasting primitive and civilized thought. They were wrong only in assuming natural laws of linear cultural development applicable to all humanity and the parallelism of the historical stages of development in diverse societies. If there is to be any cultural evolution whatsoever, one must assume that the earlier stages of thought somehow logically determine or condition the later stages, so that the former constitute a necessary, but not sufficient, condition of the latter. Such evolutionary, psychocultural determinism is compatible with a certain degree of contingency, since there is no a priori necessity that a given society will pass through all possible stages of cultural development. One may speak of an evolution of thought, or mentality, from primitive, animistic, mythological thought to that of modern rational and empirical science, from the prescientific to the scientific mentality. But there is no ground for assuming any parallel between the logical, normative evolution of humanity and the actual, historical evolution of any given society. In the former instance we are speaking of logical norms of development; in the latter, of contingent historical processes.

My thesis, then, is that there is mental evolution along with cultural evolution and that the two types of phenomena may not be separated on principle. Hitherto the historical ethnologists have attempted to differentiate between the objective, evolutionary character of culture and the non-evolutionary character of subjective psychological phenomena. This has led to eclecticism in theory. It may be illustrated by the following note from Goldenweiser, which states:

Those who insist on the social being a phenomenon *sui generis,* and on culture being in its nature historical, base their opinion on a real fact. While the content of culture, in so far as it counts, lies in the psychological level and can only be understood and interpreted through the attitudes and tendencies in that level, it cannot be derived from it or from the attitudes and tendencies embedded in it. A psychological interpretation of a culture can explain its content (explanation here standing for interpretative description) but it cannot account for it. This is a corollary of the fact that the cultural content is a heritage of the past, and that it is cumulative. This cumulation is a historical and objective phenomenon.[50]

Here we see Goldenweiser attempting to reconcile the theory of the cultural superorganic with a psychological interpretation of the content of culture. According to my thesis, one may account for the cumulative character of culture as a psychocultural phenomenon involving the epistemic products of the cognitive process. There is no need to contrast the evolutionary character of objective culture with the non-

[50] *History, Psychology, and Culture,* p. 10n.

evolutionary character of subjective psychological processes which somehow underlie this cultural content. Cultural phenomena are both subjective and objective, psychological, as well as epistemic, social, and historical. Psychological experiences, as well as cultural phenomena, may be historically acquired, for the simple reason that the two processes are in practice inseparable.

According to the theory of psychocultural evolution here proposed there is no incompatibility between the postulate of a metabiological human nature and human nature as historically given. We may begin with cultural man as historically known and analyze the empirical differences in psychocultural mentality which may be observed in diverse cultures. It is unnecessary to rationalize cultural differences in the interests of psychic uniformity, on the one hand, or to neglect fundamental cultural similarities by unduly emphasizing cultural disparities, on the other. While the actual effective powers and capabilities of men as manifested historically are products of psychocultural conditioning, the innate biological potentialities of human nature may remain more or less constant. Each type of culture develops certain potentialities of human nature and neglects others. This explains why actual historical man appears to vary with the cultural conditions which affect him and why the modes of behavior and thought of the adherents of one culture often appear so unintelligible to the adherents of another. No one culture system completely satisfies all human needs and potentialities; each system has defects corresponding to its virtues. Underlying historical, cultivated human nature we may assume a metabiological human nature which contains a reservoir of potentialities and capabilities which are available for future cultural exploitation.

It should be noted, furthermore, that the concept of a metabiological or metacultural human nature is not a derivative or an abstraction from a comparative study of cultures; it is not merely the common factors presupposed by universal cultural patterns. Human nature is metacultural in the sense that it is an ontological postulate which transcends cultural experience and is assumed as the ground or condition of cultural experience. For the cultural positivist, as well as the historical idealist and the materialist, human nature is an abstraction from cultural humanity and may not be conceived apart from culture history. According to my thesis, metabiological human nature is logically prior to historical culture and underlies all forms of cultural selection and social conditioning.

This ontological human nature provides the basis for human perfectibility and cultural progress. Perfectibility as applied to human nature means potentiality for cultural development under adequate historical conditions. Cultural evolution may be understood as the unfolding or activating of the potentialities of human nature through a process of self-conditioning and education in relation to a given environment. Cultural evolution is possible because man is capable of acquiring in time new actual psychocultural powers and abilities by means of the processes of education, social conditioning, and individual creative efforts. This unique type of cultural perfectibility also explains the possibility of cultural continuity and discontinuity, and hence of progress. Cultural patterns are not only repeated but also improved upon and surpassed by later generations. It is not necessary to introduce a disparity between the constant universal culture patterns and the changing historical content, as the historical ethnologists did, since both the patterns and the contents of culture vary together in the process of cultural evolution.

Whatever may be the shortcomings of the Lamarckian theory of evolution as applied to biology, in the sphere of culture, at least, it is more nearly adequate than the Darwinian type of theory, which relies upon chance variations and the determining influence of the environment. According to my thesis, cultural evolution and cultural progress are direct consequences of human efforts in self-cultivation and the cultivation of the natural environment and depend upon the possibility of transmitting the biocultural traits so acquired through the process of education and historical, social conditioning. Cultural evolution is contingent upon human effort and rational selection; it is not an inevitable product of natural selection and chance variation in relation to a given environment. Darwinian evolution allows no place for human effort, and when applied to the human situation it leads to a kind of cultural fatalism, as may be seen in Spencer's and Sumner's evolutionary sociology. By contrast, the Lamarckian theory allows scope for human effort and initiative in the evolutionary process. From this perspective, the Marxian philosophy of historical materialism may be understood as an eclectic synthesis of Darwinism and Lamarckism, since it advocates human effort in the form of class revolutionary struggle and yet predicts the outcome as a necessary inevitable result of the "laws" of the evolutionary process. In the end, it would appear that the Marxian approach has proved the more realistic, since human efforts create the cultural conditions which serve to justify these efforts. By contrast, the Darwinian type of theory serves to justify the *status quo* and proves ineffectual in the face of social crises. A genuinely humanistic theory of culture takes into consideration the role of human effort and rational selection without recourse to fatalism.

Our distinction between metabiological or metacultural human nature and historically acquired, biocultural human nature enables us to avoid the extremes of biological determinism and historical determinism. We can allow for actual racial or social differences without committing the fallacy of racism, since we postulate the potential biological equality of man as the foundation for culturally acquired differences. On the other hand, we are not committed to any form of positivistic, historical determinism, since we postulate a metacultural self-determined human nature which is independent of cultural conditioning and constitutes the necessary condition for all cultural processes. Cultural evolution occurs under the limiting conditions of biology and historical circumstances, but the cultural process itself requires the active self-determination of man in cultivating the potentialities of human nature and of the geographical environment by rational selection. In brief, my theory of psychocultural evolution is in complete accord with the biological determinism of modern genetics, but allows scope for the active intervention of man in utilizing his biological inheritance in accordance with his cultural requirements and preferences.[51]

Finally, the full import of the psychocultural approach for the theory of cultural and social evolution may be demonstrated by contrasting the traditional sociological and ethnological approaches to this problem. For Comte, the founder of sociology, the concept of evolution was closely linked with the theory of the perfectibility of humanity which he derived from Condorcet and other eighteenth-century philosophers. Humanity signified both a normative ideal and that which was common to the aggregate of mankind. Hence, he could speak of the evolution of humanity as well as of the evolution toward humanity. Furthermore, the evolution of humanity implies the perfectibility of mankind, the possibility of the realization in time by all societies of the highest state of human perfection. As developed by Durkheim, the Comtean sociological approach led to the thesis that all culture is a function of society and social interaction and that there is no evolution

[51] Darlington and Mather, *The Elements of Genetics*, p. 354.

of culture independent of the evolution and perfectibility of society. The evolutionary school of ethnology added the principle of natural laws of cultural development through fixed stages applicable to all societies. This implied that there is an evolution of culture independent of the evolution of society. Culture was understood as the product of social exercise and interaction, but its development did not depend on a corresponding evolution in social mentality. The historical ethnologists who rejected the theory of linear, progressive, and parallel evolution, retained, nevertheless, this novel ethnological approach in continuing to separate cultural from social and psychological evolution. Culture was conceived by them as a superorganic, historical phenomenon, independent, in a sense, of both the individual and society, though carried by them.

From this perspective, the theory of psychocultural evolution is an attempt to retain the principle of social and psychological evolution and that of cultural evolution, while dropping the assumption of natural laws of cultural and social development. As indicated earlier, my thesis is that culture apart from the individual and society is an epistemic abstraction of forms. There is no cultural evolution apart from mental and social evolution. In practice, this means that cultural evolution is linked with the education and the evolution of humanity. Culture, understood as the art of human self-cultivation and self-conditioning, requires an integral approach which takes into consideration the evolution of man as well. The concept of a cultural evolution independent of man is as fallacious as the notion of an actual human nature independent of culture. In the last analysis, culture is not a reality *sui generis*, but an instrument or function of man, and its significance and value must be measured by its utility in promoting the psychocultural evolution of man in the interests of human welfare.

# 4

# Society and Culture

IN ORDER that we may more clearly understand the significance of the concept of culture and that of the ethnological method which has dominated anthropological thought for the past fifty years or so, it is essential that we take into consideration the basic ideas and presuppositions which went into the development of sociology as a distinct discipline. After all, modern anthropology was in many respects an outgrowth of sociology, and even to date many sociologists continue to think of anthropology as a subdivision of sociology, namely, that part of sociology which deals with the institutions of primitive societies. A careful analysis of the thought of Comte and Durkheim will reveal an essential similarity between the approach of the sociologists and that of the ethnologists or cultural anthropologists, for the same period.

## 1. THE SOCIOLOGY OF AUGUSTE COMTE

As noted earlier, Comte's distinction as the founder of the science of sociology lies in his discernment that social phenomena constitute a distinct level supervening upon biological phenomena. Similarly, Spencer distinguished the superorganic, or social, level of phenomena from the inorganic and organic. For both authors superorganic or social phenomena were extensions, so to speak, of organic phenomena and were dependent upon the latter. Hence, Comte, in particular, conceived of sociology as a kind of "social physics," subject to laws of its own, which could be known as definitely as could those of physics. His famous law of the three stages in the development of society, from the theological, through the metaphysical, to the positive, was taken by him to establish the new science of sociology upon a sure foundation of fact. Henceforth human history in its social and intellectual aspects was to be conceived as a natural science subject to its own dynamic laws, as well as a normative science which defined the inevitable goal of the progress of humanity. As against the classical metaphysical approach of the philosophical anthropologists of the eighteenth century,

Comte maintained that man was to be known through a study of humanity, not humanity through a study of man or human nature. Comte, it should be noted, posited a theory of cultural evolution through fixed stages, but still adhered to the nonevolutionary theory of the fixity of species in the realm of biology. By contrast, Spencer accepted the Darwinian theory of biological evolution, but did not posit Comte's particular law of the three stages in the development of thought.

For Comte, it should be noted furthermore, sociology was conceived broadly as a philosophy of human culture and history; there was no sharp antithesis between science and philosophy. Positivism as a philosophy claimed to be scientific in the sense of being based on facts and laws derived from the analysis of facts. What was significant in Comte was his vision of human culture and history as a natural phenomenon subject to natural laws comparable to the laws of the natural sciences, though not reducible to the latter. Comte posited the "autonomy of the historical world" as the sphere of his new science of sociology.[1]

It is important to bear in mind the metacultural significance of the concept of humanity as employed by Comte. Humanity is conceived by him as the supreme reality and plays the same role in his system as the concept of God or substance in classical metaphysics. For man humanity is God; it is the source of his being and the object of worship. As Lévy-Bruhl put it, "once we are thoroughly persuaded that we live in humanity and by humanity, we shall also become convinced that we must live for humanity." [2]

Humanity conceived as the Great Being is a kind of hypostasis of the functions by which man tends to become distinguished from the animal. It is the progressive realisation through time of the intellectual and moral potentialities contained in human nature; it is also its ideal impersonation. In this last sense, it becomes an object of love and adoration.[3]

Human evolution, Comte agrees with the eighteenth-century philosophers, is progressive in the sense that human culture history is a natural, necessary development toward the realization of the ideal of humanity in accordance with the law of the three stages. Humanity, for Comte, is a kind of Platonic ideal; we are said to be men only by our

---

[1] Cassirer, *The Problem of Knowledge*, ch. xiv; Lévy-Bruhl, *The Philosophy of Auguste Comte*, tr. by F. Harrison.
[2] Lévy-Bruhl, *The Philosophy of Auguste Comte*, p. 335.
[3] *Ibid.*, p. 339.

historical participation in humanity. For man it is the absolute principle of intelligibility, as well as the moral ideal.

Comte's positive philosophy, particularly his concept of a science of sociology embracing the whole of humanity, exercised a tremendous influence upon the thought of the latter half of the nineteenth century in both Europe and America. In France especially, as Cassirer has noted, Comte's *Course of Positive Philosophy* was comparable in its role to that of Kant's *Critique of Pure Reason* in Germany.

## 2. EMILE DURKHEIM AND THE PROBLEM OF SOCIOLOGICAL METHOD

Emile Durkheim, as Lévy-Bruhl has pointed out, is the real heir of Comte so far as the French tradition is concerned. In his *Rules of Sociological Method* and *The Elementary Forms of the Religious Life* Durkheim developed and refined Comte's vision of a science of sociology into a potent instrument of scientific research. Durkheim provided a systematic, logical analysis of the methodology of the new science of sociology and at the same time tended to sharpen the disparity between sociology and philosophy. In insisting upon a strict empirical approach, he was especially interested in ethnography, with a view to discovering universal laws of social processes. Durkheim's *Rules of Sociological Method* has become a classic of modern sociological and anthropological thought. Here we find the first systematic analysis of the grounds for the autonomy of sociology as a science distinct from biology and psychology.

The basic concept introduced by Durkheim is "social facts." "A social fact" is defined as "every way of acting, fixed or not, capable of exercising on the individual an external constraint; or again, every way of acting which is general throughout a given society, while at the same time existing in its own right independent of its individual manifestations." [4] A social fact is, then, thought of as a *thing* having power to act upon an individual so as to coerce him into conforming to its pattern.

There are two essential characteristics to be noted concerning social facts. First, a social fact is a product of a given society or group of individuals; social facts are either the "collective representations," or modes of thought of a given society or else the practices and institu-

[4] Durkheim, *The Rules of Sociological Method,* p. 13.

tions which follow from given collective representations. It is postulated, in this connection, that a society is a primary entity in its own right and is not to be reduced to the sum of individuals who happen to comprise it. Any genuine whole is more than the sum of its parts, since the totality formed by their union is something new; for example, the living cell is a new kind of entity which may not be reduced to the mineral particles of which it is composed.[5] Similarly, a society constitutes a new kind of phenomenon or entity which is capable of functions other than those of which the individuals taken separately may be capable. Collective representations are modes of thought which are produced by societies only and differ from the individual psychological representations produced by individuals taken separately. Thus, a crowd manifests collective thoughts and sentiments which differ in character from those of the individuals taken alone. Social, or collective, representations may manifest themselves in individual consciousness and become general throughout a given society; but they are social facts primarily because they are products of the group mind of a given society, not because they are general or manifested in the consciousness of the individuals who comprise that society.[6]

Secondly, a social fact is said to be independent of the consciousness of the individual, although it may be exemplified or manifested in the individual's consciousness. Social facts are, in other words, superpsychic and hence are to be distinguished from psychological facts. Social facts are thought of as real entities, having all the characteristics or properties of a real object or thing capable of existing in its own right independent of a given subject. As Durkheim puts it: "These ways of thinking and acting exist in their own right. The individual finds them completely formed, and he cannot evade or change them. He is therefore obliged to reckon with them."[7] Since psychology is defined as "properly the science of the mind of the individual," it follows logically that sociology, which is the science of social facts, is to be separated from psychology.[8] This conception of psychology as concerned with the conscious processes of the mind of the individual is one that cultural anthropologists of the last generation took over, and it was used by them in turn as an argument for the separation of ethnology and psychology.

In Durkheim's thought these two theses, namely, the notion of collective representations as typical products of society and the reality of social facts as superpsychic entities are not clearly differentiated, and

[5] Durkheim, *The Rules of Sociological Method*, p. xlvii.     [6] *Ibid.*, pp. 3–13.
[7] *Ibid.*, p. lvi.     [8] *Ibid.*, p. xlix.

this accounts for the inherent ambiguity of his analysis. If we take the first thesis, that collective representations are functions of society, then it follows logically that only societies are the active agents or efficient causes of collective representations. Society may then be thought of as logically prior to the individual and as therefore capable of coercing the individual to conform to its modes of thought and action. Collective representations do not act of themselves upon the individual, but only through the superior power and authority of the society which originated them. If we take the second thesis, that social facts are superpsychic entities having a reality of their own independent of the consciousness of the individual, then it would appear "as if" social facts themselves are things or powers capable of acting and reacting upon the individual without reference to the society which originated them. There is, then, an inherent ambiguity in Durkheim's thought as to the *locus* of social power. It is one proposition to assert that society is prior to the individual and that we must begin by positing society as the ultimate reality and the individual as but an abstraction apart from society. It is quite another matter to assert that social facts constitute a new sphere of reality which transcends psychological phenomena and is independent of the latter. According to the latter thesis, social facts are treated as reified, independent forces, which, though originated by society, are nevertheless capable of acting and reacting upon the individual in their own right. The problem is ultimately metaphysical, or metacultural: Are there two kinds of social reality, namely, society as well as social facts, each capable of efficient causality in relation to the individual, or is there but one ultimate social reality, society, which is alone capable of efficient causality? Durkheim, as has been said, is not at all clear on this issue and tends to confuse the coercive power of society with that of its collective representations or social facts. Thus, he writes:

And, fundamentally, this is the very essence of the idea of social constraint; for it merely implies that collective ways of acting or thinking have a reality outside the individuals who, at every moment of time, conform to it. . . . It is difficult (we do not say impossible) for him to modify them in direct proportion to the extent that they share in the material and moral supremacy of society over its members.[9]

Here Durkheim refers to the supremacy of society over its members by way of validating his notion of the coercive power of social facts.

[9] *Ibid.*, p. lvi.

The methodological implications of Durkheim's two theses are quite disparate and tend to lead in opposite directions. If we begin with the primacy of society over the individual, then, as noted, society is regarded as the ultimate reality. Thus, in his treatise *The Elementary Forms of the Religious Life* [10] he states: "Society is a reality *sui generis;* it has its own peculiar characteristics, which are not found elsewhere and which are not met with again in the same form in all the rest of the universe." On this premise sociological explanation means referring any social or cultural fact to the society wherein it originated. A social fact is explained if we can demonstrate its origin or genesis in a given type of society as well as the function or end which it serves in that society. As Durkheim writes:

*When, then, the explanation of a social phenomenon is undertaken, we must seek separately the efficient cause which produces it and the function it fulfils.* We use the word "function" in preference to "end" or "purpose" precisely because social phenomena do not generally exist for the useful results they produce. We must determine whether there is a correspondence between the fact under consideration and the general needs of the social organism, and in what this correspondence consists, without occupying ourselves with whether it has been intentional or not. All these questions of intention are too subjective to allow of scientific treatment.[11]

And again,

When the individual has been eliminated, society alone remains. We must, then, seek the explanation of social life in the nature of society itself. It is quite evident that, since it infinitely surpasses the individual in time as well as in space, it is in a position to impose upon him ways of acting and thinking which it has consecrated with its prestige.[12]

*The first origins of all social processes of any importance should be sought in the internal constitution of the social group.*[13]

Here we see that explanation of a social phenomenon consists in seeking the ground of its origin in the structure or social constitution of the social group and its function in the useful effects it produces with reference to the general needs of the social organism. Society is said to be the efficient causes of social facts, as well as the source of all coercive power over the individual. So preponderant is the power and authority of society over the individual that Durkheim is inclined to maintain that society is the ultimate object of religious worship, just

[10] Durkheim, *The Elementary Forms of the Religious Life*, p. 16.
[11] *Rules of Sociological Method*, p. 95.
[12] *Ibid.*, p. 102.          [13] *Ibid.*, p. 113.

as Comte had previously maintained that an idealized humanity was the only fitting object of religious devotion. For Durkheim, however, not humanity in general, but particular societies are the concrete universal forms of human reality. Social facts are products or functions of society, and therefore, in the last analysis, society is the ultimate reality *sui generis* which renders intelligible both the individual and the social facts which govern him. This basic assumption underlies the position of modern sociologists, who tend to treat culture in general as a function or product of society to be understood by reference to social structure.

On the other hand, if we take the second thesis, that social facts are independent realities, entities capable of acting and reacting upon the individual, then these social facts tend to be regarded as a closed, autonomous system intelligible in itself. Thus, we are informed that *"the determining cause of a social fact should be sought among the social facts preceding it and not among the states of the individual consciousness."* [14] And again,

A thing is a force which can be engendered only by another force. In rendering an account of social facts, we seek then, energies capable of producing them. . . . We have shown that a social fact can be explained only by another social fact; and, at the same time, we have shown how this sort of explanation is possible by pointing out, in the internal social milieu, the principle factor in collective evolution. Sociology is, then, not an auxiliary of any other science, it is a distinct and autonomous science, and the feeling of the specificity of social reality is indeed so necessary to the sociologist that only distinctly sociological training can prepare him to grasp social facts intelligently.[15]

Here it appears that social facts constitute an autonomous science of sociology; social facts are explainable only by reference to preceding social facts and most certainly not by reference to psychological facts. Durkheim does, indeed, state that social facts are ultimately to be referred to the "social milieu" in which they originated, particularly if we are to understand their end or function. But in the short run any given social facts are explainable by reference to other social conditions.

Durkheim never regards social facts as constituting an autonomous level of reality independent of society. He does speak at times "as if" social facts were capable of acting efficiently without society and "as if" they were social forces capable of being engendered only by other,

---

[14] Durkheim, *The Rules of Sociological Method*, p. 110.
[15] *Ibid.*, pp. 144–45.

similar social forces. On this premise, society becomes almost a superfluous reality, no longer required to explain the development of
the social process. In other words, Durkheim does not distinguish
clearly and sharply between society and the culture or civilization which
it engenders in the form of social facts and institutions, although he
implicitly does tend to separate them and to speak sometimes of society
and sometimes of reified social facts as the primary social agencies. He
states explicitly: "For a society is not made up merely of the mass of
individuals who compose it, the ground which they occupy, the things
which they use and the movements which they perform, but above
all is the idea which it forms of itself." [16] Society is, then, not only a
given community of individuals but also the collective consciousness or
representations which they possess. In other words, a society comprises
the individuals, as well as their culture.

Durkheim's position may, then, be summarized somewhat as follows:
A society manifests a collective consciousness, or group mind, which
gives rise to collective representations and the institutions which depend on the latter. The laws of the activity of the social, or collective,
mind are to be studied independently through an analysis of its collective representations. It must not be assumed that the laws of individual psychology are identical with those of social psychology. [17]
To the individual who is confronted with the collective representations
of a given society the latter appear as social facts or things with coercive
powers which he can scarcely resist. Social facts, or collective representations, are originated by society, but apparently have a life of their
own and are capable of acting and developing according to laws of
evolution of their own. [18] What the relationship is between the collective mind and its collective representations, we are not told. Logically,
we should expect, to learn that social facts are products of collective
thought and hence are to be explained in part by reference to the laws
of social psychology. But at the time Durkheim wrote, the latter science
was not in existence although it was envisaged by him. Instead, he
proceeded to write as if social facts were subject to autonomous laws
which required no reference at all to psychology. Sociology is said to be
an autonomous science, and all social facts are to be explained by
reference to the internal structure of a given society or by reference to
other social facts and conditions.

[16] Durkheim, *The Elementary Forms of the Religious Life*, p. 422.
[17] *The Rules of Sociological Method*, pp. xlix, li.
[18] *The Elementary Forms of the Religious Life*, pp. 423–24.

### 3. THE DRIFT OF LANGUAGE AND THE WAYS OF FASHION

As noted in Chapter 3, Rivers, in agreement with Durkheim, had also argued for an independent science of sociology and had come to similar conclusions. At first, in his lectures, *Kinship and Social Organization,* Rivers maintained that social facts are self-intelligible and require no reference to psychology. In his later essays, *Psychology and Ethnology,* he revised his thesis and maintained only that a provisional, methodological separation of sociology from social psychology was necessary as a means of securing scientific accuracy. The two disciplines were to be kept apart "as though" they were independent, but the final objective of the study of society was the explanation of social behavior in terms of psychology. Rivers, as noted, did not clearly distinguish between the purely methodological, pragmatic separation of sociology from psychology, on the one hand, and the ontological, meta-cultural thesis of the autonomy of social and psychological facts, on the other.

Under the influence of Durkheim and Rivers, American ethnologists were at first inclined to accept the general position that culture consisted of social facts and that ethnology or cultural anthropology was an autonomous science independent of psychology. Difficulties arose, however, when Kroeber, in his classic paper on "The Superorganic," attempted to explain culture, or civilization, as a superpsychic reality *sui generis.* Contemporary ethnologists were inclined to accept the methodological separation of ethnology from psychology, but were not at all prepared to postulate a superorganic, superpsychic cultural level of reality, although they continued to profess the thesis that cultural phenomena constituted a closed system.

As a special case in point, we may refer to Edward Sapir. In a sense, Sapir may be said to represent an extreme position among American anthropologists, since no one insisted more strongly than he upon the individual nature of "genuine" culture and upon the close interrelation of personality and culture. Yet, in essential agreement with the prevalent climate of opinion, he maintained that language manifested a "drift," or long-range historical trend, which transcended the conscious efforts of the individuals who utilized a given language. Thus he writes:

The linguistic drift has direction. In other words, only those individual variations embody it or carry it which move in a certain direction, just as only certain wave movements in the bay outline the tide. The drift of a language is constituted by the unconscious selection on the part of its speakers of those individual variations that are cumulative in some special direction. This direction may be inferred, in the main from the past history of the language. In the long run any new feature of the drift becomes part and parcel of the common, accepted speech, but for a long time it may exist as a mere tendency in the speech of a few, perhaps of a despised few. As we look about us and observe current usage, it is not likely to occur to us that our language has a "slope," that the changes of the next few centuries are in a sense prefigured in certain obscure tendencies of the present and that these changes, when consummated, will be seen to be but continuations of changes that have been already affected. . . . Sometimes we can feel where the drift is taking us even while we struggle against it . . . . knowledge of the general drift of a language is insufficient to enable us to see clearly what the drift is heading for. We need to know something of the relative potencies and speeds of the components of the drift.[19]

Sapir writes as if language were a superpsychic social fact which "drifts" independently of the individuals who utilize it as a medium of communication. Like the social facts of which Durkheim spoke, language is something objective which confronts the individual and resists his efforts at modification. Language is, as it were, a tide which has a direction of its own and carries the individuals who use it along in its momentum. Thus, for Sapir language came very close to being the very kind of superorganic entity which Kroeber thought culture was. He did, in fact, have some misgivings on that score and wondered whether he was not imputing to language "a certain mystical quality" and "giving language a power to change of its own accord over and above the involuntary tendency of individuals to vary the norm." [20] In a later essay, "Language," Sapir returned to the concept of drift but explained the phenomenon in psychological, idealistic terms. "These 'drifts,' " he explains, "are powerfully conditioned by unconscious formal feelings and are made necessary by the inability of human beings to actualize ideal patterns in a permanently set fashion." [21] Here the reference is to the social unconscious and to ideal patterns which the unconscious mind strives to realize in language. On this basis language may be superindividual, but not superpsychic. Still, it is not clear what the relation is between the ideal patterns of a language and the unconscious mind which is said to underlie them.

Kroeber continued to uphold the theory of the superorganic nature

[19] Sapir, *Language*, pp. 165–66, 174.          [20] *Ibid.*, p. 165.
[21] *Selected Writings of Edward Sapir*, ed. by David G. Mandelbaum, p. 23.

of culture with admirable consistency over a period of twenty-five years at least. As late as 1940 he collaborated in making a quantitative analysis of "Three Centuries of Women's Dress Fashions" to demonstrate empirically his basic thesis.[22] He concludes that

the rôle of particular individuals in molding basic dress style is slight. The influence of creative or important individuals is probably largely exerted on the accessories of transient mode. . . . The reverse is much more likely, that individuals conform to the style which they find in existence, operate in minor ways within its configuration, and at times of coincidence receive false credit for 'causing' one or more of its features." [23]

Kroeber does not deny that psychological motivations may be operative, but maintains that as explanations they are conjectural and "scientifically useless." That is why he prefers to utilize purely behavioristic and inductive procedures "operating wholly within the sociocultural level." [24] The role of cultural ideology in sanctioning basic dress fashions for women over given historical periods is not considered. In complete agreement with his earlier concept of culture as superpsychic he prefers to consider only the products of sociocultural life without regard to the psychological and philosophical motivations which may underlie them.

As Kroeber saw the issue at that time, the alternatives were either a theory of cultural determinism which minimized the role of individual persons, or else adherence to the thesis that history is but a series of accidents depending on the free will of individuals. He preferred the former alternative as the only one compatible with a scientific approach to culture history.[25]

It is noteworthy, however, that in the revised edition of his *Anthropology* (1948) Kroeber interpreted both language and dress in psychological, as well as historical-cultural, terms. In speaking of "style patterns" he asserts that

a style, then, may be said to be a way of achieving definiteness and effectiveness in human relations by choosing or evolving one line of procedure out of several possible ones, and sticking to it. That means, psychologically, that habits become channeled, facility and skill acquired, and that this skill can then be extended to larger situations or to somewhat altered ones.[26]

Here we see that culture patterns and configurations are not the impersonal, superpsychic entities they were formerly supposed to be,

[22] Richardson and Kroeber, *Three Centuries of Women's Dress Fashions: A Quantitative Analysis;* also Kroeber, "On the Principle of Order in Civilization as Exemplified by Changes of Fashion," *American Anthropologist,* XXI, 235–63.
[23] *Ibid.,* p. 148.   [24] *Ibid.,* p. 150.   [25] *Ibid.,* p. 152.   [26] *Ibid.,* p. 329.

but products of human choice and intelligence subject to human direction.

Still, the original thesis of Durkheim and Kroeber continues to find new and strong supporters. Recently the leading French social anthropologist, Claude Lévi-Strauss, has brought forward an impressive array of evidence to substantiate the thesis of the essential autonomy and integration of language and culture.[27] In essential agreement with the approach of Durkheim, Lévi-Strauss has formulated a coherent theory of the homogeneity and morphological identity of linguistic and social configurations. In his paper on "Language and the Analysis of Social Laws" he refers to Kroeber's monograph on women's dress fashions as an example of "a phenomenon which depends on the unconscious activity of the mind."[28] Kroeber, he maintains, has demonstrated "that this seemingly arbitrary evolution follows definite laws." As a matter of record, however, Kroeber is careful to indicate that he "was not claiming to have found laws comparable to those of physics." In fact, he wishes the reader to "consider all statements on this score as withdrawn."[29]

### 4. THE SOCIOLOGICAL VERSUS THE CULTUROLOGICAL APPROACH

We are now in a position to reconsider the significance of the concept of the cultural superorganic as discussed earlier. It appears that most of what the sociologists claimed on behalf of society and the new science of sociology the anthropologists, in turn, claimed on behalf of culture and the new science of ethnology, or, as some would now call it, culturology. For the anthropologists, culture was the ultimate reality *sui generis* and society was but the vehicle of culture, a necessary, but not sufficient, condition of culture. For the sociologists, on the contrary, society was the ultimate reality which rendered intelligible the nature of man and of the social institutions by which he is governed. Both sociologists and ethnologists agreed that culture is the product of social intercourse and independent of psychology; they differed only as regards the metaphysical or metascientific issue of the ontological priority of society and culture. As we have seen, Durkheim's position was rather equivocal or ambivalent, and one may, therefore, find support in his

---

[27] Lévi-Strauss, *Les Structures élémentaires de la parenté;* "Language and the Analysis of Social Laws," *American Anthropologist,* LIII (1951), 155–63; "Histoire et ethnologie," *Revue de Métaphysique et de Morale,* LIV (1949), 363–91.

[28] *Ibid.,* p. 158.

[29] Richardson and Kroeber, "Three Centuries of Women's Dress Fashions," p. 151.

work for either approach. Durkheim's "social facts," considered as autonomous social forces, are comparable to Kroeber's superpsychic cultural phenomena and to the "cultural facts" of which the ethnologists spoke. In fact, and as a matter of record, the anthropologists of the preceding generation tended to identify cultural and social phenomena.

Now that anthropologists are taking an active interest in contemporary literate cultures in addition to the cultures of preliterate tribal societies, it is being asked how anthropology is related to sociology. As Kroeber has recently put it, "sociology tends to be concerned with society, anthropology with *anthropos,* man, and his specifically human product, culture. All in all, these are differences only in emphasis. In principle, sociology and anthropology are hard to keep apart." [30] My point is that as a matter of historical fact the two disciplines are based upon radically different ontological premises and that this accounts for the emphasis on society in the case of sociology and on culture in the case of ethnology. Even when sociologists and anthropologists appear to be treating the same general subject matter their perspectives and methods of interpretation differ essentially.

In contemporary ethnological theory the disparity of the sociological and culturological approaches appears most clearly in the different viewpoints and emphases of British and American anthropologists. British anthropologists, following the sociological functionalism of Malinowski and Radcliffe-Brown, tend to regard themselves as primarily "social anthropologists." The sociological functionalists tend to assume that cultural achievements are thoroughly integrated with the social structure of a given society and hence are to be conceived as functions of the particular society to which they minister. The cultural anthropologists or culturologists, on the other hand, consider culture apart from society as an entity independent of society and having an objective reality and intelligibility of its own. [31]

In his recent lectures on *Social Anthropology* [32] Evans-Pritchard has pointed up the issue between British and American anthropologists. He refers to Radcliffe-Brown and Malinowski as "the two men who have shaped social anthropology into what it is in England today." [33] British

---

[30] Kroeber, *Anthropology,* p. 12.

[31] Radcliffe-Brown, "Evolution, Social or Cultural?" in *American Anthropologist,* XLIX (1947), 78–83; Bidney, "The Problem of Social and Cultural Evolution: a Reply to A. R. Radcliffe-Brown," *American Anthropologist,* XLIX (1947), 524–27.

[32] Evans-Pritchard, *Social Anthropology,* chs. i–iii.

[33] *Ibid.,* p. 53.

anthropologists, he points out, are inclined to distinguish social anthropology from ethnology and to criticize anthropologists of the last century and American anthropologists of the present for failing to make this distinction. Social anthropology is said to study social relations rather than culture, social institutions and their relations to social systems rather than isolated customs and culture traits.[34] By contrast, "the task of ethnology is to classify peoples on the basis of their racial and cultural characteristics and then to explain their distribution at the present time, or in past times, by the movement and mixture of peoples and the diffusion of cultures." [35] Ethnology, according to Evans-Pritchard, leads to problems of psychology and history, whereas the problems of social anthropology are primarily sociological and are to be treated independently (in part, at least) of psychology or history.[36] American anthropologists do not appear to have learned this elementary lesson and still continue to confuse ethnology and social anthropology by discussing cultural problems "in that mixture of behaviouristic and psycho-analytical psychologies which is called personality psychology or the psychology of motivations and attitudes." [37]

While agreeing in principle with the social anthropologists and orthodox functionalists upon the methodological separation of social anthropology and psychology, Evans-Pritchard is inclined to disagree with them on the relevance of history to anthropology. He is inclined to question their assumption that societies are natural systems and that social life can be reduced to scientific laws which allow prediction, together with the corollary that the history of social institutions is irrelevant to an inquiry into their nature.[38] This thesis of the functionalists, he maintains, is "doctrinaire positivism at its worst." Instead, Evans-Pritchard holds that social anthropology belongs rather to the humanities than to the natural sciences and that the study of history is essential for a fuller understanding of social life.[39] In this respect he finds himself closer to the American anthropologists—whom his English colleagues regard as primarily ethnologists—than to the British functionalistic social anthropologists.[40]

Evans-Pritchard has, then, clearly grasped the fact of the difference in the British and American points of view, but has not clearly explained the reason for this disparity. He notes that Morgan, Spencer,

[34] Evans-Pritchard, *Social Anthropology*, pp. 5, 40, 45.
[35] *Ibid.*, p. 4.          [36] *Ibid.*, p. 19.          [37] *Ibid.*, p. 45.
[38] *Ibid.*, p. 49.          [39] *Ibid.*, p. 60.          [40] *Ibid.*, p. 59.

and Durkheim conceived the aim of what is now called social anthropology to be the classification and functional analysis of social structures. On the other hand, Tylor and other ethnologists, particularly Americans, conceived its aim to be the classification and analysis of cultures.[41] Why the ethnologists conceived the aim of "social anthropology" to be the analysis of cultures rather than social institutions and structures is not explained. He does suggest that the reason for the dominant ethnological interests of American anthropologists is to be found in "the fractionized and disintegrated Indian societies on which their research had been concentrated," which "lend themselves more easily to studies of culture than of social structure; partly because the absence of a tradition of intensive field work through the native languages and for long periods of time, such as we have in England, also tends towards studies of custom or culture rather than of social relations; and partly for other reasons." [42] The answer is probably to be found in those "other reasons" to which Evans-Pritchard refers, since the characterization of American anthropological research which he offers is simply amusing and bears hardly any resemblance to actual facts. He speaks as if Boas, Kroeber, Sapir, Lowie, Linton, Spier, and many other well-known American cultural anthropologists had never existed.

As indicated, the main reason for this divergence in perspectives is to be found in the diverse intellectual traditions from which they originated. The sociological tradition assumed the primacy of society and of social behavior, and those who adhered to it interpreted cultural data as functions of a social system. The culturological, or ethnological, approach was based on the assumption of the objective reality of the stream of social products or achievements termed culture, or civilization, which manifested itself in the process of history. In the beginning society and culture were not clearly differentiated and tended to be confused, as appears from our study of Comte, Spencer, and Durkheim. In time, however, those who regarded themselves as sociologists tended to emphasize the primacy of society and of social systems, while the ethnologists, following the culture-historians, comparative linguists, and evolutionary anthropologists, thought of cultural phenomena as constituting an objective, self-intelligible system subject to its own laws of development. Thus, the divergence between the classical sociological and culturological approaches is not due to any superficial misunder-

[41] *Ibid.*, p. 17.                [42] *Ibid.*

standing on the part of the ethnologists or to the alleged absence of field work; it is owing rather to a fundamental difference in theoretical assumptions, or postulates, which gradually emerged in the course of nineteenth-century thought.

In a recent review of "British Social Anthropology" Murdock has come to the "startling conclusion" that the British school "are actually not anthropologists but professionals of another category." [43] "In their fundamental objectives and theoretical orientation," he remarks, "they are affiliated rather with the sociologists. Like other sociologists, they are interested primarily in social groups and the structuring of inter-personal relationships rather than in culture, and in synchronic rather than diachronic correlations."

In commenting on Murdock's paper Firth remarks dryly that the former's startling discovery is hardly news, "for he has been well warned." [44] Firth admits that "The more general theory of the anthropologists, then, is hardly distinguishable in its scope from that of the professed theoretical sociologists, though its different ethnographic base gives it a different illustrative content and a different—sometimes sharper—focus." [45]

There is real danger of a blurring, deadening eclecticism on the part of "those who are not afraid to be called eclectic." To admit, as Firth does, that social anthropology and classical theoretical sociology are scarcely distinguishable and at the same time to insist that there are no essential differences between contemporary British social anthropology and "the best American work" is to be eclectic in the sense of attempting to combine incompatible concepts and methodologies. If the "primary connections" of the social anthropologists are not with the physical anthropologists or with the students of primitive technology and archeology, then indeed there are significant differences between the British and the American anthropological approaches. Firth is all for strengthening the linkage between social anthropology and other social sciences, such as sociology, psychology, economics, jurisprudence, and history, but he does not indicate under what theoretical conditions this is to be accomplished. If the linkage is to be achieved on the pre-

[43] Murdock, "British Social Anthropolgy," *American Anthropologist*, LIII (1951), 465–73.

[44] Firth, "Contemporary British Social Anthropology," *American Anthropologist*, LIII (1951), 474–89.

[45] *Ibid.*, p. 477.

supposition of the primacy of social structure, cultural anthropologists and the culture historians would scarcely feel inclined to participate in this unilateral form of integration.

If it were simply a matter of "different levels of abstraction," one might regard the distinction between social anthropology and ethnology as valid, having practical heuristic value. Both social anthropology and cultural anthropology, or ethnology, would then be regarded as complementary branches of a more general science of anthropology. A significant theoretical issue arises only if the social anthropologist, like the sociologist, insists upon the primacy of society and social structure as the focus of integration of all cultural phenomena. Then he is confronted with the contrary thesis of the culturologist or ethnologist to the effect that culture is, or is to be conceived "as if" it were, a historical reality *sui generis*, requiring no reference to social structure or function. In general, American cultural anthropologists recognize their common affinity in regarding the category of culture as primary and object to any restriction of their sphere of interest and research, such as the exclusion of technology, culture changes, and culture history. In sum, the metascientific, or philosophical, presupposition as to the ontological primacy of either society or culture does make a pragmatic, significant difference in the scope and methodology of anthropological research. Once the issue is clearly faced, not dismissed as being merely verbal or academic, then the way will be prepared for a *rapprochement* between British and American anthropological research.

There are signs that such a reconciliation is in the making. There is an increasing awareness on the part of British anthropologists of the complementary nature of society and culture. As Nadel has stated, "Actually, neither 'social' nor 'cultural' anthropology defines our subject matter satisfactorily; as I hope to show, it is essentially two-dimensional, being always both 'cultural' and 'social.'" [46] Similarly Firth states,

The terms "society" and "culture" are used to express the idea of totality, but each can express only a few of the qualities of the subject-matter. They tend to be contrasted. But they represent different facets or components in the same basic human situations. "Society" emphasizes the human component, the people and the relations between them; "culture" emphasizes the component of accumulated resources, non-material and material, which the people through social learning have acquired and use, modify and transmit. But

[46] Nadel, *The Foundations of Social Anthropology*, p. 21.

the study of either must involve the study of social relations and values, through examination of human behavior.[47]

It is being realized that one cannot study social structure without reference to cultural material any more than one can study culture without some reference to the principles of social structure. Firth, like Nadel and Fortes, is therefore opposed to those among his colleagues who would separate social anthropologists from students of human culture. When, furthermore, he grants the relevance of history and psychology to the study of social anthropology and acknowledges that the elimination of psychology from social anthropology "solves no problems," then, indeed, he has gone a long way toward resolving the problem of a unified approach to the study of man and his cultures.

In the interest of mutual understanding among anthropologists, care must be taken lest a priori definitions of the scope of anthropology preclude the possibility of a cooperative approach from the outset. If, for example, one states, as does Murdock, that "The special province of anthropology in relation to its sister disciplines is the study of culture," [48] he arbitrarily excludes the study of social structure and social systems from the sphere of anthropology, unless he reduces social systems to culture. One is then confronted with the amusing situation in which this recognized anthropologist who has written a volume on *Social Structure* asserts that he is not a social anthropologist, but rather a cultural anthropologist. On the other hand, if social anthropology is limited by definition to the study of social systems to the exclusion of cultural and psychological phenomena, social anthropology ceases to be distinguishable from classical sociology, except for its different ethnographic base. The study of culture then becomes of secondary interest, and cultural phenomena are viewed merely as functions of social organization. In this way anthropology and sociology are pictured as antithetical or at best as independent disciplines, each with its own distinct subject matter, so that a social anthropologist is regarded as belonging professionally in the camp of the sociologists rather than in the camp of the anthropologists.

If, however, one were not to grant the assumption that anthropology need be limited to the study of culture on the ground that such limitation is impractical and unintelligible and were to maintain instead

[47] "Contemporary British Social Anthropology," *American Anthropologist,* LIII (1951), 483.

[48] "British Social Anthropology," *American Anthropologist,* LIII (1951), 471.

that cultural phenomena and social systems are internally related, then the way would be prepared for a holistic approach which studies human social and cultural phenomena as functional wholes. Social anthropology and cultural anthropology are then understood as two branches of a common discipline of anthropology concerned with the study of man and his cultures in society. Neither society nor culture is viewed as comprising the whole of the human situation, and neither is treated "as if" it were a reality *sui generis,* requiring no reference to the other. Hitherto the study of man in society has suffered from the arbitrary philosophical assumptions of the primacy of either society or culture. There is no valid reason, however, for continuing a conflict of disciplines brought about by historic accident into a "holy war" based on alleged principles and eternal spheres of interest. In the future, a unified discipline of anthropology, comprising social anthropology and cultural anthropology, is bound to replace the segmented pseudosciences of social anthropology and culturology.

## 5. THE RELATION OF SOCIETY AND CULTURE

In the revised edition of his *Anthropology* (1948) Kroeber raises anew the problem of the relation of society to culture and points up the basic issue involved. Thus, he writes:

Society without culture exists on the subhuman level. But culture, which exists only through man, who is also a social animal, presupposes society. . . . A further complication arises from the fact that human societies are more than merely innate or instinctual associations like beehives or anthills, but are also culturally shaped and modelled. . . . In short, specific human societies are more determined by culture than the reverse, even though some kind of social life is a precondition of culture. And therewith social forms become part of culture! This seemingly contradictory situation is intellectually difficult. It touches the heart of the most fundamental social theorizing.[49]

If culture be understood in terms of Kroeber's earlier position, as a superorganic, superpsychic entity subject to is own impersonal laws of development, then it follows that culture is the condition of society. Culture may then be thought of as logically prior to society, as that which gives a society its determinate social structure and institutions. The society, as has been said, is to be regarded as the vehicle of the culture, as the instrument which a culture employs to objectify itself; the culture itself constitutes a new and distinct level of reality other and higher than society. If, on the other hand, one adopts the position

[49] *Ibid.,* pp. 9, 10n.

of the sociologists, then society is regarded as the ultimate reality and culture is explained as a product and function of society. For sociologists such as Sumner and Keller sociology is the science of human society and the latter is concerned with mass-phenomena *"sui generis."* "To the science of society, which studies mores and institutions, what goes on in the mind of the individual is pretty much a matter of indifference; what enchains its interest is not guesses as to what individual men *think* but knowledge of what societies of men *do.*" [50] For the sociologist, folkways and mores are functions and products of society in its efforts to win subsistence and perpetuate the species.[51] The individual is looked upon as the agency of variation, but it is owing to society that selection of variations and transmission by tradition occur. Thus, what the anthropologist calls culture is interpreted by the sociologist as an expression of "societal evolution."

My own position is that if one acknowledges the priority of man in society, as the author of his culture, one is logically bound to accept the ontological priority of social man to culture. Once begun, the process becomes cyclical, societies developing cultures, and the cultures in turn affecting their societies. There is no a priori logical necessity for setting up a linear, one-way cultural or societal determinism and to regard either culture or society as the primary determinant of the other. Hence, evolution may be thought of as both social and cultural. There may be social evolution without corresponding cultural evolution, and *vice versa. There is, I maintain, a relation of polarity between social and cultural evolution which allows for a measure of independence, as well as mutual interdependence.*[52] It is as fallacious to regard cultural evolution as an inherent phase of social evolution (as the followers of Comte, Spencer, Durkheim and Sumner are inclined to do) as to regard culture as an autonomous process independent of the individual and society, as do the culturologists. The sociologists tend to go to one extreme in assuming a priori that cultural achievements are thoroughly integrated with the social structure of a given society and can be conceived only as a function of the particular society to which they minister. The culturologists tend to go to the opposite extreme in disregarding the partial dependence of culture upon the organic nature of the individual and the structure of society. Actually, it appears, diverse

[50] Keller, *Net Impressions,* p. 12.
[51] *Ibid.,* p. 100.
[52] Bidney, "The Problem of Social and Cultural Evolution: a Reply to A. R. Radcliffe-Brown," *American Anthropologist,* XLIX (1947), pp. 524–27.

societies may have similar cultural achievements, and cultures are not necessarily integrated functionally with their corresponding societies. Otherwise, if cultural processes and achievements are considered as functions of the social order, the significance of cultural patterns and configurations in formally molding the life of the individual and in maintaining the self-identity of a given society is lost. On this point the cultural anthropologist is not likely to yield to the sociologist.

While Kroeber shows a keen appreciation of the theoretical issue at stake regarding the relation of culture to society, he himself appears undecided at present. Under the influence of recent criticism,[53] he has revised his own conception of the superorganic sufficiently to admit that the efficient cause in the cultural process is always man in society and that culture is not to be understood as a superpsychic reality *sui generis*. In a recent paper [54] we find him writing:

I have been under fire, long ago from Boas and Benedict for mysticism, and subsequently from Bidney for idealism, in reifying culture. White has cited several such criticisms. I take this opportunity of formally and publicly recanting any extravagances and overstatements of which I have been guilty through overardor of conviction, in my "Superorganic" and since. As of 1948, it seems to me both unnecessary and productive of new difficulties, if, in order to account for the phenomena of culture, one assumes any entity, substance, kind of being or set of separate, autonomous, and wholly self-sufficient forces.

And again,

The partial solution which I propose I owe to Bidney and his bringing the four Aristotelian kinds of "causes" to bear on the problem. The efficient causes of cultural phenomena unquestionably are men; individual personalities who are in interpersonal and social relations. It seems to me that this cannot be denied, and that there is neither use nor honesty in trying to whittle any of it away.[55]

Having admitted this much, Kroeber still feels compelled to maintain that cultural forms can only be explained in relation to other cultural patterns. Psychic mechanisms do not explain the variety of cultural forms with all their "specificities." [56]

This argument leads back to cultural determinism. If all culture forms are to be explained through other culture forms, then culture con-

[53] Bidney, "On the Concept of Culture and Some Cultural Fallacies," *American Anthropologist*, XLVI (1944), 30–44.

[54] Kroeber, "White's View of Culture," *American Anthropologist*, L (1948), 405–15.

[55] *Ibid.*, p. 407–8, 410.        [56] *Ibid.*, p. 411.

stitutes a closed system. Yet Kroeber is now prepared to admit that the levels of reality are interrelated and that there is no chasm, no "leap," from the organic to the superorganic. He is, therefore, faced with a dilemma: on the one hand, man in society is the efficient cause of his culture; on the other hand, neither the concept of human nature nor of society appears to be able to account for the variety of human culture forms and institutions, and hence we are compelled to treat culture "as if" it were a closed, self-determined system or level of reality. In practice, therefore, we must take the persons involved in the cultural process for granted and proceed to investigate "the interrelations of super-personal forms of culture."

Kroeber is conscious of the disparity or conflict to which his attitude leads in practical life. "I am aware," he reflects, "that in living my practical life I must necessarily, if I am to act at all, do so *as if* I enjoyed freedom of will, even though intellectually and impersonally I choose to remain a determinist." [57] As an anthropologist therefore, he "chooses" to remain a determinist, but as a man he accepts the fiction and acts "as if" he possessed freedom of will. In the last analysis, this means that his scientific theory and actual practice in everyday experience are not in agreement—an attitude which is reminiscent of the similar predicament of the philosopher David Hume.

## 6. THE CONCEPT OF "AS IF" AND METHODOLOGICAL ABSTRACTION

As was noted in our discussion of "Levels of Reality," [58] it is important that we distinguish between epistemic, methodological levels of abstraction, on the one hand, and metaphysical or ontological levels of reality, on the other. As a methodological device it is frequently useful to abstract certain phenomena for systematic treatment and to ignore the individuals, with their motivations, who were undoubtedly involved. Thus, the historian may consider the history of ideas, of political or social institutions, as a sequence of forms without bothering too much about the individuals who initiated and championed these movements. In this sense there is a certain rhythm in the progression of historical thought; certain configurations emerge and recur which it is possible to demonstrate in the large by abstracting the universal forms from the concrete matter of the personal and social contexts in which they occurred. Natural science has developed greatly as a result of this method of abstraction. Epistemic abstraction as a methodological in-

[57] Kroeber, "White's View of Culture," *American Anthropologist*, L (1948), p. 413. [58] See ch. 2.

vention is a fiction of the logical imagination. For given purposes it is thought appropriate to act and think "as if" certain forms or patterns of phenomena could occur independently of the particular individuals and societies which initiated them. All impersonal historical writing is based on this methodological fiction of the "as if." On the other hand, the postulation of ontological levels of reality may carry with it the methodological implication that certain levels of phenomena are to be treated "as if" they are intelligible in themselves and "as if" they constituted a closed system requiring no reference to levels of phenomena below them. It would seem, therefore, that the term "as if," as employed in contemporary ethnology, is equivocal and may refer either to a logical, epistemic fiction or to an ontological, metaphysical postulate. As has been said, the culturalistic fallacy is committed only when one mistakes this epistemic, fictional abstraction for an ontological level of reality or autonomous order of nature.

Thus, Kroeber, as of 1948, is employing the concept of the "as if" as a purely methodological pragmatic device in order to express the possibility of investigating culture forms in relation to one another without reference to the individuals and societies which constitute their efficient causes. Thus, he writes: [59]

To the investigator of culture, as long as he remains merely such, it seems irrelevant for the time being where culture resides, or whether it exists autonomously or not, as long as he has genuinely cultural data to operate with and is free to operate upon them with the methods he finds most productive. The locus and reality of culture are irrelevant in the sense that they do not affect this specific cultural problem nor his specific method of dealing therewith. . . . If to do this necessitates the provisional freezing of cultural phenomena as such on the cultural level, and acting as if culture were an autonomous realm, well and good; for except by so doing we shall never find out how much autonomy cultural phenomena have or have not, nor what kind of autonomy. The *as if* attitude gives us a perfectly adequate way to proceed; and White's acceptance of this attitude seems much more fruitful than his denunciation of Simmel as stubborn, mired, and blinded by an obsolete metaphysics. White's two positions on this point are, of course, not wholly consistent: if Simmel is just perversely wrong, then culture does really "exist" on its own level and we do not have to fall back on any "as if" attitude.

Thus, for Kroeber the term "as if" refers to a purely pragmatic, methodological device, to a scientific fiction whereby the practical, field anthropologist may proceed *provisionally* and act "as if" culture

[59] Kroeber, "White's View of Culture," *American Anthropologist*, L (1948), 410.

were an autonomous realm, without committing himself to any formal
position regarding the ontological reality of culture. Whether the
adoption of this "as if" attitude and the treatment of culture as independent of individuals and societies does or does not affect the investigator's cultural problems and his method of dealing with them is a
serious question, which I should be inclined to answer in the affirmative. I do not think, as Kroeber apparently assumes, that the fiction of
the "as if" attitude will enable the cultural anthropologist to carry on
in practice just as efficiently because the problem of the locus and
reality of culture is "irrelevant" to his main task and method. I think
the problem of the locus and reality of culture is highly relevant to the
practicing anthropologist and will directly affect the area and method
of his investigations, for example, whether to engage in studies of
cultural personality or not.[60] At any rate, there can be no doubt that
Kroeber employs the concept of the "as if" to enable him to straddle
provisionally the metacultural issue as to the locus and reality of culture.

For White, on the other hand, the "as if" attitude is used to support
an accepted ontological position. As a culturologist, he treats culture
"as if" it actually did constitute a distinct level of reality, with a causal
efficacy of its own. As against Comte's thesis and Kroeber's present
thesis as to the necessary connection of the sciences, White maintains
that "the scientist must always abstract a certain segment of reality, a
certain class of phenomena, from all others, and deal with them *as if*
it existed by itself, independent of the rest." [61] Thus, White uses the term
"as if" to refer to a scientific, ontological postulate which renders intelligible the notion of an autonomous, superpsychic and supersocial
science of culturology; it is not for him merely a fiction to be employed
provisionally. White is conscious of his explanatory, ontological use of
the term when he states:

Similarly the culturologist knows full well that culture traits do not go walk-
ing about like disembodied souls interacting with each other. But he realizes
that he can explain cultural phenomena *as cultural phenomena* only when
he treats them *as if* they had a life of their own, quite apart from the glands,
nerves, muscles, etc., of human organisms. . . . It is only the traditional
habit of thinking anthropomorphically which still clings to "social science"
that keeps one from seeing that in the man-culture *system,* it is the cultural

[60] See Chapter 11.
[61] *The Science of Culture,* p. 61.

rather than the organic, factor that is the *determinant* of the events within this system.[62]

White feels, therefore, that he, as a culturologist, not only can, but must explain culture "as if" it had an autonomous reality of its own.[63] For him the "as if" attitude is not merely a logical fiction to enable him to avoid committing himself to a definite position regarding the locus and reality of culture as it is for Kroeber; it is, rather, a logical necessity growing out of his basic philosophical presuppositions.

In his essay "The Expansion of the Scope of Science" White refers to the argument that

it was one of Durkheim's chief theses that culture traits have an existence prior to, and independent of, the individual human organism, and that these traits impinge upon man from the outside and profoundly affect his behavior. And it is, of course, obvious that this is the case.[64]

Yet a little later on, in the same essay, we find this statement:

Thus we see that, although culture traits have no existence, and hence can do nothing without the agency of human beings, we can treat them scientifically *as if* they had an independent existence. . . . The physicist may treat falling bodies *as if* they fell in a perfect vacuum; or imagine an airplane passing without friction through the atmosphere.[65]

Here we see that White begins by accepting Durkheim's thesis that culture traits or social facts do have an existence independent of the human organism, but soon changes the argument and affirms instead that culture traits have no existence independent of human organisms. Nevertheless, we must, he reasons, treat them for scientific purposes "as if" they actually had such an independent existence.

White does not distinguish between the purely hypothetical use of mental constructs of the physicist, such as the concept of the perfect vacuum, and the explanatory use of the concept of an autonomous sphere of social or cultural facts of Durkheim and himself. The explanatory use of the concept of an autonomous cultural reality is not merely a hypothesis or fiction; it represents an established scientific truth for the culturologist. It is only because White's assumption of the causality or determinancy of culture traits conflicts with the anthropomorphic usage of causality by some "reactionary" sociologists and anthropologists that he is compelled to employ the term "as if" in order

[62] *Ibid.*, pp. 100–101.     [63] *Ibid.*, p. 86.     [64] *Ibid.*, p. 97.
[65] *Ibid.*, pp. 99–100.

to reconcile his scientific usage with the nonscientific usage of his opponents. In principle, however, he does postulate the independent existence and causal efficacy of culture traits and processes and hence maintains that "it is the individual who is explained in terms of his culture, not the other way round." [66] No wonder Kroeber was puzzled by White's use of the term "as if" and accused him of inconsistency. There certainly is an inconsistency in his use of the term and his changing attitude with reference to the existence or nonexistence of culture traits independent of the human organism.

It is rather amusing to reflect that it is precisely those culturologists, such as Leslie White, who are most concerned to avoid the charge of animism and to attribute it to their opponents, who in fact are most guilty of this primitive mode of thought. I agree completely with Kroeber's remark that "the last citadel of animism lies in the domain of culture," but for reasons entirely different from his and White's. [67] To attribute independent causal efficacy or powers to culture forms and traits, to reify cultural abstractions, is to engage in animistic thought. For the essence of animism is the tendency to attribute life and mind to what we, from our scientific point of view, regard as lifeless physical entities or else as a mere mode of thought, an *ens rationis*. I see no difference in principle between the so-called animism of primitive man in endowing natural forces and sometimes figments of his own imagination with life and power, and the mentality of modern culturologists who attribute to their own mental constructs autonomous superpsychic powers of action and reaction. The only difference that I can detect is that whereas native man tends to think in animistic terms in critical situations and by way of validating his magical and religious rituals, the modern culturologist utilizes a similar mode of thought in the name of a new science.

It is of interest to note in this connection that White completely misinterprets the significance and basic assumptions of modern sociology by reducing sociology to social psychology. As he puts it, "In short, sociology merely rounded out the science of psychology by making it the study of the collective aspect of behavior as well as of the individual aspect." [68] This, it would appear, is contrary to the facts and tradition of sociology since the time of Comte, Durkheim, Spencer, and Sumner.

[66] *The Science of Culture*, p. 168.
[67] White's View of Culture," *American Anthropologist*, L (1948), 409.
[68] *The Science of Culture*, p. 76.

Notwithstanding his reduction of sociology to social psychology, White has no scruples in subscribing to the basic thesis of Marxian sociology, namely, historical materialism. In agreement with historical materialism he, too, postulates that economic-technological conditions are the primary, integrating factors in cultural evolution. As against all "idealistic" or "spiritualistic" theories of culture which acknowledge the existence of mind in man and the role of ideas in the development of culture systems, White proposes a thoroughgoing mechanistic and materialistic interpretation. According to his philosophy of culture, "social systems, philosophies and art are functions of an evolving technology. Progress in cultural development is an objective concept; progress can be measured and the measurements can be expressed in mathematical terms." [69] White, therefore, tends to assume a priori the total integration of any given culture about its technology and would explain the social system and all social institutions and classes as means of perpetuating and promoting the technological system. In this respect he even goes beyond the classical sociologists, such as Durkheim and Spencer, who were prepared to start with society as a primary datum. White, on the contrary, begins with technology and then explains social organization as an effect or function of a given stage of technology. In accordance with his materialistic philosophy, everything in the cosmos is said to be interpreted in terms of matter and energy. Hence, "Culture is merely the name we give to matter-and-energy in symbolic form." [70] And again: "We may view a cultural system as a series of three horizontal strata: the technological layer on the bottom, the philosophical on the top, the sociological stratum in between. These positions express their respective roles in the culture process. The technological system is basic and primary." [71] Cultural progress is then evaluated by him "objectively" and quantitatively as "the amount of energy harnessed per capita per year." Cultural progress, in other words, can be measured in terms of horsepower.

Unlike the orthodox Marxian historical materialists, White allows no scope for revolutionary activity in terms of a class struggle, since to do so would be tantamount to admitting a subjective, human factor as a source of cultural change. To admit that culture is determined by man, even in part, would undermine the absolute determinism and

---

[69] "Ethnological Theory," in *Philosophy for the Future*, ed. by Sellars and others, pp. 357–84.

[70] *Ibid.*, p. 375.  [71] *Science of Culture*, p. 366.

mechanism of his culturology. That is why he even takes V. Gordon Childe to task for having suggested that changes in culture can be initiated, controlled, or delayed by conscious and deliberate choice of human authors.[72]

I mention this aspect of White's culture theory in order to distinguish between culturology as a theory of the autonomy of culture and as connoting a science of culture and White's particular version of the philosophy of historical materialism with which it happens to be associated. Culturology as a scientific theory of culture and cultural reality has been adhered to long before White took up the term, and that is why men of the stature of Kroeber have been prepared to express a large measure of accord with him. What seems to have been overlooked is that White's culturology also involves a materialistic philosophy of culture history which reduces the whole concept of a science of culture to absurdity. It is one thing to treat cultural phenomena provisionally "as if" they were independent of other types of phenomena and to proceed with the survey of the relations and sequences of culture forms, as Kroeber is prepared to do; it is another, and very objectionable, matter to assume dogmatically and simplistically that culturology necessarily involves a theory of the primacy of technology and of the totalitarian integration of culture on this materialistic basis. To proceed in practice "as if" this were the case is not to entertain a scientific, methodological fiction, but rather to accept, in the name of science, a sophisticated twentieth-century myth.

To return to our discussion of Kroeber's argument in favor of regarding cultural phenomena as a closed, self-intelligible system, it seems to me that the basic assumption underlying his argument is, as he himself suggests in his text,[73] that human nature is a constant, whereas culture is a variable. Hence, he maintains that the great variety of culture forms cannot be deduced or inferred from the concept of a universal human nature. In this respect, therefore, cultural anthropologists find themselves in agreement with sociologists that psychology does not explain social or cultural phenomena. To seek an explanation of cultural phenomena in terms of psychology would be to commit the *fallacy of reductionism*.[74]

I think, however, that the above assumption as to the constancy of human nature is groundless. Human nature is a constant only with

---

[72] "Ethnological Theory," in Sellars and others, eds., p. 373.
[73] *Anthropology* (1948), pp. 12–13.    [74] *Ibid.*, p. 576.

regard to its universal potentialities. Actually, human nature as a functional entity varies a great deal from culture to culture.[75] The elements of human nature which are activated and the manner in which they function vary considerably both in space and in time. We may, therefore, achieve some understanding of the origin of a given cultural phenomenon by indicating its psychological motivation and the mental processes involved in its occurrence. Psychological universals will then serve to explain the recurrence of universal cultural institutions, such as domestication, marriage, religion, and so forth. Psychological particulars, that is, particular modes of psychological activity, will throw light upon the origin and function of specific cultural traits, for example, the relation of disease to magical rituals.

## 7. DESCRIPTION, EXPLANATION, AND DEDUCTION OF CULTURAL PHENOMENA

Furthermore, we must distinguish between description, explanation, and deduction. Cultural phenomena must be described as given. We do not know, in the sense of being acquainted with, a given cultural phenomenon unless we experience and describe it as a unique or particular kind of phenomenon. In this sense it is true that psychological and cultural phenomena differ. We may explain magic, for example, as being motivated by fear of the unknown, but we still shall not know what is unique and significant about magic unless we describe it as a practical, cultural phenomenon. Explanation and deduction are not, however, the same thing. To explain the origin of a phenomenon is to indicate the conditions which produced it. Deduction, however, is a logical process whereby a particular is inferred from a universal. Thus, in offering an explanation of a given cultural phenomenon we are not deducing it from its antecedent conditions, but indicating the sufficient conditions for its emergence. Explanation, in other words, is inductive; it simply indicates, by way of experience, what is the actual sequence of events and conditions which bring about a certain new phenomenon. Deduction, on the other hand, is always a process of reduction, that is, of reducing a given particular to the status of some more general phenomenon or principle.

Thus, when we seek to explain given cultural phenomena we must first describe them as given within the context of their culture. We may seek then to understand their origin by investigating the social

[75] See Chapter 2.

conditions under which they arose and the functions they tend to fulfill in a given society. We may further investigate the probable ideological and psychological motivations which underlie them. Of course, since cultural phenomena are part of a historical process, we may facilitate our understanding of a given cultural phenomenon by studying the antecedent historical, cultural, and social conditions which brought it about. Much of historical and cultural explanation is of this sort. But ultimately we come upon cultural traits and institutions for which no further historical data are available. In other words, the historical process is not one of infinite regress. In the last analysis, we must fall back upon man in society in a given environment as the ultimate source of his culture. We do not, then, explain a given culture by deducing it from human nature or society, but by pointing out the probable or necessary and sufficient conditions for its emergence. When we say that culture constitutes a new level of phenomena, what we mean is that logically culture cannot be inferred or deduced; it can only be described as it is in itself and by reference to the conditions which brought it about. If culture could be inferred or deduced from some other set of phenomena, it would no longer be unique. Ultimately, as indicated in our discussion of human freedom,[76] culture is to be conceived as the gift or invention of human freedom. We cannot deduce it or infer it as a necessary consequence from antecedent conditions; we can only posit it as given and then try to indicate the factors involved in its historical evolution.

The only other alternative, the one adopted traditionally by cultural anthropologists and ethnologists, has been to argue that cultural phenomena constitute a closed system and that explanation of cultural phenomena consists in pointing out the historical, social, and cultural antecedents from which it evolved. The fear of reducing social or cultural phenomena to the lower levels of psychology or biology has led anthropologists and sociologists alike to reify or hypostatize social facts and cultural facts into autonomous forces capable of acting upon one another, as well as upon individuals and societies, in complete independence of man. This, in my opinion, is metaphysical nonsense and involves the *fallacy of misplaced concreteness*. If the social scientist is prepared to admit an ultimate discontinuity in the social process, if he is prepared to admit that at some point cultures emerged as a novelty in nature, then the magic circle of social and cultural phenomena will

[76] Chapter I.

be broken and they will cease to be considered as autonomous things or forces to be explained only in terms of other cultural and social phenomena. Anthropologists have recognized that there may be discontinuities in culture and hence, like Boas and Lowie, have stressed the uniqueness of culture systems. If they would go one step farther and grant that the cultural process as a whole is unique, involving a discontinuity in nature, then they would see that the methodological fear of reductionism is nothing but a groundless delusion. The alternatives are not either reductionism or complete autonomy. There is a third alternative, namely, a *relative autonomy* which maintains the distinctiveness of cultural phenomena, while indicating the noncultural, or metacultural, factors, including those of biology, psychology, human freedom, and experience in relation to a given environment, which may have conditioned the emergence of universal and special cultural phenomena in all their varieties. This will not preclude the investigation of the historical and cultural conditions which may have produced certain cultural institutions and customs, where such historical data is available or may be reconstructed.

### 8. THE FALLACY OF REDUCTIONISM AND THE THEORY OF CAUSALITY

It seems to me that modern social scientists, in their anxiety to avoid the fallacy of reductionism, have presupposed it all along by reducing effect to cause. A cultural effect, they argue, is to be explained only through a cultural cause; the cultural present is to be explained through the cultural past; if culture were to be explained through some noncultural process or phenomenon, that would mean the reduction of cultural to noncultural phenomena. The whole argument presupposes the classic notion so clearly formulated in Spinoza's *Ethics,* namely, that a knowledge of the effect involves a knowledge of the cause, so that an effect may be deduced from its cause. This basic assumption leads straight to monistic, causal determinism and involves ultimately the reduction of all given phenomena to some one underlying causal principle or substance.

If, instead, one were to adopt an emergent theory of causality, according to which a cause is but the limiting condition of an effect, then one avoids the danger and fallacy of reductionism entirely. On this basis, an effect is a newly emergent novelty requiring certain necessary and sufficient conditions for its existence, but the effect cannot be deduced from the cause. There is no a priori logical necessity, as Hume pointed out long ago, for a given cause to produce a given effect; the effect is known only a posteriori, as given in experience. Thus, water, for example, is the effect of a synthesis of hydrogen and oxygen in proper proportions, but the phenotype "water" cannot be deduced from either of these elements taken separately. Similarly, given a human organism and a viable environment, the human being will proceed in time to invent a system of artifacts to minister to his needs, for example, fire, utensils, and so forth. The given artifacts may be explained as the effects of natural causes—man in society working upon the materials of his environment—but these artifacts may not be deduced from these antecedent conditions. Similarly, culture as a whole may be understood as the emergent effect of certain noncultural, causal conditions, but culture would not thereby be reduced to human nature, society, or the environment, since it cannot be deduced from them.

The paradox of modern culture theory lies in the fact that modern ethnologists began by postulating the emergent character of cultural phenomena and insisting upon their autonomy, as may be seen from Kroeber's classic paper on "The Superorganic," but then employed a reductionistic logic or methodology in order to justify their thesis. On this basis, a cultural effect could be explained only through a cultural cause, since to introduce noncultural explanatory factors would be to reduce cultural to noncultural phenomena. Thus, culture became a transcendental entity without roots in the nature of man and society, and yet exercising, a strange all-determining power or influence upon both man and society. How this was possible was never explained, since, as has been said, culture was thought of as a closed system and the culture-historical method was incapable of explaining the origin and function of culture itself.

By adopting the theory of causality suggested here, namely, the position that an effect is an emergent of certain necessary and sufficient conditions, but cannot be deduced from a knowledge of the cause, one could safeguard the uniqueness and relative autonomy of cultural phenomena without subscribing to an absolute cultural and historical determinism. Human freedom and cultural determinism may then be reconciled, since it will no longer be necessary, in the interests of a science of culture or of society, to exclude man and society from an active, efficient role as the originators and directors of the cultural process.

## 9. CULTURE AS ENTITY AND AS PROCESS

The essential point of my criticism of the concept of culture as an autonomous level of reality centers in the argument that culture is not a new kind of entity or substance, but only a new kind of process and human achievement. Ontologically speaking, only substances, that is, things capable of independent existence, are to be conceived as constituting an order, or level, of reality. One may speak of an inorganic level of reality precisely because one may postulate an order of physical things and forces. Similarly, one may refer to an organic level of reality because empirically one may perceive biological entities or organisms capable of existing as distinct entities. Among biological or organic substances one may distinguish between those capable of conceptual thought and language, such as man, and those incapable of it. Ontologically and empirically, there is no distinct psychological or cultural level of reality, although there are distinct psychological and cultural phenomena. In other words, one must not assume a complete identity between empirical phenomena and ontological reality. A psychological process is something we attribute to some kinds of animals, but psychological processes, the so-called minds of animals, are not empirically observable entities comparable to those of physics or biology. Similarly, cultural processes may be attributed to man in particular, but cultural phenomena, like mental processes in general, do not have a substantial, independent reality of their own. Culture is an attribute of man, a mode of acting and thinking which we attribute to human enterprise; it is not, therefore, to be thought of as an entity *sui generis*.

Historically, the notion that social or cultural facts constitute a new, autonomous level of reality was introduced by Comte and Durkheim. They argued that because society was to be regarded as a new kind of entity, not reducible to the aggregates of individuals who compose it, therefore the products of society and social life, namely, what Durkheim called collective representations and social facts, were also new kinds of entities, comparable to those of physics and biology and subject to their own laws of development. By confusing society with the cultural achievements of society, they were led to postulate natural evolution of social facts according to fixed laws corresponding to the evolution of society. This tendency to identify the social and the cultural was continued by the anthropologists, long after they isolated the culture concept for independent treatment. The notion that there were distinct levels of social reality and autonomous sciences corresponding to them seemed very plausible and attractive, as this thought opened the way for the founding of new sciences. At last man and his culture were to be brought under the scope of natural science, and the last citadel of animism and freedom would be brought under orderly control and subjected to the laws of nature. Any one who opposed this mechanistic, naturalistic approach was henceforth regarded as a reactionary and an opponent of scientific evolution.

Thus, the last ghost of "animism" was laid low. Animistic forces were eliminated not only from the sphere of physical and biological nature but from the human sphere as well. Not only nature but man also was deprived of his "anima." The notion that man was a being capable of freedom of initiative or that the development of his culture had anything to do with what men in particular thought and willed and strove for was henceforth dismissed as the outmoded delusions of reactionaries such as philosophers and theologians; social scientists knew better.

While the impetus to investigate the origin and function of human institutions and other cultural achievements has added greatly to our store of knowledge and has provided modern scholars with a degree of insight into human affairs which previous generations lacked, the grandiose claims on behalf of the science of society and the science of man have not been realized. After some one hundred years, the alibi is still brought forward that the "youth" of these new sciences is responsible for their failure to obtain the necessary information and to establish the promised "laws," but that given sufficient funds and encouragement the promised results would certainly be forthcoming.

The fallacious assumptions underlying these universal claims were scarcely examined. The absurdity of eliminating man himself from the social and cultural process did not seem to matter; all that mattered was the establishment of the reign of law in human affairs—at least in theory. Meanwhile, human affairs have gone from bad to worse, and the past few generations have witnessed a series of social crises such as the apostles of social law and social progress hardly dreamed of in their theoretical utopian schemes.

It is high time, therefore, that we stop to reconsider the foundations of modern sociology and anthropology and to expose some of the fallacious assumptions and arguments upon which they are based. The foremost theoretical assumptions are that every new kind or type of phenomena requires the postulation of an autonomous level of reality subject to its own laws of development and that social and cultural facts require the postulation of distinct levels of social and cultural reality, each of which is *sui generis.* In opposition, I have urged, first, that neither social nor cultural facts constitute a distinct ontological level of reality intelligible through itself alone. As processes involving the active efforts of man in society, cultural and social facts are not ultimately intelligible through themselves alone, although they may be treated as abstractions for immediate purposes of investigation. The notion of the autonomy of social and cultural reality is based on nothing more than a misleading analogy initiated by Comte and Durkheim, whereby empirical kinds of phenomena and levels of reality became identified and confused. This had led to the fallacy of misplaced concreteness, whereby a category of phenomena properly termed an attribute of man in society became converted into an autonomous entity independent of man and society.

Ultimately culture is not intelligible by itself, for the simple reason that culture is a correlative phenomenon, always involving some reference to nature, including man and his geographical environment. One may distinguish at least four variables in the cultural process, namely, human nature, society, geography, and historical experience. Any cultural explanation is an attempt to indicate the limiting conditions of a given cultural phenomenon or pattern by reference to the interrelations of these factors. Because psychology, biology, sociology, or geography may be insufficient, when taken separately, to account adequately for the specificity of a given cultural phenomenon, it does not follow that therefore culture or culture history is sufficient by itself to account for it. In practice, the so-called autonomy of culture leads to the elimination of all explanation of cultural phenomena other than historical. Thus the present meaning of a given cultural process is always "reduced" to the past in an indefinite regress. This leads to an impoverishment of cultural explanation, since the origin of culture itself still remains a mystery not subject to explanation by the historical method. By contrast, I should say that cultural phenomena constitute the most open of systems, requiring complex explanations in terms of many variables. All one can do under given circumstances is to indicate the most probable conditions which underlie a given process or institution, including historical conditions, when these are known or can be reconstructed. Under no circumstances will one be able to "deduce" cultural phenomena from these limiting conditions, but only to indicate how they emerged. The assumption of a universal determinism leads to the confusion of explanation with deduction and prepares the way for a monistic "reduction" of effects to their causes. On the other hand, the postulate that culture is an emergent product of human freedom and creativity in relation to human potentialities and those of the geographical environment precludes the danger of reductionism and deductionism and leaves us free to take into consideration all the complex and variable factors which condition the cultural process.

## 10. THE SOCIOLOGISTIC AND THE CULTURALISTIC FALLACIES

The assumption that culture is explainable in terms of some one ultimate factor leads to a whole series of fallacies. If one assumes that society is the ultimate ontological entity *sui generis* and that all cultural processes and institutions are to be explained by reference to their functions in relation to this self-intelligible reality, then one commits what may be called the *sociologistic fallacy*. This corresponds to the *culturalistic fallacy* of the culturologists, who, in turn, regard culture as an autonomous, superorganic, self-explanatory entity transcending man and society. Thirdly, if one should attempt to deduce culture from biology, psychology, or geography, then one would commit the *naturalistic fallacy*. In every instance determinism by reference to some closed, ontological, self-explanatory system is fallacious. An adequate explanation of cultural phenomena is complex, since it must take into consideration all the factors mentioned above. Moreover, the postulate that culture is a process depending upon the causal efficacy of man in society permits us to regard culture as a unique phenomenon subject to a series of limiting conditions which preclude human omnipotence and yet allow sufficient scope for human freedom and creativity in time. The first prerequisite of a science of culture is respect for the facts as verified by experience. And the fact remains that man is an animated creature, capable of initiating cultural processes. The fallacy of animism is committed only in attributing life to the lifeless; there is no fallacy in attributing life and mind to man and in regarding him as the author of his culture. Only a perverted, dehumanized sociology and culturology would attempt to eliminate man himself from a study of culture and society.

## 11. HUMAN FREEDOM AND CAUSAL DETERMINISM

Perhaps the problem concerning the role of man and society in the development of culture may be more clearly formulated somewhat as follows: Hitherto sociologists and culturologists have been inclined to think as if there were only two alternatives, namely, human freedom or causal determinism. If one admits the postulate that man is endowed with freedom of will, it was argued, then a science of culture or of society becomes impossible, since free will implies an essential arbitrariness or causelessness in human affairs and hence the omnipotence of man over nature. The only acceptable alternative, it would appear, is to posit a thorough determinism, which regards man and society, as well as their cultural achievements as equally subject to natural law or causal determinism. Thus Tylor writes:

But other obstacles to the investigation of laws of human nature arise from considerations of metaphysics and theology. The popular notion of free human will involves not only freedom to act in accordance with motive, but also a power of breaking loose from continuity and acting without cause— a combination which may be roughly illustrated by the simile of a balance sometimes acting in the usual way, but also possessed of the faculty of turning by itself without or against its weights. This view of an anomalous action of the will, which it need hardly be said is incompatible with scientific argument, subsists as an opinion, patent or latent in men's minds, and strongly affecting their theoretic views of history, though it is not, as a rule, brought prominently forward in systematic reasoning.[77]

Similarly Durkheim states,

It displeases man to renounce the unlimited power over the social order he has so long attributed to himself; and on the other hand, it seems to him that, if collective forces really exist, he is necessarily obliged to submit to them without being able to modify them. This makes him inclined to deny their existence. In vain have repeated experiences taught him that this omnipotence, the illusion of which he complacently entertains, has always been a cause of weakness in him; that his power over things really began only when he recognized that they have a nature of their own, and resigned himself to learning this nature from them. Rejected by all other sciences, this deplorable prejudice stubbornly maintains itself in sociology. Nothing is more urgent than to liberate our science from it, and this is the principal purpose of our efforts.[78]

Thus, both Durkheim and Tylor are in agreement that human society and culture are subject to natural law and that the notion of an arbitrary, causeless free will or of human omnipotence must be rejected as incompatible with the scientific enterprise.

As against this line of thought I maintain that human freedom and causality are compatible. To posit human freedom is not to assume some completely causeless factor which may contravene natural law.

[77] Tylor, *Primitive Culture*, I, 3.
[78] Durkheim, *The Rules of Sociological Method*, Author's Preface tr. 2d ed., p. lviii.

Human freedom is always subject to natural law and to cultural authority. The concept of a motiveless human will is a delusion which no philosopher of any standing, so far as I know, has ever maintained. As man is part of the order of nature, all his actions must necessarily be in conformity with the laws of nature. Nevertheless, human freedom is possible in the sense that man is free to act and express himself in accordance with his natural powers.[79] Intellectually, man is free in that he may conceive ideas about himself and nature as a whole and create a new order of phenomena, the artifacts, mentifacts, socifacts, and all the products of the arts and sciences, which would not exist but for him. One may readily grant, as Spinoza, and later Durkheim, insisted, following Francis Bacon, that to be commanded and controlled human nature and society, like nature as a whole must first be obeyed. But let us not forget the possibility of self-control and self-command subject to the conditions of natural law. A science of man, society, and culture does not preclude the possibility of human direction and control, no more than a science of physics precludes human control or adaptation of natural forces to promote human welfare.

It is of historic interest to note here that Tylor, notwithstanding his criticism of the notion of free will as antithetical to a science of culture, did not himself go to the extreme of denying the role of man in general and of the individual in particular in the reformation or transformation of human culture. He was really only opposed to the notion of an anomalous, causeless spontaneity not subject to natural law. Thus, we find Tylor contrasting "those who cannot see the forest for the trees"—who see only the separate life of individuals, but cannot grasp the notion of the action of a community as a whole—with those, on the other hand, who "cannot see the trees for the forest," who see only societies and culture, but not individuals.

The philosopher [he observes] may be so intent upon his general laws of society, as to neglect the individual actors of whom that society is made up, and of him it may be said that he cannot see the trees for the forest. We know how arts, customs and ideas are shaped among ourselves by the combined actions of many individuals, of which actions both motive and effect often come quite distinctly within our view. The history of an invention, an opinion, a ceremony, is a history of suggestion and modification, encouragement and opposition, personal gain and party prejudice, and the individuals concerned act each according to his motives, as determined by his character and circumstances. Thus sometimes we watch individuals acting for their own ends

[79] See Chapter I.

with little thought of their effect on society at large, and sometimes we have to study movements of national life as a whole, where the individuals co-operating in them are utterly beyond our observation. But seeing that collective social action is the mere resultant of many individual actions, it is clear that these two methods of enquiry, if rightly followed, must be absolutely consistent.[80]

This passage is obviously directed against Comte and Buckle, whom Tylor read carefully and to whom he refers in the text. Tylor is opposed to the notion that society constitutes a new kind of reality *sui generis* and that a knowledge of the individual is useless for an understanding of social facts. Collective social action, he maintains, is merely the resultant of many individual actions. The two methods of inquiry, that is, from the perspective of the individual or of the society as a whole, are not antithetical, but rather complementary; it is not necessary to prefer the social approach to the exclusion of the individualistic psychological approach. Tylor had no fear of reductionism, such as later ethnologists were obsessed with, and hence saw no inconsistency in attempting to understand the laws of mental development from a study of the collective facts of culture, on the one hand, and to postulate determinate mental processes as underlying the universal characteristics of such phenomena as myths, on the other.

Thus, while Tylor insisted that ethnology is a natural science leading to the discovery of the laws of the evolution of human thought, he also maintained that the science of culture was "essentially a reformer's science," "active at once in aiding progress and in removing hindrance." [81] The science of culture had a practical import in that by revealing to the student the course of cultural development, it pointed out the way of progress and exposed "survivals" of superstition and myth which no longer possess any functional value or authority. One is impressed with Tylor's eminent sanity and with his ability to avoid the extremes of later sociologists and culturologists, who found it necessary to eliminate the individual person in the so-called interests of scientific objectivity and determinism.

The issue, then, is not whether man's "will" is free, in the sense of being undetermined or causeless, but whether man as a whole is or is not to a limited extent the active agent and efficient cause of the cultural process and whether culture, if its historical conditions are understood, is subject to human control in the interests of human well-being.

[80] Tylor, *Primitive Culture*, I, 12–13.     [81] *Primitive Culture*, II, 410.

I maintain that human freedom and causal determinism are quite compatible and that no irreconcilable conflict is involved. Man is not free, in the primitive, animistic sense, to exercise omnipotent control over the powers of nature and to bend them to his arbitrary will. Primitive animism, in other words, is an abuse of the human powers of thought in that it attributes to man and to nature preternatural powers of which they are not, in fact, capable. But surely this is no reason why one should exclude, in the name of animism, all reference to human power and freedom of initiative in the cultural sphere as well. Man does happen to be an animated creature endowed with life and mind, and one must reckon with these powers as given by nature and not explain them away as of no practical import in the interests of "scientific" simplicity.

Human freedom may be conceived as the human power of action, subject to the determination of intelligence in relation to a given environment. Intelligence and the cultural products of intelligence provide man with ideas of possible alternative courses of action. The ability to exercise choice or preference with reference to possible alternatives constitutes the so-called freedom of willing. Thus, free will is involved in the exercise of human power as subject to natural law. There is no autocratic, anomalous entity called "will" which exercises its arbitrary powers independently of, or contrary to, natural law. Man's will is manifested by his powers of choosing or preferring one alternative rather than another, and this implies that the human will is subject to intelligence and to all those natural conditions which affect human power of action. Free will, so conceived, is not only compatible with a science of man or of culture but is, in fact, a necessary postulate for an understanding of human life and history.

# 5

# *Human Nature and the*
# *Cultural Process*[1]

THE BASIC CONCEPT of contemporary social science is undoubtedly that of culture. We are indebted to anthropologists especially for having distinguished explicitly the category of culture from that of society and for having drawn attention to the role of the cultural process and the "cultural heritage" in molding the life of the individual within society. There is, moreover, general agreement among social scientists that culture is historically acquired by man as a member of society and that it is communicated largely by language or symbolic forms and through participation in social institutions. There is, however, considerable disagreement regarding the ontological status of culture, that is to say, regarding the sense in which culture may be understood as real and the conception of human nature in relation to the cultural process. These problems we shall endeavor to investigate.

## 1. THE GENESIS OF THE CULTURAL PROCESS

The concept of culture is best understood from a genetic and functional point of view. To cultivate an object is to develop the potentialities of its nature in a specific manner with a view to a definite end or result. Thus, for example, agriculture is the process whereby the potentialities of the earth and of seeds are cultivated with a view to the growing of edible plants. In like manner, "anthropoculture," [2] as it may be called, comprises the various ways in which man has tended his nature so as to make it grow or develop.[3] But human culture differs from agriculture in that every stage and phase of the anthropocultural process is to some extent supervised and directed and either consciously

[1] Reprinted in part from *American Anthropologist*, XLIX (1947), 375–99.
[2] Bidney, "On the Philosophy of Culture in the Social Sciences," *Journal of Philosophy*, XXXIX (1942), 449–57; also Chapter 2.
[3] Marett, *Man in the Making*; also, "Anthropology and Religion," in *The Social Sciences and Their Interrelation*, ed. by Ogburn and Goldenweiser.

or unconsciously imitated, with a view to producing a type of man and society which is adjusted to its geographic and social environment. Anthropoculture so conceived refers to the dynamic process of human self-cultivation, whether from conscious or largely unconscious motives, and is identical with education in the original sense of that term. The cultural process, as applied to man, differs from other natural processes in that the former is not autonomous and does not guide itself, but requires constant and deliberate selection and effort on the part of its actual and potential adherents. This process of conscious selection and conditioning does not preclude unpremeditated and unconscious imitation through social suggestion. For example, what language a child shall speak is a matter not left to chance, but is determined for it by its sociocultural milieu and by the deliberate educational efforts of the community. As Sapir observed, much of linguistic behavior is unconsciously patterned so that the people who utilize a given language are hardly conscious themselves of its intricate patterns. But language, in common with the cultural pattern as a whole, involves deliberate selection and direction on the part of its adherents in order to insure continuity in cultural life.

From a historical point of view it is easy to understand why, as men came to attach greater importance to the cultivation of their mental natures, or "souls," the term "culture" came to refer specifically to the latter, and culture became identified with *cultura animi*. But genetically, integral culture refers to the education, or cultivation, of the whole man considered as an organism, not merely to the mental or spiritual aspects of his nature and behavior.

Man is by nature a cultural animal, since he is a self-cultivating, self-reflective, self-conditioning animal and attains to the full development of his natural potentialities only insofar as he lives a cultural life. As contrasted with other animals whose range of development is biologically limited, man is largely a self-formed animal capable of the most diverse types of activity and personality. This point is no new discovery of modern ethnologists and was commented upon by the Spanish humanist Juan Luis Vives in his "Fable about Man" and by Pico della Mirandola in his classic "Oration on the Dignity of Man." Man's special dignity is said to consist in this, that he is of indeterminate nature and may exercise freedom of choice as though he were "the maker and molder" of himself.

On man when he came into life the Father conferred the seeds of all kinds and the germs of every way of life. Whatever seeds each man cultivates will grow to maturity and bear in him their own fruit. . . . It is man who Asclepius of Athens, arguing from his mutability of character and from his self-transforming nature, on just grounds says was symbolized by Proteus in the mysteries.[4]

Man as compared with other animals compensates for his biological deficiencies by his inventive ability, particularly by his technical ingenuity and his ability to invent linguistic symbols for the purpose of communication. All animals which are capable of learning and teaching one another by precept or example are capable of acquiring culture. Hence, not culture in general, but human culture, as manifested in systems of artifacts, social institutions, and symbolic forms of expression, is peculiar to man. This implies an evolutionary approach to the concept of culture which recognizes degrees of culture from the subhuman to the human level. There is continuity in cultural evolution as well as in biological evolution and there is no basis, therefore, either in fact, or in theory, for assuming a leap from the organic to the cultural level. It is encouraging to note that some American cultural anthropologists and linguists, notably Hallowell and Voegelin,[5] have recently found themselves in basic agreement with this point of view.

By a logical transition of thought, the term "culture" has come to refer to the direct product of the process of self-cultivation. Hence, functionally and secondarily culture refers to the acquired forms of technique, behavior, feeling, and thought of individuals within society and to the social institutions in which they cooperate for the attainment of common ends. Since different societies have acquired diverse forms of cultural behavior and thought, anthropologists have designated each system or configuration of actual forms as constituting a culture. Thus, by "culture" in general, or human culture, we refer to the abstract, morphological character of the culture of man considered as a species of animal; by "a culture" we refer to the specific modes of behavior and thought, of theory and practice, of social ideals and institutions, together with the products of these cultural activities which are shared in whole or in part by the members of a given society.

[4] Pico, "Oration on the Dignity of Man," in *The Renaissance Philosophy of Man,* ed. by Cassirer, Kristeller, and Randall, p. 225.

[5] Hallowell, "Personality Structure and the Evolution of Man," *American Anthropologist,* LII (1950), 168; Voegelin, "Culture, Language and the Human Organism," *Southwestern Journal of Anthropology,* VII (1951), 357–73.

## 2. THE NOTION CULTURE AS A "LOGICAL CONSTRUCT"

Some contemporary anthropologists, notably Clyde Kluckhohn and John Gillin, find difficulty with the above notion of culture. They would rather differentiate between actual behavior and the patterns or forms of behavior, reserving the term "culture" for the latter. Thus, Gillin states that "culture is to be regarded as the patterning of activity, not activity itself." Similarly, Kluckhohn writes that "culture is not behavior—it is an abstraction from behavior." [6] And again:

Behavior is never culture. Rather, concrete behavior or habits are part of the raw data from which we infer and abstract culture. Behavioral products (artifacts) comprise our other class of raw data. Culture, thus, is not something which is seen but an inferential construct. . . . Culture, it must be repeated, is a logical construct. It may be manifested either in men's acts or in the products of these acts.[7]

From the above quotations it appear that Gillin and Kluckhohn agree that culture in general is to be defined connotatively by pattern, structure, or form conceived as a logical abstraction or construct, but that it must not be identified with actual behavior or with the instrumental products of the cultural process.

It is interesting to note in this connection that Kluckhohn, while maintaining that culture is a logical construct, also describes it as "historically created, selective processes which channel men's reactions both to internal and to external stimuli." [8] He fails to realize that logically the idea of culture as a dynamic process is a realistic concept, contrary to the idealistic notion of culture understood as a conceptual construct other than the actual activities and processes which comprise human behavior.

The aforementioned writers, in common with many other anthropologists and sociologists, fail to differentiate, it seems to me, between the notion of culture as an "essence" conceived by the investigator and culture as a mode of "existence" of a given society. The field anthropologist, reporting on his findings or telling others about his observations, is interested in the distinctive "patterns" or forms of activity

[6] Gillin, "Cultural Adjustment," *American Anthropologist,* XLVI (1944), 429–47; Kluckhohn, "Patterning as Exemplified in Navaho Culture," in *Language, Culture and Personality, Essays in Memory of Edward Sapir,* ed. by Spier and others.

[7] Kluckhohn, review of A. L. Kroeber's *Configurations of Culture Growth, American Journal of Sociology,* LI (1946), 336–41.

[8] Kluckhohn, "The Concept of Culture," *The Science of Man in the World Crisis,* ed. by Linton, p. 84.

and may construct a typical or average pattern of activity by which the diverse individual activities may be imagined and classified. The anthropologist's concept of a given culture so understood is, indeed, an abstraction or construct, since he has abstracted the form from the actually formed behavior. But the anthropologist's construct of a culture and the same culture as a mode of living or existing are two entirely distinct objects and should not be confused. In an earlier publication I drew attention to the distinction between the realistic and the idealistic aspects of culture and pointed out that "an adequate conception of culture requires the union of both the realistic and the idealistic theses. A culture consists of the acquired or cultivated behavior and thought of individuals within a society, as well as of the intellectual, artistic, and social ideals which the members of the society profess and to which they strive to conform. In other words, a culture must be understood in its practical and theoretical aspects." [9]

It is especially noteworthy that Ralph Linton, who formerly shared the views of Kluckhohn and Gillin, has since modified his position.[10] In his *Cultural Background of Personality* he, too, now distinguishes the "culture construct" from the "real culture" and from the "ideal patterns." [11] He does not, however, reveal the source of his new inspiration.

### 3. THE IDEA OF CULTURE AS SUPERORGANIC

In the preceding analysis we have noted that culture refers not only to the process of education or human self-cultivation but also to the resultant state or product of cultivation. Understood in the latter sense human culture refers to the forms and processes of behavior and thought acquired by man through the development of his innate potentialities. Culture as an acquired state of being (as distinct from the process of becoming, which is cultivation) is essentially a subjective or personal attribute, since it is a state or quality attributed to an actual organism.

The cultural process is, however, polaristic. Man cultivates not only himself or his own natural potentialities but also the natural objects of his environment. Thus, we have a second class of cultural products,

[9] Bidney, "On the Philosophy of Culture in the Social Sciences," *Journal of Philosophy*, XXXIX (1942), 449–57.

[10] Bidney, "On the Concept of Culture and Some Cultural Fallacies," *American Anthropologist*, XLVI (1944), 30–44; Linton, *Study of Man;* also Linton, "Culture, Society and the Individual," *Journal of Abnormal and Social Psychology*, XXXIII (1938), 425–36.

[11] Linton, *The Cultural Background of Personality,* pp. 43–52.

namely, artifacts, or instruments invented by man for the better satisfaction of his needs and wants. Logically, the objective products of
the cultural process are also designated constituents of culture, and
anthropologists, accepting uncritically a dualistic metaphysics, commonly employ the term "material culture" to refer to the aggregate of
artifacts produced by a given society. Furthermore, since objects or
artifacts exist independently of the organism, all such culture products
may be described, in Herbert Spencer's term, as "superorganic."

Further reflection reveals that there is more than one type of superorganic product of the cultural process. In addition to material artifacts
and "agrofacts" there are conceptual symbols, or "mentifacts," comprising language, traditions, literature, and moral, aesthetic, and religious
ideals, as well as the various intellectual instruments of scientific research which are valid and objective for the mind which conceives
them and reflects upon them as mental phenomena. There are also
the social norms and organizations, which we may term "socifacts" and
which serve to regulate the conduct of the individual within society, as
well as the society as a whole in relation to other societies. These ideational symbols and axiological norms are also properly regarded as
superorganic, since they are not primarily attributes of human behavior,
but objects whose validity and subsistence are phenomenologically real
and independent of the individual organism, even though they could
never be thought of and practically realized without organic effort. The
sum total of the artifacts, socifacts, and mentifacts which comprise
superorganic culture are commonly referred to as the "social heritage."
Besides his geographical environment, man is said to be born into a
given social environment, as well as into a cumulative, cultural tradition
and inheritance to which he is trained to adapt himself and in which
he participates as a member of a given society.

It is of interest to note in this connection that philosophical realists
and idealists have different conceptions of the social heritage. The
realists, as exemplified by Franz Boas,[12] maintain that culture consists
of the body of artifacts plus customs and traditions. The idealists, as exemplified implicitly by Marett,[13] Redfield,[14] and Cassirer,[15] maintain that
the cultural heritage consists primarily of ideas or communicated intelligence and symbolic expressions, since they hold that only ideas or

[12] Boas, "Anthropology" *Encyclopedia of Social Sciences*, II, 73–110.
[13] Marett, *Man in the Making.*
[14] Redfield, *The Folk Culture of Yucutan.*
[15] Cassirer, *An Essay on Man.*

symbols may be communicated and transmitted. For the cultural idealists, therefore, so-called material culture is a contradiction in terms,
since for them the real cultural entities, or units, are the conceptual
ideas, or norms, not the particular artifacts which exemplify or embody
them. This idealistic presupposition apparently also serves to explain
the position of those who maintain that culture consists of logical constructs, but not of the actual behavior itself. Logically, the idealistic
position leads to the conclusion that the study of culture is concerned
primarily with the description and phenomenological analysis of concepts or symbols and with the stages of the evolution of cultural mentality.[16]

### 4. THE ORGANIC AND THE SUPERORGANIC VIEWS OF CULTURE

The point I would emphasize at this stage is that culture conceived
as identical with cultural products has been and may be interpreted
in a personalistic, realistic sense as the state of behavior and thought
which is the direct result of the process of education. In a secondary
sense, culture may be conceived as an impersonal, superorganic tradition comprising the aggregate of material and/or ideal products of a
given society or of mankind as a whole. One reason for the confusion
in contemporary culture theory is the failure on the part of social scientists to distinguish adequately between the dynamic, personal conception of culture and the static, impersonal conception involved in
the notion of the cultural heritage. The issue, as I see it, is whether culture is to be understood primarily as a state, or mode, of living exemplified in the personalities of the individuals who comprise society or
is to be regarded historically and idealistically as a tradition which man
acquires from his ancestors. The issue becomes confused when the
impersonal, superorganic cultural products are implicitly endowed,
following the Hegelian and Comtian tradition, with efficient power
"as if" they were dynamic entities which somehow make or develop
themselves according to natural laws of their own—a tendency which
I have previously designated as "the culturalistic fallacy." Logically, it
should be noted, there need be no contradiction between the organic
and the superorganic views of culture, provided it be kept in mind
that we are dealing with different levels of abstraction and that organic, or personal, culture is logically and genetically prior to superorganic, impersonal culture. The recent development of interest on

[16] *Ibid.*, p. 52; Sorokin, *Social and Cultural Dynamics*, IV, 19n.

the part of social psychologists and anthropologists concerning the interrelation of personality and culture is owing to an intentional reaction against the superorganic view of culture [17]—a reaction which is decried by the conservative superorganicists as a "reduction" of culture to social psychology.

The actual conflicts which have developed in contemporary culture theory have arisen because of the extreme positions adopted by both "organicists" and "superorganicists," which have led partisans of both views to deny the element of truth in the other's position. Morris E. Opler, for example, has written of the "Cultural and Organic Conceptions in Contemporary World History" [18] and has interpreted the Second World War as a "phase of the overshadowing struggle between two world conceptions, the organic and the cultural." Contrary to the complacent attitude of so many anthropologists and sociologists who were taught to worship social "facts" and to distrust theoretical issues as merely "verbal" or philosophic casuistry, Opler, at least, has appreciated the serious social import of the cultural problem for our times and has drawn attention to the existential crises which result when extreme organicist views are put into practice on an international scale. I maintain, however, contrary to his basic thesis, that the organicist and the superorganicist views may be reconciled and that it is fallacious to oppose the category of the organic to the superorganic, or "cultural," view.

As Malinowski [19] has shown, human culture is organic in the sense that it is initiated for the purpose of satisfying man's psychobiological needs and aspirations. There is, accordingly, an organic connection between the type of culture which an organism manifests, or lives by and for, and the type of biological structure it possesses and psychosomatic functions which it is capable of exercising.[20] Monkey culture,

---

[17] Young, *Social Psychology;* Kardiner, *The Individual and His Society;* Thompson and Joseph, *The Hopi Way;* MacGregor, *Warriors without Weapons;* Du Bois, *The People of Alor;* Hallowell, "The Rorschach Technique in the Study of Personality and Culture," *American Anthropologist,* XLVII (1945), 195–210; Hallowell, "Personality Structure and the Evolution of Man," *ibid.,* LII (1950), 159–73.

[18] Opler, "Cultural and Organic Conceptions in Contemporary World History," *American Anthropologist,* XLVI (1944), 448–59.

[19] Malinowski, "Culture," in *Encyclopaedia of the Social Sciences,* IV, 621–45; *A Scientific Theory of Culture.*

[20] Greenman, "Material Culture and the Organism," *American Anthropologist,* XLVII (1945), 211–31; Sheldon, *The Varieties of Temperament;* Mead, "The Concept of Culture and the Psychosomatic Approach," in D. G. Haring, ed., *Personal Character and Cultural Milieu,* pp. 518–38.

for example, differs from human culture because the psychobiological potentialities and needs of the monkey organism differ from those of man. Thus, as was said previously, not culture in general, but human culture, with its symbolic constructs and artifacts, is peculiar to man. All human systems of culture have universal traits [21] in common, such as systems of artifacts, social institutions, language, and traditions which differentiate them radically from animal cultures. All human cultures are communicable to human beings, but not to other animal species. Monkeys and dogs may be taught a few cultural tricks, but apparently they are incapable by nature of participating fully in a human system of culture or becoming humanized. In sum, it may be stated that there is an organic, neurological, a priori structure [22] which limits the type of culture of which any animal, including man, is capable in relation to a given environment.

Furthermore, I maintain, in agreement with previous writers,[23] that there is an element of truth in the position of Huntington [24] that geographical factors, such as climate, do affect the energy-potential of man that is available for cultural achievement. The climate and the geographical resources of a country do affect the type of culture which it is possible for man to realize and maintain in a given environment.[25] One need not go to the extreme of regarding climate as the primary or dominant factor in cultural development, but it is certainly a significant contributing factor.

Similarly, with reference to the races of mankind, there may be some significant differences which may account, in part at least, for some of the diversities in human culture systems. Otto Klineberg,[26] for instance, is prepared to grant that "among the members of relatively small, isolated and therefore inbred communities, we may expect a marked degree of homogeneity in physical features and an accompanying 'typical' psychology, genetically determined." [27] According to Shapiro,

[21] Murdock, "The Common Denominator of Cultures," in Linton, *The Science of Man in the World Crisis*, pp. 123–42.

[22] McCulloch, "A Heterarchy of Values Determined by the Topology of Nervous Sets," *Bulletin of Mathematical Biophysics*, VII (1945), 89–93.

[23] Shapiro, "Society and Biological Man," in Linton, ed., *The Science of Man in the World Crisis*, pp. 19–37.

[24] Huntington, *Climate and Civilization;* also *Mainsprings of Civilization.*

[25] Markham, *Climate and the Energy of Nations.*

[26] Klineberg, "Racial Psychology," in Linton, ed., *The Science of Man in the World Crisis.*

[27] *Ibid.,* p. 67.

While all the arguments for racial correlations with innate capacity may be explained away, a tantalizing but elusive conviction that races or peoples are in some degree differentiated by their inherited abilities lingers on. My own inclination is to regard the extreme, all or nothing, hypothesis as eventually unsatisfactory in clarifying the relationship of race, capacity and civilization. Just as the racist explanation of every minutia of culture behavior and capacity is obviously maleficent and untenable before the facts, so the tendency to interpret all aspects of civilization and society as based on factors outside and beyond the genes seems only a partial explanation of an extraordinarily complex relationship.[28]

Furthermore, from a medical point of view, it would appear that the state of health or disease in a society affects its general vitality and therefore its cultural creativity. Here, too, as in the case of geographical determinism, one need not go to the extreme of maintaining with Hooton[29] and some medical historians that biological constitution or the state of health is the primary determining factor in culture history. All that is necessary for our present thesis is to recognize the roles of health and disease as providing organic conditions which help or retard the cultural evolution of a society. As Ackerknecht has reasoned:

Of course, it would be foolish to deny to malaria any influence on history, and we have no intention of doing so. The problem under discussion is whether or not malaria is a *primary* factor in history. In this respect malaria seems rather to be "man-made" everywhere, to be caused by history (a complex of social, economic and moral factors), rather than to cause history.[30]

On occasion, disease may dramatically affect the course of culture history in reducing the efficiency of armies and their prospects of military conquest.[31] It is a commonplace of ethnohistory that native peoples have had to give way before the white man not merely because they lacked the latter's mechanical equipment, but more because they had no immunity to most of the diseases which the white man brought with him. According to Ashburn, it is an open question whether, in the coming centuries, machinery and science or immunity to disease will most influence racial dominance.[32]

Thus, from the perspectives of biology, physical anthropology, and medicine one must reckon with the organic foundations of human culture as basic for an understanding of its general patterns and contingent

[28] "Society and Biological Man," *ibid.*, p. 30.
[29] Hooton, *Man's Poor Relations;* also *Why Men Behave Like Apes and Vice Versa.*
[30] Ackerknecht, "Malaria," in *Ciba Symposia,* VII (1945), 51–56; Sigerist, *Civilization and Disease.*
[31] Zinsser, *Rats, Lice and History.*
[32] Ashburn, *The Ranks of Death,* p. 212.

variations. In general it may be said that the organic foundations of human culture provide the material conditions for the cultural process, the universal as well as special conditions which limit the course of human development and cultural change. The organic factor is an essential one, but it is not sufficient of itself to account for the diversity of cultural traits and patterns.

Organicism becomes mythological only when it is arbitrarily assumed that biological factors are the primary ones and that cultural diversity among human societies implies fixed metabiological differences which set one race permanently above or beneath others in the scale of biological evolution. Certainly "racism" as a pseudo-explanation of socio-cultural prejudice has no basis in established fact. For cultural purposes mankind must be considered as a unit, since all groups of men have common potentialities for participating in human culture.[33] Racism as a metabiological doctrine, on the other hand, presupposes that some societies of men have advanced farther in the scale of biological evolution than others and that the former are naturally selected or "chosen" for permament cultural dominance over others. The "organic" tie-up between culture and "blood and soil" makes of a given culture system a monadic, solipsistic affair which automatically precludes participation by any other group, so that different societies of men are treated as if they belonged to different species of animals. On this mythological assumption there can be no peaceful resolution of political differences, and force, rather than persuasion, becomes the primary means of "settling" disputes. In this sense the Second World War is but a lesson in applied logic.

As a reaction to the extreme biological myths of the nineteenth and twentieth centuries,[34] the doctrine of superorganicism draws attention to the communicable nature of human culture and to its independence of comparable, biological evolution. But superorganicism represents the opposite extreme in that its proponents tend to neglect the organic conditions of culture altogether and to concentrate exclusively upon historical and environmental factors, such as "diffusion" and the autonomous laws of cultural development. Culture and society (the two are often confused by positivistic sociologists) are regarded by superorganicists as if they were superpsychic entities that follow independ-

[33] Montagu, *Man's Most Dangerous Myth: the Fallacy of Race;* Benedict, *Race, Science and Politics;* Krogman, "The Concept of Race," in Linton, ed., *The Science of Man in the World Crisis,* pp. 38–62.
[34] Chandler, *Rosenberg's Nazi Myth.*

ent laws of their own and require no reference to the psychobiological nature of the individuals who participate in them. In this way a superorganic fatalism is substituted for the equally objectionable organic fatalism which they oppose.

The thesis I am concerned to emphasize here is that from a logical and genetic perspective organicism and superorganicism represent two extreme positions, since the organic, as well as the superorganic, factors in culture must both be recognized as integral elements in the cultural process. Either factor taken separately is an abstraction from the total cultural situation. Positively, it may be said, the organic conditions determine culture, and culture as a superorganic achievement in turn affects organic conditions. The process appears to be cyclical and two-dimensional rather than linear and one-dimensional.

## 5. CULTURE AS THE SOCIAL HERITAGE

The contrast between the personalistic, humanistic view of culture, on the one hand, and the impersonal, transcendental view of culture, on the other, may be pointed up further by analyzing the notion of "the social heritage." As applied to culture the latter term implies that the essential feature of culture is the fact of transmission and communication. The individual is thought of as being born into a man-made world of artifacts, symbols, and social institutions which he acquires from his ancestors. This superorganic, sociocultural world is then said to mold the individual in conformity with the prevailing cultural patterns and to determine the nature of his mentality. On this basis, it is asserted, we can understand the nature and mind of the individual only through the society of which he is a member, according to George Mead,[35] John Dewey,[36] Charles H. Cooley,[37] and Ellsworth Faris,[38] or through humanity as a whole, according to Comte [39] and Ernst Cassirer.[40] Furthermore, once culture is hypostatized into a transcendental force, it is but a short step, although a very significant one, to regard it as an autonomous process which evolves according to fixed laws and molds not only individuals but also whole societies and even all hu-

[35] Mead, *Mind, Self and Society.*
[36] Dewey, *Human Nature and Conduct;* "Human Nature," in *Encyclopedia of the Social Sciences,* VIII, 531–36.
[37] Cooley, *Human Nature and the Social Order.*
[38] Faris, *The Nature of Human Nature.*
[39] Lévy-Bruhl, *The Philosophy of Auguste Comte.*
[40] Cassirer, *An Essay on Man.*

manity—a thesis which such diverse social thinkers as Hegel, Comte, and Marx, Spengler and Sorokin have developed at length. Culture, on this basis, becomes the primary, impersonal "agent," or cause, of cultural history, and men become relegated to the role of passive vehicles which embody the great cultural ideas, forms, or forces in history. Thus, superorganic culture has come to be regarded as a kind of Fate which in the name of Social Science has superseded metaphysical Providence. Beginning as an inheritance from the past, culture has gradually acquired the status of a transcendental social force which molds the future of man as well.

On the other hand, according to the personalistic, organic, humanistic theory of culture advocated here, the term "social heritage" is inadequate and even misleading as a synonym for culture. First, it may be pointed out that cultural objects *per se*, whether artifacts, socifacts, or mentifacts, are but inert, static matériel, or capital, for cultural life and that of themselves they exert no efficient creative power. Only individuals or societies of men can spontaneously initiate and perpetuate cultural processes which may result in superorganic cultural achievements, and hence there can be no autonomous cultural process independent of human intelligence and voluntary effort. To think otherwise is to mistake a conceptual abstraction for an actual vital agent; and to attribute power of activity to cultural ideals or forms is to commit the metaphysical fallacy,[41] or the fallacy of "misplaced concreteness," for which Aristotle originally criticized Plato, namely, the fallacy of attributing efficient causality to conceptual forms. Cultural achievements are (to use Aristotelian terms) the material and formal causes or conditions of cultural development, but they are not the efficient causes or active agents. And since culture is not an efficient cause, it cannot make or develop itself or "interact" with members of society. This is not to deny that cultural achievements do constitute a part of the human environment and provide the conditions for social life; all I deny is that these superorganic phenomena constitute an autonomous, ontological realm which man is incapable of transcending or shaping. Only by surreptitiously introducing the attribute of regulating activity (which pertains only to organisms) into the notion of the superorganic does one come to regard it as a dynamic, autonomous force which supersedes human agents. If we bear in mind that culture, in its primary sense, is

[41] Bidney, "On the Concept of Culture and Some Cultural Fallacies," *American Anthropologist*, XLVI (1944), 30–44.

logically and genetically an acquired attribute of human nature and that it is for us as human beings to determine which cultural heritage is to be conserved and fostered and which is to be allowed to wither away through desuetude, then we shall be rid permanently of fatalistic delusions concerning the cultural superorganic.

Furthermore, the notion of the social heritage fails to take into account the facts of novelty and change in cultural life. Culture is not merely given; it is literally always "in the making." Human culture is historical because it involves change as well as continuity, creation of novelty together with conservation of tradition. We do not understand the presence of pattern or configuration in history unless we take into consideration the factor of continuity and tradition. Cultural history is not the record of a merely fortuitous sequence of events; it has meaning precisely because we do recognize some inner continuity and logical connection between events.[42] But history also involves the emergence of new events and novel formations which are not to be accounted for on the basis of inertial, cultural forces. Ultimately we must have recourse to the dynamic human agents whose creative inventions and insights, as well as persevering determination, are the sources of all cultural processes. Comte notwithstanding, in the human sphere at least we cannot eliminate the category of human agents as efficient and final or motivating causes so as to rely solely upon abstract, positivistic, formal laws to explain the evolution of cultural phenomena. We require a metacultural principle or agent to render intelligible the genesis and diverse configurations of the cultural process.

Finally, the personal, humanistic, and the impersonal, transcendental views of culture may be contrasted in terms of their "genuineness," or "authenticity." Edward Sapir,[43] it will be recalled, distinguished "genuine' from "spurious" culture by pointing out that genuine culture is integrated and meaningful to the individual, whereas nongenuine culture is atomized and personally meaningless, since it fails to satisfy the individual's desire for complete participation in his social culture. On this basis, he argues, preliterate tribal cultures are much more genuine than modern literate Western cultures, since in the latter human relations are depersonalized and mechanized and rarely provide sufficient outlet for the average individual, whereas in the former the individual

---

[42] Kroeber, *Configurations of Culture Growth;* "History and Evolution," *Southwestern Journal of Anthropology,* II (1946), 1–15.

[43] Sapir, "Culture, Genuine and Spurious," in *Selected Writings of Edward Sapir,* ed. by David G. Mandelbaum.

can participate in all the manifold integrated activities of his society. Recently José Ortega y Gasset contrasted the authentic, original needs felt by individuals with the unauthentic, impersonal, social and collective mode of existence. As he puts it in his essays:

Anything social is intrinsically, and not by chance, a human phenomenon in its unauthentic form; and social existence is a defective—albeit inevitable— mode of being-a-man which belongs to every personality. . . . When human dealings establish themselves as social facts, they become mechanical and unauthentic—ideas grow hackneyed—but thanks to such transformations they are also freed from the whims, the frailty and the arbitrariness of individuals.[44]

For culture to become authentic, therefore, it must be individualized and personalized so that the individual may become aware of its intrinsic importance to his existence.

Thus, it appears, both Sapir and Ortega y Gasset regard individual, existential culture as genuine or authentic and impersonal, mechanical culture as nongenuine, or unauthentic. Contrary to the sociological approach which regards superorganic culture as logically and genetically prior to the individual, they would assert the primacy and "plenary mode" of individual culture, and the secondary, defective character of superorganic, impersonal culture. This is not meant as a denial of the reality and restrictive influence of social traditions. All it does mean is that impersonal, sociocultural facts have to be and can be evaluated in terms of their import for the lives of the individuals who are confronted with them and that in the last analysis, it is the personal importance of culture in the life crises of the individual [45] and his society which determine its final validity and influence. This point may be illustrated by the oft-proclaimed futility of relying on new institutions or new legislation so long as the proper "good will" and "change of heart" are lacking to make their enforcement effectual. The point has special relevance for us in connection with survival and axiological crises [46] which now confront the world after the Second World War and with the problem of building an enduring peace. As the New York *Times* has put it:

For the democracies, working on the principle of government by the consent of the governed, know that, even though it takes force to enforce a law or treaty against the recalcitrant, nevertheless, in the long run, neither laws nor

[44] Ortega y Gasset, *Concord and Liberty and Other Essays,* pp. 109n., 109–10.
[45] Bidney, "On the Concept of Cultural Crisis," *American Anthropologist,* XLVIII (1946), 534–52; Arendt, "What Is Existenz Philosophy?" *Partisan Review,* XIII (1946), 34–56.
[46] See Chapter 12.

treaties can endure unless they are sanctioned by the great majority of the people, and that bad laws and bad treaties which do not find such sanction are usually nullified, sometimes with explosive consequences.[47]

In sum, this means that impersonal "laws" and social arrangements are not effective unless they gain the adherence and sanction of the people who acknowledge their validity and put them into practice. In other words, impersonal, superorganic culture is an abstraction; personal, individualized culture is the ultimate, existential reality in the sphere of social life.

### 6. THE POLARITY OF NATURE AND CULTURE

The general thesis I have sought to establish up to this point is that human culture in general may be understood as the dynamic process and product of the self-cultivation of human nature, as well as of the natural environment, and involves the development of selected potentialities of nature for the attainment of individual and social ends of living. By means of the cultural process the potentialities of human nature and of cosmic nature are adapted to one another for the purpose of promoting human existence and welfare. I am especially concerned to make it clear that culture is an essentially correlative, polar concept and is unintelligible apart from its reference to nature. A scientific theory of culture is one that reckons seriously with the polar factors of culture and the data derived from an immediate experience of nature. While it is possible to abstract either factor from the total context for the purpose of logical analysis, I do not think that either factor alone is intrinsically intelligible. Human nature is the *locus* of culture, and the potentialities of human nature may be said to set limits to the kind of cultural processes which may be introduced and encouraged. The phrase "contrary to nature" often employed by moralists implies that a given cultural custom or institution may be practically incompatible with some of the basic psychobiological and social needs and aspirations of human nature taken individually or collectively. As Aristotle said, speaking of moral virtue, "neither by nature, then, nor contrary to nature do the virtues arise in us; rather we are adapted by nature to receive them, and are made perfect by habit." [48]

The polarity, or complementarity, of nature and culture implies that while there is some degree of independence, or autonomy, of

[47] New York *Times,* July 8, 1946.
[48] Aristotle, *Nicomachean Ethics,* 1103a.

natural and cultural factors, there is also some degree of interdependence, or mutual dependence.[49] If there were no determinate human
nature and natural environment for man to cultivate and transform
there would be no cultural process or product. Similarly, if human nature
were completely unmodifiable, if man were incapable of determining
for himself the direction or particular form of his development through
the process of conditioning and education, there could be no culture.
The cultural process requires as its indispensable condition a determinate human nature and environment that is subject to transformation
by man himself.

Furthermore, culture may be thought of as a natural process in the
sense that it is ultimately a spontaneous expression evolved in the
exercise of man's natural potentialities and in response to his felt psychobiological and social needs and the stimulus of his geographical
environment. This, however, does not make natural and cultural processes any the less disparate. "Natural selection" alone does not explain
either the great diversity of cultural forms of expression or the reason
for the conservation of some forms in preference to others. For that we
have to introduce the supplementary notion of normative "cultural
selection," which is often at variance with so-called natural, or biological, selection. Natural selection works largely through survival
crises; cultural selection works primarily through axiological crises.
The attempt on the part of the organic and superorganic determinists
to reduce the cultural process to an automatic, autonomous process
of natural selection disregards the essentially human and rational element in the cultural process, namely, the normative selection of cultural values.

The point at issue here is of the utmost importance and underlies
many of the basic problems of theoretical anthropology. As a result
of the attempts of evolutionary ethnologists of the nineteenth century
to view culture as having a "natural history," there has developed a
tendency on the part of modern anthropologists to regard culture itself
as a part of the order of nature. Academically this is demonstrated by
the fact that anthropologists alone are usually classed with the "natural
scientists" and admitted into scientific societies from which other social
scientists are excluded.

My thesis is that the reduction of cultural processes to natural processes involves "the naturalistic fallacy" of which the fallacy of racism,

---

[49] Sheldon, *Process and Polarity.*

discussed earlier, is but a special example. Culture is natural in the sense that it is a product of human discovery and invention and does not require the assumption of "supernatural" agencies and powers. But culture and nature are, nevertheless, two radically disparate factors and may not be reduced to one another without serious impoverishment and confusion of thought. "Anthropoculture" is a human achievement and demonstrates the perfectibility of man and his freedom of creativity. It is a "natural" consequence of human potentiality, but has no primary reality of its own other than that of being an attribute of man's activity. Cultural processes presuppose natural processes, but the converse does not hold.

In the history of Western philosophical thought many attempts have been made to reduce culture to nature, especially in the field of ethics and law, such as Aristotle's assumption of a "natural law" transcending moral conventions, and the Stoic doctrine of "living in conformity with nature." The theory of the evolutionary ethnologists that culture is a natural process with a natural history of its own was but a modification of an ancient approach. When evolutionary ethnology was combined with Darwinian evolutionary biology, culture was then viewed as an autonomous system subject to laws comparable to those of biology and not subject to human interference. For the "social Darwinists" cultural phenomena, like biological phenomena, were thought to be subject to a process of "natural selection" which was independent of subjective human purposes and goals.

As against this entire school of thought, which still has its adherents in contemporary anthropology and sociology, I have argued for the polarity and relative independence of natural and cultural processes. Culture as a free creation of man is not to be evaluated by the universal laws of physical and biological phenomena. Cultural values are human norms instituted by man for the enhancement of human life in particular, and their validity cannot be determined by the degree of their conformity to the universal processes of cosmic nature. Normative ethics, for example, is based in large measure upon what Albert Schweitzer has called the principle of "reverence for life." This principle is the antithesis of the Darwinian law of natural selection and the struggle for existence. All that is distinctively human in civilized ethics is based upon this "contravention" of the rule which apparently prevails in the biological sphere. From this perspective it seems true to say that one phase of the universal, perpetual crisis of our times is the fact that some of the nations of the world have attempted to justify international aggression by appealing to the Darwinian principle of natural selection and the "right" of the strong to subjugate the weak irrespective of human costs and human ideals.

It is high time, therefore, that as students of human culture anthropologists awaken to their responsibility as human beings and break with the lingering tradition of social Darwinism and its correlate, the theory of the superorganic autonomy of culture. In the sphere of culture, at least, we require a humanistic approach to account for the facts of human experience and human history. Cultural variation, unlike natural variation, depends in large measure upon the rational, normative selection of man. Whether or not there be a providential "life force" which pushes man to ever higher levels of achievement, man must live and act to realize ideal goals in the faith that if nature does not guarantee the success of his efforts, she will not, in any event, oppose them and doom them to failure if he persist in being humane. If mankind so believes and is prepared to enforce its ideals, those who are morally "fittest" to survive may also be biologically competent to do so.

In order to realize the common objectives of social life, man has at all times endeavored to regulate and standardize the expression of his natural affects and appetites. By encouraging the development of some human potentialities and impulses, the cultural process makes for an actual increase in liberty or power of achievement and thereby enables man individually and collectively to engage in a multitude of enterprises which he would otherwise be unable to undertake, or carry through, successfully. In this sense we may accept Cassirer's statement to the effect that "human culture taken as a whole may be described as the process of man's progressive self-liberation." [50] On the other hand, the cultural process is also a restraining discipline which checks or suppresses the individual's impulses in the interests of society—a point which Freud and his followers have stressed.[51] Accordingly, there is in all cultural systems some degree of tension between the individual and his society, between the egoistic impulses one would fain indulge and the altruistic ideals one is more or less conditioned, or compelled, to obey. The essential weakness of culturalistic theories of human nature lies in their failure to render intelligible individual differences,

[50] Cassirer, *An Essay on Man*, p. 228.
[51] Freud, *Civilization and Its Discontents;* Kardiner, *The Individual and His Society;* Róheim, *The Origin and Function of Culture.*

as well as the perpetual tension, between individuals and their society. If, for example, one were to accept Cooley's thesis that "society and individuals do not denote separable phenomena but are simply collective and distributive aspects of the same thing," [52] then it is difficult to see how one could logically account for class conflicts and the prevalence of criminals in all human societies.

The tension between individuals and their society is of necessity increased and may reach the limit of endurance when there is gross social injustice. When opportunities and restraints do not affect all members of a society equally or in equal proportion, minority groups are bound to feel resentful and to cease to conform to common social ideals and practices. A stable society requires a cultural system so organized as to provide a maximum of opportunity for the development of human potentialities and the perfection of the individual with a minimum of social constraint. A society may fail in its cultural objective because its culture may be grounded on inadequate, unscientific knowledge of man's nature and cosmic environment and therefore appear unable to satisfy basic psychobiological needs and aspirations. Such a culture may then be said to be unrealistic, or "contrary to nature." Historically, it seems that the development of human culture is the record of man's attempts to devise cultural systems which are in harmony with nature, human and cosmic. And when the cultural ideals and institutions fail to satisfy universal human needs, the cry always goes up, "back to nature."

This point is well illustrated by the Western doctrine of natural rights. It is no accident of history that the reformers and revolutionists of every generation appeal to the inalienable natural rights of the individual to "life, liberty and the pursuit of happiness," to "freedom from want and freedom from fear," in opposition to those sociocultural forces which would deprive the individual of those privileges and securities. The historical error in the doctrine of natural rights lies in the tendency of its seventeenth- and eighteenth-century protagonists, such as Hobbes, Spinoza, Locke, and Jefferson, to contrast nature and culture instead of viewing them as the correlative poles of a single process. They failed to realize, in spite of acquaintance with the cultures of native societies through contemporary travelers' tales, that there are no precultural peoples living in "a state of nature." The accounts of these pseudoprimitive peoples of the Americas only served to confirm each

[52] Cooley, *Human Nature and the Social Order;* Young, *Social Psychology.*

philosopher in his own preconceived notions of human nature. Under the influence of Stoic philosophy the philosophers of the Enlightenment sought to discover principles of ethics, politics, and law which were in agreement with nature and reason. The idea arose that a rational, analytic science of man and society based on the verifiable facts of experience and history is possible. Hence, we find them speaking of a natural ethics, natural religion, and natural law and politics, discoverable by reason and yet based on and in agreement with the essential nature of things. Theoretical, rational anthropology was to provide the philosopher and statesman with guiding principles in the light of which he could reform society and establish institutions in harmony with reason. The great paradox of rationalism is that the very thinkers and reformers who in the name of reason sought to abolish historical cultures, succeeded only in instituting cultural changes which were often even more arbitrary and unrealistic than those they endeavored to replace, since they failed to appreciate the cultural attachment and inertia of the very peoples they sought to reform and liberate, as, for example, in the French Revolution. Nevertheless, it remains true that these liberal, humanistic philosophers laid the foundations of the modern democratic state and the constitutional rights of the individual protected by law.

The excesses of the rationalists led to the opposite reaction of historians, romanticists, sociologists, and ethnologists of the eighteenth and nineteenth centuries, who justified cultural customs on the ground that they proved their worth in the historical process. By denying natural rights and substituting historical, social rights they sanctioned every social institution they preferred and deprived the individual of any criterion by which to evaluate critically and objectively the actual role and ideal function of the social institutions to which he was required to submit.[53] William Graham Sumner crystallized this positivistic attitude when he stated that "in the folkways, whatever is, is right . . . For the men of the time there are no 'bad' mores. What is traditional and current is the standard of what ought to be." [54] This positivistic, cynical acceptance of social, historical culture led logically to the growth of the totalitarian states of our generation, which proclaimed a new version of the ancient doctrine that "justice is the interest of the stronger" by endowing the state with absolute rights and the individ-

[53] Stapleton, *Justice and World Society.*
[54] Sumner, *Folkways,* pp. 28, 59.

ual with those occasional privileges which it pleased those in power to grant him.[55]

In terms of our analysis, the way out of this dilemma is to recognize that all moral and political rights are based on sociocultural acknowledgment, but that this need not preclude the admission that these culturally based rights have also a natural, ontological basis in man and the cosmos which renders their cultural acceptance intelligible. This resolution of the problem would avoid the naturalistic fallacy of deducing cultural norms from nature and of assuming any actual precultural rights—a fallacy which leads in practice to unscrupulous neglect of one's social duties and responsibilities to other members of human society. It would also avoid the positivistic fallacy of identifying the "is" and the "ought" for a given culture and would thereby obviate the cultural relativism and social dictatorship which are the logical consequences of this fallacy in practice. Only by putting into practice the balanced, polar theory of the natural potential basis of individual rights and the sociocultural origin and recognition of actual, "natural rights" do we preserve a proper equilibrium between the individual and his society, between the perennial claims of the individual and the historically changing conditions under which his claims are recognized and supported by the state.

## 7. CULTURAL TYPES AND THE CONCEPT OF THE NORMAL

Actual positive, or historical, cultures differ markedly from one another in the selection of possible forms of activity and organization, and every society, therefore, has the defects corresponding to its cultural virtues. This cultural selection and integration is manifested by the ideal type of man which the members of a given society prefer and by the social institutions they provide to make it possible for the average individual to approximate this ideal. Thus, one society idealizes the warrior type; another, the man of wealth; a third, the scholar; a fourth, the cooperative individual who performs his social duties easily.[56] Each ideal type calls for the development of some human potentialities and the suppression or restraint of others. As there are a limited number of natural human propensities and basic impulses, there are necessarily a limited number of cultural configurations and cultural personality types.

[55] Cobban, *The Crisis of Civilization.*
[56] Benedict, *Patterns of Culture;* Mead, *Cooperation and Competition among Primitive Peoples.*

On the other hand, if one were to begin with the postulate of the extreme culturalist that human nature is an abstraction from or function of culture, then it would follow logically that there is no limit to the number of cultural personality types and no objective way in which the normal type may be distinguished from the abnormal. On this basis, the concept of "normality" is culturally defined as relative to the context of a given culture and society, since there is no absolute or precultural human nature which may serve as referent for normality.[57] Ultimately such a relativistic concept of normality would preclude the possibility of a transcultural science of medicine or psychiatry. While it is advisable to take into consideration the effects of cultural conditioning upon the individual's state of health and upon the socially acceptable conditions of "normality," one must still postulate a transcultural or metacultural biological and psychiatrical standard of normality which transcends the purely relative, highly variable cultural norms.[58]

### 8. HUMAN NATURE AND THE ORIGIN OF HUMAN CULTURE

The significance of the polarity of human nature and culture may also be demonstrated by contrast with the position of Ellsworth Faris. He states:

The primordial origin of human culture is a problem to the solution of which it is impossible to bring any facts. Sociology is in the same position on this point as that in which biology finds itself with respect to the problem of the origin of life. And just as the biologist came at last to utter the dictum: "all life comes from the living," so the student of culture declares: *Omnis cultura ex cultura.* And if all culture comes from antecedent culture then no culture comes from the operation of the instinctive activities of individuals. . . . Grammars are not contrived, vocabularies were not invented, and the semantic changes in language take place without the awareness of those in whose mouths the process is going on. This is a super-individualistic phenomenon and so also are other characteristic aspects of human life, such as changes in fashions or alterations of the mores.[59]

Faris's argument, which is reminiscent of Kroeber's original position, is that since human cultures may not be deduced from the so-called

---

[57] Benedict, "Anthropology and the Abnormal," *Journal of General Psychology,* X (1934), 59–82; Mead, "The Concept of Culture and the Psychosomatic Approach," in *Personal Character and Cultural Milieu,* ed. by D. G. Haring.

[58] Wegrocki, "A Critique of Cultural and Statistical Concepts of Abnormality," in *Personality in Nature, Society and Culture,* ed. by Kluckhohn and Murray, pp. 551–61.

[59] Faris, *The Nature of Human Nature,* pp. 22–23.

instinctive endowment of individuals or racial groups, and since cultural development is not bound up with improvement in mental capacity, it is argued that the only logical alternative is to assume that culture is a process *sui generis,* a transcendental social process which genetically precedes the individual and determines the type of human nature he is to acquire. By identifying cultural personality with human nature Faris concludes that "human nature is not to be ascribed to the newborn." [60]

In answer to the argument of Faris, the point I would stress is that there is no mystery regarding the primordial origin of human culture. We do know that cultural achievements are the product of human discovery and invention and can trace the course of their development beyond the horizon of recorded history. Culture, we can say a priori, is coeval with the existence of man, if it be granted that man is by nature a cultural animal. And thus, as against the superorganicist position of Faris I maintain: *Omnis cultura ex natura.* By this we do not mean that the specific forms of culture may be deduced from any so-called instincts or innate action patterns; all that is meant is that ultimately the cultural process is to be understood as a spontaneous expression and discovery of human nature and human creative intelligence. On this point, therefore, we find ourselves in agreement with Clark Wissler's statement [61] to the effect that "in the last analysis, it is the behavior of man as a functioning individual that results in culture, though just what detailed form the culture of the group takes is determined by the circumstances of the time and place in which the specific culture traits arise." Cultural forms of expression may, indeed, be evolved without any corresponding evolution in innate human capacity, since the educational process does not alter one's innate ability, but develops and activates one's abilities so as to promote the creative power and freedom of the individual. The cultural process as a method, or way, of thinking and living provides material and intellectual instruments for utilizing human powers and actualizing them in relation to given geographical and social environments. For this reason the cultural process is self-perpetuating and cumulative, since past achievements may be utilized as steps to further creative advance. In this limited sense culture may be said to arise from culture, just as one mode of thinking arises from another. But the process of thinking is not

[60] *Ibid.,* p. 35.
[61] Wissler, *An Introduction to Social Anthropology,* p. 359.

intelligible apart from a thinker, a mind capable of conceiving ideas, and the cultural process can be understood only by reference to the metacultural creative potentialities and limitations of human nature.

It should be noted here that logically, or theoretically, there need be no incompatibility between the maxims *cultura ex cultura* and *cultura ex natura*, once we distinguish between the ontological relation of nature and culture, on the one hand, and the historical process of cultural development, on the other.

The cultural problem is in this respect similar to the biological issue of biogenesis *versus* abiogenesis. Modern biological research is now coming around to the position that such factors as enzymes may serve as a bridge between the quick and the dead. As Northrup has put it:

The criterion of reproduction, which has long been used to distinguish the quick from the dead, has failed, and the problem of defining a living thing, always a difficult one, has become even more difficult. It begins to look as though this difficulty is inherent in the subject and may be due to the fact that there exists no fundamental distinction between living things and inanimate things. Thus the modern biochemist finds that in some cases it is very difficult to make any very fundamental distinction, these days, between the quick and the dead.[62]

Similarly Woodruff writes:

Apparently our well-worn and well-liked antithesis between the inorganic and the organic does not exhaust the possibilities. The molecular unit of the non-living world seems to approach the cellular unit of the living. Philosophers in little things are revealing an intermediate microcosm which may partially bridge the enormous gap between the quick and the dead.[63]

Similarly, with regard to cultural phenomena one may grant that diverse cultural configurations are to be explained in part by historical and environmental factors, while still maintaining that ultimately cultural phenomena are not intelligible apart from the structure and the functions of human nature. For example, it is no accident or mystery that one may find, as Wissler,[64] Malinowski,[65] and Warden[66] have pointed out, certain universal cultural institutions in all types of human society which answer to the universal needs for food, shelter, protec-

[62] Northrup, "The Quick and the Dead," in *Serving through Science Series,* Radio Broadcast, 1946, published by U.S. Rubber Company.
[63] Woodruff, "Biology," *The Development of the Sciences,* Second series, ed. by L. L. Woodruff.
[64] Wissler, *Man and Culture.*
[65] Malinowski, *A Scientific Theory of Culture.*
[66] Warden, *The Emergence of Human Culture.*

tion, communication, social relations, and the psychobiological crises of life, such as birth, puberty, marriage, and death. The precise form which these universal institutions and mores take is in turn determined by various factors, such as the nature of the geographical and social environment, as well as by the more or less unique historical experiences and cultural contacts of the various societies. One cannot predict with certainty just what new forms of cultural expression may be evolved inasmuch as cultural forms are not determined exclusively by the exigencies of the function they fulfill. According to Malinowski, "form is always determined by function," [67] and that is why he claims that a natural science of culture based on the determinism of cultural form by function is possible. I am not convinced that he has established his thesis. Form is not always determined by function, since one and the same form may be utilized for different cultural functions, and different forms may subserve similar functions in diverse cultures. Therefore, I maintain instead that this formal cultural indeterminancy renders a precise predictive science of cultural forms impossible of achievement, since human creativity and imagination simply will not be bound down to any one formula, and the unpredictability of historical processes upsets one's calculations.

### 9. THE EXTREMES OF NATURALISM AND CULTURALISM

Briefly put, the point I am concerned to make is that by taking the view of the polarity of human nature and culture we may avoid the extremes of naturalism and culturalism. The former group tends to attribute to innate human nature, taken individually and collectively, modes of thought and action which are in fact cultural products and achievements. This I have designated the "naturalistic fallacy," since it involves the attempt to deduce cultural forms from nature. On the other hand, the culturalists have gone to the opposite extreme and tend to attribute to culture a role which minimizes or ignores the element of nature, a tendency which I have designated as the "culturalistic fallacy." The notion that culture is a transcendental, superpsychic process which molds the individual while developing according to natural laws of its own is in my opinion the prime example of the culturalistic fallacy, since it ignores the question of the human origin of culture and regards cultural phenomena as if they were autonomous, efficient agents of themselves.[68]

[67] Malinowski, *A Scientific Theory of Culture*, p. 149.
[68] See Chapter 2.

The extreme position to which the positivistic culturalists are driven by their own presuppositions may be illustrated by the following passage from La Piere and Farnsworth's *Social Psychology*.

The behaviors that are typical of the Japanese differ from those that are typical of Americans. Japanese and Americans have, in other words, different human natures. Earlier students endeavored to find norms of behavior that would hold true for all of mankind throughout all of human history. But no specific pattern of action possessing any such universality has, as yet, been discovered. When we get beyond broad generalizations, such as that human beings eat and that they take care of their offspring, there is nothing that can be said of mankind as a whole. . . . The similarities that exist among the members of a given society cannot, therefore, be traced to something inherent in the nature of man. They are the result of the fact that the majority of the members of a given society have had much the same set of social experiences. Thus likenesses that can be observed in the behavior of members of a society exist largely because this mode of behavior is characteristic for that society. The fact that human nature varies from society to society, and in lesser degree between different groups within the society, is the basis for the layman's classification of people into fixed categories. . . . Human nature defined as the typical behavior for members of a given social grouping conforms to general usage.[69]

The authors' basic assumption is that human nature is to be inferred from positive cultural phenomena. Since the latter reveal no universal patterns (notwithstanding ethnological evidence to the contrary), they conclude that there is no universal human nature. According to their thesis there are as many types of human nature as there are types of cultural personality. Far from disagreeing with the common tendency of the unsophisticated among ourselves, as well as among primitive tribal societies, to set up sharp reservations regarding the human nature of other groups because of culture-personality differences, these social psychologists use such prejudices as evidence to corroborate their position. Logically, it would seem, their position should lead to a denial of the possibility of any universal social psychology, since it is meaningless to distinguish natural from cultural processes once nature has been reduced to culture. The thesis I am concerned to establish is that the postulate of an ontological human nature is a prerequisite of both individual and social psychology.[70] The mechanisms involved in interindividual relations may then be distinguished from the cultural forms in which they are expressed.

Another illustration of the culturalistic theory of human nature, but

[69] La Piere and Farnsworth, *Social Psychology*, p. 148.
[70] See Chapter 1.

from a Neo-Kantian, idealistic point of view, is furnished by Ernst Cassirer's work. He writes:

The philosophy of symbolic forms starts from the presupposition that, if there is any definition of the nature or "essence" of man, this definition can only be understood as a functional one, not a substantial one. We cannot define man by any inherent principle which constitutes his metaphysical essence—nor can we define him by any inborn faculty or instinct that may be ascertained by empirical observation. Man's outstanding characteristic, his distinguishing mark, is not his metaphysical or physical nature—but his work. It is this work, it is the system of human activities, which defines and determines the circle of "humanity." [71]

Cassirer, in conformity with the Neo-Kantian doctrine of Hermann Cohen and Wilhelm Dilthey, denies the possibility of an ontological or substantial knowledge of human nature.[72] In agreement also with contemporary existentialists, such as Sartre,[73] he maintains that man may be known only existentially and functionally through the cultural symbols which he creates progressively in time. The consciousness of man is the locus, the point of synthesis of the various types of cultural symbols, and is thus the functional bond between them. Cassirer is able to speak of a universal human nature because he maintains, in agreement with Comte, that the individual is to be understood only through "humanity," through an analysis of the historical intellectual achievements of mankind.

It is of interest to note here that Neo-Kantian historical idealists and Neo-Freudian cultural psychoanalysts agree in interpreting culture as essentially a symbolical process. For the Freudian, or Neo-Freudian, the real meaning of a symbol is always understood regressively by reduction to the primordial mother-child relation and the delayed infancy of human nature. For the Neo-Kantian culturologist the cultural symbol is not a sublimation of the infantile condition, but is analyzed phenomenologically for its actual logical content; the symbol is said to carry its meaning within itself and is known by intellectual intuition. Thus, whereas the Freudian psychoanalyst tends to view cultural symbolic constructs as strictly determined by the genetic, psychological experience of the individual or of the race, the Neo-Kantian philosopher interprets symbolic constructs as free expressions of the historic con-

---

[71] Cassirer, *An Essay on Man*, pp. 67–68.

[72] See Bidney, "The Philosophical Anthropology of Ernst Cassirer," in *The Philosophy of Ernst Cassirer*, ed. by P. A. Schilpp; also Kuhn, Review of Cassirer's *Essay on Man, Journal of Philosophy*, XLII (1945), 497–504.

[73] Sartre, *L'Existentialisme est un humanisme*.

sciousness of man. If, on the one hand, the Freudian psychoanalysts tend to reduce cultural symbols to expressions of innate, unconscious human impulses, the historical idealists, on the other hand, tend to ignore the biological basis of the cultural process and to focus attention upon the autonomous evolution of historical experience.

The major difficulty in Cassirer's theory of human nature is that, having reduced man and nature to symbolic constructs, there remains nothing for the cultural symbols to symbolize. Man is said to be an "animal symbolicum" subsisting within a symbolic universe.[74] Of man and nature as substantive, active agents there can be neither experience nor conceptual knowledge. Man knows himself, as well as nature, only as a cultural essence or form, but not as an ontological existence. Hence, on this assumption, the philosophical anthropologist may concern himself only with a "phenomenology of human culture," with a critical analysis of the types of cultural meanings revealed in historical experience. The dynamics of cultural change find no place in his philosophy, since he denies the very ontological and existential presuppositions which could render such problems significant.

In general, it may be said that psychological and sociological positivists in common with Neo-Kantian historical idealists tend to reduce the category of nature to that of culture, thereby turning epistemology and ontology into cultural anthropology or sociology.[75] Thus, while the historical idealists object to the naturalistic method and "social physics" of the positivists and insist upon the unique subjective approach required for a proper "understanding" (*verstehen*) of human phenomena, nevertheless, they agree in their respective conclusions, since they both share a common anti-metaphysical perspective.

## 10. CONCLUSION

The basic issue regarding the relation of human nature and culture is whether the cultural process is to be understood as forming or constituting human nature, on the one hand, or whether it is to be conceived as an instrument for regulating a human nature which has a substantial being and determinate, innate form of its own. Cultural idealists and materialists of the Hegelian and Marxian schools have, on the whole, made common cause with extreme empiricists such as Locke and

[74] Cassirer, *An Essay on Man*, p. 26.
[75] See Bidney, "The Philosophical Anthropology of Ernst Cassirer," in *The Philosophy of Ernst Cassirer*, ed. by P. A. Schilpp.

Hume, and social behaviorists, such as George Mead, in advocating the first position. On the other hand, ever since the time of Plato and throughout medieval and modern times there have been those who contended that an ontological or metaphysical knowledge of human nature is possible and that there are innate factors of mental structure and function which are not derived from experience and culture. In modern times Descartes, Spinoza, and Leibnitz continued this tradition. Kant is at the cross-roads, retaining the notion of an a priori mental structure, while denying the possibility of any ontological knowledge. The Neo-Kantians, following Dilthey and Hermann Cohen and their critique of historical reason, have cast off Kant's scruples regarding the retention of an ontological thing-in-itself and have made common cause with the Comtean culturalists by asserting the primacy and autonomy of cultural phenomena. On the other hand, the defection of the Neo-Kantians has been compensated for by psychologists such as William James and William McDougall and by Freudian psychoanalysts, who have argued for innate action-patterns or specific human instincts as underlying cultural activity. The classical evolutionists, such as Herbert Spencer, Lewis H. Morgan, Tylor, and Frazer, who linked up the stages of cultural evolution with corresponding stages in mental development [76] are essentially in the same ontological tradition.

According to the polaristic position adopted here, culture is to be understood primarily as a regulative process initiated by man for the development and organization of his determinate, substantive potentialities. Nevertheless, human nature is logically and genetically prior to culture, since we must postulate human agents with psychobiological powers and impulses capable of initiating the cultural process as a means of adjusting to their environment and as a form of symbolic expression. In other words, the determinate nature of man is manifested functionally through culture, but is not reducible to culture. Thus, one need not say with Ortega y Gasset that "man has no nature; he has history." [77] It is not necessary according to fact or logic to choose between nature and history. Man has a substantive, ontological nature, which may be investigated by the methods of natural science, as well as a cultural history, which may be studied by the methods of social science and humanistic scholarship. Adequate self-knowledge requires a comprehension of both nature and history. The theory of the polarity

[76] See Chapter 7.
[77] Ortega y Gasset, *Concord and Liberty, and Other Essays*, p. 148.

of nature and culture would do justice to both factors by allowing for the ontological conditions of the historical cultural process. There is an important distinction to be made, however, between the ontological conditions of the human cultural process and the ontological conditions, or presuppositions, of given historical systems of culture. Sorokin, for example, in his *Social and Cultural Dynamics,* and Northrop, in his *The Meeting of East and West,* have discussed some of the views of reality implicit in diverse Eastern and Western cultural systems. In this study my concern is with the metacultural presuppositions of any system of culture whatsoever. The problem, it seems to me, was soundly appraised by the Neo-Kantian philosophical anthropologists; my disagreement is solely with their particular idealistic approach.

## 11. POSTSCRIPT

In their joint monograph entitled *Culture: a Critical Review of Concepts and Definitions* Kroeber and Kluckhohn have now reached a consensus of opinion. It is interesting to note that Kroeber shares Kluckhohn's thesis that "the logical construct, culture, is based upon the study of behavior and behavioral products. . . . But culture is not behavior nor the investigation of behavior in all its concrete completeness." [78] Kroeber has apparently gone from one extreme to another while continuing in the idealistic tradition. He began by defining culture as an emergent, autonomous reality *sui generis;* but under the influence of Kluckhohn he has come to regard culture as a conceptual, logical construct other than behavior. Culture has been reduced from the highest level of phenomena to an *ens rationis,* to a thing of reason in the mind of the ethnologist.

My own position is that while culture patterns may well be considered in abstraction from actual behavior for the purpose of comparative study and analysis, this does not imply that culture is *nothing but* a logical construct of patterns or forms. The polaristic theory of culture which I advocate implies that the unit of culture is the *patterned process* and that culture comprises the patterned behavior of man in society. Only by combining pattern and process as distinguishable but inseparable elements of cultural behavior will it be possible to discover and understand the "dynamic mechanisms" which Kroeber finds it so "very hard to find."

[78] *Culture: a Critical Review of Concepts and Definitions,* p. 189.

# 6

# *Metaanthropology and Anthropological Science*[1]

MODERN SCIENTIFIC THOUGHT has not been favorably disposed toward metaphysics. Owing largely to the empiricism of Francis Bacon, John Locke, and David Hume, the critical idealism of Immanuel Kant, and the positivism of Auguste Comte metaphysical theory has come to be regarded generally as the antithesis of the scientific approach. Even philosophers themselves, the custodians of the metaphysical tradition, are not in agreement as to the role and validity of metaphysical concepts, the general tendency since Kant and outside Catholic circles being to relegate metaphysical postulates to the realm of religion and faith, while denying their significance for empirical or verifiable knowledge.

## 1. THEORIES OF THE RELATION OF SCIENCE TO METAPHYSICS

On the whole, one may distinguish three main positions as regards the relation of science to metaphysics.

First, one may mention the positivistic, evolutionary position of Comte, according to which metaphysics is said to be prescientific. Metaphysical thought is held to be a stage intermediate between primitive, animistic, theological thought, on the one hand, and positive, empirical, scientific thought, on the other. Metaphysical thought shares with animistic thought the acceptance of nonobservable entities, but differs from the latter in being critical and in formulating distinct logical categories. On this basis, cultural progress is measured by the extent to which the last vestiges of metaphysics have been successfully eradicated from systematic thought and by the effort which has been made to promote a positivistic, scientific mentality, especially in dealing with human affairs. Sociology, according to Comte, is the last frontier of

[1] Reprinted in part from *Ideological Differences and World Order,* ed. by F. S. C. Northrop, pp. 323–55.

natural science and was envisaged by him as a study of society whereby the laws of sociocultural development may be discovered and human life regulated in accordance with these progressive laws.

Emile Durkheim and Lucien Lévy-Bruhl applied Comte's positivistic approach to the comparative study of "social facts" in literate, as well as preliterate, cultures. Lévy-Bruhl in particular made a thorough survey of the extant ethnographical literature and as a result of his wide research set up the distinction between the "prelogical" character of the "collective representations" of native peoples, on the one hand, and the logical, scientific character of the civilized, collective mentality, on the other.[2] In characterizing the native mentality as "prelogical" he was careful to note that he did not mean that it was illogical, or contrary to logic, but only that it was indifferent to our accepted logical categories. The native mentality, in its collective representations, accepted a pattern of thought which permitted natives to think in terms which apparently violated our Western principles of logic. Thus, instead of the principle of contradiction and identity, which is fundamental to our accepted mode of thought, they implicitly utilized the notion of "participation," which contradicts our notion of discrete entities and permits them to think of one and the same thing as participating in the very essence of things other than itself.

Lévy-Bruhl's choice of the term "prelogical" was not a happy one and has given rise to much misunderstanding and criticism of his position. By identifying the logical with the scientific mentality, he led his critics to believe that native thought was illogical, notwithstanding his constant reiteration that such was not his meaning at all. Even Cassirer[3] took Lévy-Bruhl to task for his conception of the prelogical and once more pointed out that native thought and custom were logical and "rational" provided one understood their basic premises and presuppositions. Cassirer failed to realize that Lévy-Bruhl's own published works provided a wealth of material to demonstrate this very thesis; namely, that native mentality as manifested in its social or collective representations operated, on the whole, from premises that differ radically from those accepted in modern European cultures, although it was quite logical in terms of its own assumptions.

What Lévy-Bruhl really meant by his use of the unfortunate term

[2] Lévy-Bruhl, *How Natives Think.*
[3] Cassirer, *An Essay on Man;* also *The Myth of the State;* Bidney, "The Philosophical Anthropology of Ernst Cassirer," in *The Philosophy of Ernst Cassirer,* ed. by P. A. Schilpp, pp. 517–27.

"prelogical" was, as may be gathered from the context of his works, that native thought was prescientific in the sense that it did not clearly distinguish the sphere of empirical, verified knowledge and practice from myth and magic. He agreed that native culture did comprise many data that were based on empirical observation, but pointed out that the natives themselves failed to differentiate clearly and consistently between the sphere of the empirical and that of the nonempirical, between verifiable and nonverifiable notions, and hence were indifferent to the scientific and logical categories which characterize our scientific and rational modes of thinking. In this respect native mentality may be compared with the folklore of civilized peoples, which may be said to be prescientific in the sense .that folklore is a mixture of empirical observation and uncritical imagination. The distinction between the prescientific and scientific mentality is not psychological, but rather cultural, and does not reflect upon the inherent ability of a group of people to think logically.

Furthermore, owing to a positivistic, antimetaphysical bias, Lévy-Bruhl failed to appreciate the point that the disparity between native and civilized mentalities depends upon ontological factors rather than purely logical procedures. In other words, what appear at first sight as differences in psychology and logic are in fact differences in metaphysical or ontological perspective, the native mind manifesting an uncritical acceptance of a "natural metaphysic" which presupposed the unity of all life and the inherent interrelatedness of things, while the scientific mind tends to assume a uniform order of nature which precluded psychical or mystical influence on physical events. Lévy-Bruhl himself exhibited an ethnocentric perspective in assuming that only the positivistic, antimetaphysical position current in his time was scientific and logical and that metaphysical postulates were prelogical, as well as prescientific. Had he not made this assumption, he would have been able to grant that native mentality is logical without being scientific, thereby obviating a great deal of unnecessary criticism. In his posthumously published notebooks Lévy-Bruhl conceded his use of the term "prelogical" in describing native thought was not justified.[4]

A second approach to the problem of the relation between science and metaphysics may be described as postscientific and is the position which regards metaphysics as supplementing science, as stepping in,

[4] *Les Carnets de Lucien Lévy-Bruhl,* Preface by Maurice Leenhardt; see also ch. 10.

so to speak, where the scientific angels fear to tread. The classical expression of this view is undoubtedly that of Kant, who in his *Critique of Practical Reason* acknowledges the validity of such nonempirical entities as God and the human soul as regulative ideas or postulates essential for morality and faith, while denying any scientific knowledge of a metaphysical or noumenal reality.

Among anthropologists Bronislaw Malinowski comes closest to the above view. In opposition to Lévy-Bruhl, with his evolutionary conception of the prelogical cultural mentality of the native, Malinowski maintains that natives do clearly distinguish between natural and secular phenomena, on the one hand, and supernatural and holy phenomena, on the other. The native is said to resort to myth and magic, not because he fails to differentiate the objects of scientific knowledge from those of magic and mythology, but precisely because he does, in fact, make this distinction. In his lectures on *The Foundations of Faith and Morals* Malinowski states explicitly:

Primitive Man has his science as well as his religion; a myth does not serve to explain phenomena but rather to regulate human actions. . . . It is rather the recognition of his practical and intellectual limitations and not the illusion of the "omnipotence of thought" which leads man into ritualism; which makes him re-enact miracles, the feasibility of which he has accepted from his mythology. . . . In short, myth is not a pseudo-science of nature; it is a history of the Supernatural. It invariably refers to a unique break in the history of the world and mankind.[5]

According to Malinowski there is no need to assume a mythical mentality which gradually evolved into the logical, civilized mentality. Myths are expressions of faith in the existence of supernatural forces and are characteristic of man at all stages of human culture. As beliefs in the supernatural, myths supplement or complement scientific knowledge and practice; they are neither a substitute for science, nor are they antithetical to scientific thought. Thus, he writes:

Mythology is definitely the complement of what might be called the ordinary knowledge or science of primitive man, but not its substitute. . . . Since they have their own science, mythology cannot be their system of explanation in the scientific sense of the word. Myth serves as a foundation for belief and establishes a precedent for the miracles of ritual and magic.[6]

Thus, metaphysical myth may be said to begin where scientific knowledge ends, and yet myth is pragmatically significant in providing as-

[5] Malinowski, *The Foundations of Faith and Morals.*
[6] *Ibid.*

surance of and faith in the harmony of man and his cosmic environment. Although the philosopher William James would not have used
the word "myth," his religious "will to believe" is an instance of this
position in a sophisticated modern Western culture.

Malinowski apparently comes close to affirming that the native has
an implicit theory of double truth and double reality, one for his
intellect, which is empirical and logical, and the other for his heart,
which is nonempirical and emotional. The native is said to recognize
clearly the difference between his rational, secular knowledge and his
sacred, emotional beliefs involved in his myth, ritual, and magic. Thus,
native science and "pseudoscience," or magic, may exist side by side,
since they are incorporated in different traditions and applied to different spheres of activity.[7]

I find it difficult to reconcile this conception of native thought as
involving a scientific and a pseudoscientific, or magical, epistemology
at one and the same time. It is one thing to maintain that myth com-
plements scientific knowledge in the sense that it transcends, but does
not contradict, scientific knowledge. It is another and conflicting proposition to maintain that the native differentiates clearly between scientific and nonscientific knowledge and yet retains his belief in a
spurious pseudoscience called magic. Belief in and practice of magic
are contrary to science, whereas belief in metaphysical reality is, as
Kant realized, quite compatible with scientific theory and practice.
The former position involves an epistemology of double truth which is
essentially self-contradictory; the latter position implies a monistic
epistemology which is logically coherent.

In a paper entitled "Historical Relations of Religion and Science"
Charles Singer questions whether the native has any science, but his
answer differs fundamentally from that of Malinowski, notwithstanding the former's polite attempt to minimize the difference as "almost
entirely verbal." According to Singer:

The scientific motive is provided by a conscious faith in the existence of general laws underlying the multiplicity of phenomena. Science is the purposeful search for such general laws that can be used to link together the observed phenomena. The savage has none of this faith, this aspiration. This
faith, we have said, is a thing consciously held. It is something moreover
which is by no means necessarily implied when the savage resorts, as he

---

[7] Malinowski, "Magic, Science and Religion," in *Science, Religion and Reality,* ed.
by Joseph Needham, p. 80; also reprinted in *Magic, Science and Religion and Other
Essays,* ed. by Robert Redfield.

often does, to reason. While many modern anthropologists are disposed to deny the existence of a pre-logical stage of human development, they must, we believe, admit a pre-scientific stage. Where there is no science or where science is not yet differentiated, we cannot hope to trace anything which concerns us here.[8]

In a footnote to this passage Singer remarks:

Dr. Malinowski regards science as a very early development. The difference between us is, however, almost entirely verbal. It is due to the fact that I have interpreted *science* as the self-conscious investigation of nature with the direct and avowed object of educing general laws. Such is science as we know it today and as the Greeks knew it. Dr. Malinowski, however, rightly considers that there are certain scientific elements even in the most primitive culture and it is these *elements* that he calls *science*. I should describe this early stage as *science in the making*. If the reader will bear these terminological differences in mind, he will perceive that there is little or no difference between Dr. Malinowski and myself.

Notwithstanding the fact that Singer here tends to minimize the difference between his position and that of Malinowski, I still think that the issue involved goes much deeper than he apparently realizes.[9] The issue is not whether native culture comprises empirical and rational elements of knowledge, but whether the native clearly differentiates between this type of evidence and nonempirical, irrational thought. According to Singer and Lévy-Bruhl the native does not yet clearly distinguish empirical from nonempirical knowledge, even though he undoubtedly does utilize empirical observations and logical thought in his theoretical and practical constructions. If the native were conscious of the radical difference between these two modes of thought, he could not possibly retain his belief in magic; modern civilized man gave up his belief in magic once he became aware of the scientific method and the uniform causal interrelations obtaining among natural phenomena. The scientifically trained ethnologist, for example, may make a scientific study of the folklore and magical practices of his preliterate contemporaries, but he can scarcely share their beliefs or follow their practices, since to do so he would have to cease being a scientist. According to Malinowski, science and pseudoscience may be compatible for the native, but apparently not for the scientific anthropologist. The issue, then, far from being "merely verbal," is of fundamental importance,

---

[8] Singer, "Historical Relations of Religion and Science," in Needham, ed., *Science, Religion and Reality*, p. 89.

[9] Ackerknecht, "Natural Diseases and Rational Treatment in Primitive Medicine," *Bulletin of the History of Medicine*, XIX (1946), 467–97.

since the answer one gives has a bearing on one's interpretation of native culture, as well as culture history.

Since Malinowski mentions Frazer in his interpretation of primitive magic as pseudoscience, it is well to recall that the latter, in agreement with Tylor, maintained that native magic and myth were to be explained in rational, intellectualistic terms. The native mind was said to be essentially rational, or logical, and myths were interpreted as rational constructions, motivated in part by intellectual wonder, but based on erroneous major premises. Thus, animism, according to Tylor, is a logical theory which offers a plausible explanation of death on the analogy of sleep and dreams and represents a primitive philosophy. Malinowski apparently seeks to combine this rationalistic theory of Frazer and Tylor with the mystical, prelogical interpretation of Lévy-Bruhl, and therefore he holds that the native mind is both rational and irrational in different contexts of experience. The native is said to be empirical and rational in his secular everyday experience and practices, but emotional and prone to wishful thinking in times of individual and social crises, when his rational knowledge proves to be inadequate. As against Tylor, he holds that native myth, magic, and religion are not the products of intellectual wonder and do not originate as etiological explanations of natural phenomena. He agrees, rather, with Lévy-Bruhl and Durkheim that the functions of native myth and magic are primarily sociological and that the latter are to be understood as rationalizations of emotional needs introduced to promote social solidarity and a feeling of cosmic harmony. But then Malinowski reverts to the rationalistic approach of Tylor and Frazer, maintaining that natives are conscious of the difference between rational-empirical knowledge, applicable to the sphere of nature only, and mystical, sacred traditions, applicable to the sphere of the supernatural. Hence, he holds, the native mentality, far from being prelogical, as Lévy-Bruhl asserts, is essentially logical, even when it has recourse to magic and myth. On this basis, therefore, the distinction between rational and irrational thought tends to disappear, since even apparently irrational thought and practice serve rational social functions.

A third approach to the problem of the relation of metaphysics to science may be described as superscientific. According to the classic formulation of Henri Bergson,[10] intuition provides genuine insight into the fundamental reality of nature and life, whereas the scientific in-

[10] Bergson, *Creative Evolution.*

tellect, while providing useful pragmatic tools, tends to falsify the nature of reality. Metaphysical intuition provides insight into the "vital impetus" (*élan vital*) which underlies the evolutionary processes of nature. The scientific intellect, by abstracting the static forms and structures from the cosmic flux and processes, enables man to contemplate and to measure natural phenomena in their spatial relations, but fails to grasp the fundamental duration of things. In setting up the dichotomy of metaphysical intuition and intellectual abstraction, Bergson rendered indirect support to the mystics and romanticists who posited superrational faculties which transcended the evidence of reason and science. From the supposition of a superrational sphere of experience it was a short, though very important, step to the realm of the irrational, since in either instance the validity of reason and science is questioned. Thus, in seeking to combat the excessive mechanism and materialism of his day, which he identified with the scientific approach, Bergson went to the opposite extreme by divorcing metaphysics and science and accusing science of falsification. As subsequent developments in relativity theory and the philosophy of science have demonstrated, the concept of process and the historical view of nature may be adequately comprehended in scientific terms without recourse to a superior faculty of intuition. Bergson apparently mistook the limitations of the science of his day for an inherent defect of the human intellect and of science in general, and while he himself was much too close to the scientific tradition and to the moral values of Hebrew-Christian culture to realize the full significance of the divorce between metaphysics and science, he unwittingly gave support and comfort to the very ethnocentrism and mythology of the state [11] which he personally abhorred so sincerely. In accusing science of inherent falsification, he implicitly helped prepare the way for a "science" of myth-making whose value was to be measured by its pragmatic consequences in achieving given objectives.

## 2. THE CONCEPT OF METAANTHROPOLOGY

As against the view that metaphysics is either prescientific, postscientific, or superscientific, the thesis is here advanced that metaphysics is or may be the theoretically postulated aspect of science, as well as postscientific ontological speculation compatible with science, though not an integral part thereof. Insofar as metaphysics is scientific it may

[11] Bergson, *The Two Sources of Morality and Religion.*

be subjected to indirect verification and validation, and hence the concept of a scientific metaphysics, far from being a contradiction in terms, is a genuinely valid notion. Each science may be thought of as having its own metaphysical aspect, and thus one may speak of metaphysics, metabiology, metaethnography,[12] and metalinguistics.[13] It is merely an accident of the history of philosophical thought that the term "metaphysics," originally employed by the editors of Aristotle's works to indicate the book which came after the physics, has come to comprise the whole of ontological thought, thereby obscuring the fact that ontological postulates constitute an indispensable element in every one of the sciences.

It should be noted, however, that metaphysics as an aspect of a given science is not simply to be identified with theory in general, but only with ontological theory. Thus, metaanthropology, for example, is not merely another name for anthropological theory, but refers to a special kind of theory, namely, the theory concerned with the problems of cultural reality and the nature of man. One may also discuss anthropological theories which are not ontological, such as that of independent invention versus diffusion of culture traits. Similarly, the study of cultural *leitmotifs*, exemplified in Ruth Benedict's *Patterns of Culture*, is not metascientific in the sense here used. In general, it may be said that purely descriptive theories may be regarded as scientific theories which are not essentially ontological or metascientific. In the last analysis, an ontological, metascientific theory is an attempt to explain why phenomena are related in a given manner by referring to some aspect of reality which provides an intelligible ground for their occurrence and interrelation.

It is implied in the above that the category of the logical and that of the scientific are not identical.[14] In the first place, as has been noted, metaphysical thought may be postscientific in the sense of going beyond the data of science and being compatible with scientific thought. The concept of God, for example, is not a scientific concept and is not subject to empirical verification, though it may be a postulate of thought and of faith quite compatible with all available scientific evidence. Furthermore, any system of metaphysical thought may be logical in the sense that it is a deductive system which may be deduced from given

[12] Lowie, *The History of Ethnological Theory*, p. 274.
[13] Whorf, *Four Articles on Metalinguistics*.
[14] See Chapter 10.

premises, and hence it may be argued that there is no "prelogical" meta-physics, no matter how primitive the stage of cultural development. Only those metaphysical postulates are genuinely scientific which have been subjected to indirect, empirical verification and are in accord with the facts of the sciences. Metascientific thought is an achievement of our Western scientific culture which began with the ancient Greeks, but has really taken on its modern forms after the time of the Renaissance. Prescientific, or nonscientific, metaphysical theories are characteristic of most human cultural thought, whether it be literate or preliterate.

With reference to the problem of native thought in particular, it would seem more in accord with the facts of ethnology to accept the thesis of Charles Singer that native culture is prescientific. Notwith-standing the empirical and rational elements to be found in native cultures, especially as regards the manufacture and utilization of artifacts, native thought, like the folklore of the peasants of modern states, does not yet differentiate clearly between scientific and nonscientific evidence. The folk practices of all peoples, whether literate or pre-literate, provide ample demonstration of the uncritical mentality which permits them to follow rational and irrational procedures indiscriminately. Thus, natives will avail themselves of modern medical hospital services only *in extremis* and after having exhausted their own traditional expedients, thereby demonstrating that they have little faith in and attach a minimum of practical importance to strictly scientific procedures. This, of course, is not to say that the mentality of natives or of peasant folk is prelogical in the sense of being indifferent to the principle of contradiction, but only that such folk, in their uncritical, pragmatic frame of mind, are indifferent to scientific methodology and do not yet realize the logical incompatibility of their empirical-rational procedures, on the one hand, and their magical rituals and supersti-tions, on the other.

It would seem more in accord with ethnographic evidence to say that natives do differentiate between secular, everyday experience and sacred, superhuman tales and traditions about gods and spirits, since they have special terms to designate the different categories of narra-tive and tradition.[15] This, however, does not mean that they distinguish

---

[15] Radin, *The Road of Life and Death; A Ritual Drama of the American Indians*, p. 54; Boas, "Mythology and Folk-Tales of the North American Indians" in Boas and others, *Anthropology in North America*; Bidney, review of Radin's *The Road of Life and Death* in *Journal of the Histor of Medicine*, II (1947), 406–7.

clearly between the sphere of the natural and that of the supernatural, since gods and spirits are just as much a part of the order of "nature" as are men and animals. The dichotomy of the natural and the supernatural implies a scientific epistemology and critical, metaphysical sophistication which must not be assumed without reliable evidence. And modern ethnography does abound in evidence that sacred, as well as secular, traditions are equally credible to the native mind and differ only with regard to the motivations for belief.

Strictly speaking, natives, like other peoples at a prescientific stage of thought, do not regard themselves as believing in myths, since the distinction between scientific knowledge and myth, which the scientific ethnologist has constructed in his analysis of native cultures, is unknown to the natives themselves. This point may be demonstrated in everyday experience even with reference to our own culture, for it may easily be shown that the concept of "myth" is relative to one's accepted beliefs and convictions, so that what is gospel truth for the believer is sheer "myth" and "fiction" for the nonbeliever or skeptic; for example, compare the typical Freudian or Marxian position on religion with that of the firm believer in any one of the major religious faiths. Once the relativity of the category of myth to scientific evidence and rational demonstration is recognized, it becomes apparent that there is no fixed category of myth pertaining to some prehistoric era only and that the very notion of myth itself presupposes a scientific consciousness which may not be attributed to the prescientific mentality.[16] Myths and magical tales and practices are accepted precisely because prescientific folk do not consider them as merely "myths" or "magic," since once the distinction between myth and science is consciously accepted, the acquired critical insight precludes the belief in and acceptance of magic and myth.

One may make a scientific study of folklore and of prescientific cultures in general precisely because the dividing line between science and folklore is real and significant. The fact that what is sometimes presumed to be scientifically established turns out, upon later evidence or more critical analysis, to be fictitious and mythical merely shows how narrow is the margin between our scientific and prescientific mentalities and how much of the latter still lingers even in our sophisticated critical minds. But in all such instances the very fact that one is able to re-examine critically "the folklore of science" and to record the history

[16] See Chapter 10.

of human error is ground for optimism and trust in man's faltering rationality and in his ability to transcend gradually the limitations of past perspectives and cultural traditions. It is, as Conant has pointed out so clearly in his study of the methodology of science,[17] this self-corrective function of scientific method which has enabled the scientist to transcend the self-perpetuating myths of primitive, or uncritical, prescientific thought and has put the modern scientist in touch with immense resources of power which the native magician and uncritical metaphysician could scarcely imagine.

There is, indeed, a logic or method in native ideology, as there is in all forms of irrationality and madness—a method which the rational mind may come to understand and utilize—but this does not obviate the radical and irreducible distinction between the category of the rational and scientific, on the one hand, and that of the irrational and mythical, on the other. There may be a reason for everything in a given cultural ideology, but not everything therein is in accord with reason and much of it may be contrary to reason and scientific evidence. The genuinely rational mind may understand the "logic" of the irrational mind, but the converse does not hold. Ernst Cassirer has demonstrated this thesis in *The Myth of the State* by pointing up the conflict between the quest for rationality and the modern resurgence of irrationalism consciously brought about by those who have made a "science" of mythical propaganda.

It is worth noting in this connection that there is a strong tendency among contemporary cultural anthropologists, sociologists, and social psychologists to assume that native ideology, as well as modern ideologies in general, are to be understood primarily from a sociofunctional perspective. Native thought is said to be a function of a given social organization and to provide rationalizations for social needs and requirements. Furthermore, owing to the impact of contemporary psychoanalysis a concerted effort is being made to explain genetically the pattern of social institutions and the ideology which sustains them by reference to the child-training programs and the family relations which prevail in a given society. Thus, the sociological, as well as the psychoanalytical, approach tends to stress the relativity of native ideology either to a specific social context or to a given pattern of child conditioning. The adherents of both these positions tend to assume a unitary motivation for native ideology and agree implicitly in precluding ob-

[17] Conant, *On Understanding Science*.

jective, intellectual wonder and the free play of imagination as significant factors in the formation of native ideology.

It seems to me, however, that the sociological and psychoanalytical
approaches tend to go to extremes in their reaction against the intellectualistic, philosophical approach. If some of the nineteenth-century
ethnologists and sociologists tended to go to one extreme by attempting
to explain native thought in intellectualistic terms, the modern tendency
is to go to the opposite extreme by failing to reckon with intellectual
wonder and theoretical speculation as significant factors in the development of native thought. Both the nineteenth-century rationalists and the
twentieth-century irrationalists make the mistake of assuming a single
basic motivation for native ideologies, thereby setting up superficial
antitheses and promoting futile controversies. As Boas pointed out long
ago,[18] there is no single motivation for native thought in general, and
one may, therefore, acknowledge objective and subjective, rational and
irrational, sources of native thought.

### 3. THE METACULTURAL BASES OF CULTURAL IDEOLOGIES

One of the important tasks of the student of metaethnology is the
investigation of the basic, logically primitive assumptions as to the
nature of the world and of man involved in any one given cultural system. The task of rendering explicit these fundamental ontological postulates and assumptions is said to be metaethnological, since the reality
with which the investigator is here concerned is metacultural, that is,
it is presupposed as given and ultimate by the adherents of any given
culture, as something to which their empirical cultural institutions and
behavior must conform and with which it must reckon, rather than as
the product of their own creation and invention. Nature as a whole
may be said to be metacultural, because it provides an indispensable
condition for the cultural process and may not therefore be regarded
as derived from culture alone.[19] There is nothing mystical about this
concept of metacultural reality; it connotes simply that ontological
factor within experience which provides the precultural conditions for
any cultural processes whatsoever. The analysis of the metacultural
postulates of a given culture, whether deductively inferred or intuitively
conceived, is essentially a philosophical, or metaanthropological, under-

[18] Boas, "The Origin of Totemism," *American Anthropologist*, XVIII (1916),
319–26.
[19] See Chapter 5.

taking and as necessary a part of anthropological science as is the collecting of empirical data. To appreciate properly the philosophy of life and *Weltanschauung* which serve as leitmotifs for a given culture requires some measure of philosophical discipline and insight, which necessitates that there be professionally trained philosophers working in the social sciences as well as philosophically minded social scientists.

The notion that the philosophy of a culture determines the general pattern of its empirical traits and institutions and provides it with a unity of meaning is one that modern, historically minded philosophers such as Nietzsche, Dilthey, and Cassirer, and historians such as Burckhardt and Spengler, have explicitly recognized and expounded. The concept of philosophy as a "way of life" has been an integral part of the occidental, as well as the oriental, philosophical traditions, although this view has often been stated in individualistic, rather than in social, terms. The point is one, however, which requires restatement for our times, because social scientists, in their ill-considered attempts to imitate the radical positivism and empiricism of the natural sciences, have largely tended to neglect this philosophical perspective.

It is highly significant, therefore, that a sociologist of the stature of Sorokin has endeavored to introduce this metacultural perspective into contemporary sociology. His *Social and Cultural Dynamics* is based upon the major premise that the "presuppositions of a culture determine its empirical manifestations and institutions." His analysis of all cultures into the supertypes sensate, ideational, and idealistic is an attempt to provide a "logico-meaningful" basis for the integration of any given culture (insofar as it is integrated) in terms of its ultimate epistemological-metaphysical presuppositions. The point I am concerned to make here is that there is a real functional difference between the philosophical tasks of the metaanthropologist and the metasociologist, on the one hand, and that of the empirical anthropologist and sociologist, on the other. The fact that so few sociologists have been inclined to follow the path indicated by Sorokin demonstrates how exceptional is his philosophical interpretation of the role of the sociologist.[20]

Northrop's study of world cultures entitled *The Meeting of East and West* amply demonstrates that the professional philosopher has something significant to say on questions of cultural presuppositions. In

[20] See Sorokin's comment on Northrop's essay "Philosophy and World Peace," in *Approaches to World Peace*, pp. 678–80.

common with other contemporary philosophers, such as Whitehead, Cassirer, and Dewey, he maintains that the major cultures of the Western and the Eastern worlds involve basic theoretical assumptions from which the social institutions and practices that they value proceed. What is especially novel and thought-provoking in Northrop's approach is his particular thesis as to the nature of these basic theoretical assumptions, which are said to underlie all historical cultures and which serve in each instance as a focus of integration. This thesis, as expounded in the aforementioned work, as well as in his collected essays *The Logic of the Sciences and the Humanities,* is that the philosophy of natural science which is presupposed by the adherents of a given culture determines largely, though not entirely, the particular character of their cultural ideology, together with its practical and empirical manifestations. The philosophy of science underlying any given historical culture is a composite of the data of empirical observation and intuition supplemented by logical inferences and constructs suggested by these data. All cultures are said to have their philosophies of science, the differences between cultural ideologies being ascribed either to the diversity of the empirical data of which cognizance is taken in a given culture or to the disparate logical inferences which are drawn to supplement these data.

Northrop's thesis apparently implies a relativistic conception of science which blurs the distinction between the scientific and the pre-scientific stages in the evolution of human thought. In this respect it is the antithesis of the evolutionary approach of modern anthropology and sociology according to which science marks a late stage in the development of culture. Since all cultures are thought to presuppose a given philosophy of science, cultural progress may be said to lie in the extension of empirical observation and intuition and in the refinement of logical theory so as to include and explain the totality of phenomena— a process which does not require any significant change in methodology, but only in content. As Northrop puts it:

The difference between a modern Western society and a society of natives in the South Sea Islands is not that the ideology of the former is scientifically grounded, whereas that of the latter is nonsensical hocus pocus and illogical. The ideologies of both express logical thinking, once one discovers the conceptual standpoint of each. Furthermore, both conceptual standpoints are empirically and hence scientifically verified. The difference is that the native South Sea islanders pass to their generalization with a particular group of observable factors in nature and the natural man attracting their attention, whereas modern Westerners have come upon different empirical natural facts and have achieved empirically verified generalizations which perhaps include a larger number of observable facts. Even so, as *The Meeting of East and West* has demonstrated, our traditional modern Western scientific and philosophical theories overlook or neglect certain facts of nature, especially those in the realm of aesthetic immediacy, which the empirically supported philosophies of the Orient and the Native South Sea islanders, such as the Balinese, take into account.[21]

Northrop's point is that it must not be assumed uncritically, as Westerners tend to do, that Western scientific culture is superior in all respects to that of the East and to native cultures. The Western mentality, in neglecting the element of esthetic intuition and the ontological esthetic continuum which it presupposes, presents a one-sided perspective of nature, and the Oriental and native mentalities are impoverished because of their neglect of the theoretically postulated and verified constructs of modern technological science. Both types of culture are equally scientific in the sense of being empirically verified and differ only as regards the phenomena which they recognize.

Northrop's concept of the philosophy of science implies a monistic epistemology which comprehends the whole of human knowledge under the category of science. Whereas critics such as Sorokin regard science as only one epistemological approach, which requires to be supplemented by those of religion and philosophy, Northrop does not, however, admit any special "truths of reason" or "truths of extrasensory and metalogical intuition" in addition to those of natural science.[22] His thesis is that once the philosophy of science of a given culture undergoes radical change, its social and political philosophies, together with its theory of religion, must change likewise, since the latter are but functions of the former. Northrop's philosophy of culture is monistic in the sense that he postulates one predominant factor, namely, the philosophy of natural science of a given culture, as the focus of integration, and in this respect his position may be compared with other monistic cultural theories, such as those of the Freudian psychoanalysts and the Marxian materialists. Unlike the latter theories, however, Northrop's philosophy of culture tends to fall into the ideational tradition, since the major emphasis is upon the role of ideas rather than upon social movements and institutions, although parenthetically he does acknowledge that other factors are also involved.

[21] Northrop, *The Logic of the Sciences and the Humanities,* p. 337.
[22] See Northrop's reply to Sorokin in *Approaches to World Peace,* p. 683.

Northrop's work has excited a great deal of scholarly attention and has met with sincere praise, as well as vigorous opposition.[23] Anthropologists and sociologists are inclined to question whether philosophical presuppositions, even if present in every culture, do exercise so predominant a role in cultural dynamics as this theory prescribes and whether nonideational social and technological factors may not be equally or more significant. The social scientists are also disturbed by the central, predominant position ascribed to the philosopher and the natural scientist, especially since this theory would exclude the former from participating on an equal footing in the task of formulating normative social theories and objectives.

With reference to ethnological theory in particular, Northrop's interpretation of the role of a philosophy of science in native cultures is reminiscent of the intellectualistic approach of Tylor and Frazer. But whereas Frazer, for example, adopts an evolutionary approach and traces the stages of cultural thought from magic, through religion,[24] to science, Northrop allows for no such evolutionary development. There is, according to Northrop, quantitative progress as regards the accumulation of the data of experience and qualitative progress as regards the logical constructs and theoretical concepts by which they are supplemented, but with respect to method there is said to be evolution within scientific procedure from one state of scientific inquiry to another. Northrop's position may be regarded as the opposite extreme to that of Lévy-Bruhl, since the former affirms that native thought is both logical and scientific, while the latter denies that it is either logical or scientific.

It is important at this stage to distinguish between the general thesis that native cultures reveal basic philosophical or metacultural presuppositions which serve to integrate their cultural perspectives, and the special contention that any given native ideology is based upon a specific philosophy of natural science. The general thesis is acceptable to most anthropologists, whereas the special theory is not. Northrop's analytical study of contemporary cultures, like that of Sorokin, has rendered significant service to contemporary culture theory in making explicit the metacultural presuppositions of some contemporary cultural ideologies and in counteracting those sociological and psychoanalytical approaches which tend to ignore the objective, intellectual element in the cultural process. In reacting against the excessive in-

---

[23] See Kroeber's review in *American Anthropologist*, XLIX (1947), 306–9.
[24] Frazer, *The Golden Bough*, one volume edition, chaps. iv, lxix.

tellectualism of the nineteenth-century social scientists, modern anthropologists and sociologists have apparently gone to the opposite
extreme by neglecting the "logico-meaningful" postulates which serve
as a focus of integration for a given culture. Northrop has undoubtedly
made a strong case for the recognition of th.e ideational factor in
the study of human cultures, and there are signs that this point of
view is winning some measure of serious consideration among social scientists. The question remains, however, whether in maintaining that native cultures, together with other historical cultures, are
based upon determinate philosophies of science he has not claimed
too much and has not gone beyond the available ethnological evidence.

One of the major sources of difficulty for readers of Northrop's work
concerns the relation of the factual to the normative conception of
science. On the one hand, he employs science in a purely historical,
relativistic sense as pertaining to all types of culture. On the other hand,
he conceives of science in a normative sense as a theory of truth about
nature which alone is capable of winning universal assent and transcending the limitations of contemporary cultural traditions. Insofar
as he employs the historical, relativistic concept of science, the question
of "historical fact" as to whether science does play the role he assigns
to is in the history of culture is highly relevant. But insofar as he employs the normative concept of science, the question whether historical
cultures have been scientifically rounded is not directly relevant.[25] As
may be gathered from the context of this analysis, I find myself in basic
agreement, in part at least, with the thesis of the normative function
of science, but differ as regards the historical, relativistic conception of
science and its role in the formation of cultural ideologies in the past.

In a later essay [26] Northrop reaffirms his basic thesis that all historical
cultures, whether literate or preliterate, are based upon empirically
verified facts of nature.

I question [he writes] whether there has ever been a society that had myth
in any sense other than that of a metaphorical or aesthetic expression of what
was to it a literal empirically verified basic conception of nature. It is not
an accident that the early gods are connected with thunder, lightning, rain,
and the sun.[27]

[25] Northrop, *The Logic of the Sciences and the Humanities*, p. 346.
[26] Northrop, "Ethics and the Integration of Natural Knowledge," in *The Nature
of Concepts, Their Inter-relation and Role in Social Structure* (Proceedings of The
Stillwater Conference Conducted by The Foundation for Integrated Education), pp.
116–39.
[27] *Ibid.*, p. 127.

Thus, in order to justify his thesis that all cultures are rationally integrated systems based on a philosophy of science, Northrop is apparently prepared to rationalize primitive myths as being scientific allegories, thereby returning to the type of mythological interpretation originally maintained by the Stoic philosophers, Francis Bacon, and the German nature-mythologists of the late nineteenth century.[28]

### 4. THE PROBLEM OF CULTURAL REALITY

The most significant contribution of modern ethnology to contemporary thought has been the objective insight it has provided into the diversity of human cultures and the role of cultural conditioning in the development of the potentialities of human nature. Tendencies of behavior of thought once regarded as grounded in the instinctive nature of man or in the character of a race are now seen to be due largely to historical, cultural factors. There is, in short, general acceptance among social scientists of the predominant role of cultural conditioning and of the sociocultural environment in shaping the life of man both individually and collectively.

There is serious disagreement, however, as to the connotation of cultural reality and the nature and number of the primary agencies involved in the cultural process.[29] It is asked, in what sense is culture real? Is it essentially an autonomous form or level of reality, or is it an abstract pattern and configuration other than human behavior? In general, it appears, cultural anthropologists have tended to adopt either of five types of approach.

First, there is the realistic position according to which culture is defined as the aggregate of acquired customs, folkways, and thoughtways, together with the manufacture and utilization of artifacts and agrofacts, or products of agriculture. This implies that culture is a quality or attribute of actual overt and covert social and individual behavior.

A second group, impressed with the role of linguistic symbols in the communication and acquisition of knowledge and experience, has been inclined to adopt an idealistic, or ideational, position. Culture is thus conceived as the aggregate and historical continuity of communicated ideas or meanings exemplified in artifacts, institutions, and the behavior of persons.

Others, regarding society as the locus of culture, maintain that social

---

[28] See Chapter 10.     [29] See Chapters 2 and 5.

forces are the primary sources of cultural ideologies and that ideological systems are reflections of these primary social forces. Contemporary Marxism may be regarded as a variant of this general sociological approach inasmuch as it is based on the assumption that economic-technological institutions constitute the primary, dynamic factors in determining the emergence of and the changes in cultural ideologies.

A fourth group regard culture as a kind of *ens rationis,* as a logical construct derived by abstraction from social behavior and thought. According to the latter position a culture is a configuration of patterns or forms abstracted by the mind of the ethnologist and is to be differentiated from the actual behavior and instrumental products of human behavior from which it is abstracted.

Finally, there is the instrumental, functionalistic view of culture associated with the names of Malinowski and Radcliffe-Brown. The functionalists point out that the unit of culture is not the trait, or pattern, but rather the institution and tend to look upon culture as an apparatus designed to serve the collective needs of a society in relation to a given environment.

The issue between the cultural realists and functionalists, on the one hand, and the impersonal, transcendental idealists and materialists, on the other, assumes practical import when we turn to the conflicting philosophies of culture history to which they lead. The transcendental idealists (exemplified by Kroeber and Sorokin) together with the historical materialists (for example, Leslie A. White) view culture as an impersonal, "superorganic" entity or force which makes or develops itself in the course of the evolutionary process. The cultural realists and functionalists, on the other hand, insofar as they take an individualistic position, tend to take into consideration the voluntary directives and self-determination of the human agents themselves in selecting the goals they would pursue. By contrast, both idealistic and materialistic superorganicists tend to adopt a fatalistic philosophy of culture history and to regard man, individually and collectively, in the role of cultural puppets or robots.

Cultural fatalism as a philosophy of cultural evolution owes its plausibility to the abstraction of human achievements from the psychodynamic human agents and activities by which they are produced. Once human ideals, social institutions, and technical inventions are regarded as impersonal, superorganic entities and endowed with a force of persistence and development of their own, "as if" they were their own causal agents, then it seems logical to disregard their human creators and initiators—a tendency which I have designated as the culturalistic fallacy.[30] In this manner it has come about that what began as a scientific quest for empirical factors and conditions involved in the cultural process has ended by becoming a transcendental metaphysics in which impersonal cultural forces are presumed to shape human destiny in accordance with their own special laws of development.

In practice, however, as recent history has demonstrated, cultural fatalism and humanism tend to be fused, since human effort and initiative are bound to assert themselves, notwithstanding the subtleties and learned, logical fictions of the "as if" theoreticians which are designed to exclude them in the name of "culturology." [31] In this connection it is interesting to note that Sorokin, in his more recent *Society, Culture, and Personality* has emphasized the role of persons as human agents of cultural change. Similarly, Kroeber, in the newly revised edition of his *Anthropology,* has come to recognize the psychological motivations of the cultural process as manifested in personality structure.

The culture of contemporary Soviet Russia is of especial interest in this connection, since it involves an impressive attempt to combine a doctrine of humanism with Marxian historical materialism. As George Reavey has recorded in his *Soviet Literature To-day,*[32] the new Soviet humanism is a social and historical humanism which, unlike the individualistic humanism of the Renaissance and of the eighteenth-century rationalists, refers "to the positive, social man, to the maker of history, to the man who transforms social conditions and who has the lever of history in his grasp, to the man building a new world society." It is this faith in man, particularly in Russian man, as the agent of history in the transformation of the world which gives Soviet humanism its particular religious intensity and dynamic character. It is a humanism which takes time very seriously, because nature itself is held to be subject to perpetual change in accordance with the theory of dialectical materialism and because social life also is subject to laws of development in time in agreement with the principles of historical materialism.

This, too, is the conclusion of Raymond A. Bauer's comprehensive

[30] See Chapter 2.

[31] White, "Culturological vs. Psychological Interpretations of Human Behavior," *American Sociological Review,* XII (1947), 686–98.

[32] Reavey, *Soviet Literature To-day,* chap. x, "The New Demiurge and the Window of Europe."

study entitled *The New Man in Soviet Psychology*. Man, and especially Soviet man, is said to be infinitely capable of controlling the universe which he inhabits, and any propositions, no matter how seriously held in the past, which imply limitations on man's ability to control his destiny have been rejected. In the new Soviet psychology responsibility, rationalism, and individualism are stressed and the thesis of traditional Marxism that society, not the individual, is responsible for antisocial behavior has been quietly discarded and superseded. The newly emergent concept of man in Soviet psychology as well as in political practice is one which defines man as being primarily conscious, rational, and purposive.

## 5. CULTURAL ANTHROPOLOGY AS NATURAL SCIENCE AND HUMANITY

In the development of modern cultural anthropology one may discern two major "themes." On the one hand, there is the theme derived from the naturalistic, positivistic, evolutionary tradition of the nineteenth century that cultural reality represents an autonomous, superorganic, superpsychic level of reality subject to its own laws and stages of evolution. On the other hand, there is the recurring theme, which dates back to the humanistic tradition of Greek philosophy, the Renaissance, and the rationalism of the eighteenth-century philosophers, that human culture is the product of human discovery and creativity and is subject to human regulation.

According to the superorganic view culture is a level of reality which is, as it were, a *causa sui,* a process which is conceived through itself alone and which molds the experience of man as a member of society. The humanistic, personalistic approach, with which I here identify myself, stresses human freedom and intelligence and the role of persons, taken individually and collectively, in determining their cultural destiny. Thus, while both schools of thought affirm a belief in human progress, the superorganic evolutionists tend to assume that cultural progress comes about by natural selection and by the inherent logic of the cultural process itself, whereas the humanistic school maintains that progress is a function of human voluntary effort and thought as guided by normative ideals. The superorganicists proclaim that the study of man and his culture is a natural science capable of revealing natural laws of cultural development comparable to those found in the sphere of the biological and physical sciences. The humanists reply that in an empirical social science there is a radical disparity between natural facts and normative ideals and that this disparity of facts and ideals renders a natural science of human culture impossible of realization. The humanists grant that society and culture are subject to evolution and that there are necessary conditions of cultural development which it is the function of the social scientists to investigate. But it should not be forgotten, they would add, that the thesis of cultural evolution is quite compatible with the admission of human freedom in the sense of self-determination and originality, since human freedom is not something absolute, but is limited by human power and intelligence in relation to a given natural and social environment.[33] Thus, the humanists would maintain, the scientific study of human culture is for the most part a historical, critical, and comparative study which, while it may reveal significant regularities and parallels, is by its very nature precluded from attaining the status of a precise, predictive natural science.

√ The above analysis should make it clear that the problems of the ontological status of culture and the methodology of cultural anthropology are major metaanthropological issues which cannot be resolved by reference to empirical data of ethnography alone, since the problems concern the very conditions of the cultural process itself. They are problems in the philosophy of culture which must be resolved by logical analysis of metacultural presuppositions and by appeal to the history of human experience.

### 6. IDEOLOGICAL DETERMINISM AND FREEDOM OF THOUGHT

The problem of the nature of the cultural process is closely bound up with the metapsychological problem as to the nature of human thought. The basic issue is whether human thought is in essence culturally determined or whether one may still acknowledge the mind's inherent capacity for self-determination and creative invention.

If, on the one hand, one were to assume, as Nietzsche and Marx do, that moral values and ideals always serve the special interests or will to power of some dominant group or minority group, then it would follow that thought is necessarily determined by sociopolitical and economic conditions. According to this assumption there is no logical way of overcoming cultural relativity and class perspective. The "logic of power" takes the place of the power of logic and reason. Instead of

[33] Briffault, *Rational Evolution*, ch. i; see also chs. 1 and 16.

power in the service of ideals, we have the doctrine of ideals in the service of power.

On the other hand, if one were to agree with Aristotle and Einstein in postulating the fundamental creativity of the human intellect and imagination, then it would follow that man is inherently capable of transcending the limitations of his sociocultural environment, notwithstanding the very considerable influence which the latter exerts upon him.

For many historians, sociologists, and anthropologists the attraction of the theory of thought-determinism lies in the fact that it purports to explain scientifically the natural laws of cultural development and to predict human behavior. They seem to think that social science, unlike natural science, requires a radical determinism of the human mentality and that to admit any significant self-determinism or creative spontaneity in human thought would preclude the possibility of a science of society and culture. Thus, the social scientist tends to outdo the natural scientist, inasmuch as the latter is content to postulate determinism for physical phenomena only, but is prepared to acknowledge the mind's freedom in constructing postulates and theories for the understanding of nature and in devising plans for adapting nature to human needs.

But this antithesis of absolute determinism versus freedom of thought is not at all necessary. The paradox of science is that there could be no science unless the mind were free to reflect upon the evidence of nature and to formulate its own concepts. To deny freedom of thought in the alleged interests of science is to undermine the very condition of the scientific process. The scientific intellect is capable of reflecting upon the phenomena of nature precisely because it transcends, or stands outside and apart from, the phenomena it comprehends, since otherwise the process of observation and the method of verification would have no meaning. Thus, freedom of scientific thought is a prerequisite of science considered as the investigation of phenomena subject to natural law. The scientific mind which denies its own freedom is denying itself and undermining its very foundations.

Ideological determinists inconsistently assume their own ability to transcend the ideological relativism they discern in the historical process and envisage some cultural state which somehow has an absolute, timeless validity obviating the necessity of further historical development. Hegel's idealization of the Prussian state of his day and Marx's ideal of a classless society are cases in point. In brief, historical relativism, whether it takes the form of historical idealism or of historical materialism, tends to be accepted as a scientific theory of cultural development because its adherents claim a timeless, or absolute, perspective which transcends its own limitations. In practice this means that cultural relativists tend to deny the objective validity and ideal universality of any system of thought other than their own and hence treat their opponents as deluded victims of their respective cultural institutions and historical traditions. Thus, theoretical historical relativism leads in practice to rigid intellectual dogmatism and authoritarian intolerance of dissent which precludes any respect for opposing views.

### 7. THE METACULTURAL PRESUPPOSITIONS OF ONE WORLD

We of the twentieth century, living in this age of science and technology, are especially conscious of the unity of the world from a functional and geographic point of view. Modern means of communication and travel have made geographical isolation a thing of the past. Economically, too, the development of specialized industries and of world trade has made all nations dependent upon one another for their very subsistence and for the maintenance of their civilized standards of living. This lesson is brought home to us very vividly when normal trade relations are suspended and it becomes impossible to carry on the highly mechanized industrial life to which we have become accustomed.

Ideationally, however, we are still living in ethnocentric worlds of our own imagination, worlds which are the products of our diverse historical experiences and traditions. Because of the prevalence of mythological, prescientific views of man and nature, the nations of the world tend to live in private cultural worlds of their own, somewhat like a dreamer who dwells in a world of his own imagination and does not participate in the common-sense world of wide-awake men. The question then, arises, is it possible for men to emerge from their ethnocentric, imaginary, and mythological worlds and to participate in a common cultural world?

The answer to this problem seems to be, as Plato originally discerned and as Northrop's *The Meeting of East and West* has lately reminded us, that it is possible for mankind to emerge from its cultural caves and behold a common, rational world in the light of human intelligence, provided men learn to distinguish knowledge based on reason and experience of nature from the subjective opinions and mythological notions derived from their limited, traditional, cultural environments. This world of reason and of science is one and the same for all precisely because it is the world of common reason and common sense. Thus, the world of culture may become one and the same for all, in essentials at least, provided it is based upon a scientific and rational knowledge of the nature of man and his world and of the sociocultural conditions of civilized life. Mere functional and geographic interdependence of cultures is a mechanical kind of unity which would apply to any kind of world organization or lack of organization. A genuine and significant world unity is one characterized by the mutual acknowledgement of common values; it is a teleological unity leading to harmonious relations among the peoples of the world. Only in such a world of common values can there be a real and enduring peace, a peace which is more than a temporary armistice between conflicting factions.

From an ontological perspective the indispensable presupposition of a common world is the assumption of an objective, ontological, metacultural order of nature which is independent of man but which man may discover and conceive through his own logical constructs.[34] If one adheres to the subjective, idealistic view that "the world exists only with reference to the knowing mind, and the mental activity of the subject determines the form in which the world appears,"[35] then, indeed, one is logically compelled to oppose as "ontological dogmatism" the position that the world exists independently of us. From the position of Kantian idealism it is but a short step to the relativistic, historical idealism of the Neo-Kantians and the historical materialism of the Marxists. As Karl Mannheim argues in his *Ideology and Utopia*, ideological relativity leads logically to a "sociology of knowledge" which postulates a total "relationism" of all ideological perspectives and denies any one ideology a privileged position as regards truth-value.

The basic assumption of sociological relationism is "that there are spheres of thought in which it is impossible to conceive of absolute truth existing independently of the values and position of the subject and unrelated to the social context."[36] On this premise there is no meaning to the concept of "one world," since there are as many worlds as there are disparate sociocultural contexts. One cannot arrive at the

[34] See Chapter 1.  [35] Mannheim, *Ideology and Utopia*, pp. 58–59.
[36] *Ibid.*, pp. 70–71.

notion of "one world" through a summation of ideological perspectives, since there is no basis for assuming a common denominator. It is only on the assumption that man is able to transcend his limited, historical ideological perspectives and to achieve a rational and scientifically verified knowledge of a metacultural, or transcultural, ontological reality that the concept of "one world" becomes intelligible as an epistemological, as well as an axiological, ideal.

Upon the social scientists and humanists especially falls the task of providing a common ideological frame of reference for the relative perspectives of the contemporary world. Such a "general theory of relativity" for the human world is a formidable undertaking and will require the united efforts of the world's best minds in the years to come. For in the world of culture, as in the political world, the crucial practical problem of our time is not so much whether unity is desirable, as what kind of unity shall we have. A cultural unity which impoverishes human life and thought by excluding whole areas of cultural experience as meaningless may have the virtue of simplicity, but will fail, nevertheless, of general acceptance, regardless of the learned support it may receive. We must remind ourselves constantly that cultural integration, like political unification, is not an unqualified good and that everything depends upon the nature of the final composition. For me the problem of cultural integration is essentially the harmonizing of diverse, polar interests and disciplines, each of which must enjoy a measure of autonomy to ensure its own creative advance. There is always the danger that the adherents of some one discipline, or class, will arrogate to themselves a "mission" to dictate to the rest in the alleged interests of "integration." A genuinely scientific and realistic view of cultural dynamics will be based upon a healthy respect for the complexity of cultural life and for the reciprocal influence of subjective and objective factors. Only by keeping in mind the Platonic vision that integration, whether of culture or of society, depends essentially upon harmonizing the one and the many can this objective be approximated.

# 7

# Evolutionary Ethnology and Natural History

ONE OF the outstanding problems of contemporary ethnological theory concerns the relation of ethnology to history. This may be demonstrated by the caustic comments of Paul Radin in writing a review of a recent symposium on personality and culture:

Some two generations ago the great English legal historian declared that anthropology would very shortly have to choose between being history or nothing. He was not alone among anthropological thinkers in feeling that its data were in no sense separate and distinct from history. . . . Maitland was wrong. Anthropology did not become history nor did it ostensibly become nothing. In fact, it became everything and seemed to have taken its etymological meaning literally.[1]

Radin's remarks are certainly challenging and point up the issue which seems to divide contemporary anthropological thought. Is anthropology primarily a historical science, or is it an integrative science concerned with all aspects of the human sciences? Radin reminds us that some two generations ago Maitland drew attention to this problem and decided in favor of the historical thesis. Modern "culturologists" are inclined to agree with Maitland that anthropology must either be understood as essentially a historical science—the history of human culture—or else it becomes nothing more than a name for a general interest in the study of man, with no distinct subject matter of its own.

By way of surveying this problem in historical perspective I propose to examine the approach of Tylor which Maitland probably had in mind and to indicate briefly how the conception of the nature and function of a science of culture has changed since his day, particularly in the United States, under the influence of Boas and Kroeber.

[1] Radin, "What Is Anthropology?" a review of Kluckhohn's *Mirror for Man* and *Personality in Nature, Society and Culture* (ed. by Kluckhohn and Murray), *Kenyon Review*, XI (1949), 523–26.

1. TYLOR ON THE SCIENCE OF CULTURE HISTORY

It is significant to note that Tylor entitled his first work, published in 1865, *Researches into the Early History of Mankind and the Development of Civilization*. The title of this work serves to indicate that the founder of the modern science of ethnology looked upon ethnology as essentially a historical discipline, concerned with tracing the development of culture or civilization from prehistoric to modern times. For Tylor the very term "culture" was but a shorter version of the German term *Kulturgeschichte,* or "culture history." He explains that "in the remote times and places where direct history is at fault, the study of Civilization, Culture-History as it is conveniently called in Germany, becomes itself an important aid to the historian, as a means of reconstructing the lost records of early or barbarous times." [2] Similarly in his work *Primitive Culture* he states:

If the field of inquiry be narrowed from History as a whole to that branch of it which is here called culture, the history, not of tribes or nations, but of the condition of knowledge, religion, art, custom, and the like among them, the task of investigation proves to lie within far more moderate compass. . . . This may appear from a brief preliminary examination of the problem, how the phenomena of Culture may be classified and arranged, stage by stage, in a probable order of evolution.[3]

The study of culture history, or culture, is essentially a historical study, because culture is intrinsically a historical process. Anthropology is the study of man's development in the course of history. This I take to be the significance of Tylor's classic definition of culture, namely, "Culture or Civilization, taken in its widest ethnographic sense, is that complex whole which includes knowledge, belief, art, morals, law, custom, and any other capabilities and habits acquired by man as a member of society." [4] Culture is an attribute of man acquired by him in time as a member of society. One cannot, therefore, understand the culture history of mankind as a whole or of any given society, except by viewing it as a continuous, historical process involving development from some primitive condition to some more advanced state. For Tylor, culture is always the culture of a given society or community, and hence does not refer directly to the individual as such. This does not mean, however, that culture may be understood apart from or independently of the individual's mental processes, since "collective social action is

[2] *Researches*, p. 5.     [3] *Primitive Culture*, I, 5–6.
[4] *Ibid.*, p. 1.

the mere resultant of many individual actions." [5] In brief, the study of culture is the historical study of man's development in society, and culture is the actual historical process of man's evolution, as manifested by his acquired habits and capabilities, from a primitive state to a more advanced state.

Tylor's conception of culture as culture history may be best understood as involving the intellectual vision of a philosophy of cultural progress comparable in many respects to those of Vico and Herder, of the French philosophers of the eighteenth century, such as Condorcet, and especially comparable to that of Comte. He states explicitly: "Auguste Comte scarcely overstated the necessity of this study of development, when he declared at the beginning of his 'Positive Philosophy' that 'no conception can be understood except through its history,' and his phrase will bear extension to culture at large." [6]

Tylor's vision of a science of culture history is based upon a philosophy of cultural progress involving three stages of development, but instead of Comte's triad of theological-metaphysical-positive stages, he postulates savagery-barbarism-civilization as the three universal stages of cultural progress. Unlike Comte, however, he does not proclaim these three stages as a "law" of the development of society, but simply maintains the thesis of the progressive development of culture as an inductive, empirical fact.[7]

The basic *motif* underlying Tylor's ethnological theory is the continuity of culture history as involving a process of development from a lower to a higher degree of culture. Mankind as a whole may be viewed as having passed through these phases of cultural development, and each civilized society may be similarly imagined to have evolved from a more primitive condition of which there is no extant record.

## 2. THE CONCEPT OF THE CONTINUITY OF CULTURE HISTORY

As has been said, this conception of the continuity of culture history, involving progressive development from a lower to a higher degree of culture, was not original with Tylor and may be traced back to the rationalists of the Age of Enlightenment. Their characteristic doctrine of the perfectibility of man in time implied that cultural progress was dependent upon man's rational efforts to perfect himself and his institutions. Culture, or civilization, was recognized as the instrument evolved by man, under divine Providence, for perfecting humanity.

[5] *Ibid.*, p. 13.  [6] *Ibid.*, p. 19.  [7] *Ibid.*, p. 26.

Man was conceived as the creator of his cultural destiny, and there were thought to be no limits to his ability to transform the inherited, historical cultural order in the light of newly emerging moral ideals. By living in harmony with the fixed laws of human nature and the order of nature as a whole, man could regulate his individual and social life in accordance with the dictates of reason so as to promote universal peace and the general happiness of mankind.[8] Rousseau notwithstanding, the arts and sciences were appreciated as instruments which make for the progress of humanity, rather than as impediments which corrupt and hinder it. In Germany, in particular, the concept of culture (*Cultur* or *Kultur*) was contrasted with Rousseau's deification of nature and the cult of sophisticated primitivism.

This humanistic conception of man as the creator and transformer of his culture implied a distinction between the fixed order of nature and the variable order of human culture. While nature herself was conceived as increasing in perfection through divine creativity in time, this meant only a gradual increment of forms of being, but no essential transformation in the order of nature as a whole.[9] But in the sphere of human culture, which was man-made, there was constant progress and transformation in the very organization of human life and society, as well as in the number and variety of human inventions and discoveries.

In Kant's work we find a point of transition from the humanistic, voluntaristic approach, which the eighteenth-century philosophers inherited from the Renaissance thinkers, such as Pico della Mirandola, to the naturalistic approach of the nineteenth-century sociologists and ethnologists. While Kant postulated man as individually and morally free, as a being capable of legislating for himself in obedience to the categorical imperative, he thought, nevertheless, that social phenomena could be interpreted "as if" they were subject to natural laws of their own. In his essay "Idea for a Universal History with Cosmopolitan Intent," published in 1784, we find that he distinguishes between the metaphysical conception of the freedom of the will and the "phenomenal appearance" of the will as manifested in human actions. Human actions appear to be determined by general laws of nature, as are other classes of events in nature. Thus, the statistics of marriages in the major countries show that they occur according to stable natural "laws,"

---

[8] Becker, *The Heavenly City of the Eighteenth-Century Philosophers.*
[9] Lovejoy, *The Great Chain of Being,* ch. ix.

comparable to those which regulate the weather or the seasons. Kant therefore concludes:

Individual human beings, each pursuing his own ends according to his inclination and often one against another (and even one entire people against another) rarely unintentionally promote, as if it were their guide, an end of nature which is unknown to them. They thus work to promote that which they would care little for if they knew about it.[10]

What appears to be nothing more than a senseless march of events may reveal, upon further study, "an end of nature." "A history of creatures who proceed without a plan would be possible in keeping with such an end; the history would proceed according to such an end of nature." Kant thought that it would take the equivalent of a Kepler and a Newton to figure out and explain the end, or plan, of nature in the progressive development of the original endowments of the entire human species in the course of history, and he himself did not feel equal to the task.[11] All Kant suggested at that time was a regulative idea, or principle of interpretation, by means of which the historian may look at human history "as if" it were a process determined according to some law or plan of nature.[12] The nineteenth-century social philosophers and historians attempted to construct such a scientific philosophy of history as Kant had envisaged and what was for Kant only a regulative idea became for them a necessary law of progress and cultural evolution.

In Fichte's work on *The Vocation of Man,* published in 1800, one finds a clear conception of the idea of culture as an ideal of humanity, together with the ideal of historical cultural progress from savagery to civilization. Thus, he writes:

It cannot be intended that those savage tribes should always remain savage; no race can be born with all the capacities of perfect humanity (*volkommene Menschheit*), and yet be destined never to develop these capacities, never to become more than that which a sagacious animal by its own proper nature might become. Those savages must be destined to be the progenitors of more powerful, cultivated (*gebildeten*) and virtuous generations;—otherwise, it is impossible to conceive of a purpose in their existence, or even of the possibility of their existence in a world ordered and arranged by reason. Savage races may become civilized (*cultiviert werden*), for this has already occurred;—the most cultivated nations of modern times are the descendants of savages. Whether civilization (*Bildung*) is a direct and natural develop-

---

[10] *The Philosophy of Kant,* ed. by Carl J. Friedrich, p. 117.
[11] *Ibid.,* pp. 116–17.
[12] Collingwood, *The Idea of History,* p. 94.

ment of human society, or is invariably brought about through instruction and example from without, and the primary source of all human culture (*Cultur*) must be sought in a superhuman guidance,—by the same way in which nations which once were savage have emerged into civilization (*Cultur*), will those who are yet uncivilized gradually attain it. They must, no doubt, at first pass through the same dangers and corruptions of a merely sensual civilization (*sinnlichen Cultur*) by which the civilized nations (*gebildeten Völker*) are still oppressed, but they will thereby be brought into union with the great whole of humanity (*Menschheit*) and be made capable of taking part in its further progress (*Fortschritten*). It is the vocation of our race to unite itself into one single body, all the parts of which shall be thoroughly known to each other, and all possessed of similar culture.[13]

It is highly instructive to note that Fichte here puts forward the two alternative theses which Tylor struggled with more than fifty years later, namely, that of the natural development of culture and that of supernatural guidance, but does not express any marked preference for the former, as did Tylor. In accordance with the metaphysical postulates of divine providence and the perfectibility of man, Fichte is convinced that savages are destined to pass to a higher stage of civilization, just as civilized man may, in time, move forward "to a higher culture of which we can at present form no conception.[14] He infers that the most cultivated nations of modern times are the descendants of savages —a point which Tylor still found it necessary to argue. It should be noted, furthermore, that Fichte, in common with the eighteenth-century philosophers and with Tylor also, contrasts the uncultured savage with the cultured or civilized man, although he admits degrees of culture, varying from the sensual to the ideal and spiritual. Fichte's liberalism and cosmopolitanism may be contrasted with the ethnocentric doctrine of Germanic *Kultur* developed during the course of the nineteenth century and utilized for political purposes to justify cultural and political absolutism.[15]

The cultural cosmopolitanism of the European Enlightenment, with its ideal of the culture of humanity and vision of rational progress based on divine Providence and human effort, was kept alive in the traditions of the French and the American revolutions. The real and the ideal were not identified as they were in Hegelian idealism and later in Marxist historical materialism, and scope was allowed for human initiative in transforming the historical cultural order in the light of

[13] Fichte, *The Vocation of Man*, pp. 119–20.
[14] *Ibid.*, p. 122.
[15] Dewey, *German Philosophy and Politics*, pp. 62–63, 89, 91 ff.

newly emerging ideals. In brief, cosmopolitan, or democratic, culture, as it may be called, was humanistic, rationalistic, and voluntaristic, as contrasted with the metaphysical culture of historical idealism, and historical materialism which was transcendental and deterministic.

The nineteenth-century French philosophers in particular, such as Saint-Simon and Auguste Comte, added the notion that historical development and progress were natural developments subject to natural laws and hence did not require the metaphysical postulate of divine Providence, or superhuman guidance. As Bury has noted,[16] the "law" which Saint-Simon educed from history was that "epochs of organisation or construction and epochs of criticism or revolution succeed each other alternately." As our knowledge becomes more positive and less conjectural, society will become transformed accordingly. The first step in the goal of transforming human society in order to promote human happiness was the amelioration of the lot of the working class which constituted the majority of modern society—a thesis which Marx later developed into a powerful weapon of revolution.

Auguste Comte, who was for a time closely associated with Saint-Simon, developed the concept of sociology as a science concerned with the laws of the development of society. While Comte owed to Saint-Simon the idea of a positive philosophy and to Turgot the concept of the three stages in the development of human thought (theological-metaphysical-scientific), he developed these ideas far more systematically. Especially, the concept of the three stages was transformed by him into the basic law of social dynamics. Every branch of knowledge was said to pass successively through these three states, and since history is ultimately governed by man's ideas, all human history was considered subject to this epistemic law. All phenomena of social life are integrated about these fundamental intellectual changes. Following Condorcet, Comte conceived of humanity as a single individual subject to development in time, with the most advanced societies or nations representing humanity at a given historical epoch. Humanity so conceived led to ethnocentrism and to the belief that the culture of a given nation was especially qualified to represent humanity. In fact, Comte's philosophy of culture history suffered from the outset from European ethnocentrism, inasmuch as he based his synthesis upon the movement of European history to the exclusion of Oriental history and the data of primitive cultures. Furthermore, Comte's philosophy

[16] Bury, *The Idea of Progress*, p. 284.

of history represented a fixed, closed system in that the positive stage represented the ultimate goal of development. Like Hegel, Comte ended with a fixed absolute idea which was not subject to historical development. This point was early detected by his more critical followers, who, like Durkheim, thought that "it is entirely arbitrary to consider the third stage as the definitive state of humanity." "Who knows," he asked, "whether another will not emerge from it in the future?" [17] Comte's ideal of progress was not indefinite, as was that of the eighteenth-century philosophers, but fixed and determinate in accordance with his own idea of the absolute limit of human achievement.

In Buckle's *History of Civilization in England* the idea of history as subject to general laws received popular expression. In support of his Comtean thesis, he referred to statistical studies as indicating the regularity of social phenomena, such as crimes and accidents. Buckle used his statistical approach to demonstrate the thesis that the individual does not determine social processes, but that society determines the acts and thoughts of the individual.

Modern ethnological thought has been built largely upon the foundations of Comtean positivism. Tylor, we have seen, was much influenced by Comte's conception of a natural history of mankind subject to laws of growth comparable to those of physics. He spoke approvingly of Buckle's interest in seeking "the great laws of human development." Tylor felt, however, that in the present state of knowledge the data were insufficient for the construction of a general philosophy of history, "explaining the past and predicting the future," although he admitted in principle the possibility of a natural science of human history.[18] He preferred to follow an inductive method, basing his theses and hypotheses on a careful comparative study of ethnographic evidence, thereby avoiding a priori generalizations and purely speculative inferences.

The Darwinian theory of biological evolution strengthened Tylor's naturalistic approach to the study of human history. Henceforth it appeared that nature as a whole had a history and was subject to a process of evolution. For Comte, nature as a whole was static and retained its fixed forms, while human history was progressive within fixed limits. For the evolutionary ethnologist, human history was but part of the history of nature, both being subject to transformation in time and to

[17] Durkheim, *The Rules of Sociological Method*, p. 119.
[18] *Primitive Culture*, I, 5.

natural laws. As Tylor put it, "if law is anywhere, it is everywhere." [19]

Thus, the laws of nature as manifested in history replaced the wisdom of man and the Providence of God as the condition of human evolution and progress. Like the Stoics of old, the social scientists urged man to conform to nature, but the nature they asked man to conform to was a historical nature, not one fixed and eternal. By conforming to the laws of history and to the rational, scientific ideals indicated by a study of culture history, man would be certain of achieving the ultimate goal of civilization as a self-conscious agent of nature. Culture history was a natural process subject to natural law, and by happy coincidence man's freedom consisted in conforming to this rational natural law.

As an evolutionary ethnologist, Tylor adhered to the position of the continuity of the phenomena of culture history. Ethnographic evidence, including historical reconstruction of the prehistoric data of archaeology, led him to the conclusion that mankind as a whole must have passed, by a process of cultural evolution, from a primitive, prehistoric stage through a middle stage, and finally to the more advanced civilized state which it has now attained among European nations. In his *Anthropology*, published in 1881, Tylor attempted a brief description of these three stages. The "savage" stage is characterized by subsistence on wild plants and animals and the utilization of stone age implements; the "barbaric" stage emerges when man takes to agriculture and metalwork and establishes some form of community life in villages and towns; and the "civilized" stage dawns when men begin to acquire the art of writing.[20] His conclusion is that

so far as the evidence goes it seems that civilization has actually grown up in the world through these three stages, so that to look at a savage of the Brazilian forests, a barbarous New Zealander or Dahoman, and a civilized European, may be the student's best guide to understanding the progress of civilization, only he must be cautioned that the comparison is but a guide, not a full explanation.[21]

It should be noted that these three stages in the process of culture history were understood by Tylor, not as "laws" governing the historical process, but as empirical generalizations which enabled the ethnographer to comprehend the continuity of culture. There is no a priori necessity for all peoples alike to pass through these three stages and to attain the same degree of civilization, as Fichte had maintained. All

[19] *Ibid.*, p. 22.    [20] *Anthropology*, I, 18.    [21] *Ibid.*, p. 19.

one can assume on the basis of ethnographic evidence is that all extant civilized peoples must have passed through a primitive savage state and a barbaric phase of culture history before attaining their present state. Every civilized society, he maintained, has evolved from a less advanced state, and ultimately from a primitive, prehistoric stage of culture, either by its own inventive efforts or aided by social contacts and cultural diffusion. The guiding principle of Tylor's philosophy of culture history is progressive development from the primitive to the civilized state in contrast to any theory of degeneration from a more advanced to a primitive stage.

### 3. CULTURE HISTORY AND PSYCHOLOGY

According to Tylor the causal laws underlying the process of cultural evolution are to be sought in the unchanging laws of human nature from which all cultural phenomena are ultimately derived, not in the cultural phenomena themselves. Thus, Tylor states repeatedly that he is concerned with "the study of human thought and action," with "the laws of human nature," and "the general laws of intellectual movement." [22] He had in mind the physical sciences which postulate an unchanging physical nature in order to explain changing physical phenomena, and hence he assumed that there must be similar unchanging laws of human nature to explain the course of culture history. Thus he writes:

It is no more reasonable to suppose the laws of mind differently constituted in Australia and in England, in the time of the cave-dwellers and in the time of the builders of sheet-iron houses, than to suppose that the laws of chemical combination were of one sort in the time of the coal-measures, and are of another now. The thing that has been will be; and we are to study savages and old nations to learn the laws that under new circumstances are working for good or ill in our own development. [23]

Thus, the historical science of culture was closely bound up for Tylor with the psychological study of man. The two poles of his approach are culture history and psychology. On the one hand, he was concerned to trace the basic stages of cultural evolution; on the other hand, he wished to discover the nonhistoric, unchanging laws of human nature which underlie culture history. Contrary to the sociological approach of Comte, who sought to establish purely sociological and historical

[22] *Primitive Culture*, Vol. I, chs. i, iv.
[23] *Ibid.*, pp. 158–59.

laws of human development, Tylor looked for psychological laws as the source of intelligibility of culture history.

For Tylor, the processes of culture history were not intelligible in themselves and were to be explained ultimately by reference to the universal metacultural principles of human nature, the laws of mental development. Human nature was not, however, conceived as static, but rather as a dynamic entity whose mode of functioning was subject to development in time. The study of culture history provides important clues to the various mental conditions of different peoples and hence ethnography is at the same time a study of "mental history." [24] One comes to understand man through a critical comparative study of the culture history of mankind, and the consequent discovery of the laws of mind, in turn, serves to explain the course and development of cultural phenomena. The primitive human mind, for example, expressed itself in what we regard as mythical thought because it failed to distinguish between subjective and objective data of experience and hence confused images and words with objective reality. Thus, by combining the study of culture history with critical comparative analysis of the species of cultural phenomena, the ethnologist achieved insight into the natural laws which govern the functioning of the human mind through the various stages of its cultural evolution. It was because the ethnologist was able to reconstruct the mental processes which underlie primitive cultural phenomena by studying myths and "survivals" in modern culture that he could explain their origin and function at a given stage of cultural development and yet retain a certain measure of detachment and objectivity in evaluating their significance for their historical originators, on the one hand, and for the modern scientist, on the other.

#### 4. TYLOR ON THE CONCEPT OF CULTURAL PROGRESS

As said, Tylor's minimal thesis is that culture is a historical process subject to development in time. Unlike the theoretical system of Comte, Tylor's scheme did not postulate any fixed limits or goals for the ethno-historical process. The phases of human culture as a whole were simply evaluated in relation to the contemporary culture of Europe and America. As Tylor puts it: "The educated world of Europe and America practically settles a standard by simply placing its own nations at one end

24 *Ibid.*, II, 446.

of the social series and savage tribes at the other, arranging the rest of mankind between these limits according as they correspond more closely to savage or to cultured life." [25]

This meant that, while the process of cultural development was characterized by progress, the latter was understood in a relative, comparative sense. On this basis there were said to be degrees or grades of culture. Hence, in order to evaluate the degrees of progress in the development of culture Tylor was led to employ the concept of culture in two distinct ways, namely, in a normative, ideal sense, as well as in a relative, historical sense. Tylor's classic definition of culture as comprising all the capabilities and habits acquired by man as a member of society refers to culture in this relative sense; any human society whatsoever may be said to possess a culture, or some degree of culture. On this basis, there are no uncultured peoples, no matter how primitive. On the other hand, he also states that "from an ideal point of view, civilization may be looked upon as the general improvement of mankind by higher organization of the individual and society, to the end of promoting at once man's goodness, power, and happiness." [26] According to this definition, only the most highly developed peoples may be said to be civilized, the remainder being savages, or barbarians. This ideal, normative concept of culture or civilization is reminiscent of the philosophical use of the term in the eighteenth century.

The inherent ambivalency of Tylor's use of the term "civilization" may be pointed up by noting that the term "civilization" refers to a positive stage in the development of culture, namely, that characterized by the art of writing, as well as to a moral ideal comprising "man's goodness, power and happiness." From the positive, factual point of view, a society may be said to be civilized once it has become literate, regardless of its state of virtue and happiness. From the moral point of view, mere literacy is not enough to merit the attribute "civilized"; what is more essential is the state of virtue and intelligence. Progress towards civilization is measured by moral achievements and the general welfare of the society as a whole and not merely by the proportion of literacy. Literacy is a means to virtue and intelligence inasmuch as it facilitates the preservation of knowledge and the communication of traditions, ensuring the continuity of intellectual and moral progress. Literacy in and by itself does not bring about the beginning of social virtue, since preliterate societies are obviously not lacking in moral ideals and prac-

[25] *Ibid.*, I, 26.          [26] *Ibid.*, p. 27.

tices. On the other hand, as Tylor admits, literate peoples may degenerate in virtue and be guilty of a degree of immorality not found among savages or barbarians. Tylor's use of the term "civilization" to connote the achievement of literacy, as well as a moral standard of culture, leads to confusion and equivocation.

A survey of Tylor's works reveals that he was not at all consistent in his use of the concept of culture, shifting constantly from the positive and relativistic to the normative and moral sense of the term. Thus, he refers to "uncultured man" as compared with "cultured modern men" and contrasts "barbaric hordes" with "cultured men." [27] On the other hand, he also refers to the development of culture and civilization and speaks of grades, or stages, of culture as if there were no sharp line of demarcation between the state of culture and the so-called precultural stage of human life. [28]

The concept of degrees, or stages, of culture would seem to imply the notion of an ideal, absolute culture to which given historical cultures approximate more or less. On the assumption of such a Platonic norm of culture one could speak coherently of progress toward culture or civilization. While this absolute notion is, in part, implicit in Tylor's work the fact remains that he does not employ the term "ideal" in this absolute sense. For Tylor civilization is an ideal only in the relative sense that as compared with some lower forms of society and culture it marks an improvement. Thus, for him a given form of civilization is an ideal, as well as an actual, mode of social life. In speaking of progress toward civilization, he does not mean progress toward an absolute ideal, but progress as measured empirically and comparatively by reference to actual forms of society. Tylor states explicitly that:

The present comparatively narrow argument on the development of culture at any rate avoids this greatest perplexity. It takes cognizance principally of knowledge, art, and custom, and indeed only very partial cognizance within this field, the vast range of physical, political, social and ethical considerations being left all but untouched. Its standard of reckoning progress and decline is not that of an ideal good and evil, but of movement along a measured line from grade to grade of actual savagery, barbarism and civilization. [29]

It appears, therefore, that Tylor is here distinguishing between an absolute ideal of good and evil and a relative ideal by which one may evaluate comparatively the actual grades of culture. His identification

---

[27] *Ibid.*, II, 443, 453.  [28] *Ibid.*, I, 7.
[29] *Ibid.*, p. 32.

of the ideal with the actual in speaking of civilization is highly confusing, since it leads him to an equivocal use of the concept of civilization. Because civilization is for him an ideal, as well as an actual, historic form of social life, he is led to contrast civilization with savagery
and barbarism and to speak of cultured and uncultured peoples. At
the same time he postulates a scale of culture and refers to the development of culture from lower to higher grades, thereby implicitly assuming the unity of human culture and the relativity of actual historical
cultures. Modern ethnologists have, on the whole, accepted his relativistic historical definition of culture, while ignoring his normative
definition as irrelevant to the science of culture.

## 5. THE PROBLEM OF A SCALE OF CULTURE

Tylor points out that

among naturalists it is an open question whether a theory of development
from species to species is a record of transitions which actually took place, or
a mere ideal scheme serviceable in the classification of species whose origin
was really independent. But among ethnographers, there is no such question
as to the possibility of species of implements or habits or beliefs being developed one out of another, for development in Culture is recognized by our
most familiar knowledge.[30]

While according to Tylor there can be no question of the reality of
development in the realm of cultural phenomena, it is extremely difficult to determine how this evolution is to be conceived and evaluated.
In biology there is said to be a hierarchical "scale of nature" involving
the evolution of higher forms from lower forms. There is an empirical,
as well as ontological, basis for grading species by reference to the
kinds of function which they manifest. Biological evolution may, therefore, be said to be progressive. The problem remains whether there is
a similar "scale of culture." With reference to the technical arts there
is evolution and progress insofar as there is an increase in the efficiency,
quantity, and quality of artifacts. Similarly, there is unquestionable
progress in the evolution of man's scientific knowledge of nature. The
criteria of progress in the technical arts and in scientific knowledge are
objective and quantitative.

But in speaking of civilization from an ideal point of view, Tylor
refers to the "general improvement of mankind by higher organization
of the individual and society, to the end of promoting at once man's

[30] *Ibid.*, pp. 14–15.

goodness, power and happiness." The criterion of progress is seen to be largely subjective, since man's goodness and happiness may not be evaluated with any degree of scientific accuracy. Tylor here introduces a eudaimonistic, moralistic criterion of progress which is not subject to scientific verification, or formulation.

The difficulty inherent in Tylor's moralistic conception of progress in culture or civilization may be pointed up by reference to his notion of retrogression. He admits that "there actually have to be taken into account developments of science and art which tend directly against culture." [31] The development of the art of poisoning, of corrupt literature, of means of arresting freedom of thought and expression, and other harmful arts and inventions are not conducive to the good of society and hence are said to be "contrary to culture." Tylor here presupposes the ideology of nineteenth-century English liberalism and individualism as the moral criterion for evaluating progress and retrogression in culture.

We must distinguish, therefore, between Tylor's ethnological views and his moralistic, philosophical presuppositions. While he disclaims any ideal standard of good and evil in his evaluation of savagery, barbarism, and civilization, he is in fact presupposing such a moral ideal in evaluating cultural progress. His statement that antiliberal arts are "against culture" would, if followed out, lead to the exclusion of whole segments, or departments, of contemporary culture, including much scientific research on the atomic bomb, as anticultural.

The problem remains, then, whether the notion of a scale of culture is to be rejected as irrelevant to or incompatible with a science of culture. Tylor himself acknowledged the difficulty of setting up an absolute scale.

If not only knowledge and art, but at the same time moral and political excellence be taken into consideration, it becomes yet harder to reckon on an ideal scale the advance or decline from stage to stage of culture. In fact, a combined intellectual and moral measure of human condition is an instrument which no student has as yet learnt properly to handle.[32]

Tylor, therefore, contented himself with a limited, comparative, pragmatic and moral evaluation of the three stages of culture, while disclaiming any knowledge of an absolute scale.

Tylor, it would appear, confused the whole issue of cultural evolution by failing to distinguish clearly between cultural evolution and

[31] *Ibid.*, p. 28.                    [32] *Ibid.*, p. 28.

progress. This does not mean that we must reject entirely the notion of a scale of culture; but it does mean that the scale of culture must be factual and capable of scientific verification.

As a preliminary to any possible evaluation of cultural progress, it is necessary for the ethnologist to continue with his historical and comparative research in order to determine the facts of cultural evolution and the various processes by which it has been and may be brought about. Tylor's thesis that culture is an essentially historical process subject to evolution from a primitive, prehistorical to a more advanced state and that this process may be studied without reference to biological or racial differences still remains a sound basis for future ethnological research. In rejecting his moralistic appraisal of culture history and his value-charged conception of culture, the ethnologist need not, and indeed must not, reject his general historical perspective and his vision of the unity of culture as a possession of mankind which is subject to continuous development in time. Otherwise, without the connecting links and continuity provided by the historical perspective, ethnology becomes the study of cultures of particular peoples, and the anthropologist loses sight of the forest of culture because of the trees. As the science of culture history, ethnology is not, as Tylor held it was, "essentially a reformer's science," [33] any more than history in general is essentially a reformer's science, although a critical evaluation of culture history within the context of particular societies may well motivate the potential reformer to act in accordance with his evaluation.

6. TYLOR ON CULTURAL EVOLUTION AND CULTURAL DIFFUSION

In view of the criticism to which the theory of cultural evolution, particularly as formulated by Tylor, has been subjected, it is important to note here that the concept of evolution utilized by him was thoroughly compatible with cultural diffusion. All he was concerned to establish was the thesis of cultural evolution from savagery to civilization as against a doctrine of cultural retrogression. It did not affect his thesis in any way that cultural diffusion, as well as independent invention, was involved in the process of development. After all, it should be remembered that it was Tylor who said, "Civilization is a plant much oftener propagated than developed." [34] In his *Researches into the Early History of Mankind* we find him indicating explicitly the various modes of cultural development.

[33] *Ibid.,* II, 453.  [34] *Ibid.,* I, 53.

Three ways are open, independent invention, inheritance from ancestors in a distant region, transmission from one race to another; but between these three ways the choice is commonly a difficult one.[35]

Later in the same work he recognizes the important role of cultural diffusion.

On the whole, it does not seem unreasonable, or even an over-sanguine view, that the mass of analogies in Art, and Knowledge, Mythology and Custom, confused and indistinct as they at present are, may already be taken to indicate that the civilizations of many races, whose history even the evidence of Language has not succeeded in bringing into connexion, have really grown up under one another's influences or derived material from a common source. But that such lines of argument should ever be found to converge in the last instance towards a single point, so as to enable the student to infer from reasoning on a basis of observed facts that the civilization of the whole world has its origin in one parent stock, is, in the present state of our knowledge, rather a theoretical possibility than a state of things of which even the most dim and distant view is to be obtained.[36]

This is a prophetic passage, in that Tylor here clearly anticipates the type of thesis later put forward by arch-diffusionists, such as Elliot Smith and W. J. Perry, as to the monistic origin of civilization and rejects it. In brief, Tylor held that culture probably originated independently more than once, owing to the psychic similarity of man the world over, but that actual historical development involved numerous instances of cultural diffusion, or inheritance from a common tradition.

Furthermore, it is of great interest to bear in mind that Tylor himself ✓ recognized that no extant "primitive" peoples represent the actual primordial state of man, but are themselves the products of a long, historic process of development. As he put it:

But if we may judge that the present condition of savage tribes is the complex result of not only a long but an eventful history, in which development of culture may have been more or less interfered with by degradation caused by war, disease, oppression and other mishaps, it does not seem likely that any tribe known to modern observers should be anything like a fair representative of primary conditions. Still, positive evidence of anything lower than the known state of savages is scarce in the extreme.[37]

Judging from this passage, it would seem that Tylor appreciated fully the fact of historical development and accident underlying contemporary savagery and did not mistake any extant tribe as being actually aboriginal. Original or primitive culture is a prehistoric phenomenon below that of any known tribes. Even savages, he thought,

[35] *Researches*, p. 374.   [36] *Ibid.*, p. 377.   [37] *Ibid.*, p. 378.

had but the remains of the magical state of mind which they inherited from ancestors of yet lower culture. The "primary condition of the human race" may be conjectured and inferred from the culture of known savages, but is not identical with the latter.

As a first step in the study of cultural evolution, Tylor suggested the necessity of studying or analyzing the basic "details," or "culture traits," as they were later called, and to chart their distribution, just as the geographer or botanist or zoologist studies the distribution of species of plants or animals.[38]

How good a working analogy [Tylor remarks] there really is between the diffusion of plants and animals and the diffusion of civilization, comes well into view when we notice how far the same causes have produced both at once. In district after district the same causes which have introduced the cultivated plants and domesticated animals of civilization, have brought in with them a corresponding art and knowledge. The course of events which carried horses and wheat to America carried with them the use of the gun and iron hatchet, while in return the old world received not only maize, potatoes, and turkeys, but the habit of smoking and the sailor's hammock.[39]

There can be no doubt, then, that Tylor did, in fact, explicitly recognize the role of cultural diffusion in the process of cultural development—a process which, he clearly saw, worked both ways between savages and civilized men. Before attempting any classification of cultures in terms of their typical traits and customs, he counseled the ethnographer to investigate as far as possible the actual distribution and diffusion of these "species" and the possible historical events which led to their present distribution.

I do not find any disparity whatsoever between Tylor's first published work, the *Researches into the Early History of Mankind*, on the one hand, and his *Primitive Culture* and *Anthropology*, on the other. But A. C. Haddon, in his "Introduction" to Tylor's *Anthropology*, asserts that

in the earlier book Dr. Tylor's attitude was on the whole clearly in favour of the diffusion of culture, and tended more to a theory of the borrowing of myths and folk-tales than Andrew Lang, for example, had ever been disposed to accept. In his Preface to the second edition (1873) of the later book [*Primitive Culture*] the author describes it as a "work on civilization insisting so strenuously on a theory of development or evolution." [40]

Haddon implies that in *Primitive Culture* Tylor had switched to the evolutionary theory of culture, whereas in the earlier *Researches* he

38 *Primitive Culture*, I, pp. 7–8.  39 *Ibid.*, pp. 8–9.
40 *Anthropology*, I, vi–vii.

had held to a theory of cultural diffusion. I find nothing in the texts to substantiate this assertion. The mere fact that Tylor refers to the evolution of culture in the later work, whereas he employed the term "development" exclusively in the earlier work, is no indication of any significant change in his point of view.

Of the two alternatives, namely, independent invention and borrowing from others, Tylor was inclined to favor the former except where there was historic evidence to indicate diffusion or borrowing. This is tied up with his psychological approach and his belief in the universality of the laws of human nature. The decision, however, whether a given custom or trait was due to independent invention or to diffusion was to be based upon available ethnographic evidence and comparative analysis.

### 7. TYLOR AND BASTIAN ON CULTURAL EVOLUTION

In his "Introduction" to Tylor's *Anthropology* Haddon quotes Elliot Smith's statement to the effect that

the late Sir Edward Tylor, perhaps more than any other scholar, was responsible for securing recognition for the speculations of Waitz and Bastian claiming the independent evolution of customs and beliefs. . . . Without Tylor's persistent advocacy such doctrines would not have received credence on the part of serious men, but would have lapsed into the oblivion from which they should never have emerged.[41]

According to Elliot Smith, Tylor's advocacy of the theory of cultural evolution was an "unfortunate disservice to ethnology."

Elsewhere Elliot Smith refers to the alleged disparity between Tylor's *Researches* and his *Primitive Culture* and suggests Tylor's dependence upon Waitz and Bastian for the idea of cultural evolution. According to Smith,

The modern hypothesis of the independent development of culture which Sir Edward Tylor adopted from Adolf Bastian subsequently became known as 'evolution.' The irony involved in the misuse of this irrelevant label cannot be fully appreciated unless the reader is reminded of the fact that Adolf Bastian was the friend and collaborator of Virchow in his reckless opposition to the whole conception of biological evolution. . . . The choice in ethnology is between accepting diffusion or the confusion of Bastian. Dr. Rivers announced his decision in 1911.[42]

This is an extraordinary statement and bears little resemblance to actual historical facts. In the first place, Smith confuses the principle

[41] Haddon, in Tylor, *Anthropology*, I, vii.
[42] Smith, in "Introduction" to Rivers, *Psychology and Ethnology*, p. xxvii.

of evolution with that of independent development. There is nothing in Tylor which warrants any such identification. As has been said, Tylor's chief concern was to establish the thesis of cultural evolution and progress from a hypothetical primary or primitive condition of savagery to modern civilization. It was immaterial to his thesis whether independent invention or mutual cultural dissemination was the primary factor. All he did suggest, some fifty years before Elliot Smith advocated the thesis, was the improbability of reducing all forms of civilization to a single origin.

Secondly, Smith's suggestion that Tylor simply borrowed, or took over, the concept of cultural evolution from Bastian is, to say the least, highly misleading. Smith himself points out the irony of attributing the theory of cultural evolution to an antievolutionist such as Bastian. But instead of re-examining his interpretation of Bastian, he prefers to retain his own absurd suggestion. It is true that Bastian's own theory of *Elementargedanken* was, as Boas recognized, antievolutionary in that Bastian adopted the view of the "permanence of forms of thought" and of "the fundamental sameness of forms of human thought." [43] This was a position which influenced Boas a great deal and led him to oppose the evolutionary approach of Tylor and Morgan. Bastian's position was psychological, rather than historical, since the basic elemental ideas were not affected by the historical process and were not subject to development in time. It is, therefore, indeed absurd and ironical for Elliot Smith to attribute Tylor's evolutionary theory of culture history to Bastian, since they represented antithetical positions. Tylor's evolutionary approach goes back to Comte and Buckle, to the *Kulturgeschichte* of Klemm and Waitz, to whom he refers, and to the philosophy of progress of the eighteenth-century European Enlightenment.

In his paper "The Ethnological Analysis of Culture," which, Elliot Smith maintains "marked an epoch not only in Dr. Rivers' own career, but also in the history of ethnology," [44] Rivers presents his interpretation of the theory of cultural evolution, which probably influenced Smith's evaluation of it too. According to Rivers:

The theoretical anthropology of this country is inspired primarily by the idea of evolution founded on a psychology common to mankind as a whole, and further, a psychology differing in no way from that of civilized man. . . . Where similarities are found in different parts of the world, it is assumed,

[43] Boas, *Anthropology*.
[44] *Psychology and Ethnology*, p. xxvi; the paper was first delivered as a presidential address by Rivers in 1911.

almost as an axiom, that they are due to independent origin and development, and this in its turn is ascribed to the fundamental similarity of the workings of the human mind all over the world, so that, given similar conditions, similar customs and institutions will come into existence and develop on the same lines. . . . It is when we come to Germany that we find the most fundamental difference in standpoint and method. It is true that in Adolf Bastian Germany produced a scholar thoroughly familiar with the evolutionary standpoint, and the *Elementargedanke* of that worker forms a most convenient expression for the psychological means whereby evolution is supposed to have proceeded. In recent years, however, there has been a very decided movement opposed to Bastian and the whole evolutionary school. . . . This movement . . . was orginated by Ratzel. . . . Ratzel believed that the resemblances he found could only be explained by direct transmission from one people to another and was led by further study to become an untiring opponent of the *Elementargedanke* of Bastian and of the idea of independent evolution based on a community of thought.[45]

Here, I believe, we may find a clue to the reason that Boas, Smith, Haddon, Lowie, and others were led to confuse cultural evolution and the theory of the independent development of culture. Bastian's theory of *Elementargedanken* did, indeed, imply the principle of independent development, since he asserted as a general law that the psychic unity of mankind everywhere produced similar "elementary ideas." [46] As Lowie has noted, it was Bastian's belief in independent development that most directly affected his contemporaries. Once Bastian's theory was interpreted as essentially "evolutionary," then the notion of independent development became linked with the concept of evolution. The fact remains, however, that Bastian himself put the major emphasis upon his theory of elementary ideas as basic for an understanding of folk thought (*Völkergedanke*); culture development proper (*eigentliche Kulturentwicklung*) became significant only at the higher stages of culture history and is, therefore, of subordinate importance as compared with this nonhistorical factor.[47] Bastian's own contemporaries, such as Ratzel, did interpret his approach as essentially nonhistorical, and Bastian himself certainly did not regard himself as an evolutionist. And so, by one of those queer pranks of historical scholarship this nonhistorian, this nonevolutionist, came to be labeled by a later generation as an "evolutionist," and the theory of independent development of basic folk ideas became associated with the theory of cultural evolution.

[45] *Ibid.*, pp. 121, 122, 123.
[46] Lowie, *History of Ethnological Theory*, pp. 35–36.
[47] *Ibid.*, p. 36.

What made the association of the idea of independent development with the theory of evolution appear plausible was the fact that cultural evolutionists, such as Tylor, did accept and advocate a measure of independent, parallel invention with reference to the savage state of culture—even though Tylor and his British and American followers did not subscribe to Bastian's psychological determinism. The fact that Tylor himself put forward the postulate of independent invention as but one mode of cultural evolution and did not subscribe to the idealistic Herbartian and Leibnitzian theory of innate ideas, such as Bastian presupposed, was entirely overlooked.[48]

Another factor which made the confusion of Bastian's and Tylor's views seem plausible was that both of them adhered to the principle of the psychic unity of mankind and therefore both held to the psychological determinism of cultural development. The fact that Tylor assumed a basic identity of the potentialities of human nature, conceived in individualistic terms, whereas Bastian assumed the actual identity of the social psyche or mind of different peoples was again overlooked. Tylor did not assume any a priori identity of mental content, but only a similar potentiality for conceiving similar ideas and making similar inventions at a given stage of mental and cultural development. For Tylor, mind was subject to evolution or development in time, and hence he could speak of ethnology as concerned with mental laws and mental history.

Thus, the term "psychic unity of mankind" turns out to be ambiguous and capable of being interpreted either in an evolutionary or a non-evolutionary sense. Bastian's *Elementargedanken* were innate predetermined expressions of the social psyche common to all *Naturvölker*. His conception of growth was Aristotelian and Stoic rather than Darwinian and involved the notion of the development of innate forms, such as the *logoi spermatikoi* of the Stoics, not the transformation of organic forms which is presupposed by the theory of organic evolution. Bastian's idea of psychic unity involved the assumption of the identity of the *Elementargedanken* of all peoples, whether primitive or civilized, and hence was antithetical to a theory of mental and cultural evolution. On the other hand, it was precisely the principle of transformism as applied to culture history which constituted the essence of Tylor's theory of mental and cultural evolution. To associate Tylor with Bastian and to call them both evolutionists is to abuse the term. There is noth-

[48] Schmidt, *The Culture Historical Method of Ethnology*, p. 5.

ing in the theory of cultural evolution as envisaged by Tylor which involves the dogma of universal independent development of culture or the total psychological determinism of cultural thought.

Boas, as has been noted, did not confuse Bastian's theory of *Elementargedanken* with the evolutionism of Tylor, and he contrasted their approaches. He did, however, regard independent development and psychological determinism as essential elements of the theory of cultural evolution. Later historians added to the confusion by identifying Bastian's views with those of the evolutionists and with Tylor's thought in particular.

For example, T. K. Penniman states:

Thus in his [Bastian's] work are united two 'schools' of anthropological study, the evolutionary, and the historical or diffusionist, which ought never to have been separated, for they are complementary to each other, and any reasonable worker must take account of both. . . . Tylor, like Bastian, dealt with beliefs that underlie institutions. The approach of both was the psychological. The main difference between the two was in the power of organization and clarity of presentation.[49]

Penniman apparently sees no essential difference between the approach of Tylor and that of Bastian; both are said to be evolutionary, as well as historical and diffusionist. The fact that for Bastian there was no inherent difference between the innate mentality of primitive men and that of civilized man, while for Tylor there was a marked difference between the mythopoeic mind of the savage and that of civilized man, is not taken into consideration in arriving at this conclusion. The "elementary ideas" of Bastian were said to be common to all mankind and hence not subject to evolution. That was why "it was evident to him that similar ideas and cultural traits rose independently in various tribes and regions and were originally confined to them, the material conditions determining the form, and differences varying with the environment."[50] On the other hand, Penniman says of Tylor that he is extremely careful not to admit the independent origin of similar inventions in different parts of the world until he has exhausted every possibility of diffusion or culture contact.[51] Surely that would seem to indicate a fundamental difference in approach which goes beyond the stylistic differences of clarity and mode of expression.

Lowie's account does serve to correct Penniman's blurred comparison of Bastian and Tylor. According to Lowie, Bastian did not deny

[49] Penniman, *A Hundred Years of Anthropology*, pp. 150–51, 184.
[50] *Ibid.*, p. 148.     [51] *Ibid.*, p. 177.

the principle of diffusion, "but he insisted that in each case it must be proved by detailed evidence . . . . since he contended that by a general law the psychic unity of mankind everywhere produced similar 'elementary ideas.' " [52] This point, in itself, would serve to differentiate Bastian's position from that of Tylor, who postulated no such general law of the identity of universal, elementary ideas.

Lowie, however, goes on to state that "Bastian's faith in supposedly uniform laws of growth, in a 'genetic principle' through which lower and simpler phenomena become higher and complex, shows that cultural evolutionism may very well go hand in hand with a repudiation of biological transformism." [53] Lowie does not appear to take into consideration that Bastian's conception of growth or development was Aristotelian and involved the principle of entelechy, or immanent final cause, which predetermined the direction and course of development of an organism from beginning to end. The social organism, like the individual organism, is conceived as developing in stages under the stimulus of the geographical environment which actualizes its potentialities. Thus, the elementary ideas serve as a kind of "cultural entelechy" which predetermines the development and expression of culture forms under the stimulus of the environment. Bastian's distinction between *Naturvolk* and *Kulturvolk* indicates that for him the social elementary ideas were products of innate natural development, whereas historical diffusion was secondary and only affected some later phases of cultural development. [54]

This serves to explain why diffusionists and anthropogeographers, such as Ratzel, found themselves in opposition to Bastian's approach and were inclined to stress the role of historical diffusion and the influence of the environment as primary factors, whereas Bastian emphasized independent internal development of folk cultures. That is why Graebner and others of the *Kulturkreise* school rejected Bastian's *Elementargedanken* and set out to trace the historical connections of diverse culture complexes. The adherents of this "culture historical method" assumed ultimate psychological differences among peoples and ultimate diverse culture complexes. According to these culture historians it was the similarities between cultures that required explanation, and these were accounted for by diffusion and the migration of

[52] Lowie, *History of Ethnological Theory*, pp. 35–36.
[53] *Ibid.*, p. 36.
[54] Schwarz, *Adolph Bastian's Lehre vom Elementar und Völkergedanken*. Bastian, *Ethnische Elementargedanken in der Lehre vom Menschen*, pp. ix, 15.

peoples. For Bastian, on the other hand, similarities were taken for granted as results of the identity of *Elementargedanken* and the underlying psychic uniformity of peoples, and only differences required explanation in terms of environmental influence and culture contacts. For Tylor, however, similarities could be explained either by a common mentality or the diffusion of culture traits, according to the available evidence and maximum probability under given circumstances.

Thus, we are confronted with the paradoxical situation that the theory of cultural evolution, which as set forth by Tylor was essentially a philosophy of culture history involving the concepts of cultural progress and degrees of cultural development in the course of time, was understood at the turn of the century to be essentially nonhistorical and even antihistorical. This was, indeed, a perversion of the very idea of cultural evolution understood as transformism in culture history, since a nonhistorical cultural evolution is a contradiction in terms. Some of the assumptions of the cultural evolutionists were, indeed, nonhistorical, or pseudohistorical, as, for example, the alleged stages in the evolution of religion, morality, and art, but the theory of cultural evolution as a whole was essentially a philosophy of the culture history of mankind from prehistoric to modern times. The thesis that evolutionary method in ethnology is antithetic to historical method is mistaken and false.

Rivers's "momentous" discovery in the course of his work in Oceania that Melanesian society is not really primitive in the sense of being primordial but is the result of historical cultural contacts and diffusion was anticipated by Tylor's express statement that "the present condition of savage tribes is the complex result of not only a long but an eventful history." [55] It was only on the mistaken assumption that evolutionary theory necessarily requires the postulation of independent development from innate elementary ideas that Rivers was led to contrast the evolutionary with the historical approach and to prefer the latter. He was, in fact, in complete agreement with Tylor in his insistence upon the necessity of preliminary historical and ethnological analysis of cultures before engaging in speculations concerning the evolution of culture and society. He also implicitly followed Tylor in stressing the need for the study of the psychology of customs and institutions. Tylor would have endorsed this statement that "it is only by the combination of ethnological and psychological analysis that we shall make any real advance." When Rivers finally asserts that "to me the analysis

[55] *Researches,* p. 378.

of culture is merely the means to an end which would have little interest if it did not show us the way to the proper understanding of the history of human institutions," he is back again in the Tylorian camp and speaking the language of cultural evolution.[56]

### 8. MAINE'S *Ancient Law* AND ETHNOHISTORICAL PERSPECTIVE

Maine's *Ancient Law,* published in 1861, was among the works which undoubtedly influenced Tylor. In the 1871 edition of *Primitive Culture* one finds reference to Maine's work and the latter's criticism of Blackstone's *Commentaries* by way of illustration of the thesis that a knowledge of culture history is essential for an understanding of contemporary law and custom. It is interesting to note, however, that in later editions, beginning with the edition of 1891, all reference to Maine is omitted and a fresh example is cited of Blackstone's limitations in attempting "to explain by the light of reason things which want the light of history." "It is always unsafe," Tylor concludes, "to detach a custom from its hold on past events, treating it as an isolated fact to be simply disposed of by some plausible explanation." [57] This represents also the basic thesis of Maine and may be characterized as ethnohistorical functionalism. It is an approach which combines a keen appreciation of the necessity of ethnohistorical perspective in evaluating the function and the significance of contemporary customs and institutions together with an understanding of the functional interrelations of cultural traits in both time and place, thereby avoiding the fallacies of modern sociological functionalism, such as that of Radcliffe-Brown and Malinowski, which depreciate the value of historical research.

What Tylor attempted to do in the field of ethnology, namely, to present a natural history of the development of culture, Maine had attempted previously in the field of law. As against the philosophical nonhistorical approach of jurists such as Bentham and Austin and philosophers such as Hobbes and Locke, Maine demonstrated the fallacy of reading "history" backward by attributing to early man conceptions and institutions which were in fact products of later historical achievement. As against the social contract theory in particular, Maine pointed out the primacy of custom over legislation and of society over the individual. Maine was among the first to stress the need for a study of comparative jurisprudence in order to establish the stages in

[56] Rivers, "Ethnological Analysis of Culture," in his *Psychology and Ethnology,* pp. 132, 139.

[57] Tylor, *Primitive Culture,* ed. of 1871, I, 18; *ibid.,* ed. of 1913, pp. 19–20.

the development of custom and law from "the primeval condition of the human race" to the state of modern civilization. His major thesis is the continuity of civilization. Thus, he writes:

The lofty contempt which a civilized people entertains for barbarous neighbors has caused a remarkable negligence in observing them, and this carelessness has been aggravated at times by fear, by religious prejudice, and even by the use of these very terms—civilisation and barbarism—which convey to most persons the impression of a difference not merely in degree but in kind.[58]

The notion of degrees of civilization from ancient to modern times prepared the way for the ethnological conception of culture, or civilization, as a relative historical phenomenon. Although Maine's particular thesis, "that the movement of the progressive societies has hitherto been a movement from status to contract," [59] has been discredited by later investigators, the historical approach which he initiated in the comparative study of social and legal institutions has been of lasting value.

### 9. LEWIS H. MORGAN ON THE LINES OF HUMAN PROGRESS

It is of interest to note that the subtitle of Morgan's *Ancient Society*, published in 1877, is "Researches in the Lines of Human Progress from Savagery through Barbarism to Civilization." This would indicate that Morgan modeled his work upon Tylor's *Researches into the Early History of Mankind and the Development of Civilization*. Morgan does, in fact, refer to Tylor's *Researches* in his text, although he does not mention the latter's *Primitive Culture*, where the three phases, or stages, in the development of culture are explicitly mentioned.

A comparative analysis of Morgan's *Ancient Society* and Tylor's *Researches* and *Primitive Culture* reveals some basic similarities, as well as some significant differences. In general it may be said that Morgan shares Tylor's thesis of the development, or evolution, of civilization from a primitive state of savagery, through a middle state of barbarism to modern civilization. It is similarly presupposed that progress is linear and is to be measured by setting up nineteenth-century civilization of Europe and America as the norm. By both writers the stages in the evolution of civilization are reckoned by reference to technological achievement, Morgan limiting himself to a detailed survey of the development of the arts and social institutions, and avoiding moral evaluations such as Tylor had indulged in.

[58] *Ancient Law*, p. 71.  [59] *Ibid.*, p. 100.

Like Tylor, Morgan also confused evolution and progress. Hence his chief preoccupation was to set up a scale of culture or civilization by arranging a fixed order, or sequence, in the development of the arts and social institutions. Much of this was a priori and was based upon logical analysis in terms of simplicity and complexity, although the evolutionary scheme also purported to be an account of the actual historical development of mankind. It is this confusion of logic and history which later motivated much of the criticism directed against the evolutionary school by Boas and his followers. Morgan's speculations on the development of the forms of the family from the "consanguine" to the "monogamian" was particularly vulnerable to this criticism.

The presupposition of fixed, determinate stages in the evolution of material and social culture led to the "reconstruction" that there was a prehistory of cultures for which no direct evidence was available. Thus, what was devised as a logical scheme of evolutionary development was also utilized as presumptive historical evidence. Morgan is explicit on this point:

The remote ancestors of the Aryan nations presumptively passed through an experience similar to that of existing barbarous and savage tribes. Though the experience of these nations embodies all the information necessary to illustrate the periods of civilization, both ancient and modern, together with a part of that in the Later period of barbarism, their anterior experience must be deduced, in the main, from the traceable connection between the elements of their existing institutions and inventions, and similar elements still preserved in those of savage and barbarous tribes.[60]

Having set up the basic stages in the evolution of culture, time and actual history were no longer considered relevant, since it could be assumed a priori that what was true of one stage of culture was true of all the particular, historic cultures at a similar stage. As Morgan puts it,

It does not affect the main result that different tribes and nations on the same continent, and even of the same linguistic family, are in different conditions at the same time, since for our purpose, the *condition* of each is the material fact, the *time* being immaterial.[61]

The condition of relative advancement, as determined by the state of the arts of subsistence and the art of writing, is what gives each ethnic period or stage its distinct culture and enables the student of culture

---

[60] *Ancient Society*, pp. 7–8.       [61] *Ibid.*, p. 13.

history to reconstruct the details when no direct historical evidence is available.

So essentially identical [Morgan remarks,] are the arts, institutions and mode of life in the same status upon all the continents, that the archaic form of the principal domestic institutions of the Greeks and Romans must even now be sought in the corresponding institutions of the American aborigines, as will be shown in the course of this volume.[62]

In agreement with Tylor, Morgan accepts the principle of the development and progress of culture from the primitive to the civilized stage, as against any theory of cultural degradation which would explain the existence of barbarians and savages. "It was never," he observes, "a scientific proposition supported by facts," as is the contrary theory of cultural evolution.[63]

Morgan, however, expresses his disagreement with the thesis of Maine's *Ancient Law* to the effect that the patriarchal family of the Hebrew and Latin types is the oldest form of the family and the source of organized society. The patriarchal family, Morgan argues, corresponds to the "Upper Status of barbarism, leaving at least four entire ethnical periods untouched." [64]

According to Morgan there is a "law of progress" according to which cultural and social progress is manifested "in a geometrical ratio." As he states it,

Human progress, from first to last, has been in ratio not rigorously but essentially geometrical. This is plain on the face of the facts; and it could not, theoretically, have occurred in any other way. . . . Consequently, while progress was slowest in time in the first period, and most rapid in the last, the relative amount may have been greatest in the first, when the achievements of either period are considered in their relations to the sum.[65] It is a conclusion of deep importance in ethnology that the experience of mankind in savagery was longer in duration than all their subsequent experience, and that the period of civilization covers but a fragment of the life of the race.[66]

It is important to note here that neither Tylor nor Morgan maintained the thesis that all societies are destined to pass through similar phases of cultural development from savagery to civilization. They did maintain that those societies which attained the status of civilization passed through two prior historical stages, namely, savagery and barbarism (with their subdivisions). The concept of cultural stages was applied retroactively as a means of explaining the evolution of particular, his-

[62] *Ibid.*, pp. 17–18.     [63] *Ibid.*, p. 513.     [64] *Ibid.*, p. 514.
[65] *Ibid.*, p. 37.     [66] *Ibid.*, p. 38.

torical cultures which were known to have attained the level of civilization. This meant, in effect, that the concept of cultural stages was first
utilized as a phylogenetic concept applicable to mankind as a whole
and then applied as an ontogenetic principle of historical reconstruction to historic forms of civilization. Both Morgan and Tylor were well
aware of the facts of cultural diffusion, Tylor, in particular, actually
using the term "diffusion" to indicate one source of culture change,
especially with reference to the distribution of myths. Hence, it is
erroneous to argue that the acknowledgment of the process of cultural
diffusion undermines the theory of cultural evolution. Tylor and Morgan
did not maintain that all societies are destined to pass through the
same phases in similar chronological order, as if the contact of peoples
and acculturation did not affect the processes of cultural change. All
they were concerned to establish was the historical principle of cultural
development and cultural progress from savagery to civilization as
against any theory of cultural retrogression or degradation. There were
no laws which determined a priori that all lower cultures had to pass
through the same stages in the future as the higher cultures had in the
past. The thesis of cultural predestination was, indeed, put forward by
some of the philosophers of the European Enlightenment, especially
by Fichte, as a postulate of divine Providence and the principle of sufficient reason. A similar thesis was maintained by Comte in accordance
with his law of the three stages. But the culture historians or ethnologists, such as Tylor and Morgan, did not make any such assertions.
The laws for which Tylor looked were psychological, not historical, and
the only law mentioned by Morgan was the general law of cultural
progress in accordance with geometrical ratio.

In the past, cultural evolution occurred along similar lines because
of similar human conditions and because of the specific identity of the
brain of all the races of mankind.[67] According to Morgan,

The accumulating evidence [shows] that the principal institutions of mankind
have been developed from a few primary germs of thought; and that the
course and manner of their development was predetermined, as well as
restricted within narrow limits of divergence, by the natural logic of the human mind and the necessary limitations of its powers. . . . The argument
when extended tends to establish the unity of origin of mankind.[68]

Thus, for Morgan also cultural uniformity was ultimately based
upon universal psychological and biological determinism. There were

[67] *Ibid.*, p. 8.     [68] *Ibid.*, p. 18; also p. 562.

no specifically cultural or historical laws independent of human nature which determined the course of cultural development.

Morgan differs from Tylor in that the former suggests a specific correlation between cultural development and biological development, whereas Tylor treated cultural evolution as a process independent of biological evolution. Thus, Morgan asserts that "with the production of inventions and discoveries, and with the growth of institutions, the human mind necessarily grew and expanded; and we are led to recognize a gradual enlargement of the brain itself, particularly of the cerebral portion." [69] He adduces no evidence to substantiate his assertion that the growth of culture produced a corresponding growth of cerebral structure.

From an ethnic point of view, Morgan observes that two families only, the Semitic and the Aryan, reached the status of civilization "through unassisted self-development." "The Aryan family represents the central stream of human progress, because it produced the highest type of mankind, and because it has proved its intrinsic superiority by gradually assuming the control of the earth." [70] In the light of later claims made in behalf of Aryan "superiority" as a justification for world conquest, this assertion is no longer as obvious as it once appeared.

For the strict materialistic culturologist Morgan's work is vitiated finally by the fact that he brings in God and Providence to account for the emergence of civilization some five thousand years ago. According to Morgan:

When we recognize the duration of man's existence upon the earth, the wide vicissitudes through which he has passed in savagery and in barbarism, and the progress he was compelled to make, civilization might as naturally have been delayed for several thousand years in the future, as to have occurred when it did in the good providence of God. We are forced to the conclusion that it was the result, at the time of its achievement, of a series of fortuitous circumstances. It may well serve to remind us that we owe our present condition, with its multiplied means of safety and of happiness, to the struggles, the sufferings, the heroic exertions and the patient toil of our barbarous, and more remotely, of our savage ancestors. Their labors, their trials and their successes were a part of the plan of the Supreme Intelligence to develop a barbarian out of a savage, and a civilized man out of this barbarian.[71]

Thus, for Morgan a science of culture does not preclude acknowledgment of divine Providence and the role of contingent human efforts in bringing about the historical development of culture. It is rather

[69] *Ibid.*, p. 36.    [70] *Ibid.*, pp. 562–63.    [71] *Ibid.*, p. 563.

ironical to reflect that this American ethnologist who, through his influence upon Marx and Engels, has won a special place of honor among
Marxian communist sociologists did not himself adhere to any narrow
theory of materialistic and historical determinism.

# 8

# *Cultural Dynamics and the Quest for Origins*

Boas devoted much time and effort throughout his long life to a critique of the theory of cultural evolution as he understood it. For this he has often been criticized as being anti-evolutionist and nonhistorical. This criticism is not valid, since he was not opposed to the notion of cultural evolution in general, but only to the particular version of the theory put forward by some nineteenth-century ethnologists.

## 1. BOAS AND THE CRITIQUE OF CULTURAL EVOLUTIONISM

Boas was opposed to the assumption that there was one fixed formula for cultural evolution applicable either to the past or to the future of all societies; but he was not opposed to the concept of evolution within the context of a given culture or to the idea of limited progress within certain spheres of culture, such as technology. As early as 1908 he wrote: "Notwithstanding this serious criticism much of the older theory seems plausible; but presumably a thorough revision and a more individualized aspect of the development of civilization in different parts of the world will become necessary." [1]

Specifically, Boas was opposed to the thesis of the cultural evolutionists that cultural development is always from the simple to the complex and that there are definite stages of cultural evolution making for cultural progress. In reacting against the tendency of the evolutionists to set up scales of cultural development applicable to all mankind and serving as a criterion of progress, Boas was inclined to limit himself to the study of particular cultures and the diffusion of culture traits over given areas. Thus, history took on for him a rather limited significance and became the study of the culture history of a given society rather than the culture history of mankind as a whole. Similarly, in practice

[1] *Anthropology.*

anthropology was understood as the study of particular cultures conceived as functional, integrated wholes rather than as the study of the evolution of human culture and the stages of cultural development.

In a paper entitled "The Methods of Ethnology," [2] Boas defined his attitude succinctly as follows:

American scholars are primarily interested in the dynamic phenomena of cultural change, and try to elucidate cultural history by the application of the results of their studies; . . . they relegate the solution of the ultimate question of the relative importance of parallelism of cultural development in distinct areas, as against worldwide diffusion, and stability of cultural traits over long periods to a future time when the actual conditions of cultural change are better known. . . . It may seem to the distant observer that American students are engaged in a mass of detailed investigations without much bearing upon the solution of the ultimate problems of a philosophic history of human civilization. I think this interpretation of the American attitude would be unjust because the ultimate questions are as near to our hearts as they are to those of other scholars, only we do not hope to be able to solve an intricate historical problem by a formula.

Here we see that Boas does not disclaim a general interest in a philosophical history of human civilization, but argues only that the time is not yet ripe for such a synthesis. The primary and immediate objective is, he maintains, the study of cultural dynamics, of actual processes of culture change, within the context of given cultures. After a detailed comparative analysis of the processes of culture change in particular cultures, the ethnologist will be in a position to solve such general problems as the relative significance of independent cultural development versus cultural diffusion and the basic types of culture evolved in the culture history of mankind.

In short [Boas concludes] the method which we try to develop is based on a study of the dynamic changes in society that may be observed at the present time. We refrain from the attempt to solve the fundamental problem of the general development of civilization until we have been able to unravel the processes that are going on under our eyes.[3]

Thus, as has been said, Boas reduced anthropology from the study of the evolution and progress of human culture to the study of particular cultures conceived as unique functional, integrated wholes. "Each cultural group," he observes, "has its own unique history, dependent partly upon the peculiar inner development of the social group, and partly upon the foreign influences to which it has been subjected." [4] No

---

[2] Reprinted in *Race, Language and Culture*, pp. 281–89; see especially pp. 283–84.
[3] *Ibid.*, p. 285.          [4] *Ibid.*, p. 286.

single evolutionary scheme, he argues, would explain the unique culture history of any particular society. There is no "psychological necessity" that leads to a uniform evolution the world over.

As Boas understood the theory of cultural evolution,

The evolutionary point of view presupposes that the course of historical changes in the cultural life of mankind follows definite laws which are applicable everywhere, and which bring it about that cultural development is, in its main lines, the same among all races and all peoples. This idea is clearly expressed by Tylor in the introductory pages of his classic work "Primitive Culture." [5]

As indicated in our analysis of Tylor and Morgan, a careful examination of their writings does not bear out Boas' understanding of their basic thesis. Neither Tylor nor Morgan postulated "definite laws" which determine that cultural development should be the same among all races and all peoples. Tylor's main thesis, as he repeatedly informs us, is "simply this, that the savage state in some measure represents an early condition of mankind, out of which the higher culture has gradually been developed or evolved, by processes still in regular operation as of old, the result showing that, on the whole, progress has far prevailed over relapse." [6] The laws which Tylor postulated and which he sought to determine were psychological laws, not historical or cultural laws. And while Morgan does mention a law of progress, the latter refers to the geometric proportion of cultural development. For Morgan, as for Tylor, cultural evolution was ultimately determined "by the natural logic of the human mind."

It appears, therefore, that the notion of laws of cultural development is not at all essential to the basic thesis of cultural evolution. The basic theses that occur in the work of Tylor and Morgan are: first, the unity of human culture and the concept of a scale of culture such that culture may be understood as subject to linear progress from a lower to a higher stage; secondly, the similarity of all historical cultures for the same stage of development.

The second thesis as to the similarity of historical cultures at the same stage of development is open to serious question. The concept of a scale of culture is, after all, a logical abstraction from culture history. It is possible to arrange a series of culture traits, abstracted from diverse cultures and areas, in a hierarchical order, but this would not necessarily imply their actual realization in the culture history of any given

[5] *Ibid.*, p. 281.  [6] *Primitive Culture.* I, 32.

society in that particular sequence. There is, indeed, a very limited area in which logic and history appear to coincide, namely, at the very beginning of the cultural process. It is logical, and probably historically true, as well, that food gathering and hunting preceded agriculture and settled community life. Similarly, in the sphere of technology the simpler, more obvious invention probably preceded the more complex and less obvious, especially in those instances in which the later invention marks an improvement upon the earlier, for example, in modes of making fire and in the construction of the bow and arrow. Beyond this limited area, in the sphere of intellectual culture in particular, cultural evolution takes the form of a gradual clarification of thought from the complex to the "simpler," in the sense of the clearer and more rational.

In a broad morphological sense it is, therefore, possible to postulate universal stages in the evolution of culture from a primitive, prehistorical state to the more advanced states of the historical cultures. This assumption would not, however, imply that all cultures at the same stage of development possessed the same culture traits and institutions. If there is cultural diversity at all, it must be postulated at all stages of cultural development. We are not obliged to choose between complete identity of culture traits and institutions at the same stage of cultural development or complete diversity. Just as in modern cultures we find both elements of similarity, as regards the basic institutions, and elements of difference as well, so in the prehistoric and primitive cultures we are bound to find elements of similarity and elements of diversity. It is fallacious to argue from the morphological similarity of a given stage of cultural development to complete substantial identity of culture traits and processes for the same stage, regardless of space, time, and social circumstances. The uniformity of culture history for a given stage of development is an unwarranted assumption and may be termed the "evolutionistic fallacy." Boas and his followers have done valuable service in the cause of ethnology in demonstrating, by appealing to ethnographic facts, that no single formula of cultural evolution will serve to account for the actual historical sequence of cultural phenomena in all given cultures at similar stages of development. Boas demonstrated that in the case of art, in particular, it was impossible to determine a priori whether the course of development was from representational to geometric or vice versa. Boas' *The Mind of Primitive Man* is a sustained argument against a uniform, systematic history of all cultures or categories of culture.

This thesis implies that historical reconstruction of culture history must be undertaken with great caution, since it must not be assumed without evidence that all the phases of a given prehistoric culture corresponded to the traits of some extant primitive culture. It is a valid argument to maintain that given historic civilizations must have passed through, or evolved from, some less advanced condition. By a careful study of the culture history of a given society, including its relations to other culture systems, it is possible to reconstruct some of its non-recorded culture history, for example, from a study of its myths and legends it is possible to reconstruct the thought and beliefs of a previous age. But it is hazardous to assume, as Morgan, for instance, does, that the archaic form of Greek and Roman institutions corresponded to those of the American aborigines or that all historic cultures passed through similar technological substages, regardless of geographical and temporal circumstances. Boas' reluctance to indulge in, or accept, historical reconstruction without substantial evidence indicating a high degree of probability is therefore understandable.

The thesis of the unity of human culture and the concept of a scale of culture is another matter and is to be evaluated independently of the problem of the specific phases in the development of a given category of culture. The philosophy of history underlying the concept of the unity of human culture and linear progress derives from the Hebrew-Christian tradition of the unity of mankind and the Providence of God in human history. This philosophy may be contrasted with the Greek cyclical philosophy of history, which envisages a cycle of development for a given civilization with a fixed beginning and end. The modern theory of cultural progress is a synthesis of the Hebrew-Christian notion of the evolution of mankind under divine Providence together with the rationalistic, philosophical idea of the indefinite perfectibility of man in time, as put forward at the time of the European Renaissance and the Enlightenment. This theory was opposed by the theological theory of divine revelation and human retrogression and both Tylor and Morgan found it necessary to argue on behalf of the progressive development and continuity of human civilization. While the latter could not answer the debated question as to why some peoples were left behind in "the race of progress," they were sure the disparity was not due to retrogression. In agreement with Condorcet and Comte, culture historians found it sufficient to assert that at each epoch of human history some peoples represented humanity as its highest and best and thereby assured the continuity and progress of civilization or culture. As a result, Morgan concluded that, "the history of the human race is one in source, one in experience, one in progress." [7]

Logically, it should be noted, one may differentiate between cultural evolution and progress. If one accepts a cyclical theory of culture history, one could then retain a belief in cultural evolution within fixed limits, while denying, or excluding, the possibility of indefinite progress in time. The modern historical and ethnological theory of indefinite progress presupposes a linear, orthogenetic conception of history, as well as the unity of mankind.

The thesis of the progress of human culture also presupposes a normative or ideal culture which particular actual cultures approximate more or less. Thus, the postulate of the progressive evolution of culture and the postulate of a scale of culture are to be differentiated. The concept of a scale of culture is a logical, ideal scheme or classification which may be accepted or assumed regardless of the actual course of culture history. The validity of a scale of culture does not depend upon its actual realization in given historical cultures. The actual, historical evolution of human cultures may or may not be progressive in comparison with this logical value-scale; there is no a priori reason, other than metaphysical faith, as to why it should be progressive and promote human virtue and happiness rather than the contrary. Empirically, it is the function of the ethnologist as culture historian to trace the actual evolution of given cultures and the diverse course of human culture in general, without committing himself a priori to any philosophy of progress or retrogression. How to evaluate cultural progress is a profound metaethnological problem which involves a systematic theory of values which the ethnologist as such does not necessarily possess.

The problem of the evolution and progress of culture is, then, highly complex. The philosophy of historical cultural progress is based on the assumption of the unity and continuity of human cultural experience and involves comparison with an ideal or normative culture. If, however, one denies this orthogenetic conception of human history and the essential unity of mankind, as well as an ideal of culture, then he is left with the notion of a plurality of cultures, each with its own unique culture history and evolution, but with no over-all philosophy of culture history or measure of cultural progress.

[7] *Ancient Society,* Preface, p. vi.

Boas, it appears, chose the latter alternative. In contrast to a monistic theory of cultural evolution, involving mankind as a whole, he preferred a pluralistic theory of the evolution of cultures. "It is clear," he writes, "that if we admit that there may be different ultimate and co-existing types of civilization, the hypothesis of one single general line of development cannot be maintained." [8] While Boas continued to avow an abstract, theoretical interest in the ultimate problems of a philosophic history of human civilization, in practice he preferred a pluralistic approach and concentrated his attention upon the investigation of specific cultures with a view to ascertaining the processes of cultural change, while postponing indefinitely any attempt to formulate a theory of the general development of civilization. The notion, accepted by Tylor and Morgan, that our own Western European civilization represents the highest cultural development seemed to him ethnocentric. Rather than identify our actual civilization with the ideal or norm of cultural progress, he preferred the alternative of cultural pluralism and cultural relativity. In view of the experience of twentieth-century society with two world wars brought on by Western civilized powers, Boas' aversion to the acceptance of European civilization as the norm of progress appears to have been amply justified.

It is worth noting at this point that Boas, notwithstanding his criticism of Tylor, ended by postulating psychological laws in order to explain cultural similarities. Thus, he writes:

While on the whole the unique historical character of cultural growth in each area stands out as a salient element in the history of cultural development, we may recognize at the same time that certain typical parallelisms do occur. We are, however, not so much inclined to look for these similarities in detailed customs as rather in certain dynamic conditions which are due to social or psychological causes that are liable to lead to similar results. . . . In short, if we look for laws, the laws relate to the effects of physiological, psychological and social conditions, not to sequences of cultural achievement.[9]

And again:

On account of the uniqueness of cultural phenomena and their complexity nothing will ever be found that deserves the name of a law excepting those psychological, biologically determined characteristics which are common to all cultures and appear in a multitude of forms according to the particular culture in which they manifest themselves.[10]

[8] "The Methods of Ethnology," in *Race, Language and Culture*, p. 282.
[9] *Ibid.*, p. 287.　　　　　　　　　　[10] *Ibid.*, p. 311.

This is precisely the position of Tylor and Morgan, neither of whom ever maintained the theory of laws of cultural development which Boas wrongly attributed to them. To postulate certain stages in the process of cultural development as regards mankind as a whole does not necessarily imply that all peoples everywhere necessarily passed through all of the same stages or were likely to do so.

Boas agrees with the cultural evolutionists that the sequence of industrial inventions in the Old World and in America were similar and independent. In each instance "a period of food gathering and of the use of stone was followed by the invention of agriculture, of pottery and finally of the use of metals." [11] There is, then, a "limited parallelism" in the cultural development of the two continents, but this does not imply complete identity in all phases of culture for any given stage. Morgan himself admitted "the adoption of equivalents," such as the domestication of animals in the Eastern hemisphere and the cultivation of maize and plants in the Western, but this admission did not lead him to revise his conception of the essential similarity of the arts, institutions, and modes of life in the same status upon all the continents. For Boas, on the other hand, such disparity in cultural arts in different localities precluded an identity of culture traits and institutions at any given stage of development. Nevertheless, we find that Boas is far more in agreement with the basic conceptions of Tylor and Morgan than his repeated criticism of the theory of cultural evolution would seem to indicate.

As was said of Tylor, so now it may be said of Boas, that the two poles of his anthropological interest were culture history and psychology. In the case of Boas, however, owing to his opposition to the philosophy of evolutionary progress through fixed stages, there is greater emphasis upon functional, psychological, and sociological processes, upon the dynamics of culture change as manifested in acculturation and diffusion, than upon history. Furthermore, the study of culture history tended to be limited to that of a given society, or the relation between particular societies, since history as he understood it tended to be unique for each culture. A systematic philosophy of culture history, while desirable as an ultimate objective, was something he avoided on principle. "Absolute systems of phenomena," he held, "as complex as those of culture are impossible. They will always be reflections of our own culture." [12] In sum, there can be no denying the fact, which Boas reiterated, that

[11] *Ibid.*, p. 287.
[12] "History and Science in Anthropology: A Reply," *ibid.*, p. 311.

his approach was thoroughly historical insofar as he understood every given culture as the product of historical growth, but for him history did not mean total historical determinism which leaves no scope for the element of chance and for the role of the individual in affecting culture change. Being essentially a polemicist, he tended to stress sometimes the necessity for historical perspective, and on other occasions the need for the study of actual cultural processes within the context of a given culture as prior to and the condition of historical change. The two polar interests were there all the time, but as the *advocatus diaboli* he changed his emphasis in opposition to the dominant tendencies of a particular period during the course of the last half century. As against the *Kulturkreise* theory, he emphasized the need for psychological and sociological analysis; as against the doctrine of evolutionary uniformity he stressed the study of acculturation and diffusion.[13] In short, Boas had a healthy respect for the complexity of cultural phenomena and was always on guard against some oversimplification and oversystematization. He could certainly see the trees as clearly as anyone, but his caution prevented him from surveying the forest as a whole.

## 2. MALINOWSKI ON THE CONCEPT OF ORIGIN AND THE SCIENCE OF CULTURE

In the foregoing discussion we noted that anthropology began as the study of the evolution of the culture of mankind and that under the influence of Boas it became the science of particular cultures conceived as functional wholes. Instead of surveying the culture history of humanity, the cultural anthropologist was interested in comprehending the unique culture history of a given society in relation to its neighbors. Contrary to a monistic theory of cultural evolution comprising mankind as a whole, American ethnologists, in common with other culture historians opposed to a unilinear theory of evolution, tended to think in terms of a pluralistic theory of the evolution of cultures and were inclined to eliminate the concept of progress from their perspective. Under the stimulus of Boas, greater emphasis was put on the study of cultural dynamics, on the actual process of culture change as a prerequisite for an understanding of culture history. The laws which the anthropologist hoped to ascertain were psychological and sociological rather than purely cultural or historical.

Bronislaw Malinowski may be said to have carried this antihistorical

13 *Ibid.*, pp. 310–11.

tendency to an extreme. From being the science of culture history, ethnology became the science of cultural dynamics. Instead of the concept of history, "function" became the integrating key concept. The change in perspective may, perhaps, best be pointed up by reference to the concept of "origin" as interpreted by Malinowski. Whereas the cultural evolutionists were interested in the origins of culture and sought to establish the most primitive conditions of mankind in order to demonstrate the evolution of culture, Malinowski reinterpreted the concept of origin so as to eliminate entirely any association with temporal historical sequence. Thus, he writes:

By origins we mean the conditions, primeval and enduring, which determine the occurrence of a culturally established response, the conditions which, limited by scientific determinism, define the nature of an act, device, custom and institution. . . . The search for origins thus becomes really an analysis of cultural phenomena in relation, on the one hand, to man's biological endowment, and on the other, to his relationship to the environment.[14]

Here we see that Malinowski determines origin by logical analysis of biological, social, and geographical needs and conditions. The origin of any cultural phenomenon or institution lies in those enduring, timeless conditions which necessitated its invention; it is the universal stimulus or motivation which produces the cultural response.

The all-important point to notice here is that Malinowski identifies function and origin. By indicating the function, end, or useful purpose which a given artifact or custom subserves, we are said to understand its origin as well. Since neither end nor function can be understood without reference to the satisfaction of some need, or requirement, any explanation of origin necessarily comprises a description of the function which a given cultural object fulfills in the satisfaction of basic needs and requirements. For example, he defines a fork as an "instrument for the conveyance of a solid morsel from plate to mouth."

It is obvious [Malinowski remarks] that once we define its function within the domain of observable cultures, we have *de facto* reached the maximum of evidence concerning its "first origins." This momentous act in human history—for the historian and evolutionist are usually profoundly excited over exactly such trivialities as the origin of the fork or a drum or a backscratcher —arose under the determinism of very much the same forces which keep the instrument, its uses, and its function alive in the working cultures of today.[15]

[14] Malinowski, *A Scientific Theory of Culture and Other Essays,* pp. 202–3.
[15] *Ibid.,* p. 118.

Here it appears clearly that actual function is identical with *de facto* origin. The "original" function of an artifact and its present function are said to be one and the same. We can never be certain of the actual course of events in prehistoric times, and it is futile, therefore, to engage in a search for "origins" and "historic causes," since no decisive evidence is available. "History explains nothing unless it can be shown that an historical happening has had full scientific determination, and that we can demonstrate this determination on the basis of well-documented data." [16]

In comparing his own conception of origins with that of his predecessors, Malinowski observes that the concept of origins has seldom been defined by the classical evolutionists. What is usually meant by the term is "what occurred when the ape was struggling to become a man." He points out that "one of the favorite tricks of establishing origins consists in a more-or-less arbitrary assumption that this or that tribe or type of humanity is the standard primitive survival of earliest mankind. Whatever is found in such a tribe or group of tribes is assumed as most primitive." [17] All such attempts at identifying the prehistoric primitive with some actual primitive tribe are not scientifically verifiable and do nothing more than reveal "the fertility of an ethnologist's imagination." [18]

By way of example he cites Frazer's views concerning the origin of marriage. In *Totemism and Exogamy* Frazer had accepted Morgan's assumption that the origin of marriage is to be found in complete sexual and parental promiscuity. According to Malinowski, the fallacy involved in the assumption of primitive promiscuity lies in an erroneous analysis of the institution of marriage. If, he argues, we take into consideration the needs of man, whether primitive or civilized, it becomes apparent that the family as an institution fulfills these needs and that marriage had to be regulated to fulfill these family functions. Thus, it follows that primitive promiscuity could not have been the original state of society, as such a condition could never have fulfilled the function of producing legitimate children. The origins of the family and of marriage are to be found in man's universal needs for a mate and for children. All other assumptions as to the origin of the family are but idle speculation.

Thus, Malinowski differentiates between the concept of origin and that of primitive condition. We have no knowledge of the prehistorical

[16] *Ibid.,* p. 117.     [17] *Ibid.,* p. 204.     [18] *Ibid.*

or primeval condition of man, and it is not legitimate to identify any particular extant tribe as exemplifying the original condition of man when culture was first introduced. But granting this point, which Tylor had made earlier, does it follow that the relatively primitive culture traits and customs of contemporary natives have no bearing on the study of culture history and cultural development? Is there no connection between the culturally primitive and the historically original? The basic, underlying assumption of the cultural evolutionists has been that the culturally primitive or less advanced is also historically antecedent to the more advanced stages of culture or civilization, so that stages in cultural evolution also correspond to the actual course of culture history. By separating the notion of origin from that of antecedent historical condition, Malinowski was, in effect, undermining the whole evolutionary hypothesis. The fact that we do not know the absolutely original, prehistoric condition of mankind is taken by him as an argument against employing *any* primitive data to explain the probable origin of later developments in culture.

For Malinowski, therefore, explanation of origin took the form of logical analysis and description of function in relation to need. Logic and culture history were separated, and logic became a substitute for history. Culture history became irrelevant to an understanding of cultural origins. The origins of culture were to be sought in noncultural, biological, and social needs without reference to the historical sequence of forms.

Malinowski, it seems, confused psychological and pragmatic social function with temporal, historic origin. Of course, underlying the basic types of cultural invention and custom there is always some psychobiological need or social requirement which they are introduced to satisfy. The fact remains, however, that one cultural function may be subserved by various cultural means; a psychological need may be satisfied in a variety of ways. For example, food satisfies a biological need, but the need does not prescribe how the food is to be prepared and consumed. The cultural anthropologist informs us of the diverse ways in which man has satisfied his basic needs in the course of his cultural development. No abstract, logical analysis of the function of a given artifact will explain its particular historic form and the conditions under which it originated. Culture forms have a history of their own, which cannot be deduced from their functional utility and consequences. Hence the origins which the ethnologist seeks are cultural antecedents of later cultural developments, not the psychobiological motivations and objectives which may tell him why a given type or category of cultural instruments was invented and utilized. In brief, biological and social conditions are the necessary, but not sufficient, causes of cultural invention and change. For an adequate explanation of origins we require a combination of psychobiological, social, and purely historical factors.

It appears, therefore, that the term "origin" is ambiguous and has been used to refer to end or final cause, as well as to antecedent historical conditions. In seeking for origins, the cultural evolutionists, for example, were concerned to trace the sequence of culture forms and the course of cultural evolution from some extant primitive stage to the more advanced stage of modern civilization. Malinowski, on the other hand, thought that the analysis of the probable end or final cause, as judged by present utility, was sufficient for an understanding of all culture forms, regardless of their historical sequence. Functionalism, as advocated by Malinowski, tends to involve the reduction of cultural to psychological and social phenomena, in spite of the fact that no one excelled him in proclaiming the "autonomy" of cultural phenomena.

The confusion involved in Malinowski's identification of function with historical origin may be pointed up by referring to the acute analysis of origin and function provided by Durkheim. According to the latter, "To show how a fact is useful is not to explain how it originated or why it is what it is. The uses which it serves presuppose the specific properties characterizing it but do not create them. The need we have of things cannot give them existence, nor can it confer their specific nature upon them.[19]

Durkheim, in brief, questions the very thesis which Malinowski was to introduce some half a century later. Origin in the sense of "cause of existence" and end or function are said to be independent of one another. This he demonstrates by pointing out that a social "fact can exist without being at all useful, either because it has never been adjusted to any vital end or because, after having been useful, it has lost all utility while continuing to exist by the inertia of habit alone."[20] In agreement with Tylor, he concedes that there are more "survivals" in society than in biological organisms. Furthermore, he observes, a practice or social institution may change its function without thereby

[19] *The Rules of Sociological Method*, p. 90.
[20] *Ibid.*, p. 91.

changing its form or nature, for example, religious dogmas and rites in medieval and modern times. Durkheim, therefore, lays down the rule that *"When, then, the explanation of a social phenomenon is undertaken, we must seek separately the efficient cause which produces it and the function it fulfils."* [21]

This is precisely what Malinowski failed to do. He assumes that origin in the sense of efficient cause of existence and function or utility are identical. Any attempt to seek for independent historic causes of a cultural phenomenon is dismissed as a "prescientific craving for first causes or 'true causes.' " [22]

It is rather ironical to reflect that Tylor applied a functional criterion by which to distinguish between cultural "survivals" and actually meaningful and effective culture forms, whereas Malinowski, with all his clamor for a functionalistic approach, failed to provide an adequate standard for differentiating genuine functional culture forms from pseudo-functional cultural survivals, or residues. According to Tylor,

It seems scarcely too much to assert, once for all, that meaningless customs must be survivals, that they had practical, or at least ceremonial intention when and where they first arose, but are now fallen into absurdity from having been carried on into a new state of society, where their original sense has been discarded. Of course, new customs introduced in particular ages may be ridiculous or wicked, but as a rule, they have discernible motives. [23]

Tylor distinguishes between culture traits and institutions which are functionally integrated with a given historic culture and those which in their present cultural context are obsolete survivals lingering on through cultural inertia or lag into a new state of culture and society. The practical import of Tylor's doctrine of cultural survivals is that it provides the ethnologist with historical perspective, as well as a functional criterion, by which to evaluate contemporary culture and to indicate which traits and institutions have degenerated into harmful superstitions or cultural impediments. That was why Tylor called the science of culture history essentially a "reformer's science."

On the other hand, in assuming that present function and original historical function and motivation were identical, Malinowski was led to attribute alleged rational and integrative functions to all cultural customs and institutions alike, whether primitive or civilized, using his own fertile imagination to improvise psychological or sociological functions without reference to actual historical facts and conditions. His

[21] *Ibid.*, p. 95; italics in text.   [22] *A Scientific Theory of Culture*, p. 117.
[23] *Primitive Culture*, I, 94.

underlying assumption is that all extant culture forms are rational responses to human needs, primary or derived, and may therefore be assumed to have functional value in promoting the existence of the individual and his society. Had he taken into consideration the fact, which Tylor, Maine, and Durkheim understood, that cultural function is not a constant, but is subject to historical transvaluation, then he would not have identified cultural origin and social function to the exclusion of historical conditions.

My position is that a truly functional approach must also be ethnohistorical and reckon with historical cultural changes in order to evaluate present cultural functions. Just as past functions do not necessarily indicate present values, so present functions do not measure and account for original forms and meanings. The fact that one cultural object or activity may serve a variety of cultural functions in the course of culture history and that various culture forms may have the same function in different cultures at diverse times requires from the ethnologist the greatest caution in discriminating between actual, empirical functions and historical motivations and functions of cultural phenomena.

The problem of "survivals" is one that Malinowski considered carefully, since it was basic for his whole functionalistic approach. In his essay "Concepts and Methods of Anthropology," which represents his mature views on contemporary ethnology, he writes:

There is, however, one point on which the various older schools have committed a sin of commission, rather than omission. This is the uncritical and, at times, even anti-scientific concept of "dead-weights" or cultural fossils in human culture. By this I mean the principle that cultures harbor to a considerable extent, and in positions of strategic importance, ideas, beliefs, institutions, customs, and objects which do not really belong in their context. In evolutionary theories, such dead-weights appear under the guise of "survivals." [24]

If by survival be meant any element of culture which has no proper function and does not fit in with its cultural medium, then Malinowski denies outright that there is such a thing as a survival. Cultural traits and objects may change their function, but this, he argues, does not mean that they fail to harmonize with their culture. Cultural objects and practices survive because they have a function in the context of a given society; they do not acquire a function simply because they happen to survive.

Actually, according to Malinowski, survivals in the sense of func-

[24] *A Scientific Theory of Culture*, pp. 27–28.

tionless "cultural fossils" simply do not exist. The concept of survivals is a fiction introduced by Tylor and the cultural evolutionists to bolster their theory of primitive origins and stages of development. The function of these so-called survivals is at present entirely negative—the theory of cultural survivals is itself a "survival" of an outmoded ethnological theory.

The real harm done by the concept of survivals in anthropology consists in that it functions on the one hand as a spurious methodological device in the reconstruction of evolutionary series; and, worse than that, it is an effective means of short-circuiting observation in field-work.[25]

The real harm done by this concept was to retard effective field-work. Instead of searching for the present-day function of any cultural fact, the observer was merely satisfied in reaching a rigid, self-contained entity.[26]

In all instances of so-called survivals, he argues, there is an actual function which is not apparent owing to an incomplete analysis of the facts.

The point may be granted that insofar as the concept of survivals was used to validate the notion of fixed stages of cultural development it was subject to Malinowski's criticism that it retarded effective empirical observation. But it does not follow that the concept of survivals is nothing but a fiction without any basis in ethnographic fact. A cultural survival is not merely a kind of "fossil" or dead-weight, but rather some element of culture which, for the present, may have lost its original function without acquiring a new one. Some survivals may be nothing more than obsolete customs which simply persist through inertia in our modern folkways, for example, customs associated with sneezing. It was for this reason that Andrew Lang proposed that folklore be defined as "the study of survivals." [27] The student of folklore is aware that there are many irrational, obsolete traits which persist long after the original meaning has been forgotten and in spite of the fact that their adherents cannot explain the practical import of the custom.

Of course, every historically acquired culture trait and custom may be said to have some function. The question at issue is, what is the nature and significance of that function? It is for the student of culture history to decide whether the alleged function is based on fact or superstition, whether it is a subjective delusion based on traditional lore, or whether it has an objective foundation in empirically observable consequences. Malinowski apparently explains away all cultural survivals by stating that all surviving culture traits are "fit" for something,

[25] *Ibid.*, p. 29.     [26] *Ibid.*, pp. 30–31.     [27] Marett, *Tylor*, p. 26.

but he neglects to take into account the ethnographic fact that in the sphere of culture many elements survive and persist even though they are no longer fit to survive or worthy of survival in a rationally organized culture. Ultimately, the concept of survivals is relative to a theory of cultural development and progress. If this historical perspective be lacking, there is no basis for differentiating between obsolete pseudo-functional survivals and other genuinely functional traits.

As a student of contemporary life intensely interested in a peaceful democratic world order, Malinowski could not but adopt a normative, critical approach toward some aspects of modern culture, particularly the problem of war as an institution. Thus, notwithstanding his functionalistic dogmas as to the identity of origin and function and the nonexistence of cultural survivals, we find him stating, within the context of the same essay in which he had criticized the traditional concept of origins, that "as the science of human beginnings and of human evolution, it [anthropology] can and it must answer the question whether war is primeval." [28] He then goes on to explain:

This is not a matter of "origins" in the somewhat naïve sense of what occurred to the man-ape at the beginning of culture. It is rather the question whether war, like family, marriage, law and education, can be found in all human cultures at every stage of development, and more specifically whether it played an indispensable part at the earliest beginnings of mankind. For if it can be shown that war, that is, the collective settlement of intertribal problems by armed force, is not to be found at the beginnings of culture, this is a proof that war is not indispensable to the conduct of human affairs.[29]

Malinowski then suggests that war is neither primeval nor biologically founded and that it makes its appearance very late in human evolution. A comparative study of human institutions, he remarks, demonstrates "that most of the constructive and positive functions of war have been superseded by other agencies in our modern world, and that only its calamitous, destructive rôle persists."

Here we see Malinowski adopting the very point of view of the cultural evolutionists, whom he professed to criticize. Anthropology is now understood as the science of human beginnings and of human evolution, that is, as essentially a historical science in Tylor's sense of the term. As an ethnologist, he is now interested in the historical origin of war and in learning whether it played a significant part in the earliest beginnings of mankind. His conclusion is that the constructive func-

[28] *A Scientific Theory of Culture,* pp. 215–16.
[29] *Ibid.,* p. 216.

tions of war as an institution have been superseded and hence that war in modern culture is nothing but a destructive residue of an institution which appeared very late in human evolution. This analysis is worthy of Tylor at his best, but it is completely antithetical to Malinowski's arguments against the concept of historical origins and survivals. To the student of culture history his self-contradiction is of interest in that it reveals his perverse attempts to deny and explain away established ethnographical facts in the heat of controversy, as well as his fundamental common sense and pragmatic realism in utilizing whatever data and ethnological methods may advance the cause of peace and the progress of civilization. No one in modern times did more than he to revive Tylor's conception of ethnology as essentially a reformer's science capable of being directly applied to the regulation of human affairs. But no one raised more dust in the process by denying the validity of a comparative study of cultures and of a historical evolutionary perspective.

In his posthumously published work, *The Dynamics of Culture Change*, Malinowski devotes a chapter to a consideration of "The Value of History and Its Limitations." Here we find him belatedly giving some recognition to the value of historical studies in ethnology. He now concedes that "to oppose history and science is futile. To neglect either of them makes any humanistic pursuit incomplete. . . . From this point of view, I think that so-called functionalism is not, and cannot be, opposed to the historical approach but is indeed its necessary complement." [30] The context of time, as well as the context of culture, is said to be essential to the functional approach. Functionalism and historical reconstruction are now held to be in harmony.

Of particular interest to the student of Malinowski's thought is the fact that he came to utilize the very concept of survivals which he had hitherto labeled unscientific. He recognizes the "practical relevance of surviving historical residues" [31] and the relation of cultural function to that of cultural change. He now informs us that "it is the history surviving either in live tradition or in institutional working which is important." [32]

Of course, Malinowski rationalizes, he is not interested in the study of culture history and surviving historical residues for the sake of understanding man's past or the course of human development; he is

[30] *The Dynamics of Culture Change*, p. 34.     [31] *Ibid.*     [32] *Ibid.*, p. 37.

strictly interested, as he has always been, in understanding the present functions of institutions. As he puts it:

The point at issue here, however, is that it is the vitality and present-day working of this institution [initiation rites] which really matter, and not the institution at any stage in the past, however brilliantly and completely we might be able to reconstruct it. . . . Therefore questions of the present function of an institution, its vitality and adaptability and not the shape and trappings of the past, are important for the student of culture change in its theoretical and practical aspects.[33]

Thus, whereas Tylor was concerned to demonstrate how apparently meaningless and irrational practices of the present could be understood as survivals of a past state of culture and society in which they had practical significance and rational meaning, Malinowski was interested in showing that "surviving historical residues" are not merely obsolete but may, with slight change of form and function, continue to be a potent force in the actual working of a society. In Africa, for example, under the impact of European contact, native institutions have been driven underground, adapted or suppressed, but yet managed to retain a certain measure of vitality and influence,[34] for example, witchcraft and ancestor worship. Thus, Malinowski's approach continued to be positivistic and sociological, in contrast to Tylor's perspective, which was normative and evolutionary.

Closely connected with the problem of cultural survivals and their functional evaluation is the general problem of method in ethnographic research. Evolutionary ethnology is associated with the so-called comparative method whereby culture traits from different cultural contexts were isolated, compared, and arranged in sequence with reference to the fixed stages of cultural evolution. Now the distinctive feature of the functional approach is the thesis that a culture trait is to be understood only within the context of a given culture and that culture forms apart from functions within a given sociocultural context are meaningless. According to Malinowski, "from the point of view of method and theory of field work, the most important principle lies in the functional conception of culture. This declares that to study details detached from their setting must inevitably stultify theory, field work, and practical handling alike." [35] Each culture is thought of as an integrated, unique whole, the parts of which subserve definite functions in relation to one

[33] *Ibid.*, p. 38.                    [34] *Ibid.*, p. 39.
[35] *Ibid.*, p. 41.

another. Each culture system as a whole is an "instrumental reality, an apparatus for the satisfaction of fundamental needs, that is, organic survival, environmental adaptation, and continuity in the biological sense." [36]

In agreement with Boas, Malinowski was interested in the actual functions of particular cultures rather than in the history and evolution of human culture as a whole. But Malinowski went farther than Boas in this direction by insisting upon the primacy of function over form, a position which does not permit any independent status to culture forms apart from the context of given cultural institutions. For him a really scientific culture history would be one that reconstructed the changes in the institutions of a given culture over a period of centuries and showed how these changes occurred and how they were determined.[37] On this premise, the ethnohistory of the evolutionists and cultural diffusionists does not meet the test of a scientifically reconstructed history.

The basic point at issue concerns the status of culture forms and traits. According to Kroeber, whom he quotes, the implicit assumption of most modern anthropologists has been that "all traits can occur independently of each other" and that traits can be isolated as realities and made comparable in observation and theory. To this Malinowski replies: "I am deeply convinced that there is a fundamental misunderstanding in any attempt at isolation of separate traits." [38] For the latter, the ultimate ethnographic unit is the institution, and he therefore regards any attempt to study culture traits apart from their function in a given institutional context as nonscientific. In the last analysis, therefore, one may study institutions comparatively,[39] but not technology as such or any rites, customs, and similar traditional material. This puts an effective limit on the scope of culture history.

Logically, however, it may be asked whether according to Malinowski even institutions may be studied historically and comparatively. Since the function of an institution may vary with its cultural context, one can never be certain that historical institutions which are designated by the same term are really comparable. We are, then, left with a theory of cultural nominalism which allows no scope for a comparative historical study of human culture as a whole. The science of human culture is thereby reduced to an analysis of the universal biological

[36] *Ibid.*, p. 44.          [37] *A Scientific Theory of Culture*, pp. 19, 20.
[38] *Ibid.*, p. 34.          [39] *Ibid.*, p. 216.

and social conditions of culture, and the problems of the development of culture and the stages of culture history which were central in the ethnology of the evolutionists become insignificant.

Nevertheless, Malinowski continued to pay lip service to evolutionism and diffusionism and professed "the need of a synthesis of anthropological methods." [40] In theory, he admitted, "the comparative method must remain the basis of any generalization, any theoretical principle, or any universal law applicable to our subject matter." [41] Finally, he conceded that anthropology is "the science of human beginnings and of human evolution" and that "evolution deals above all with the influence of any type of 'origins.'" [42] This admission marked a return to the original insight of Tylor, but was antithetical to Malinowski's thesis of the identity of origin and function.

Malinowski was a controversial figure, whose final position was an eclectic synthesis of views which he had subjected to harsh, often unfair, criticism. No one insisted more than he upon the "instrumental reality" of culture, yet without being conscious of any contradiction he did assert in the name of functionalism that "culture is a reality *sui generis* and must be studied as such." [43] He apparently saw no contradiction in stating that

if culture, that is, the organized, implemented and purposeful behavior of man, carries its own determinism, then we can have a science of culture, we can establish laws of culture, and without rejecting evolutionary or comparative studies in any way, we have to link them up with the scientific pursuit of understanding culture in general.[44]

Almost in the same breath culture is described as the purposeful behavior of man and as an entity subject to its own laws, and the science of culture is said to be an evolutionary and comparative study which is somehow linked up with a nonhistorical functionalistic approach. In the end, functionalism became a label for whatever views Malinowski chose to incorporate under that term.

✓ The distinctive features of functionalism, its emphasis upon the study of cultures as functional wholes, and the correlation of cultural forms with biological, psychological, and societal needs and imperatives were constructive, often original, insights which focused attention upon problems of cultural dynamics and applied anthropology. But as a

[40] *Ibid.*, p. 215.    [41] *Ibid.*, p. 18.    [42] *Ibid.*, pp. 214, 215.
[43] "Culture," in *Encyclopaedia of the Social Sciences*, III, 623; also "Social Anthropology," in *Encyclopaedia Britannica*, XX, 862–70.
[44] *A Scientific Theory of Culture*, p. 203.

polemicist, Malinowski erred most in what he attacked in the views of others, particularly in his perverse criticism of the concepts of origin and survivals and his attack upon the historical approach to the study of culture forms.[45]

### 3. NATURAL HISTORY AND THE QUEST FOR ORIGINS

In view of the great influence exercised by Boas and Malinowski on the development of contemporary anthropological thought, it is of especial interest to consider further the significance of the quest for origins in modern anthropology. I believe there is a striking parallel between the quest for a systematic science of man in the twentieth century and in the eighteenth century.

During the seventeenth and eighteenth century philosophers, such as Hobbes, Spinoza, and Locke, postulated a "state of nature" antecedent to the state of civilization or "civil society." This postulate was based on the implicit assumption that civilization was artificial, conventional, or "adventitious" and was superimposed upon a precultural state of man. Following the geographical discoveries in the New World, philosophers tended to identify the state of nature with the condition of native peoples in the Americas and in the islands of the Pacific. To philosophers such as Hobbes, Locke, and Rousseau it seemed evident that the savages of the New World represented a state of nature from which civilized European man had emerged.[46] The "social contract" symbolized for them the fact that the political state was a historical, temporal achievement of men who found the anarchic state of nature intolerable and then proceeded to establish a political organization and government with common laws and institutions. Thus, the state of nature was at first not only a logical postulate but also a historical reality and served to validate political authority and the democratic principle that the origin of the state rests upon the consent of the governed.

Rousseau, especially, realized that the "state of nature" of which his predecessors wrote was largely fictitious and mythical, since it presupposed a whole cultural apparatus of language, rational thought, and social institutions, such as the family. In his essay "On the Origin and Foundation of the Inequality of Mankind" [47] he argued that the genuine

---

[45] Gluckman, *Malinowski's Sociological Theories*, pp. 2–5.
[46] Myres, "The Influence of Anthropology on the Course of Political Science," *University of California Publications in History*, IV (1916–17), 1–81.
[47] In *The Social Contract and Discourses*.

historic state of nature had to be not only prepolitical but also pre-cultural. Primitive, original man is to be imagined as an individual comparable to the apes and monkeys whom he resembles so closely anatomically,[48] living a precarious life in the forest, without symbolic language, artifacts, and social institutions. The story of wild Peter discovered in the Hanoverian forests in 1724 served as a prototype of man in the state of nature.[49] According to Rousseau, the essential characteristics of primitive man which differentiated him from other animals were the human quality of "free-agency" and the "faculty of self-improvement," or perfectibility.[50]

Thus, man evolved in time through a process of self-perfection and self-cultivation from a prehistoric, precultural state of nature to a cultural state characterized by basic cultural traits, namely, language, the family, and morality. The ideal and happiest state of mankind, according to Rousseau, was that in which men had arrived at a state of society subject to moral restrictions but prior to the establishment of the political state.

The example of savages, most of whom have been found in this state, seems to prove that men were meant to remain in it, that it is the real youth of the world, and that all subsequent advances have been apparently so many steps towards the perfection of the individual, but in reality towards the decrepitude of the species.[51]

Rousseau still retained, however, the philosophical fiction of the "social contract" as supervening upon the cultural state of prepolitical society. This meant that for him, as for his predecessors, the political state was not a natural historic development comparable to other cultural achievements, but a dramatic, social convention introduced primarily to validate and strengthen the power of the minority and the private property they had acquired at the expense of the majority—[52] a thesis which the followers of Marx, Engels, and Lenin have since developed into a powerful political dogma and myth. Later, in his *Social Contract,* Rousseau himself sought to establish the authority of the state upon the postulate of the General Will, which he introduced to reconcile individual liberty with the highest good of the community. Whether the concept of the General Will really fulfilled this function

[48] Lovejoy, "Monboddo and Rousseau," in his *Essays in the History of Ideas.*
[49] Myres, "The Influence of Anthropology on the Course of Political Science," *loc. cit.,* p. 42.
[50] "The Origin of Inequality," *loc. cit.,* pp. 184–85.
[51] *Ibid.,* p. 214.          [52] *Ibid.,* p. 221.

is open to serious question,[53] but it does demonstrate that Rousseau came to appreciate the inadequacy of his materialistic hypothesis concerning the origin and function of the state.

Incidentally, one of the most striking paradoxes of modern times is to be found in the fact that whereas Rousseau never advocated a return to a prepolitical state,[54] the modern followers of Marx, Engels, and Lenin prophesy, in the name of scientific historic materialism, a return to this utopian state of society. When, in the course of time, mankind will have abolished private property and liquidated all private capital and capitalists, then man will have attained a degree of perfection which will render the political state unnecessary and obsolete so that it will simply "wither away." In the meantime, and for generations to come, the individual is asked to submit to the "dictatorship of the proletariat" and to permit the state to force him to be free.

In essential agreement with the suggestions of Rousseau and Montesquieu, other eighteenth-century philosophers adopted the thesis that human culture has a "natural history" and is subject to a process of limited evolutionary development. It was soon realized, however, that the hypothesis of a natural history of culture rendered the concept of a state of nature obsolete, since it was no longer necessary to contrast the state of nature and the state of culture, or "civil society." The "state of nature" came to be understood, not as an original prehistorical state, from which man somehow had emerged, but as an actual universal historical state, in which men everywhere and at all times find themselves. This inference was most clearly stated by the Scottish philosopher Adam Ferguson.

If we are asked therefore, where the state of nature is to be found? We may answer, it is here; and it matters not whether we are understood to speak in the island of Great Britain, at the Cape of Good Hope, or the Straits of Magellan. While this active being is in the train of employing his talents, and of operating on the subjects around him, all situations are equally natural. If we are told, that vice, at least, is contrary to nature; we may answer, it is worse; it is folly and wretchedness. But if nature is only opposed to art, in what situation of the human race are the footsteps of art unknown? In the condition of the savage, as well as in that of the citizen, are many proofs of human invention; and in either is not in any permanent station, but a mere stage through which this travelling being is destined to pass. If the palace be unnatural, the cottage is so no less; and the highest refinements of political and moral apprehension, are not more artificial in their kind, than the first

[53] See Chapter 16.
[54] "The Origin of Inequality," *loc. cit.,* p. 246.

operations of sentiment and reason. If we admit that man is susceptible of improvement, and has in himself a principle of progression, and a desire of perfection, it appears improper to say, that he has quitted the state of his nature, when he has begun to proceed; or that he finds a station for which he was not intended, while, like other animals, he only follows the disposition, and employs the powers that nature has given.[55]

Once it became apparent that culture was a "natural" process and that man was by nature a self-perfecting, culture-producing animal, then philosopher-historians attempted to describe the natural history of man "from rudeness to civilization."

The concept of natural history as originally utilized by Vico, Herder, Rousseau, and Ferguson involved the assumption of the continuity of cultural development from savagery to civilization. Culture history was progressive precisely because it was continuous and did not involve any radical breaks with the past. This meant also that time was an essential factor in the evolution of human culture and that time made for progress.

The idea of progress, which the eighteenth-century philosophers generally accepted, was also combined with an antithetical theory of history which assumed the essential discontinuity of the history and the comparatively stationary character of time. As rationalists, they glorified their own Age of Enlightenment and prophesied an even greater era of human progress in the future, while deploring the vice, ignorance, and superstition of the past, such as the Middle Ages. Man was, indeed, perfectible, but progress was not inevitable and required eternal vigilance and constantly renewed effort, lest the opposing forces of darkness and deception gain the ascendancy once more. Gibbon had demonstrated in his *Decline and Fall* how civilization had declined from the high point it had reached in the second century and how long and difficult had been the task of recovering from the triumph of barbarism and superstition. The constant factor in human history was human nature and it was conceived to be the task of the historian to demonstrate "the constant and universal principles of human nature" as they manifest themselves in the course of historical experience.[56]

These two approaches to the study of history corresponded to two different interpretations of the concept of the "state of nature." As used by the seventeenth- and early eighteenth-century philosophers, the "state of nature" signified an original condition from which man had

---

[55] Ferguson, *An Essay on the History of Civil Society*, pp. 12–13.
[56] Becker, *The Heavenly City of the Eighteenth-Century Philosophers*, ch. iii.

emerged into a state of "civil society." This postulate motivated philosophers and historians to seek for the origins of man's natural state in the savage tribes of the newly discovered Western hemisphere. By learning the original and primitive condition of man one could evaluate the validity and authority of the institutions of civilized life. If, on the other hand, the "state of nature" is not a genetic ethnohistorical state, but a universal, timeless condition of man, then the significant question is no longer one of human natural origins, but of ends. The "proper state" of man's nature is an ideal rational state which man may attain in the future by the application of his faculties of reason and experience, not one which he is supposed to have been born into prior to the exercise of his faculties. As Adam Ferguson put it: "Whatever may have been the original state of our species, it is more important to know the condition to which we ourselves should aspire, than that which our ancestors may be supposed to have left." [57] On this premise, history became a reformer's science interested in the future improvement of mankind rather than in the discovery of the past.

In agreement with this rationalistic, Aristotelian, and Stoic interpretation of the state of man's nature as being an ideal rational state conforming to the dictates of reason and morality, the eighteenth-century philosopher could also reinterpret the concept of natural history. Following the Stoic maxim that to live in conformity with nature is to live in accord with the dictates of reason, one may argue that "natural history" is rational history. Natural history and morality and reason tend to coincide, so that the historian may differentiate those historical processes and institutions which are "natural" in the sense of being in accord with the requirements of human nature and reason from those which he designates as "unnatural" because he evaluates them as being contrary to human nature and reason. In this way, the philosopher-historian can moralize about "progress" and "retrogression" in culture history and can appeal to history for justification of his moral principles. Thus, in place of the old dichotomy of the state of nature versus the state of civilization, there is implicitly introduced the duality of natural cultural history and "natural laws," on the one hand, and arbitrary, unnatural cultural conventions which interfere with and contravene natural law and history, on the other.

This mode of thought may be exemplified by reference to Adam

[57] Ferguson, *An Essay on the History of Civil Society,* p. 15.

Smith's *Wealth of Nations.* In discussing "the natural progress of opulence" he writes:

According to the natural course of things, therefore, the greater part of the capital of every growing society is, first, directed to agriculture, afterwards to manufactures, and last of all to foreign commerce. This order of things is so very natural that in every society that had any territory it has always, I believe, been in some degree observed. Some of their lands must have been cultivated before any considerable towns could be established, and some sort of coarse industry of the manufacturing kind must have been carried on in those towns, before they could well think of employing themselves in foreign commerce. But though this natural order of things must have taken place in some degree in every such society, it has, in all the modern states of Europe, been, in many respects, entirely inverted. The foreign commerce of some of their cities has introduced all their finer manufactures, or such as were fit for distant sale; and manufactures and foreign commerce together have given birth to the principal improvements of agriculture. The manners and customs which the nature of their original government introduced, and which remained after that government was greatly altered, necessarily forced them into this unnatural and retrograde order.[58]

Smith was apparently prepared to generalize that the natural course of things invariably led to similar stages of cultural development from agriculture, through manufacturing, to foreign trade in every society. Natural necessity and the natural inclinations of man combined to produce this natural, rational cultural sequence, but governments tend to interfere with this natural order and to produce an unnatural and retrograde order which gives precedence to manufactures and foreign trade.

Thus, we have the beginning of what Dugald Stewart called "theoretical or conjectural history" which deduces the probable stages of culture history from a psychological analysis of the normal lines of development for rational men.[59] This comparative method of historical "reconstruction" was developed systematically by the nineteenth-century cultural anthropologists.

On the whole, the predominant tendency of eighteenth-century philosophical thought was to emphasize the discontinuities of culture history and to abstract historical experiences in order to illustrate, or demonstrate, their various theoretical analyses. The chronological order of events and actual historical origins were not essential, and hypo-

[58] Smith, *Wealth of Nations,* I, 340.
[59] Gladys Bryson, *Man and Society,* p. 90.

thetical history would do where actual records were not available. Their
ultimate objective was a normative moral science of man, based upon
inductive generalizations concerning the nature of man, which would
prescribe the ideal conditions of human virtue and happiness suitable
to the "proper state of man's nature."

The eighteenth-century concept of a science of man was that of a
systematic discipline comparable to Newton's *Principia* and based on
the factual data of experience and history and on the logical inferences
deduced therefrom. The origins of human conduct were to be sought
in the universal laws of psychology, not in prehistoric events in a state
of nature and not in any "forced and uncommon condition," such as
that of a wild boy caught in the woods.[60] The history of mankind as a
whole, that is, the comparative historical experiences of societies
throughout the world, would provide source material for such a systematic science of man. Particular experiments were precluded on the
ground that they could hardly provide convincing general evidence
comparable to that provided by the wide range of historical experience.

It should be noted, furthermore, that the concept of human nature
was also understood by the eighteenth-century natural philosophers
from a historical perspective. Man as an organism was considered as
part of the order of nature and subject to the universal laws of physical
nature. According to the monogenetic theory of Buffon and Blumenbach, mankind is said to consist of one species and the various races
are thought to owe their origin to changes induced upon the "stem
genus" through the influence of climate, food and general mode of living
in a given environment.[61] This biological thesis was amplified by
Montesquieu, who utilized it to explain also the variety of human laws
and social institutions. As the latter states, "it is the variety of wants
in different climates that first occasion a difference in the manner of
living, and this gave rise to a variety of laws." [62] On this assumption,
human nature taken collectively is a historical product of geographical
determinism, and its varieties are due to historical accidents of migration. Buffon even inferred that racial characteristics, such as color, may
be gradually effaced by a radical change of temperature; for example,
if a colony of Negroes were transplanted into a cold climate, their de-

---

[60] Ferguson, *An Essay on the History of Civil Society*, p. 5.

[61] Buffon, "A Natural History, General and Particular," in Count, *This Is Race*,
p. 15; Blumenbach, "On the Natural Variety of Mankind," in Count, *op. cit.*, p. 28.

[62] Montesquieu, *The Spirit of the Laws*, I, 229.

scendants of the eighth, tenth, or twelfth generation might become as white as the natives of the climate.[63]

On the other hand, Kant, following Leibnitz, maintained that there were elemental determinants, germs (*Keime*), in an organic body which determined its potential development. External factors, such as climate, he argued, may evoke or occasion the actualization of one potentiality rather than another, but they can neither generate these "germs" nor reproduce them. According to Kant:

Man was disposed for all climates and every constitution of ground; it follows that there must have lain in him many sorts of germs and natural dispositions, ready on occasion either to be developed or held back, in order that he might be fitted to his place in the world, and that he might appear in the course of generations to have been born to that place and made for it.[64]

Man's adaptation to his environment is, then, to be understood, not as a result of chance and common physical laws, but as the product of "the foresight of Nature to equip her creation with hidden inner furnishings against all sorts of future circumstances." [65] Kant's teleological biological thesis that there were innate elemental germs (genes) was later apparently adopted by Bastian in the nineteenth century and represented in his doctrine of "*Elementargedanken*." That is, Bastian conceived of "germs of thought" which predetermined the course of psychocultural development in all peoples comparable to the organic psychophysical germs which predetermined the potential evolution of the varieties of a given species of animal.[66] Historically, it is of interest to note that Kant's biological thesis has found support among modern ethnologists, such as Boas and his followers, while Bastian's cultural thesis has become outmoded among ethnologists, but has found new adherents among psychoanalysts such as Roheim and Jung.

Of the two biological theses, that of geographical determinism proved the more attractive to the eighteenth-century social philosophers. It led Montesquieu to integrate cultural institutions with the laws of cosmic nature, politics with physics, and to demonstrate the natural relative basis of the patterns of human culture. In generalizing about national character and temperament he tended to confuse nature and culture by attributing to biological temperament stereotyped traits of culture and personality which happened to impress him, for example,

---

[63] Buffon, in Count, *This Is Race,* p. 13.
[64] Kant, "On the Distinctiveness of the Races in General," in Count, *op. cit.,* p. 20.
[65] *Ibid.,* p. 19.         [66] See Chapter 7.

the alleged tendency of the English to commit suicide.[67] Nevertheless, Montesquieu did appreciate the fact that culture and personality are closely interrelated, although he was inclined to regard natural temperament as the primary factor and did not evaluate adequately the role of cultural conditioning in the formation of personality.

Montesquieu was in advance of his times in his awareness of the close interrelation of cultural phenomena among themselves and of their function in fulfilling the wants and needs of society in relation to a given geographical environment. He was primarily concerned to demonstrate the "spirit of the laws," that is, the various relations which laws actually bear to social character and geographical environment. His implicit thesis is that men do, in fact, live according to the laws of their nature and that a comparative, historical study of positive laws and institutions demonstrates this functional relativity. Montesquieu's approach may be characterized as historical and geographical functionalism to distinguish it from the psychobiological and sociological functionalism of Malinowski and Radcliffe-Brown. He warned that in order to comprehend the spirit of a given law or custom one must take into consideration its historical function and the original intention of the lawgivers in the context of a given historical society. "The laws which appear the same have not always the same effect" and were not always made through the same motive.[68] "Wherefore to determine which of those systems is most agreeable to reason, we must take them each as a whole and compare them in their entirety." [69] He cautioned that the civil law of another nation must not be adopted without prior examination of its institutions and political laws in order to determine the degree of similarity between them. Thus, all that Malinowski and Radcliffe-Brown have insisted upon in the name of their doctrine of functionalism has been anticipated by Montesquieu, but without the former's prejudice against a historical approach.

The general impression one derives from a study of Montesquieu's *The Spirit of the Laws* is that he, in common with his contemporaries, attempted to combine a descriptive, naturalistic approach to the study of man with a prescriptive, normative, and moral approach, often without realizing their incompatibility. This led him, as it did Adam Smith, to commit what I have termed the naturalistic fallacy, that is, the fallacy of attempting to deduce cultural norms directly from na-

---

[67] Montesquieu, *The Spirit of the Laws*, I, 231.
[68] *Ibid.*, II, 158, 159.          [69] *Ibid.*, p. 161.

ture.[70] Insofar as he followed the first thesis, he attempted to demonstrate that human positive laws and customs were functionally and historically determined by the requirements of human nature in a given geographical environment. On the other hand, as a moralist and legislator he was also a rationalist in the Stoic tradition who prescribed laws of reason, as his contemporary Rousseau did, to counteract the natural tendencies of human temperament and the influence of the environment with a view to promoting moral virtue and character. He pointed out that "man, as a physical being, is like other bodies governed by invariable laws. As an intelligent being, he incessantly transgresses the laws established by God, and changes those of his own instituting." [71] That is, man as an intelligent being is capable of self-determination and is not merely a part of the order of nature whose nature and functions are determined by physical law. In dealing with man as a rational intelligent being, Montesquieu prescribes what the "wise legislator" should do to counteract the natural tendencies and impulses of man.[72] Thus, whereas the natural, positive spirit of human laws is to be understood as a function of physical nature, the moral spirit of rational laws is governed by the imperatives and ideals of reason, often in opposition to the natural inclinations of a given people. In laying the foundations for a science of man, Montesquieu did not distinguish clearly between these antithetical approaches.

It was not until the nineteenth-century poets, linguists, historians, and philosophers, under the influence of romanticism, revived interest in primitive and folk cultures that the ethnohistorical approach together with *Kulturgeschichte* [73] came to occupy the attention of scholars once more. Through the influence of Vico and Herder the culture history of classical times, as well as that of contemporary folk cultures, was studied as an end in itself. Each epoch and each people was thought to have intrinsic value of its own which it was the task of the culture historian to discover and interpret.[74]

With the advent of the Darwinian theory of biological evolution and with the introduction of new archeological evidence bearing upon the antiquity of man, the quest for human origins was revived.[75] Unlike the seventeenth- and early eighteenth-century thinkers, the nine-

---

[70] See Chapter 2.   [71] Montesquieu, *The Spirit of the Laws,* I, 3.   [72] *Ibid.,* p. 86.
[73] Gooch, *History and Historians in the Nineteenth Century,* ch. xxviii.
[74] Cassirer, *The Philosophy of the Enlightenment,* ch. v; also Cassirer, *The Problem of Knowledge,* chs. xii–xiii.
[75] Casson, *The Discovery of Man,* ch. iv.

teenth-century culture historians and ethnologists were interested in the natural history of cultural development as an end in itself. Ethnology, as Tylor, Lubbock, Maine, and Morgan understood it, was essentially a historical discipline and was that part of culture history especially concerned with the culture of preliterate peoples.

Under the influence of the positivistic philosophy of science deriving from Comte, evolutionary ethnologists, such as Tylor and Morgan, professed an interest in discovering the psychological laws underlying the culture history of mankind. That is, the nineteenth-century ethnologists, unlike the eighteenth-century philosophers, did not appeal to the empirical and introspective evidence of individual psychological experience or to selected records of history for inductive generalizations concerning human nature. Like Comte's approach, theirs was rather primarily historical and social, and they hoped to arrive at a knowledge of man's nature through a comparative study of culture history. Psychological laws were to be the final products of the study of comparative culture history, not the presupposition of historical study. Man was to be discovered through a study of culture history, not culture history through a study of man.

Furthermore, the ethnologists sought to evaluate the natural history of culture and the stages of cultural progress. They were interested not only in the mental or spiritual development of mankind but also in the comparative development of the arts, customs, and social institutions. While Tylor still spoke of ethnology as essentially a reformer's science, as the eighteenth-century philosophers had thought, the primary interest of the evolutionary ethnologists was in theory rather than in practice. Their first objective was to describe and evaluate the stages of cultural evolution and the historical sequence of modes of thought in the various types of societies and cultures. In the course of his historical researches Tylor came upon cultural phenomena which he termed "survivals" of a previous age in which they had ethnofunctional significance. This meant that the ethnologist could, after all, though indirectly, exercise a practical function by indicating the ethnohistorical origins of extant folkloristic myths, superstitions, and obsolete customs. By making people conscious of the anachronistic character of these cultural survivals the way would be prepared for eventual cultural reform. But the cultural anthropologist considered himself primarily a natural scientist interested in the cultural evolution of man and in the mental laws of cultural development.

The evolutionary ethnologists were preoccupied with the study of the origins of human culture because they considered culture essentially a historical process subject to progressive development. In practice, this preoccupation led them to engage in a great deal of historical "reconstruction" of the prehistoric origins of cultural institutions, such as the family and religion. Their fundamental presupposition was that cultural evolution developed from the simple to the complex, and they therefore exercised their fertile imaginations to envisage a primordial primitive man and simple culture unlike any given in historical experience. Similarly, on the assumption of independent, parallel stages of cultural development, they attempted to reconstruct phases of culture history for which no direct empirical evidence was available. It was against these pseudohistorical reconstructions that Boas and the diffusionists directed their criticism.

From the perspective of the present, it appears that these attempts at historical reconstruction of the mind of primitive man and of the origins of culture were comparable to the speculations of the seventeenth- and eighteenth-century philosophers concerning the state of nature antecedent to the state of society and civilization. Both approaches were pseudohistorical and mythical. The fact that Tylor himself warned against the assumption that any of the extant native peoples were ethnologically primitive did not discourage his followers from identifying various native societies, such as those of Australia and the Andaman Islands, with primitive man and using data derived from their cultures as a source of evolutionary speculation.

The historical abuses of the evolutionary ethnologists led to a reaction in the twentieth century strikingly parallel to that which occurred in the latter part of the eighteenth century. Once more in the twentieth century the study of man was said to deal with cultural dynamics and the psychological laws underlying cultural change. Boas, it is true, was not anti-historical, or even unhistorical, but he was inclined to restrict ethnohistory to the study of given societies and to trace the diffusion of specific culture traits, such as folktales, over given areas. His primary interest, however, was in discovering the dynamic laws governing cultural changes, and this meant discovering the universal psychological and biological laws which accounted for cultural uniformities. The "mind of primitive man" was, he thought, essentially similar to that of civilized man, and, in agreement with Bastian, he was inclined to minimize the differences in mentality which the evolutionary ethnologists and sociologists professed to observe, attributing such apparent differences to diversity of practical needs and historical cultural conditioning.

Malinowski, however, went to the opposite extreme and disparaged the historical approach as unscientific. By identifying psychological motivation, social function, and historical origins he unwittingly repeated the argument of the eighteenth-century philosophers, who reasoned that since culture was natural, therefore all cultural origins were to be determined by a priori analysis of human nature in society. This explains why contemporary British social anthropologists, under the influence of Malinowski and Radcliffe-Brown, have tended to neglect historical studies of culture and have instead concentrated their attention upon functional studies of social structure and cultural dynamics. For them the concept of a science of anthropology has come to mean a systematic analysis of social organization and of the functional interrelations of cultural institutions and social structures, rather than a study of culture history and cultural origins. Under the indirect influence of Durkheim, modern social anthropologists are inclined to accept the primacy of society and to interpret culture as a function of social structure,[76] rather than as a function of human nature, as Boas and the eighteenth-century thinkers assumed. Malinowski himself attempted to combine a psychological with a sociological approach, but Radcliffe-Brown and his followers are wont to provide sociological interpretations of cultural institutions. Primitive societies are now studied, not for the sake of discovering the origins of social institutions and customs, but because they are "simpler" and smaller than the large and complex societies of civilized societies and might, therefore, provide clues for an understanding of the latter.

The lesson to be derived from a study of modern anthropological thought is that a science of cultural anthropology must be historical if it is not to be reduced to a branch of psychology or sociology. As Tylor, Maine, and Maitland have demonstrated, the cultural historian can make a significant theoretical and practical contribution to the study of man when he deals with factual evidence and illuminates the ethnohistorical functions of given cultural traits and institutions within the context of their time and place. We are not compelled to choose between a nonhistorical functionalism, on the one hand, and a nonfunctional historicism, on the other. The cultural anthropologist or

[76] See Chapter 4.

ethnologist can deal adequately with his data only by combining both approaches into an ethnohistorical functionalism which evaluates cultural functions in the perspective of history and historical cultures as functional wholes. Only in this way will the cultural anthropologist avoid the naturalistic fallacy of attempting to derive culture forms from an a priori analysis of human nature in society, on the one hand, and the culturalistic fallacy [77] of treating culture as an autonomous level of reality independent of man and society, on the other.

[77] See Chapter 2.

# 9

# Culture History, the Humanities, and Natural Science

IN ORDER TO UNDERSTAND more recent approaches to the problem of the relation of ethnology and history, such as those of Kroeber and Evans-Pritchard, we must consider next the development of Neo-Kantian thought, with special reference to the philosophy of culture.

## 1. THE NEO-KANTIAN APPROACH TO CULTURE HISTORY

In Germany, in the nineteenth century, we find a continuation of the humanistic philosophy of history which originated in France in the eighteenth century. Kant had contrasted the sphere of nature, governed by necessary laws, and the moral sphere of human freedom, wherein man was his own lawgiver.[1] Neo-Kantians, such as Windelband, generalized this distinction and contrasted the methods of history and natural science. History was said to be an expression of human freedom and ideal values; science was thought to have for its object the discovery of natural law. Dilthey and later Windelband designated two kinds of science, namely, "nomothetic" science, concerned with natural, universal laws, and "idiographic" science, which deals with the individual and is purely descriptive.

Dilthey, especially, distinguished between *Geisteswissenschaften* and *Naturwissenschaften*. The former were said to deal with life forms which had to be "understood" (*verstehen*) through actual experience of the values involved therein, whereas the natural sciences had for their objects abstract, value-free phenomena which could be "explained" causally. Rickert criticized Dilthey's use of the term *Geisteswissenschaft*, arguing that the dualism of *Geist* and *Natur* was unwarranted, since the ensemble of physical artifacts comprised neither

[1] Bidney, "The Philosophical Anthropology of Ernst Cassirer and Its Significance in Relation to the History of Anthropological Thought," in *The Philosophy of Ernst Cassirer*, ed. by P. A. Schilpp, p. 487.

natural products nor spiritual entities. Instead, Rickert suggested the term *Kulturwissenschaft,* because *Kultur* indicates the processes of cultivation and valuation whereby its products could be clearly differentiated from those of *Natur* which were self-originated and value-free.[2] This Neo-Kantian conception of culture has been accepted by contemporary idealistic philosophers of culture, such as Ernst Cassirer.

The Neo-Kantian philosophers held that the *Kulturwissenschaften,* the human and historical sciences, required a subjective approach which would yield understanding (*Verstand*) and provide concrete idiographic insight into the mental symbolism involved—a type of knowledge which no amount of external objective observation and causal explanation could possibly supply. That is why they were opposed to the reduction of history to natural science and to the thesis that culture history was a kind of social physics subject to natural laws. The method of the human sciences and that of the natural sciences were thought to be antithetical. As Collingwood has stated the position:

Thus genuine historical knowledge is an inward experience (*Erlebnis*) of its own object, whereas scientific knowledge is the attempt to understand (*begreifen*) phenomena presented to him as outward spectacles. This conception of the historian as living his object, or rather making his object live in him, is a great advance on anything achieved by any of Dilthey's German contemporaries.[3]

For the positivists the mind of man was part of the order of nature, and its cultural achievements were thought to be subject to natural law. For the idealists, on the other hand, culture and nature were distinct and required different methods for their interpretation.

If we bear in mind the close connection between the philosophical and scientific thought in the Germany of the nineteenth century, it will enable us to understand the significance of the concept of *Kultur* and of culture history as employed by anthropologists such as Bastian. For the latter, *Kultur* was an expression of *Geist,* and *Kultur* was therefore a spiritual expression subject to processes of development which do not pertain to the sphere of natural phenomena. By contrast, Tylor thought of culture history as a natural science, just as Comte had conceived sociology to be, and his evolutionary theory of culture history was based on the assumption of the unity of the natural sciences and the universality of the scientific method.

[2] Rickert, *Kulturwissenschaft und Naturwissenschaft.*
[3] Collingwood, *The Idea of History,* p. 172.

## 2. KROEBER ON CULTURE HISTORY AND NATURAL SCIENCE

Among American anthropologists, Kroeber, in particular, approximates most closely the Neo-Kantian position in distinguishing between the historical method and that of natural science. In his paper "History and Science in Anthropology" [4] Kroeber maintains that the distinctive feature of the historical approach is not the dealing with time sequences, but "an endeavor at descriptive integration." By contrast, the scientific approach aims to analyze processes in quantitative terms. This corresponds to Rickert's and Dilthey's distinction between nomothetic natural science and idiographic, descriptive historical science. Kroeber seems to sharpen the distinction by speaking of science and history as if they involve two different, but complementary, methods. There is said to be a historical attitude and approach, as well as a scientific one. Ethnologists, he points out, have been most successful in providing historic patterns of cultural phenomena and in presenting an integrated view of a given culture as a whole. In their quest for scientific processes and laws they have not been successful. Kroeber characterized Boas as primarily interested in scientific processes and functions rather than in culture history, notwithstanding the psychological fact that Boas may have thought that he was following a historical method.

The master made a devastating reply to Kroeber and expressed his "complete disagreement with his interpretation." [5] For Boas the mere description of a culture and of its "working" is not history. For historical interpretation, the descriptive material must be supplemented by archeological, biological, linguistic, and ethnographic comparisons. Boas maintained that throughout his academic career he had tried to understand the culture he was studying "as the result of historical growth" and could not see how his interest in cultural processes affected his historical approach. On the contrary, he felt that a knowledge of the dynamic processes underlying culture history and culture change were of direct value to the study of culture history. He concludes that

what Kroeber and Redfield call the "history" of a tribe appears to me as a penetrating analysis of a unique culture describing its form, the dynamic reactions of the individual to the culture and of the culture to the individual.

[4] Kroeber, "History and Science in Anthropology," *American Anthropologist,* XXXVII (1935), 539–69.

[5] Boas, "History and Science in Anthropology: a Reply," reprinted in his *Race, Language and Culture,* pp. 305–11.

It obtains its full meaning only when the historical development of the present form is known.[6]

In brief, functional ethnographic accounts were not history unless supplemented by a study of the temporal sequence of forms and conditions which led to the present state of a culture. Cultural description without some reference to a temporal process of change simply was not history for Boas.

The fact is that Boas understood the concept of history in the positivistic, naturalistic sense as referring to any sequence of forms viewed in temporal perspective. History was essentially a process of change or development; to eliminate process and temporal sequence was to deprive history of its essential properties. In this respect Boas's position was essentially similar to that of Tylor, who adopted the concept of natural history and saw no contradiction in maintaining the possibility of laws of culture history. Kroeber, on the other hand, by accepting the dichotomy of history versus science was led to separate process from descriptive integration and to identify history with the latter. No wonder Boas, who was no philosopher and had no understanding of Neo-Kantian epistemology, was rather bewildered and shocked by his former student's new definition of history and simply confessed "that to me this does not give sense."

In a subsequent article,[7] published some eleven years later, Kroeber returned to the subject of history and expressed substantially similar views. He explicitly states that he is "basing on Rickert but going beyond him." Referring to Boas' criticism of his earlier statement, he writes:

I realize that this concept of synchronic historical treatment is so contrary to habitual thinking that it is likely to seem unintelligible, as it did to Boas in 1936. On the contrary, I am convinced that the essence of the process of historical thought will continue to fail of being grasped as long as time is considered most important in that essence. This essence is the characterizing delineation of groups of phenomena in context, into which both time and space factors enter; but, with spatiotemporal place once established, either of these two considerations can be temporarily suppressed by being held constant by the historian, if circumstances or his objective warrant.[8]

According to Kroeber's thesis, the essence of history is not the time element; space determination is equally important. Since either space

[6] *Ibid.*, pp. 310–11.
[7] Kroeber, "History and Evolution," *Southwestern Journal of Anthropology*, II (1946), 1–15; reprinted in *The Nature of Culture*, pp. 95–103.
[8] *Ibid.*, p. 13.

or time may be held constant in a particular history, neither element can be regarded as essential. The essential factor is an "analytic-synthetic characterizing description." The basic historical method is the qualitative description of a given set of cultural phenomena in context, into which both time and space factors may enter or be held constant. Thus, an ethnographic study of a given community is essentially "a timeless piece of history."

On the contrary, science is not concerned with the space-time continuum, with the singularity of quality, or with style. Science is said to be "nomothetic," or systematic, and its essence is the method of abstraction, "the resolution of phenomena into metaphenomenal formulations." Science is concerned with quantitative, rather than qualitative, precision. Thus, science is a quest for laws, for exactness of measurable findings and verifiability by experiment. The method of history, on the other hand, prevents it from ever attaining to laws or general theory and exact prediction. Ultimately history recognizes patterns or stylistic formulations, "the physiognomy of events." Science provides a knowledge of the universal, repetitive, predictive character of events and processes to the exclusion of concrete details of pattern or style.

Kroeber's thesis is that the method of history and the method of science are two approaches applicable to any kind of phenomena, although actually the scientific method has been most successful on the level of inorganic phenomena, and the historical method on the level of psycho-socio-cultural phenomena. Thus, the study of culture may be viewed, on the one hand, as a historic discipline devoted to the description of cultural phenomena and their characteristic styles or configurations in the context of space and time, the time factor being held to either a synchronic or a diachronic dimension. On the other hand, the study of culture may be approached with the intention of developing a science of culture, "which is slated to be erected some time," and then attention will be focused upon the abstracted cultural processes underlying the qualitative, stylistic culture configurations, without further reference to particular space-time contexts. Thus, cultural anthropology may be viewed as a historical, humanistic discipline, as well as a natural science, depending upon the method or approach which is utilized in studying cultural phenomena.

From this it is apparent that the attempts of the cultural evolutionists to establish laws of culture history or of historical evolution were fundamentally mistaken, since they confused history and science and looked for laws where none could possibly be found. History is not an exact science, and it is therefore futile to seek for laws of culture history. In his *Configurations of Culture Growth* Kroeber has given us a strictly historical survey of the development of the basic branches of modern culture, as well as of "the growth of nations" without reference to the dynamic processes underlying the sequence of culture configurations. It is not surprising to find him concluding that he sees "no evidence of any true law in the phenomena dealt with; nothing cyclical, regularly repetitive, or necessary." [9] Having excluded, on principle, any reference to psychocultural processes and to psychological motivations from his historical survey, he could scarcely expect to find any evidence of true law in the phenomena with which he dealt.

In his paper "The Concept of Culture in Science" [10] Kroeber has returned once more to the same theme. In evident approval of the basic approach of the Neo-Kantian philosophers of science he writes:

The neo-Kantian philosophers have long since pointed out that, while a strictly scientific approach is generalizing and nomothetic, a historical approach is idiographic, in that it remains much more attached to the particular phenomena *per se*. Instead of dissolving them away into laws or generalizations, the historical approach preserves its phenomena, on whatever level it happens to be operating, and finds its intellectual satisfaction in putting each preserved phenomenon into a relation of ever widening context with the phenomenal cosmos.[11]

Kroeber remarks that the Neo-Kantian philosophers did not take the next steps which would follow logically from their premises. First, "the contextual relations which a historical approach determines involve relations of absolute space equally with absolute time—not of time alone or primarily, as is so often asserted for history." Here, as in his earlier paper, he maintains the thesis that the differentiation into synchronic and diachronic treatment is secondary and that the essence of the historical approach, as contrasted with the scientific, nomothetic one, is characterized by "superindividuality, patterning, relative nonconcern with cause." Secondly, history and science should not be regarded as disciplines operating on different levels of phenomena. Rather, it should be assumed that the scientific, as well as historical, approach is applicable "to all levels of phenomena, though with a sliding degree of fruitfulness."

[9] Kroeber, *Configurations of Culture Growth*, p. 761.
[10] Kroeber, "The Concept of Culture in Science," *The Journal of General Education*, III (April, 1949), 182–96; reprinted in *The Nature of Culture*, pp. 118–35.
[11] *Ibid.*, p. 186.

It is with reference to the latter point that his critical comment on Rickert may be understood:

After brilliantly showing that the *Geisteswissenschaften,* as so called in nineteenth-century Germany, were really disciplines dealing not with spirit or soul as such but with culture and that their *de facto* approach was essentially historical, the neo-Kantian Rickert blocked his farther progress with a simplistic dichotomy, to wit: Culture, historically intelligible, versus Nature, scientifically intelligible. Here the antithesis, culture: nature, is a relic of the older idealistic antithesis, spirit: nature, as this in its turn had been a softening modernization of theological soul: body opposition. And it is the same sharp antithesis which led Rickert to misappraise thoroughly the genuinely historical component in the sciences of astronomy, geology and biology.[12]

Kroeber in effect suggests that history and science are methods of approach applicable to all levels of phenomena, such as geology, astronomy, and biology, not to specific classes or levels of phenomena. In actual inquiry, however, he admitted that on the whole the two methods tend to apply to different levels of phenomena, thereby granting the main premise of the Neo-Kantian position. With reference to culture theory in particular, this meant that the study of culture could be approached from either a scientific or a historical point of view. Cultural anthropology was not exclusively either history or science, but a complementary synthesis of both approaches.

In my opinion the basic, unresolved difficulty in Kroeber's ethnological position is the relation of scientific processes to historical forms in culture. He recognizes culture history minus cultural process and cultural process minus culture history as two aspects of culture, but does not show us how they are related in actual cultural experience. The assumption of the classical evolutionary ethnologists was that culture history was essentially a temporal process, subject to stages of development from primeval to modern times. For them ethnology was the science of culture history, and the ethnologist sought for specific cultural and mental laws to explain the processes of culture history. If, however, one were to begin with Kroeber's Neo-Kantian postulate that culture history is essentially an integrative, descriptive study of cultural configurations, or styles, leading to the recognition of values, then the concept of a science of culture history would become a contradiction in terms, because culture history as such has nothing to do with actual temporal processes. To say that ethnology may be viewed sometimes as

12 *Ibid.,* pp. 186–87.

culture history and sometimes as natural science leaves unresolved the basic problems whether there is a natural history of culture and in what the interrelation of culture history and cultural process consists.

The issue, as I see it, comes down to this: If there is to be a science of culture history, or a systematic science of culture, then there must be specific, significant cultural uniformities and regular correlations of cultural phenomena. If one abstracts the integrative description of concrete cultural phenomena in their qualitative configurations and functional interrelations as pertaining to the sphere of culture history, all that can possibly remain are the abstract, psychological, and biological processes which underlie them. The study of these processes pertain primarily to psychology and biology, and hence any significant laws or generalizations will be accredited to these disciplines rather than to ethnology. Logically, therefore, on this premise ethnology becomes the study of culture history and is to be classified as a nonscientific, humanistic discipline, along with history in general. As a matter of record, Kroeber seems prepared to grant precisely this conclusion. We find him now writing:

It is true that it is customary to relegate many such studies to what are named the "humanities" and therewith to read them out of the so-called "social sciences." But what of that—provided that the phenomena considered and the forces in them are regarded as natural, as part of the rest of nature and in no sense supernatural? And provided also that they are subjected to dissection, recombination, and inference according to the basic rules of evidence followed in the investigation of other parts or realms of nature, without admittance of bias, personal advantage, self-superiority, or ethnocentricity.[13]

Certainly this idealistic interpretation of culture history is the antithesis of the naturalistic, positivistic approach with which Kroeber began his ethnological studies. Prior to the revised edition of his *Anthropology*, in 1948, Kroeber postulated the concept of the cultural Superorganic as referring to an autonomous level of phenomena independent of psychology and biology. In his classic paper "The Superorganic," [14] Kroeber explicitly refers to culture, or civilization, as a process *causa sui*, involving a deterministic view of history. Culture was said to be subject to a process of emergent evolution without antecedents in the beginnings of organic evolution. "The point is," he stated, "that there was an addition of something new in kind, an initiation of that

[13] *Ibid.*, p. 191.
[14] *American Anthropologist*, XIX (1917), 162–213.

which was to run a course of its own." [15] In summary, Kroeber's original concept of the cultural superorganic was in fundamental agreement with the positivistic, naturalistic concept of history as held by the classical evolutionists and evolutionary sociologists. According to this view, which he shared with other contemporary anthropologists, ethnology was essentially the science of culture history; there were not two aspects or approaches to the study of culture, namely, a historical and a scientific one, but only a single approach, which comprised both history and science, because culture history itself was considered a natural science. In fact, as discussed earlier, Kroeber's approach to the study of culture was so thoroughly sociological, evolutionary, and historical that he found himself opposed to Boas' more orthodox students, who were not inclined to accept the superpsychic interpretation of culture which he put forth and which allowed so little scope for psychological motivation and initiative in culture history.[16]

It seems fair, therefore, to conclude that Kroeber has been, and to a certain extent still is, working with two antithetical conceptions of history, namely, natural positivism and Neo-Kantian idealism. Insofar as he adopted the naturalistic, evolutionary approach to the study of culture, ethnology was for him essentially the science of culture history, and cultural phenomena were regarded as constituting an autonomous level of reality subject to its own historical laws. Since he adopted the humanistic, idealistic Neo-Kantian position of Rickert and Dilthey, he has tended to set up a dichotomy of history and science and to contrast the idiographic approach of the historical method with the abstract, nomothetic approach of the scientific method. Ethnology then becomes a dual discipline with a historic, as well as a scientific, aspect. Instead of asserting unequivocally, as he had done in the past, that culture constitutes an autonomous level of historical phenomena, Kroeber now compromised by suggesting cautiously that culture history is to be regarded "as if" individual personalities did not have a hand in cultural events—an artifice which he avowedly adopted from White, not from Kant. Henceforth the so-called "autonomy of culture" became nothing more than a logical fiction, a pragmatic, temporary device for continuing to study culture history "as if" it were independent of the individual persons who may have been the efficient causes of cultural change.[17] From a long-range perspective, we are now told, one

[15] *Ibid.*, p. 210.     [16] See Chapter 2.
[17] "The Concept of Culture in Science," *The Journal of General Education*, III (1949), 194; see also Chapter 4.

may study culture history without reference to the men who initiated its processes; from a short-range perspective, one may not eliminate the individual, whose role looms so much larger. Both methods of study are said to be equally legitimate.[18]

Psychologically, Kroeber's attitude is very understandable. The fictional device of the "as if" enables him to adhere to his long-cherished cultural superorganic and to pursue the study of culture history as before without reference to the motivations of individuals. On the other hand, he has admittedly been sufficiently affected by recent criticism and the trend of modern culture-personality studies so that he is no longer prepared to maintain the rigid autonomy of culture history and is willing to recognize the role of the individual as the efficient cause of culture. He now compromises and would embrace both concepts at once; he would eat his cake and have it too. It is all, he now holds, a matter of "perspective"—not of principle. Similarly, with reference to the concept of history his Neo-Kantian approach prevents him from continuing to regard history as a natural science as he once did. And so he again compromises; ethnology is both history and science. Here he was carried away by a false analogy between natural sciences—such as geology, astronomy, and biology—and ethnology. The fact that the data of these natural sciences may to some extent be studied historically, because their phenomena are subject to natural processes of development, does not imply that these sciences may be converted into historical disciplines comparable to culture history.

It is rather amusing to reflect that Kroeber once ruled Boas out of culture history by an a priori definition of history as being essentially timeless and descriptive, notwithstanding the fact that Boas and the "American historical school" were intensely interested in the processes of acculturation and diffusion. Now, by theoretically divorcing the study of culture history from that of cultural processes, Kroeber it appears, has split ethnology into a humanistic study of cultural configurations and values, on the one hand, and a scientific, psychobiological study of processes, on the other. The classical ethnologist's dream of a unified systematic science of culture and of culture history has all but disappeared from his thought. It is scarcely surprising to realize that ethnologists of the most disparate views are finding it difficult to accept his new thesis, even though it is in spirit a compromise which would do justice to all points of view. Extreme culturologists,

[18] *Ibid.*, p. 194.

such as White, cannot reconcile his recognition of the role of the individual and his idealistic conception of history with the traditional superorganic, superpsychic approach to culture.[19] And functionalists, such as Malinowski, even when prepared to recognize the complementary character of historical studies of culture, feel that "the hackneyed distinction between nomothetic and idiographic disciplines is a philosophical red herring which a simple consideration of what it means to observe, to reconstruct or to state an historic fact ought to have annihilated long ago." [20]

### 3. EVANS-PRITCHARD ON SOCIAL ANTHROPOLOGY AS A KIND OF HISTORIOGRAPHY

While apparently Kroeber's Neo-Kantian conception of the methodology of history and science has had no significant influence upon American ethnologists, it is beginning to affect anthropological thought in England. In a recent paper,[21] E. E. Evans-Pritchard has explicitly recorded his agreement with Kroeber's basic position:

I agree with Professor Kroeber that the fundamental characteristic of the historical method is not chronological relation of events but descriptive integration of them; and this characteristic historiography shares with social anthropology. . . . Nor does the anthropologist's determination to view every institution as a functioning part of a whole society make a methodological difference. Any good modern historian aims—if I may be allowed to judge the matter—at the same kind of synthesis. . . . I conclude, therefore, following Professor Kroeber, that while there are, of course, many differences between social anthropology and historiography they are differences of technique, of emphasis and of perspective, and not differences of method and aim.

Evans-Pritchard's paper is of exceptional interest in relation to our discussion of Kroeber in that he recognizes more clearly than the latter the nature of the theoretical issue involved. He contrasts the approach of positivistic natural history with his own humanistic historiographical approach. Whereas Kroeber had maintained that cultural anthropology is both a natural science and a historical discipline, depending upon which aspect of culture is selected for study by either of

---

[19] White, "Kroeber's 'Configurations of Culture Growth,'" *American Anthropologist*, XLVIII (1946), 78–93.

[20] Malinowski, *A Scientific Theory of Culture*, pp. 7–8.

[21] Evans-Pritchard, "Social Anthropology: Past and Present," *Man*, L (1950), 118–24.

the two methods, Evans-Pritchard draws the logical inference that social anthropology is primarily a kind of historiography and must not seek
to emulate the natural sciences in their quest for laws. Thus, what appears as only one alternative method in Kroeber, becomes the essential
objective in Evans-Pritchard. For the latter, ethnology has finally been
reduced to a species of historiography, to one of the humanities, and
even the possibility of a science of culture has been precluded. He summarizes his position clearly as follows.

The thesis I have put before you, that social anthropology is a kind of
historiography, and therefore ultimately of philosophy or art, implies that
it studies societies as moral systems and not as natural systems, that it is
interested in design rather than in process, and that it therefore seeks patterns and not scientific laws, and interprets rather than explains. These are
conceptual and not merely verbal, differences. The concepts of natural system
and natural law, modelled on the constructs of the natural sciences, have
dominated anthropology from its beginnings, and as we look back over the
course of its growth I think we can see that they have been responsible for a
false scholasticism which has led to one rigid and ambitious formulation
after another. Regarded as a special kind of historiography, that is as one
of the humanities, social anthropology is released from these essentially
philosophical dogmas and given the opportunity, though it may seem paradoxical to say so, to be really empirical and, in the true sense of the word,
scientific. This, I presume, is what Maitland had in mind when he said that
"by and by anthropology will have the choice between becoming history or
nothing."

Here we see that while Evans-Pritchard apparently reiterates
Kroeber's position, he does so with an important difference. He says
not only that history is the study of design and pattern, rather than
of process and law, as Kroeber does, but also that social anthropology
is essentially a kind of historiography, or art. This is a conceptual difference, not merely verbal. Social anthropology is said to deal, not with
a natural system of phenomena subject to natural law, as Tylor and
the cultural evolutionists held, but with moral or value systems which
are to be interpreted rather than explained causally. Evans-Pritchard
here approximates closely the original position of Rickert and Dilthey
in separating the historical, cultural "sciences" from the natural sciences—a thesis which Kroeber had gone out of his way to criticize.

Evans-Pritchard's reference to Maitland's classic prophesy merits
further comment. It will be recalled that we began this study of ethnology and history with a quotation from Paul Radin in which the latter

also appealed to Maitland. This leads us to ask what Maitland did mean by his statement that "by and by anthropology will have the choice between being history and being nothing."

Maitland expressed this conviction in the course of his address "The Body Politic," [22] delivered about 1899. A careful reading of this address reveals that what he is there examining critically is Spencer's thesis that there is a science of history comparable to any of the natural sciences, such as biology. The natural sciences, he suggests, may well supply the historian with some useful and fruitful metaphors, but the historian would do well not to hand himself over "body and soul" to the professor of any one science. In particular, the notion that society is an organism, as Spencer suggested, subject to laws of evolution comparable to those which prevail in biology, has not been proven. Our sociologists, he points out, too frequently attempt to obtain a set of "laws" by studying one class of phenomena, as if one could detach one kind of social phenomenon from all other kinds and obtain by induction a law for the phenomena of that class, for example, the notion that there is an evolutionary law for the development of the family from a state of promiscuity to monogamy, or that there is a similar evolution of property. When the historical, ethnographic evidence is examined by one trained "in a severe school of history" to look upon all the social phenomena as interdependent, one gets the impression that the sociologists and anthropologists have been "far too hasty with their laws." For the scientific historian each case begins to look "very unique," and a law which deduces a fixed sequence of social structures and institutions looks improbable. There is rarely any direct evidence of the passage of a barbarous nation from one state to another. It is in this context that Maitland concludes with the statement: "My own belief is that by and by anthropology will have the choice between being history and being nothing." [23]

The fact that the social and cultural development of each nation has a unique history of its own precludes the possibility, according to Maitland, of conceiving any kind of idea of the normal life of a body politic. Societies may imitate one another and thereby promote a certain measure of cultural similarity, but there is no proof that if left to themselves they would invariably have achieved the same inventions and institutions independently. There is no universal natural his-

[22] Maitland, *Selected Essays*, pp. 240–56.
[23] *Ibid.*, p. 249.

tory of social institutions or cultural inventions. There is no empirical basis, therefore, for attempting to reconstruct the past of civilized peoples by transferring data from contemporary barbarian tribes. These tribes are not on the normal highroad of progress and can offer no precise indication of the earlier stages of civilized nations. A study of primitive peoples may tell the historian what to look for, but never what he will find.[24] Since we do not know what is normal or what is abnormal in social history, one can hardly speak of a "political science," or of a science of social and cultural history comparable to our knowledge of the processes studied by the natural sciences.

Maitland's thesis, proposed from the perspective of a historian of law, anticipates clearly the criticism advanced later by Boas and his followers, and reiterated by Evans-Pritchard. The anthropologists and sociologists of the nineteenth century employed the so-called comparative historical method and purported to show the origin and development of social institutions and cultural inventions according to logical fixed stages. Boas and the extreme diffusionists introduced historical ethnographic evidence to demonstrate that the notion of fixed "procrustean stages" of cultural evolution, or of laws of the natural history of culture was not valid. That is why the so-called "genetic approach," as well as the historical comparative method, fell into discredit. Functionalists, such as Malinowski, then went to the opposite extreme and decried the historical approach as largely irrelevant to a science of culture. A society, like any other natural system, it was argued, could be described and explained in terms of natural law without reference to the past, that is, to history. Evans-Pritchard diagnoses the cause, or source, of the evolutionists' fallacy and confusion as due to their assumption "that societies are natural systems or organisms which have a necessary course of development that can be reduced to general principles or laws." This is putting the case from a sociological point of view. If the statement were altered to read "that cultures are natural systems having a natural history subject to a necessary course of development," the indictment would apply to culturology, or cultural anthropology, as well.

The point of Maitland's criticism and prophesy is, then, that the anthropologists and sociologists who are seeking for a universal natural history of society and culture as subject to natural law simply are not reckoning with the empirical facts of history. Anthropology is

[24] *Ibid.,* p. 253.

essentially, he held, the study of social history and each society must be studied empirically without any preconceived notions as to what will be found. "I do regret the suggestion," he concluded, "that at the present time the student of history should hope for and aim at ever wider and wider generalizations."

Maitland would, therefore, restrict anthropology to the case-by-case study of social history and discourage any attempt at generalization on a more or less universal scale. Anthropology, on this assumption, is a branch of general history and its method and objectives are not essentially different from those of history so understood. Anthropology is history—not in the sense of natural history—but in the restricted positive sense of a factual record to be determined by a critical study of the unique course of events and social changes which characterize a given society. Maitland's approach, like that of his nineteenth-century contemporaries in France and Germany, was that of a positivist interested in the minute collection of fragmentary facts, but opposed to the sociological and anthropological assumption of "laws" of sociocultural history. For him, anthropology must, as must history in general, aim at producing, "not aesthetic satisfaction but intellectual hunger." [25]

We are now in a position to return to Evans-Pritchard's statement as to what Maitland presumably meant when he confronted anthropology with the choice of being history or nothing. I think there can be little doubt that the former is right in his inference that for Maitland anthropology is a kind of humanistic historiography, not an autonomous natural science. What Evans-Pritchard fails to see, however, is that Maitland's positivistic conception of history and his own borrowed Neo-Kantian, idealistic conception are antithetical. For the idealist, history, including culture history, is a matter of interpretation and evaluation and hence is essentially subjective; for the positivist, history, like natural science, is an objective record of man's past yielding an organized body of established knowledge. Furthermore, Maitland's historian was interested in ascertaining the actual facts of the processes of social life as they occurred in the context of a given spatio-temporal situation; he was not interested in a subjective description and evaluation of institutions as types independent of given social contexts. As Collingwood puts it: "The best historian, like Mommsen or Maitland, became the greatest master of detail. . . . The ideal of universal history was swept aside as a vain dream, and the ideal of historical litera-

[25] *Ibid.*, p. 248.

ture became the monograph." [26] By contrast, Evans-Pritchard thinks that the description of the culture of a given society, whether synchronic or diachronic, is but the first phase of the anthropological historian's work. In the second phase, the anthropologist is supposed to seek by analysis the latent forms of a society and culture, and in the third phase he is to compare the social structures his analysis has revealed in a wide range of societies. This last phase, in particular, is not at all in agreement with Maitland's position, which discouraged generalizations and comparative analyses.

We are now confronted with this paradoxical situation: old-fashioned positivistic historians such as Maitland viewed history as the factual record of objective natural processes and sequences of social events, but were not interested in seeking general laws or universal generalizations. Idealistic ethnohistorians, on the other hand, profess to view *"* history subjectively, as interpretations of the patterns and values of a given culture, to the exclusion of processes, but yet are interested in ever-wider generalizations and comparative analyses of social structures and their functions. This is precisely what the naturalistic cultural evolutionists, with their positivistic historical comparative method, ventured to do and for which the professional historians, both positivistic and idealistic, criticized them. The only difference between idealistic ethnohistorians and naturalistic evolutionary ethnologists seems to be that the former professes an interest in establishing or constructing "significant patterns" without reference to actual processes, whereas the latter professes to be seeking for "laws" which he has not yet discovered. Pragmatically, so far as actual methods of research are concerned, there appears to be no significant difference at all. According to Evans-Pritchard, "it does not follow from regarding social anthropology as a special kind of historiography rather than as a special kind of natural science that its researches and theory are any the less systematic." [27] The point at issue is, however, that one has a right to expect that differences in theory, if they are at all significant and not merely verbal, should lead to pragmatic differences in practice and methodology.

At this stage it is important to distinguish two theses which are not differentiated clearly in Evans-Pritchard's paper, namely, the idealistic conception of history and the humanistic anthropocentric philosophy

[26] Collingwood, *The Idea of History*, p. 127.
[27] Evans-Pritchard, "Social Anthropology," *Man*, L (1950), p. 123.

of culture. The two theses are not logically or necessarily connected. I have maintained elsewhere in this book, the thesis of a humanistic approach to the study of culture, one that is compatible with the concept of human freedom and a normative evaluation of culture. Logically, however, it is possible to maintain this thesis without accepting an idealistic theory of history which would set up a dichotomy of historical and scientific method. One may, instead, maintain the inseparability of pattern and process in culture history, as I am inclined to do, and urge that the historian is, and should be, interested in analyzing objective historical processes, as well as in evaluating significant patterns, without subscribing to the uncritical assumption that there are natural laws of culture history. It is my impression that the Neo-Kantian ethnohistorians tend to reintroduce implicitly the very processes they profess to exclude from history by speaking of structures and functions as essential to an integrative description of a culture. By subordinating function to structure and pattern, as if pattern and form were primary and function and process were secondary, they manage to conceal from themselves the fact they too are dealing with cultural processes, as well as with forms or configurations.

I find myself, therefore, in sympathy with Evans-Pritchard's humanistic philosophy of culture, while rejecting his Neo-Kantian conception of the methodology of history and science, which he derived from Kroeber. I find myself in complete accord with him when he writes:

Social anthropologists, dominated consciously or unconsciously, from the beginnings of their subject, by positivist philosophy, have aimed, explicitly or implicitly, and for the most part still aim—for this is what it comes to—at proving that man is an automaton and at discovering the sociological laws in terms of which his actions, ideas and beliefs can be explained and in the light of which they are controlled. This approach implies that human societies are natural systems which can be reduced to variables.[28]

It is, I maintain, only a dogma of modern positivistic and materialistic sociologists and culturologists that a scientific study of culture involves a denial of human freedom or power of self-determination in the directing of cultural processes and goals.

On the other hand, there is nothing in the so-called historical method as such which leads necessarily either to a humanistic or to a naturalistic and deterministic approach to the data of culture history; what

[28] *Ibid.*, p. 123.

that approach happens to be depends upon one's metahistorical presuppositions, or philosophy of history and science. History does not
eschew, as Evans-Pritchard seems to think, "rigid formulations of
any kind"; otherwise competent historians would never have attempted to envisage a natural philosophy of history. Turning from
science to history will not of itself change one's interpretation of cultural phenomena, unless one happens to have a special kind or type of
philosophy of history and of historical method whose pragmatic consequences are such as to lead away from naturalistic determinism in
culture. The Neo-Kantian, idealistic conception of history is but one
particular interpretation or theory of the method of history; one may
accept, instead, a more realistic approach, as suggested here, which
would be in even greater accord with the ethnographic data and with
a humanistic and normative philosophy of culture.

In this connection it is of interest to note the comments of Daryll
Forde on Evans-Pritchard's paper. In a communication entitled "Anthropology, Science and History" [29] Forde makes the point that

Kroeber recognizes the dependence of certain histories on scientific knowledge, referring to the extensive "use" which astronomers make of physics, and
natural historians of theories of biological process. But the essential point is
that interpretative or integrative advances in history in all fields including
the socio-cultural are dependent not only on the accumulation of new data
concerning events but equally, and often more crucially, on advances in
relevant analytical knowledge and on the application to the concrete data
new or old of the concepts and criteria these afford. . . . The relation, it
should also be pointed out, is complementary or reciprocal in that historical
advances in the determination and presentation of new data concerning
events provide new analytical problems for solution.

I think that Forde's criticism is well taken. As indicated earlier, for
Kroeber cultural anthropology or ethnology is both a natural science
and a historical discipline, depending upon which method is used and
which phenomena are selected. The two methods are supposed to be
complementary, in that historical description provides a holistic survey
of the actual functioning of a culture, and scientific analysis of the
structure and function of sociocultural phenomena leads to wider generalizations. Conversely, a knowledge of basic concepts and processes
serves to provide the historian with a profounder understanding of
historical integrations—a point Boas, in particular, had stressed. By
identifying social anthropology with historiography, Evans-Pritchard

[29] *Man*, L (1950), 155–56.

was really departing from Kroeber's thesis, even while he was invoking Kroeber's statement in support of his reduction of culture to history. Kroeber is not at all prepared to say with Maitland that anthropology is either history or nothing; for him it is partly history and partly science.

Furthermore, I find myself in agreement with Forde's criticism to the effect that professional historians do not, as Maitland did not, undertake comparative analyses of cultural institutions. The philosophical historian to whom Evans-Pritchard refers is really a theoretical ethnologist concerned with the study of abstract structures and processes. In this sense, too, anthropology is more than historiography.

On the other hand, Forde does not seem to appreciate the fact that Evans-Pritchard is proposing a revolutionary approach to the study of social anthropology in urging anthropologists to turn away from the natural sciences and to turn toward the humanistic disciplines, especially the history of ideas and social history in general. Evans-Pritchard is proposing a break with the positivistic philosophy of science underlying contemporary anthropology and with the cultural determinism of contemporary culturology which would reduce man to an automaton incapable of affecting significant cultural changes. These theoretical propositions are of immediate, direct concern to the anthropologist and are not to be dismissed, as Forde is inclined to do, as irrelevant to scientific analysis.

### 4. WHITE ON CULTURE HISTORY AND CULTURAL EVOLUTION

In contrast to the Neo-Kantian idealistic conception of culture history proposed by Kroeber and supported by Evans-Pritchard, we turn next to a brief analysis of the historical materialism of Leslie A. White. In agreement with cultural evolutionists of an earlier period, White accepts the thesis of the evolution of human culture and of natural laws of cultural development through fixed stages. He differs, however, from the classical evolutionists, such as Tylor and Morgan, in distinguishing sharply between the sphere of culture history and that of cultural evolution. History is said to deal with the particular, unique, and contingent, while evolution refers to the stages of the development of culture as subject to universal necessary law, irrespective of the actual historical sequence in any given culture.

It is important to bear in mind, as was noted earlier, that for Tylor culture history was a branch of natural history subject to natural law. Tylor's main thesis was that of the progressive evolution of human culture from the primitive to the civilized state as conditioned by the laws of mind. His minimal thesis was that culture is a historical process subject to evolution in time, but without any fixed goal or limit. The hypothesis of progressive evolution and the continuity of culture history was his contribution to a philosophy of culture history. Evolution, so understood, was Tylor's formula for the interpretation of the culture history of mankind as a whole and for the evaluation of the basic cultural achievements of mankind in the course of the historical process. The theory of cultural evolution enabled Tylor, as it did Morgan, to // reconstruct the past history of civilized nations for which no direct records were available. The laborious attempts by the adherents of this theory of unilinear development to reconstruct the prehistory of peoples such as the Greeks and the Hebrews by a comparative study of contemporary preliterate peoples are evidence of the method of this school. The facts of historical diffusion and spontaneous variations were not taken as a refutation of cultural determinism and linear progress, but rather as an indication of interference with these assumed stages of cultural evolution.

The basic lesson to be derived from a direct study of the works of the classical evolutionists is that the theory of evolution provided formulas of culture history applicable to all peoples. This explains the opposition of the culture historians, whether monistic diffusionists or *Kulturkreise* pluralists, to the fixed evolutionary formulas which were proposed to illuminate the actual historical sequence of social institutions, such as marriage, law, and so forth. The general fact of evolution in the sense of the development of culture from a primitive to a more advanced stage was not disputed at all, and hence the issue was not one of "diffusion versus evolution," but rather of diffusion versus one particular type, or formula, of culture history and cultural evolution.[30] The so-called "anti-evolutionists" simply denied that there was any one fixed formula for cultural evolution applicable either to the past or the future of all societies, but they did not deny that there was some kind of cultural development among all historical societies. It was the assumption of the uniformity of the historical stages of cultural evolution of unrelated societies which evoked the criticism of historians such as Maitland and of ethnologists such as Boas, who pointed to

[30] Lowie, "Professor White and 'Anti-Evolutionist Schools,'" *Southwestern Journal of Anthropology*, II (1946), 240–41; Bidney, "On the So-Called Anti-evolutionist Fallacy: a Reply to Leslie A. White," *American Anthropologist*, XLVIII (1946), 293–97.

ethnographic evidence to controvert the hypothesis of unilinear development.

White's attempt to separate culture history from cultural evolution, thus, does not reckon with the facts of the history of modern ethnology. If culture history and cultural evolution were as distinct and disparate as he says they are, there would have been no point at all to the prolonged debate over the concepts of natural history and natural evolution of culture.

The basic assumption underlying White's distinction between history and evolution is the superorganic, superpsychic nature of cultural phenomena. For White culture is still a reality *sui generis,* subject to its autonomous processes and laws. Hence, culture must be explained, not by reference to man or to the fact of human biology and psychology, but through itself alone as a distinct level of reality. Hence, the evolution of any one category of culture must be viewed as subject to fixed, predetermined, logical stages of development. Cultural evolution is a temporal process involving the sequence of forms of culture, as well as a logical, irreversible sequence of stages. As a temporal process, evolution occurs and is manifested within the culture of mankind in the course of time. But this does not mean, for White at least, that mankind may be said to have a culture history, as Tylor and the classical evolutionists maintained. By a priori definition he has delimited the sphere of history as comprising the contingent relations of specific, unique temporal events.[31] By similar a priori definition, evolution is said to deal only with "temporal-formal processes" [32] which are thoroughly deterministic and not subject to human control. Hence, while evolution may be said to occur in time, it is nevertheless nonhistorical, since only the temporal, chance, sequence of specific events—not of forms which are universal types—may be regarded as historical. As White puts it: "The historic process and the evolutionary process are alike in being temporal in character, i.e., non-repetitive and irreversible. But, whereas the historic process is merely temporal, the evolutionary process is formal as well: it is a *temporal-sequence-of-forms.*" [33]

White does not explain what the relation is between the history of a given class of phenomena and their evolution. He merely informs us that in evolution we are dealing with the development of the stages of a class of phenomena, for example, writing, whereas in history the

[31] White, *The Science of Culture,* p. 8.
[32] *Ibid.,* p. 11.                    [33] *Ibid.,* p. 13.

emphasis is upon the single event, unique in time and space, for example, it is a historical fact that in a certain place, at a certain time, a certain form of writing was found.[34] On his own admission, however, it would appear that one may speak of the history of forms of phenomena, such as of writing, and if so, it follows that history, as well as evolution, may deal with forms of cultural phenomena. Hence, the question still remains, what is the relation between the history of a given culture form and its evolution? Could there be any evolution apart from actual history? If there can be cultural evolution apart from history, how is culture history relevant to evolution? Are they merely two parallel series independent of one another?

The dilemma with which White is confronted is this: If evolution is a concept pertaining to the data of the culture history of mankind, then it follows, as the classical evolutionists maintained, that the laws, or formulas, of evolutionary sequences may serve to reconstruct and predict the actual history of particular societies. In culture history law would have the same function as does law in other natural sciences, namely, to explain and predict the sequence of natural events in time and space. But if, as White maintains, evolution is nonhistorical and has no bearing on historical processes, what function may, then, be assigned to the so-called evolutionary laws? If evolution does not explain or help us to reconstruct particular histories, what does it do for the ethnologist? Every law in the natural sciences is repetitive in the sense that it is a universal formula applicable to many instances. But White has stated that the evolutionary process is nonrepetitive and that hence evolutionary laws may not be regarded as re-exemplified in the historical process. A nonrepetitive law is, however, a contradiction in terms. Theoretically, White might have said that while the evolutionary process is nonrepetitive in the sense that the evolution of the culture of mankind is a single, progressive movement, the historical processes in which evolution is exemplified may be repetitive. But he has ruled out this possibility in advance by stating explicitly that history, too, is nonrepetitive.

One is perforce led to the conclusion that White's divorce of history from evolution renders history unintelligible and evolutionary processes of no pragmatic value to the ethnologist. White's postulation of two independent orders of culture, namely, the logical-temporal order of

[34] White, " 'Diffusion vs. Evolution': an Anti-evolutionist Fallacy," *American Anthropologist*, XLVII (1945), 339–56.

cultural evolution and the contingent variable order of culture history, is reminiscent of the Platonic dualism of the realm of Ideas and the contingent order of phenomenal nature. Aristotle's original criticism of Plato's philosophy of science in the first book of his *Metaphysics*, to the effect that such duplication was superfluous and forever rendered a science of nature impossible, seems to be equally applicable to the dualism of normative laws of cultural evolution versus contingent, nonrepetitive culture history. If the laws of cultural evolution do not serve to explain and predict the actual historic processes of given cultures, then they are of no scientific use.

In his critical discussion of White's views on history and evolution, Kroeber contrasts his own duality with regard to the methods of history and science with White's trinity of history, evolution, and science.[35] Kroeber is particularly critical of White's notion of history as a record of the unique, chronological sequence of events. All history, he points out, deals with relations, functions, and meanings and hence is not merely the annalistic tracing of discrete events. History, he maintains, is always interpretative and is therefore concerned with functional relations. As he puts it, "All real history is nothing but an interpretation by means of description in terms of context." [36]

Of especial interest in Kroeber's paper "History and Evolution" is the fact that here, for the first time, one encounters the change in his general theory of culture which he later developed at length in the revised edition of his *Anthropology*. Instead of citing the phenomenon of written language as an example of the superorganic, superpsychic character of culture, Kroeber actually explains the stages in the development of writing by reference to psychological facts and historic tendencies. The stages of writing are logically distinguishable, but this, he argues, does not mean that they normally or necessarily succeed each other. As Kroeber states his argument:

Not only do the historical facts show that the succession of styles has been pictograph-ideogram-rebus-phonogram in the known instances, but an argument could well be adduced that that order is psychologically irreversible in a free internal development uninfluenced by alien inventions. . . . Such a step-by-step transference is wholly conceivable psychologically, whereas the direct or immediate use of a visual figure as symbol for a sound-cluster makes no psychological sense. It is in this way that we may legitimately

[35] White, "History, Evolutionism and Functionalism," *Southwestern Journal of Anthropology*, I (1945), 221–48; Kroeber, "History and Evolution," *Southwestern Journal of Anthropology*, II (1946), 1–15.

[36] "History and Evolution," *ibid.*, p. 4.

speak of the developmental process implied in the three stages as being irreversible: the one-wayness is on the psychological, not on the cultural level.[37]

Here we have an explicit statement to the effect that the stages in the evolution of writing do not indicate the autonomous working out of the cultural process, but are to be explained by psychological processes and psychological conditions of thought transference. What appears to be an irreversible process of evolution is in fact a psychological process completed only once and spread by a process of historical diffusion. If by evolution is meant, as White appears to mean, a process which is fixed, necessary, and predetermined, an "unfolding of immanences," then Kroeber will no longer have anything to do with the concept, since he now finds "a simple causal explanation in terms of psychological association." [38]

Thus, Kroeber can find no basis for distinguishing evolution as a valid method intermediate between history and science. What White calls "evolution" is a mixture of history and science. The nonrepetitive parts of cultural evolution are merely large histories or summarized culture history; the repetitive parts are parts of the findings of science. It is only because White arbitrarily limits history to tracing the movements of discrete culture items in the continuum of time and excludes all interpretation and causal relations from its assigned task that he proceeds as if history and evolution were temporal processes independent of one another. Furthermore, as we have seen, Kroeber maintains that the essence of history is not chronological temporal sequence, but rather descriptive integration and that hence there is no need to postulate a separate evolutionary method in addition to that of history, since the study of cultural achievements, quite apart from their diachronic sequence, is said to be intrinsically historical.

It is noteworthy that Kroeber, even in the first edition of his *Anthropology,* when he still adhered to the notion of the superorganic nature of culture as a reality *sui generis*—the view which White yet proclaims —rejected linear evolution through fixed stages leading to inevitable progress.[39] In this respect he showed himself to be at one with his teacher Boas, although he departed radically from the latter in his conception of the autonomous nature of culture. The concept of the cultural superorganic led Kroeber to a theory of cultural determinism and historical determinism, but under the influence of Boas he always

[37] *Ibid.,* pp. 7–8.　　　[38] *Ibid.,* p. 9.　　　[39] *Anthropology* (1923), p. 8.

shied away from any simplistic schemes of evolutionary progress. White, curiously enough, accepts chance and contingency in the realm of culture history—but affirms a rigid, narrow, materialistic determinism in the context of cultural evolution. Kroeber was, at least, consistent and coherent. By comparison, White's view is eclectic and incoherent.

5. HERSKOVITS ON ETHNOHISTORY AND CULTURAL LAWS

Our survey of the history of modern ethnology has revealed various approaches to the problem of the relation of ethnology to history. First, we examined the theory, associated with Tylor, Morgan, and the evolutionary ethnologists and sociologists in general, that anthropology is the natural science of culture history and that the ultimate objective of the anthropologist is to discover the laws of history and to formulate a philosophy of cultural progress. Secondly, we discussed the view of Boas that ethnology is the science of cultural processes involving a study of ethnohistory. Boas implicitly contrasts history with science, and apparently his thesis is that while each culture must be understood as the product of historical growth and development, the essential aim of the ethnologist is to study the universal cultural processes and psychological conditions underlying culture changes. Thirdly, we examined the view of Kroeber that anthropology is both history and science, history being understood in the Neo-Kantian sense as the integrative description of given cultures, irrespective of time. For Kroeber, then, ethnology is both a humanity and a science, depending upon which method of approach is utilized. Historical description provides a holistic survey of the actual functioning of a culture, and scientific analysis of cultural processes leads to wider generalizations. On this basis, the study of culture forms, undertaken synchronically and diachronically, constitutes the sphere of history and may be pursued independently of the study of cultural processes. It was because Boas had put the primary emphasis upon the study of cultural processes rather than upon forms that Kroeber regarded the former's approach as primarily scientific rather than historical. Fourthly, we noted that Evans-Pritchard accepts Kroeber's distinction between the method of history and the method of science, but infers that anthropology is essentially a kind of historiography and not to be classified among the natural sciences. Fifthly, according to White, ethnology, or culturology, is the science of cultural evolution. Evolution and history are now contrasted, evolution being the process of the temporal development of culture forms, and history the contingent sequence of particular events. Evolution is said to be subject to natural laws, but history, since it deals with the unique and the contingent, is not a science. Thus, while White distinguishes between history and science, as do Boas and Kroeber, his conception of an evolutionary science is one which they do not share. Sixthly, we found that Malinowski developed the thesis of a science of culture, independent of history and involving the establishment of laws of culture. The science of culture, so understood, comprised the analysis of the universal biological and societal conditions of culture, without reference to historical or evolutionary development. There is no place in Malinowski for an independent study of the history of culture forms, such as Kroeber advocates and practices, since he does not concede that forms are intelligible apart from sociocultural functions. If Kroeber may be said to put the primary emphasis upon culture history as the study of culture forms, Malinowski may be viewed as going to the opposite extreme, by making function primary and form secondary and by failing to recognize the significance of culture history as an integral part of anthropology.

In relation to the above survey, the thesis proposed by Melville J. Herskovits in *Man and His Works* appears to be an eclectic synthesis of various approaches. As does Boas, whose student he was, Herskovits stresses the importance of ethnohistory and historical processes, such as acculturation. But whereas Boas looked for the possibility of "laws" and of causal determinism in the ultimate effects of physiological, psychological, and social conditions upon cultural patterns and processes, Herskovits, in agreement with Malinowski and Radcliffe-Brown, asserts that there are, in fact, purely cultural laws governing cultural processes. Kroeber, too, professed in theory the possibility of a science of cultural processes, as distinguished from a history of culture forms, but he thought that such a science is still in the making and did not therefore venture to cite any examples of cultural laws. According to Herskovits, the study of ethnohistory—that is, the culture history of particular peoples, not the history of culture forms as independent of personal agents—is significant and important pragmatically, because it enables the ethnologist to abstract and infer general laws governing the types of cultural processes revealed by ethnohistory. History is said to be "the laboratory in which the scientist of culture works," [40]

[40] Herskovits, *Man and His Works,* p. 619.

and from which he derives insights into the nature and processes of culture. Herskovits summarizes his thesis by stating: "Cultural forms are the expression of unique sequences of historical events, but they are the result of underlying processes that represent constants in human experience." [41]

We are, then, left with the functionalist thesis that cultural forms are unique owing to unique historical sequences of events, but cultural processes are universals and therefore constant. This thesis goes contrary to the views of culture historians, such as Kroeber, who recognize that cultural forms may be viewed as universals independent of cultural processes. According to Herskovits, each culture is unique as regards its historical forms, but the processes underlying these forms are constant and general. Judging from the context of his work, he appears to be following the view of Radcliffe-Brown, whom he quotes at length, and who differentiates between ethnology and "comparative sociology." [42] For the latter, ethnology, which is concerned with the historical relations of particular peoples, is not a generalizing science, but comparative sociology is "a science that applies the generalizing method of the natural sciences to the phenomena of the social life of man and to everything that we include under the term culture or civilization." If for "ethnology" we substitute the term "ethnohistory" and for "comparative sociology" the "science of culture," then Herskovits's views appear to be identical with those of Radcliffe-Brown. Only the comparative sociologist or culturologist, it appears, is able to formulate "laws," or generalizations, of processes; the ethnohistorian can provide no generalizations, since cultural forms are, by a priori definition, unique historical products.

The problem then remains: How does one correlate general processes with particular historical forms of culture? If the cultural processes are uniform, why are not the resultant forms uniform too? We are confronted here, it would seem, with the same type of problem which arose in connection with our analysis of the views of White. There we noted that by separating the universal evolutionary process from the unique, contingent sequences of history, White rendered history unintelligible and the evolutionary process of no pragmatic value for an understanding of actual cultures. The same criticism applies with reference to Herskovits' dichotomy of history and scientific culture theory. If the so-called cultural laws do not serve to explain ethnic

[41] *Ibid.*      [42] *Ibid.*, pp. 611–12.

history, what then is their function? If one cultural law can give rise to various culture forms, what is the correlation obtaining between cultural process and cultural form? Herskovits does, in fact, suggest that "cultural form is but the expression of cultural process, and that any generalizations about form must, in the final analysis, derive from hypotheses regarding process," [43] and hence implies the possibility of generalizing about forms, but he does not explain just what the correlation is. All we can gather is that function, or process, is primary, while form is secondary and derivative.

When we turn to his text for examples of the much-heralded cultural laws, we find some of them to be restatements of cultural postulates, well known to every student of anthropology, which no anthropologist had considered worthy of being designated as "laws." Thus, the proposition that "culture is learned and not inborn," which all ethnologists since the time of Tylor have accepted as axiomatic, is now put forth as a "law." Another such generalization, but this one derived from Marxian historical materialism, is that "culture responds to its natural setting in accordance with the forms of its technology." Still another example is the proposition that "given two cultures in contact, borrowing will not go beyond the limits of form described by the differences between the elements and institutions of the cultures concerned." [44] From these examples it appears that practically any generalization whatsoever which the ethnologist may make concerning culture and cultural processes may be regarded as a "law." On this assumption, it may indeed be granted that the number of "laws" is "very considerable" and far exceeds the number of laws to be found in the physical sciences.

Herskovits, one gathers from his text, assumes that "law" and generalization are identical and hence does not distinguish between postulates, axioms, hypotheses, and laws. In fact, he himself uses the term "postulates" as equivalent to law. Thus, he states:

The generalization that through the learning process the developing human organism becomes a being whose behavior is overwhelmingly in consonance with the sanctioned patterns of his culture, leads to an acceptance of the further postulate that we can predict the behavior of the individual conditioned to live in accordance with these patterns.[45]

To reduce the concept of law to that of any generalization about phenomena is to render the term meaningless and to make any resemblance between "law" as so used and laws in the physical sciences nothing more

[43] *Ibid.,* p. 619.    [44] *Ibid.,* pp. 620–21.    [45] *Ibid.,* p. 621.

than a homology. Law as used in the natural sciences prescribes some fixed rule governing the sequence and relation of phenomena; but a "law" which allows us to infer in general what to expect but does not prescribe or anticipate the precise nature of the phenomena to be experienced is no law in the scientific sense of the term. What Herskovits terms "laws" appear to be vague generalizations barely exceeding ethnological platitudes. In attempting to reconcile the assertion that each society has its own unique ethnohistory with the assumption that culture and society are natural systems subject to natural law, Herskovits appears to be working with two antithetical concepts—a criticism which Evans-Pritchard applies to the functionalists in general. The assumption of the uniqueness of each ethnohistory leads him to cultural relativism, while the so-called "laws" lead him to assume purely formal, abstract cultural universals.

Herskovits declares that "once full account is taken of the fact of variation, the reconciliation of range in cultural form with regularity in process is well in hand." [46] The notion of regularity in process precludes purely "historic accident"; every accidental occurrence is seen to be subject to law, while its apparent uniqueness is attributed to the variety of ethnic experiences and ethnic ways of life. Ethnic history will enable the student to understand the particular experiences of given peoples and how processes of acculturation have affected their historical development. The constant factors, or general principles, which characterize cultural processes will, however, enable the ethnologist to predict in general, but not in detail, the behavior of individuals and groups subject to these cultural conditions.[47]

Thus, Herskovits would substitute ethnohistory for the culture history which Tylor, Kroeber, and Evans-Pritchard, among ethnologists, regarded as essential tasks of modern ethnology. Instead of the study of the relation and sequence of culture forms in the context of given cultures and societies, he advocates the study of particular ethnic groups in their ecological settings. In agreement with functionalists, such as Malinowski, he disparages the study of historic culture forms apart from their institutional functions in given societies. Taking as his example the case of the classical evolutionists, with their assumption of a fixed series of forms of cultural development, Herskovits apparently goes to the opposite extreme and denies that any generalizations concerning cultural forms *per se* are significant. Cultural forms are said to be unique historic "accidents," determined by the unique ethnic his-

[46] *Ibid.*, p. 620.　　　　　　　　[47] *Ibid.*, pp. 620–21.

tory and cultural experiences of diverse peoples; only cultural processes are universals capable of generalization. Thus, by definition culture history as an independent study of cultural forms is precluded—notwithstanding the considerable achievements of historical ethnologists in tracing the development and diffusion of culture forms.

When we turn to Herskovits' text for an example showing how ethnohistory may be utilized as a laboratory for the ethnologist, we find him drawing up "a scale of intensity of Africanism" with reference to New World Negro cultures. This scale, he points out, is based on the assumption that "culture can be studied as the series of related but independent variables we term aspects." [48] What he has done, in effect, is to select a series of categories of culture, such as technology, economic life, social organization, religion, magic, art, folklore, and language, and to compare these forms of behavior with reference to European ways of life so as to determine the degree of acculturation. Thus, in practice Herskovits' method turns out to be essentially similar to that employed by Kroeber and other culture historians in tracing the distribution of culture traits in given areas. This method implies that traits can be isolated as realities more or less independent of one another and made comparable. This, we have seen, was the thesis which Malinowski rejected as essentially incompatible with the functionalistic method. Herskovits is apparently prepared to follow in practice the method of the culture historians in tracing the distribution of culture traits and forms, but denies in theory the validity of historical descriptions of culture forms apart from cultural processes and social experiences.

Herskovits' approach is eclectic in the sense that he attempts to combine Boas' concept of history as a unique ethnic process of development in time involving acculturation, the functionalism of Radcliffe-Brown and Malinowski, with their thesis of the primacy of function over form and their concept of laws of cultural process, and the comparative historical method of trait distribution employed by the culture historians. While he is thereby saved from a narrow simplistic dogmatism, the net result is not coherent.

## 6. TOWARD A REALISTIC CONCEPTION OF CULTURE HISTORY

During the course of this critical and historical analysis of the relation of the concept of history to modern ethnological thought I have ventured to offer some positive suggestions as to the way in which

[48] *Ibid.*, p. 615.

some of the difficulties inherent in the positions under consideration may be obviated. By way of conclusion, I propose to state in summary form some of the positive theses to which I have been led as a result of this study.

First, it seems clear from our analysis that unless the ethnologist defines clearly his concept of history and the philosophical or meta-anthropological presuppositions which it entails, there can be little prospect of arriving at any agreement on this problem or making any progress toward a coherent ethnological theory. Some conservative anthropologists say, "anthropology is history or nothing." Others, such as the functionalists, counter, "anthropology is the scientific study of cultural processes." Still others would say that anthropology is both history and science. With the exception of Kroeber, hardly any anthropologists have ventured to define what they meant by history and the relation of history to a science of ethnology.

The realistic concept of history which I propose, as against the idealistic concept introduced by Kroeber, is that *history is our human description and interpretation of any natural process or sequence of events in the context of space and time.* This definition has some important implications: First, it implies that culture history in particular comprises a study of both patterns, or forms, and processes and that it is fallacious to limit the study of history to forms without processes. Secondly, the notion of a "timeless history," proposed by Kroeber, is a contradiction in terms. Mere descriptive analysis of a given culture is, as Boas maintained, ethnology, but not history. Thirdly, it is entirely arbitrary to separate process from form and to assign form to history and process to science. History, as well as science, deals with processes, even though the processes are of different kinds. In history the interest is in the continuity of processes over more or less lengthy time intervals; in science the primary emphasis is upon discrete processes affecting the relations of types of phenomena.

Fourthly, history involves a subjective, as well as an objective, element. Unless there were objective processes in nature and in the social life of man, there would be no history. On the other hand, unless some human mind describes that which has occurred and interprets and evaluates its significance, there would also be no history. Subjectively, it may be said that all history is human history in the sense that man or the human mind is the measure of history. The positivists treat history, as they do natural science, as if history were nothing but the record of objective facts independent of the observer. What they fail to see is that the "facts" of history require reconstruction and evaluation by the human mind in order that they may be comprehended as a continuity, or causally connected series of events. Furthermore, in the human sphere facts and events must be evaluated and interpreted with reference to psychological motivations and symbolic significance in a given spatio-temporal context.

The idealistic historians, such as the Neo-Kantians, have firmly grasped the point that human history requires an act of understanding and interpretation, but they have arbitrarily limited the sphere of history to that of human society and culture and excluded the sphere of nature from historic discourse. Only man, they say, has a history; nature is subject to universal processes, but has no history. By making descriptive, idiographic integration and interpretation the essential property of historical method, they exclude time and process as nonessential characteristics of history, thereby setting up a dichotomy of the spheres of history and science corresponding to the duality of culture and nature. As against the idealistic conception of history and historical method, it may be argued that while historical method does in fact require interpretation and evaluation, there is no valid ground for excluding a historical study of purely natural phenomena as well. Kroeber, it may be noted, grants that historical method may be applied to the study of natural phenomena, but he interprets historical method in idealistic terms. The scientist-historian, he says, may study the history of the earth or of astronomical phenomena, but insofar as he is a historian he will limit himself to the sequence of forms and their integrations. Similarly, the culture historian is said to study the forms of cultural phenomena and the configurations of culture growth, but not cultural processes, since the latter pertain to the domain of a science of culture.

My thesis is that historical method requires no such limitation; the historian, as well as the natural scientist, is concerned with processes and forms, but from a different perspective. The historian is primarily interested in recording and interpreting a given spatio-temporal sequence of events as a causally connected continuum. The natural scientist is interested in discovering the constant, uniform relations between types of phenomena. Both are interested in processes, the historian in understanding the origin and development of a series of forms and social institutions leading to a contemporary situation, while the natural scientist is interested primarily in the repetitive character of natural processes and in the universal principles which govern the relations between natural phenomena. This does not mean that the historian may not arrive at certain generalizations concerning the basic factors which determine the course of social and cultural history, and he may even be convinced that in certain respects history, too, repeats itself. But the historian grants that in the sphere of human history there are many more variables than constants, while for the natural scientist it is the constants that matter and the regularities are the objects of research. That is why the historian may well profit from the researches of the scientist in that he may come to understand certain historic changes in terms of underlying universal laws, while others will remain in the category of the unique and the unpredictable. It is because both historian and scientist are concerned with processes that their work often proves complementary and mutually beneficial.

One source of confusion in modern ethnological thought is the failure to distinguish between natural and cultural history. As has been noted, the classical cultural evolutionists, following eighteenth- and nineteenth-century conceptions of a natural history, confused natural history and cultural history by assuming that there were natural laws of historical development and evolution comparable to those of physics. The self-assigned task of the ethnologist was the discovery of the natural laws of culture history which determined the course of cultural progress. It was this notion that there is a natural history of social institutions and cultural inventions which Maitland attacked and which empirically-minded, inductive ethnologists, such as Boas, criticized so persistently and finally undermined. In attacking the notion of fixed, unilinear stages of culture history and cultural evolution these critics were not attacking the idea of evolution itself as a method of studying cultural phenomena. Since Darwin the concept of evolution has been recognized by scientists as a universal principle, and no scientist, unless constrained by dogma, now questions the validity of this principle. How evolution is to be conceived in the sphere of culture is still to be determined. That there has been cultural evolution from a primitive state to that of modern civilization is not doubted. But how to evaluate cultural progress is in doubt, and the assumption that there are fixed, necessary laws governing the development of all peoples is rejected.

Kroeber's Neo-Kantian humanistic concept of culture history may, then, be understood as a substitute for the concept of a natural science of culture history involving natural laws. Evans-Pritchard, we have seen, realized most clearly the humanistic implications of this Neo-Kantian approach and contrasted it with the positivistic and naturalistic assumption of a science of culture history. The naturalistic, deterministic approach, he holds, leads to the thesis that man is an automaton incapable of self-determination. Kroeber, however, still adheres to a deterministic philosophy of history, although he admits that in practice he has to act "as if" he were a free agent.

One reason for Kroeber's hesitation is the fact that he, in common with others, contrasts the natural with the supernatural. To deny the notion of a natural science of culture history would, it is argued, lead to the introduction of theological supernaturalism, and this, of course, must be avoided at all costs if we are to have a science of ethnology. There is, however, a third alternative. Culture is natural in the sense that it is a human achievement in accord with natural law. But the naturalness of culture does not mean that its phenomena are independent of man in the same sense that physical phenomena are governed by laws independent of man. Culture is natural, and yet is an achievement whose processes supervene upon and utilize those of nature without being reducible to those of nature. A form of marriage is natural, since it depends upon natural organisms, but it may not be deduced from "human nature," since it is an invention of man in many forms which vary historically with social conditions.

It is for this reason that an explicit recognition of the disparity between natural history and cultural history would do much to clear up current confusions in ethnological theory. In the natural history of the earth or the sun the scientist-historian traces the stages in the development of these natural bodies; for the scientist they have a history, since they have a genesis in time through the operation of natural forces. Cultural history, on the other hand, is the study of the cultural selection and of the cultural evolution of mankind. There is no predetermined, immanent necessity or teleology in the evolution of human culture, taken phylogenetically or ontogenetically, since culture is not a natural organism, subject to predetermined stages of growth. As was discussed in another context, culture may be viewed as an expression of human freedom of creativity, while subject to the limitations of nature. While there are certain cultural universals, namely, institutions which subserve universal human needs, such as family organization, religion, and so forth, the variety of the forms of culture consonant with the satisfaction of human needs is almost limitless, and they are not subject to any fixed formula. The ethnohistory of the various peoples of the world shows remarkable disparities, as well as parallels, and therefore, without committing serious errors of historical fact one may not assume uniformity in all stages of development.

This would mean that culture history in the sense of a comparative study of the sequence of culture forms, together with ethnohistory or the sociocultural history of a given people and political history or the study of states in their relations to one another are all essentially humanistic studies, differing only in the selection of some particular aspect of the human situation. The positivists were right in one respect: either all human history is subject to natural law and is comparable to the natural sciences, or else all history is a humanistic study differing essentially from natural science. To make an exception of culture history, or cultural evolution and to regard the latter as a natural science while leaving history in general to the humanists and the philosophers is an arbitrary and inconsistent procedure.

The ethnological study of history, to be scientific, must be empirical and without any restraining preconceptions derived from positivistic philosophies of science as to the nature of the order and processes to be found therein. Cultural determinism is a fact of history and the historian must reckon with it in explaining human motivations and social movements. But culture history is also the expression of human freedom and human ideals. Culture history is neither a record of unique and incoherent events, without rhyme or reason, nor is it a rigidly determined sequence of forms. The degree of regularity and uniformity is something to be determined empirically. While there may be a reason for every detail the historian may discover in the course of his researches, he would be foolhardy to assume that everything that happens is in accord with predetermined reason and law. It is not the business of a scientist to discover "laws" where none exist.

The assumption of an earlier day, which is still echoed by some contemporary ethnologists, that anthropology is history or nothing was originally based upon the uncritical acceptance of the Comtean philosophy of society as a natural system subject to natural, historical law.

If this assumption be denied, then the way is left open to recognize the disparity of natural and cultural history and for the challenging role of the ethnologist in preparing the way for the exercise of human freedom in the progressive, creative transformation and evolution of human culture. To reduce anthropology to history, or to separate it from history, is to impoverish it.

# 10

# *The Concept of Myth*[1]

CULTURAL EVOLUTIONISTS speak as if there were a "mythopoeic," or myth-making, stage of human thought in which primitive peoples lived. There is general agreement among ethnologists that myths deal with a supersensuous, supernatural sphere of reality and refer to some prehistoric time. On this assumption myths have been defined as "stories of anonymous origin, prevalent among primitive peoples and by them accepted as true, concerning supernatural beings and events, or natural beings and events influenced by supernatural agencies." [2]

## 1. EVOLUTIONARY APPROACHES TO THE INTERPRETATION OF MYTH

According to Tylor, "First and foremost among the causes which transfigure into myths the facts of daily experience, is the belief in the animation of all nature rising at its highest pitch to personification." [3] Tylor, however, explicitly recognized the relativity of myth to one's criterion of possibility and noted that "the ordinary standards of possibility, as applied to the credibility of tradition, have indeed changed vastly in the course of culture through its savage, barbaric and civilized stages." [4] He drew attention to the fact that the doctrine of miracles commonly accepted in the Middle Ages became, as it were, a bridge along which mythology traveled from the lower into the higher culture. "Principles of myth-formation, belonging properly to the mental state of the savage, were by its aid continued in strong action in the civilized world." [5] The real source of myth in all ages, Tylor maintained, has been the "pragmatizer" who, because of his incapacity to hold abstract ideas is forced to embody them in material incidents and to clothe every thought in concrete shape.[6] He believed, however, that the growth of myth has been checked by science and that myth is,

---

[1] Reprinted in part from *American Anthropologist*, LII (1950), 16–26.
[2] Gayley, *The Classic Myths in English Literature and in Art*, p. 1.
[3] Tylor, *Primitive Culture*, I, 285.　　[4] *Ibid.*, p. 371.
[5] *Ibid.*　　　　　　　　　　　　　[6] *Ibid.*, p. 407.

therefore, to be considered a primitive ethnology expressed in poetic form.[7]

Similarly, Wundt,[8] following Vico, maintained that there has been an evolution of myth corresponding to the main stages of cultural development. Parallel to the Totemic Age, he postulates the *Märchen* myth, a narrative resembling the fairy tale, which centers about magical agencies, demons, and gods. In the Heroic Age myths arose which deal with the exploits of culture heroes, who, though aided by magic and supernatural agencies, are primarily dependent upon their own efforts. Theogonic and cosmogonic myths are also held to be characteristic of this period. Finally, in the age of reason and development to humanity man is said to have attained a large measure of rational, critical thought and a cosmopolitan perspective which enabled him to transcend the limitations of the mythical mentality.

Susanne K. Langer has struck a new note by putting forward a theory of the emergence of myth as a distinct category of primitive thought. Unlike the evolutionary ethnologists and in contrast to philosophers such as Cassirer, she does not assume that primitive thought is mythological, but maintains that mythological thought is itself the product of an evolutionary process of development.

According to Langer,[9] myth begins in fantasy, and to this extent it shares a common origin with dreams and the dream-narrative. As the dream-narrative is recounted, it undergoes various modifications in the interests of coherence and public appeal. As a result, higher fictional modes of story emerge, namely, the animal fable, the trickster story, and the ghost story, and these develop into the fairy tale. The fairy tales, in turn, are motivated by wishful thinking and reflect the cultural frustrations of a given society. It is perennially attractive, yet never quite believed by adults even in the telling.

The myth, according to Langer, is not to be understood as a development of the fairy tale, or *Volksmärchen*, as Wundt and other German scholars have suggested, but rather as something newly emerging which involves a "thematic shift" in function. Myth is said to be motivated, not by subjective, wishful thinking, but rather by the quest for an understanding of the significance of nature and life. Hence, unlike fairy tales, myths are taken with "religious seriousness" either as historic facts or as mystic truths. The typical theme of myth is tragic, not utopian, and

[7] *Ibid.*, pp. 317, 413 ff.     [8] Wundt, *Elements of Folk Psychology.*
[9] Langer, *Philosophy in a New Key,* p. 139.

its characters tend to become stable personalities of a supernatural order. Thus, although both myth and fairy tale are said to originate in fantasy and to involve the identification of a mental symbol with the object to which it refers, the functions of the two differ radically. Whereas fairy tales are held to be the expression of wishful thinking and personal gratification, myths, at their best, are to be regarded as a recognition of the drama of human existence. Their ultimate aim is not the wishful distortion of the world, but rather serious comprehension and envisagement of its fundamental nature. Myths are regarded as representing metaphorically a world-picture and insight into life generally and may, therefore, be considered primitive philosophy or metaphysical thought.

As Langer reconstructs the evolution of human thought, the legend which produces the culture hero constitutes an intermediate link between the fairy tale and the full-fledged nature myth. The culture hero narrative represents a transitional stage between the egocentric interest of the folk tale and the objective, universal interest of the nature myth. The culture hero may be interpreted as "man, overcoming the superior forces that threaten him." Man thus becomes a hero among his gods. "The highest development of which myth is capable is the exhibition of human life and cosmic order that epic poetry reveals." [10] When man begins to abstract his concepts and to examine them critically, when he inquires into the literal truth of a myth, then myth becomes superseded by discursive philosophy and science. Religion, as is myth, is said to rest on a provisional mode of thought which is inevitably succeeded by science and a philosophy of nature. Myth and religion are provisional, poetic products of the creative imagination when confronted with the mysteries of nature and life. In this sense they may be regarded as recurrent phenomena of historical experience.

The problem of the evolution of myth thus involves two distinct issues. First, there is the question whether all primitive thought is to be identified with the so-called "mythopoeic," or "prelogical" mentality, or whether myth constitutes but one phase or element of primitive thought. Secondly, there is the issue whether mythical thought itself is subject to a process of evolution, or is a passing, or provisional, mode of thinking characteristic of the primitive mind only.

On the whole, classical cultural evolutionists have taken the position

[10] *Ibid.*, pp. 163–64.

that primitive thought is to be identified with mythological thought. In opposition to this position, nonevolutionists, such as Boas and Malinowski, have maintained that historical, primitive cultures as we know them provide no ground for holding to this thesis. Whether or not primitive, prehistorical man had a mythopoeic mentality and constantly mistook mental symbols and images for the objects of reality is something we can only conjecture, since we have no evidence on the subject. But historical men, as represented by our culturally primitive contemporaries, do distinguish clearly between fictional folk tales, historical legends, and supersensuous, cosmogonic, and theogonic narratives, as well as between practical, empirical experience and magical arts. There is no basis, according to these students, for assuming that the precritical, irrational narratives which we designate as myths, but which nonliterate man holds as historical truth or sacred tradition, are outgrowths of some more elementary mode of mythical thought, such as the mundane folk tales. From the perspective of the natives themselves there is no doubt that the narratives we regard as myth do involve a "thematic shift" and that their function in native thought and culture differs essentially from that of the fictional tales told for entertainment.

As to the problem whether mythological thought itself is subject to evolutionary development or is a passing phase of primitive thought only, here, too, we find considerable disagreement. The cultural evolutionists were inclined to hold that mythological thought itself was subject to evolutionary development and that the character of myth varied with the cultural standard of credibility, as did Tylor, or with the mode of sociopolitical organization, as did Wundt. They tended to assume, however, that with the growth and dissemination of science, mythical thought was bound to disappear almost entirely. In contrast to this position, Malinowski [11] maintained that myth, like religion, fills a universal human need and is therefore indispensable to human culture at all stages of development. Myth, he contends, is to be understood as a postscientific mode of thought, as supplementing scientific thought by rationalization and wishful thinking, or by what William James has called "the will to believe" in the face of recurrent crises all men must face, such as death. With the growth of scientific thought, he realizes, the sphere of mythological extrapolation becomes restricted, especially with regard to myths of magic. But myth remains as a vital influence

[11] Malinowski, *Magic, Science and Religion*.

in civilized life, closely allied with religious faith. The function of myth is thus held to be the validation, or justification of cultural beliefs and practices, rather than to explain the causes of natural phenomena.

## 2. FRANZ BOAS ON FOLK TALES AND MYTHS

It is of interest to note in this connection that Boas found it difficult to define the scope of myth. "It is fairly clear," he states, "that stories are unhesitatingly classed as myths if they account for the origin of the world and if they may be said to have happened in a mythical period different from the one in which we now live. The difference is clearly recognized by many tribes, such as the North American Indians, the Andaman Islanders, and the native Australians." [12] A problem arises, however, when one attempts to distinguish between myths and folk tales, since the same tales or plots appear in both.

Boas attempted, therefore, to define "mythological concepts" while by-passing the difficult question of the classification of myths and folk tales. Thus, he explains:

Definition of mythological concepts is much easier than definition of mythological tales. Mythological concepts are the fundamental views of the constitution of the world and of its origin. These enter into tales relating to incidents in the lives of mythical beings, and into folk tales referring to the exploits and sufferings of our contemporaries, often of known individuals. Thus the African tells of encounters with ancestral ghosts and of the misdeeds of witches; the Koryak shaman recounts his fights with evil spirits; the European relates the incidents of the lives of the saints and dealings with the devil; the Oriental listens to stories of demons controlled by magic rings, and the American Indian to visits to the land of ghosts. In all these legends the mythological concepts appear as part and parcel of the tales.[13]

Boas does not explain why fundamental views of the constitution of the world are said to mythological, but we may infer, since he cites Wundt in a footnote, that it is because such concepts are supersensuous, or metaphysical. By contrast, folk tales are said to deal almost throughout "with events that may occur in human society, with human passions, virtues and vices."

The most important characteristic of mythological concepts is said to be personification (a point Tylor had made), yet tales involving personified animals are sometimes regarded as folk tales when the

[12] Boas, "Mythology and Folklore," in *General Anthropology*, ed. by Boas, pp. 609–10.

[13] *Ibid.*, p. 609; also Thompson, *The Folktale*, pp. 303, 389–90.

natives themselves do not take such stories seriously and recount them merely for entertainment. Tales dealing with the personification of natural phenomena, such as the sun and the moon, are, on the other hand, evaluated by Boas as myths. In other words, while all mythological concepts are personifications, either of animals or of natural phenomena, not all tales involving mythological concepts are myths. According to Boas, the only tales that are clearly mythological are those concerned with the personification of natural phenomena and referring to some prehistoric epoch. Folk tales, on the other hand, are to be considered as analogous to modern fiction or novelistic literature. "The free play of imagination operating with everyday experience is sufficient to account for their origin." Thus, folk tales may utilize mythological concepts without themselves being regarded, or interpreted, as myths.

Psychologically and from the perspective of the adherents of a given culture, the difference between mythical tales and folk tales is that the former are taken seriously, while the latter are not. As Boas puts it:

It would not be fair to assume that the myths dealing with the origin of the world or of the gift of arts and ceremonials to mankind were the result of a light play of imagination, as we suppose the rather insignificant animal tales to have been. The importance of the subject matter and the seriousness with which they are treated suggest that they are the result of thought about the origin of the world and of wonder about cultural achievements and the meaning of sacred rites. The only causality known in an anthropomorphic world is the one prevailing in human society, and thus it comes about that the incidents of human life that result in achievements are transferred to the mythical beings.[14]

Boas, unlike Malinowski, grants that myths have an explanatory function and are motivated in part by wonder and intellectual reflection. Myths are said to be taken seriously in the sense that they deal with subjects of the utmost importance to native life and constitute primitive man's beliefs as to the nature and origin of his world and the cosmic significance of his rites and customs.

Boas distinguishes sharply between the novelistic, fictional folk tale and the explanatory myth with which it happens to be associated. The relation between the folk tale, or novelistic plot, on the one hand, and the explanatory, mythological interpretation attached to it, on the other, is said to be "very loose." The same tale often appears associated with a great variety of explanatory myths, and this would seem to indicate that

[14] Boas, "Mythology and Folklore," in *General Anthropology*, p. 616.

the folk story has an independent existence and is prior to the mytho-logical, explanatory after-thoughts suggested by its contents.

Similarly, Boas distinguishes between rites or customs and the myth-ical interpretations associated with them. "The uniformity of many such rituals over large areas," he points out, "and the diversity of mytho-logical explanations shows clearly that the ritual itself is the stimulus for the formation of the myth. . . . The ritual existed, and the tale originated from the desire to account for it." [15] Just as the novelistic folk story, or plot, is held to be prior in time to the mythological inter-pretation associated with it, so rituals are thought to be prior to the variable, cultural myths which validate their origin and significance.

From this it would appear that according to Boas empirical, practical rites, customs, and folk tales preceded mythological interpretation and explanation. Mythological concepts and narratives are, so to speak, rationalizations introduced after folk tales, rites, and cultural arts had been invented and diffused. In this respect Boas' view may be under-stood as the antithesis of the classical evolutionary approach of Tylor and Wundt, both of whom presupposed that mythological thought preceded or was associated with empirical concepts from the beginning. Boas assumes implicitly that primitive man clearly distinguishes be-tween fictional, imaginary folk tales and empirical concepts, on the one hand, and supersensuous, metaphysical concepts and tales on the other. He is then left with the difficult problem of explaining how the novelistic plot became associated with a mythological interpretation. "The in-vestigation of the reason for this association," he admits, "is an attractive problem, the solution of which can only in part be surmised." [16]

Boas' dilemma may be summarized somewhat as follows: Though all attempts to differentiate between myths and folk tales on the basis of subject matter are bound to fail, since similar supersensuous, meta-physical concepts enter into both, yet cultural rituals and novelistic folk stories are said to precede the various mythological narratives with which they become associated. Myths, that is, are said to be rationaliza-tions or after-thoughts attached to rituals and folk tales. On this as-sumption, there would apparently be a clear, scientific basis for dis-tinguishing myths from folk tales—a thesis later developed by Mal-inowski. But if the association between empirical rituals and folk tales, on the one hand, and myths, on the other, is secondary, then the prob-

[15] *Ibid.*, p. 617.
[16] Boas, *The Mind of Primitive Man*, p. 242.

lem remains how they ever became associated in the first place. As Boas himself acknowledges, "The essential problem regarding the ultimate origin of mythologies remains—why human tales are preferably attached to animals, celestial bodies, and other personified phenomena of nature." [17] Furthermore, once it is granted that mythological concepts "enter into" folk tales, the problem whether folk tales precede myths or *vice versa* becomes meaningless.

### 3. THE PSYCHOCULTURAL APPROACH TO MYTH

From the perspective of the psychocultural approach advanced here, Boas' objection that the same tale could not be classed at one time as a myth and at another time as a folk tale is not insurmountable. Since the object of myth, as Tylor noted, varies with the social standard of possibility, it follows that a given tale may at one time be classed as myth and at another as a folk tale, depending upon the degree of credence attached to it by a given society. Lowie, in particular, has noted [18] that folk tales are sometimes utilized for purposes of etiological rationalization of rites and that priestly adaptation may convert fiction into sacred myth. Conversely, in the process of time myths can become folk tales, which may then be refashioned by the creative artist into great literature having lasting symbolic value for subsequent generations, for example, Goethe's *Faust*, Cervantes' *Don Quixote*, and Melville's *Moby Dick*.

Boas himself has noted that folk tales are taken lightly by their originators, while myths are taken seriously, but he interpreted this psychological observation in a static, fixed sense rather than from a changing, relativistic psychocultural perspective. By natives tales are taken seriously not because they are myths; they are evaluated by us as myths because they are, or were, taken seriously by those who recounted them. It is not only the nature of the metaphysical concepts involved or the distance of the prehistoric space-time in which the events narrated occurred which determines whether or not a given tale is to be regarded as a myth; it is rather the psychocultural attitude or degree of belief of those who recount them. Thus, the accepted belief or subjective truth of one epoch may become myth for the next. In all instances, it is the psychocultural context, rather than the subject matter, which determines how a given narrative is to be classified.

[17] Boas, "Mythology and Folk-Tales of the North American Indians," in *Anthropology in North America*, ed. by Franz Boas.
[18] Lowie, *Primitive Religion*.

According to my thesis, the term "belief" is an epistemically neutral term in the sense of being beyond truth and falsity. To say that one believes a given statement tells us nothing of its scientific or objective validity, that is, whether the given statement is in accordance with empirically established facts. But myth is not a scientifically neutral term; on the contrary, it is a value-charged term and implies a negative evaluation concerning the validity of a given narrative. In other words, myth is correlative to belief and implies a priori that the narrative or explanation described as mythological is not true or credible. It is important to note, furthermore, that a myth is evaluated as such only from the perspective of those who do not share the ideas and beliefs under consideration. From the perspective of those who accept the ideas and beliefs as true or valid, the latter are not myths at all. What we may regard as "myths" are, psychologically, charters of belief for those who accept them and live by them. Belief is essential to the acceptance of "myth" and accounts for its effectiveness in a given cultural context, but the very fact of belief implies that subjectively, that is, for the believer, the object of belief is not mythological. Hence, nonbelief in a given narrative, tradition, or explanation is essential for its evaluation as myth, just as belief in its truth and validity is essential for its acceptance as an effective element of culture. In this way, the distinction between belief, myth, and truth is retained, while the relativity of myth to belief and an accepted cultural standard of credibility is recognized.

We must distinguish, furthermore, between myth and superstition. Myth involves a belief of a special kind, namely, an incredible belief or the idea of a credible impossibility. A superstition, on the other hand, is a mode of fear based on some irrational or mythological belief and usually involves some taboo in practice. Myths may give rise to superstitions, and the latter may stimulate the invention of myths. Superstitions may, however, arise from any irrational association of ideas, whether speculative or empirical, such as the idea of a black cat as an omen of bad luck, and hence do not necessarily arise from mythical narratives or notions of the supernatural. Furthermore, since a superstition is essentially an irrational fear, it is to be distinguished from precritical folk beliefs in general, some of which may comprise elements of empirical knowledge. Some recent collections of "superstitions" apparently do not make this distinction.[19]

[19] De Lys, *A Treasury of American Superstitions.*

Since belief may be objectively either true or false, it follows that what a given individual regards as myth may reflect his own unbelief rather than objective truth, just as his subjective "truth" may be objective myth. In this sense myth is a function of cultural belief and unbelief. Since Nietzsche and Kierkegaard, many modern philosophers, theologians, and social scientists have tended to evaluate "truth" subjectively or "existentially" and to deny the validity of any objective metaphysical truth. In particular, moral values have been explained as functions and mythological rationalizations of a "will to power" on the part of social classes. Thus, the "transvaluation of all values" by Nietzsche has led many modern thinkers to regard traditional metaphysical and moral truths as a "mythology of dangerous ancient ideas." The term "myth" has become a term of abuse whereby to discredit the liberal, democratic tradition, with its rational "ascetic ideals" and belief in a common humanity. Instead, we have the "truth" of the new "supermen" which posits a new morality in the interests of political power. Contemporary political propaganda and the "cold war" between the East and the West provide many instances of this relativistic interpretation of myth.

The relativity of myth to belief in general renders intelligible the continuous change in the evaluation of a particular myth, or mythological system, to be found at different periods of culture history. The firm faith of one generation becomes the myth of the next. Thus, the Greek folk deities and religious traditions have become the myths of the classical scholars. Where belief is not guided by critical, self-correcting, scientific intelligence, the fortunes of a given myth vary from time to time and culture to culture, depending upon the changing psychocultural orientation of the society concerned. Thus, it may happen that what one society regards as mere fable or legend unworthy of credence may become the accepted faith, or dogma, of another. In the process of historical acculturation, it may be shown, many primitive religious traditions have become folktales, while the folktales of one culture have often been used to rationalize or validate the ritual and customs of another.

Objectively and normatively, however, myth is relative to established knowledge, and to this extent myth may be described as belief, usually expressed in narrative form, that is incompatible with scientific and rational knowledge. Insofar as knowledge is demonstrable and potentially universal, the category of myth may be said to refer, by comparison, to propositions and narratives which, though once accepted and believed, are no longer worthy of rational credence. For example, theories of disease which explain disease as due to evil spirits are mythological because they are incompatible with scientific medicine, not merely because they are no longer believed by civilized societies.

This explains why so many scientists and philosophers belittle and regret myth-making, although they recognize its great influence in sociocultural life. Insofar as it is acknowledged that there is a normative body of well-authenticated truth and that human reason is capable of distinguishing truth from falsity and fiction, responsible and mature minds will prefer objective truth and well-founded faith to fictions and myths, regardless of the latter's so-called pragmatic value. To regard myth as a neutral term beyond truth and falsity and to interpret the culture of scientific rationalism as if it also were based on myth, is to undermine the very basis of rational and scientific thought. From this perspective, the greatest myth of the twentieth-century is the identification of all cultural ideology with myth in the name of social science.

The position here taken may be contrasted with that of Robert MacIver. According to MacIver:

By *myths* we mean the value-impregnated beliefs and notions that men hold, that they live by and for. Every society is held together by a myth-system, a complex of dominating thought-forms that determines and sustains all its activities. All social relations, the very texture of human society, are myth-born and myth-sustained. . . . We use the word in an entirely neutral sense. Whether its content be revelation or superstition, insight or prejudice, is not here in question. We need a term that abjures all reference to truth or falsity. We include equally under the term "myth" the most penetrating philosophies of life, the most profound intimations of religion, the most subtle renditions of experience, along with the most grotesque imaginations of the most benighted savage. . . . Whatever valuational responses men give to the circumstances and trials of their lot, whatever conceptions guide their behavior, spur their ambitions or render existence tolerable—all alike fall within our ample category of myth.[20]

As against this thesis, I maintain that in the term "belief" we already have a neutral term indifferent to truth and falsity. Myth, on the other hand, by common usage is a value-charged term and implies a negative evaluation of the truth of a given belief. MacIver admits that myths

[20] MacIver, *The Web of Government*, pp. 4–5.

are "value-impregnated beliefs" and yet holds that they are neutral, or beyond truth and falsity. My point is that that it is not possible to separate the social and cultural values of myths from their truth-value. The force of a "myth" in a given culture is due to its uncritical acceptance by its adherents as true or valid for themselves; the moment this belief is questioned it becomes a myth and ceases to be effective as a guide to conduct. MacIver's use of the term "myth" blurs the distinction between philosophy, religion, and superstition.

A similar criticism applies to Kimball Young's statements concerning the relation of myth and ideology. In essential agreement with Malinowski, Young reasons that there is no difference in value between the "myths" and "legends" of primitive man and those of civilized man; both alike are imaginative interpretations of events designed to resolve some social crisis.[21] As Young has put it:

Myths and legends are considered true by the believers. We are conscious of our own myths and legends, not as strange or foreign stories devised for amusement, but as accounts of actual events and meanings. It is evident that savage myths and legends mean little to us largely because they are outside our culture.[22]

The commonly accepted thesis of Malinowski subscribed to by Young, namely, that myths are "charters of belief" whose function it is to validate custom and rite, seems to confuse the subjective perspective of the native with the objective perspective of the ethnologist. Insofar as given narratives are charters of belief they are not "myths" to those who accept these beliefs; they are myths only to those who do not acknowledge their validity. Malinowski was undoubtedly right in stressing the pragmatic, effective role of myths in primitive culture, but he overlooked the fact that the effectiveness of myths depends on their acceptance as true or valid, that is, on their not being treated as "myths" at all. It were better, therefore, to say that what we call myths are, in fact, charters of belief for those who accept them and live by them.

Young, like Malinowski, recognizes the relative character of myth, but fails to differentiate between myth and valid belief. He observes that myths and legends are considered true by the believers, but does not explain the difference between the myths of the believers and those of the unbelievers. According to Gomme, whom he quotes, "it is just this belief in the truth of the myth or legend which sets it distinctly

[21] Young, *Social Psychology*, p. 199.    [22] *Ibid.*, p. 200.

apart from romance or fiction." But the question still remains, how do we distinguish between "a true belief" and "belief in the truth of a myth?" For Young, as for Malinowski, all ideological beliefs are on the same level and all are equally mythic products of fantasy thinking invented to stabilize some critical situation. The question may be raised, however, what does belief contribute to myth? Is it essential for a myth to be believed in order to be a myth? If it is answered that belief is essential to myth, we are left with two kinds of myth, namely, myths which are believed and those which are not believed. The difficulty then remains how to distinguish credible and incredible myths.

In the last analysis, Young accepts an operational theory of fictions according to which the concepts of science, art, and religion are fictions devised to aid us in controlling practical problems. Thus he writes:

The most significant myths and legends emerge out of recurrent problems of adjustment to our physical and social-cultural world. They are part of our value system and are closely related to the devices of social control. The more common situations in which myths and legends have arisen and still arise involve religion and supernaturalism, economic matters and political problems. Much of what passes for history is loaded with myths and legends of various sorts, and writers have repeatedly tried to characterize whole epochs in terms of their basic myths or ideologies.[23]

Examples of potent ideological myths are the Christian dogma of the fall of man, the myths of economic utopias, such as that of Marx, the political myth of fascism, and the doctrine of social progress.

According to Young, the problem is not to eliminate myth but to regulate it so as to provide a stimulus for moral action and social idealism. As against those who would eliminate myth he writes:

Many earnest persons belittle or regret myth-making. They consider it foolish or pathological and somehow a bit devilish or evil. This very attitude is an illustration of the persistence of the eighteenth century cult of rationalism and of its myth that man is largely an intellectual, deliberate and scientific creature. . . . but myth and legend are as inevitable in human society and culture as are mechanical inventions and the use of rational instruments for bending the physical universe to our utilitarian purposes. . . . As we shall note, the problem is not to try to prevent heroics and myths and legends but to control them within a moral framework which will prevent their abuse in the hands of unscrupulous men. . . . We must remind ourselves that man does not live in a colorless universe of passive objectivity but in a subjective, emotionally toned world of attitudes and images, and that myth, ideology and legend determine his conduct more than does the purely physical universe.[24]

[23] *Ibid.*, p. 210.     [24] *Ibid.*, pp. 220–21.

Young's theory of myth as social fiction having pragmatic value for social control bears a close affinity also to Hans Vaihinger's *Philosophy of the "As If"* to which he refers. Vaihinger's basic thesis is that ideas are instruments for finding our way about more easily in the world and that "truth is merely the most expedient degree of error, and error the least expedient degree of ideation, of fiction." [25] This implies that the boundary between truth and error is not rigid, since truth is only the most expedient error. Historically, he finds that there is a process of development from myths, the products of the inventive imagination, to hypotheses, and finally to dogmas. Similarly, there is a regressive process which leads from dogmas, through hypotheses, to myths and fictions. The Greek folk deities were dogmas for the people, hypotheses for Aristotle, and fictions or myths for later thinkers.

Vaihinger's philosophy of the "As If" was the direct outcome of his study of Kant. According to Vaihinger, Kant had discovered that the categories of thought were fictions, but he obscured the point by attributing them to the ego as innate forms and by assuming a metaphysical "thing-in-itself" (*Ding an Sich*). In Friedrich Nietzsche, Vaihinger found the intellectual predecessor of his philosophy. Nietzsche had the courage of his convictions to proclaim that the will to appearance, to illusion, to deception is deeper, more metaphysical, than the will to truth. For Nietzsche, myth and illusion were of more value than truth for thought and life. As Vaihinger notes, Nietzsche admitted in his posthumous writing that his philosophy was an "inverted Platonism," according to which "living in illusion" was the ideal.

In sum, I have tried to show that there is a gradual and subtle process of thought which leads from the notion that myth is a neutral term beyond truth and falsity to the skeptical, pragmatic doctrine which reduces all ideology to myth and social delusion. Both MacIver and Young identify ideology and mythology, but the former is not prepared to reduce mythology to social fictions. For MacIver myths are epistemically neutral, but for Young they are noble fictions. According to the thesis which I am prepared to uphold, the term "belief" is epistemically neutral, but "myth" is not neutral. Nonbelief in a given tradition is essential to its interpretation as myth, just as belief is essential for its acceptance as true narrative.

Insofar as belief is founded on critical and scientific thought the type of objects placed in the category of myth remains fairly constant,

[25] Vaihinger, *The Philosophy of the 'As If,'* tr. by C. K. Ogden, p. 108.

although the number of such objects tends to increase with time.[26] Belief in demons and magicians is categorized as mythological, and there is little probability of any revision in our evaluation so long as we adhere to our scientific mode of thought. Similarly, the Ptolemaic theory in astronomy is now mythological and with the scientific knowledge now available it is likely to remain so. Historically, however, there is always the possibility that some of the scientific theories now found acceptable may turn out to have been erroneous or false, and in this sense science, in the process of self-correction, may condemn some of its own former doctrines as mythological. That is why the cautious scientist is inclined to view his theoretical speculations as hypothetical views subject to constant revision rather than as final, absolute truths. In the sphere of the social sciences, it would appear, there is now danger that in reducing ideology to mythology and in denying the objective validity of social values, science itself becomes a kind of mythology. The process of myth-making has turned back on itself to create the "myth of science" after pursuing the "science of myth."

According to the thesis which I have sought to maintain there is a sense in which the relativity of myth may be explained and also a sense in which the objective, normative evaluation may be retained. Insofar as myth is a function of belief and disbelief, it is relative to given sociocultural contexts in space and time. On the other hand, if we retain the concept of an ontological reality and an objective truth which it is the function of science to discover and approximate, then the category of myth refers to a class of beliefs which are now considered irrational or erroneous. In this latter sense the object of myth does not vary with the historical cultural context, but is transcultural, since the validity of scientific truth does not vary with the sociocultural context.

✓ I should distinguish, then, three categories of belief. First, there is scientific belief which may be verified. Secondly, there is myth which refers relatively to any belief which we discredit, although acceptable to others in the past or the present. Objectively and normatively, myth refers to belief incompatible with scientific fact. Thirdly, there is a sphere of belief which lies between science and myth. Religious beliefs, such as the belief in God, are neither scientific nor mythological. The concept of God is not a scientific concept, because it does not refer to an object which may be empirically verified. Neither does the con-

[26] Read Bain, "Man, the Myth-Maker," *Scientific Monthly*, LXV (1947), 61–69.

cept of God refer to a mythological entity, since there is nothing in scientific knowledge to disprove the existence of such a being. That is why religion is essentially the sphere of faith—faith which may be in accord with scientific knowledge, but may not be reduced to scientific truth or disproved by scientific knowledge. Some aspects of religious belief may be found to be incompatible with scientific knowledge, such as belief in a multitude of anthropomorphic gods constantly intervening in natural processes, and hence there is bound to be a close relation between historical religions and mythology. There may, in other words, be said to be a continuous growth in religious belief comparable to the development in human knowledge and experience in general. I see no valid ground, however, for setting up a narrow dichotomy, as the positivists are inclined to do, of science, on the one hand, and myth, superstition, and fiction, on the other. There is, I should say, a realm of rational belief which may be in accord with scientific knowledge and which goes beyond strict empirical verification. There are postulates of experience which we introduce to render experience intelligible and significant, and these are metascientific presuppositions which we can never verify empirically. Philosophy and religion belong in this general sphere.

### 4. MYTH, SYMBOLISM, AND DEGREES OF TRUTH

While all myths may be evaluated as incredible beliefs, there are, nevertheless, various degrees of truth in diverse types of myth. The great myths are those to which we moderns ascribe an implicit, or latent, symbolic truth-value which may never have been intended by their originators. The great myths lend themselves to a variety of symbolic interpretations, and their greatness lies precisely in their prolific suggestiveness for the creative imagination of the sensitive artist. Thus, although the narrative of Genesis concerning Adam and Eve and the forbidden fruit is regarded nowadays by critical scholars as mythological,[27] it still continues to have for them significant symbolic value as great literature, notwithstanding the fact that even the symbolic interpretations vary greatly—for example, the often conflicting "obvious" interpretations of the fall of man given by Freudians, Neo-Freudians, and Jungian psychoanalysts. I am inclined, therefore, to the view that there is no one single symbolic interpretation of a given myth which is necessarily the correct one and that all attempts at a

[27] Frazer, *Folklore in the Old Testament.*

monistic, "scientific" mythology designed to reduce all myths to a single type are bound to be discredited eventually. In their attempts to rationalize the symbolic significance of ancient myths, philosophers, theologians, ethnologists, folklorists, and psychoanalysts have sought for a single type of reality, or a single type of truth, underlying the variety of mythological expressions and thereby have only succeeded in inventing "scientific" myths of their own.

A historical survey of mythological theory reveals that there have been two basic approaches to the interpretation of myth, namely, the literal and the symbolic. For those who interpret myth literally, myth is understood either as an evolutionary mode of thought characteristic of the mind of primitive man, or else as a universal mode of thought originating in man's will to believe in the face of natural crises. On the other hand, there has been a strong tendency from ancient to modern times to interpret myth symbolically as referring to an esoteric reality other than, or in addition to, the apparent, exoteric reality.

It is important at this point to distinguish between allegory and myth. An allegory may be defined as a narrative consciously invented for the purpose of illustrating some philosophical truth. An allegory is, therefore, not to be taken literally, because its essential function is to symbolize a timeless truth suggested by the events it describes. A myth, by contrast, is a traditional narrative, considered by us as pseudohistorical, which is accepted by its adherents as literally true. A myth may have an esoteric, symbolic meaning in addition to the literal, exoteric meaning, but the latter is primary and constant, whereas the symbolic interpretation is highly variable and changes with the cultural context. Thus, modifying Robertson-Smith's and Boas's thesis, I agree that rite is more constant than the mythological interpretation associated with it, but from this it does not necessarily follow that rite preceded myth chronologically. It may well be that the association between rite and myth is synchronic, rite being the constant and myth the variable factor. Similarly, a narrative, such as a folktale, may have many symbolic, mythological interpretations associated with it in the course of its cultural diffusion, but its literal meaning and symbolic interpretation may be synchronic, the literal meaning remaining constant. My thesis does not require a chronological sequence from rite and literal narrative to symbolic allegorical interpretation, since such a historical sequence may not be demonstrable in all instances. Historically, it may be demonstrated that in the culture of the West there has been such a sequence from the literal to the allegorical interpretation of myth, but I am prepared to grant that there probably always has been some symbolic interpretation associated with mythical narrative. But where the narrative ceases to be taken literally, then myth is reduced to allegory and thereby ceases to be myth.

Historically, it may be shown that some allegories have been treated as myths by later generations, such as the Neo-Platonists, and conversely that myths have been reduced to allegories. The process works both ways, and there is, therefore, no necessary chronological sequence from myth to allegory. It is important, nevertheless, to keep in mind the categorical distinctiveness of allegory and myth and not to confuse the two categories. Otherwise, there is a tendency to reduce myth to allegory. This may be demonstrated by the recurrent attempts of scholars, particularly philosophers, to explain away the traditional, literal significance of religious scriptures and to retain only an allegorical, poetic interpretation. In this way traditional religion is reduced to moral truth, and religious faith in the literal, historical sense ceases to function, although lip service continues to be paid to the traditional formulas.

The culture of ancient Greece provides most interesting examples of the historic relations between allegory and myths. On the one hand, there were the poets and the dramatists who systematized and gave artistic expression to the traditional myths of gods and heroes. On the other hand, there were the critical philosophers and sophists who found it difficult to accept the folk myths as given literally and sought either to reinterpret them so as to provide them with a more rational meaning, or else to modify them radically so as to eliminate the irrational and immoral elements. It was, indeed, a revolutionary event in the history of human culture when the Greek philosophers of the sixth century first began to question the folk traditions and to appeal to *logos* against *mythos*. A struggle ensued between the mythopoeic poets and the critical philosophers in which the latter were often held up to ridicule. The dialogues of Plato represent a dramatic expression of this conflict between the mythological poets and the rationalistic philosophers in which Plato takes his revenge upon the myth-makers by excluding them from his ideal state.

It is of interest to note in this connection that Plato, notwithstanding his opposition to the mythological poets, endeavored to retain as much of the theological myth of Homer as he thought compatible with sound reason and morality and even considered inventing a few "noble fictions" for the instruction of the children. Furthermore, it should be noted, Plato systematically employed fictional, allegorical narratives of his own for the purpose of illustrating some abstract intellectual truth or epistemic distinction. The famous allegory of the cave in the *Republic* is an instance of his poetic and dramatic use of allegory in the interests of philosophic analysis.

Thus, Plato distinguished between myth and allegory. A myth was a traditional narrative about the gods or some culture hero which purported to give instruction concerning the life of the gods and their relations to men. An allegory, by contrast, was a fictional narrative with symbolic meaning; it was deliberately invented for its symbolic truth and was not intended to be taken literally. Plato was not opposed to poetry and the arts, but insisted that they were to be subservient to philosophical and scientific truth. Poets, left to themselves, were inclined to be carried away by their emotions and imagination and therefore required the supervision of an intellectual class in order that the minds of young people should not be corrupted.[28]

The work of Aristotle furnishes us with another example of how a critical philosopher attempted to reconcile traditional myth with rational science and metaphysics. The following passage is of special interest:

Our forefathers in the most remote ages have handed down to us their posterity a tradition, in the form of a myth, that these substances [the stars] are gods and that the divine encloses the whole of nature. The rest of the tradition has been added later in mythical form with a view to the persuasion of the multitude and to its legal and utilitarian expediency; they say these gods are in the form of men or like some of the other animals, and they say other things consequent on and similar to these which we have mentioned. But if we were to separate the first point from these additions and take it alone— that they thought the first substances to be gods, we must regard this as an inspired utterance, and reflect that, while probably each art and science has often been developed as far as possible and has again perished, these opinions have been preserved until the present, like relics of the ancient treasure. Only thus far, then, is the opinion of our ancestors and our earliest predecessors clear to us.[29]

Here, within the limits of a single paragraph, we find in nuclear form, some of the basic suggestions for the interpretation of myth which

[28] See Bidney, "The Philosophical Anthropology of Ernst Cassirer," in *The Philosophy of Ernst Cassirer*, pp. 465–544.
[29] Aristotle, *Metaphysics*, 1075–76.

have been developed in the subsequent history of thought. Ancient myth is thought to contain a rational, scientific element as well as an irrational, corrupt element added for the purpose of expediency in order to persuade the multitude. The purely anthropomorphic narratives of the gods are said to be later additions suited to the mentality of the folk and the requirements of local custom. Thus, Aristotle reconciles philosophy and mythology by treating myth both as primitive symbolic philosophy and as pragmatic social fiction.

The Neo-Platonic and Stoic philosophers continued the symbolic interpretation of myth, but tended to reduce myth to allegory. That is, the literal narrative was explained away and only the symbolic, philosophic interpretation was retained. They sought to identify the various Greek deities with the primary cosmic elements of their philosophy. Thus, whereas Plato endeavored to retain the literal meaning of the sacred myths and invented fictional allegories of his own to exemplify basic philosophical insights, the Stoics and Neo-Platonists attempted uncritically to reinterpret the myths so as to read into them their own philosophy of nature. In the early centuries of this era pagans, Jews, and Christians vied with one another in providing allegorical interpretations of their respective myths, each maintaining that their own traditions contained an absolute esoteric truth. What Sallustius [30] did for the Roman mythology, Philo the Neo-Platonist did for the Old Testament.[31]

The allegorical method of interpreting myths has continued to attract philosophers, linguists, and ethnologists in modern times as well. Francis Bacon, the prophet of modern science, who did so much to discredit traditional Greek and scholastic philosophy, sought to rehabilitate Greek mythology as the repository of an esoteric wisdom. According to Bacon, the mythological poets expressed allegorically and in veiled form, a true wisdom which later philosophical speculation corrupted. It is not surprising to find, however, that the profound philosophical truths which he presumes to have discovered in the Greek myths turn out to be nothing other than Bacon's own materialistic philosophy of science and truisms of ethics and education.[32] In this respect Aristotle, whom Bacon criticized so severely, appears to have been much more

---

[30] Sallustius, "On the Gods and the World," in Murray, *Five Stages of Greek Religion.*

[31] Philo, *On the Account of the World's Creation Given by Moses,* tr. by Colson and Whitaker.

[32] Bacon, *The Wisdom of the Ancients; Advancement of Learning.*

cautious and critical. Aristotle was prepared to grant that some elements of myth, such as the belief that the stars were divine, contained philosophic truth, but he was careful to suggest that he considered the anthropomorphic tales of the gods as later additions having no philosophical value. Bacon, however, is prepared to accept the Greek myths in their entirety, finding some ingenious rational allegory hidden beneath every irrational legend. As Tylor has remarked, "the fault of the rationalizer lay in taking allegory beyond its proper action and applying it as a universal solvent to reduce dark stories to transparent sense." [33]

In his *New Science* Giambattista Vico sought to establish a science of ethnohistory which would apply to the "civil affairs" of mankind the scientific method which Bacon thought to apply to the realm of nature. [34] Like Bacon, Vico also maintains that myth contains an essential symbolic truth, but differs from him in that the truth of myth is said to be historical rather than philosophical. "For the wisdom of the ancients was the vulgar wisdom of the lawgivers who founded the human race, not the esoteric wisdom of great and rare philosophers." [35] According to Vico, "the fables in their origin were true and severe narrations (whence *mythos*, fable, was defined as *vera narratio*). But because for the most part they were originally monstrous, they were later misappropriated, then altered, subsequently became improbable, after that obscure, then scandalous and finally incredible." [36] The first fables were histories, and the poets must be considered the first historians of the nations. [37]

In order to rediscover the historical reality behind the later versions of primitive myth, Vico, as did Bacon, resorts to allegorical interpretation. His method of interpretation may be described as "ethnic Euhemerism," since he attempts to reduce the culture heroes of myth to class concepts, or symbols, of the society which they represented at a given period of history. Even the gods of classic myth are only symbols of sociocultural conditions. Thus, Homer is said to be "an idea or a heroic character of Grecian men insofar as they told their history in song." [38] Homer's epic poems are to be considered as "treasure stores of the customs of early Greece," rather than as legendary tales of culture heroes and gods. [39] When, for example, the myth states that Vulcan split the

---

[33] Tylor, *Primitive Culture*, Vol. I, ch. viii.
[34] Vico, *The New Science*, tr. by Bergin and Fisch, #163.
[35] *Ibid.*, #384.  [36] *Ibid.*, #814.  [37] *Ibid.*, #817, #820.
[38] *Ibid.*, #873.  [39] *Ibid.*, #904.

forehead of Jove with an ax, whence sprang Minerva, it really meant
to signify that the multitude of *famuli* practicing servile arts broke the
rule of the patricians or heroes.[40]

Vico appreciated the cultural value of myths as containing valuable
historic records of the evolution of human thought and social institutions. But instead of treating myth empirically and literally as an expression of given historical cultures, he proceeded to interpret myth
allegorically, as if it were nothing but a vehicle for the expression of
ethnohistoric facts. Thus, notwithstanding his criticism of the philosophers who thought to find esoteric philosophic wisdom in myth, Vico
followed their rationalistic, allegorical approach in seeking to abstract
historic and ethnic truth from the same sources. He confused the objective, ethnological value of myth as a record of primitive thought,
with its subjective, symbolic value for the critical mind which could
not take the myths literally.

## 5. MYTH, POETRY, AND ROMANTICISM

Vico's ethnohistorical evaluation of myth was not in harmony with
the rationalistic and critical approach of the eighteenth century, which
was inclined to evaluate myth negatively as mere superstition, or deceit.
Vico's thought may be said to have by-passed the eighteenth century
and to have exercised its full influence during the nineteenth century
in the development of romanticism. Through Herder and Goethe, his
appreciation of myth as a source of prehistory and of linguistic etymol-
ogy as a key to culture history led to a new approach to the study of
history as essentially an organic process subject to natural stages of
development.

With the development of romanticism, myth was evaluated as essentially a poetic expression, and poetic truth was identified with myth.
Myth was appreciated not only for is ethnohistoric value but also for
its intrinsic positive value as a vehicle of expression of poetic truth.
In complete antithesis to the critical rationalism of the Age of Enlightenment, the romanticists put myth at the top of the cultural disciplines as an independent source of artistic truth-values, as well as a key
to the understanding of a people's culture. As Ernst Cassirer has stated:

According to this metaphysical conception the *value* of myth is completely
changed. To all the thinkers of the Enlightenment myth had been a barbarous thing, a strange and uncouth mass of confused ideas and gross super-

[40] *Ibid.*, #589.

stitions, a mere monstrosity. Between myth and philosophy there could be no point of contact. Myth ends where philosophy begins—as darkness gives way to the rising sun. This view undergoes a radical change as soon as we pass to the romantic philosophers. In the system of these philosophers myth becomes not only a subject of the highest intellectual interest but also a subject of awe and veneration. It is regarded as the mainspring of human culture. Art, history, and poetry originate in myth. A philosophy which overlooks or neglects this origin is declared to be shallow and inadequate. It was one of the principal aims of Schelling's system to give myth its right and legitimate place in human civilization. In his works we find for the first time a *philosophy of mythology* side by side with his philosophy of nature, history and art. Eventually all his interest seems to be concentrated upon this problem. Instead of being the opposite of philosophic thought myth has become its ally; and, in a sense, its consummation.[41]

For the romantic poet, myth served as a model of poetic expression and indicated the type of symbolic language which the poet was to cultivate. As opposed to the critical idealism of Kant, Novalis, in agreement with Schlegel and Schelling, put forth the concept of "magic idealism" in which feeling, rather than intellectually clear concepts, formed the basis of thought.[42] In the historical idealism of Ernst Cassirer an attempt was made to synthesize the categorial, critical approach of Kant with the historical, evolutionary perspective of the romanticists and ethnologists. Cassirer recognized myth as an autonomous form, or organ, of symbolic expression of the human spirit which manifested in the course of its historic development the free, creative power of the human imagination and served as a mainspring for the development of human thought in general.[43] For Cassirer, as for the romantic philosophers in general, history was the process of the progressive, self-revelation of spirit, but the former limited himself, as did the positivists, to empirical analysis of the achievements of the human spirit and did not venture to discern the mind of "absolute spirit" as did Schelling, Hegel, and the romantic mythologists who followed them.[44]

### 6. MYTH, POETRY, AND RELIGION

As may be gathered from the preceding analysis, the concept of the symbolic character of myth is equivocal. Historically, myths were said to be "symbolic" because they were thought to refer to esoteric

[41] Cassirer, *The Myth of the State*, pp. 182–83.
[42] *Ibid.*, p. 183.
[43] See Bidney, "The Philosophical Anthropology of Ernst Cassirer," in *The Philosophy of Ernst Cassirer*, ed. by P. A. Schilpp.
[44] Dawson, *Religion and Culture*, p. 14.

cosmic metaphysical forces and powers other than the phenomenal, imaginary beings explicitly mentioned in the narratives. In the philosophy of romanticism and in historical idealism, myths are said to be "symbolic" in the linguistic sense that they are direct expressions or representations of thought comparable to other linguistic symbols. On this assumption, there are no transcendental, ontological forms of reality other than the thought-forms which the myth may be said to symbolize. A myth is symbolic because it comprises a special type of linguistic symbol whereby the human mind, or spirit, expresses itself. Its symbolic value is inherent in is subjective meaning. The mythic symbols may be thought of as "free-floating" forms of thought which require no reference beyond themselves to be intelligible. These symbol-forms have only an ideal reality as expressions of thought and do not refer to substantial forms of reality other than themselves. Hence, the "truth" of myth is something inherent in itself which may be intuited by the creative imagination and sympathetic understanding. Mythic truth is independent of scientific verification and demonstration. Mythic truth is poetic truth and is not subject to the same criteria as is scientific truth.

The problem of the interrelation of factual and symbolic truth in myth may be pointed up by reference to the following statement by Susanne K. Langer.

In a book called *La genese des mythes,* A. H. Krappe declares categorically that myths are made up out of whole cloth by poets, are purely aesthetic productions, and are not believed unless they happen to be incorporated in some sacred book. But this is to confuse the myth-making stage of thought with the literal stage. Belief and doubt belong essentially to the latter; the myth-making consciousness knows only the appeal of ideas, and uses or forgets them. Only the development of literal-mindedness throws doubt upon them and raises the question of religious *belief*. Those great conceptions which can only dawn on us in a vast poetic symbolism are not propositions to which one says yea or nay; but neither are they literary toys of a mind that "knows better." The Homeric Greeks probably did not "believe in" Apollo as an American fundamentalist "believes in" Jonah and the whale, yet Apollo was not a literary fancy, a pure figment, to Homer as he was to Milton. He was one of the prime realities—the Sun, the God, the Spirit from which men received inspirations. Whether any one "believed" in all his deeds and amours does not matter; they were expressions of his character and seemed perfectly rational. Surely the Greeks believed in their gods just as we believe in ours; but they had no dogma concerning the gods, because in the average mind no matter-of-fact doubts of divine story had yet arisen, to cloud the significance of those remote or invisible beings. Common sense had never asserted itself *against* such stories to make them look like fairytales or suggest that they are figures of speech. They were *figures of thought,* and the only figures that really bold and creative thought knew.[45]

Here the author distinguishes between fictions, literal or factual truth, and symbolic, poetic, mythological truth. Myths are said to be figures of thought, not mere figures of speech, representing symbolic truth only. The moment one raises the question of the literal or factual worth of myth, it ceases to function as myth and gives way to philosophy and science. Belief, according to Miss Langer, is not essential to myth; belief pertains only to literal, factual truth. Myths are expressions of a poetic mode of thought prior to the development of rational, discursive thought. "The first inquiry as to the literal truth of a myth marks the change from poetic to discursive thinking. As soon as the interest in factual values awakes, the mythical mode of world-envisagement is on the wane." [46]

I see no basis, however, for Miss Langer's statement that the Homeric Greeks probably did not believe in Apollo in a literal sense. It seems to me that she is inclined to attribute to the ancient Greeks a degree of philosophical sophistication which the common folk never possessed. What we now regard as myths were not myths to the Greeks at all, but traditional religious narratives which were accepted literally and formed the validation for their rites and religious institutions. Otherwise, one cannot explain the conflict between philosophy and religion in classic Greek culture.

I am in agreement with Langer's argument, as against Krappe's position, that myths are not merely poetic fictions created by ancient poets, since the poets themselves utilized ancient traditions which were common knowledge among the folk. On the other hand, I hold that it is indeed significant to raise the question as to the factual truth and credibility of a narrative, as the Greek philosophers did, since otherwise one has no means of distinguishing true narrative and tradition from false and fictitious legends. Thus, myths are neither beyond factual truth nor merely symbolic poetry or poetic religion. If the mythical figures of thought symbolize a reality other than themselves, then it is significant to ask what is the philosophical basis for belief in the existence of this form of reality. Langer would set up a provisional category of symbolic, religious truth which is between fiction and factual

[45] Langer, *Philosophy in a New Key,* pp. 158–59.
[46] *Ibid.,* p. 164.

truth. I agree that religious belief is to be distinguished from scientific knowledge, on the one hand, and pure fiction, on the other. But I maintain that religion is not to be identified with poetic vision and that the truth or falsity of religious belief is a highly pertinent matter which ought not to be dismissed lightly.

According to Langer,

there is the silly conflict of religion and science, in which science must triumph, not because what it says about religion is just, but because religion rests on a young and provisional form of thought, to which philosophy of nature—proudly called "science" or "knowledge"—must succeed if thinking is to go on. There must be a rationalistic period from this point onward. Some day when the vision is totally rationalized, the ideas exploited and exhausted, there will be another vision, a new mythology.[47]

I do not think that the history of the conflict between religion and science ought to be dismissed as "silly," as if there were no problem there at all. Insofar as religious belief has been incompatible with scientific knowledge such conflict was inevitable and necessary. The conflict is futile only to the extent that partisans of science reject totally the validity of religious experience and partisans of religion presume to dictate what should be accepted as true concerning the order of nature. To reduce religious belief to the level of poetic vision, to a provisional mode of thought which rational thought is bound to supersede, is to explain away its prime significance and validity for the religious believer.

Another example of a similar approach to the problem of myth and symbolic, poetic truth is to be found in Santayana's essays on *Poetry and Religion*. For Santayana religion is a kind of poetry that expresses moral values and reacts beneficently upon life.[48] While the sincere believer acceps the literal and empirical reality of all that his sacred scriptures contain, the philosopher may accept a given religious tradition and epic, such as the Christian epic, only as the poetic transformation of an experience.[49] For Santayana what is significant in a given historical religion, such as Christianity, is its allegorical and moral significance, not its literal dogma. "Poetry is called religion when it intervenes in life." Religion is deflected from its course when it is confused with a record of facts or of natural laws, and poetry is arrested in its development if it remains an unmeaning play of fancy without relevance to

[47] *Ibid.*, pp. 164–65.
[48] Santayana, *Poetry and Religion*, p. 105.
[49] *Ibid.*, p. 106.

the ideals and purposes of life.[50] Thus, the position expressed in Langer's work turns out to be substantially identical with that of Santayana, although the latter grants that the common adherents of a historical religion, such as the Greek religion, believed in the literal and factual truth of their epics or myths.

In his scholarly work *The Myths of Plato* J. A. Stewart arrives at a similar evaluation of myth and poetry from a Kantian point of view. According to Stewart, "the essential charm of all Poetry, for the sake of which in the last resort it exists, lies in its power of inducing, satisfying, and regulating what may be called Transcendental Feeling, especially that form of Transcendental Feeling which manifests itself as a solemn sense of Timeless Being." [51] This transcendental feeling is manifested normally as faith in the eternal values of life. Since myths in general, and the Platonic myths in particular, evoke this transcendental feeling, Stewart is inclined to identify myth and poetry. The Platonic myths are said to be "dreams expressive of Transcendental Feeling, told in such a manner and such a context that the telling of them regulates, for the service of conduct and science, the feeling expressed." [52] Unlike Santayana and Langer, Stewart does not isolate the object of myth from that of science, but, following Kant, he regards the object of myth as an "idea of reason" not given by scientific knowledge and yet necessary as a postulate of thought which validates our human aspirations and ideals. We must act "as if" there were such objects, even though they are not to be verified by scientific experience. Myth, so understood, is in the service of science, and yet goes beyond scientific knowledge. This, according to Stewart, was the function of myth in the thought of Plato, and that is why Plato constantly resorted to myths and allegories in order to illustrate his philosophical speculations. "Plato's Myths induce and regulate Transcendental Feeling for the service of conduct and knowledge by setting forth the *a priori* conditions of conduct and knowledge." [53]

In evaluating Stewart's argument, I should say that he was reading too much of Kant into Plato. Furthermore, Stewart does not differentiate, as Plato did, between myth and allegory. Plato used allegories and tales to illustrate some basic philosophic thesis, but he did not attempt to interpret the traditional religious myths "as if" they were philosophical allegories. It is true that, in the third book of the *Republic*

[50] *Ibid.*, pp. v, vi.
[52] *Ibid.*, p. 42.

[51] Stewart, *The Myths of Plato*, p. 22.
[53] *Ibid.*, p. 49.

Plato does refer to myths as "noble fictions" suitable for the instruction of the young, but then he is careful to distinguish his censored and revised "myths" from the traditionally accepted tales. Stewart's interpretation of "myth" in Plato is reminiscent of the approach of Vaihinger, since, as we have seen, the latter also derives from Kant the principle of the "as if" (*als ob*) as an essential postulate of reason. In view of the historical fact that Plato's epistemology and metaphysics differ so radically from the critical idealism of Kant, it is far-fetched to identify the function of myth in Plato with its possible, pragmatic function in the Kantian system. In Plato "myths," or rather, allegories, were employed as logical fictions to illustrate philosophic suggestions tentatively submitted; they were not meant as a warrant of faith or transcendental guide to conduct.

It is implicitly assumed by the aforementioned writers that poetic truth and scientific truth pertain to disparate categories of thought and that the two are not connected. Poetic truth is for them, as for the romanticists in general, identified with myth and is thought of as a product of the imagination whose function it is to evoke transcendental feelings concerning the ultimate meaning and values of life. Poetic truth is moral truth having pragmatic value for life; like myth, it is independent of factual or scientific truth. Thus, Dante's *Divine Comedy* and Milton's *Paradise Lost* are considered Christian poetic myths, comparable to the Homeric myths, because they are products of the creative imagination of great poets and deal with the themes of human origin and destiny.

My own position is that poetry, myth, and religious belief are not to be reduced to, or identified with, one another. Dante's *Divine Comedy* is not a myth, comparable to the Homeric myths, simply because of its subject matter. A given religious belief, whether in poetic form or not, becomes mythological for the skeptic who questions its validity. Similarly, poetry is mythological if one questions the beliefs expressed therein. For Dante, however, the *Divine Comedy* was not a myth, because he accepted the validity of the Christian faith on which he based it; for him the poem was an artistic, imaginative expression of a fundamental religious truth warranted by divine revelation. It is true, he also intended that his poem be understood allegorically as well as literally. But Dante, as did Plato, distinguished allegory from myth, since allegory was a commonly accepted method of dramatizing religious truth. In sum, the poem of Dante is not to be regarded as a myth simply because it expresses a moral truth in imaginative form; it is a myth only for those who question the underlying Christian faith of Dante concerning the fall of man and the relation of God to man in history.

In a discussion of "Dante and Myth" [54] Charles S. Singleton characterizes Dante's great poem as a myth. The *Divine Comedy* is said to be a myth because it is a "true lie," a poem based on religious faith and yet fictional in that it purports to describe a reality which the poet has only imagined. A significant myth is "faith seeking vision," the vision of an objective order of things in its goodness and rightness. Genesis, Plato, and Dante provide examples of poetic-religious myths; in each instance faith precedes and vision follows. "If Plato had recognized as the truth what Dante embraces as the truth, and if he could have known Dante, he would surely have found him *his* poet."

Singleton apparently identifies allegory and myth, although Plato and Dante did not. The *Divine Comedy* is an allegorical poem consciously constructed for the purpose of expressing literally and imaginatively Dante's vision of the state of souls after death and at the same time symbolically, or anagogically, his belief in divine retribution. Dante accepts literally the truth of the existence of souls after death and of the ensuing divine judgment; the imaginative elaboration of this basic faith does not convert the poem into a "true lie." A deliberate fiction is not a lie unless it is intended to deceive, and Dante certainly intended no deception. Dante is not saying that divine retribution is to be taught "as if" it were true because of its pragmatic value in regulating conduct; on the contrary, he accepts the truth of this tradition on faith and imagines the state of sinners afterward. This is the antithesis of the deliberate "noble fictions" which Plato suggested as suitable for the education of the young in the third book of his *Republic*. In sum, I stress the point that in myth there is vision seeking faith; in allegory there is faith seeking vision. Far from being identical, myth and allegory are complementary.

Singleton's interpretation, as do Santayana's and Langer's, puts all faiths on an equal level and rates all religious belief, past or present, as equally mythological. This implies a relativistic theory of religious truth as a function of faith. Yet in speaking of "the true lie" and the "untrue lie" he also implies that there is an objective, normative truth which the poet may know. Myth, as is religion, is said to be based on the presupposition of the identity of thought and being and to involve

[54] Singleton, "Dante and Myth," *Journal of the History of Ideas*, X, 482–502.

belief in the possibility of transcending the world of history and change. That is why he evaluates myth positively as an essential of human culture akin to poetry and religion. Myth presupposes a timeless truth known by faith and envisaged by the poet.

We are, then, confronted with these alternatives: If religious, metaphysical truth is a relative function of faith, then all faiths are equally valid, since their validity is independent of their philosophical, or rational, credibility. If, on the other hand, religious and metaphysical truths are objective and normative and may be known by the poet, then we must differentiate valid from invalid faith. On the latter assumption, we must set up two categories of myth, namely, myth based on valid faith and myth demonstrably false and invalid. Singleton apparently employs the term "myth" to refer to the first category of myth, namely, to myth as involving a true faith in an objective order of values. Nevertheless, in classing Dante with Plato and Homer he also implies a purely relativistic notion of faith and a relativistic theory of myth. Singleton wished to have it both ways at once: myth is said to exemplify a timeless symbolic truth and yet to remain, in part, a lie. Hence, he describes myth as a "true lie." My conclusion is that he confused myth, allegory, and religion.

Among contemporary philosophers, Ernst Cassirer has been most concerned with the problem of myth and has undoubtedly influenced philosophical thought in this connection. According to Cassirer, myth, religion, and art were historicaly very closely connected, but tended to develop independently in the course of cultural evolution. From a functional perspective he maintains that art, such as poetry, and myth differ in that the artist is indifferent to the existence or nonexistence of his object, whereas "in mythical imagination there is always implied an act of *belief*." "Without belief in the reality of its object, myth would lose its ground." [55] In art there is always an element of make-believe, of conscious or unconscious fiction, which is lacking in genuine myth. That is why Cassirer considers the Platonic "myths" not genuine, since Plato created them in an entirely free spirit. "Genuine myth does not possess this philosophical freedom; for the images in which it lives are not *known* as images. They are not regarded as symbols but as realities." [56] Thus, for Cassirer an art of myth-making is a contradiction in terms, and that is the basic reason why he does not identify the poetic

[55] *An Essay on Man,* p. 75.

[56] *Myth of the State,* p. 47; see also Müller, *Introduction to a Scientific System of Mythology,* pp. 51–52. Cassirer was apparently following Müller rather closely on this point.

with mythic imagination. In this respect, therefore, his position differs radically from that of Santayana and Langer, both of whom tend to identify the function of myth with that of poetry.

Cassirer recognizes, however, a close affinity between the language of poetry and that of myth. In both types of symbolism one expresses the "physiognomic characters" of objects and evaluates them emotionally and dramatically as conflicting powers which affect the welfare of man.[57] This mode of experiencing nature continues to retain its anthropological value in spite of the ideal of truth introduced by science, which denies to myth any objective or cosmological value. The physiognomic characters attributed to objects by the mythic and poetic imagination retain their reality in social life.[58] Cassirer is, therefore, opposed to any attempt to reduce myth to scientific allegorical truth; the language and function of myth and science have nothing in common.

Cassirer recognizes the closest affinity between myth and religion. Both myth and religion originate in feeling, and their common function is to promote a feeling of the solidarity and unity of all forms of life. "To mythical and religious feeling nature becomes one great society, the *society of life.*" [59] "Religion and myth begin with the awareness of the universality and fundamental identity of life." [60] This presupposes that the common object of myth and religion is metaphysical and involves an internal, essential interrelatedness of all forms of life which renders "the law of metamorphosis" intelligible.[61]

On the other hand, Cassirer finds himself in complete agreement with the sociological school of Durkheim on the proposition that "society is the true model of myth." [62] On this assumption, or premise, the object of myth is the social, religious rite. Hence, following Robertson-Smith's thesis as developed in *The Religion of the Semites,* Cassirer now accepts the maxim that in order to understand myth, we must begin with the study of rites.[63] Rite is a more fundamental element in man's religious life than myth, and the latter merely serves to rationalize and symbolize the former. "Myth is the *epic* element in primitive religious life; rite is the *dramatic* element." [64] Myths are nothing but the interpretations of rites. This explains why Cassirer does not find himself in sympathy with any theories, such as that of Tylor, which tend to

[57] *Essay on Man,* pp. 76–77.
[58] *Ibid.,* p. 77.
[59] *Ibid.,* p. 83.
[60] *Myth of the State,* p. 37.
[61] *Essay on Man,* p. 81.
[62] *Ibid.,* p. 79.
[63] *Myth of the State,* p. 24.
[64] *Ibid.,* p. 28.

describe myth as a savage philosophy. For Cassirer myth involves predominantly an emotional rather than intellectual response; it is a means of representing and expressing emotions in symbolic forms. That is why he finds Malinowski's approach so congenial and repeatedly quotes him with approval.[65] In myth man organizes and expresses his hopes and fears and finds solace in explaining away and denying death.[66]

Cassirer saw no contradiction or incompatibility in following simultaneously both a metaphysical and a sociological approach. According to the metaphysical approach, there is some intellectual motivation in myth and religion and he therefore speaks of the evolution of religious thought and of progress in the development of individual, social, and moral consciousness. On this basis "myth is from its very beginning potential religion," [67] but "religious sympathy is of a different kind from the mythical and magical. It gives scope for a new feeling, that of individuality." [68] Cassirer was, apparently, more influenced by Bergson's *The Two Sources of Morality and Religion* than his critical comments upon it would lead one to believe. For him, as for Bergson, the higher ethical religions are expressions of a new positive ideal of human freedom and of a positive power of inspiration and aspiration.[69]

On the other hand, insofar as Cassirer follows the sociological approach of Durkheim and Malinowski, he tends to identify myth and religion in their origin and present function. Myth is said to rationalize and validate ritual and to organize man's hopes and fears. In this respect religion remains "indissolubly connected and penetrated with mythical elements" throughout the whole course of its history.[70] On this premise there can be no progress in religious thought, any more than one can speak of progress in religious rites and the myths that symbolize them. The idea of progress involves some objective criterion of truth and moral values in relation to which religion may be compared, but such an objective, ontological standard is denied on principle by the sociological approach. That is why I have been led to the conclusion that Cassirer's philosophical thought on religion and mythology is inherently incoherent and that he has attempted to combine two antithetical approaches to the evaluation of myth and religion.[71]

[65] *Essay on Man*, pp. 74–75, 80; *Myth of the State*, p. 48.
[66] *Myth of the State*, pp. 48–49.      [67] *Essay on Man*, p. 87.
[68] *Ibid.*, pp. 95–96.          [69] *Ibid.*, p. 108.
[70] *Ibid.*, p. 87.
[71] See also Bidney, "The Philosophical Anthropology of Ernst Cassirer," in *The Philosophy of Ernst Cassirer*, ed. by P. A. Schilpp.

### 7. MYTH AND SYMBOLISM IN FREUDIAN PSYCHOANALYTICAL THEORY

At the beginning of the previous section I contrasted two conceptions of symbolism with reference to myth, namely, the symbol as referring to an ontological, metaphysical reality and the symbol as a free-floating form of thought whose meaning is inherent in itself. According to the latter meaning, we have found, myths were said to symbolize certain moral and religious values whose validity was independent of philosophic truth and scientific fact.

When we examine the presuppositions of Freud's psychoanalytical theory we find that myth has a symbolic value also, but the reality which is symbolized is psychological and ethnohistorical. The symbol in dreams and in myth is regressive, and its significance is determined by the genetic and ethnohistorical experiences of the individual and the race.[72] Freud has fused a symbolic interpretation of the Oedipus myth of Sophocles with a Darwinian, ethnological myth of his own invention to account for the universal presence in the unconscious mind of man of an "Oedipus complex."

In brief, as outlined in *Totem and Taboo* his position may be summarized as follows: Following suggestions of Darwin and Robertson Smith, Freud assumes that primitive man lived with his fellows in a "primal horde," wherein a jealous father kept all the females for himself and drove away the growing sons. "One day" the expelled brothers slew and ate the father, as "cannibalistic savages" are wont to do. The totem feast is the repetition and commemoration of this first criminal act, which marked the beginning of social organization, moral restrictions, and religion.[73] Thus, they created the two fundamental taboos of totemism out of a sense of guilt, namely, the sacredness of the totem and exogamy. Murder and incest, the two basic crimes of primitive society, correspond with the two repressed wishes of the Oedipus complex. The inherited Oedipus complex, in turn, rests on the Lamarckian assumption of the inheritance of acquired, historical traits.

Stanch followers of Freud, such as Geza Roheim, have been inclined to question the scientific validity of Freud's hypothesis of the origin of totemism and of the phylogenetic, ethnohistorical basis of the

[72] See Chapter 5.

[73] Freud, "Totem and Taboo," in his *The Basic Writings of Sigmund Freud*, pp. 915–16.

Oedipus complex.[74] Ethnologically, Freud's assumptions as to the condition of primitive society and the origin of totemism have not been substantiated and must, therefore, be considered mythological. His theory of the primal horde is reminiscent of the precultural "state of nature" which the philosophers of the seventeenth and eighteenth centuries imagined.

Regardless of the difficulties inherent in Freud's ethnohistorical speculations his followers in the psychoanalytical movement tend to agree in correlating the phenomena of dreams with mythological narratives and in interpreting the content of myths by reference to the genetic, psychological experience of the race.

Thus, according to Brill,[75] the myth of Adam and Eve represents the infancy of humanity. In its infancy the child is in paradise, but as soon as it grows to the age of puberty it is driven out of paradise and must now live by the sweat of its brow. The snake is the symbol of sex. According to Leon J. Saul the story of Adam and Eve symbolizes the theme of growth in the grasp of reality which comes with maturity. Here prime significance is attached to the symbolic value of the fruit of the tree of knowledge.[76]

On the whole, psychoanalysts agree that myth is the road to understanding the unconscious processes of the human psyche. Symbolic language is held to be the only common language of the human race. In myth primitive, innate impulses are expressed in disguised form. Ethnologically myths portray the social relations of the individual in the family and the relations of the family in the tribe. In all instances, the symbolism of myth is regressive and refers to the primordial genetic experience of man, his delayed infancy, and the consequent Oedipus complex.[77]

For the orthodox follower of Freud religion is based on illusion, and hence all religious beliefs are mythological. In his study *The Future of an Illusion* Freud contrasts the "education to reality" which science provides and the illusions, products of wish-fulfillment, fostered by religion.[78] His god is *Logos,* and he would, therefore, dispense with the system of "wish-illusions, incompatible with reality" represented in religion.[79]

---

[74] See Chapter 1.
[75] Brill, *Basic Principles of Psychoanalysis,* p. 57.
[76] Saul, *Emotional Maturity,* ch. viii.
[77] Mullahy, *Oedipus; Myth and Complex.*
[78] Freud, *The Future of an Illusion,* pp. 54–55, 86.
[79] *Ibid.,* p. 76.

### 8. JUNG ON MYTHS AND THE COLLECTIVE UNCONSCIOUS

All analytic or depth psychologists agree that myth has a symbolic value and refers to the unconscious processes of the human psyche. They differ as regards the nature of the reality which myth symbolizes.

Whereas accoding to Freud the symbol in dreams and myth is a product of the unconscious mind of the individual, for Jung and his followers the symbol in myth is a product of the collective unconscious. The reality symbolized by myth, according to the Freudians, is some form of sexual experience based upon the Oedipus complex; for the followers of Jung, on the other hand, the symbols expressed in dream and myth refer to a variety of "archetypes," or elemental forms, whereby the collective unconscious of humanity expresses itself.[80] Jung's concept of the collective unconscious is reminiscent of the "collective representations" of Durkheim and of the *Elementargedanken* of Bastian.[81]

For the followers of Jung, therefore, myth is an autonomous expression of the collective unconscious having a primordial spiritual value of its own. Myth and religion are essentials of the cultural life of the individual and society and are not to be superseded by education to a scientific, myth-free reality. Religion, in its beginning, is a coherent and organic pattern of myths, and the mythic symbols represent a dynamic and living relatedness to the eternal, typical forms of expression of the collective unconscious.[82] The story of paradise in Genesis is a myth symbolizing the psychological truth that man may not be like God, knowing and being conscious. Man commits the tragic crime of claiming consciousness for himself, and he is driven out of paradise, out of the preconscious participation in God and the divine harmony. The story of Adam and Eve expresses the fear of the enormous burden which consciousness brought to man. In the dreams and phantasies of patients the symbol of paradise represents the craving for the blissful state in which they were children without responsibility and when they could trust the "omniscience" of their parents.[83]

Jung's approach may be characterized as psychological and allegorical. Ultimately all significant myths symbolize some archetype, or form, of psychological experience emerging from the collective unconscious into consciousness. A myth symbolizes some elemental psychological,

---

[80] Jung and Kerenyi, *Essays on a Science of Mythology*, p. 100.
[81] See Chapter 7.
[82] Adler, *Studies in Analytical Psychology*, p. 198.
[83] *Ibid.*, p. 180.

or spiritual, truth; its perennial significance lies in its allegorical, symbolic reference. Thus, Kerenyi interprets classic Greek myths as symbolizing the "primordial child in primordial times," [84] as well as "Kore," the type of the maiden.[85] The "science of mythology" consists of phenomenological, analytical studies of the primordial, innate human types symbolized by mythical narratives regardless of the variety of cultural contexts. In this respect, therefore, Jung's and Kerenyi's approaches are continuations of the allegorical tradition in mythology and differ from previous historical attempts in that the former recognize an irreducible plurality of mythological *motifs* or archetypes and are opposed to a monistic interpretation which would reduce the reality symbolized in myth to a single prototype. As Jung puts it,

Contents of an archetypal character are manifestations of processes in the collective unconscious. Hence they do not refer to anything that is or has been conscious, but to something essentially unconscious. In the last analysis, therefore, it is impossible to say what they refer to. Every interpretation necessarily remains an "as-if". . . . If, then, we proceed in accordance with the above principle, there is no longer any question of whether myth refers to the sun or the moon, the father or the mother, sexuality or fire or water; all we can do is to circumscribe and give an approximate description of an unconscious core of meaning.[86]

All attempts to define precisely the "truth" behind myth are, therefore, doomed to failure, since the unconscious core of meaning is always a "figure of speech" which eludes definition. As against Freud's attempt in *Totem and Taboo* to reconstruct the ethnohistory of mankind in order to account for the Oedipus complex, Jung maintains that to reconstruct the contents of the unconscious by reference to previous conscious events in the history of the race is futile, since the unconscious never was conscious in the first place. At every new stage of civilization one may find a new interpretation of a given mythological archetype in order to connect the life of the past with the life of the present. Otherwise, if we attempt to cut loose from our "archetypal foundations" we are left with a "rootless consciousness" which succumbs helplessly to neuroses and psychic epidemics.[87]

There are, however, a limited number of archetypal *motifs,* or "primordial images," which appear in myths and fairy tales, as well as in dreams and the products of psychotic fantasy.[88] There are types of

[84] Jung and Kerenyi, *Essays on a Science of Mythology,* ch. i.
[85] *Ibid.,* ch. iii.     [86] *Ibid.,* p. 104.
[87] *Ibid.,* pp. 105–6.     [88] *Ibid.,* p. 100.

situations and types of figures that are repeated frequently and have a corresponding meaning. Among the typical human figures Jung lists the shadow, the wise old man, the child (including the child-hero), the mother (primordial mother or earth mother) and her counterpart the maiden, and lastly the *anima* in man and the *animus* in woman.[89] These are typical figures of the unconscious, forms existing a priori, or biological norms of psychic activity.[90] The unconscious component of the self can only be partially expressed through human figures; the other part of it has to be expressed through objective, abstract symbols, such as powerful animals, insects, plants, and geometrical figures.[91]

Contrary to the thesis of Malinowski, Kerenyi and Jung maintain that myth is essentially symbolical and aetiological. They admit that for its adherents the myth expresses literally what it relates—something that happened in primordial times. But this, they urge, does not preclude the possibility that myth has a symbolic, universal significance also. Myth is said to "lay a foundation" (*begründen*) for the world and indicates the *archai,* or first principles, to which everything individual goes back and out of which it is made.[92] "Myths are original revelations of the preconscious psyche, involuntary statements about unconscious psychic happenings, and anything but allegories of physical processes." [93] Hence, myth and religion are said to have a common origin and a common function, in that both originate in the unconscious and serve to link the conscious life of man with psychic processes independent of and beyond consciousness.[94]

## 9. SYMBOLISM, ART, AND SCIENCE

Our survey of the history of mythological theory has demonstrated that there have been two basic approaches to the interpretation of myth, the literal and the symbolic. On the whole, ethnologists, whether evolutionists or functionalists, have been inclined to interpret myth literally. Evolutionary ethnologists, such as Tylor, and classical scholars, such as C. O. Müller, sought to evaluate myth as an expression of primitive thought and as a mode of thinking destined to be superseded by scientific thought. The functionalists, such as Malinowski, evaluate myth as a universal human phenomenon having a pragmatic function in resolving critical problems not amenable to empirical investigation and scientific procedures. Myth deals with the sphere of the supernatural

[89] *Ibid.,* pp. 218–19.     [90] *Ibid.,* p. 219 n.     [91] *Ibid.,* p. 224.
[92] *Ibid.,* pp. 8–9.     [93] *Ibid.,* p. 101.     [94] *Ibid.,* p. 102.

and supersensuous, as does religion; both have a vital meaning for their adherents and serve to validate their cultural institutions. On the other hand, philosophers, historians, theologians, and psychologists from ancient to modern times have been inclined to evaluate myths as expressing some absolute metaphysical, historical, or psychological truth which underlies the apparently irrational and absurd tales. Philosophers have been inclined to see their own philosophical systems reflected in the myths, and contemporary analytical psychologists find that myths reflect the psychological processes and types which they have conceived quite independently. Those who have adopted a symbolical interpretation have been wont to select some one single kind or reality as the referent of myth and the object of its truth. On the whole, it may be said that the latter have tended to reduce myth to a kind of allegory, since they were concerned to reduce the mythical narrative to some form of timeless truth and to minimize the literal significance of the narrative itself.

Thus, the phrase "a science of mythology" turns out to be ambiguous. For the ethnologist it usually means a scientific study of the origin and function of myth in the history of human culture. Here scientific, empirical method is applied to the study of myth, but no attempt is made to reduce myth itself to science. On the other hand, for those who interpret myth symbolically, the term "science of myth" has been interpreted to mean the scientific knowledge to be found in the analysis of myth. For the latter, therefore, a science of myth involves the application of scientific method for the purpose of ascertaining the cross-cultural, scientific validity, or significance, of myth regardless of the variety of cultural contexts. In this way myth is reduced to science and the dividing line between science and myth is eliminated. This may be compared with the implicit, converse attempt to reduce science itself to myth by evaluating scientific concepts and cultural ideologies as fictions of the imagination serving a pragmatic function.

My own thesis is that a scientific study of myth should refer to the study of myth from an ethnological point of view. Myths are elements of culture and are to be investigated with the same empirical and critical methods employed in the study of culture in general. Such a scientific approach does not preclude a symbolical interpretation of myth provided it is clearly understood that in doing so one is engaging in literary art. The great myths suggest to each critical reader some moral or psychological truth which may not even have occurred to their original adherents. Thus, a later generation may find degrees of truth in mythological narratives beyond the perspective of their originators, who accepted them literally. What one finds in myth depends upon the content of the mind one brings to it.

Thus, myth may have an artistic, allegorical, and philosophical value for critical thought which it did not have for its poetic originators, and in this sense myth may have timeless value as a work of art, even though it may no longer be believed literally. As noted, the myth of Adam and Eve still exercises a potent charm over the imagination of thoughtful men, who discern in it, each according to his own insight, some imaginative psychological, moral, or philosophical truth. Myth, like great fictional and dramatic literature in general, may have profound symbolic or allegorical value for us of a later generation, not because myth necessarily contains such latent wisdom, but because the plot or theme suggests universal patterns of action where comparable problems arise. That is, the original and literal value of a myth in a given historical culture and its symbolic value for the adherents of a later culture are two entirely different evaluations which must not be confused. It must not be assumed that the symbolic value of a myth for us and the actual historical significance of the myth for its poetic originators are identical. The nature and degree of truth found in a given myth will vary with the cultural context and the special intuitive insight of its interpreters.

My point is that myths are not "higher" forms of latent, unconscious truth which the conscious mind, through labored analysis, may abstract and delineate in part. Myths are the first approximations to truth in a primitive culture which, because they are reflections upon elemental problems, continue to retain a measure of artistic value as marking the dawn of human intelligence. Myths have an objective ethnological truth-value and a subjective, artistic symbolic value in spite of the fact that we evaluate them as myths.

From the perspective of culture theory the concept of natural, universal, biologically conditioned mythological symbols which emerge into consciousness from the collective unconscious is not tenable. If culture is not biologically inherited, then the concept of innate cultural symbols is self-contradictory and involves the naturalistic fallacy of attempting to deduce culture from nature. Mythological symbols are historically and ontogenetically acquired, as are cultural symbols in general, and their significance, therefore, will vary with their cultural contexts. Through the processes of suggestion and cultural diffusion some culturally acquired symbols may, in time, become generally accepted and may affect the artistic achievements and psychological experiences of individuals of other cultures also. In this sense, as Roheim has suggested, cultural symbols are potentially universal, but never actually so. The fact that cultural symbols are products of the creative intelligence of man leads me to deny the validity of all attempts at a monistic reductionistic interpretation of mythological symbols. As C. O. Müller noted long ago, "we have no ground whatever for excluding beforehand any class of thoughts and ideas from the mythic representation, if it can be at all supposed that they lay within the sphere of intellectual activity in those primitive ages." [95] Besides, as Müller has also shown, there is no exact correspondence between symbolic objects and particular ideas in classical mythology. The connotation of symbols varies with cultural modes of intuition.

### 10. MYTH AND THE PSYCHOCULTURAL EVOLUTION OF THOUGHT

If it be granted that myth is a universal cultural phenomenon originating in a plurality of motives and involving all mental faculties which may contribute to social illusion and delusion, then it seems reasonable to accept the thesis of the continuity of precritical, critical, and scientific thought. A comparative, psychocultural and ethnohistorical study of human thought reveals the essential similarity of the processes at work in the formation of myth, while allowing for differences in the types of myth which prevail at different times and cultures. From the perspective of modern critical thought, animistic thought is "mythopoeic" because it represents a mode of thinking which is no longer characteristic of our age. In reality, all that has changed is the mode of expression. In precritical cultures animistic tales of culture heroes and of magic and epic cosmogonic and theogonic myths tend to prevail. In critical, prescientific cultures myths of the miraculous and supernatural gain currency. In scientific thought, there is a tendency to discount narratives of the miraculous and supernatural, but to accept secular myths instead. In our so-called scientific culture we have the secular beliefs of pseudo-science, such as the myths of racial superiority and the stereotypes of racial and national character. That is why the struggle of man against myth [96] demands such ceaseless vigilance

[95] Müller, *Introduction to a Scientific System of Mythology*, p. 19; for a discussion of the variety of symbolic connotations of a single object see pp. 219 ff.
[96] Dunham, *Man against Myth*.

and self-conscious analysis. Myth is most potent when it is assumed complacently that one is free from it.

The sociopolitical myths of our time are the products of the divorce of scientific thought from the social values which underlie our effective social beliefs and institutions. In fact, modern social scientists and philosophers have encouraged this trend by putting a new positive value upon myth. In order to safeguard the "autonomy" of moral and religious values they have made the validity of the latter independent of scientific truth-values. In this way rational thought has proved itself capable of undermining its own foundations by espousing myth as a "higher" form of truth in the interests of personal "peace of mind" and of national "solidarity." The "myth of modernity," with its glorification of the present age, has replaced the "myth of progress," which envisaged a better world in the future.[97] The modern "myth of the proletariat" has served to sanction revolutionary activity with a view to realizing in our time the eschatological myth of a stateless and classless society.[98] Normative, critical, and scientific thought provides the only tested, self-correcting means of combatting the growth of myth, but it may do so only on condition that it retain its own integrity and does not mistake reason for rationalization. Otherwise, in order to preserve life we may cast away the reasons for living.[99]

[97] Baudouin, *The Myth of Modernity*, ch. i.
[98] Berdyaev, *The Russian Idea*, p. 249.
[99] Baudouin, *The Myth of Modernity*, p. 19.

# 11

# *The Concept of Personality*
# *in Modern Ethnology*[1]

ONE of the outstanding characteristics of contemporary cultural anthropology is its serious concern with the study of the personality of the individuals participating in a given culture. Whereas anthropologists of a previous generation were primarily concerned with an impersonal factual survey of the traits and institutions of a given culture and paid little attention to the subjective, or inner, life of the carriers of the culture, the present tendency is to reverse this trend and to put the major emphasis upon the influence of given cultural institutions and patterns on the personality and character of their adherents.

## 1. THE SIGNIFICANCE OF THE CONCEPT OF CULTURE FOR THE STUDY OF PERSONALITY

One reason for this change in perspective on the part of cultural anthropologists is to be found in their altered view of the nature of culture. The older anthropologists tended to conceive culture in general as an impersonal, "superorganic" tradition and environment comprising the aggregate of material and ideal achievements of historical human society. They assumed, furthermore, more or less explicitly, that culture comprised a distinct conceptual level of reality, a discrete order of purely cultural phenomena which develop according to laws of their own. Culture was said to be a process *sui generis* requiring no reference to other orders of phenomena for an explanation of its origin and stages of development. Hence, a sharp boundary line was drawn between the sphere of culture, on the one hand, and that of organic biology or psychology, on the other. The study of personality was thought to pertain to the domain of psychology and psychiatry, but was considered beyond the province of the cultural anthropologist. Otherwise, it was

[1] Originally prepared as a paper for the Viking Fund Conference on Culture and Personality, held in New York City, November 7, 1947.

thought, there was grave danger that culture, which constituted the highest level of the orders of natural phenomena, might be "reduced" to the level of psychology, and the purity of cultural phenomena corrupted by uniting orders of events which by nature and science ought to remain separated.

On the other hand, there has been a persistent, though minor, tendency to regard culture realistically as referring to acquired forms of technique, behavior, feeling, and thought of individuals within society. From this point of view, culture is essentially a subjective, or personal, attribute of individuals, since it is a state or quality acquired by and attributed to individuals participating in a given cultural configuration and specific cultural institutions. Cultural forms are said to be abstractions from cultural behavior and experience, and as such they have no concrete reality apart from the individuals who have produced them. On this basis, the cultural anthropologist may be interested in all forms of human expression insofar as they have been affected by cultural influence. There can be no sharp line of demarcation between the sphere of culture, on the one hand, and that of organic and psychological phenomena, on the other. Culture is an attribute of human behavior and is therefore to be studied as an integral part of human behavior, not as if it were a dynamic entity capable of acting and developing apart from the organisms which express themselves through it.

Logically, it should be noted, there need be no conflict between the realistic, individualistic approach and the idealistic, superorganic approach, provided it is realized that we are dealing with different levels of abstraction.[2] Actual, or concrete, culture is primarily that state or modification of the behavior and thought of individuals within society which is the direct result of the process of education and of participation in the life of a community. Abstract, or ideal, culture is an impersonal, superorganic aggregate and configuration of forms of experience transmitted by human society and embodied in the sum total of human artifacts, socifacts (institutions), and mentifacts (ideas and ideals) produced by human effort. In actual concrete culture the major emphasis is upon the real cultural processes manifested in the life and experience of individuals within society; in abstract culture the emphasis is upon the cultural forms and achievements apart from the human agents who produced them. Obviously, from the point of view of methodology one need not quarrel with the attempt to study the sequence of

[2] See Chapter 5.

forms or patterns of cultural products or achievements, while taking for granted the human agents involved. One becomes involved in what I have termed *the culturalistic fallacy* [3] only when these cultural abstractions are reified, or hypostatized, so that culture is regarded as a process *sui generis*, subject to its own natural laws of development. It is the mistaking of an epistemological abstraction for a concrete reality and of an abstract form for a concrete process which constitutes the culturalistic fallacy. But obviously there is no fallacy involved in the abstraction of cultural forms as such for the purpose of separate analysis. One may be said to commit the culturalistic fallacy only insofar as he confuses the abstract and the concrete in attributing to epistemological cultural abstractions an efficient causality and dynamic power which only pertain to concrete human agents.

## 2. THE CONCEPT OF THE SUPERORGANIC

It is important to bear in mind in this connection that the concept of the cultural superorganic may be and has been conceived in at least three distinct senses.[4] First, as originally used by Herbert Spencer the term "superorganic" refers to the cumulative aggregate of human achievements which constitute the artificial hereditary environment of man. Secondly, culture is said to be superorganic in the sense that man's psychological capacity for cultural invention and symbolization enables him to develop new cultural forms without any corresponding change in his organic and mental structure. In other words, culture is superorganic in the psychological sense that human mental functions are to some degree independent of man's organic structure, since cultures vary, while the organism remains constant. Thirdly, there is the concept of the superorganic as originally formulated by Kroeber and subsequently modified by L. A. White,[5] according to which cultural phenomena are regarded as "superpsychic" in the sense that they require no reference to the psychological nature of man. Cultural phenomena are said to constitute an independent level of reality which is intelligible in itself and which it is the special task of the "culturologist" to investigate.

It is gratifying to note in this connection that Kroeber has now

[3] See Chapter 2.

[4] *Ibid.*; also Bidney, "The Problem of Social and Cultural Evolution: a Reply to A. R. Radcliffe-Brown," *American Anthropologist*, XLIX (1947), 524–27.

[5] White, "Culturological vs. Psychological Interpretations of Human Behavior," *American Sociological Review*, XII (1947), 686–98; also White, "Kroeber's 'Configurations of Culture Growth,'" *American Anthropologist*, XLVIII (1946), 78–93.

modified his original idealistic view of the superorganic and that in the revised edition of his *Anthropology* he employs the term in the second sense, as referring to man's psychological capacity for cultural invention and communication. Thus, he writes:

In one sense culture is both superindividual and superorganic. But it is necessary to know what is meant by these terms so as not to misunderstand their implications. "Superorganic" does not mean nonorganic, or free of organic influence and causation; nor does it mean that culture is an entity independent of organic life in the sense that some theologians might assert that there is a soul which is or can become independent of the living body. "Superorganic" means simply that when we consider culture we are dealing with something that is organic but which must also be viewed as something more than organic if it is to be fully intelligible to us. In the same way when we say that plants and animals are "organic" we do not thereby try to place them outside the laws of matter and energy in general. We only affirm that fully to understand organic beings and how they behave, we have to recognize certain kinds of phenomena or properties—such as the powers of reproduction, assimilation, irritability—as added to those which we encounter in inorganic substances. Just so, there are certain properties of culture—such as transmissibility, high variability, cumulativeness, value standards, influence on individuals—which it is difficult to explain, or to see much significance in, strictly in terms of the organic composition of personalities or individuals. These properties or qualities of culture evidently attach not to the organic individual man as such, but to the actions and the behavior products of societies of men—that is, to culture. In short, culture is superorganic and superindividual in that, although carried, participated in, and produced by organic individuals, it is acquired; and it is acquired by learning. What is learned is the existent culture.[6]

This passage is historically significant, especially in view of the author's great influence upon American anthropologists and sociologists, in that it shows that Kroeber no longer identifies the superorganic with the superpsychic as he did in the earlier edition of his *Anthropology* and in subsequent papers, but rather holds that there need be no conflict between the organic and the superorganic views of culture, provided culture is not regarded as an entity or process *sui generis*. As evidence of his conciliatory attitude, Kroeber has accordingly added a chapter on "Cultural Psychology" to the revised version of his *Anthropology*, which takes up the problem of "Personality in Culture." While he still retains some reservations and maintains "a certain caution" in face of the alleged danger of "intellectual reductionism" which may reduce cul-

[6] Kroeber, *Anthropology*, rev. ed., pp. 253–54; see also pp. 574–77 for references to personality and culture.

tural to psychological phenomena, he is, nevertheless, prepared to concede that "anthropology is now in a position to call such a halt and review the tie-up with psychology."

The contrast between the superpsychic and the psychological conceptions of the superorganic may be pointed up by reference to Pitirim A. Sorokin's analysis in his recent work *Society, Culture and Personality*.

According to Sorokin: [7]

The superorganic is equivalent to mind in all its clearly developed manifestations. Superorganic phenomena embrace language; science and philosophy; religion; the fine arts (painting, sculpture, architecture, music, literature, and drama); law and ethics; mores and manners; technological inventions and processes from the simplest tools to the most intricate machinery; road-making; building construction; the cultivation of fields and gardens; the domestication and training of animals, etc.; and social organizations. These are all superorganic phenomena because they are the articulations of mind in various forms; none of them arise mainly in response to blind reflexes or instincts.

In a footnote to the above passage he continues:

The best definition of the superorganic is given by E. De Roberty. He rightly indicates that the transition from the inorganic to the organic and then to the superorganic is gradual. Vital phenomena have rudimentary mental processes like irritability, sensation, feeling, emotion, and association of images. But no species except man has the highest forms of mind represented by four main classes of social thought: (*a*) abstract concepts and laws of scientific thought; (*b*) generalizations of philosophy and religion; (*c*) symbolic thought of the fine arts; and (*d*) rational applied thought, in all disciplines from technology, agronomy, and medicine, up to ethics, social planning, and engineering. This superorganic thought is the "stuff" of sociocultural phenomena. Concrete historical events and sociocultural phenomena always represent a mixture of physical, biological and superorganic phenomena. See E. De Roberty, *Nouveau Programme de Sociologie* (Paris, 1904). Social scientists who state that social phenomena are in their nature psychological or mental say, in a less distinct form, the same thing. This means that practically all representatives of the psychological and sociologistic schools in sociology (and they make up the main streams of social thought) are in implicit or explicit agreement with the thesis of this work. . . . See also A. L. Kroeber, 'The Superorganic.' " [8]

Sorokin, it appears, employs the concept of the superorganic as referring to those distinctively human mental functions involved in abstract symbolic thought and distinguishes this human superorganic

[7] Sorokin, *Society, Culture, and Personality*, pp. 3–4.
[8] *Ibid.*, p. 4.

thought from the organic thought which is the product of blind reflexes or instincts. Thus, he is inclined to accept the position that sociocultural phenomena are in their essential nature psychological, or
mental, and finds it difficult to draw any sharp boundary line between
psychological and sociologistic studies.[9] It is of interest to note in this
connection that in referring to Kroeber's paper on "The Superorganic"
Sorokin appears to be unaware that the latter was committed to a superpsychic view of the superorganic.

Nevertheless, Sorokin does not appear very happy about his identification of the superorganic with the mental, and later he differentiates between "the psychological school" and the "sociologistic or sociocultural
school." [10] The former is said to take some psychological element as an
independent variable and to trace its effect in sociocultural life with a
view to establishing a causal connection between the psychological and
the social aspects of cultural life. The sociocultural school, on the other
hand, is said to study sociocultural phenomena in all their essential aspects. "Consequently," he maintains, "only this school gives us real sociology in the strict sense of the term. The other schools surveyed—
namely, cosmosociology, biosociology, and psychosociology—are but
peripheral and derivative disciplines." In fact, Sorokin explicitly takes
the position that sociocultural phenomena are more significant than
psychological ones for an understanding of human personality. Thus he
states:

Consequently, sociocultural phenomena do not require explanation from
the standpoint of the psychological properties of their members, quite the
reverse; psychological characteristics need to be elucidated from the standpoint of the properties of the sociocultural interaction into whose matrix they
are embedded. Without a knowledge of the society and culture into which
a given individual was born and reared none of his personality traits—beliefs,
ideas, convictions, tastes, likes and dislikes—can be understood; his whole
mentality, his manners and mores, his ways of conduct and life, are entirely
incomprehensible. Not only his whole psychosocial personality but many of
his biological properties are molded and conditioned by the sociocultural universe in which he is reared.[11]

Sorokin's dilemma, it appears, has been brought about by the fact
that he is employing the concept of the superorganic in two distinct
senses. On the one hand, he has identified the superorganic with the
mental in its higher forms of expression and is thus committed to the

[9] Sorokin, *Society, Culture, and Personality*, p. 25.
[10] *Ibid.*, pp. 25–26.                         [11] *Ibid.*, p. 27.

position that human culture and personality are to be explained in terms of psychological, symbolic thought, or mental processes. On the other hand, he reverts to the older sociological position that sociocultural phenomena are unique and primary and that the latter are to be differentiated from the psychological processes which underlie them. This implies that sociocultural phenomena are superorganic in the sense that they are superpsychic. Hence, Sorokin maintains that sociocultural phenomena are to be conceived and explained through themselves alone and do not require psychological data for their explanation; on the contrary, sociological data serve to render intelligible the psychological characteristics of the personality of the individuals who are subjected to their influence.

Sorokin's position is instructive precisely because it serves to render explicit the underlying issue in contemporary sociological and anthropological culture theory which has given rise to conflicting approaches to the problem of human personality. In actual practice, an eclectic compromise has been reached, many social scientists accepting the superpsychic view of sociocultural phenomena while they engage in or promote studies of personality which imply or presuppose an antithetical, psychological interpretation of the concept of the superorganic.

### 3. THE POLARITY OF CULTURAL PHENOMENA

The opposition to the study of personality on the part of the adherents of the superorganic, superpsychic view of culture is owing in large measure to their extreme view of the autonomy of cultural phenomena. Historically, this opposition is understandable, since the superorganic view of culture was originally formulated (by Kroeber in particular) in opposition to the extreme claims of organicists, who failed to differentiate cultural phenomena from biological, psychological, and racial phenomena and attempted to derive cultural phenomena directly from the latter. But instead of maintaining simply that cultural phenomena involve a new element of historical experience which, while it presupposes biological, psychological, and societal conditions, is not entirely explicable in terms of the latter, the superorganicists went to the opposite extreme by claiming that culture constitutes a new level of reality which is to be conceived through itself alone. Any attempt to correlate psychological or psychiatrical data with cultural processes was, therefore, regarded with suspicion as undermining the autonomy of cultural anthropology or as a reduction of culture to psychology.

By way of reconciling the historically antithetical organic and super-organic approaches to the study of human culture, I have elsewhere,[12] developed the thesis of the polarity of cultural phenomena.[13] Briefly put, my thesis is that culture in general may be understood as the dynamic process and product of the self-cultivation of human nature, as well as of the natural, geographical environment, and involves the development of selected potentialities of nature for the attainment of individual and social ends of communal life. Culture is essentially a polar concept in the sense that it is unintelligible apart from nature. The polarity, or complementarity, of nature and culture implies that while there is some degree of independence, or autonomy, of natural and cultural phenomena, there is also an essential interdependence, or mutual dependence. The cultural process requires as its indispensable conditions a determinate human nature and natural environment that are subject to transformation by man himself.

The polarity of nature and culture implies, furthermore, that natural selection and cultural selection are disparate processes. Cultural selection is normative and ultimately involves the active choice of the human agents of a given culture system. Natural selection alone does not explain either the great diversity of cultural forms of expression or the adherence to given forms of culture by certain societies notwithstanding the biological cost. Creative, normative cultural selection is often at variance with, or opposed to, natural, biological selection. The attempt on the part of the organic, as well as superorganic, determinists to reduce the cultural process to an automatic process of natural selection disregards the essentially human and unpredictable element in the cultural process, namely, the normative choice of distinctively human cultural values.

In brief, all cultural phenomena are composed of two disparate elements, namely, the element of nature, conceived in physical, biological, psychological, or social terms, and the element of human creativity and choice. There are purely natural phenomena, but there are no purely cultural phenomena which are conceived through themselves alone. All cultural phenomena are natural phenomena modified by human effort and interaction.

#### 4. HUMAN NATURE, THE PERSON, AND PERSONALITY

The cultural anthropologist, as distinct from the psychologist, is concerned with the cultural expression of human nature. He is indebted to

---

[12] See Chapter 12.          [13] See also Chapter 5.

the psychologist for data as to the psychological conditions and processes underlying cultural forms and attempts to correlate these cultural phenomena with given psychological processes. A knowledge of psychology enables him to understand the universal patterns and motivations of cultural phenomena and to appreciate the distinctive, special role of historical experience and tradition in relation to a given society.

As Durkheim has noted,[14] there are two egos in every individual, namely, a psychobiological ego, with which he is endowed by nature, and a sociocultural ego, which he acquires through participation in a given society and culture system. These two egos are in a constant state of tension and never quite harmonize. By encouraging the development of some human potentialities and impulses, the cultural process makes for an actual increase in individual liberty and power of activity and thereby enables men, individually and collectively, to engage in a multitude of enterprises which they would otherwise be unable to pursue. On the other hand, the cultural process is also a restraining discipline which checks or suppresses the individual's impulses in the interests of society. Therefore, in all cultures there is some degree of tension between the individual and his society, between the egoistic impulses one would fain indulge and the altruistic ideals one is more or less compelled to obey. Hence, there arises the problem of the "fitness" of a given culture for its adherents, on the one hand, and of the adjustment of its adherents to a given culture, on the other.

Actual historical cultures differ markedly from one another in the selection of possible forms of activity and organization, and therefore every society has the defects corresponding to its self-imposed virtues. This cultural selection is manifested by the ideal type of person which the members of a given society prefer relative to the ages of life and the sex of the individual. At a given stage of development, each ideal type calls for the expression of some human potentialities and the suppression or restraint of others.

Insofar as an individual (or an aggregate of individuals) carries out a given culture role, or ideal, he may be said to be a person (*persona*). A person is simply one who performs a function in the cultural life of a given society. Apart from sociocultural life there are organisms and psychobiological egos, but no persons.[15] Personality is an attribute which human nature acquires through participation in a given culture;

---

[14] In Le Dualisme de la nature humaine (*Scientia*, XV, 206–21) as quoted by Sorokin in his *Society, Culture, and Personality*, p. 346.

[15] See also Angyal's *Foundations for a Science of Personality*, p. 199.

it is the product of sociocultural participation and recognition. A person may be described as the product and agent of the sociocultural process.

&#10003; It is implied in the foregoing propositions that human nature is logically and genetically prior to personality. Personality is an attribute which man acquires historically through participation in sociocultural life; human nature is a precultural or metacultural notion in the sense that it is postulated as the condition of the cultural process and is therefore not to be explained in terms of the latter. Otherwise, if one attempts to explain human nature in terms of culture, as La Piere and Farnsworth have done in their *Social Psychology*,[16] one commits the culturalistic fallacy of reducing nature to culture.[17] If, as the culturologists maintain, it is fallacious to reduce cultural phenomena to psychology, it is equally fallacious to reduce psychology to cultural processes. Personality is a cultural attribute of human nature, but is not identical with the latter.

### 5. SOME PSYCHOLOGICAL DEFINITIONS OF PERSONALITY IN CONTEMPORARY PERSONALITY AND CULTURE STUDIES.

Although contemporary cultural anthropologists are keenly aware of the influence of culture on the formation of personality, they are still inclined to define personality in purely psychological terms. They tend to imply that the concept of personality is primarily a psychological notion, but that one must take into consideration the cultural background of personality in order to provide an adequate analysis of the structure and functions of given personality types. Thus, we find that Ralph Linton, in his *Cultural Background of Personality*, writes:

For the purpose of the present discussion, personality will be taken to mean: "The organized aggregate of psychological processes and states pertaining to the individual." This definition includes the common element in most of the definitions now current. At the same time it excludes many orders of phenomena which have been included in one or another of these definitions. Thus, it rules out the overt behavior resulting from the operation of these processes and states, although it is only from such behavior that their nature and even existence can be deduced. It also excludes from consideration the effects of this behavior upon the individual's environment, even that part of it which consists of other individuals. Lastly, it excludes from the personality concept the physical structure of the individual and his physiological processes. This final limitation will appear too drastic to many students of

[16] LaPiere and Farnsworth, *Social Psychology*, 2d ed.
[17] See Chapter 5.

personality, but it has a pragmatic, if not a logical, justification. We know so little about the physiological accompaniments of psychological phenomena that attempts to deal with the latter in physiological terms still lead to more confusion than clarification.[18]

Linton's definition of personality is essentially psychological and idealistic, and it bears a close similarity to the structuralistic, mentalistic psychology of Titchener and Wundt. By excluding from his concept of personality overt behavior and the effects of this behavior on others, as well as the physical structure and physiological processes of the individual, he is left with the introspected, inferred covert responses and value attitudes. It is of interest to the student of cultural anthropology to observe in this connection that while Linton has modified his former idealistic concept of culture and now adopts a realistic approach which includes overt behavior, he still retains an idealistic, mentalistic position as regards the concept of personality.

Similarly, John Gillin states: "We shall regard a personality, for present purposes, as an internal organization of emotions, attitudes, idea patterns, and tendencies to overt action. This internal organization is empirically manifested in a continuity which may be called the 'style of life.'"[19]

Gillin's definition of personality is essentially identical with that of Linton, since the former explicitly agrees that personality is an "internal organization" of psychological states and tendencies to action. Nevertheless, Gillin later explains that

The difference between an *individual* and a *person* is that the latter is an individual who has been socialized, who has absorbed and organized internally to some extent the tenets of his culture so that he is recognized by other individuals as a personal integration, the cultural components of which, at least, are commonly understood in the group.[20]

This statement implies that a person is essentially a cultural product and hence may not be conceived in purely psychological terms, as may an individual. Actually, however, Gillin, like Linton, provides a psychological definition of an individual while claiming to present a definition of personality.

Kluckhohn and Mowrer also provide a psychological definition of personality, but unlike Linton, they adopt the approach of social behaviorism and define personality in terms of "social stimulus value."

[18] Linton, *The Cultural Background of Personality*, p. 84.
[19] John Philip Gillin, *The Ways of Men*, p. 573.
[20] *Ibid.*, p. 577.

In their paper "Culture and Personality: a Conceptual Scheme" they explain:

We follow May in assuming that the parameters of a personality may be defined by a human organism's effects upon others. All attempts to describe an individual "as he really is" must be regarded as extra-scientific unless they are firmly based upon the regularities in the stimulus value which this individual has for others. The only way an observer can "know" other personalities is by noting and making inferences of their social stimulus value—whether in casual social relationships, in controlled interviews, or as manifested in more refined experimental situations such as those provided by the various projective techniques. A subject's own statement of his needs, motives, etc., will normally constitute an important part of the data but can never be taken at their face value without critical evaluation—they must always be interpreted in terms of the reactions of one or more observers. The definition of personality as social stimulus value seems to us one which will permit relatively objective operations.[21]

As contrasted with the Watsonian behavioristic approach, wherein personality is defined as "the sum total of habit systems," Mark May shifts the emphasis from the individual's response, or reactions, to the stimulus value or effects of his behavior upon others.[22] The nature of one's personality is said to be determined by how one is responded to, by how one is treated, so to speak, rather than by one's own responses or self-estimation. In accepting May's position, Kluckhohn and Mowrer have thus adopted a social, behavioristic approach which is the antithesis of the introspective, subjective approach of Linton, who explicitly excludes overt behavior and its effects upon others from his definition of personality. It is of interest, furthermore, to note here that whereas Kluckhohn's concept of culture is idealistic, inasmuch as he holds culture to be "a mental construct," his definition of personality is objective and behavioristic. For Linton, on the other hand, the situation is reversed, since he now accepts a realistic view of culture, but still retains an idealistic concept of personality.

In their paper "Dynamic Theory of Personality," written a little earlier, Kluckhohn and Mowrer reject the position that personality is to be defined as identical with social-stimulus value. Thus, they write:

Although we thus recognize the two-fold meaning of the term, we shall employ "personality" in this chapter to refer to the individual as an organized,

[21] Kluckhohn and Mowrer, "Culture and Personality: A Conceptual Scheme," *American Anthropologist*, XLVI, 1944, pp. 1–29.
[22] See May, "The Foundations of Personality," ch. iv of *Psychology at Work*, ed. by P. S. Achilles, pp. 82–83.

adjusting, behaving entity, not to the way in which this individual may influence other individuals (or things). We acknowledge that before any "personality" can become an object of scientific study, that individual must indeed *have* "social stimulus value" i.e., other human beings must be able to observe and make coherent statements about him; but this is not to say that this "social stimulus value" *is* the individual's personality. The order of effects which an object of scientific study has upon the observing scientist is very different from the type of effects, namely, the rewards and punishments, which are instrumental in determining both an individual's "reputation" with others and his own habit structure. It is, we believe, in the latter sense that clinicians most often use the term personality; and this definition is also most consistent with our emphasis on learning; for what an individual is or becomes is determined, not primarily by the way in which his actions reward or punish others, but by the way in which these actions directly or indirectly affect the individual himself.[23]

Here the authors acknowledge that while an individual as a person does indeed have social stimulus value, the latter is not to be identified with his personality, because the order of effects varies so greatly. Instead, they prefer to employ the term "personality" in the clinicians' sense as referring to an individual's habit structure acquired through the process of learning.

In a footnote to the above publication, Kluckhohn and Mowrer refer to the disparity in their concepts of personality. They remark:

Elsewhere an attempt has been made to explore and elaborate the concept of personality as "social stimulus value." In adopting a different conception for the purposes of this chapter, we make no judgment as to which is ultimately "right," i.e., most generally useful. Such a judgment would demand an analysis of the nature of *observation of* vs. *participation in* social events and of the factor of reciprocity in relation to all social roles which would take us far beyond the scope of this chapter.[24]

Again, in another footnote to their paper "Culture and Personality: a Conceptual Scheme" they explain:

Second, we are addressing ourselves to two different sets of questions in our two publications. In this article the interest centers upon classificatory abstractions and upon the query: how do we attain our knowledge of personality? The other paper has a point of view which might be designated as "clinical"; the central question is more nearly: what *is* personality? Here personality is seen largely from the standpoint of the reactor; there we try to see personality as it may be imputed to the actor. Perhaps a philosopher might say that the point of view of this paper approaches the "epistemological," that of the other the "ontological." The history of science permits

[23] *Personality and the Behavior Disorders*, ed. by McV. Hunt, I, 77–78.
[24] *Ibid.*, p. 78.

two inductions: 1. it is useful to behave experimentally with respect to conceptual schemes without necessarily claiming "truth" for one to the exclusion of another. 2. a conceptual scheme may be appropriate for analyzing one group of problems, utterly inappropriate for treating the same set of data with a view to a different group of equally legitimate questions.[25]

These candid comments are significant in that they explicitly raise the problem of the validity of scientific definitions. In general, it appears that Kluckhohn and Mowrer, as well as Linton, take the position that a scientific definition is to be evaluated by its pragmatic utility in a given context of research. "Truth," as defined, is taken as the equivalent of general utility for a given purpose, and hence it is maintained that the scientist is not bound to accept any one definition as the "true" or "right" one. This explains why Kluckhohn, in collaboration with Henry A. Murray, provides still another definition of personality in terms of physiology. In their introduction to an anthology of essays entitled *Personality in Nature, Society, and Culture* the authors define personality as "the continuity of functional forces and forms manifested through sequences of organized regnant processes in the brain from birth to death" (p. 32).

As opposed to this pragmatic position it may be pointed out that a real, or scientific, definition is supposed to define the universal, or logical, essence of an object—that in virtue of which a thing is what it is. A scientifically valid and adequate definition, as distinct from a purely conventional or arbitrary one, is one that delimits the nature of an object as a whole and does not identify the properties which pertain to a part only with the object as a whole. A scientific definition is one that may be epistemologically verified in every instance of the object's presence and has ontological import as well, in the sense that it defines the essence or principle of being of its object so that, granted the actual presence of a given form or set of properties, the object in question is also present. Thus, the attempt made on the part of Kluckhohn and Mowrer to differentiate between an epistemological and an ontological definition appears to be invalid, since a valid definition has both epistemological and ontological import.

Furthermore, while it may be granted that a scientific definition is one that may be pragmatically verified and leads to specific practical consequences, as pragmatists since Charles Peirce and William James

[25] Kluckhohn and Mowrer, *American Anthropologist*, XLVI (1944), 1–29.

have maintained, the fact remains that unless a definition provides a universal, logically coherent concept, there is no way of determining whether one is dealing with only one type of object. That is, an adequate scientific definition is one that provides a coherent, universal, logical concept which in practice may be verified by the consequences to which it leads. The primary factor, however, is the universal, logical concept. Otherwise, if one accepts the pragmatic criterion as primary, then he becomes involved in an arbitrary pluralism and nominalism so that it becomes impossible to obtain any common measure of agreement as to what a thing is or how it is to be conceived. Thus, a pragmatic investigator finds himself providing many definitions of the same object, each of which he asserts is pragmatically justified in a given context. The situation becomes truly scandalous when two or more "scientific" pragmatists provide conflicting definitions, as in the case of Linton's and Kluckhohn's definitions of personality, and find that they have no common measure of "truth" and "rightness" beyond their own preferences. The only way out of this impasse, apparently, is for scholars to acknowledge that an adequate and scientific definition is one that provides a logically coherent, as well as practically verifiable, concept —one which connotes the essential properties of an object and at the same time denotes the practical epistemological means of its own verification.[26]

## 6. PERSONS AND PERSONALITY AS POLARISTIC, PSYCHOCULTURAL CONCEPTS

The implicit assumption underlying the attempts of contemporary cultural anthropologists to provide psychological definitions of personality is that there is a duality of personality and culture, that each is intelligible in itself, and that it is the task of the ethnologist to demonstrate their interrelation in given sociocultural systems. This explains why anthropologists such as Linton, Gillin, and Kluckhohn, while fully cognizant of the role of culture in the formation of personality, nevertheless proceed in their formal definitions of personality to exclude culture entirely.

In contrast to this basic current assumption, my thesis is that the concept of personality is a priori a psychocultural notion. It is not

[26] See Timasheff, "Definitions in the Social Sciences," *American Journal of Sociology,* LIII (1947), 201–9.

merely that there is a cultural element or aspect to personality, as Margaret Mead,[27] for instance, has maintained, but that the concept of personality connotes logically and essentially a polaristic, psychocultural entity. Hence, it does not make sense to provide a purely psychological definition of personality, since psychology tells us nothing about the special attitude and mode of activity of a person in a given sociocultural context.

By way of concise and systematic formulation, I wish to submit the following definitions of person and personality together with some inferential comments.

1. A person may be defined as the socially recognized subject, or agent, of psychocultural interaction. A person may be either an individual or a corporation, such as the state. Any one who performs a given cultural role in society involving duties and rights is a person.

2. A personality is a determinate psychocultural action and reaction pattern, whether overt or covert, which is typical or characteristic of an individual (or organization of individuals) in the performance of his sociocultural role at a given stage of development. Personality is an attribute of persons; it is a property which is the product of sociocultural participation and recognition. Personality refers to the form, or structure, of a person and hence implies the prior existence of a person. Only persons are the agents, or patients, of the cultural process.[28]

Personality is something historically acquired by an individual in the course of sociocultural life in society and hence requires social recognition. A person depends for his very existence upon the sociocultural recognition he receives. Hence, there can be no persons apart from human society.

A person is a polaristic entity in the sense that he comprises two distinct elements, namely, the element of human nature and that of culture. As noted earlier, human nature and personality may not be identified, since human nature is precultural, or metacultural. The polarity of personality is manifested by the fact of tension between the individual and his society which gives rise to deviants, or nonconformists, who fail to conform to the modal personality type.

Furthermore, since the personality of an individual changes with his cultural role, as well as his psychosomatic constitution, as he passes

[27] Mead, "The Cultural Approach to Personality" in Harriman, ed., *Encyclopedia of Psychology*, pp. 477–87.
[28] Compare Murphy, *Personality*, pp. 7–8.

through the ages of life, any one individual may be said to have a plurality of personalities at a given time or in a sequence of times. There may be a plurality of persons in one individual, and many individuals may unite to form a single corporate person, such as the state, with a distinct personality over and above the personalities of its participant members.

The uniqueness of any given person is the product of the special constitutional, social, and cultural factors which have combined to make him what he is. Every personality may be said to have its special, as well as its general, aspects, which it shares with other personality structures. In general, the psychologists have tended to stress the uniqueness of the person, while the cultural anthropologists have drawn attention to the common elements, or traits, to the "basic personality structure," or "modal personality," which the individual shares with the other members of his cultural community. Either approach taken by itself is an abstraction, since the concrete person manifests both particular, or special, as well as general, or universal, personality traits. For general purposes, however, such as the evaluation of a person's political rights, the uniqueness of personality may be ignored, and the "equality" of all persons before the law proclaimed. All men are not born equal, but persons may be treated and recognized as equals.

It is important to differentiate in this connection between the general, ideal personality structure and the real personality structure. The ideal personality structure is a product of the cultural ideals one has acquired and professes. The real personality structure is an inference from the observable behavior or practices of the average member of a given sociocultural group and only partially corresponds to the social ideals professed. A major source of prejudice and misunderstanding may be traced to the tendency to evaluate the "social character" of one's own ethnic group in terms of the ideal personality structure and to form "stereotypes" of alien ethnic groups, especially minority groups in one's midst, which are based on partial observation of the behavior of a few individuals and hence do not correspond to actual social facts and norms.

As a member of a particular group, or class, an individual also acquires a class, or status, personality which may be in conflict with the class, or status, personality of other groups. One of the fundamental issues of contemporary political thought and practice is whether the individual as a citizen may participate in a common, or communal, personality whose interests transcend those of his class personality, whether the state as a person is to govern in the common interests of all classes or whether it must necessarily govern in the interests of some one class. In my opinion that is the basic issue between democracy and totalitarianism (whether of the left or the right) with regard to personality and culture.

Finally, with the progress of cultural ideals and cultural diffusion there is gradually emerging the notion of a fundamental, universal culture for humanity as a whole. Insofar as men come to regard themselves as citizens of a common cultural world they may acquire a cosmopolitan, or universal, personality and recognize universal human rights. At present the concept of a universal ideal personality is far from realization, nevertheless it is significant as a norm and objective which the social scientists of the world may help mankind to attain in the future. The Universal Declaration of Human Rights approved by a committee of the United Nations is a step forward in this direction.

# 12

# *The Concept of Cultural Crisis*[1]

CONTEMPORARY THINKERS in all walks of life are acutely aware that this is an age of crises and that all the resources of human intelligence and wisdom should be utilized to provide basic diagnoses and to indicate directions of resolution. An analysis of contemporary social thought reveals, however, that there is radical disagreement among social scientists and philosophers with regard to the nature and origin of cultural crises and their relation to the cultural process as a whole.

## 1. IDEALISTIC AND MATERIALISTIC THEORIES OF CULTURAL CRISIS

Idealistic writers, such as Sorokin, maintain that the crisis of our age is the reflection of its mental and spiritual disintegration and that the social ordeal, or actual social conflict among societies, is but the external consequence of the more fundamental, underlying ideological transition.[2] On the other hand, for positivists and Marxian materialists the crisis proper is to be found in the socio-economic anarchy and strife between classes, while the ideological conflict is considered merely as a projection or reflection of this clash of technological and social interests. Among both cultural idealists and materialists there is a tendency to adopt a fatalistic philosophy of cultural history and to regard cultural crises as inevitable natural phenomena. Those who adopt such a fatalistic attitude tend to wait, more or less passively, for the predestined crises to take their inevitable courses and to usher in an era either of catastrophe or of unlimited progress, depending on their faith as to the final outcome. Sorokin, for example, believes in the unity of human culture and adduces historical, statistical evidence to support his optimistic faith in the cyclical recurrence of the basic types of culture. Spengler, on the other hand, with his monadic, organic theory of undiffusable culture types, logically maintains that each culture type is destined to extinction without hope of resurrection in some new form,

---

[1] Reprinted in part from my paper "On the Concept of Cultural Crisis," *American Anthropologist*, XLVIII (1946), 534–52.

[2] Sorokin, *The Crisis of Our Age*.

and he finds it impossible to say "whether and when a new culture shall be."[3] Some, believing in ultimate cultural and social progress, take the position that the inevitable is also the desirable, and therefore they decide to accelerate the blessed process in order to help make the long run just a little shorter. Thus, as Arthur Koestler has observed, so-called war criminals may be punished for their part in putting obstacles in the way of human progress and causing temporary grief and suffering, but not because their deeds could conceivably make any appreciable difference in the historical process.[4]

Cultural fatalism as a philosophy of cultural evolution owes its plausibility to the divorce, or abstraction, of human achievements from the psychobiological processes by which they are produced. Once human ideals, social institutions, and technical inventions are regarded as impersonal, "superorganic" entities with a force of persistence and development of their own, independent of their human creators, it seems plausible to disregard human agents as the primary determining factors. In this manner, what began as a scientific quest for empirical factors involved in the cultural process ends by being a mystical metaphysics of fate in which nonempirical forces are presumed to shape human destiny in accordance with their own laws of development.

## 2. THE POLAR CONCEPT OF CULTURE

The view of culture here submitted is opposed to the superorganic theory of culture, whether it be conceived in materialistic or idealistic terms. Culture is here understood as a polar concept, comprising human creativity and the postulated potentialities of nature, human and cosmic. On this basis human culture may be defined as the process and product of the cultivation of the potentialities of human nature and the natural environment for the satisfaction of basic psychosocial needs and aspirations.[5] The cultural process thus provides the instrumental means, as well as the normative ends, of social life; it is a process of creation and discovery by which men live, as well as an ideal for which they live.

Since theory and practice are the ultimate, irreducible categories of culture, it follows that an integral, or holistic, concept of culture comprises the acquired, or cultivated, behavior, feeling, and thought of in-

[3] Spengler, *The Decline of the West;* Frank, *Fate and Freedom.*
[4] Koestler, *The Yogi and the Commissar,* p. 184.
[5] See Chapter 5, "Human Nature and the Cultural Process."

dividuals within a society, as well as the patterns or forms of intellectual, social, and artistic ideals which human societies have professed historically. A given historical society may be said to possess a well-integrated culture insofar as its constituent members live more or less consistently and compatibly in conformity with the ideal norms of truth, beauty, and goodness which they profess and which they have embodied more or less perfectly in their system of institutions. Subjectively, the integration of a culture is manifested in the personality structure and dynamic processes of the individuals who live in conformity with it, and is exhibited by their co-ordinated habits and attitudes of mind in relation to one another. On this basis normative, ideational culture has no actual existence as a cultural force unless it is practiced and influences men's behavior as members of a society. Similarly, practical culture is not intelligible apart from the epistemic, moral, and aesthetic postulates and ideals which men have created or discovered for themselves and which have an objective meaning and validity independent of the practices to which they lead. Furthermore, there appears to be a relation of polarity between cultural theory and practice which allows for some degree of independence, as well as of mutual interdependence. If this be the case, it follows that one may not assume a priori that either theory or practice is logically prior to the other, since in any given situation the factor which happens to be predominant in initiating or providing the occasion for social and cultural change must be determined empirically.

From this standpoint we can indicate how the apparently conflicting claims of cultural materialism and idealism may be reconciled. The realistic materialists, it would appear, have apparently stressed the role of economic and social practices as the primary factors in cultural evolution and have therefore tended to relegate ideas to the position of *post hoc* reflections or rationalizations of events in the sociocultural world. The idealists, on the other hand, have emphasized the primacy of theoretical ideas and ideals as the "final causes," capable of occasioning or initiating purposive action in an intelligent being, and have therefore regarded actual social practices and institutions as "objectifications" or "vehicles" of these predominant ideas. According to the position here maintained, both materialists and idealists are right in their affirmations as to the independent roles of cultural theory and practice, but they are wrong in claiming the absolute primacy of either factor. Theory and practice are relatively and conditionally predominant in any given historical situation, and under all circumstances they exercise reciprocal influence.

### 3. NATURAL AND CULTURAL CRISES

Since a cultural crisis is the negative counterpart of cultural integration, it follows that the former involves the disintegration, destruction, or suspension of some basic elements of sociocultural life. There are, however, various types of cultural crises which may be classified according to the factors or conditions which give rise to them.

Since culture is intrinsically a polar concept involving the interdependence of natural potentialities and human creativity, it appears that crises may be classified in the first instance into two groups, namely, natural and cultural crises.

Natural crises are those suspensions of sociocultural life brought about by factors more or less beyond human control. Thus, the basic transitions in the life cycle of man from birth to death give rise to natural crises which are accompanied in all societies by some forms of cultural rite and ceremony. Similarly, such phenomena as floods, storms, earthquakes, drought, and so forth tend to disrupt cultural routine and to produce states of emergency requiring desperate measures. Although the number and extent of such natural crises tend to diminish with the progress of science, there are always bound to be the inevitable biological crises which are an inherent part of our mortal nature, as well as environmental catastrophes against which there can be no certain protection.

A cultural crisis, properly speaking, is the direct result of some disfunction inherent in the very form and dynamics of a given mode of culture. Cultural crises may originate either within or outside a given society and may affect all or some of its members. For example, industrial strife and civil war are internal cultural crises, while international wars are external cultural crises.

Natural crises tend to unite people, regardless of their racial and cultural differences, in the face of some common catastrophe or potential danger. Nature appears under such circumstances as the common enemy of mankind, and in this sense one touch of natural crisis "makes the whole world kin." An appeal to aid the victims of an earthquake, epidemic, or famine usually meets with generous response on the part of most people, irrespective of racial origin or cultural creed. Natural crises tend to unite men as members of the same species, whereas cultural differences tend to produce crises and to separate them into conflicting groups, as if they were members of different species. The basic social problem of our time is, undoubtedly, how to produce a sense of cultural human kinship which may be instrumental in obviating cultural conflicts, to parallel the sense of natural kinship in the face of natural crises.

All crises have both subjective and objective aspects. From the perspective of the human victims involved, a cultural crisis is a summons to decision and action and may mark a radical parting of the ways or directions of living. So long as the members of a given society are content with their mode of living, even though actual objective conditions may be far from satisfactory, they do not themselves experience a state of crisis. It is only when they come to feel, whether of their own accord or through external propaganda, that their present condition is intolerable, in the sense that it cannot be or ought not to be, tolerated, that they begin to face a potentially or actually critical situation. Psychologically, a cultural crisis is experienced as a state of indecision or uncertainty regarding two or more significant alternatives which may affect the destiny of the individual. Objectively, a cultural crisis manifests itself as a state of emergency brought about by the suspension of normal, or previously prevailing, technological, social, or ideological conditions. From this standpoint the crisis situation is one in which things and events are "in the balance" and presents open possibilities for the better or the worse with regard to the final outcome. Whether viewed from the subjective or the objective pole, a cultural crisis may be regarded as a state of transition, as an unstable, or passing, condition, since man abhors living in a state of cultural suspension or in a cultural vacuum and no society can maintain itself for long in a condition of cultural suspension or chaos. Once a decision has been reached or events have changed for the better, the crisis is regarded as in the process of resolution.

Every genuine cultural crisis marks a point of transition from an old to some new form of cultural life, but does not of itself provide any indication as to the direction which events will take. Crises may be either constructive or destructive, reformative or deformative. Insofar as the crisis situation indicates a revolt by human agents against self-destructive cultural inertia and is intended to prepare the way for constructive cultural reforms, it may be a decided good. Furthermore, a society may "drift" into a critical situation, such as an economic depression, or the crisis may be deliberately provoked by a minority who find prevailing conditions intolerable. But whatever the origin of the crisis, it may be converted from a potential evil into a potential good. The good envisaged may be the restoration of the *status quo* or some radical reform designed to prevent recurrence of critical conditions. The issue between conservatives and radicals is, in many instances, whether the *status quo* is to be retained or whether the time has come for some basic change, the conservatives demanding absolute proof that change is necessary, while the radicals assert that change is desirable if there is no indisputable evidence to the contrary.[6] The phrase "to restore law and order," so often used in times of trouble, is for this reason highly ambiguous, since the primary questions are what kind, or form, of law and order shall we have and under whose auspices is it to be administered? Law and order may be "restored" either by returning to the *status quo* or by instituting desired reforms.

## 4. THEORETICAL AND PRACTICAL CRISES

From the perspective of theory and practice, in the ideational-affective experience of individuals a cultural crisis may appear as a basic conflict or incoherency of thought and emotion which occasions a suspension of voluntary and intellectual activities. Thus, one speaks of scientific, moral, or religious crises when he wishes to refer to the fact that commonly accepted theories, ideals, and beliefs have broken down and are no longer regarded as tenable because contradicted by new evidence or found incompatible with new conditions. Similarly, a practical crisis may be demonstrated by the unworkability or incompatibility of prevailing institutions or customs and by the suspension, because of active or passive resistance, of normal, or routine, cultural behavior.

Within limits, theoretical and practical crises may occur independently of one another. For example, a crisis in abstract theoretical physics or in metaphysical speculation need not be accompanied by social unrest, since there are few individuals competent to appreciate the issues involved and these issues have no immediate or direct bearing on social conduct. Similarly, there may be general agreement in theory, but no harmony in practice, since the difficulty may be to adjust proper social and technological means to agreed ends—a situation frequently encountered in a democratic society. Every crisis in

[6] Calhoun, "William Graham Sumner," *Social Forces*, XXIV (1945), 15–32.

theory, if it is at all significant, is bound sooner or later to have practical import within some limited sphere; for example, a crisis in scientific theory is bound to affect experimental and field techniques and hence to determine the character of the data which are supplied. However, the presupposition that facts and field techniques are not affected by one's theoretical assumptions is one that dies hard, since it is so much easier to adopt a "pragmatic" attitude and accept "results" without bothering to examine the origin of one's methodology and the means to be taken to render that methodology more coherent. My point is that theories are not merely pragmatic descriptions of established facts, but are themselves a factor in determining the selection of data and their organization into meaningful wholes.

Historically it may be shown that owing to general cultural inertia, the active resistance of vested interests and the unwillingness of leaders of society to admit radical departure from sanctioned tradition, even after such changes have actually taken place, there is usually considerable "lag" in the conformity of practice to theory, radical changes in theory not being immediately accompanied by corresponding changes in practice, while reactionary practices are often misrepresented as conforming to traditional theory. In this manner many Quislings and Lavals, who have betrayed their nations, have sought to justify their conduct in terms of the professed ideal traditions of their countries. In general, it appears, it is difficult to differentiate between progress and reaction, especially for those living in an era of transition, since each party always represents its own position as progressive and that of its opponent's as reactionary. Frequently it takes a critical practical situation to reveal men's real, or actual, beliefs as distinct from those they profess when they are not obliged to act. In this sense, as Thomas Paine observed, "times of trouble" do "try men's souls." [7] Only critical, particularized thinking, as distinct from stereotyped slogan-thinking, an unbiased eye for correlating labels with pragmatic consequences, and a measure of historical perspective on the part of individuals and governments alike can protect a society from unwittingly promoting cultural corruption and eventual self-destruction.

In the long run, however, especially in the sphere of social culture, the theoretical and practical elements are bound to be correlated, a

[7] Paine, "The Crisis Papers," *The Selected Work of Tom Paine,* ed. by Howard Fast.

crisis in practice leading to dissatisfaction with prevailing theory or ideology, particularly on the part of the articulate intellectuals, or else some radical innovation in theory undermining accepted social norms. It is significant that in democratic cultures, especially at election time, social radicals, as well as reactionaries, have a tendency to develop what may be termed "a crisis complex" and to envisage either the introduction of certain reforms or the failure to introduce new legislation, as probable potentials for a social crisis—an eventuality which is intended to arouse public emotions of anxiety and to win partisan adherents for a particular platform. On the other hand, in nondemocratic cultures and in "socialistic" democratic cultures governments tend to supervise the education of their subjects and to institute various forms of "thought control" to make certain that no subversive ideas penetrate the social mind, thereby admitting implicitly that ideas do have a significant power to influence and initiate cultural change. While in general societies seem to be more likely to accept radical changes in times of trouble and transition, the crisis acting as a kind of cultural catalyst, totalitarian, or monistic, societies must depend on such practical emergencies to a much greater extent than do individualistic, democratic societies, since the former make no provision for peaceful changes and "loyal opposition" and must rely on the initiative and will of those in power.

Societies, it appears, as well as individuals, differ markedly in their attitudes toward change. Native societies, in common with most preindustrial societies, adhere to cultural traditions and folkways much more rigidly than do modern, industrialized peoples. Novelty is not worshiped for its own sake, as it tends to be among us, and a new cultural trait is usually accepted only when its functional utility has been demonstrated or when it fits easily into the established culture pattern.[8] Moreover, among natives there is no organized research for technological improvement or for scientific, verifiable knowledge, since the concept of scientific method as a means of progressive increase of knowledge and adaptation of natural forces to human control seems to be peculiar to our Western culture.[9] Under the circumstances, cultural change is comparatively slow and usually occurs when the natives are compelled to make some new adjustment to their natural or social environment.

[8] Fejos, *Ethnography of the Yagua;* Thompson and Joseph, *The Hopi Way.*
[9] Ackerknecht, "Natural Diseases and Rational Treatment in Primitive Medicine," *Bulletin of the History of Medicine,* XIX (1946), 467–97.

For natives in particular, therefore, necessity is not only the mother of invention, which is rare enough, but is, moreover, in the form of cultural crises, the primary stimulus toward the acceptance of cultural innovations acquired by acculturation and diffusion. As Linton writes:

The crisis situations in which the inventor receives the highest degree of recognition and reward seem to be those in which the very existence of a society and culture are threatened by some other society. The situation of the Plains Indian tribes after their final defeat and confinement to reservations would be a case in point. Although the white culture made available a new set of culture patterns which were adapted to the new conditions, acceptance of these would have meant the destruction of the whole of Indian culture and society. The Indians realized this, and the result was a frantic search for some way out. Messiahs such as the founder of the Ghost Dance religion were welcomed and honored, and their social and religious inventions were immediately accepted by tens of thousands of individuals. . . . Prior to the sudden onslaught of the whites such crisis situations must have been rare.[10]

This, however, should not be taken to imply that without, or apart from, such crises there would be complete cultural inertia and that culture otherwise reproduces itself true to type.[11] One must allow for "spontaneous variations" in the cultural sphere, as well as in the biological sphere. Natural increase or decrease in population, for example, or gradual cultural diffusion and acculturation may bring about changes without the stimulus of crises. The process appears to be cyclical, change, whether of society, culture, or environment, inducing cultural crises, and cultural crises, in turn, stimulating cultural invention and acculturation. The comparative frequency of cultural crises among modern societies is owing largely to the rapidity of cultural and social change, which, while it is progressive on its technological and scientific side, tends to be regressive on its social, interpersonal, and intersocietal side. The crises of our Western culture are largely internal and are, in effect, the symptoms of diseases produced by our opportunistic, aggressive, pragmatic way of living. Native peoples, on the other hand, like the common folk among civilized peoples, live at a much slower cultural tempo, and their crises are primarily external, the product of their geographical environment and the aggression of hostile societies.

Finally, it should be noted that one's theory as to the nature and

[10] Linton, *Study of Man,* pp. 308–9.
[11] Faris, *The Nature of Human Nature,* p. 287.

origin of cultural crises is itself a major factor in the resolution of such crises. If one were to adhere to the view that cultural crises are fated, whether by some power of Destiny, as the Greek dramatists imagined, or by the modern impersonal laws of cultural evolution and natural selection, then logically one would do nothing but drift from one crisis to another, hoping that fate or necessity may see the race through to happier times or waiting pessimistically for the inevitable doom. If, on the other hand, one were to adhere to the humanistic view submitted here, that man under God or Nature controls his own cultural destiny and in the long run is free to choose and realize the ends he would achieve, then he could be certain that much thought and effort will be expended by all who share this view to bring about an improvement in our human condition. Prayer, as is well recognized, is also a form of activity which may function as a psychological incentive to human effort by providing the individual in society with a common faith in the cosmic basis of his ideals and in their eventual successful realization. Religious faith may, however, also tend to identify providence with fate, as may be seen among the Mohammedan Arabs of the Near East, and this may result in a paralysis of cultural effort and initiative.[12] It is precisely because of our belief that man can and ought to decide for himself the form of his future cultural development that we can predict within limits and with some measure of certainty the course of events in the near future, since it is for us collectively to decide and determine whether they shall take place in our time. On the other hand, belief in so-called impersonal, inevitable, laws of cultural development tends to paralyze human initiative (unless, indeed, one decides, in spite of his theory, to help along and accelerate "the wave of the future") and, moreover, provides no empirical criterion for predicting the direction or pattern of cultural changes to come. In human affairs, then, we are confronted with the paradoxical situation that man's freedom, or power of self-determination, is the source of his cultural "laws" of social behavior. All cultural trends are conditional or hypothetical, since they depend on human intelligence, will, and initiative for their inception and maintenance, and there is no a priori certainty, or guarantee, other than human faith and determination, that development will follow one direction rather than another. The concept of "natural laws of cul-

---

[12] Tannous, "Extension Work among the Arab Fellahin," *Applied Anthropology*, III (1944), 1–12.

tural development" which is presupposed by the naturalistic positivists and transcendental idealists simply has no basis in fact.

### 5. SURVIVAL AND AXIOLOGICAL CRISES

Since, as has been noted, the cultural process provides both the means and the ends of social living, one may distinguish two corresponding types of crises, namely, survival, or existential, crises and axiological,[13] or value, crises. Survival crises involve the preservation of social existence; axiological crises refer to transformations in the form or system of values of a given culture. In a survival crisis the question is: To be or not to be. In an axiological crisis, the problem is how to be; what kind of life is worth living and preserving. Put in Darwinian terms, the issue is the survival of the fittest in contrast to the normative problem of who or what is fittest or most worthy to survive.

Survival crises may originate from either natural or cultural causes. All natural crises, such as the processes of birth and death, earthquakes, floods, drought, famine, and so forth, are survival crises, since they affect primarily the very possibility of the existence of the individual and his society. From a cultural perspective, war, whatever its motives and objectives, for a minority of the participants at least, even under the most favorable circumstances, is a survival crisis. Similarly, a society may also experience survival crises when its culture is inadequate to cope with the problems of its social or natural environment, especially when confronted by rapid or sudden changes. In all instances survival crises are practical emergencies.

Axiological crises, on the other hand, originate primarily from cultural causes, such as the assumed incompatibility of two or more cultural systems, or conflicting social interests. Axiological crises may be both theoretical and practical, internal, as well as external. In extreme instances an axiological crisis may be a reflection of value nihilism, of the anarchic cultural state in which there are no established, socially recognized standards, and all parties act without scruples and with a view solely to their own immediate advantage. In the sphere of international relations, such cynical and unrestrained disregard of the ideal rights and interests of other peoples soon becomes intolerable and inevitably leads to open conflict and survival crises—a sequence of events with which the Second World War has made us all too familiar.

[13] Urban, *The Intelligible World.*

Similarly, within a given society the unwillingness of various groups to co-operate for the common good soon makes for the suspension of normal, social life and imperils the life of the community. The rise of crime statistics and the widespread industrial strife of the postwar era in American life are all indicative of the temporary axiological crises of our society.

The tragedy of axiological crises is that so many of them need never have occurred if only the disputants had not regarded opposite polar values, which may, and ought to, complement one another, as if they were logical and practical contraries and hence mutually exclusive. In the political sphere there is always the temptation on the part of those in power to exclude the opposition or to govern in the interest of one class, even though the opposition represents a polar interest essential for the well-being of the state as a whole. Thus, to cite but one example from contemporary American politics, individual freedom and social planning are pragmatically compatible social ideals which are represented in the heat of political controversy as if they were contraries between which we are compelled to choose. The real issues are, *freedom for whom* and *planning for what.* If cultural institutions be viewed functionally and evaluated in terms of their contribution to the social welfare rather than abstractly and impersonally as absolute entities which must be retained regardless of the human cost, then the political and social issues of our society can be readily resolved.[14]

In all such axiological issues it is not a question of either-or, of all-or-none, but of both-and, of the proper proportion of each. There are indeed instances of genuinely opposed and contrary values, of good versus evil, such as social democracy versus racial and religious intolerance, or government by arbitrary will and force versus government by objective law and rational persuasion, which require decisive, uncompromising action. Democracies in particular have in the past, at least, allowed themselves to condone obvious evil practices on the assumption that interference with such "self-expression" would be a violation of individual freedom, thereby endangering their very existence as democracies. But while it may be admitted theoretically that our main problems involve the harmonizing of two genuine, positive goods, a resolution of the conflict in practice is most difficult and requires a degree of practical wisdom which is rarely found among political leaders. That is why, as history demonstrates, it is not difficult to reach agreement

[14] Schlesinger, *The Age of Jackson,* especially ch. xxxvii.

as to the existence of a survival crisis and the means to be taken to remove it, but it is extremely difficult to obtain agreement as to the existence and nature of value crises. Democratic statesmen, in particular, who require the support of public opinion for their policies, find it advisable to wait for the opportunity to win popular support in a war of defense, rather than take the initiative themselves on ideological grounds and risk public disapproval and internal strife. Only after the struggle has begun is the ideological import of the struggle publicized in order to win additional public support. The manner in which the late President Roosevelt rallied public opinion and led a united nation to participate in the Second World War after the Japanese attack on Pearl Harbor illustrates this point.

In historical experience axiological and survival crises are closely interrelated, since man is prepared to sacrifice his existence, if need be, for the values and institutions which render his life meaningful. Man, it appears, is not content with mere self-preservation in the biological sense, since the self he is most concerned to preserve is his cultural and spiritual self, the one expressed in his moral, religious, and scientific aspirations.[15] A life deprived of freedom in the practice of one's cultural traditions is for the majority of men not worth living, and they are therefore prepared to resist all attempts to deprive them of cultural autonomy—a fundamental, ideological motivation which unscrupulous, dictatorial governments of modern times have tended to underestimate. Negatively, a society, like an individual, when confronted with social forces with which it cannot cope, may lose its self-respect and in frustration yield its will to live in order to escape the burden of an existence which it finds uninteresting and intolerable. The decline of many native societies when they are brought into contact with Western peoples points up this social attitude.[16] Modern Zionism, on the other hand, is at bottom the expression of a cultural renaissance among the Jewish people and of their determination to live a cultural life of their own in a national home of their own. The recognition by the United Nations of the newly created state of Israel marked the fulfillment of a messianic dream and was, in part, a tribute to the unconquerable courage and idealistic faith of the Jewish people in the face of the catastrophic survival crises which confronted its members, especially during the

[15] Bidney, *The Psychology and Ethics of Spinoza.*
[16] Pitt-Rivers, *The Clash of Culture and the Contact of Races;* Reed, *The Making of Modern New Guinea.*

Second World War and in the ensuing war with the Arab states.[17]

The close connection between axiological and survival crises may be further illustrated by the changing relations between cultural majorities and cultural minorities. In times of war, when the life of the nation is at stake, there is a degree of social harmony and mutual co-operation which rarely prevails in times of peace. In times of peace, survival crises, such as strikes and economic depressions, frequently provide the occasion for a breakdown of traditional values and the violation of minority rights, notwithstanding all the liberal sentiments inculcated in the schools and professed by the majority in times of prosperity. This would indicate that one may not divorce social ideals from prevailing economic and social conditions and that insofar as a society suffers from economic or political insecurity one may expect prejudicial discrimination against the cultural minorities. As a rule, a given so-called cultural minority problem is really a reflection of chronic majority prejudice and insecurity.

Axiological and survival values are also brought into close relation by the struggle for power between groups within a society or between diverse societies. Since Nietzsche [18] and Marx, it has become commonly recognized that the profession of universal social ideals may serve the special interests of some dominant group, or of a subservient group who wish to weaken those in power. Thus, it has not been difficult to show that the advocates of freedom and laissez faire during the nineteenth century usually fought for economic privileges without corresponding social responsibilities. Similarly, most wars of the past have been to some extent, at least, motivated by a quest for power, although indirectly and as a by-product they may have in some instances resulted in social reforms and increased social welfare.

This close association of partisan interests and social ideals has led many of the sophisticated to conclude that there is no objective basis in the nature of things for human values and that all values are ultimately relative to one's social and economic class.[19] What is overlooked in the name of realism and positivism is that although one may be deceived into believing that given parties mean their universal, idealistic professions to be taken literally, the fact that such appeals are, and can

[17] Weizmann, *Trial and Error;* Steinberg, *A Partisan Guide to the Jewish Problem.*

[18] Nietzsche, "The Genealogy of Morals," in his *Philosophy of Nietzsche.*

[19] See Chapter 6.

be, made successfully is itself proof of man's ability to transcend his class interests and to envision objective values in harmony with scientific reality. The cultural evolution of man reveals a striking tendency toward the universalizing, or "democratizing," of human values and institutions, notwithstanding all the temporary setbacks and reactionary attempts to "nationalize" or tribalize cultural values.

From a broad philosophical perspective, one's theory of social values and cultural dynamics constitutes a most significant factor in the production or elimination of a "perpetual crisis complex." If, for example, one adheres to the positivistic and relativistic doctrine that sociocultural conflicts and crises are inevitable because there is no rational way of reconciling opposite social values, then, indeed, one is bound to act as if every cultural difference of opinion constituted a major threat to one's way of life. On this basis the state of peace is but a truce between rival factions within or outside given societies which enables both sides to build up their strength for the inevitable decisive struggle. In the end, on this premise, there can be but one dominant power in a world of cultural uniformity devoid of social classes. In this manner, what begins as sociocultural relativism and pluralism ends by sanctioning the most ruthless cultural monism.

The Neo-Darwinian theory of cultural evolution has been a significant factor in promoting a perpetual crisis complex. The basic premise of this biocultural theory is that in the sphere of culture—as in that of biology—"the struggle for existence" leads naturally to "the survival of the fittest." From a simplistic, practical point of view, one must admit, the position seems plausible. One must first live in order to lead any chosen form of life. This would seem to imply that survival values are logically and actually prior to axiological, cultural values and that all normative values are rooted ultimately in the desire for self-preservation and demonstrate their validity by the practical power of their adherents in the struggle for existence. The cultural process and the realization of cultural ideals is not, on this basis, an end in itself, but always, and primarily, a means for the preservation of life in the struggle for existence in competition with others and with the forces of nature. Everything cultural needs justification in terms of life, but life itself requires no justification.

Critics of this naturalistic theory of cultural evolution and cultural validity have demonstrated repeatedly that there is no inherent connection between biological struggle for existence and axiological, normative fitness for survival.[20] Besides, for cultural man mere life, or self-preservation in the biological sense, is no longer sufficient as a motive for living, as may be seen from the frequency of suicides among individuals with a maximum of economic security. Whatever may have been the case in really primitive societies (of which we have no record), modern civilized man is concerned to live a normative, cultural life and is prepared to sacrifice his existence, when required, in order that his society and his children may continue to enjoy the amenities of a civilized life. Cultural values are "superorganic" in the sense that they transcend biological, organic values and are not deduced from them, even though they are rooted in the natural needs and potentialities of the human organism and are dependent on human initiative. Thus, although one must, indeed, first live in order to live well or in accordance with one's ideal of the good life, it does not follow that life under any or all circumstances is the primary end-in-itself of human striving. In a sense, cultural man reverses the natural biological order and determines for himself the conditions and standards of a tolerable and desirable existence.

## 6. THE CRISES OF ACCULTURATION

One of the most widespread forms of axiological crisis is exemplified by the process of acculturation. For many native peoples brought involuntarily and reluctantly into contact with Western civilization, acculturation is all too often "deculturation," since the old, partially discarded cultural forms and institutions are not superseded by functional new forms. Such cultural crises may be regarded as the products of cultural inertia and of the withering away of native institutions when brought into contact with alien patterns of culture which they can neither resist nor assimilate. More often, however, an axiological crisis is the product of a negative reaction of active resistance to some of the sociocultural changes brought about by the introduction of new industrial techniques. Thus, as Chinese sociologists have noted,[21] the transition in China from an argicultural to an industrial age has been accompanied by resistance on the part of workers and peasants who were more or less compelled by the exigencies of the war to undergo these changes. In such instances the axiological crises are brought

[20] Sorokin, *Contemporary Sociological Theories;* Urban, *The Intelligible World.*
[21] Shih, *China Enters the Machine Age.*

about by the personal dissatisfaction of the human victims with the impersonal processes and demoralizing social by-products of technological changes. For many peoples of the East, technological efficiency is often thought to be obtained at too high a price in social well-being, especially since its most articulate advocates tend to regard efficiency as an end in itself rather than as a means to the end of gracious living.

It should be noted, however, that positive acculturation, as well as negative acculturation, on the part of native peoples may also lead to social unrest because of the very attempt to imitate some of the cultural ideals and practices introduced by the dominant group. In contemporary China the initial success of the communist revolution may well accelerate the process of acculturation regardless of internal resistance and human costs. In the case of dependencies and colonies, natives, on learning the implications of the democratic way of life, have come to resent the disparity between idealistic, equalitarian ideology and their subservient status as colonials.[22] Where, as in the case of India and the Dutch East Indies, virtual independence has been granted, the axiological crisis is being successfully resolved and the process of acculturation continues peacefully. Elsewhere, as in the protectorates and mandated areas of North and Central Africa and Indonesia, the struggle continues. In South Africa the present government of the insecure white minority has embarked on a program of reactionary legislation designed to keep the native majority in perpetual subservience as a cultural minority. Under such conditions of enduring tension any power, whatever its ulterior motives, which offers support and sympathy to the suppressed minority is bound to exercise considerable influence. It may well be part of what Vico has called historic providence and Hegel "the cunning of reason" that the struggle for the democratization of social values continues and may be brought to a successful conclusion in time in spite of the antagonists and by means never intended by their protagonists.

Undoubtedly the Second World War must be regarded in this connection as the most potent factor in promoting culture change on a scale never before put into practice. The destruction and devastation of the war has compelled the survivors in Europe and Asia to build anew, not only in the material sense but also in the cultural sense of

[22] Kennedy, "The Colonial Crisis and the Future," in Linton, ed., *The Science of Man in the World Crisis;* Wirth, "The Problem of Minority Groups," in *ibid.;* Keesing, "Applied Anthropology in Colonial Administration," in *ibid.;* Wilson, *The Analysis of Social Change.*

revising their traditional institutions and patterns of thought. Acculturation will proceed voluntarily and more or less coercively. In a sense,
the victors in this war, the Anglo-Americans, on the one hand, and the
Russian peoples, on the other, are now engaged in a vast secular mis-
sionary enterprise, whose objective is the winning of converts to their
ideological faiths. The democratization of Japan by the Americans and
the communizing of Eastern Europe and China by Russia are manifestations of the new process of planned world acculturation. Whatever
may be the material rewards, the Great Powers are now concerned to
establish "empires of the mind" [23] and to build the world of the future
in their own images.

## 7. THE CONCEPT OF PERPETUAL CRISES

There is profound truth, apparently, in the symbolical account in
Genesis of the Fall of Man. Man, it seems, prefers to win his way to a
paradise on earth through a knowledge of good and evil, through a long
process of survival and axiological crises, rather than accept a cultural
order whose benefits and advantages he does not appreciate and which
he has had no share in creating "by the sweat of his brow." Human
failure to achieve lasting social stability and peace is owing chiefly
to the psychological fact that men are drawn together more by fear of
some crisis, some imminent danger which threatens their very existence
or cherished privileges, than by pure love of the universal, ideal good
—a truth which Thomas Hobbes implied in his classic *Leviathan*. According to Hobbes, man was compelled to forego the liberty of exercising his "natural rights" or powers in the "state of nature" and to
combine with his fellows in a civil or cultural state, because he found
the perpetual threat to his security intolerable. The basic truth of this
hypothesis—apart from its historical inaccuracies—is demonstrated by
our contemporary democratic societies, where one finds a maximum
of social cohesion and communal effort in times of survival crises, such
as war or famine, while in so-called normal times of peace nature, in
the form of unscrupulous egoism and unceasing industrial struggles,
is allowed to take its blind course, irrespective of the social maladjust-
ment thereby produced. Historically, too, most governments have been
quick to realize the value of survival crises as a means of maintaining
themselves in power and overriding all opposition to their iron-clad

[23] McCormick, "Empire Moving in Opposite Directions," New York *Times*, March
16, 1946.

control, on the pretext of some national emergency. The modern totalitarian governments have simply carried to an extreme the notion that life is a perpetual crisis in which the end of national survival and power justifies any kind of means, regardless of the human and cultural costs. In this way individual freedom is sacrificed to "the higher freedom" of unconditional surrender to the categorical dictates of the state.

Our modern states are at one with the so-called primitive societies in seeking to maintain the unity and cohesion of the in-group by drawing attention to the actual or imaginary dangers which threaten them from some out-group of "barbarian" strangers.[24] Where such useful and indispensable foreign enemies are lacking, both primitive and civilized societies manage to fixate upon some convenient scapegoat in their midst, some natural evil spirit or sorcerer in the case of the former,[25] and some helpless minority in the case of the latter. Thus, native peoples, although they enjoy considerable cultural stability when left to themselves, live in a state of perpetual crises because of their belief in the malevolence of the natural forces of their environment and their fear of other societies which do not recognize the human rights of alien strangers. Native peoples therefore tend to possess a predominantly tragic outlook upon life rather than a care-free one,[26] since they imagine nature to be an organic whole in which all forces and events interact and "participate" [27] in diverse ways so as to promote or hinder human welfare. The severe trials and ordeals which many native societies sanction in the course of the critical "rites of passage" [28] marking the human life-cycle from birth to death are evidences of their perpetual fear and concern for their survival and social welfare.

So-called civilized peoples, on the other hand, having conquered their fear of malevolent gods and spirits through acquisition of the scientific point of view, suffer instead from chronic cultural instability and an apparently insatiable desire for dominion over others less "advanced" than themselves in the art of war. Owing to the development of ever-more-powerful weapons of human destruction, our civilized societies are beset by perpetual fear of mutual annihilation and feel compelled, therefore, to prepare themselves for the defense of their vital interests.

[24] Sumner, *Folkways*, ch. i.
[25] Frazer, *The Golden Bough*, chs. lvi, lvii, lviii.
[26] Radin, *Primitive Man as a Philosopher*, chs. viii, xi.
[27] Lévy-Bruhl, *Primitives and the Supernatural.*
[28] Tozzer, *Social Origins and Social Continuities*; Malinowski, "Culture," in *Encyclopaedia of the Social Sciences*, IV, 621–45, especially p. 642.

The development of atomic energy as a weapon of destruction has revolutionized the whole process of war and upset the traditional concept of "the balance of power." Man's ability to induce atomic, or nuclear, disintegration has also made it possible for him to produce cultural disintegration on a scale never imagined before. War may no longer be compared to a chemical reaction which produces new compounds, but leaves the original elements unchanged. Atomic war is essentially war of annihilation, just as the release of atomic energy involves the transmutation of elements and the conversion of matter into radiant energy.[29] The atomic revolution, therefore, necessitates a corresponding social and axiological revolution to meet this new crisis of humanity.

The nations of this postwar world, especially the victorious Big Powers, are now faced with a crucial decision: whether to acknowledge their obligation to participate in one intelligible world of primary, universal values, or to go on competing with one another within their conflicting cultural worlds; whether to seek their mutual welfare within the framework of a democratic world order, or to promote their own interests and sovereign power irrespective of the social cost to themselves and other peoples. The latter alternative has been tried throughout recorded history by the so-called practical statesmen and has led mankind into a series of ever-increasing disasters. Perhaps now, with the advent of the age of atomic energy and atomic destruction and with the imminent threat of planetary annihilation,[30] the former alternative, envisaged by the great prophets and utopian dreamers of all ages, may yet be put to the test. In this manner, out of the greatest potential crisis may come the greatest actual progress for all mankind.

In the meantime the world crisis continues unresolved. The very finality of atomic warfare and the constant threat of mutual annihilation, now that both sides have the atom bomb, have made the great powers wary about embarking on a Third World War. Instead we have the "peace" of a perpetual world crisis, commonly called "the cold war," in which the opposing powers impoverish themselves in making preparations for total war, while their peoples hope and pray that it may not come to pass. The tragedy of this world crisis is that both the democratic and the communist nations find themselves in op-

[29] Masters, Dexter, and Way, eds., *One World or None.*

[30] Einstein, "Einstein on the Atomic Bomb as Told to Raymond Swing," *Atlantic Monthly,* CLXXVI (1945), 43–45.

position because of mutual fear and distrust. As a citizen of a great democracy, I cannot but feel that this country and its allies in the United Nations desire peace and international harmony above all else. Yet if its opponents have no faith in its professed ideals and prefer to put their trust in unilateral military and economic power this country, too, must prepare for war in the interest of self-preservation. It is a vicious circle, created by fear and mythological ideology, from which there appears at present to be no escape. I cannot help hoping, nevertheless, that where pure idealism may not prevail, the interest of mutual self-preservation may do so in the long run, since men are most likely to invoke universal ideals when it is to their special interest to do so. It is rational, therefore, to believe and assume that in the course of time the nations of the world may consent to give up some of their "natural rights" and refrain from exercising their "sovereign power," in order to emerge from the insecurity of the international "state of nature" and to participate, instead, in a world cultural community which would guarantee to all alike security with liberty and justice.

# 13

# Modes of Cultural Integration

UNDOUBTEDLY cultural integration is one of the basic social problems of our age. The ever-increasing specialization of our cultural life has made educators, scholars, and scientists keenly aware of the need for some principle of unification whereby to comprehend our culture as a whole and to provide a common meaning and objective for the multitude of diverse interests and values. Practically, the Second World War, even more than any theoretical argument, has led thinking men to realize that genuine, enduring peace requires a harmony of world cultures which may enable all the peoples of the world to live together in peace, assured of their common human rights and opportunities for progressive development.

## 1. THE CONCEPT OF FUNCTIONAL INTEGRATION

Beginning with the empirical, comparative study of culture traits and cultural institutions for the purpose of reconstructing the stages of evolutionary development, anthropologists have gradually adopted the holistic perspective of the psychologists, physicists, philosophers, and biologists and have begun to view cultural phenomena as interrelated wholes which are more than the sum of their parts. Although Boas and his followers made implicit use of the category of function in their field investigations of particular cultures, it remained for Malinowski and Radcliffe-Brown to make "functionalism" a fighting term in contemporary anthropology. From a philosophical point of view this theory may be understood best as the application to ethnology and social anthropology of the current naturalistic, instrumental approach developed by John Dewey. The functionalists define the nature of a thing by its activities, or effects, within a given social context. The functionalists insist also that a culture is an organic whole and that any attempt to study its parts in isolation or abstraction from one another is bound to give a distorted view of the culture. They are opposed, therefore, to the comparative study of aggregates of culture traits and forms abstracted from their cultural context. Notwithstanding some lip service to the importance of historical studies, the functionalists have tended to emphasize the study of cultural processes and institutions within a given culture rather than the ethnohistorical study of diffusion and acculturation.

In common with philosophical instrumentalism, ethnological functionalism rests on the assumption that function is logically prior to form and determines the latter. Malinowski explicitly states that "form is always determined by function, and that in so far as we can not establish such a determinism, elements of form cannot be used in a scientific argument."[1]

As I see it, the really significant difference between cultural functionalism and cultural historicism is essentially metacultural and concerns the ontological status of culture.

According to the sociocultural approach derived from nineteenth-century evolutionism, culture is said to be a "superorganic" entity independent of the facts of biology and psychology. The superorganic level of reality is thought to be an emergent reality which requires no reference to the levels below it and is intelligible in itself without regard to the nature of man. On the other hand, functionalistic theory insists upon the instrumental reality of culture and indicates its utility in the satisfaction of primary and derived human needs. For the functionalist, cultural phenomena are not intelligible apart from their relation to psychobiological phenomena and social needs and imperatives. Malinowski himself drew attention to this issue.

But it might be maintained, as is done by some sociologists, for instance Durkheim, that the subject matter of social science and that of physiology have to be kept strictly apart. This is not possible. For although human beings are animals, they are animals that live not by physiological drives alone, but by physiological drives molded and modified by the conditions of culture.[2]

From this point of view, culture appears as a vast conditioning apparatus which, through training, the imparting of skills, the teaching of norms, and the development of tastes, amalgamates nurture with nature, and produces beings whose behavior cannot be determined by the study of anatomy and physiology alone.[3]

Functionalism, as represented by Malinowski, involves a humanistic, psychobiological conception of culture and in this respect may be

[1] Malinowski, *A Scientific Theory of Culture*, p. 149.
[2] Malinowski, *The Dynamics of Culture Change*, p. 42.
[3] *Ibid.*, p. 43.

contrasted with the impersonal, superorganic theory of some culture historians and social anthropologists.

The issue between functionalism and historical superorganicism may be demonstrated also by reference to the positions taken as regards cultural unity and cultural pluralism. Insofar as culture is held to be a superorganic reality, human culture is thought of as a universal, unitary tradition, or "stream," in which particular cultures participate. As Lowie has put it:

> There is only one natural unit for the ethnologist—the culture of all humanity at all periods and in all places; only when the functionalist has, at least implicitly, defined his particular culture within that frame of reference, does he know what he is talking about. . . . In short, spurning isolated facts as superciliously as does Malinowski, we shall seek meaningful relations in all directions, not within the supposedly watertight compartment of a single body of social tradition.[4]

> A science of culture must, in principle, register every item of social tradition, correlating it significantly with any other aspect of reality, *whether that lies within the same culture or outside*. In defiance of the dogma that any one culture forms a closed system, we must insist that such a culture is invariably an artificial unit segregated for purposes of expediency.[5]

According to Lowie, culture is a concrete, historical universal and all particular cultures are abstractions therefrom. On the other hand, Malinowski's position may be characterized as cultural pluralism, or nominalism. For the latter only particular cultural wholes are real units and the concept of universal, human culture is an abstract generalization derived from the imagination of many particular, concrete cultures. According to this nominalistic and pluralistic thesis, it may be said that there is a universal human culture, inasmuch as one finds in all human societies institutions which have identical functions in satisfying individual and social needs. This morphological universality of cultural institutions is compatible with an actual plurality of cultures. Logically, the universalistic and nominalistic, or pluralistic, views of culture may be reconciled by a concept of culture which recognizes some degree of historical continuity in human culture, as well as an actual plurality of cultures. In practice, however, these two positions are usually presented as antithetical, since each denies the element of truth in the other.

Malinowski, in particular, has stressed the thesis that the elements

[4] Lowie, *History of Ethnological Theory*, p. 236.
[5] *Ibid.*, p. 235.

of a culture are closely interrelated and has drawn attention to the dangers of meddling with its functional pattern of interdependent institutions. In his general axioms of functionalism he states that culture "is an integral in which the various elements are interdependent." [6] Cultures are said to be functionally integrated in the sense that all their elements serve as means to the satisfaction of psychobiological needs and that the institutions of a culture are interdependent.

Malinowski points out that cultural integration may be accounted for on a series of principles.

Culture is an integral composed of partly autonomous, partly coördinated institutions. It is integrated on a series of principles such as the community of blood through procreation; the contiguity in space related to coöperation; the specialization in activities; and last but not least, the use of power in political organization. Each culture owes its completeness and self-sufficiency to the fact that it satisfies the whole range of basic, instrumental and integrative needs. To suggest, therefore, as has been recently done, that each culture only covers a small segment of its potential compass, is at least in one sense radically wrong.[7]

For Malinowski there are, therefore, no cultural "survivals," that is, traits and customs which are not functionally related to their culture. Each culture is a complete, self-sufficient entity. Malinowski assumes that the actual function and the ideal, as well as historical, function of an institution, or custom, are identical and maintains, therefore, that each culture satisfies the whole range of basic, instrumental and integrative needs. On this assumption, there can be no obsolete culture traits or instances of culture "lag." He assumes a priori that all institutions and customs are equally satisfactory and does not recognize the possibility of disfunctional, reactionary tendencies within the context of a given culture. That is why he is prepared to criticize those anthropologists who grant that each historical culture comprises but a small segment of human potentialities.

Furthermore, according to Malinowski a culture may be integrated as far as the satisfaction of basic human needs is concerned, but this does not imply the coordination of all its institutions. A culture is not to be thought of as if it were one great integrated institution comprising many subordinate institutions. A culture is an aggregate of institutions, not an organized system. Malinowski apparently goes along with the sociologists far enough to adopt the institution as the basic unit of cul-

[6] Malinowski, *A Scientific Theory of Culture*, p. 150.
[7] *Ibid.*, p. 40.

ture, but parts company with them when it comes to interpreting cultural phenomena as functions of society.

Malinowski's failure to provide any principle of integration for a culture as a whole goes back to his conception of the individual. Man, as conceived by him, is an aggregate of needs and impulses which lacks any unifying principle or over-all coherent character. Each human need is said to be incorporated in a specific type of institution, but the culture as a whole lacks a principle of integration capable of integrating the many diverse functions and motivations. At most, we are told, that all the institutions of a culture are interdependent, but no genuine explanation is offered as to the nature and extent of this interdependence. In the end, we are really not much further ahead of the old school of anthropologists, with their much-maligned trait complexes, since the functionalist's "integrative imperative" does not manifest itself in the culture as a whole.

When we turn to Radcliffe-Brown, we find that he, like Durkheim, interprets the functional significance of institutions by reference to the postulated unity and solidarity of the social group. That is, he assumes social integration as a fact, as well as an ideal, and interprets cultural phenomena as products of society designed to promote social rather than individual needs. Thus, he writes:

The function of any recurrent activity, such as the punishment of a crime or a funeral ceremony, is the part it plays in the social life as a whole and therefore the contribution it makes to the maintenance of the structural continuity. . . . The function of a particular social usage is the contribution it makes to the total social life as the functioning of the total social system. Such a view implies that a social system . . . . has a certain kind of unity, which we may speak of as a functional unity. We may define it as a condition in which all parts of the social system work together with a sufficient degree of harmony or internal consistency, i.e., without producing persistent conflicts which can neither be resolved nor regulated.[8]

From this it appears that Radcliffe-Brown regards the society as the ultimate functional unity and interprets all cultural phenomena as means of promoting this social unity. In this respect his position is fundamentally similar to that of the sociologists rather than that of the cultural anthropologists, since the latter do not acknowledge the primacy of society over culture.

[8] Radcliffe-Brown, "On the Concept of Function in Social Science," *American Anthropologist*, XXXVII (1935), 394–402; reprinted in his *Structure and Function in Primitive Society*, pp. 178–87.

## 2. THE AESTHETIC, OR FORMALISTIC, INTEGRATION OF CULTURE

While Boas may be said to have introduced the concept of "pattern" in his description of culture areas, Sapir merits the credit for having systematically transferred the concept of "pattern" from his linguistic studies to those of culture and personality.[9] Sapir's paper "The Unconscious Patterning of Behavior in Society," [10] made explicit use of this concept long before Ruth Benedict popularized the term in her study *Patterns of Culture*. In this paper he explicitly distinguished between the form and the function of cultural patterns, indicating that the formal, or structural, element of cultural patterns is often adhered to actually, as in the speaking of a language, without any awareness on the part of individuals that they are doing so. Similarly, the function of a given pattern often becomes obscure, and yet people continue to perform acts whose functional significance escapes them. In this respect he was in complete agreement with Boas and Leslie Spier, who had noted the disparity of form and function and had demonstrated how a ceremony, such as the Sun Dance, may change its functional significance without corresponding change of form.

Some contemporary ethnologists have held the position that culture is a "construct" and an abstraction from actual behavior. Kluckhohn, in particular, has drawn a sharp distinction between cultural patterns, or "designs for living," on the one hand, and cultural behavior, on the other, the former being identified with culture proper. Thus, he states:

Culture is not a disembodied force. It is created and transmitted by people. However, culture, like well-known concepts of the physical sciences, is a convenient abstraction. . . . What is seen are regularities in the behavior or artifacts of a group that has adhered to a common tradition. The regularities in style and technique of ancient Inca tapestries or stone axes from Melanesian islands are due to the existence of mental blueprints for the group.[11]

Culture is a *way* of thinking, feeling, believing. It is the group's knowledge stored up (in memories of men; in books and objects) for future use.[12]

Since Culture is an abstraction, it is important not to confuse culture and society. A "society" refers to a group of people who interact more with each

[9] See the comprehensive review by Zellig S. Harris of *Selected Writings of Edward Sapir, Language*, XXVII (1951), 288–333.
[10] Sapir, "The Unconscious Patterning of Behavior in Society," in *The Unconscious: a Symposium*, ed. by E. S. Dummer; reprinted in *Selected Writings of Edward Sapir*, ed. by D. G. Mandelbaum, 544–59.
[11] Kluckhohn, *Mirror for Man*, p. 22.      [12] *Ibid.*, p. 23.

other than they do with other individuals—who cooperate with each other for the attainment of certain ends. You can see and indeed count the individuals who make up a society. A "Culture" refers to the distinctive ways of life of such a group of people.[13]

Similarly, Gillin holds that "culture is to be regarded as the patterning of activity, not the activity itself." [14]

Historically, ethnologists may be thought of as having gone from one extreme to another. Beginning with an empirical, comparative study of culture traits, they have gradually paid less and less attention to the content of culture and more to the aesthetic patterns and forms, so that now culture pattern has been identified with culture, and the actual behavior and traits are thought of as only the exemplifications of the construct, or abstraction, called "culture."

Insofar as pattern, or form, is said to be the unit of culture, then any given culture is conceived as a configuration of culture patterns. Historical cultures are thought to be characterized by an over-all configuration, or "superstyle," which serves to differentiate it from other pattern systems. Thus, the unity of a culture is manifested by its aesthetic form, or style, rather than by an interdependence of functional institutions. Integration of culture is manifested by aesthetic coherency, rather than by social solidarity.

It is of interest to note in this connection that Kroeber, in his *Configurations of Culture Growth,* has drawn attention to the danger of abstracting pattern and form from content of culture:

I have spoken in the foregoing paragraphs of culture patterns and culture content as if they are easily contrastable phenomena: the form and the substance of culture, so to speak. I am fully aware that this distinction is beset with difficulties: cultural form and content are both merely aspects of the same phenomena as they occur in nature. With analysis a point is soon reached where distinction becomes ambiguous. We can abstract an art style or an intellectual process, in the more favorable cases, and deal with it as pattern or form. We can also extract from the body of a culture individual items like the wearing or not wearing of shoes, or the lighting of candles as a religious offering, and treat these as if they were pure content or substance. Nevertheless, it is obvious that culture form can exist only with reference to culture content. A style can exist only in the presence of certain techniques. A way of thinking can be applied only upon a body of factual knowledge. And, on the other side, there is always a tendency for the items of culture

[13] *Ibid.,* p. 24.

[14] Gillin, "Cultural Adjustment," *American Anthropologist,* XLVI (1944), 429–47.

content, as they come in contact with one another, to form associations or complexes which in turn inevitably have form. We simply have no rigid criterion by which we can say that this cultural phenomenon is form and that is content. The two are necessarily in relation and must be considered as no more than useful abstractions of phenomena. At times we can fruitfully separate these aspects and give consideration chiefly to the one or the other; but this does not mean that they are separate realities. They occur interwoven.[15]

While Kroeber obviously has an adequate theoretical appreciation of the inherent relation of culture patterns and content, his actual procedure in writing this volume is to separate culture patterns from the dynamic, cultural processes with which they are actually associated in culture history. He traces the historical evolution of the great cultural configurations, but fails to render intelligible the cultural processes which made these changes possible and necessary.

As indicated earlier, my own position is that integral culture is not an abstract conceptual construct, but rather a concrete unity of form and content, pattern and process, in actual, inseparable unity and that either element when taken in abstraction from the other lacks the reality of actual culture. It is legitimate to abstract the form, or style, of a given artifact, or custom, for specific study; but one must not identify this patterned abstraction with cultural reality to the exclusion of empirical content and processes.

It is amusing to reflect that contemporary American anthropologists are divided over the ontological issue whether culture should be regarded as an abstraction or considered a reality *sui generis,* as of a superorganic level of phenomena. That is, culture is thought to be either a construct, or mental abstraction, lacking in concrete reality, or else it is said to be the supreme reality which renders all human life intelligible. Both conceptions are fallacious. The superorganicists tend to commit what I have termed elsewhere "the culturalistic fallacy"; the abstractionists, on the other side, commit what I should call "the conceptualistic fallacy" by failing to differentiate between a conceptual construct and the ontological object to which it refers.

One may illustrate the conceptualistic fallacy by reference to the method of natural science. In physics one postulates entities, such as atoms and the force of gravity, by means of conceptual constructs. The objects to which these concepts refer are not perceived, yet their existence in nature may be verified indirectly and their modes of opera-

---

[15] Kroeber, *Configurations of Culture Growth,* pp. 798–99.

tion may be described and predicted. Truth in science is not merely "the most expedient form of error," [16] as Vaihinger concluded, since the logical constructs of the scientist are not mere fictions, but hypotheses subject to indirect empirical verification by the method of epistemic correlations.[17] Similarly, the concept of culture is abstract, just as all concepts are, but this does not imply that cultural reality, to which this concept refers, is nothing but an abstraction in the ethnologist's mind, or a mental blueprint of behavior in society. Actual cultural reality is a concrete union of pattern and process, form and content, structure and events, each element of which may be abstracted for separate analysis by the intellect. The conceptual construct of culture and the actual process of culture may correspond epistemically in a scientific theory of culture but they are not identical and must not be confused.

### 3. THE CONCEPT OF INTEGRAL CULTURE

So far I have been concerned to point out that cultural reality comprises both process and pattern and is to be conceived as an ontological synthesis of both elements. Apparently there is a relation of polarity between cultural forms and processes, such that each factor is to some degree independent of the other and also essentially interdependent. The anthropological functionalists go to one extreme by maintaining the complete dependence of cultural form upon social function, while the formalists, or patternists, go to the opposite extreme by disregarding partly the varying functional significance of a given cultural form.

An ontologically integrated culture is one in which both form and function are mutually adapted so as to produce logical coherency and social harmony. An integral, holistic culture may be connotatively defined as the process and product of forms of life and thought acquired by man in society by virtue of which a society functions as a unit for the attainment of the common ends of self-preservation and self-realization.

*The significant cultural unit is the historically acquired form of activity, or patterned process,* rather than the pattern of which Ruth Benedict speaks or the social institution which Malinowski selects. A cultural pattern is an abstraction and is, therefore, scarcely to be regarded as the unit of concrete culture. Similarly, a culture is more than

---

[16] Vaihinger, *The Philosophy of 'As If,'* ch. xxv.
[17] Northrop, *The Logic of the Sciences and Humanities.*

the sum of its institutions, since many ideal culture traits are not institutionalized. Unless, therefore, one is prepared to exclude all individual habits as "precultural" achievements, as Malinowski [18] does, he must reject the thesis that the institution is the ultimate unit of culture.

Furthermore, I maintain that culture is essentially a polar concept and is unintelligible apart from a reference to nature, human and cosmic. From a genetic point of view culture in general may be understood as the dynamic process and product of human self-cultivation and involves the integral development of the potentialities of human nature, as well as of the cosmic environment, with a view of fitting man to nature and nature to man. The cultural process is begun to fulfill human psychobiological, intellectual, and social needs and is developed beyond the necessities of survival so as to provide the amenities of a good or perfect life. Integral culture, conceived as a normative ideal, satisfies man's biological, as well as his social, intellectual, and emotional, needs and aspirations by providing adequate expression for his potentialities and interests.

By developing human potentialities the cultural process makes for an actual increase in human power of achievement, often at the expense of the individual. As a restraining discipline, culture prepares the individual for life in society and achieves this objective by modifying and suppressing the individual's natural impulses in the interests of group welfare. Accordingly, there is in all societies some degree of tension between the individual and his society, between the egoistic impulses one would gratify and the altruistic ideals and social imperatives one acknowledges and is constrained to obey. The well-organized community, as well as the well-governed state, is one in which the interests of both the individual and society are protected, the society recognizing the individual's personal rights to freedom of self-expression in action and thought, while the individual identifies himself with his society and seeks to conform as far as possible to its time-tested ideals and indispensable requirements.

An integrated culture is a moving equilibrium, an ever-changing harmony regulated in accordance with the requirements of individual and social life. How to provide for this homeostatic, self-balancing equilibrium of sociocultural life is a problem which requires a maximum of practical wisdom and political statesmanship. In actual culture

[18] Malinowski, A Scientific Theory of Culture, p. 135.

history one may discern a tendency for states to go to either of two extremes: either to attempt to keep their culture in a more or less static condition by rigid adherence to tradition, or else to tolerate anarchistic movements which are contrary to the common interest. How to maintain cultural continuity along with cultural change is a perpetual challenge which every generation has had to face anew, but which, under the critical conditions of our times, confronts us with special urgency. We are being asked to choose between social security and individual freedom, as if these were logical alternatives rather than polar interests requiring mutual satisfaction.

To say that a normative, integral culture is a moving equilibrium is to imply that it is a homeostatic system analogous to a living organism. Integral culture is an open, rather than a closed, system, such that the system as a whole remains in a steady state, though there is a continuous flow of component materials.[19] Just as living systems maintain themselves in a steady state by utilizing materials rich in free energy, thereby avoiding the increase of entropy which cannot be averted in closed systems, so in cultural systems a steady homeostatic condition is maintained insofar as provision is made for the utilization of free invention, initiative, and novelty. Complete sociocultural conformity may be compared to a state of entropy which follows upon the leveling down of differences in a closed system. Cultural diversity and heterogeneity counteracts the tendency to cultural entropy and makes for a dynamic, self-feeding system, which maintains itself in a steady state while constantly making adjustments to environmental changes.

Instead of regarding culture systems as if they were organisms subject to morphological stages of inevitable growth and decay, as Spengler and Toynbee have done, it seems necessary to revise our conception of the cultural process upon the analogy of the open systems characteristic of physical and biological phenomena. Such a revision would enable us to comprehend the fact of cultural continuity and to avoid the pessimistic conclusions of cultural fate which have been put forward in the name of history and science. If there is to be a constant renewal of cultural life, then culture systems must be treated normatively as open systems capable of self-maintenance while undergoing change and creative evolution.

Both the social and the individual aspects of culture represent es-

[19] Bertalanffy, "The Theory of Open Systems in Physics and Biology," *Science,* CXI (1950), 23–29.

sential polar factors which exert a reciprocal influence upon one another. To suppress the individualistic, minority element of culture is to deprive cultural life of an indispensable source of development. Non-socialized culture, it must be emphasized, is still culture and is not to be excluded as "precultural," as Malinowski and other social anthropologists are wont to do. To identify culture with the "social heritage" is to assume that any given culture system is a closed system rather than a historical, ever-changing, open system subject to modification in a changing world.

In the course of time every culture, no matter how adequate it may have been, ceases to satisfy the universal and special needs of its adherents because of changing social and environmental conditions. People then become the slaves of their own creations and rationalize their enslavement by regarding culture as a "superorganic" entity over which they have no control. But sooner or later there is a humanistic reaction, and men arise, happily ignorant of the superorganic cultural determinism to which they are supposed to submit, whose rallying cry is "back to nature" and who appeal to the underprivileged to free themselves from the chains of their cultural past. Then, for a while men live in the faith that this time they will build to bring heaven down to earth. But the reality always falls short of the mythical dream and the process is repeated again. The history of human culture may be thought of as the record of man's attempts to devise culture systems which function in harmony with natural law.

## 4. THE EPISTEMIC INTEGRATION OF CULTURE

From an epistemological point of view holistic, or integral, culture may be described denotatively as comprising the historically acquired actual and ideal forms of behavior, feeling, and thought of members of society, as well as the products of these processes, such as artifacts, agrofacts (the products of agriculture), socifacts and mentifacts. Normative, ideational culture has no effective existence unless it is practiced and influences social behavior. Practical culture, the actual behavior and thought of persons, is not intelligible apart from the postulates and ideals which men have conceived for themselves. Epistemically, a culture as a whole is said to be integrated insofar as there is conformity between the actual behavior of its adherents and their professed ideals, between their theory and their practice. The ideational element of a culture is integrated insofar as the ideas and ideals which it comprises are logically coherent and aesthetically harmonious. The practical element of a culture is integrated when its customs and institutions are mutually compatible and viable. In a well-integrated culture people live more or less consistently and harmoniously with one another and approximate the ideal norms of their cultural tradition.

Theory and practice are to be understood as correlative, polar opposites, each of which involves the other, yet is partially independent of the other. Theory without practice is vain; practice without theory is blind and irrational. A rational life requires a happy combination of both elements. Overemphasis upon either element of human culture tends to produce fanatical dogmatists or unprincipled opportunists. Morally, we must judge theory by its practical consequences for human life and welfare, and practice by its theoretical implications. A theory which enables a man to be a good citizen cannot be entirely wrong, however erroneous it may appear. The fact that there is no exact correspondence between theory and practice is a basic argument in favor of freedom of thought in the political state, since the state's concern is with practical conformity to its laws and institutions rather than with theoretical consistency. Conversely, a theory which leads to harmful social consequences is socially suspect, notwithstanding its apparent rationality and coherency. In actual cultural and social life "integration" is not an unmixed good and may be pursued too efficiently. If the well-being of society is our criterion, rather than logical consistency or blind conformity, the way will be left open for freedom of thought and for a measure of social deviation and nonconformity.

Culturally, we must distinguish two separate factors in all theory, namely, the ideal formal principle and the actual varying content. For example, the ideal of justice may be conceived as a universal absolute ideal, but the empirical, historical content of that ideal, what is and may be regarded just under given circumstances, may well vary with time and conditions. Absolute ideals and varying cultural content are quite compatible in theory and practice. It is fallacious to assume that absolute ideals imply fixed modes of action regardless of the human situation. Morality and government are arts precisely because the moral man and the statesman must evaluate the changing requirements of the particular situation while adhering to basic fixed principles. Theoretically, we are not compelled to choose between a fixed absolutism which does not allow for cultural adjustment to the psychobiological needs of individuals and an anarchic opportunistic relativism which recognizes no fixed principles.[20] It is the narrowly practical people, who are always intent on doing something and do not stop to consider the significance and consequences of their acts, that are in the end among the most impractical. It is because people who pride themselves on their "practicality" neglect this elemental distinction that so much intolerance and abuse still prevail. It is usually the so-called conservative "practical" people, who persist in acts and customs which no longer serve the purpose for which they were originally intended, that corrupt morality and law. In our culture, especially, the "practical" men who are concerned with amassing wealth regardless of the human cost of their economic pursuits are responsible for a large measure of our social and economic problems.

In natural science speculative theory constantly enlarges the area of practical endeavor by revealing new prospects and spheres of research and application. In other words, scientific theory not only serves to render nature more intelligible but ultimately leads to practical discoveries and inventions. The atom bomb is but the most dramatic instance of the practical import of theoretical research. Similarly, culture theory suggests sociocultural inventions and adjustments which make possible a more efficient organization of society and a greater degree of harmony between societies.

In the realm of culture, however, the concept of the practical refers not only to what can be done but also to what ought to be done in order to achieve a given end. From this point of view what is practical is relative to one's theory of cultural values. What is practical for a member of a preliterate culture is impractical for a member of modern society. The significant changes in the history of human culture have brought about a transvaluation of the effective practical values of human conduct. The ideal of what ought to be done and what we are capable of doing suggests what can be done in the future.

Both theory and the practical requirements of social life provide the stimuli for cultural change. Historically, it may be shown that men have visualized ideal values which transcended the prevailing norms and customs of their time. That is, the ends, or values, which the intellect conceives are not mere abstractions and rationalizations of actual cultural conditions, though they are often suggested by cultural experiences, but creative constructs which have a reality and validity independent of their cultural context. Hence, the value of a cultural ideal

[20] See Chapter 15.

does not consist only in its being a means to action; practice may be the means of realizing ultimate ideals whose validity is intrinsic to themselves alone. Similarly, the horizons of social theory may be enlarged through experience gained in critical situations; social practice may, therefore, also lead to a revision of theory in the interests of cultural change. The doctrine of the polarity of theory and practice would do justice to both factors as essential elements in cultural life.

## 5. THE PSYCHOLOGICAL INTEGRATION OF CULTURE

Psychologically, cultural integration is manifested by the coordinated behavior habits, ideals, attitudes, and interests of the members of a given society. From an interindividual perspective, cultural integration is exemplified by the efficient functioning and harmonious interaction of the classes which constitute society. Negatively, it is shown by the absence of social crises which endanger the community. Thus, if one keeps in mind the polarity of the individual and his society, it appears that neither one alone is to be considered as the locus, or focal point, of cultural integration.

Modern ethnologists and psychiatrists who have been concerned with the study of personality and culture, such as Linton and Kardiner, have suggested the concept of "basic personality structure" as a means of evaluating cultural integration. The important point to note at the outset is that both Linton and Kardiner admit that they presuppose the notion that culture is an abstraction, or conceptual construct. On this premise culture can be said to exist only within the ego, or mind, of the individual. From this it is inferred that the common cultural ego, the basic personality structure, provides the locus of cultural integration. This thesis is clearly stated by Linton:

Basic personality structure, as the term is used here, represents the constellation of personality characteristics which would appear to be congenial with the total range of institutions comprised within a given culture. It has been deduced from a study of culture content and organization and is, therefore, an abstraction of the same order as culture itself. . . . By employing the concept of a societal personality structure it becomes possible to place the focal point of culture integration in the common denominator of the personalities of the individuals who participate in the culture. Culture is, in the last analysis, a matter of modes within the distributional ranges of the individual's responses with respect to various repetitive situations.[21]

[21] Linton, Foreword to Kardiner's *The Individual and His Society*.

Similarly, in the same work Kardiner quotes with approval Linton's statement that "culture insofar as it is anything more than an abstraction made by the investigator, exists only in the minds of the individuals who compose a society." [22]

Subsequently we find that Linton, taking into consideration the criticism of his concept of culture,[23] differentiates between "real culture patterns," "ideal culture patterns," and "culture constructs." In *The Cultural Background of Personality* he writes:

> To sum up, a *real culture* consists of the sum total of the behaviors of a society's members in so far as these behaviors are learned and shared. A *real culture pattern* represents a limited range of behaviors within which the responses of a society's members to a particular situation will normally fall. . . . A *culture construct pattern* corresponds to the mode of the variations within a real culture pattern.[24]

> In addition to real culture patterns and the culture construct patterns developed on the basis of the investigator's observation and plotting of behavior, all cultures include a certain number of what be called *ideal patterns.* These are abstractions which have been developed by the members of a society themselves. They represent the consensus of opinion on the part of the society's members as to how people should behave in particular situations.[25]

If one were to adopt this triadic classification of culture patterns, it would follow logically that there are also three types of personality structure corresponding to them, namely, a real personality structure, a modal personality structure, and an ideal personality structure. What Linton and Kardiner call the "basic personality structure" is, in fact, the average or modal personality structure which corresponds to the culture construct pattern. Linton explicitly states that "the basic personality type for any society is a matter of averages." [26] What is needed, therefore, is the concept of a "real personality type" to represent the lowest common cultural denominator, and an "ideal personality type" to connote the "value-attitude systems" which the members of a society profess. In fact, Linton implicitly makes use of a real and an ideal personality type, while believing that he is still talking about the basic, or construct, personality type. Thus, he speaks of "common personality elements" and of "common understandings and values" as

[22] Linton, *The Study of Man*, p. 8.

[23] Bidney, "On the Concept of Culture and Some Cultural Fallacies," *American Anthropologist*, XLVI (1944), 30–44.

[24] Linton, *The Cultural Background of Personality*, p. 46.

[25] *Ibid.*, p. 52.          [26] *Ibid.*, p. 137.

characterizing the "basic personality type for the society as a whole." [27] A basic source of difficulty in Linton's analysis of personality may be traced to his failure to distinguish the three types of personality which correspond to the three types of culture patterns.

The problem still remains to determine in what sense the basic personality structure is the locus and focal point of cultural integration. According to Linton:

The outstanding contribution which the *basic personality structure* approach makes to integrational studies is that it provides a logical place for cultures which are not dominated by an *idée fixé*. . . . When such a personality structure is recognized as the focus of the institutions comprised within a given culture, it can be seen that such institutions need not be mutually consistent, except to the degree required for their actual functioning, as long as they are individually consistent with various aspects of the personality structure involved. Thus, as in the Marquesan case, one series of institutions may be oriented about a basic food anxiety, another about what are to us peculiar attitudes regarding sex, and still another about certain hostilities engendered by what are here common childhood experiences. The phenomenon of culture integration becomes three-dimensional, with its foundations firmly rooted in the complex though similar personalities of the individuals whose desires and responses constitute the ultimate reality in the whole culture construct.[28]

Thus, Linton grants that the basic personality structure is not logically coherent, since it reflects the association of basic institutions which constitute the culture construct as a whole. For Linton and Kardiner, as for Malinowski, a culture is a functionally integrated whole and need not be logically coherent. The functionalist, we found, failed to provide any principle of integration for a culture as a whole, because he conceived human nature as an aggregate of needs and impulses without any unifying principle. Each type of sociobiological need was said to be satisfied through a specific type of cultural institution, but the aggregate of institutions lacked an over-all integrating principle. Since Kardiner accepts the institution as the unit of culture and lists the "key integrational systems," he is confronted with a similar problem. Thus, the criticism which Linton levels at the functionalists, namely, that "the integration dealt with by the functionalists is primarily a matter of the mutual adaptation and working interdependence of patterns" and that "the picture which emerges is that of a mass of gears all turn-

[27] *Ibid.*, p. 129; also, Linton, in "Foreword" to Kardiner's *The Psychological Frontiers of Society*.

[28] Linton, "Foreword" to Kardiner's *The Individual and His Society*.

ing and grinding each other," applies equally to his and to Kardiner's approach. Linton assumes, but does not prove, that the basic personality type is "fairly well-integrated" [29] and that the "status personalities" which are superimposed upon a given basic personality type are "thoroughly integrated with the latter." [30]

The problem of the locus, or focal point, of a culture should be clearly differentiated from that of the problem of cultural integration. As Linton has implicitly demonstrated, a culture may be said to have a focus without necessarily being coherently integrated. Linton and Kardiner posit the basic personality structure of the ego as reflecting the institutions of a culture, but this does not mean that the personality is any more integrated than the culture. Insofar as culture is thought to be an abstraction, or logical construct, then the locus of any given culture is necessarily the ego, mind, or personality of the individual. If, however, culture is understood realistically and sociologically as an aggregate of interdependent institutions, then the locus of culture is to be found in the society rather than in the individual. Furthermore, if culture were to be viewed as a superorganic entity independent of egos, then culture may not be said to have any locus at all. Finally, according to the polaristic theory of culture here advocated cultural integration may be manifested either subjectively or objectively, individually or socially, and there is no one preeminent locus of culture as a whole.

### 6. THE PHENOMENOLOGICAL INTEGRATION OF CULTURE

The problem of the integration of culture may also be considered from the perspective of a phenomenology of culture. According to this point of view a culture is understood as a system of symbols, or meanings, as, for example, in the sociology of Sorokin and the philosophical anthropology of Cassirer. Culture is, then, a value-charged term connoting the spiritual life of man and comprising all moral, aesthetic, and intellectual achievements. All technological processes and products, as well as social institutions, are on this idealistic premise reduced to the status of "embodiments," or vehicles, of cultural symbols and values. Thus, the German sociological idealists sharply differentiate between "culture" and "civilization," between the system of meanings and values, on the one side, and the outer sphere of techno-

[29] Linton, *The Cultural Background of Personality*, p. 129.
[30] *Ibid.*, p. 130.

logical phenomena and social institutions which serve as means and instruments of cultural life. Among American sociologists MacIver represents this position.[31]

This thesis of the duality of culture and civilization has attained some popularity through the influence of Oswald Spengler's *The Decline of the West*. According to Spengler's well-known theory of culture history, a society may pass through precultural (unintegrated), cultural (integrated), and postcultural (disintegrated) stages of development. Primitive peoples are said to be in the precultural stage, since their life and thought do not bear the influence of a single, dominant *leitmotif*, such as characterizes a society possessed of genuine culture. The peoples of the West are said to be in a postcultural, decadent stage of civilization.

Spengler's theory of culture history presupposes the Hegelian metaphysical notion that a system of culture is the necessary product of a special type of Idea, which fulfills its historical destiny in accordance with its own predetermined organic logic. Each cultural type is a monadic unity predestined to pass through its universal, morphological phases from birth, through maturity, to decline and final extinction. The types of "soul," or mentality, which he mentions, namely, Apollonian, Magian, and Faustian, seem to represent a mixture of aesthetic, moral, and metaphysical categories.

The most comprehensive analysis of the problem of cultural integration in contemporary sociological literature is undoubtedly to be found in Sorokin's *Social and Cultural Dynamics*. Sorokin rejects the duality of culture versus civilization, but his fundamental philosophy of culture is, nevertheless, essentially in the idealistic tradition of Hegel. Like the idealists, he, too, distinguishes between the inner, or immaterial, meanings and values of culture and the external, material "shell" which embodies these cultural meanings in the space-time continuum.

The full import of Sorokin's idealistic conception of culture is demonstrated in his theory of the "logico-meaningful integration of culture," which he contrasts with causal, or functional, integration. Since he identifies a culture with a given set of objective, phenomenological meanings, which are intellectually intuited, it follows that a culture, to be integrated, must be logically consistent and coherent. Furthermore, since any logical system must begin with definite major premises, or

[31] MacIver, *Society: a Textbook of Sociology.*

postulates, it follows that the basic logical and metaphysical postulates of a culture system determine the character of the cultural, phenomenal expressions which are derived from them. It is these basic meanings and values which enable us to comprehend the style, spirit, or mentality of a given culture and make it possible for us to conceive it as an intelligible whole, rather than as an aggregate of atomic traits.

Sorokin maintains that there are three basic types of cultural mentality, namely, sensate, ideational, and idealistic, each of which has various subdivisions. For the sensate mentality, the ultimate reality is materialistic, truth is derived from sense experience, and human values are hedonistic and utilitarian. The ideational mentality goes to the opposite extreme and regards fundamental reality as spiritual, truth as derived from intellectual intuition and faith, and human values as absolute and spiritual. Finally, the idealistic mentality is a synthesis of the sensate and ideational approaches. It allows for both sensation and intellectual intuition in the conception of truth and reality, admits both material and spiritual reality, and acknowledges eternal, spiritual, as well as temporal, material values.

Unlike Spengler, Sorokin believes in the unity of human culture and adduces historical, statistical evidence to support his optimistic faith in the cyclical recurrence of these three basic types of cultural mentality. Whereas Spengler, with his monadic, pluralistic theory of undiffusable cultural types, maintains that each culture type is destined to extinction without hope of resurrection in a new form, Sorokin has faith in the historical continuity of cultural life. They agree, however, in maintaining that there is an "organic" logic in the life of culture which predetermines its autonomous development and that societies are merely the instruments or vehicles of the culture forms by which they are possessed.[32] Sorokin, like other cultural idealists, presupposes a "superorganic" theory of culture, according to which culture is said to act as if it were a kind of spiritual automaton operating in conformity with its own "organic" laws and logic independently of its human carriers.

The theory of the logico-meaningful integration of culture is not necessarily connected with a deterministic philosophy of culture history, such as Sorokin's. Northrop's *The Meeting of East and West* provides an instance of a philosophical approach to the problem of cultural integration which does make such a separation. By uncovering the

[32] Sorokin, *Social and Cultural Dynamics*, I, 51, 53.

basic epistemological premises of a culture and analyzing its philosophy of science Northrop maintains that one is able to understand it as a coherent whole without committing oneself to a deterministic philosophy of culture history. For both Sorokin and Northrop cultures are logically integrated wholes whose underlying epistemological and ontological premises provide the key to an understanding of their empirical expressions and institutions.

Kroeber's *Configurations of Culture Growth* is the ethnological counterpart to Sorokin's *Social and Cultural Dynamics*. From a purely culturological standpoint and without any metaphysical preconceptions as to the dynamics of culture history, Kroeber has arrived at conclusions which synthesize some of the theses of Spengler and Sorokin. He begins with the premise that a culture, or civilization (he does not differentiate them) is a configuration of style patterns and that each civilization is characterized by a "superstyle," or dominant pattern, which serves to integrate its various elements. Each civilization has a consistency and coherency of its own which is both logical and aesthetic. In agreement with Spengler he regards each civilization as subject to growth and decline in an irreversible process, but unlike the former he also maintains that a civilization may be reconstituted by the incorporation of new elements from other civilizations. All civilizations are said to be subject to change in time; they must either be reorganized or else perish and become dissolved because of "the exhaustion of their potentialities." Kroeber sees evidence in European culture history of such a process of reconstitution at the time of the Renaissance and interprets our contemporary critical period, not as marking a decline of the West similar to that of Graeco-Roman culture, but rather as the beginning of a new phase of reconstruction and the emergence of European Culture III.

For Kroeber there is no uniform morphological destiny universally applicable to all civilizations, as Spengler held. He acknowledges the possibility of cultural alternatives and possible choices at critical moments of history. Such an alternative confronted Western man upon the consummation of the High Medieval phase of culture, about 1250 A.D., when he had to decide whether to continue with his medieval culture until all its potentialities became exhausted or else to revitalize it with new elements and so enlarge and alter its scope and pattern. Western medieval man chose the latter alternative, and the period of 1400–1500 marked a time of growth and reorientation which led to the emergence of our modern culture, or Western Civilization II. Thus, from an analysis of the records of culture history Kroeber is led to deny a completely deterministic philosophy of culture history, such as Spengler and Sorokin maintain, by allowing for cultural alternatives and the effective significance of human choice at critical periods. This humanistic interpretation of culture history is the antithesis of the superorganic theory of the autonomy of cultural reality which he formerly held in common with Spengler and Sorokin.

Practically, the problem remains how to determine whether a given culture phase indicates exhaustion of cultural potentialities and imminent dissolution, the reconstitution of an old culture in a larger pattern, or the emergence of a new culture. One may ask, for example, whether, if contemporary culture is not doomed to destruction, a new world culture is emerging, as Northrop suggests, or whether what is emerging is Western Culture III. This is not merely a semantic difference, but involves a difference in evaluation of the direction of contemporary culture history. It is easy to pronounce a postmortem judgment, as in the case of ancient Egyptian culture, that a given culture had exhausted its potentialities; but how to determine in the case of any living culture whether it has exhausted its potentialities or is capable of renewing its energies and advancing creatively is not a simple factual question, but a normative question of evaluation and interpretation which admits of no easy resolution. This, in turn, raises the question whether a purely factual approach to the study of culture history will resolve for us the normative problems as to the direction of culture history in the past and the teleology of the future. Perhaps more consideration needs to be given to the factor of contingency in human culture history and the role of human will in the realization of cultural alternatives.

7. THE MYTHOLOGICAL AND RELIGIOUS INTEGRATION OF CULTURE

In the phenomenological approach to the problem of cultural integration the general assumption is made that the unit of culture is the symbol, or conceptual meaning, and that a culture is a logically coherent system of ideas manifesting a distinctive logical-aesthetic pattern, or style. Cultures are implicitly thought to be rational, integrated entities whose essential structures can be analyzed in terms of basic underlying symbols of reality and value. Closely allied with this approach is the nineteenth-century assumption, derived from Hegel and Comte, that history is essentially a rational process subject to necessary laws and that historical cultures are rational constructs of ideas and institutions.

In the mythological approach to cultural integration the initial assumption is that a cultural ideology is not entirely the product of rational thought and objective experience of nature, but is also the subjective, irrational product of human imagination and wishful thinking. While functionalistic ethnologists, such as Malinowski, have stressed the point that mythical thought serves to validate culture and provides sanctions for rituals and institutions, they have not appreciated the significance of the pragmatic role of myth in their theory of cultural integration. It is not enough to point out that the various elements of a culture are interdependent; the problem is to explain why they are interdependent and why the modes of interdependence vary with different cultures. By taking into consideration the mythological idea-pattern of a culture it is possible to reach an understanding of some of the underlying motivations of its adherents. It makes little difference from this perspective whether the myth originated prior to the cultural practices or whether the myth originated later and serves to rationalize accepted rituals and institutions. In either case the myth-complex of a given culture is significant as providing insight into the acknowledged norms of behavior and thought.

The important point to bear in mind here is that the effectiveness of myth depends upon its acceptance by a given society, irrespective of its rational foundation in fact and experience. While all men may be capable of rational thought, very few engage in critical logical analysis, especially in matters affecting their common political and religious interests. In societal affairs, as Tarde and Sorel have observed, collective thought tends to be indifferent to the principle of contradiction. It is not the truth-value of an ideal or principle which determines its acceptability by a given society, but rather its relevance to emotional needs, common aspirations, and wish-fulfillment. This is a fact which modern political leaders have kept in mind, and by utilizing all the technological means of mass communication, such as the radio and the press, they have succeeded in obtaining credence for their mythological propaganda. The rise of Hitler and the Nazi party in Germany is a case in point. By exercising efficient thought control to eliminate all contrary factual evidence or critical analysis, the modern state is capable of imposing any ideological myth which it regards as necessary in order to maintain itself and to carry on its struggle with other states. The Italy of Mussolini and the government of Japan in the interval between the First World War and the Second World War illustrate the role of the myth of the state in modern political action and thought.

Modern man lives, as did his ancestors, not by science and rational thought alone but also by faith, by belief in a variety of creeds, secular and religious. A given ideological creed is a complex of beliefs historically acquired in the experience of a given society. It comprises rational, as well as irrational, ideas which have become hallowed by tradition, and is largely impervious to critical analysis. The common culture complex, as it may be called, which comprises ideational, affective, and behavioral traits, is not a logically integrated whole, but rather a historical association of traits affecting the individuals participating in a given culture and may reveal upon analysis all the contradictions and anachronisms of its accumulated traditions. This explains why "common sense," to which we, with our rationalistic tradition, constantly appeal, is so often irrational, but socially acceptable, and why the common sense of one culture is so often the nonsense of another.

The logical integration of culture, far from being a fact of historical experience, is largely an ideal of the philosophers and the social scientists. To achieve a logical integration of culture in practice requires ruthless dictatorship and the elimination of cultural minorities by discrimination and persecution. What we are witnessing in our time is the political integration of culture by means of myths with a view to promoting national efficiency and the quest for power. The modern totalitarian state is certainly "integrated" for efficiency of action and thought, irrespective of the wishes of the individual or of the minority. Scientific knowledge is utilized in exploiting, often plundering, natural resources and for technological inventions. This synthesis of mythology and scientific technology is the peculiar characteristic of twentieth-century culture. Far from being logical and rational, our culture is in large measure intrinsically irrational and is, therefore, peculiarly subject to perpetual crises, which manifest themselves in revolution and war. While deploring the cultural instability of our times, some of our modern social scientists sanction this bifurcation of our culture into the sphere of scientific technology and myth by identifying all cultural ideology with myth in the name of social science.[33]

[33] See Chapter 10.

## 8. THE HISTORICAL INTEGRATION OF CULTURE

So far we have discussed the problem of cultural integration from a synchronic perspective. All the various approaches which we have examined presuppose the notion of a culture as a given system of behavior and thought characteristic of a given society. This is essentially an atemporal view of culture and involves taking a cross-section of a culture without reference to its historical antecedents. This is partly because modern anthropologists have largely abandoned the historical point of view in their treatment of cultural problems and have concentrated, instead, upon a critical, analytical approach. Insofar as historical considerations have occupied their attention at all, it has been in connection with problems of cultural diffusion.

When we view the problem of cultural integration from the perspective of space-time rather than from a purely functional, formal, or ideational standpoint, then it appears that the unity of a culture consists in its continuity. Each culture is to be understood as a unique, irreversible continuum of traditions and experiences which have been acquired by a society in the course of its psychohistorical life. This provides us with an empirical criterion of the identity of a given culture. A culture may be said to be self-identical insofar as its adherents are conscious of the continuity of their cultural life and experiences. Just as an individual has a sense of personal identity to the extent of his retention of memory of his past and perceives the continuity of his present experiences with his past, so a society may be said to possess the same culture insofar as its members retain a sense of the historical continuity of their present cultural ways with those of their past. Similarly, as a victim of amnesia becomes for all practical purposes a different person in virtue of the fact that his present experiences are not correlated with his past, so a society may be said to enter upon a new way of life if there is no continuity between its present and past cultural existence. It may then be said, in Kroeber's words, that the culture has "exhausted its potentialities" and that a new culture has arisen. The Jewish people provide the outstanding example of a modern people who have retained a sense of historical continuity of cultural traditions, notwithstanding their dispersion among all the nations of the world. This accounts in part for the modern miracle by which the Jews have been able after two thousand years to reconstitute a state of Israel in Palestine after winning the recognition of the United Nations.

On the other hand, the modern Greeks and Egyptians, having lost their continuity with the cultural traditions of the ancient Egyptians and Greeks, are presumed to constitute new societies having distinctive cultures of their own. In the case of China, however, historians are justified in speaking of the different phases of Chinese culture from ancient to modern times, instead of different Chinese cultures, because of the continuity of Chinese society and culture.

One does not determine the emergence of a new culture simply by adding up the number of new traits and comparing them with the number of old ones. A culture is a spatio-temporal process and product whose essence and existence cannot be understood apart from the ethnohistorical context in which they have developed. Its unity is the unity of a process, of a social life which has been and is being lived. A culture which has no roots in the ethnohistorical past of a people remains something alien, artificial, and contingent. That is why statesmen always endeavor to incorporate revolutionary cultural changes with the cultural traditions of their country, thereby retaining a sense of cultural continuity. This has been demonstrated in modern Soviet Russia, which has recognized the necessity of combining a study of prerevolutionary Russian history and culture with a knowledge of postrevolutionary Marxism as interpreted by Lenin and Stalin. A purely international, scientific culture without a basis in the ethnohistory of a people lacks for most people the emotional appeal which is necessary for social and political solidarity. Only the intellectual revolutionary, whose loyalty is to "mankind," rather than to his own country and its traditions, can be satisfied with a supernational culture which disregards all that is unique in the cultures of peoples. On general theoretical principles, all one can say is that unless a state is allowed to adapt a new cultural ideology or new institutions to its own cultural past, it is not likely that they will become permanent features of its social life.

In stating that a culture is to be understood as an ethnohistorical process with a unique, irreversible continuity of its own, I do not mean to imply any theory of mechanical determinism of the past upon the present and future. All that is implied is the principle of historical continuity whereby the various factors which contributed to the ethnohistorical development of a culture may be properly evaluated. Man is both a dynamic principle within nature, a *natura naturans*, and a mode of nature, a *natura naturata*. Hence, the culture-historical process cannot be understood either as a necessary process subject to laws of nature as a whole or only as an expression of human freedom to be understood in terms of the autonomous human spirit. As Reinhold Niebuhr has remarked, "both freedom and necessity are involved in every human action and in every historical concretion and configuration." [34] The culture-historical process involves the freedom and creativity of man, as well as the determinism of social, cultural, and cosmic factors which affect his development.

From this it follows that the historical unity of a culture is not simply the logical unity of a system of ideas progressively evolved in time. Historical rationalism, whether of the idealistic Hegelian or of the materialistic Marxian type, assumes that the cultural process is essentially rational and may, therefore, be explained in terms of a logical sequence of ideas and institutions. Similarly, evolutionary naturalism, following the Darwinian principle of evolution, tends to regard the cultural process as subject to necessary stages of evolutionary, progressive development. Both types of theory are deterministic in the sense that they are attempts to explain the historical process in terms of universal principles which are essentially rational and logical. By contrast, the principle of the historical continuity of a culture is compatible with recognition of the contingency of the cultural process, as well as of the deterministic factors which affect its course. The cultural process is viewed as a composite of rational and irrational factors. Not all that happens is in accord with reason, although reasons may be found for all that happens. Historical continuity does not imply the determinism of the past, but only a consciousness of the past in relation to the present, which may serve to orient a given society in determining for itself the course of its future development. The very fact that man remembers his past enables him to transcend the limitations of the past so as to alter the course of his future activities.

The principle of the historical continuity of culture simply affirms the relation of the past to the present in determining the self-identity of a given culture. In order to understand objectively the predominant characteristics of a culture, we must ascertain how it functions in the present and the ends to which it is oriented. In other words, the principle of historical continuity must be supplemented by the principle of teleofunctional integration if we are to evaluate a culture realistically.

[34] Niebuhr, *Faith and History*, p. 17.

A culture may not be understood in terms of its past alone or in terms of its present functional organization alone. An adequate knowledge of a culture requires a synthesis of historical perspective with an empirical study of the actual interrelation of its cultural institutions and the ends or objectives to which it is oriented.

A knowledge of the historical continuity of a culture tells us nothing of the present state of integration of that culture except insofar as the present is identical with its past. In view of the fact, however, that modern cultures are subjected to frequent and radical changes, a knowledge of present conditions and probable directions of change is of the utmost importance. So long as anthropologists were obsessed with the theory of linear cultural evolution, a knowledge of the past as revealed by the study of primitive cultures was considered indispensable. Modern anthropological thought is more concerned with the present in order to anticipate the future and seeks to determine the actual interrelation of cultural phenomena in given cultural contexts. Primitive cultures are studied because they are thought to be "simpler" and easier to comprehend in their entirety, not because they provide insight into antecedent stages of cultural evolution. In their eagerness to understand present cultural functions, anthropologists tend to disregard the role of past conditions and traditions in the effective balance of the present. Furthermore, a positivistic preoccupation with "facts" and field observation has tended to divert attention from an appreciation of the role of cultural ideals in determining the degree of cultural integration in the future.

From a theoretical perspective, cultural integration is motivated by the quest for intelligibility, by the need for having a common program of action which is self-consistent, but not self-defeating. Unless there is a common historical bond of cultural beliefs and ideals which may serve as a guide to conduct and as a tradition to be upheld, a society or a state ceases to function effectively and drifts toward anarchy. Under changing conditions there is constant need to reevaluate and reform social practices and institutions. How to preserve a sense of historical continuity in the midst of ideational and actual social changes is a task which requires consummate statesmanship. From the perspective of history, cultural integration is an unfinished task involving renewed efforts in the light of newly emerging ideals and changing social conditions.

## 9. TELEOFUNCTIONAL INTEGRATION OF CULTURE

A major source of confusion in discussing the problem of cultural integration is the fact that the concept of integration involves both a positive, factual meaning and a normative, teleological significance. Thus, from a positive viewpoint every culture is functionally integrated in the sense that its elements are interdependent. In this sense integration is a neutral, value-free term and tells us nothing about the specific structure and institutions of a given culture system. On the other hand, integration is used also as a value-charged term, as is that shibboleth "law and order," as if any form of sociocultural integration is intrinsically good and any lack of integration is inherently evil. There is constant emphasis in press communications on the "need for integration" in the reorganization of Europe, for example, and on the necessity of "economic integration" as the first step toward the unification of Western Europe.

It should be kept in mind, however, that integration *per se* is not an absolute good and that its value depends upon the end, or objective, which integration is meant to achieve. A society organized for war and conquest may be highly integrated, but that will not appear good to those societies which desire to be left alone in peace. It is the dominant end of integration, rather than its efficiency, which enables one to evaluate it realistically. The essential problem in cultural integration, is, then, integration for what?

By the "teleofunctional integration of culture" I refer to the functional integration of the elements of a culture for the purpose of achieving a given end, or objective. Any culture whatsoever may be said to be integrated teleofunctionally if it is effectively organized for the purpose of realizing a given objective, regardless of the value of that end. Normatively, a culture is integrated teleofunctionally if its adherents are enabled to lead a happy life which gives maximum scope for individual participation in the advantages of social life. How to conceive the absolute good of man and society is a metacultural, philosophical problem which presupposes a critical, comparative study of human values.[35]

Under the influence of the theory of evolution, social anthropologists have tended to assume that society is the ultimate reality and that all cultural traits and institutions are to be evaluated by reference to

[35] See Chapter 14.

their function in promoting social survival and social solidarity. In this way the notion of function as a positive fact of social organization and function as an end or ideal are confused.

If culture and society are clearly differentiated and one does not assume uncritically that every mode of culture subserves the end of social survival and solidarity, the way is prepared for distinguishing between cultural values and social functions. The ends or values of a culture are ends-in-themselves which a society may choose to adhere to and by which it may regulate its institutions. Indirectly, the fact that the members of a society regulate their conduct by the ideals they profess may make for social solidarity, but that is a pragmatic consequence of ideals and does not explain their intrinsic value for their adherents, who may not even realize the social significance of their acts. As self-preservation is not the absolute goal of human existence, but rather the necessary condition for leading a culturally-prescribed way of life, so the preservation of a given form of society is not the chief function of culture, but only a necessary condition for the historical continuity of the cultural process and the realization of cultural values.

If culture were to be regarded as subservient to society, there would be danger of providing justification for a totalitarian view of culture, so that culture would lose its significance and validity apart from a given social organization. In my opinion the "sociological" interpretation of culture has helped prepare the way for the deification of the modern state as the supreme arbiter of cultural life. To be sure, individual democratic sociologists who have advocated such a view of culture have themselves been champions of freedom of thought and of the rights of the individual as over against the state. But given the condition wherein a political party governs in the name of the state, there is on this basis no logical alternative to accepting its right to prescribe the forms of cultural life as well. For example, the Communist sociology of culture makes culture relative to and a function of the class struggle, and it is therefore logical for its adherents to control and direct the forms of cultural expression wherever they have attained to political power. Similarly, the thesis of the sociology of culture may be utilized as justification for cultural dictatorship of the extreme right, as in the case of contemporary Spain and Argentina. Thus, what appears as a mere academic issue regarding the relative autonomy of culture and society turns out to have serious political consequences.

### 10. CULTURAL INTEGRATION AND CULTURAL DEMOCRACY

Modern anthropologists continue to speak as if a society and its culture were more or less homogeneous phenomena and tend to describe a culture as "an organized group of behavior patterns" [36] characteristic of a society, that is, "an organized group of people." It is assumed that in all but very exceptional instances there is no incompatibility between social classes and the various culture patterns associated with the basic types of social status and role. It is granted that in current society there are conflicts "because our inherited system of statuses and roles is breaking down; while a new system, compatible with the actual conditions of modern life, has not yet emerged." [37]

As I see it, the basic discovery of Marx was his appreciation of the fact of actual conflict of class interests in human societies. Instead of assuming, as his predecessors had done, that all social classes are mutually compatible and a necessary result of the division of labor, Marx maintained that there is an inherent conflict, or incompatibility, between social classes corresponding to the disparity of economic interests. From this Engels drew the conclusion that the state was instituted to prevent an open conflict between economic classes, such as the freemen and the slaves, the rich and the poor. When society involves itself in "insoluble self-contradiction and is cleft into irreconcilable antagonisms which it is powerless to exorcise," then the state is instituted as a power to preserve order in social life.[38]

According to Marx and Engels, the state is a historical phenomenon which arises at a certain stage of economic development and is destined to fall away as soon as economic classes are abolished and society organizes production on the basis of free and equal association of producers. Every state is thought of as essentially an instrument for the protection of the interests of the dominant economic class. Hence, as long as the state exists it is in a condition of perpetual crisis, since it does not resolve the conflict between classes, but only keeps them in check temporarily.

The cultural significance of this conception of society and the state lies in the fact that it denies the universal objective validity of cultural values and maintains, instead, that the latter are functions of economic class interests. Cultural ideals are regarded as weapons, or instruments,

[36] Linton, *The Cultural Background of Personality*, p. 56.
[37] *Ibid.*, p. 81.
[38] Engels, *The Origin of the Family, Private Property and the State*, pp. 156–57.

for rationalizing the will to power of the dominant economic class. Far from sharing a common value system, the economic classes which comprise a society are said to be in actual, though often hidden, conflict, since their economic and cultural values are incompatible. The state, it is true, endeavors to cover up this irreconcilable conflict "with the cloak of love and charity," thereby introducing "a conventional hypocrisy" which seeks to convince the exploited class that its exploitation is in its own best interests.[39]

While one may reject the Marx-Engels theory of the economic origin and function of the state on anthropological grounds, the fact remains that the two men drew a realistic picture of the conflicts inherent in the economic orders of the societies of their time. Just as Freud compelled reluctant students of man to reckon with the reality of neuroses and psychoses as derived from unresolved conflicts in the psychic life of the individual, so Marx and Engels have drawn attention to the reality of class conflicts based on the disparity of economic power. While one may disagree with their monistic theories as to the source of these conflicts, one must reckon with the facts to which they have so dramatically drawn attention.

What is unique and historically significant in the case of the Western democracies is that this conflict of cultural interests has become institutionalized and is now recognized as a permanent feature of national life.[40] In this way the cultural minority of one period has the opportunity of becoming the cultural majority of another. Cultural democracy receives expression through the two-party system, which enables the adherents of opposing parties to attempt to win the approval of the majority.

Thus, cultural democracy is the antithesis of authoritarian, or totalitarian, culture, which insists upon cultural uniformity in the name of the state. Instead, cultural democracy makes its appeal to the consensus of a majority of the citizens, on the assumption that cultural truth is to be determined pragmatically by the social experiences to which it leads. It is opposed to the notion of a single, absolute, all-embracing truth and implies rather the acceptance in practice of the fallibility of the human mind and the diversity of human interests. No single party, it is assumed, can be permanently right on all issues; hence the necessity for a two-party system to take into account the opposite

[39] *Ibid.*, p. 162.
[40] Trevelyan, "The Two-Party System in English Political History," in his *An Autobiography and Other Essays.*

interests and perspectives. The method of cultural democracy bears some affinity to pragmatic scientific method in that both involve a process of trial and error which allows for the testing of alternate hypotheses.

Cultural democracy is the attempt to carry out the will of the majority without destroying the cultural minority. Hence, it is a culture system which makes a prime virtue of tolerance of cultural deviation and freedom of expression. The moment the majority becomes intolerant of the cultural minority and attempts to destroy it, it ceases to function democratically and becomes, instead, a mass dictatorship. Pseudo-democracy is based upon the assumption that the will of the majority alone ought to be reckoned with and that the minority has no rights which entitle it to continue in existence. Thus pseudo-democracy always leads to political and cultural dictatorship, as has been demonstrated by the rise of the Nazi party in Germany and by the emergence of Communistic dictatorships in Eastern Europe and China in the name of the "people's democracy."

From the perspective of cultural democracy, the problem of cultural integration may be viewed dynamically as one of maintaining a balance of polar, opposite and complementary interests. As against the Marxist assumption that class interests necessarily conflict and that the ultimate alternatives are either a dictatorship of some one class or else a utopian classless society instituted by force and revolution, the faith of cultural democracy is that class interests, while real, may be complementary and need not necessarily conflict. From a theoretical perspective, the interests of capital and labor, state ownership and private enterprise, are not antithetical; they become antithetical and incompatible in practice because each party seeks a monopoly of control in order to increase is own advantages at the expense of the other class. But this does not warrant the assertion that the state, by a priori definition, is an instrument of coercion. The normative state, as in an ideal cultural democracy, is an agency for the promotion of the common welfare through the harmonization of polar, complementary interests and values. Thus, while one may recognize the actual conflict of class interests and values in the given historical state, he must not be blinded to the fact that the state, with all its imperfections, offers the only means of maintaining public order and the possibility of rectifying social abuses. The weakness of a democratic culture is also the source of its strength, since in permitting open cultural conflict by peaceful means it also offers the prospect of social harmony based upon a recognition of mutual advantages. This is a never-ending task requiring an idealistic faith in the willingness and ability of rational men to seek the general good and to promote social freedom and justice.

Cultural integration, so understood, is a dynamic balance of polar interests and values with a view to the general welfare. It is a mode of teleofunctional integration, inasmuch as it is oriented toward a determinate goal, but it is also normative integration, since it seeks to provide a maximum of coordination and satisfaction for all significant sociocultural differences insofar as they are mutually compatible. As contrasted with "logico-meaningful," or purely ideational, integration, democratic, teleofunctional integration aims, not at logical consistency, but rather at historical compatibility in the interests of cultural freedom. Such integration is not utopian, since it takes into account the actual historical continuity of cultural interests and values and seeks to combine them with newly emergent cultural institutions and processes. Every real or existential culture is an eclectic combination of traditional elements and emergent forms; what varies is the proportion of the old and the new and the effectiveness of the role of rational thought in coordinating them. In progressive societies a sustained effort is made to "rationalize" the sociocultural order so as to take into account new scientific discoveries and provide a greater measure of rational coherency. In a democratic society the process of cultural change is necessarily slow, but its effects are bound to be lasting and cumulative since it is based upon the consent and active participation of all the members of the society.

# 14

# *Normative Culture and*
# *the Categories of Value*

IN CONSIDERING what constitutes the unity of a culture it seems scarcely sufficient to point out that the elements of a culture are functionally interdependent, since the significant question concerns how the culture is unified and how it differs from other culture systems? Psychologically, it is understandable that wholeness, or unity, should be valued highly in an age which is characterized by fractionalism and social crises and that the concept of integration should appear to be a magic formula, so to speak, for resolving our sociocultural dilemmas. Upon critical analysis, however, it soon becomes apparent that integration apart from its relation to some dominant end, or objective, has no cultural significance. In evaluating any given culture the essential problems are how it is integrated and for what it is integrated, not is it integrated? The quest for wholeness and unity is not intelligible apart from some specification of the value of a given form of unity in relation to other forms.

### 1. THE CATEGORIES OF VALUE AND THE TYPES OF CULTURE

Since the meaning of a culture is to be understood teleofunctionally by reference to the end, or final objective, which its adherents strive to realize individually and collectively, we must next consider the basic types of value which it is possible for man to pursue. Ever since the time of Plato, philosophers have recognized that there are three fundamental categories of value, namely, truth, goodness, and beauty. Truth may be defined as an attribute of thought by virtue of which the mind conceives the real nature of things. The good may be understood as a property of things and acts considered desirable. Beauty may be defined as an attribute of the forms of things which renders them attractive. I think it may be demonstrated that actual historical cultures have been oriented so as to manifest the dominance of one or the other of these categories of value.

The problem of values as applied to culture may be considered from two distinct points of view. On the one hand, one may investigate the category of value which serves as a focus of integration for any given culture. On the other hand, one may inquire whether culture itself, that is, the concept of culture may not be conceived as essentially a value expression. Thus, the question as to whether a given culture is to be understood as primarily aesthetic, moral, or factual is to be differentiated from the question whether the concept of culture is to be conceived in similar terms. I think it may be shown that the concept of culture has been interpreted as if it referred primarily to aesthetic, moral, or factual-scientific phenomena. This may explain why definitions of culture in the literature of the humanities, as well as in ethnology, have been so numerous and diverse. Similarly, the ethnological perspective and evaluation of cultural phenomena will in turn depend upon the concept of culture which is utilized implicitly or explicitly. Thus, if culture be understood as essentially an aesthetic phenomenon, the student of culture will be concerned with the aesthetic aspects of the cultures he is investigating and will tend to neglect other aspects of culture. Similarly, a moralistic conception of culture will predetermine one to orient his studies with reference to moral interests to the neglect of the aesthetic and the noetic. In order to illustrate this thesis I shall begin with a brief historical survey of the philosophical and ethnological literature which treats of culture as an aesthetic norm.

## 2. CULTURE AS AN AESTHETIC NORM

We owe to the Greek Sophists and to Protagoras in particular the insight that "man is the measure of all things" and that man as a creator of culture is an artist molding himself in conformity with his beliefs and ideals. So conceived, human culture in general may be understood as "the art of living," or as the general art which comprises all the special arts of human society. Like any special artistic expression, the culture of a particular society may be contemplated as an aesthetic configuration manifested in the static artifacts of a culture, as well as in the actual modes of life and thought. In this sense aesthetic style is the final distinctive measure of man, taken individually and collectively.

Historically, this view of culture is best known to us in the West from a study of classic Greek culture, although Chinese culture also developed it to a high degree. In fact "form" and "face-saving" have much greater significance in the East than in the West—a point modern ethnologists who have participated in both types of culture have noted. In classic Greek culture the important role of music, literature, drama, the choral dance, and gymnastics, as well as the mathematical sciences, bears witness to its aesthetic orientation. Even Plato's attempt, under Socratic influence, to reorient Greek culture toward moral interests succeeded only in reaffirming the primacy of the aesthetic values, since it was the mathematical forms which served to define his Idea of the Good.

From a sociological standpoint Plato's aesthetic conception of culture may be best understood against the background of the Athenian society of his time. Greek culture was actually a culture of the leisure class made possible by the utilization of slave labor for all the menial, utilitarian tasks of social life. Thus, when Plato and Aristotle discoursed upon education and culture, they had in mind the free-born Athenian citizen and gentleman who had the social opportunity and leisure to cultivate the liberal arts and sciences. This partly explains why the natural sciences, such as physics, were scarcely developed except in a speculative way, since technology and science seemed to Greek educators antithetical. By contrast, the conceptual or theoretical sciences, such as mathematics and astronomy, reached a high stage of development in the Platonic academy.[1]

This liberal tradition of a cultural aristocracy was transmitted to the Romans, but under Stoic influence it became transformed into a universal human ideal, the ideal of *humanitas,* considered as the mark of all that is distinctively and normatively human.[2] This Roman tradition was carried on throughout the Middle Ages as the study of the "humanities," comprising the *trivium* (grammar, rhetoric, and logic) and the *quadrivium* (arithmetic, music, geometry, and astronomy). This program of education also set the pattern for the modern liberal arts and the study of the humanities.

So it has come about that culture, which for the Greeks comprised all the liberal arts and sciences as integrated in an over-all aesthetic pattern, has for the educated people of the West come to mean popularly a refinement of taste manifested in literary, emotional, and intui-

---

[1] Farrington, *Greek Science,* Vol. I, ch. ix.
[2] Bidney, "The Philosophical Anthropology of Ernst Cassirer," in *The Philosophy of Ernst Cassirer,* pp. 478–84.

tive appreciation of the fine arts, such as music and painting, together with a knowledge of classical literature and contemporary letters. Our aesthetic culture has become divorced from our daily life as an added refinement, not necessarily bearing any connection in practice to social conditions. Aesthetic culture, far from being a total vision of life, a "testament of beauty," as Robert Bridges phrased it, has become an ornament, or luxury, which enables a select few to escape from the vulgarities of daily experience. In brief, the major paradox of our contemporary democratic culture is the fact that our educational system is based upon abstract, aristocratic cultural values, whereas our social system is organized on democratic lines, and our scientific technology is geared to material wealth and national power. The incompatibility of our cultural ideals and practices is demonstrated daily by the social esteem in which our educational system is held and the distrust of the educated man in practical affairs.

In modern times Alfred North Whitehead seems to have recaptured this Greek mathematical-aesthetic vision of culture by recognizing that mathematics as the generalized study of pattern is a prerequisite of understanding good and beauty in all forms of culture. According to Whitehead:

The notion of pattern is as old as civilization. Every art is founded on the study of pattern. Also the cohesion of social systems depends on the maintenance of patterns of behaviour; and advances in civilization depend on the fortunate modification of such behaviour patterns. Thus the infusion of pattern into natural occurrences, and the stability of such patterns, and the modification of such patterns, is the necessary condition for the realization of the Good. Mathematics is the most powerful technique for the understanding of pattern, and for the analysis of the relationships of patterns. Here we reach the fundamental justification for the topic of Plato's lecture. . . . The essence of this generalized mathematics is the study of the most observable examples of the relevant patterns; and applied mathematics is the transference of this study to other examples of the realization of these patterns.[3]

Thus, for Whitehead, as for Plato, the real world is good when it is beautiful.

It is important to bear in mind that one may arrive at an aesthetic philosophy of culture and life by either of two logical approaches. One may, as in the case of Plato and Whitehead, base his philosophy of

---

[3] Whitehead, "Mathematics and the Good," in *The Philosophy of Alfred North Whitehead*, ed. by P. A. Schilpp, pp. 677–78.

culture upon a comprehensive metaphysical and scientific foundation and come to believe in the primacy of the aesthetic category. Or else, one may come to a similar conclusion by the impressionistic method of denying any metaphysical truths and by accepting the immediate aesthetic impressions of experience. According to this relativistic perspective, one philosophy and mode of life is as good and true as another, and the criterion of choice is simply the preference of the individual. In Somerset Maugham's classic story *Of Human Bondage* the author summarizes his conclusions on the meaning of life.

As the weaver elaborated his pattern for no end but the pleasure of his aesthetic sense, so might a man live his life, or if one was forced to believe that his actions were outside his choosing, so might a man look at his life, that it made a pattern. . . . Out of the manifold events of his life, his deeds, his feelings, his thoughts, he might make a design, regular, elaborate, complicated, or beautiful; and though it might be no more than an illusion that he had the power of selection, though it might be no more than a fantastic legerdemain in which appearances were interwoven with moonbeams, that did not matter; it seemed, and so to him it was. In the vast warp of life, (a river arising from no spring and flowing endlessly to no sea,) with the background of his fancies that there was no meaning and that nothing was important, a man might get a personal satisfaction in selecting the various strands that worked out the pattern. There was one pattern, the most obvious, perfect and beautiful, in which a man was born, grew to manhood, married, produced children, toiled for his bread and died; but there were others, intricate and wonderful, in which happiness did not enter and in which success was not attempted; and in them might be discovered a more troubling grace.[4]

There is obviously a vast difference between Maugham's empirical, impressionistic view of life patterns divorced from all considerations of truth and finality and the metaphysically oriented intellectual vision of Plato and Whitehead. For Maugham each pattern of life, whether it be rational or irrational, has a romantic beauty of its own, simply because it is an expression of life capable of yielding satisfaction to someone. For Whitehead, a pattern of life to be significant must be grounded in the eternal harmony of nature.

Among modern philosophers, Nietzsche was one of the first to consider the problem of a philosophy of culture and to classify cultures according to their dominant value-orientation. According to Nietzsche, all culture is a delusion of the will to life, and he distinguishes three such "planes of illusion." In *The Birth of Tragedy* he writes:

[4] Maugham, *Of Human Bondage*, p. 590.

One is chained by the Socratic love of knowledge and the delusion of being able thereby to heal the eternal wound of existence; another is ensnared by art's seductive veil of beauty fluttering before his eyes; still another by the metaphysical comfort that beneath the flux of phenomena eternal life flows on indestructibly: to say nothing of the more ordinary and almost more powerful illusions which the will has always at hand. These three planes of illusion are on the whole designed only for the more nobly formed natures, who in general feel profoundly the weight and burden of existence, and must be deluded by exquisite stimulants into forgetfulness of their sorrow. All that we call culture is made up of these stimulants; and, according to the proportion of the ingredients, we have either a dominantly *Socratic* or *artistic* or *tragic* culture; or, if historical exemplifications are wanted, there is either an Alexandrian or a Hellenic or a Buddhistic culture.[5]

When we substitute for Nietzsche's tragic type the moralistic type, then his classification corresponds to the three basic value categories.

Nietzsche prophetically rejected a predominantly theoretical, or scientific, culture of the Socratic, Alexandrian type, because, notwithstanding its inherent optimism and delusion of limitless power, it gradually "drifts towards a dreadful destruction" when the barbaric slave class comes to regard their mode of existence as an intolerable injustice. So, too, artistic, or Hellenic, culture is unsatisfactory because its underlying attitude toward existence is unrealistic and negative; it seeks to escape from the struggle and pain of existence by contemplating aesthetic forms rather than by grappling with life's problems. The only acceptable alternative for Nietzsche is tragic culture (also called Dionysian culture in his *Ecce Homo*), which expresses an affirmative, realistic attitude toward the intrinsic tragedy of existence. Tragic culture is said to symbolize a Dionysian wisdom (which takes the place of science) as to the inherent evil of life through Apollonian art media. This Dionysian-Apollonian vision gives one the courage to live resolutely and without the "effeminate" scruples of the traditional Christian ethos. Nietzsche may be thought of as accepting an ethically oriented culture expressed in Apollonian individualistic art forms and as rejecting either a positivistic type of culture, which encourages the development of technological civilization, or an artistic type which, as in Schopenhauer, seeks escape into the dream world of art forms.

It is important to note that for Nietzsche, Apollonian and Dionysian art forms are polar opposites in a metaphysical and also in an empirical sense. Apollonian culture expresses not only measured restraint but also

[5] *The Philosophy of Nietzsche,* pp. 287–88.

the principle of individuation (*principium individuationis*) as exemplified in the forms of the dream world, as well as in sculpture and the plastic arts. Dionysian culture symbolizes the "drunkenness" of spirit, the emotion of ecstasy, which enables the individual to lose self-consciousness and to experience a mystic feeling of oneness—the primordial unity—with his fellowmen and nature. This experience of unity was attained in Greek music and the Bacchic choruses. Apparently for Nietzsche the main significance of these Greek art forms lies in their deeper metaphysical and cosmic meanings, the characteristics of measured restraint and ecstatic frenzy being only the psychological concomitants. Through Apollonian culture media one gives expression to the principle of individuation, to finitude, or limitation of form; through Dionysian culture media, such as music and the dance, one attains the feeling of the infinite, of the undifferentiated unity of man and nature. These fundamental metaphysical principles were synthesized in Plato's *Timaeus* as the union of geometrical Forms or Ideas with the Receptacle or undifferentiated material ground principle, which gives rise to the empirical world of changing nature.

Ruth Benedict's *Patterns of Culture* is significant historically as an attempt by a contemporary ethnologist to apply the concept of Dionysian and Apollonian culture types, which she derived from her study of Nietzsche, to native tribal cultures. As interpreted by her, the Dionysian type of man is imbued with the desire to achieve excess in personal experience in order to attain "the illumination of frenzy." The Apollonian type of man is said to be guided in all his activities by a certain measure and norm. Benedict finds that the Zuñi Indians of the Southwest reveal an Apollonian pattern in their culture, whereas the Plains Indians, with their ecstatic visions, manifest a Dionysian mentality. The terms "Dionysian," and "Apollonian" do not represent fixed constellations of traits identical in every culture, but rather certain types or patterns compatible with diversity of empirical content.

With reference to our analysis of Nietzsche's views, it is difficult for me to understand how Benedict could have arrived at the conclusion that "Greece did not carry out, as the Pueblos have, the distrust of individualism that the Apollonian way of life implies, but which in Greece was scanted because of forces with which it came in conflict. Zuñi ideals and institutions, on the other hand, are rigorous on this point." [6] As I understand Nietzsche, the essence of Apollonian culture is pre-

[6] Benedict, *Patterns of Culture*, p. 73.

cisely its emphasis upon the principle of individuation—a factor which in practice made for extreme individualism among the Greeks, as Thucydides testifies in his history of the Peloponnesian War. By contrast, the cultural function of the Dionysian festivals and mysteries was to foster a feeling of sympathy and ecstasy which transcended individual consciousness. Thus, Dionysian art forms, far from fostering extreme individualism, actually served to merge individual differences in a transcendental feeling of cosmic unity.

In abstracting the notions of measured restraint and ecstatic community of feeling from their context in Greek culture, Benedict has retained only a nominal similarity to the original ontological meaning of the terms "Apollonian" and "Dionysian" and has in fact perverted the philosophical values intended by Nietzsche. In seeking individual supernatural visions, and in trying to shame their rivals, the Plains Indians and the Kwakiutl Indians of the Northwest coast endeavored to emphasize their individual differences. Their so-called "Dionysian excesses" are the antithesis of the Greek Dionysian rituals whose object it was to achieve ecstatic self-forgetfulness. Similarly, the so-called "Apollonian rituals" of the Indians of the Southwest tend functionally to promote a sense of the harmony of man and nature and to suppress individual competition—an attitude which is the antithesis of the Greek Apollonian. One must differentiate, therefore, between Apollonian and Dionysian "excess" so as to determine whether the excess leads to accentuation or elimination of individual differences. To attribute all excess to the Dionysian mentality and all restraint to the Apollonian mentality is not to conform to the true meaning of the concepts as employed by Nietzsche. By emptying the terms "Apollonian" and "Dionysian" of all ontological meaning, Benedict has failed to see that "excess" and "restraint" are relative terms whose ontological import varies with the objective which the adherents of a given culture seek to achieve.

### 3. CULTURE AS A MORAL NORM

Moralistic culture is culture lived and organized according to some dominant idea of the good for a given society. It is culture regarded as a "way of life" and prescribing an ideal of how one ought to live to become an acceptable member of society. As an absolute normative ideal, the concept of *humanitas,* or humanity, is to be understood as the way of life peculiar to man and involving the development of those

ethical characteristics which differentiate man from the beasts. Absolute moral culture tends to become identified with "civilization," as
when we speak of civilization versus barbarism and ask rhetorically,
"Are we civilized?" By contrast, relativistic moral culture, as described
by anthropologists and sociologists, is only the way of life characteristic
of a given people and does not involve any evaluation of its validity for
all mankind.

In a moralistic conception of culture, emphasis is placed on the functional significance of traits and institutions for the life of the individual
and his society. This, it appears, is the reason for the basic difference between the aesthetic approach to culture of Kroeber and Benedict, on
the one hand, and the functionalistic approach of Malinowski and
Radcliffe-Brown, on the other. Through his insistence that "culture
must be understood as a means to an end, that is, instrumentally or
functionally," [7] Malinowski has implicitly adopted a moralistic approach to ethnology in general. Thus, for the functionalist the unit
of culture is the social institution which fulfills basic biosocial requirements, whereas for those who adopt an aesthetic approach, as does
Benedict, the unit of culture is the pattern or configuration. The reason underlying this disparity of culture units is, I suggest, that each
party tends to conceive culture in general under a different value category.

Psychologically, the most significant characteristic of moral culture
is the fact that those who share it entertain a tragic and more or less
ascetic way of life. Metaphysically, the mores are thought to have
intrinsic connections with the processes of nature and to receive divine
sanction and support. It becomes, therefore, a matter of life and death
for the individual, as well as his society, that these mores be adhered to
strictly. This, it appears, is the ontological basis of many primitive
taboos and renders intelligible the severe trials which many native
peoples impose upon their members in the critical "rites of passage"
marking the human life cycle from birth to death. [8] These ordeals and
rituals provide meaning and dignity to native life by associating their
culture with cosmic processes and offering social recognition of the
individual's acquired status and role. Contrary to the novelistic fiction
that natives lead care-free lives, ethnologists have demonstrated that
native peoples have a predominantly tragic outlook upon life, since

---

[7] Malinowski, *A Scientific Theory of Culture,* pp. 67–68.
[8] Tozzer, *Social Origins and Social Continuities,* ch. iii.

they imagine nature as an organic whole in which all forces and events interact so as to promote or hinder human welfare.[9] This explains why *primitive religion must be understood as the integrative factor in primitive culture,* binding together all its institutions and pervading all its manifold rites and customs. It is because religion is "an everpresent dimension of experience" that native peoples fail to designate by a special term.[10]

All the Hebrew-Christian-Muslim scriptures may be described as authoritative historic revelations of the knowledge of good and evil which, it is believed, the Deity revealed to mankind for their salvation. Although Genesis relates that man was originally forbidden to partake of the tree of knowledge of good and evil, the Deity subsequently became reconciled to this perverse human curiosity and arranged to supplement human reason and experience by divine revelation and example. Henceforth this way of life became, as Hebrew and Christian theologians testify, the prime objective of human interest and a matter of vital concern calling for crucial decision and acts of faith.[11] By comparison, the detached, disengaged attitude of theoretical speculation and the leisurely enjoyment of aesthetic forms and patterns seemed to rest on a tragic misconception of human values and human destiny. Human life on earth was regarded as a series of tragic moral crises brought about by man's willful disobedience and transgression of natural and divine law.

From a philosophical perspective the culture of the West may be said to be indebted to Aristotle for its moralistic outlook, just as it is obligated to Plato to some extent for its aesthetic orientation. For it was Aristotle who was responsible for the teleological approach to the study of nature and culture and for the subsequent philosophical emphasis upon ends, or final causes. In the field of politics and ethics his naturalistic analysis of human virtue and social organization still retains much of its validity for us, since it is in accord with the biological orientation of modern thought.

Historically, it is noteworthy that the Greek term *ethos* draws attention to the process of habituation with reference to a given ideal. The Latin term *mores* tends to divert attention from habit to custom, or convention (the Greek *nomos*), and thus sharpens the contrast between

[9] Radin, *Primitive Man as a Philosopher,* ch. xi; Lévy-Bruhl, *Primitives and the Supernatural;* Thompson and Joseph, *The Hopi Way.*

[10] Lee, *Religious Perspectives in Anthropology,* p. 8.

[11] Kierkegaard, *Either/Or;* also *Concluding Unscientific Postscript.*

nature and art which the Greek term *ethos* harmonized. By indicating that ethics is natural and yet not given by nature, that we are adapted by nature for virtue, but require training and habituation to achieve it, Aristotle [12] kept in mind what I have called the polarity of nature and culture. The idea of the good was for Aristotle a practical and rational human ideal, not an impersonal, transcendental form of reality and thought, as in Plato, to be contemplated for its aesthetic value.

In the great medieval synthesis of Greek philosophy and Christian religion, moral-religious culture was intensified and integrated to a degree hitherto unknown. The *Summa theologica* of St. Thomas Aquinas and the *Divine Comedy* of Dante gave classic theoretical and poetic expression of the ideals of this culture. The essence of this way of life is the view "that this is a moral world and that sin and virtue not merely have a practical issue but an eternal significance; they not only matter but they matter infinitely, they matter eternally." [13]

The ideal man of medieval Christian culture was not, as among the Greeks, the wise man or philosopher in quest of rational wisdom, but rather the saint, the righteous man, dedicated to a life of ascetic holiness and imbued with faith in divine grace and love.[14] Life on earth was conceived as a "pilgrim's progress," as a way fraught with temptation and moral crises in which the individual prepared himself for the Day of Judgment and life after death. The whole process of living from birth to death became the direct concern of the Church, since the Church alone was the spokesman of God on earth.

Metaphysically, the final synthesis achieved by St. Thomas was the doctrine that God was to be conceived as the highest and universal good and the end which man was destined to seek. The human soul was said to achieve its consummate happiness through the beatific vision of the Divine Good, thereby transcending itself and participating in the infinite source of its being. Unlike Aristotle, St. Thomas maintains that the specific object of moral virtue is God, the supreme good from whom all beings derive their goodness. The Platonic Idea of the Good, which Aristotle found so unintelligible and for which he could provide no place in his naturalistic ethics, became, when combined with the notion of the personal God of the Hebrew-Christian tradition, the very cornerstone of the whole medieval cultural synthesis.[15] It is this latent

[12] Aristotle, *Nicomachean Ethics*, 1103a.
[13] Mumford, *The Condition of Man*, p. 146.
[14] Turner, *The Great Cultural Traditions*, II, 1144, 1161.
[15] A. E. Taylor, *Plato; the Man and His Work*, pp. 288–89.

Platonism, concealed in the Aristotelian terminology, which accounts, in my opinion, for the final Thomistic identification of theoretical and practical virtue.[16]

With the growing secularization of thought during the seventeenth and eighteenth centuries, ethical and political theories were separated largely from theology, but the essential moralistic orientation of Western culture remained. The rationalists of the period utilized the Stoic ideal of *humanitas* as a postulate of their political theory and regarded the state as a historical institution organized to serve the common interests of its component citizens. In conjunction with the doctrine of natural rights, sanctioned partly by the Christian belief in the intrinsic value of the individual soul, the universal ideal of a common humanity served as a powerful revolutionary instrument of political and social reform in the struggle against arbitrary government and outmoded institutions. This moralistic perspective was embodied later in the Constitution of the United States of America, which set forth the doctrine of the inalienable rights of the individual as against the state. Whatever discrepancies may still exist between the ideals of the Constitution and actual social and political practices, the fact remains that the ideal culture of the United States has been primarily a moral one, guided by fixed principles of right and wrong. There is, in my opinion, a necessary, logical connection between the moral orientation of American culture and the fact that the United States has intervened in two world struggles and given generously of its resources without expecting to gain dominion over others.

States organized on an amoral basis, such as Germany, Italy, and Japan in the period between the First World War and the Second World War, have always regarded themselves as "beyond good and evil" and as not bound by moral conventions of right and wrong. Such states have always underestimated the dynamic power of moral ideals, even when they are imperfectly adhered to, and in their cynical adherence to *realpolitik* they have failed to reckon with the real efficacy of the ideal as a determining cultural force. In the moral state and society might is joined with right, and power is not deliberately sought as an end in itself irrespective of the human costs. The organization of the United Nations is a profession of faith in the ideal of a common humanity, and its validity as an ideal is not impaired by the fact that the world is still divided into two blocks whose aims and methods are

[16] Gilson, *The Spirit of Mediaeval Philosophy.*

antithetical. In proclaiming anew the doctrine of the universal rights of man and in outlawing genocide, the peoples of the world are seeking to reintroduce a moral perspective into the government of men and are laying the foundations for an emergent world culture.

### 4. CULTURE AS AN IDEOLOGICAL NORM

Culture may also be viewed from an intellectual perspective as essentially an ideology, or system of ideas. Thus, some modern ethnologists have defined culture as "communicable intelligence," as "conventional understandings," and as "communicated ideas." [17] The distinguishing characteristic of all such ideational views of culture is their identification of culture with a given tradition of ideas. Whereas the aesthetic approach to culture looks at culture from the perspective of feeling and intuition, and the moral approach views culture in terms of human will and effort, the ideational view of culture regards the intellect as the primary source of cultural experience. According to this ideational view of culture, the unit of culture may be said to be the symbolic form, idea, or meaning, rather than the aesthetic pattern, or the institution.

Politically, the enthronement of the intellect may lead to the dictatorship of the "philosopher-king," as in Plato's *Republic*. If all virtue and culture are based upon scientific knowledge, it appears foolish to leave the government of the state in hands other than those of the scientist, who should know the absolute truth concerning man and society.

It is significant that in the nineteenth century another philosopher-scientist, Auguste Comte, also sought to establish a "positive polity," with a hierarchy of scientist-priests who were to impose their scientific political and social culture upon their society. Notwithstanding Comte's opposition to theological authoritarianism and to any metaphysical absolutes, he reintroduced the very political dictatorship which he opposed in others in the name of positivism.

Historically, too, when the doctrine of positivism was tried out in practice in Latin America, it served as a justification of dictatorship. As Leopold Zea has shown in his instructive survey "Positivism and Porfirism in Latin America," [18] the dictatorship of Porfirio Diaz in Mexico (1884–1911) received the active support of educators, who

---

[17] See Chapter 2.

[18] Zea, "Positivism and Porfirism in Latin America," in *Ideological Differences and World Order*, ed. by Northrop, pp. 166–91.

consciously adhered either to the "sociocracy" and "religion of humanity" of Comte or to the bourgeois liberalism of John Stuart Mill and Herbert Spencer. The only liberty allowed by the Diaz government was economic liberty; political liberty, it was assumed, would automatically be attained with the diffusion of scientific education. As Zea concludes, "Positivism had become another instrument serving the desire of power and dominion that had distinguished Spanish Americans at all times. Scientific absolutism had superseded religious absolutism." [19]

Similarly, it is not an accident of history that modern Communism, with its doctrine of the "dictatorship of the proletariat," should claim absolute scientific validity. Instead of the political positivists, we now have the Communist state, which arrogates to itself in the name of Marxism the right to determine the truth of scientific theories.[20] Political dictatorship is justified in the name of dialectical and historical materialism, just as formerly it had been proclaimed in the name of positive science.

Among contemporary American philosophers, Whitehead and Northrop have attempted to reinterpret the basic vision of Greek scientific and philosophical thought for modern life. Whitehead, we have noted, recaptured the Greek mathematical-aesthetic perspective of Plato by maintaining that mathematics provides the basis for an understanding of the good and the beautiful in a normative culture. The ultimate good is thought of as an aesthetic pattern conceived through mathematical insight. Northrop, on the other hand, seeks to achieve a synthesis of modern science and art by combining the ontological principles of finite form and the infinite, undifferentiated aesthetic continuum, as suggested in Plato's *Timaeus*. The forms are conceptual postulates indispensable for an understanding of modern science; the undifferentiated aesthetic continuum is known by immediate intuition. Thus, whereas Whitehead derives the concept of the beautiful directly from mathematical pattern, Northrop derives the experience of beauty from a distinct metaphysical and epistemological source. By identifying intellectual concepts by postulation as the distinctive contribution of Western culture and aesthetic concepts by intuition as the contribution of Oriental culture, Northrop neatly divides world culture into two opposite and complementary segments, which require only mutual ap-

[19] *Ibid.*, p. 189.
[20] Huxley, *Heredity, East and West.*

preciation to bring about an integrated, normative world culture.[21]

The important point to note in this connection is that the theory of the scientific-aesthetic integration of culture tends to reduce the category of the good to the category of the true. Northrop, in particular, has restated this Platonic thesis most explicitly:

> The good is neither a fact nor a meaning; it is a set of philosophical presuppositions. These presuppositions have nothing to do with ethics, since empirically and intellectually speaking, there is no such thing as ethics. There are no purely ethical facts as there are no purely ethical meanings. There is only the nature of things and one's basic theory concerning what is. One's philosophical presuppositions designate this basic theory. "Good" is merely a single word for this basic theory. It is one's philosophy rather than, as modern ethical teachers suppose, an item, either naturalistic or idealistic, within that philosophy.[22]

In other words, the word "good" is but a name for the deductively formulatable system of empirically verified basic common denominator concepts of natural science, when these concepts are considered not with respect to their truth as tested by natural science against nature but with respect to their implication for the fulfillment of the true nature of man when applied to an act of human behavior and to human relations. In short, ethics is not a science yet to be created; ethics is an art, the art which takes the basic common denominator concepts as determined and verified by natural science and applies them to personal behavior and social relations.[23]

According to Northrop, a knowledge of scientific facts of nature together with their philosophical presuppositions as defined in a philosophy of science is sufficient to identify the good and to provide a norm for human conduct. By identifying philosophical scientific truth with "the good" and denying any purely ethical facts or meanings, he has explained away any specifically moral problems. This position is the antithesis of the Aristotelian and Kantian positions, which specify a distinct moral good and practical reason other than scientific theory of nature and theoretical reason. Northrop's categorical position appears to be the opposite of that of the Neo-Kantians, who would reduce the category of the true to that of the good. That is, whereas Neo-Kantians, such as W. M. Urban,[24] argue that "what ought to be" is the

---

[21] Northrop, *The Meeting of East and West.*

[22] Northrop, "Philosophy and World Peace," in *Approaches to World Peace*, p. 644.

[23] Northrop, "Ethics and the Integration of Natural Knowledge," in *The Nature of Concepts, Their Inter-relation and Role in Social Structure*, p. 124.

[24] Urban, *The Intelligible World*; see also Bidney, "The Philosophical Anthropology of Ernst Cassirer," in *The Philosophy of Ernst Cassirer*, ed. by Schilpp, p. 501.

criterion of "what is" taken as factually true, Northrop holds that "what is" ontologically, as defined by a given philosophy of science, is the criterion of "what ought to be" in cultural life. The entire Kantian theory of the autonomy of ethics is dismissed as an "error," and "the assumption of British philosophy of both the Cambridge realistic and the Oxford idealistic version that ethics is moral science" is said to be "similarly misguided." [25]

## 5. FACTS AND CULTURAL VALUES

What is particularly significant about modern empirical science is its methodical exclusion of the values, such as the good and the beautiful, in its pursuit of scientific truth. For scientific purposes the world is viewed as an order of natural forces subject to mathematical measurement and manifesting universal invariant uniformities, or laws. The function of the scientist is to discover the efficient causes of natural phenomena, how things work and the principles which explain why they function as they do. The scientist is interested only in ascertaining the facts of nature; his theories are but the pragmatic instruments which he has devised to render intelligible the interrelation of the phenomena he has observed. The scientist is not concerned to praise or to blame, but to understand the invariant order of nature.

At this point it is important to indicate the inherent ambiguity of the term "fact." Facts are usually contrasted with values. Facts are said to be the data which the scientist observes in nature; they are what he discovers in nature. Hence, facts are thought to be "objective" and independent of the preferences of the observer. By comparison, values are "subjective" preferences and without any basis in the order of nature. In this way, the more man extends his scientific knowledge of nature, the less significant nature becomes to him, since his values seem to have no objective basis in nature. In brief, modern science appears to lead to value-nihilism, to the doctrine that there is no objective basis in nature for moral and aesthetic values.

As against this thesis, I maintain that the dichotomy of scientific facts and cultural values is not valid. So-called facts are really truth values, human evaluations as to the truth of one's ideas concerning the order of nature and cultural experiences. "Facts" are judgments as to what is the case and may change with one's beliefs and interpretations. This is demonstrated particularly in the constant revaluations to which

[25] Northrop, "Ethics and the Integration of Natural Knowledge," in *op. cit.*, p. 124.

historical "facts" are subjected in the course of time.[26] What the scientific method of investigation has demonstrated is the relative autonomy of truth values and their comparative independence of moral and aesthetic values in the sphere of nature. In contrast to the prescientific practice of arguing a priori from the moral or aesthetic properties of a thing to its actual existence, the critical scientist maintains that the goodness and beauty of an object are irrelevant to the truth of its existence. A priori arguments, he maintains, are contentious, provoking emotional conflicts, but not increasing our effective knowledge and power.

But this does not mean that truth values and moral and aesthetic values have nothing to do with one another. There are such things as a "true good" and a "true beauty" in contrast to a false, or apparent, good and beauty. A scientific demonstration may be "beautiful" to those who are impressed by its clarity, and the beauty of a noble deed may shine brightly notwithstanding failure to accomplish a given objective. Of the three categories of value, truth values are primary, since they underlie all other judgments of value. But each category of value has a certain relative autonomy and is not to be reduced to the others. The concepts of the true, the good, and the beautiful are phenomenologically distinct and have to be conceived independently of one another. Yet, they are also mutually related in nature and culture.

If, then, by science we mean the discipline which is concerned with the establishment of truth values by empirical methods, then obviously science is very much concerned with values. Besides, cultural values are "facts" to the social scientist who investigates them; they are observable factors effective in the cultural experience of a society. In the sphere of human culture and society the scientific observer cannot avoid studying value phenomena as such and he must apply himself to the task in the same spirit as does the natural scientist.

## 6. THE CONCEPT OF A NORMATIVE SCIENCE OF CULTURE

If it be granted that there may be a science of cultural values, then the way is prepared for the recognition of a possible normative science of human culture. By the concept of a normative science of culture I mean a science of culture concerned with the formulation of cultural ideals as possible means and ends of sociocultural life. Hitherto it has been thought that science deals only with facts, with what is the case, and cannot therefore deal with values, with what ought to be. Hence

[26] Trevelyan, "Bias in History," in his *An Autobiography and Other Essays.*

the notion of a normative science was regarded as a contradiction in terms. If, however, it be granted that the antithesis of facts and values is false, then it seems that the concept of a normative science is not at all self-contradictory.

The function of a normative science, as distinguished from a positive science, is to investigate and suggest new modes of human conduct which may serve as norms for cultural experience and experimentation. As contrasted with the old positivistic thesis that an empirical, comparative study of "social facts" will reveal moral laws comparable to the laws of physics, a normative anthropology would concern itself not only with what is the case actually and historically but also with what may be and ought to be, with possible alternative ideals suggested by the facts of cultural experience and natural science, but not given actually in any cultural system. The objective of such a normative anthropology is not to discover "laws" of cultural development, but rather to discover new cultural possibilities and potentialities which may be of practical significance in cultural invention and innovation.

The position here suggested is an attempt to avoid the extremes of either a theory which completely separates the natural sciences from the social sciences or one which reduces the social sciences to natural sciences. If the first alternative were to be adopted, as the Neo-Kantian philosophers and historians have done, then one would set up a sphere of *Geisteswissenschaften* with objects and methods of their own. In practice this division has led to a complete separation between cultural ends, or values, and scientific means, thereby reintroducing the same duality of value-free natural science and subjective values which earlier thinkers had anticipated. Even realistic philosophers, such as Bertrand Russell, tend to perpetuate the antithesis of "science" and "values" by maintaining that moral values are ultimately matters of choice and are not derived from scientific knowledge.[27] On this premise cultural ideologies are left without a basis in scientific fact, and the way is left open for the supremacy of the myth of the state.

On the other hand, if one were to adopt the second alternative and reduce the human sciences to natural sciences, then he would fail to allow for the element of human will for the realization of ideal values not given in cultural experience. Furthermore, by the identification of the ideal and the actual in culture the way is prepared for political

[27] Russell, "The Science to Save Us from Science," New York *Times* Magazine, Sunday, March 19, 1950, p. 33.

dictatorship, since no scope is afforded for the realization of ideal, alternative values not prescribed by positive science. Thus, in practice we have a meeting of extremes. Cultural and political dictatorship may be brought about in the name of positive science, as well as in the name of ethnocentric myth. Communistic "dictatorship of the proletariat" is a modern instance of a state which is validated in the name of positive natural science; the Nazi state of Hitler justified sociocultural dictatorship by reference to "the myth of the twentieth century" of Alfred Rosenberg. The Nazi doctrine lacked universal appeal because it involved the notion of a chosen people whose destiny it was to rule all others. The Communist gospel, however, since it appeals to science and the universal values of the common man, has a certain idealistic attraction and has been successful in winning converts, particularly among the more idealistic self-sacrificing individuals who were influenced by its messianic message. In practice, however, modern Communist states tend to value political solidarity and "integration" above scientific, objective integrity.

Only by recognizing the validity of a normative science of man do we avoid the dangers of both of these extremes. According to our thesis, man is envisaged as part of the order of nature subject to natural laws, but at the same time recognition is given to the factors of cultural creativity and self-determination, as well as to the role of ideals in furthering cultural enterprise.

## 7. THE DISPARITY OF THE IDEAL AND THE ACTUAL

The concept of a normative science involves the principle of the disparity of ideal and actual truth. This principle was first clearly formulated by Plato. As Cassirer has stated,

It is one of the first principles of Plato's theory of knowledge to insist upon the radical distinction between empirical and ideal truth. What experience gives is, at best, a right opinion about things; it is not real knowledge. The difference between these two types, between *doxa* and *episteme*, is ineffaceable. Facts are variable and accidental; truth is necessary and immutable.[28]

The ideal is never given in experience, but may be suggested by it. With reference to the sphere of the natural sciences, this ideal truth represents the limit of the metaphysical knowledge of nature.[29] In the sphere of the social sciences and human studies, this ideal truth rep-

[28] Cassirer, *The Myth of the State*, p. 69.
[29] See Chapter 1.

resents a norm, or goal, of human endeavor, a possibility compatible with human potentialities, but does not correspond to any actual, historical cultural situation. Here, too, cultural ideals are "social facts," but they are facts of a different order from the empirical facts of a given culture. The ideal truths of science and philosophy are products of cultural experience; yet they transcend the empirical limits of actual cultural experience. They are timeless, atemporal ideals, suggested by experience, but pointing to a metacultural reality which surpasses anything given in the context of historical experience.

Ultimately, the issue involved is a metaphysical, or metacultural, one. If the only reality is a cultural reality and relative to the experience of an organism, as cultural and sociological relativists maintain,[30] then the concept of an ideal truth other than given cultural experience becomes meaningless. As against this position, I maintain that the postulate of objective reality, independent of the observer, is a fruitful one, since it serves as a normative guide to research and presents an intelligible goal for the scientist to approximate. Our conceptual and empirical knowledge of reality varies with our interests and experiences, but reality as an ontological existent independent of man is an absolute object to which our ideas progressively conform in the course of our pursuit of knowledge by scientific methods.[31] Similarly, moral and aesthetic values are real attributes of objects, although for purposes of physical science the former may be disregarded. Moral and aesthetic values may be said to be real and objective in the sense of having a basis in nature, human and cosmic.

With this perspective one can understand the fallacy involved in asserting that virtue is knowledge or that culture is a communicated system of ideas. In either instance the ineradicable difference between the ideal and the actual is not recognized. To identify culture with a knowledge of "social facts" is to exclude all those cultural ideals which are presupposed in any historical culture and serve as regulative norms without being consistently practiced. The positivistic fallacy,[32] as it may be called, consists in the identification of the ideal with the actual, of the "ought" with the "is" of cultural experience. My point is that attempts to derive cultural ideals from actual empirical facts and in general to identify the category of truth with that of the good are bound

---

[30] Lundberg, *Foundations of Sociology*, ch. i; Znaniecki, *Cultural Sciences; Their Origin and Development.*

[31] See Chapter 1.

[32] See Chapter 2.

to lead to the positivistic fallacy, regardless of whether the "is" of fact is conceived in purely phenomenal terms or is understood in conceptual, ontological terms. The converse fallacy, the normativistic fallacy, is the reduction of the "is" of scientific fact to the "ought" of moral judgment and practical reason. The latter fallacy is best exemplified in the Neo-Kantian axiological approach. In either instance an attempt is made to explain away the ineradicable disparity of the normative ideal and actual facts.

The history of human thought demonstrates clearly the temptation to reduce ideal to factual truth. In the case of Plato himself this is shown by his *Republic,* which is a theory of the ideal state, as well as of the best state.[33] As an ideal state, the republic can admit of no compromise and must therefore exclude the poets and arists, who by definition are not concerned with the pursuit of truth and reality. As the best state under the circumstances, the republic compromises by utilizing the cultural heritage at its disposal. In the best state Plato is prepared to include the poets and myth-makers, since he admits the necessity of "noble fictions" to inspire the young with the proper moral ideals. I find that the idealistic philosopher and the practical statesman in Plato were never quite reconciled, although in his later work, such as the *Laws,* one can discern a tendency toward conservatism and practical idealism. The danger in Plato's utopia, as in all subsequent utopias, is that by making his ideal state concrete the utopian idealist inevitably tends to introduce some of the historical culture of his day, with all its local and temporal limitations. There is also danger of engaging in wishful, impractical thinking insofar as the utopian idealist fails to reckon with the facts of human nature, by imagining men as disembodied intellects interested in ideal truths and disregarding the irrational impulses and cultural limitations of actual men. In brief, since the ideal truths of culture and society transcend our immediate experience, they cannot be visualized in concrete form without serious falsification. The culture of the "world of tomorrow" is always partially beyond our grasp. To claim that the ideal has been realized, whether in the name of science or of religion, is to set up a false absolute, which by claiming perfection automatically halts and restricts cultural progress.

In historical experience the price of identifying the ideal with the

[33] See Bidney, "The Philosophical Anthropology of Ernst Cassirer," in *The Philosophy of Ernst Cassirer,* ed. by Schilpp.

actual of culture is intolerance, born of a false absolute. Once it is asserted that a given cultural system embodies all the ideal values, then the way is prepared for a justification of intolerance toward all who deviate from this absolute norm. No one is more ruthless and intolerant than a utopian idealist who believes that his particular vision provides the only means of salvation for mankind. This explains why in the sphere of religion we are confronted with the historical spectacle of an Inquisition which engaged in mass persecution in the name of a religion of love. In philosophy, we have the example of the Hegelian philosophy, which identified the real with the rational and sought to justify the Prussian state of its day as the embodiment of absolute values. Similarly, Marxism, which is an inverted Hegelianism, involves the worship of history as manifested through the processes of dialectical and historical materialism. In conformity with the utopian myth of Marxism, only the Communist state embodies all the social virtues and only the proletarian class is fit to represent mankind.

In the autobiographical accounts compiled in *The God That Failed* [34] we are given an intimate view of the experiences of some ex-Communists and Communist sympathizers. At first they regarded the Communist state of Soviet Russia as the realization of the kingdom of God on earth, until, through a slow process of disillusionment, each discovered in turn the gap between his own vision of the ideal good and the actual practice of the Communist party and state. According to the logic of the emotions, it was assumed that because contemporary capitalistic society was deficient in moral values, therefore the Communist state represented the realization of social idealism. It was a case of prior faith seeking rationalization and justification. All incompatible facts and experiences were explained away as minor imperfections which in no way impaired one's faith in the infallibility of the party and in the dialectical course of history. By this mode of reasoning, young idealists and scientists were led to betray their countries in order to serve mankind and to help realize the utopian state and world order of the future.

What is particularly noteworthy in the case of the "Soviet myth" is that here, for the first time in history, the identification of the absolute ideal with political real was undertaken in the name of a particular party and state, as well as in the so-called interests of mankind as a whole. Henceforth, it is held, all who adhere to this ideal of society and

[34] *The God That Failed*, ed. by R. Crossman.

are prepared to support the policies of this state are scientific, progressive, and the friends of mankind; all who are opposed are deluded reactionaries and the enemies of mankind. Mankind is divided into two camps, the enlightened and the saved by the grace of Marxism and the deluded and the damned by the sin of capitalism and idealism. There is no more tragic example in the whole of human history than this mythological identification of the absolute ideal and the historically real—a myth which has split the world asunder into hostile camps.

There is also the complementary danger of setting up "Democracy" as an antithetical absolute and justifying the *status quo* of our culture as the fulfillment of the ideal. To some liberal, pragmatic apologists "Democracy" has become "the religion of religions," and cultural pluralism the world's panacea.[35] By contrast, the thesis I wish to maintain is that no historical social system is free from some defects and limitations of one kind or another and that to identify the ideal and the historically given is bound to lead to a falsification of the ideal absolute. On this assumption, constructive criticism is always in order, since one may point out the disparity between professed ideals and actual accomplishments with a view to bringing them into closer accord. Otherwise, if one were complacently to accept the *status quo* of a given culture, one would be led to indulge in rationalization and mythical propaganda as the only means of reconciling the ideal and the actual, what ought to be with what actually prevails.

Criticism of any sociocultural system must consider two distinct types of deficiency in a given cultural situation: first, deficiencies inherent in the given ethos; secondly, deficiencies owing to the disparity between valid ideals and actual social practices. Among those who now abjure "the God that failed" disillusion is frequently the result of a consciousness of the disparity of ideals and practices, but the cultural idol itself is still worshiped. Complete conversion would require rejection of the ideals, as well as the practices.

A false absolutism may be effected in various ways. Historically, relative ethnocentric absolutism is the most common. This is a naïve absolutism in which it is assumed that one's own culture system and values are superior to all others. Secondly, there is classical absolutism, the notion that a particular cultural epoch marked the summit of human achievement. On this assumption, all one can do is attempt to recapture this bygone vision, whether it be "the glory that was Greece"

[35] Kallen, *The Education of Free Men,* ch. xvii.

or the great synthesis of medieval European culture in the thirteenth century. Thirdly, there is historical absolutism, which involves the belief that whatever is, is best for the time being. This is a serial absolute which the nineteenth-century doctrine of evolutionary progress rendered plausible. As Niebuhr has remarked, "the dominant note in modern culture is not so much confidence in reason as faith in history." [36] Time and history have become self-explanatory and the source of intelligibility of all cultural processes. This has led to a false optimism as regards the growth of human freedom and to tragic disillusionment when events failed to justify this mythological belief.

In contemporary ethnological theory culture has become the new absolute and self-explanatory reality, the measure of man and his works. This new cultural absolute is no longer used to justify cultural progress, but rather to justify cultural relativism. While culture is said to be the measure of all things, all historical value systems are treated as equally valid. Having set up culture as the new historical absolute and principle of intelligibility, contemporary American anthropologists have tended to deny the former faith of the nineteenth-century ethnologists in laws of cultural evolution, as well as in the validity of any absolute ideal of cultural progress.

## 8. CULTURAL REALITY AND CULTURAL RELATIVISM

Among contemporary cultural anthropologists, Herskovits in particular has articulated the thesis of cultural relativism in its most uncompromising form. In *Man and His Works* he has devoted an entire chapter to "The Problem of Cultural Relativism," and I shall, therefore, examine his main arguments in order to indicate his basic presuppositions.

Philosophically it is extremely interesting that Herskovits adopts the thesis of historical idealism and quotes Cassirer with approval to corroborate his view that "experience is culturally defined." [37] According to Herskovits, "Even the facts of the physical world are discerned through the enculturative screen so that the perception of time, distance, weight, size and other 'realities' is mediated by the conventions of any given group." [38] Thus, having adopted the thesis of cultural idealism, Herskovits finds that there is literally no other reality than cultural reality, and hence he concludes logically that the only values

[36] Niebuhr, *Faith and History*, p. 3.
[37] Herskovits, *Man and His Works*, p. 27.
[38] *Ibid.*, p. 64.

which are acceptable to the individual are those which are relatively valid for his culture at a given time.

Herskovits distinguishes between cultural absolutes and cultural universals. There are said to be cultural universals in the formal sense that there are universal types of institution, and morality in general is an example of such a universal, since it is a characteristic of all cultures. But the actual forms of morality are functions of given historical experiences of the societies that manifest them. That is why there can be no absolutes in the sense of fixed standards which admit of no historical variations.

Thus, we are asked to transcend our ethnocentrism in the name of cultural relativism. "Cultural relativism" is used as a value-charged term denoting a positive, praiseworthy attitude, while "ethnocentrism" connotes a negative value incompatible with an unbiased, objective approach. Herskovits does not explain how it is theoretically possible to have cultural relativism without ethnocentrism, in view of the fact that cultural conditioning necessarily leads the members of any given society to prefer their own value system above all others. What he apparently has in mind is a culture system which inculcates the relative validity of its own values for its own adherents, together with recognition of the equal value of other systems. He implies, therefore, an ideal cultural relativism totally different from the real cultural relativism of historic cultures, which recognize the absolute validity of their own values and deny equal recognition to other systems. A major source of confusion in Herskovits's thesis is that he fails to differentiate clearly between this implicit ideal cultural relativism which he advocates and the real, historic relativism which he posits to account for the variety of actual systems.

There are, apparently, two kinds of ethnocentrism—a vicious and a benign kind. The vicious kind of ethnocentrism involves belief in objective absolute values and hence intolerance of other codes. The benign kind involves preference for one's own value system, as well as mutual respect for those of other societies. How it is possible to transcend ethnocentrism of the intolerant variety, if there is no objective standard of comparison, is not explained. Furthermore, it is not at all clear why one should prefer his own system of cultural values rather than some other system, provided the cultural blinkers which have been imposed on him do not prevent him from envisaging some other system. It may be expedient to adhere to a given social code at a spe-

cial time and place, but it is difficult to see why one should adhere
to it exclusively or exercise moral restraint in the presence of other culture systems. The fact of cultural variations in historic cultures does
not imply the absolute value of cultural differences and the obligation to respect them. The "is" of cultural relativism does not imply the
"ought," that is, the obligation to respect other people's codes and
norms. To derive the "ought" from the "is" of culture is to commit what
I have termed "the positivistic fallacy."

As an axiological position, the doctrine of cultural relativism involves "the transvaluation of values." The absolute values of truth,
goodness, and beauty which men profess are said to have only a limited
historical validity for a given society and culture. All so-called "absolute" values are really "relative absolutes" whose validity is recognized
only within the context of a given culture. We must distinguish, however, sociological relativism from cultural relativism. According to
sociological relativism, cultural values are functions of social organization and vary with its modes. That is, the sociological relativist explains the origin of a particular value system by reference to the society
and the class interests which it fosters. Thus, Nietzsche evaluated moral
values by reference to two social classes, the masters and the slaves,
engaged in a conflict of wills to power, and Marx evaluated moral
values as reflecting the economic interests of classes, such as capitalists
and workers. By contrast, the cultural relativist does not explain the
origin of social values, but accepts them as given. Philosophically, contemporary ethnologists find historical idealism most congenial and
postulate cultural reality as a reality *sui generis* which renders all the
phenomena of experience intelligible. At most, we are informed that
cultural relativism is a fact of ethnographic experience and a necessary
product of cultural conditioning. Values are said to be conditioned by
culture, but culture itself must be taken for granted as self-explanatory.
This is what is meant by the assertion that culture is a "closed system."

The issue as interpreted by the cultural relativists apparently turns
on two alternatives: one must either accept a doctrine of fixed absolute
values or deny objective norms in favor of historic relativity and the
relative validity of values. I do not think, however, that we are necessarily limited to these two alternatives. In the sphere of natural science
there is a cumulative advance in man's knowledge of nature notwithstanding the continuous reevaluation of beliefs and postulates. The
scientist does not argue that because some former truth values have

been rejected because of new, objective evidence, therefore there is no objective criterion of truth. On the contrary, it is because of his faith in an objective order of nature amenable to gradual human discovery that he is prepared constantly to question his assumptions and generalizations and to alter them in accordance with his available empirical evidence. The natural scientist does not use objective evidence to discredit objective truth values. Similarly, in the sphere of moral truths it is not logical to reject objective moral norms simply because some alleged objective moral norms are seen to have a purely subjective validity within a given cultural context. There is no reason on principle why there may not be a cumulative increment in our knowledge and achievement of moral ideals comparable to our advance in the attainment of knowledge in the natural sciences. Murder and incest, for example, are even now instances of negative moral values which are concrete ethnological universals, even though there is considerable disparity in the range of their application in different cultures.

The social and cultural relativists maintain that society determines the ideological perspective of its members and hence can see no common measure in cultural values. For them there are only historic "relative absolutes," since each culture system is asserted to be absolutely valid. What is overlooked by the relativists is the important consideration to which Kant drew attention in his essay "Idea for a Universal History with Cosmopolitan Intent," namely, that "in man (as the only rational creature on earth) those natural faculties which aim at the use of reason shall be fully developed in the species, not in the individual." [39] That is, man has a capacity for reason which is developed in the history of human society, but not in the experience of the individual, since the life of the individual is far too short to achieve complete rationality. Mankind has the potentiality for developing rationality to its fullest extent, and rationality is, therefore, a universally valid ideal. Thus, if society, through its culture, is responsible for warping the perspective of the individual through its relative absolutes, it is also the only means for achieving in time the maximum degree of objectivity and universality of thought which man is capable of attaining. Similarly, if the perspective of the individual is a product of his culture, it is also true that individuals may in turn affect the cultural perspective of their society in the direction of greater rationality and objectivity.

Finally, the cultural relativists fail to see that cultural ideologies

[39] *The Philosophy of Kant*, ed. by Friedrich, p. 118.

are effective precisely because they are believed and acknowledged to have absolute value by their adherents for all mankind, not only for their adherents. If a given value system were not accepted as objectively valid, it would soon lose its effectiveness as a motivation for conduct. Social and cultural relativists tend to assume that men would continue to adhere to and respect their cultural values, even after they were convinced by the sophisticated ethnologists that their so-called absolute and universal values were but subjective delusions. Modern states, however, are not so impractical and have instituted rigid systems of thought control and censorship to prevent their subjects from acquiring a critical comparative judgment. They have preferred to follow the counsel of pragmatic sociologists, such as Sorel and Pareto, and regard social myths as indispensable for social action. What is important is that the myth should be believed and serve as an inspiration for heroic action.

The practical, effective alternatives are not cultural absolutism versus cultural relativism, as contemporary ethnologists are inclined to maintain, but rather rational norms with a potentiality for universal acceptance and realization versus mythological absolutes destined to lead to perpetual crises and conflicting political policies. Far from resolving our international problems, cultural relativism leads to conflicting political and social mythologies. The only effective alternative to a mythical relative absolute is a better, more rational and more objective ideal of conduct and belief capable of overcoming the limitations of the former.

In their anxiety to obviate the evils of national ethnocentrism, especially when allied with the quest for power and domination over weaker peoples, contemporary anthropologists have unwittingly tended to substitute serial ethnocentrism for the static ethnocentrism which they abhor. By "serial ethnocentrism" I mean the attitude of viewing each culture from its own perspective only, as if that were the primary virtue of the objective anthropologist. So timid and wary has the modern anthropologist become, lest he commit the fallacies of the evolutionary ethnologist of the nineteenth century, that the very thought of "the comparative method" strikes him with terror. Thus, comparative studies are viewed as unscientific adventures reminiscent of an outmoded era in cultural anthropology.

As long as anthropology remains at the descriptive stage, anthropologists may rest content with cultural pluralism and relativism on the ground that they do not wish to overstep the bounds of scientific fact. But if anthropology is to attain the stage of making significant generalizations concerning the conditions of the cultural process and the values of civilization, then comparative studies of cultures and their values must be made in order to demonstrate universal principles of cultural dynamics and concrete rational norms capable of universal realization. Hitherto the task of suggesting and prescribing normative ideals and goals has been left chiefly to utopian philosophers and theologians. I suggest that it is high time for anthropology to come of age and for anthropologists to show their respect for human reason and science by cooperating with other social scientists and scholars so as to envisage practical, progressive, rational norms worthy of winning a measure of universal recognition in the future.

For the positivists and pragmatists in philosophy and social science, this distinction between the absolute ideal and the varying historical cultural norms does not appear valid. Since the former maintain that the real is that which is given in immediate experience, or is similar to such empirical data, there can be for them no significant difference between the goal and the going, between the end and the means. Hence, to the positivist and the pragmatist "the best" and the "absolute ideal" are arbitrary terms. "It represents the preference of a person, not the perfection of a thing." [40] Ideals as they are known in experience are subject to historical change, and the concept of a timeless absolute ideal which transcends cultural experience is thought to be an invalid abstraction.

According to the position here maintained, the concept of an absolute value is a significant regulative norm. It is a fact of experience no less than the empirical data of the positivist, but it is a "fact" of a different order; it is a fact created by and as a result of experience. The absolute norm is real insofar as it is conceived as an ideal possibility whose validity is independent of its actual realization in cultural experience. Hence, the absolute ideal may serve as a goal of cultural endeavor which is radically different from the process, the going, whereby it is approximated. The concept of the best is not merely a preference of a given historical society; the normative best is a meta-cultural ideal which transcends the actually given of historical experience and yet as a regulative norm is a significant factor in molding experience. The concept of an absolute ideal truth, good, or beauty

[40] Kallen, *The Education of Free Men*, p. 304.

connotes an ideal which to some extent transcends empirical experience and yet serves to bring about a closer conformity of cultural facts and ideals. As a regulative norm and ideal possibility, it is a product of cultural experience and yet not quite a part of it; it functions within the historical process and is not subject to the historical process itself. The moment this absolute norm is given expression within the context of a given culture, it becomes in part falsified. That is why every attempt to identify the ideal with the actually existent is a delusion, a myth which sets up a false idol and hinders cultural progress. The ideal absolute is compatible with cultural freedom and diversity, since it does not dictate categorically the particular form which historical cultures must assume, but serves only as a regulative norm and measure by which to evaluate diverse cultural approaches. There may be more than one cultural way to the heaven of the ideal truth, goodness, and beauty.

### 9. THE FUNCTION OF SCIENCE IN MODERN CULTURE

The problem of normative culture and relative values may be discussed profitably by reference to the function and role of science in modern culture. There are two main approaches to the problem of the nature and function of science. On the one hand, science has been regarded as a body of authoritatively established truths based on verification by empirical evidence. On the other hand, there is the pragmatic view that science is essentially a method for pursuing truth which yields practical results and enables man to adjust successfully to his environment. The "quest for certainty" and the knowledge of an ultimate reality independent of the knower are held to be delusions, since there is no absolute certainty and no knowledge of a reality independent of the knower. The only constant is said to be the scientific method; there is no body of scientific "truth" which is fixed and established once and for all. The first, positivistic view tends to regard science as an absolute achievement, a more or less closed system, to which details may be added, but which is not subject to basic revision. According to the second, pragmatic view, nothing at all is fixed except the method, or road; the results are subject to constant revision in the light of experience and practice.

Recently, however, there have been attempts to reconcile these two antithetical views in the interests of cultural integration. Science, it is realized, is not merely an instrument for gaining mastery over the forces of nature; it has also a normative, humanizing function in determining one's entire cultural perspective. Science is not merely an instrument of technology, but also an end in itself, a humanity which determines the spirit of a culture. As the progressive quest for truth concerning nature and human culture, science must serve the interests of humanity as a whole. It is the spirit of science, at once rational, progressive, and self-corrective, which may serve as an absolute norm for culture as a whole, irrespective of its factual and technological achievements. As the rational and empirical pursuit of truth, science is an absolute value and a moral good. The use of scientific method for irrational purposes, such as the communication of irrational myths, superstitions, and prejudices, is a perversion of the spirit of science. In normative science ends and means are in harmony, since normative science involves the use of rational means to communicate verified knowledge.

It is because of this separation of ends and means in the utilization of scientific method that science has been decried as an evil which has exiled man from the Garden of Eden, in which he might otherwise dwell. There must be a will to truth, a willingness to acknowledge the absolute value of scientific truth and to utilize it for rational moral and aesthetic ends, if science is to serve to humanize mankind and in the development of a normative civilization. Science, taken in abstraction from moral and aesthetic values, tends to be abused and perverted in the service of ends incompatible with scientific pursuits. A science which is used for irrational ends is the agent of its own destruction; a science of means apart from a science of ends is self-defeating.

Thus, the proposition frequently put forth in the name of science by eminent scientists and philosophers, that science has nothing to do with moral values and aesthetic feelings, while it appears plausible in the sphere of technology, is only a half-truth concealing a great illusion. The scientific pursuit of knowledge is itself a moral good, and the scientist has his own ideal code of professional ethics to obey. Furthermore, the scientist requires a social and cultural environment suitable for the pursuit of his vocation, namely, one which permits him complete freedom of thought and experiment in the pursuit of scientific truth and cultural knowledge. That is why the scientist as scientist must be actively concerned with the preservation of the basic cultural freedoms lest he jeopardize his own enterprise. The unethical pursuit of science leads to ultimate self-destruction, as does the unscientific pursuit of ethics and aesthetics.

As against the extreme antithetical views that science is either a method without content or else a method yielding a fixed body of necessary truths, the position taken here is that normative science is a progressive, cumulative, self-critical discipline and comprises a cumulative fund of verified truths. Science is normative in the sense that it offers a criterion whereby myth and superstition may be differentiated from rational and empirical knowledge. Normative science is a cumulative process which establishes a fund of authentic knowledge, while revising some of its tentatively accepted theories. It is neither absolutely fixed nor in constant flux; it is partly fixed and partly changing. Normative science is an approximation to the ideal absolute truth and involves the postulation of a metaphysical reality which transcends our limited experience. As a historical cultural process, science is subject to constant revision; yet scientific knowledge puts man in touch with a metacultural reality which transcends the cultural limitations of any particular space-time culture.[41] In this sense normative science makes for substantial progress.

Edmund W. Sinnott has presented a vigorous argument against the extremes of intolerant absolutism and tolerant indifference. In his essay "Ten Million Scientists" he writes:

Science is by no means completely tolerant. Its goal is to seek out the truth, and its history has been one of steady progress toward this end. If truth could not be disentangled from error, science would have no meaning. So long as a particular element of truth has not been discovered or is only imperfectly known, the seeker's mind must be completely open to help from other quarters; but once a portion of the truth has been found, has been separated from error and become a part of the intellectual capital of mankind, then the conception of tolerance to ideas incompatible with it quite loses its meaning. Tolerance of what has been proved to be untrue is manifestly absurd. Thus, science builds an ever-growing body of certainty, of assured and proved truth.[42]

Thus, normative science combines freedom and tolerance in the pursuit of truth with intolerance of falsity when it has attained convictions. As Sinnott has stated, "the spirit of science, if it truly takes possession of a man, can carry him along the middle way which leads

[41] See Chapter 1.
[42] Sinnott, "Ten Million Scientists," *Science,* CXI (1950), 123–29.

both to that freedom and tolerance so necessary for the democratic way of life, and to the convictions and enthusiasms that keep life from growing flabby and stale."

The spirit of normative science is a cultural universal which is applicable to any cultural discipline, regardless of its subject matter. But normative science is more than a disembodied spirit; it is also a body of knowledge carrying conviction through empirical evidence and rational demonstration. Normative science does make for absolute standards and is also compatible with freedom of inquiry and cultural progress. The belief that the application of tolerance to cultural pluralism regardless of common values will in time lead to harmonious integration and "orchestration" of world cultures is but a pious, aesthetic delusion. Unless science can provide potentially universal cultural values capable of winning ardent adherents, other methods will be found to fill this need, such as the mythological appeal to race, class, or nationality. The choice is between "contentious knowledge" of conflicting mythological ideologies and normative scientific, rational truths capable of producing a rational consensus among the peoples of the world.[43] Only a cultural unity based upon a common core of rational values and brought into being by voluntary deliberate consent can endure indefinitely.

[43] Bidney, "The Concept of Value in Modern Anthropology," in *Anthropology Today*, edited by A. V. Kroeber, pp. 682–99.

# 15

## Ideology and Power in the Strategy of World Peace[1]

THE DEVELOPMENT of atomic energy has revolutionized the whole process of war and the concept of peace and upset the traditional concept of the balance of power among nations. Man's ability to induce nuclear disintegration has made it possible for him to produce cultural disintegration on a scale never imagined before. Atomic war is essentially a war of annihilation, just as the release of atomic energy involves the transmutation of elements and the conversion of matter into radiant energy. The atomic revolution, therefore, necessitates a corresponding social and axiological revolution.

A crisis offers the possibility of disaster, as well as an opportunity for a new creative advance. The nations of the world, especially the big powers, are now faced with a crucial decision: whether to participate in one intelligible world of universal values or to go on competing with one another within their conflicting, private cultural worlds; whether to seek their mutual welfare within the framework of a genuine democratic world order or to promote their own interests and so-called sovereign power irrespective of the social cost. The alternative of power politics has been tried exclusively throughout recorded history by "practical" statesmen and has led to a series of disasters of ever-increasing proportions. Perhaps now, with the threat of planetary destruction as a warning, the alternative of a universal human order and common civilization envisaged by the great spiritual leaders of all ages may yet be put to the test.

It is one thing, however, to point the ideal direction for a resolution of the world's basic problem; it is quite another to indicate the practical steps to bring about this consummation. It is all very well to submit the proposal that the world is in need of a supernational govern-

[1] Originally prepared for the Eighth Symposium of the Conference on Science, Philosophy and Religion. held in Philadelphia in September, 1947.

ment and of international laws.[2] But one has also to reckon with the existing cultural situation, which makes it impossible to proceed immediately with the realization of this ideal. Whether the world will respond to this "most challenging opportunity of all history" with constructive vision and achieve greatness, or whether it will find the task too difficult—that is the question of our troubled times. From a historical perspective, as Arnold Toynbee [3] has reminded us, the formula of "Challenge and Response" in all historical epochs provides the cultural conditions of human progress. Whether we of this epoch have the greatness of mind and courage to meet our challenge or whether, as has recently been asserted, "all signs indicate that we are failing to meet the challenge" [4] remains to be seen.

### 1. THE PROBLEM OF ONE WORLD IN THEORY AND PRACTICE

Politically, the quest for world unity is as old as the recorded history of man. All the empire builders were motivated by this ideal. But they all sought a unity of power and dominion, an imposed "organic" unity. The crucial question of our times, then, is not shall we have world unity? Rather, it is what kind of unity shall we have? Unity on what terms? Shall we substitute for the one world which the Nazis dreamed of, the utopian, classless world society envisaged by the Marxists? Or shall we rather strive for a voluntary, democratic world order based on the concept of a supranational government which recognizes no absolute, sovereign, national rights and is dedicated to the ideal of world peace?

Of course, we of the twentieth century are especially conscious of the unity of the world from a functional and geographic point of view. Geographical isolation is a thing of the past. Economically, too, the development of specialized industries and of world trade has made all nations dependent on one another. Culturally, however, we are still living in ethnocentric worlds of our own creation, worlds which are the products of our diverse human historical experiences and geographical environments. The question arises, is it impossible for men to emerge from their ethnocentric worlds to participate in a common cultural world? If so, how is this to be achieved?

The answer seems to be, as Plato discerned, that it is possible for

---

[2] See, for example, Reves's popular discussion *The Anatomy of Peace.*

[3] Toynbee, *A Study of History*, chap. v.

[4] Statement by Emergency Committee of Atomic Scientists, New York *Times,* June 30, 1947.

mankind to emerge from its cultural caves and behold a common world in the light of the sun, provided men learn how to distinguish scientific knowledge based on reason and experience of nature from the subjective opinions and wishful notions derived from their limited traditional cultural environments. Through scientific knowledge alone can man conceive of one world subject to universal natural laws, the same for all. Only a science of cultural phenomena capable of producing a sense of human cultural kinship, parallel to the sense of biological kinship which we have as members of the same species, can overcome the cultural isolation and conflict which is the curse of our times.

Since the common cultural world of man is primarily an ideal world of common objectives, of moral values and principles, it must necessarily depend upon the common will and efforts of mankind for its realization. Hence, we must not assume, as the positivists and functionalists tend to do, that because of the interdependence of modern societies, the human world is in fact one. Mere functional or geographic interdependence of cultures is a mechanical kind of unity which would apply to any kind of world organization or lack of organization. A genuine and significant world unity is one characterized by the mutual acknowledgment of common values or objectives; it is a teleological unity, manifested in harmonious social, political, and economic relations. Only in such a common universe of cultural participation can there be real or enduring peace. As Wendell Willkie so clearly realized in his *One World,* unless the United Nations dedicate themselves sincerely to the actualization of this wartime ideal, the Second World War, like the First World War, will have been nothing more than a "costly fight for power" ending "with an armistice, not a real peace." The ideal of one world requires that we substitute a strategy of peace for the strategy of war, since peace is not merely the absence of overt strife, but rather a positive social state and common mental attitude which must be deliberately cultivated and promoted.

## 2. THE PROBLEM OF IDEOLOGICAL AND SURVIVAL CRISES

Every genuine cultural crisis marks a transition to some new form of cultural life, but it does not of itself indicate the direction which events will take. Cultural crises may be either constructive or destructive. Insofar as the critical situation is a product of the revolt of human agents against self-destructive cultural inertia and is intended to prepare the way for constructive sociocultural reforms, it may be a decided good. On the other hand, a society may drift into a critical situation, such as an economic depression, without any prior deliberation on the part of those affected. But whatever the origin of the crisis, it may be converted from a potential evil into a potential or actual good. The good envisaged may be the restoration of the *status quo* or some radical reform. The issue between conservatives and radicals is whether the *status quo* is to be maintained until there is absolute proof that change is necessary or whether change is desirable as long as there is no indisputable evidence to the contrary. The phrase "to restore law and order," so often used in times of unrest, is for this reason highly ambiguous, since the real questions are: *What kind of law and order shall we have* and *who is to decide the form it shall take?* Law and order may be "restored" either by reinstituting the old order of social affairs or by removing the sources of discontent.

From the perspective of theory and practice, a cultural crisis may appear in the ideational-affective experience of individuals as a basic conflict, or incoherency, of thought and emotion which occasions a suspension of voluntary and intellectual activity. Thus, one may speak of scientific, moral, or religious crises when he wishes to refer to the fact that commonly accepted theories, ideals, and beliefs have broken down because contradicted by new evidence or found incompatible with new conditions. Similarly, a practical crisis may be demonstrated by the unworkability or incompatibility of prevailing institutions or customs and by the suspension, through active or passive resistance, of normal, or routine, cultural behavior.

Usually there is considerable lag in the conformity of theory and practice, a radical change in theory not being immediately accompanied by corresponding change in practice, while reactionary practice is often misrepresented as in accord with traditional theory. In this manner many Quislings and Lavals have sought to justify their conduct in terms of the professed ideal traditions of their people. In an era of transition each party represents its own position as progressive and that of its opponents as reactionary. Only critical, particularized thinking, an unbiased eye for correlating party labels with pragmatic consequences, and a measure of historical perspective can protect a society from unwitting cultural corruption and eventual self-destruction.

In the long run, theoretical and practical crises are bound to be closely correlated, a crisis in practice leading to dissatisfaction with prevailing theory or ideology, particularly on the part of the articulate intellectuals, or else some radical innovation in theory undermining accepted social institutions. In democratic societies, especially at election time, social radicals, as well as reactionaries and conservatives, have a tendency to develop what appears to be a crisis complex and to envisage the introduction of certain measures or the failure to support certain reforms as potential for a social crisis—an attitude which is expected to arouse public anxiety and to win partisan adherents for a particular platform or candidate. On the other hand, in nondemocratic societies, whether of the right or the left, governments tend to supervise the education of their subjects and to institute various modes of "thought control" to make certain that no subversive ideas penetrate the social mind or affect public opinion. While apparently in general societies are more likely to accept radical changes in times of trouble, the crisis acting as a kind of cultural catalyst, totalitarian societies must depend on such practical emergencies to a much greater extent than democratic societies, since the former make no provision for peaceful change.

One may distinguish two corresponding types of crisis, namely, survival, or existential, crises and axiological, or ideological, crises. Survival crises involve the preservation of the existence of a given society; axiological, or ideological, crises refer to transformations in the form or system of values of a given culture. In a survival crisis the question is, *to be or not to be;* in an ideological crisis the problem is, *how to be and what to be.* Put in Darwinian terms, the issue is the factual survival of the fittest in contrast to the normative determination of the fittest, or most worthy, to survive.

The tragedy of ideological crises is that so many of them need never have occurred, if only the disputants had not regarded polar values, which ought to complement one another, as if they were mutually exclusive. In the political sphere there is always the temptation on the part of those in power to govern in the interests of one class or vested interest, even though the opposition may represent a polar interest essential for the well-being of the state. In a democratic society this admittedly evil practice is mitigated somewhat by the fact that the opposition partly may look forward to governing in turn and thus either undo or offset the measures introduced by their predecessors. In totalitarian governments, however, the myth must be inculcated that the party in power alone represents the true interests of the state as a whole and that any opposition to its rule is treason.

In historical experience, ideological and survival crises are closely bound together, since man is prepared to sacrifice his very life, if need be, for the values and institutions which render his life meaningful. Man, it appears, is not content with mere self-preservation in the biological sense, since the self he is most concerned to preserve is his cultural self, the one expressed in his moral, religious, artistic, and scientific ideals and practices.

### 3. THE STRUGGLE FOR POWER AND THE IDEOLOGY OF POWER

Ideological and survival crises are brought closely together by the struggle for power between nations or classes. The closer the cultural similarity, the more intense has been the rivalry for territorial expansion and dominion—a fact which the history of modern Europe amply illustrates. Karl Marx has made the world conscious of the class struggle within society, and by thus rendering diverse economic groups class conscious has intensified the conflict. Marx has taught the workers and those intellectuals who identify themselves with the working class to distrust the profession of universal social ideals and to detect behind every idealistic principle some concealed economic interest. As a result, there has developed among large segments of contemporary society a perpetual crisis complex, since it is maintained that there is no rational or peaceful way of reconciling opposite social values and that the so-called state of peace between societies and within non-Communistic societies, is but a truce.

Whereas formerly ideological and power crises were kept distinct and the attempt was even made to justify expansionist or imperialistic tendencies by appealing to universal values, now the quest for power has become an end in itself. Ideals have become the tools, or instruments, for rationalizing the irrational will to power of some particular nation or class. The Marxists in particular now seek to "debunk" all idealism in culture history and to reduce all human ideals to symbols of economic power interests. What is new, therefore, in the present world unrest is that henceforth one may not separate ideological conflict from the quest for power, as was formerly done.[5] This is the significance of our new age of *realpolitik* and materialistic cultural "dynamics." The "logic of power" has pre-empted the place of the power of logic and reason. Instead of power in the service of ideals, we now have the

[5] See Carleton, "Ideology or Balance of Power?" *Yale Review*, XXXVI (Summer, 1947), 590–602.

doctrine of ideals in the service of power. Therein lies the ultimate metacultural issue of our times.

### 4. THE METAANTHROPOLOGICAL PROBLEM: IDEOLOGICAL DETERMINISM VERSUS FREEDOM OF THOUGHT

Underlying the new ideology of power there is a basic philosophical or metaanthropological assumption as to the nature of man and of human thought. The basic issue is one of thought determinism versus the inherent freedom and creativity of thought.

If one assumes with Nietzsche and Marx that ideals always serve the special interests or will to power of some group, then it follows that thought is necessarily determined by sociopolitical or economic conditions. On the other hand, if one agrees with Aristotle and Albert Einstein in postulating the fundamental creativity of the human imagination and intellect, then it follows that man is inherently capable of transcending the limitations of his sociocultural environment, notwithstanding the very considerable influence which they exert upon him.

The attraction of the theory of thought determinism for many historians, sociologists, and anthropologists, is owing to the fact that it purports to explain scientifically the natural laws of cultural evolution and to predict the corresponding stages of development in diverse culture systems. On the other hand, those who deny, as does the present writer, such unilinear cultural determinism contend that human affairs are not entirely a matter of science and that ample allowance must be made for the arts and humanities as independent, significant factors in the cultural process. They question, furthermore, the assertion that cultures are logically integrated wholes whose character is determined by the predominance of some one cultural element, such as economic conditions or family relations.[6]

It is significant to note that ideological historical determinists inconsistently assume their own ability to transcend the ideological relativism which they discern in the historical process. In brief, historical relativism, whether it takes the form of historical idealism or of historical materialism, tends to be accepted as a scientific theory of cultural development precisely because its adherents claim a timeless, or absolute, perspective. Hegel's idealization of the Prussian state of his day and Marx's ideal of a classless society are cases in point. In practice, this means that cultural relativists tend to deny the objective validity or ideal univer-

[6] See Reich, *The Mass Psychology of Fascism.*

sality of any system of thought other than their own. Thus, what appears to be a scientific, relativistic doctrine of the stages of mental evolution becomes in practice the justification for rigid intellectual dogmatism and authoritarian intolerance of dissent which precludes any genuine synthesis of or respect for opposing views.[7]

The contrast between the theories of ideological determinism and of intellectual freedom may be illustrated by reference to the diverse conceptions of the methodology of science to which they lead. If, for example, one adheres to Marxist theory, no scientific interpretation is allowed to contradict the absolute formula of dialectical and historical materialism. Science virtually becomes the handmaiden of a given dogmatic philosophy, and in this respect it parallels the medieval doctrine of the subordination of science and philosophy to theology. A case in point is the reception accorded to Einstein's theory of relativity, which varied according to whether it was thought to be essentially idealistic or compatible with dialectical materialism.[8]

Similarly, the arguments used by Lysenko to controvert the scientific genetic theory of the internationally acknowledged expert Vavilov reveal the subservience of Soviet science to Marxist political philosophy.[9] Thus, science tends to be subordinated to "secular myth,"[10] which coerces all thought and permits no adverse criticism.

On the other hand, the theory of the freedom and creativity of thought insists upon the primacy of fact or verified experience over theory. Science is progressive, precisely because its results are regarded as subject to revision and reinterpretation in the light of new discoveries. A scientific hypothesis is, as Einstein has maintained, a free invention of the mind to render intelligible the facts of experience within a limited field of observation and is subject to verification by empirical observation and pragmatic consequences. It is this combination of intellectual creativity and practical respect for the data of experience, this *self-corrective*[11] function of scientific method, which accounts for the advance of scientific achievement.

[7] See Kennan, "The Sources of Soviet Conduct," by X, in *Foreign Affairs*, XXV (July, 1947), 566–82.

[8] See Frank, *Einstein: His Life and Times*.

[9] Sax, "Soviet Science and Political Philosophy," LXV, *Scientific Monthly*, (July, 1947), pp. 43–47.

[10] Bain, "Man, the Myth-Maker," *Scientific Monthly*, LXV (July, 1947), 61–69.

[11] See Conant, *On Understanding Science*.

## 5. THE CONCEPT OF THE STATE AND THE PROBLEM OF WORLD ORDER

One's theory as to the nature of man and the functions of human thought also has a direct bearing upon his theory of the nature of the state and international relations. Insofar as thought is held to be determined by economic or power interests, there is no objective good common to all classes. Hence Marx and Engels [12] were consistent in regarding the state as essentially a power, or instrument, for the protection of the interests of the dominant economic class, while moderating the conflict between classes. It follows that any given state is in a condition of perpetual crisis, since any opposition to its policies may logically be construed as a threat to its dictatorial power. This overt or covert conflict inherent in the very structure of the state may eventually be overcome only when the revolutionary proletariat seizes control of the state apparatus and succeeds in "liquidating" all other classes. Only then, when the "dictatorship of the proletariat" has achieved its goal of a classless society, may one look forward to a "withering away" of the state as an instrument of coercion. According to Lenin's *State and Revolution*,[13] men will gradually "grow accustomed" to brotherly love and to self-regulation in the pursuit of common ideals and interests when there is no further economic incentive to class struggle. The conflict within the Communist party itself and the purges and treason trials of the founders of the Soviet Russian State since the death of Lenin demonstrate the fallacy of his utopian assumption.

If, however, one grants that ideas and ideals do have an objective reality and validity and that men by nature do have common interests, then it is possible to conceive of a universal good in which members of a given society may participate. On this basis it makes sense to conceive of the state as a moral person [14] which represents the true interests of all classes or groups. The state is then, not primarily an instrument of coercion, but an agency for the promotion of the common welfare and the harmonization of opposite interests. As such, its power rests on the continued assent of the governed, not upon enforced submission.

With regard to international affairs, a similar contrast prevails. Insofar as the state is thought to be primarily an instrument of economic

[12] Engels, *The Origin of the Family, Private Property and the State*, p. 155.
[13] See Lenin, *State and Revolution*, pp. 68, 73–75.
[14] See the scholarly paper "The Founding Fathers," by M. F. X. Millar, in *Foundations of Democracy*, ed. by F. E. Johnson.

power, all states must regard one another as rivals who threaten one another's security and sovereignty. The relation between states is, therefore, one of perpetual crisis. If, however, the state is held to be primarily a moral person concerned with the welfare of its members, then states, like individuals, may unite to promote their common interests without loss of their integrity and power of self-determination. A world government based on international consent is a logical consequence. The ideal of perpetual peace between nations becomes a practicable objective.

In view of this analysis, the problem confronting the United Nations becomes intelligible. The conflict between Soviet Russia and her dependencies, on the one hand, and the Anglo-American democracies on the other is owing to failure to agree upon a common theory of the state and of the nature of man. The Marxian Communists think in terms of two extremes, namely, either a dictatorial state governing in the name and interests of some economic class or else an anarchic, stateless, classless society, whose members have so altered their character structure that they have become conditioned to seek one another's welfare without governmental supervision. Since the latter alternative has not been realized and, according to Stalin,[15] is not likely to be realized in the near future, there remains only the former alternative. In the case of Soviet Russia the tension is enhanced by the alleged hostility of the capitalistic democracies to the communistic form of government.

Hence, Soviet Russia is wary of yielding any of her "sovereign rights" or of participating in good faith in any plan for world government. Thus, the "one world" objective which originally inspired the formation of the United Nations may now be seen as involving a confusion between an ideal possibility and the actual cultural reality. The tragedy of the situation is that culturally distrust soon becomes mutual and thereby creates its own justification. There can be no actual one world unless the nations of the world acknowledge its validity as an ideal compatible with diversity of group and national interests. The only alternative is the never-ending struggle for a precarious "balance of power" which has already been the source of two world wars within one generation.

## 6. IDEOLOGICAL THEORY AND POLITICAL PRACTICE

While it appears that there is no immediate prospect of reconciling the conflicting cultural and political views of the communistic states

[15] See Stalin, *Foundations of Leninism*, p. 119.

with those of the democratic capitalistic states, this does not mean that nothing can be done to alleviate present sociocultural tensions. It does mean that we must not delude ourselves into believing that the resolution of this world problem may be readily achieved through mutual good will and especially through a sympathetic "understanding" of the communistic point of view. The trouble with the counsel of "understanding" is that one party is asked to do all the understanding, while the other party apparently may do as it pleases, on the assumption that adverse criticism may be attributed to lack of understanding of its legitimate needs and intentions. This, it may be recalled, was precisely the propaganda tactics pursued by the Fascists and the Nazis preceding and during the Second World War. In view of the abuse of this weasel word, it must be emphasized that mutual understanding is not enough, since a *de facto* understanding of differences does not necessarily breed harmony; it may as well, and often does, breed mutual contempt and hostility.

There is a common tendency on the part of so-called practical men to assume that theoretical issues are not important and that the immediate task is to face practical objectives upon which agreement is possible. This practical approach assumes that reasonable people will readily agree to "self-evident" truths and that differences of opinion regarding means can be easily adjusted.

What the advocates of the practical approach fail to appreciate is that the sphere of the practical is relative to and is delimited by one's theoretical ideals.[16] The determination of the practical objective may involve an entire ideology, or philosophy, of social life which comprehends a special configuration, or hierarchy, of values. Hence, what may be practicable for a member of one society may be highly impracticable for a member of another. What is practicable for a Moslem is not at all so for a Hindu—a condition which has led to the setting up of two distinct dominions in modern India. In brief, an objective is practicable not only because it can be achieved but also because it is considered desirable.

It may be readily granted that self-interest and mutual fear of aggravating tensions may lead to some cooperation on practical issues which are not very vital or do not require any radical reorientation of one's cultural perspective. The willingness of the United States to do

[16] Bidney, "On Theory and Practice," *University of Toronto Quarterly*, VII (1937), 113–25.

business with Japan almost up to the time of Pearl Harbor is a case in point. Both parties to an ideological disagreement may yield a point here and there in the hope of gaining some greater advantage for themselves in the future. But it would be foolhardy to mistake such goodwill tactics for a genuine reconciliation or for unity of purpose. It is significant to note in this connection that Lenin [17] quotes Marx to the effect that "if you must combine, then enter into agreements to satisfy the practical aims of the movement, but do not haggle over principles, do not make concessions in theory."

Thus, while the Marxian Communists subscribe to the inseparability of theory and practice as philosophical doctrines, politically they are prepared to compromise themselves and enter into agreements with opponents in order to maintain their ultimate objective.[18] Marx was the first to proclaim the tactics of the "democratic front," and Lenin [19] later reminded the party members that "the Communists support every revolutionary movement" and that "we are obliged for that reason to emphasize general democratic tasks before the whole people." It is these tactics of combining in a "United Front" with unsuspecting liberals that have often enabled the Communists to gain control of organizations. Politically, therefore, the Communists tend to subscribe to the doctrine that their ends justify any means they consider expedient—a "practical" doctrine which has served to disillusion many a fellow traveler who has been attracted by some elements of their social idealism.

## 7. THE IDEOLOGICAL AND POLITICAL APPROACHES TO THE RESOLUTION OF SOCIOCULTURAL TENSIONS

It is implied in the preceding remarks that the resolution of international tensions may be approached from an ideological, as well as from a political, perspective. The ideological approach seeks to establish a common frame of reference, or system, of cultural values as a prerequisite for any lasting social peace. The political approach makes is appeal to the satisfaction of immediate interests. It is obvious that there is no inherent incompatibility between these two approaches, provided one is not allowed to supersede the other.[20] There is, for ex-

[17] Lenin, *What Is to Be Done?*, pp. 27, 29. See also Wolfe, "Lenin as a Philosopher," *Partisan Review*, XIV (July–August, 1947), 396–413.

[18] See Stalin, *Foundations of Leninism*, ch. vii, "Strategy and Tactics."

[19] Lenin, *What Is to Be Done?*, p. 80. For a revealing study of the application of these tactics on the American scene see *American Communism*, by Oneal and Werner.

[20] See McGill, "Northrop's *Meeting of East and West*," in *Science and Society*, XI (Summer, 1947), 249–59.

ample, need for immediate cooperation in drawing up peace treaties
and for the rehabilitation of Europe. On the other hand, there are, as
has been noted, definite limits to the direct, practical approach, since
ideological considerations soon make themselves felt. The failure of the
Truman-Marshall Plan for the economic rehabilitation of Europe to win
general acceptance is a case in point. Hence, every effort must be made
to promote common ideological objectives.

One source of hope in the contemporary situation lies in the fact that
Soviet Russia and the Western democracies have the same ultimate
ideological objective of ultimate peace and the brotherhood of man.
They differ essentially in their strategy and tactics for the realization
of this common goal. The Communists are committed to a philosophy
of perpetual crises, or "permanent revolution," until their utopian,
anarchistic ideal of social entropy, or absolute equality, is achieved.
The democrats, on the other hand, are committed to a philosophy of
harmony and rational persuasion through majority vote in the resolution of social conflicts.

The tragedy of the situation is that this unceasing ideological conflict is really one of means, not of final values. Insofar as the Communist
is a social idealist, he finds much to agree with in the democratic doctrine of the intrinsic value of the common man and the humanistic role
of scientific effort in raising the common standard of living. Politically,
the Communist stresses the fact of social responsibility, while the
individualistic democrat stresses the role of individual initiative. These
are polar interests which modern democracies recognize as mutually
complementary ideals and functions.

Hitherto both Communists and democrats have acted, consciously
or unconsciously, on the assumption of social Darwinism by supposing
that the struggle for existence within society is the condition for cultural
evolution. They differed primarily as regards the *locus* and objectives
of the social struggle. The popular spokesmen for the capitalistic democracies of the late nineteenth century and early twentieth century,
men such as the sociologists Herbert Spencer and William Graham
Sumner,[21] viewed the struggle in individualistic terms within the framework of a laissez faire economy of individual competition and opposed
major social reforms as interference with the laws of nature. The
Marxian Communists, on the other hand, have maintained that the
historical struggle is one between conflicting economic classes. To this
social Darwinism the Marxists added the Hegelian postulate of the

[21] See Hofstadter, *Social Darwinism in American Thought, 1860–1915.*

dialectic of history, thus interpreting the social struggle as a necessary, logical development. As Veblen has remarked, "even Engels, in his latter-day formulation of Marxism, is strongly affected with the notions of post-Darwinian science, and reads Darwinism into Hegel and Marx with a good deal of naïveté." [22] The Marxian philosophy of culture history, because of its Hegelian element, provided an ideal goal and a militant faith in the inevitability of final victory for the proletariat, whereas the Anglo-American Darwinian theory envisaged no final consummation and was utilized by its adherents as a justification for the *status quo* of economic practice.

Modern democracies have gone a long way since the time of Spencer and Sumner and are now prepared to recognize the responsibility of the political state for the social welfare of all its citizens. If the Communists were also prepared to discard their mythological form of social Darwinism and to replace the doctrine of the class struggle by the democratic doctrine of common interests, the way would be prepared for mutual cooperation. The present growing tension is the product of mutual fear and distrust, which, in turn, is the outgrowth of an outmoded nineteenth-century ideology. The conflict is irrational precisely because it is based, not on incompatible ideals but on outmoded philosophical theories. It is especially tragic that at the very moment when the democracies of the world are approaching most closely to the social idealism of the Communists, the political conflict between them is at its height.

The practical import of the above analysis is that every effort must be made to alleviate international tensions by stressing our common objectives. It is up to social scientists and social philosophers to clarify the cultural presuppositions of the conflicting social systems. What is needed, especially, is a synthesis of philosophical analysis with the historical perspectives and empirical methods of the social sciences.[23] This task will not be easy, inasmuch as many sociologists and anthropologists have adopted the relativistic perspective of the Marxists, while professing opposition to its economic interpretation of culture history. There is urgent need, therefore, for a complete reorientation of contemporary social theory toward the systematic universalism demanded by the ideal of a "science of man" or a "science of social relations."

In the second place, so far as our own society is concerned, we must

---

[22] Veblen, "The Socialist Economics of Karl Marx and His Followers," republished in *The Place of Science in Modern Civilization and Other Essays,* pp. 431–56.

[23] Cohen, "The Role of Science in Government," *Scientific Monthly,* LXV (1947), 155–64.

make every effort to satisfy the legitimate demands of labor for a higher standard of living and a voice in the regulation of industrial affairs. This puts the responsibility on both labor and management to recognize their common interests and complementary functions in the social order. We must demonstrate to the world, even more clearly than in the past, that class struggle is not inevitable and that class conflict need not lead to the triumph of one or the liquidation of the other.

There is grave danger at present that in our efforts to curb communism we may be led to condone fascistic tendencies. A genuinely democratic government which recognizes its social responsibilities and humanitarian industrialists who regard labor as a partner in their enterprises have nothing to fear from totalitarianism, either of the left or of the right.

In the meantime, political realism requires that we neither confuse ideals with social facts nor cease to proclaim our faith in the democratic ideal and our criticism of those who would prevent its realization. This means that we reject the *ad hominem* argument as to the obvious imperfections of our own democratic society as an excuse for the dictatorial policies of the Communists in setting up puppet governments in the countries they have occupied. "Understanding," as practiced by some of our so-called liberals, consists in adopting the party propaganda line of the critics of democracy and in attributing to their own governments motives which are alien to its ideals and policies.

A sane and realistic appraisal of factual, cultural trends is quite compatible with a rational appreciation of democratic ideals. There will always be some disparity between cultural facts and ideals. The real dangers to progress are refusing to reckon with the social realities and failure to distinguish clearly between the democratic ideal and the extremes of the right and the left which seek to march under its banner.

### 8. THE SOCIAL RESPONSIBILITY OF THE SCIENTIST

Upon the anthropological, or social, scientists in particular falls the task of providing a common ideological frame of reference for the relative perspectives of the diverse, sociocultural configurations. What is needed above all is a theory of sociocultural integration which will provide a rational, as well as empirical, foundation for the ideal of a common humanity.

The appeal for world unity must be directed primarily to the scientists of the world as the group most potentially qualified for realizing this objective. Instead of the slogan "Workers of the World unite," or the implied, but not articulated, "Politicians of the World unite," we might substitute the call "Scientists of the World unite."

The appeal to economic, class interests as a basis for world unity has failed. The assumption of Marx and Engels that the proletarian class will somehow transcend the limitations of their historical folkways and loyalties and combine to crush their capitalistic oppressors has been demonstrated as contrary to the facts of culture history. It is precisely the sort of ideal which may appeal to rationalistic political exiles, to desperate, rootless men who cannot conceive the strong cultural and emotional bonds which unite a people reared in a common tradition. The Communist leaders, furthermore, failed to reckon that class or social differences are no bar to participation in a common cultural perspective as long as all classes accept the given system of social values and their places in the social hierarchy. The peasant, for example, will not resent his feudal landlord and may even fight to protect him in order to preserve the traditional social hierarchy—a fact which was demonstrated in Hungary after the First World War, when the Hungarian peasants broke the back of the Communist revolution.[24] Cultural anthropology provides many examples of societies, such as the Australian aborigines, who tolerate gross inequalities because they accept the arrangements of their cultural folkways. It takes a complete and radical social and cultural revolution for a given class to demand the abolition of all classes but itself.

The class of scientists, on the other hand, is by its very nature the one group in modern society which is, and ought to be, dedicated to the principle of objective universal truths. I do not mean that all scientists are free of prejudice or of the limitations of their cultural environment; all I do wish to assert is that the scientist, as scientist, pursues the one method capable of achieving universal, verifiable results and thereby also a common universe of discourse and action. Science is the one cultural process which is self-corrective and progressive, precisely because it is both free and self-disciplined, free in its universal postulations and disciplined in reckoning with the data and consequences of experience.

From a social point of view, therefore, the scientist requires a democratic cultural environment which will guarantee him complete freedom of scientific thought and research. The freedom of science and political freedom are thus closely bound together. The scientist is

[24] I am indebted to Paul Fejos for this example.

logically and morally bound to resist the corruption of science which results from the practical application of the theory of the sociological determinism of thought. Such an "integration" of science and society reduces science to myth or political propaganda and renders the scientist incapable of communicating intelligibly with other scientists of different cultural backgrounds.

The scientist, especially the anthropological, or social scientist, cannot and ought not to be indifferent to the sociopolitical situation insofar as it affects his very existence as a scientist. Scientific objectivity does not imply sociocultural indifference; the Olympian attitude so often assumed by scientists is hardly appropriate to the socially conditioned animal which is man. Hence, the scientist who is aware of the humanistic implications of this vocation must be on guard against the twin extremes of ideological regimentation and social irresponsibility. Scientific idealism, like philosophical idealism in general, tends to neglect the social and material conditions of genuine scientific enterprise, and thus it helps prepare the way for the cultural irrationalism and mythological fanaticism to which it is opposed in principle.

## 9. CONCLUSION

The human world is one in fact, inasmuch as the cultural phenomena of any society and ultimately of world society are functionally interdependent. But the character, or quality, of that unity, whether it is to be a world of common humane values fit for civilized man to live in, or whether it is to be a world of social entropy, shaken by perpetual crises, is a question of value which we of this generation are required to answer. The general direction in which a resolution of the social and cultural tensions of our times is to be sought is in the main clear. What is needed above all is the active faith and the united resolution to make the ideal of a common cultural world for mankind one that will work both at home and abroad. For unless we are sincere in our conviction that the ideal of a common humanity is a practicable ideal and are prepared to make the effort to provide adequate material, social, and educational conditions for its realization, then most assuredly it will not work.

In the last analysis, the final test of sincerity is the effort one makes practically to achieve the realization of his ideals. This is the perennial challenge of human ideals to human intelligence and effort.

# 16

# The Problem of Freedom and Authority in Cultural Perspective [1]

THE PROBLEM of freedom and authority is the common concern of all men. It is an ancient philosophical problem which has received the careful attention of eminent social philosophers and philosophical anthropologists of all historical cultures. Only recently, however, have anthropologists, such as Boas and Malinowski, examined this problem from a cultural and ethnological perspective.

## 1. THE RELATIVITY OF CULTURAL FREEDOM

According to Franz Boas: "Freedom is a concept that has meaning only in a subjective sense. A person who is in complete harmony with his culture is free. For this reason, the concept of freedom can develop only in those cases where there are conflicts between the individual and the culture in which he lives." [2] Boas maintains that the concept of freedom is entirely subjective and relative to a person's conformity or lack of conformity to a given culture. A person feels free insofar as he finds himself in complete harmony with his culture; he feels "unfree" when he becomes conscious of the limitations of his culture and is no longer willing to submit to them. No person is absolutely free, because every culture imposes certain limitations upon one's conduct.

Boas unnecessarily complicated his thesis by stating that "the concept of freedom is not found in primitive society," owing to "the lack of knowledge of diverse forms of thought and action." The fact that natives may not have terms for the abstract concept of freedom does not imply their inability to conceive and understand the concept even within the limitations of their cultural experience. As Lowie has indicated, native tribes with opportunities for cultural contacts, still ad-

---

[1] Originally prepared as paper for the Twelfth Conference on Science, Philosophy and Religion, held in New York City, September, 1951.

[2] Boas, "Liberty among Primitive People," in *Freedom; Its Meaning*, ed. by R. N. Anshen, p. 51.

here to their own ethos. One may not, therefore, argue from a linguistic deficiency to a psychological and cultural deficiency. Whether or not natives have the concept of freedom would not affect Boas's main thesis that the individual in harmony with his culture feels free. The feeling of cultural freedom does depend, not upon the individual's total or comparative ignorance of other cultural alternatives, but upon his acceptance of the ethos of his culture in preference to that of other cultures. Even in primitive society the individual has occasion to experience the restraints of his culture when some of his desires are thwarted, for example, in the choice of a wife or a husband, regardless of his comparative knowledge of other cultures. The subjective feeling of freedom does not, therefore, depend entirely upon comparative ignorance of other cultural alternatives, but also upon the satisfaction which the person derives from conforming to his cultural institutions. This sound psychocultural principle apparently underlies all recent and contemporary attempts at thought control initiated by totalitarian governments. To limit a subject's knowledge of other cultural alternatives, deliberately to distort the truth concerning other peoples and to depict one's own cultural institutions as the only satisfactory and "free" institutions, is to preclude the possibility of alternative choices and to preserve the feeling of freedom in conforming to the dictates of the state.

On this basis, if the concept of freedom is entirely subjective and relative, then all peoples may be said to be free, provided they feel free, no matter what the conditions under which they live. A slave who accepts his lot without complaint is as free as his master—or freer, if the latter feels the limitations of his own position. Yet this view appears to run counter to common sense and common experience. We do seem to feel that there is also some objective basis for evaluating freedom, in addition to the purely subjective feeling resulting from conformity to a given culture. A slave is not free, even though he accepts his lot cheerfully. And the fact that a given society conforms to its culture need not prevent a student of culture from comparing the limitations of that culture in relation to others and evaluating the degrees of cultural freedom to be found in them. As Boas himself suggests, or implies, the consciousness of the concept of freedom involves a comparative knowledge of other cultural alternatives. To the extent, therefore, that one is conscious of the ideal of freedom, one may envisage cultural alternatives which enlarge the scope of freedom. The feeling of restraint under a given culture need not be conceived merely as a subjective reaction of discontent, for it may be derived from a knowledge of cultural possibilities which give fuller expression to the individual's desire for freedom. Does it not make sense to speak of the development of human freedom? And if it does, we must assume that there is some objective, rational standard for evaluating degrees of human freedom and man's progress in the quest for freedom.

## 2. TYPES OF FREEDOM

Obviously the concept of freedom is complex, rather than simple. I propose to distinguish three basic types of freedom, namely, psychobiological, cultural, and moral freedom.

Psychobiological freedom is action in accordance with one's innate abilities, powers, and inclinations. One feels free insofar as there is no external restraint or compulsion which hinders him from doing whatever he has an inclination to do. Genetically, psychobiological power is subject to development in time. The infant is not free to walk and talk at birth; only with the maturation following upon growth does he acquire the abilities and powers which he then feels free to exercise. The human organism has different freedoms relative to the ages of life and to the powers and inclinations associated with each age. This is the "natural liberty" of which the seventeenth- and eighteenth-century philosophers spoke and which they attributed to man's living in the "state of nature."

Secondly, cultural freedom comprises all those liberties of action which are permitted to man living under a given system of culture. Cultural freedom presupposes psychobiological freedom or power, but involves, in addition, the patterning of human conduct in socially recognized ways. Every culture, as anthropologists have noted, is a system of freedoms and restraints, prescribing patterns of freedom and proscribing actions which are thought to be socially harmful. Universally, theft, murder, and incest are forbidden, with reference to members of the in-group or one's own society. The kinds of cultural freedom which are permitted vary, of course, from culture to culture. The members of a given culture are usually conditioned to accept the limitations of their culture, and hence feel little or no restraint or compulsion in conforming to its imperatives. It is only the exceptional individual who is prepared to fight against the folkways and mores of his society; for the majority freedom lies in obedience to custom and cultural folkways. In all cultures there is some tension between the desires and inclinations of the individual and the respectable, socially approved norms of conduct. Where this tension is not restrained and suppressed, it gives rise to crime—to action which violates socially approved norms. Crime thus involves a conflict between the demands of psychological liberty and cultural freedom.

Thirdly, there is moral freedom which may be defined as action in accord with the rational good of the individual or his society. An individual is said to be morally free, insofar as he acts in conformity with the requirements of his "true good" and his "true self." Thus, moralists have pointed out that a man who does not curb his passions is a "slave" to them, because such a person may see the better and follow the worse. The life of the passions, as Spinoza has demonstrated, is but human bondage. From a social and political point of view, man in society is free insofar as he acts with reference to the good of his fellow citizens. The free man, as Kant has insisted, acts out of respect for the moral law and the Categorical Imperative, which enjoins him always to treat other human beings as ends and to respect their human rights. This moral law, philosophers from the time of Plato and Aristotle have regarded as the "law of nature" or the law of reason to which man is subject regardless of the civic or cultural laws of the political state. Moral freedom, both theologians and moral philosophers agree, involves a knowledge of the truth concerning the nature of man and the proper virtues of man, and action in accordance with these rational ideals. Moral freedom and rational enlightenment are thus closely bound together.

Moral freedom and cultural freedom do not coincide. Moral freedom is based upon the presupposition of a rational norm, or ideal, which may be approximated, but is never completely realized. Cultural freedom, on the other hand, is something which varies historically with different cultures and is subject to reform in accordance with changing ideologies and social circumstances. A person may feel culturally free and yet be considered as morally nonfree with reference to the kind of life he leads. What may be culturally permissible, for example, sexual fertility rites, may be morally reprehensible and intolerable.

The distinction here drawn between psychobiological, cultural, and moral freedom corresponds to the distinction drawn by Rousseau in his *Social Contract* between natural liberty, civil liberty, and moral freedom.[3] In his *Discourse on the Origin of Inequality*,[4] Rousseau

---

[3] Rousseau, *The Social Contract*, bk. 1, ch. viii.　　　　[4] *Ibid.*, p. 184.

clearly made the point which exercised such great influence upon Kant, namely, that

it is not so much the understanding that constitutes the specific difference between man and the brute, as the human quality of free-agency. Nature lays her commands on every animal, and the brute obeys her voice. Man receives the same impulsion, but at the same time knows himself at liberty to acquiesce or resist: and it is particularly in his consciousness of this liberty that the spirituality of his soul is displayed.

Man's moral freedom, he points out in his *Discourse on Political Economy*,[5] is based upon man's rational ability to formulate laws in the interests of the public good. By subjecting himself to the requirements of moral law, which he himself has instituted, man is able to enjoy a maximum of freedom in social harmony with other members of society. Rousseau, however, tends to identify moral and civil or political freedom. The general will is the expression of public reason in public law. Hence, every citizen is said to be morally, as well as politically, free insofar as he obeys the general will as expressed in civic law. From this assumption it is an easy, but inevitable, step to the conclusion that "whoever refuses to obey the general will shall be compelled to do so by the whole body. This means nothing less than that he will be forced to be free." By identifying moral and political freedom by means of the concept of the general will as embodied in the state, Rousseau tended to confuse the ideal Platonic norm of the good and the actual decrees of the state, thereby justifying political compulsion of the individual in the interests of the higher morality and freedom of the state.

It is this confusion of the metacultural ideal with positive, cultural law which has since, through the influence of Hegel and Marx, also served as a justification, or validation, of the iron discipline and intolerance of the totalitarian state, in which virtue is identified with conformity to the general will of the state.[6] Rousseau himself recognized the difficulty of determining just what the general will represents under particular circumstances. All we do know is that for him the general will is a kind of Platonic ideal; "the general will is always right and always tends to the public advantage; but it does not follow that the resolutions of the people have always the same rectitude."[7] He points out that "there is often a great deal of difference between the will of all and the general will; the latter regards only the common interest,

[5] *Ibid.*, p. 256.
[6] *Discourse on Political Economy*, p. 260.
[7] *The Social Contract*, bk. 2, ch. iii.

while the former has regard to private interests, and is merely a sum of particular wills." [8] In explaining how the general will may be known in cases in which it has not expressed itself, Rousseau writes: "for the rulers well know that the general will is always on the side which is most favorable to the public interest, that is to say, most equitable; so that it is needful only to act justly, to be certain of following the general will." [9] In practice, therefore, he leaves it to the ruler rather than to the people to decide what is the general will and the general interest. Had Rousseau recognized the disparity between the moral ideal and the cultural facts, he would not have regarded the state as a moral person actually embodying the general will and would have separated the demands of moral freedom from *de facto* cultural freedom permitted by the state. As it is, he granted the state or the sovereign power "an absolute power over all its members." [10] This doctrine, as has been noted, logically prepares the way for the modern doctrine of totalitarian state power in the name of moral freedom.

### 3. THE CONCEPT OF AUTHORITY

Closely allied to the concepts of cultural and moral freedom is the concept of authority. Cultural freedom is prescribed by a given system of culture. This means, in practice, that a given society collectively or through its leaders permits certain forms of activity and prohibits others. Similarly, as regards moral freedom there is a principle of limitation involved, but in this case the individual himself, by means of his conscience or the general consensus of public opinion, prescribes the norm of conduct. In both instances there is a principle of limitation at work which defines the sphere of individual and social freedom. This principle which regulates the freedom of the individual or of members of a given society, may be designated as the factor of authority. Authority may thus be defined as a quality which the mind attributes to a person (or principle) who is recognized as qualified to exercise a regulative, or directive, power over the behavior of others. It should be noted that the concept of authority involves two distinct ideas, namely, that of competence and that of directive power. An authority is one whom an individual or a society regards as competent, or qualified, to regulate conduct and issue directives. A principle, whether it be a law, a custom, or an ideal, is said to be endowed with

---

[8] *Ibid.*  [9] *A Discourse on Political Economy*, p. 259.
[10] *The Social Contract*, bk. 2, ch. iv.

authority insofar as its validity is recognized and it serves as a means of regulating human conduct. The measure of competence or qualification is partly relative to cultural conditioning, so that the objects of authority will vary with diverse cultures. The shaman exercises authority in primitive cultures, but would not be recognized in our culture, where the scientist enjoys high prestige. Thus, cultural authority is an attribute which may vary with cultural perspectives and social beliefs. It is only insofar as some absolute norm of value is postulated, as in normative science, ethics, and religion, that the principle of absolute, transcultural authority is also postulated.

It follows that there may be as many kinds of authority as there are spheres of competence which are socially recognized. A political authority is one who is recognized as qualified to rule over, or govern, a given state. A religious authority is one whose jurisdiction is accepted in religious matters. Some authorities are ranked higher than others, and the hierarchical order will vary with different cultural systems. Historically, it has been demonstrated that no nation or state can endure without recognizing some ultimate authority, but there is no agreement ethnologically as to the locus of that authority.

So far as Western culture is concerned, two basic trends may be observed. Owing to the influence of the Hebrew-Christian tradition and the acceptance of the Old and the New Testaments as books of divine revelation, there developed a tendency toward a theocentric culture, according to which all authority was conceived as derived from God, the author and originator of man and nature. The Bible, as the revealed will of God, was to serve as the authoritative source for the regulation of human affairs. In Christian societies, the church was the interpreter of divine revelation, and its authority was therefore recognized as supreme. The doctrine of the divine right of kings was a product of this mode of theological thought and was based upon the assumption that the authority of the king was derived from the authority of God, the author of all things.

In opposition to the doctrine which made God and divine revelation the measure of and the source of authority over all things, we have the humanistic tradition which originated among the Sophists of ancient Greece, according to which man is the measure of all things and all authority in human affairs is derived from man himself. In the sphere of political theory this humanistic thesis received its classic expression in the period following the European Renaissance during the seventeenth and eighteenth centuries. In the philosophies of Hobbes, Spinoza, Locke, Rousseau, Hume, and Kant the democratic, humanistic principle was put forward that political authority is derived from the consent of the governed and is justified by its utility in promoting the interests of society. The concept of "the state of nature," whether it was taken as referring to a supposed historical state based on contemporary ethnographical evidence or was merely a fictive, logical postulate, served to draw attention dramatically to the problem of the origin of political and cultural authority and was employed to demonstrate the purely human, historical origin of political authority and its function in the service of society. This doctrine was to have revolutionary import in Western culture and led to the development of modern democratic states, in which political authority is ultimately derived from the consent of the people and is justified by its utility in promoting the welfare of their citizens. One of the characteristics of the modern age is the general tendency to justify, or validate, political authority, whether it be democratic or autocratic and dictatorial, by appeal to the consent of the governed.

From the above analysis it appears that authority, by its very nature, requires justification, or validation, because, as said above, authority depends on recognition of competence, or qualification. With reference to primitive cultures, as Malinowski has pointed out, myths serve to provide the necessary validation for the authority of tribal rulers and the sanctity of custom, by referring the origin of cultural institutions and traditions to some remote, prehistoric past and preternatural events. Authority in civilized societies or among literate peoples is justified either by religious belief, scientific knowledge, or by some rationalistic philosophy which is just as "mythological" to those who do not accept the validity of these beliefs or rationalizations. Those who do not accept the authority of a given state are inclined to contrast "authority" and "freedom," as if they involved two opposing principles; on the other hand, those who do accept the authority of a given state or culture see no such conflict and find their freedom in conforming to the established authority. Accordingly, those who tend to oppose authority to freedom set up a false antithesis, since authority depends for its function upon the free recognition of its competence on the part of those who submit to its direction. There may be a conflict between some forms of authority and the demands of moral freedom, but such conflict is brought about because the individuals concerned recognize some different trans-cultural principle of authority.

Furthermore, authority involves not only competence but also power to regulate, or direct. Authority without regulative power is a contradiction in terms. This power may, however, be either intrinsic or extrinsic. Power is said to be intrinsic insofar as the object of authority exercises such power directly and by its very nature; for example, the authority of a doctor depends upon his actual ability to heal and cure the sick and on his actual possession of a knowledge which is valued by his community. Power is said to be extrinsic if it be adventitious or superadded to some person who of himself alone does not possess it; for example, he who commands an army has extrinsic power which he may utilize in promoting his authority. Such extrinsic power is a means to an end, in the sense that it enforces personal authority and executes its will. Political authority is complex in that it combines intrinsic and extrinsic power; the ruler must be qualified to rule and have intrinsic power in this sense, and his authority is upheld and supplemented by extrinsic power of police and soldiers. The intrinsic power of a principle or ideal is that of a final cause, or unmoved mover—its power is that of affecting some intelligence which acknowledges its authority. Ultimately, political authority is a species of moral authority designed and recognized to promote the social good, and its authority depends on its moral function rather than upon the physical force by which it may be supplemented to enforce obedience. Political authority, as Rousseau and Kant maintained, depends on respect for or recognition of the law and the general interest on which it should be based (but, contrary to Rousseau, is not necessarily based); it does not depend primarily on the physical force which may be utilized to enforce it. Extrinsic power neither confers authority nor serves to validate it. As frequently stated, might is not right. Authority is a right of governing in virtue of certain qualifications; the mere fact of exercising the extrinsic powers of government does not automatically confer the right to do so. Power without authority is tyranny.

## 4. TOTALITARIAN CULTURE AND THE CONCEPT OF THE TOTALITARIAN STATE

In the foregoing analysis the point was made that there may be as many kinds of authority as there are spheres of competence which may be socially recognized. On this assumption, political authority is but one kind of authority. Just what the scope of political authority is and what are its limits are debatable questions. According to the democratic philosophy of the eighteenth and nineteenth centuries, the function and authority of government extended only to the protection of individual rights; the function of government was to protect life, liberty, and property, and all those various cultural activities of the individual which may be comprised under "the pursuit of happiness." Government was to provide the necessary conditions of security for the exercise of individual freedom, and hence that government was best which governed least and exercised a minimum of control over the life and thought of its citizens. This meant, in practice, that the authority of the government was strictly limited, so far as the cultural life of a nation was concerned. In particular, government had no authority, or jurisdiction, over religious matters, and church and state were sharply separated. Similarly, education was not in the province of government, and educators could feel free to teach, subject only to the self-discipline of their own organizations, which set the necessary standards and qualifications. On this basis, it may be said, there was a plurality of authorities, each claiming a measure of autonomy, or freedom, in the pursuit of their own interests. This is still the creed and practice of democratic states, even though modern democracy now recognizes the obligation of government to take a more active part in promoting social justice and the economic welfare of its citizens.

As shown previously,[11] what is new in modern political theory and practice is the emergence of an ideology of power. Instead of power in the service of ideals, we now have the doctrine of ideals in the service of power. Underlying the new ideology of power is the metaanthropological assumption developed by Friedrich Nietzsche and Karl Marx that moral values always serve the special interests or will to power of some dominant group or of some subservient group in quest of power. The concept of a common good in which all members of a given state may participate is dismissed as a delusion of metaphysical idealists. The state is thought to be essentially an instrument for the protection of the interests of the dominant economic class and is a product of society at a particular stage of development.[12] Only when the "dictatorship of the proletariat" has achieved its goal of a classless society

[11] See Chapter 15.
[12] Engels, *The Origin of the Family, Private Property and the State*, p. 155.

through the liquidation, or elimination, of all opposition may one look forward to a "withering away" of the state as an instrument of coercion.[13] The modern, materialistic ideology of power is based upon the premise that cultural ideals are rationalizations of the political will to power. Hence ideological conflict is an inherent part of the struggle for power in international affairs. According to the Marxists all ideology is a function of economic conditions and every culture system is integrated about given historically determined economic institutions. Thus, contrary to the "delusion" of the liberals and the democrats that a given culture system may comprise a plurality of partially autonomous cultural interests, the Marxist sociologists maintain that every culture system constitutes an integrated cultural whole dominated by economic institutions. Every ideology is but a reflection and rationalization of the dominant economic institutions prevalent at the time and of the class whose interest they promote.

This belief in complete cultural integration and in cultural determinism tends to bring about its own verification. The belief of contemporary Communists, following in the general tradition of Marx and Engels (though Marx himself was never quite an orthodox Marxist) that every culture is an integrated whole and that its ideology is a function of its economic institutions, has led in practice to systematic efforts to make their culture conform to their theory of economic determinism. In other words, the theoretical belief in total cultural integration as a historical, cultural fact had led in practice to the elimination of individual, cultural deviation, and the effective prevention of the expression of heterodox views. Thus, the modern Communist states have embarked upon a program of cultural "integration" which embraces every aspect of the life of the individual. The modern totalitarian state is but a logical expression in practice of the theory of the total integration of culture. In conformity with their theory of the state as an instrument of coercion, they utilize all the powers of the state to bring about complete cultural uniformity and compliance. As cultural ideology is conceived as an instrument of political power, it becomes the function of the state to exercise complete, or total, political control over all aspects of cultural life, with a view to making it theoretically consistent and an instrument in the conflict of ideologies. Thus is set up a vicious cyclical process in which a totalitarian theory of culture

[13] Lenin, *State and Revolution.*

leads to totalitarian governments, and totalitarian government, in turn, leads to rigid cultural dictatorship. Underlying the whole process is the assumption of a monistic concept of authority based upon economic power. It is rather ironical to reflect that Plato, in his *Republic*, looked forward to the day when philosophers would be kings, in order that political power might be united with wisdom. In modern times, philosophers have become kings and have set themselves up as authorities over the total cultural life of their states. Obviously, it makes a great deal of difference which kind of philosophy prevails and who the philosophers in power happen to be.

It is of interest to note in this connection that the concepts of totalitarian culture and totalitarian government may be arrived at either from a materialistic or an idealistic position. We have seen that Rousseau, by conceiving the state as a moral person embodying the general will, arrived at the conclusion that the state has absolute authority over its members and may coerce them in the name of moral freedom. Thus, insofar as the state is conceived to embody the moral ideal of society, one is led to justify a political dictatorship of culture in the name of some idea of the good. Similarly, in the *Republic* Plato took it upon himself to exile the poets and the artists from his state, because they tended to deal with myths rather than with philosophical and scientific truths. As a philosopher-king, Plato thus set up a kind of intellectual dictatorship in the interests of justice and the idea of the good. Rousseau, who was much influenced by Plato, conceived of the general will as comparable to the Platonic idea of justice and the ideal social good, but without the specific content of the latter. Instead of universal ideas which have to be discovered and intellectually intuited, Rousseau posited an abstract general will which has to be willed into existence by the state. But Rousseau's general will and Plato's ideal of justice are equally absolute, infallible ideals which determine the goals of moral freedom and justify the total cultural dictatorship of the state and its absolute authority over the life of its members. In the historical materialism of Marx, on the other hand, the state is conceived as amoral, as an instrument of power in the hands of the governing class. Nevertheless, as the ultimate goal is a moral, classless society, the dictatorship of the proletariat is also justified in the interests of this moral ideal. Once more we have a philosophical-political dictatorship, only this time we have a different élite class, the proletariat, which constitutes the membership of the Communist party. Thus, we have a meeting of extremes, for both absolute idealism and absolute materialism justify totalitarian culture and totalitarian government.

## 5. ABSOLUTE FREEDOM VERSUS ABSOLUTE AUTHORITY

Historically, the modern world has been confronted by two extreme doctrines concerning the nature of man and the relation of freedom to authority. On the one hand, liberal, democratic philosophers, in their reaction against political tyranny and religious intolerance, sought to establish the inalienable rights of the individual in contrast to historically instituted political authority. The common note of their philosophical anthropology was the doctrine of the natural equality of man in opposition to the Aristotelian theory of natural inequality. The individual was said to be endowed with certain inalienable rights which it was the function of the state to protect. These natural rights were attributed to man by reference to the laws of nature, or reason, and hence did not originate with the state. Among these natural rights, according to John Locke and the Founding Fathers of the American Constitution, were life, liberty, and the protection of property. In the nineteenth century, under the influence of the theory of evolution and the emergence of a science of evolutionary sociology, the doctrine of absolute individualism was supported by appeal to the laws of cultural evolution. Thus, Herbert Spencer and William Graham Sumner found themselves in accord with Adam Smith for entirely different reasons, in insisting upon the doctrine of laissez faire and noninterference with economic enterprise, as contrary to the laws of nature and natural laws of cultural development. The basic pattern of the thought of the so-called liberal, democratic philosophers was their inclination to maintain the doctrine of the absolute rights of the individual in his economic and other cultural pursuits, as against the authority of the state.

For the great majority of the people this doctrine of absolute rights to freedom introduced a form of economic tyranny in place of the former political tyranny. With the development of the industrial revolution in the eighteenth and nineteenth centuries and the increase of population, the irresponsible freedom of the individual proved to be the right of the exploitation of the many by the few, because freedom of enterprise depended on control of economic resources. In the sphere of economics, as contrasted with the purely intellectual pursuits, the freedom of the individual in democratic society proved to be a delusion, so far as the great majority were concerned, as the right to freedom of enterprise was not joined to any effective power to implement it. Individual freedom no longer seemed to be in harmony with the general interests of society as a whole, although the liberal sociologists prophesied that in the long run it would prove to be advantageous to the progress of society.

The appeal of the Marxist doctrine of historical materialism results from the fact that it emphasized social responsibility and justice rather than the rugged individualism of the democrats. In opposition to the doctrine of the absolute rights of the individual and the fixity of human nature, Marx and Engels put forth the theory of historical materialism, according to which there is no fixed human nature or essence, because the nature of man is said to be conditioned by social and economic institutions. Hence, there can be no inalienable human rights with which so-called "human nature" may be endowed. Human nature was essentially a social product historically conditioned and molded by society, and all the so-called "rights" of man were therefore derived from the state. Because capital was the root of all evil, state ownership of economic resources was the panacea which would transform competitive, selfish man into altruistic, social man. The spurious freedom of democratic society would be replaced by the real, or effective, freedom of Communist society, for the state would provide economic security and freedom from exploitation.

During the first half of the twentieth century the socialistic doctrines of man and society, especially those of the Marxists, have exercised great influence upon the democratic societies of Europe and the Americas. Most democratic societies have now come to realize that the doctrine of the absolute rights of the individual, particularly in the economic sphere, is not compatible with the best interests of society as a whole. There has been a growing awareness that individual liberty carries with it social responsibility and that the interests of society take precedence over those of the individual. Similarly, there has been a decided change in the theory of the functions of the state toward the recognition of the responsibility of the state to promote the welfare of its citizens, not merely by providing a minimum of security for individual enterprise but also by positive leadership in ameliorating social conditions and in correcting social abuses. The democratic state is becoming increasingly a moral person concerned with the actual welfare of all classes of citizens rather than with the special interests of one class. In this way the democratic states continue to seek reform by adopting some of the economic principles of socialistic theory, while avoiding the excesses of totalitarian political and cultural dictatorship. The Communist states, on the other hand, have so far shown no similar spirit of compromise, but have, on the contrary, continued to exaggerate their ethnocentric differences, the nearer the democratic states approach some form of economic socialism. The totalitarian ideology of power and the doctrine of an "ethics of violence" and permanent revolution prevent any long-term peaceful solution, notwithstanding the repeated assertions of their proponents that they seek nothing but peace.

### 6. CONCLUSION AND SUMMARY

The basic thesis of this chapter is that freedom and authority are complementary, polaristic requirements essential for the proper functioning of any sociocultural system. Within the context of any culture, freedom and authority are complementary principles which mutually limit one another. Generally and positively, at its lowest common denominator the concept of freedom refers to the exercise of power; negatively, freedom refers to any unrestrained or unimpeded activity. One may, however, distinguish three levels, or modes, of freedom, namely, psychological, cultural, and moral freedom. Similarly, the concept of authority involves two essential elements: first, sociocultural recognition of competence, or qualification, to govern and regulate conduct; secondly, effective power to regulate this conduct.

Authority may, however, be conceived in monistic or pluralistic terms. According to the pluralistic theory, there are as many kinds of authority as there are spheres of socially recognized competence. This thesis implies the relative autonomy of spheres of authority. Historically, the Western democracies have separated the expression of political from religious and educational authority. According to the monistic theory, on the other hand, the state is the final authority in all spheres of cultural life. This presupposes the assumption that the state is the embodiment of absolute truth. What is new in modern totalitarian culture is the fact that we have here a secular absolutism and ideological intolerance instead of the religious intolerance and absolutism of an earlier age. "Philosopher-kings" have replaced the theologian-kings of the past. We now have ideological dictatorship in the interest of political dictatorship. By contrast, the basic presuppositions of modern democratic cultures, with reference to the problem of freedom and authority, are first that political authority is derived from the consent of the governed and secondly that political authority is independent of other aspects of cultural authority.

It is important to bear in mind that no matter what the political organization may be, it is still possible to have a mode of totalitarian culture. That is, even a democracy may have a form of cultural totalitarianism if its members are sufficiently intolerant of cultural minorities. The blessed term "integration" often serves to make acceptable a form of total cultural authority which its so-called liberal adherents reject when practiced by others in the name of dictatorship. That is why Democracy must not be upheld as if it were an absolute good not subject to the evils and diseases which afflict other political systems.

The great modern discovery, it seems to me, is the principle of social freedom as a prerequisite of and an integral element in social justice. This implies the utilization of political authority to promote social freedom. Authority need no longer be looked upon merely as a principle of limitation which restrains the exercise of individual freedom. What is emerging is a new, positive conception of authority as the principle of the plenitude of freedom. On this premise authority becomes the instrument of freedom rather than of restraint and coercion.

The fundamental theoretical and practical problem is to determine the limits of freedom and authority in relation to varying social and cultural conditions. There are no inalienable freedoms which are not subject to limitation in the interests of the social good under critical conditions. Cultures differ widely in the scope of freedom allowed to the individual and in the theoretical and practical sanctions they provide for the exercise of authority. We of the West must be especially careful to avoid the ethnocentric fallacy involved in setting up the individualistic standards of our capitalistic democratic society as a universal norm for all peoples. Freedom, in its various modes, is something which may not be imposed upon others; it must be experimentally acquired by the people concerned as a product of their cultural experience.

The crises of our times reveal a tendency to swing between a theory of the absolute rights of the individual and the absolute rights of the state, and between the contrary poles of cultural totalitarianism and the "dreadful freedom" of individualistic existentialism. There is a tendency to set up petrified cultural absolutes based upon the arbitrary will of given men, or to deny the authority of cultural traditions and long-established social institutions in order to affirm the will and freedom of the individual. The thesis of this chapter is that progressive freedom requires a dynamic, pluralistic conception of the relation of freedom and authority, one which recognizes the absolute authority of moral and scientific norms together with the apparent relativity and temporal character of most of our cultural and social expressions in approximating this ideal.[14] Natural science offers a model of a progressive, self-reforming discipline which combines rational authority with freedom of initiative and change. Similarly, a normative and scientific theory of culture and society would recognize the polarity of freedom and authority and would make provision for the establishment of new forms of social and individual freedom and authority in accordance with the ever-changing requirements of man in society.

[14] See Chapter 1.

# Bibliography

Achilles, P. S., ed. Psychology at Work. New York and London, 1932.

Ackerknecht, Erwin H. "Malaria," *Ciba Symposia*, Vol. VII (1945), Nos. 3 and 4; especially section on "The History of Malaria," pp. 51–56.

—— "Natural Diseases and Rational Treatment in Primitive Medicine," *Bulletin of the History of Medicine*, XIX (1946), 467–97.

Adler, Gerhard. Studies in Analytical Psychology. New York, 1948.

Alexander, Samuel. Space, Time and Deity. London, 1920.

Allport, F. H. "The Group Fallacy in Relation to Social Science," *American Journal of Sociology*, XXIX (1923–24), 688–703.

Angyal, Andras. Foundations for a Science of Personality. New York, 1941.

Arendt, Hannah. "What is Existenz Philosophy?" *Partisan Review*, XIII (1946), 34–56.

Aristotle. The Works of Aristotle; ed. by W. D. Ross. Oxford, 1908–31.

Arnold, Matthew. Culture and Anarchy. New York, 1883.

Ashburn, Percy M. The Ranks of Death; ed. by Frank D. Ashburn. New York, 1947.

Bacon, Francis. The Advancement of Learning; ed. by G. W. Kitchin. New York, 1934. Everyman's Library.

—— The Wisdom of the Ancients, Bacon, Francis, Works . . . ed. by James Spedding and others (New York, 1869), Vol. XIII.

Baine, Read. "Man the Myth-Maker," *Scientific Monthly*, LXV (1947), 61–69.

Barzun, Jacques. Of Human Freedom. Boston, 1939.

Bastian, Adolf. Ethnische Elementargedanken in der Lehre vom Menschen. Abtheilung 1. Berlin, 1895.

Baudouin, Charles. The Myth of Modernity; tr. by Bernard Miall. London, 1950.

Bauer, Raymond A. The New Man in Soviet Psychology. Cambridge, Mass., 1952.

Becker, Carl L. The Heavenly City of the Eighteenth-Century Philosophers. New Haven, Conn., 1932 and 1951.

Benedict, Ruth. "Anthropology and the Abnormal," *Journal of General Psychology*, X (1934), 59–82.

—— Patterns of Culture. New York, 1934. Pelican Books edition, 1946.

—— Race, Science and Politics. New York, 1940.

—— "The Science of Custom," in V. F. Calverton, ed., The Making of Man (New York, 1931), pp. 805–17.

Berdyaev, Nicholas. The Russian Idea; tr. by R. R. French. New York, 1948.

Bergson, Henri. Creative Evolution; tr. by Arthur Mitchell. New York, 1944.

—— The Two Sources of Morality and Religion. New York, 1935.

Bertalanffy, Ludwig von. "The Theory of Open Systems in Physics and Biology," *Science*, CXI (1950), 23–29.

Bidney, David. "The Concept of Meta-Anthropology and Its Significance for Contemporary Anthropological Science," in F. S. C. Northrop, ed., Ideological Differences and World Order (New Haven, 1949), pp. 323–55.

—— "The Concept of Myth and the Problem of Psychocultural Evolution," *American Anthropologist*, LII (1950), 16–26.

—— "The Concept of Value in Modern Anthropology," in A. L. Kroeber, ed., Anthropology Today: an Encyclopedic Inventory (Chicago, 1953), pp. 682–99.

—— "Culture Theory and the Problem of Cultural Crisis," in Lyman Bryson and others, eds., Approaches to Group Understanding (Sixth Symposium, Conference on Science, Philosophy and Religion, New York, 1947), pp. 553–73.

—— "Human Nature and Culture," in Lyman Bryson and others, eds., Conflicts of Power in Modern Culture (Seventh Symposium, Conference on Science, Philosophy and Religion, New York, 1947), pp. 179–96.

—— "Human Nature and the Cultural Process," *American Anthropologist*, XLIX (1947), 375–99.

—— "Ideology and Power in the Strategy of World Peace," in Lyman Bryson and others, eds., Learning and World Peace (Eighth Symposium, Conference on Science, Philosophy and Religion, New York, 1948), pp. 200–219.

—— "On the Concept of Cultural Crisis," *American Anthropologist*, XLVIII (1946), 534–52.

—— "On the Concept of Culture and Some Cultural Fallacies," *American Anthropologist*, XLVI (1944), 30–44.

—— "On the Philosophy of Culture in the Social Sciences," *Journal of Philosophy*, XXXIX (1942), 449–57.

—— "On the So-called Anti-evolutionist Fallacy: a Reply to Leslie A. White," *American Anthropologist*, XLVIII (1946), 293–97.

—— "On Theory and Practice." *University of Toronto Quarterly*, VII (1937), 113–25.

—— "The Philosophical Anthropology of Ernst Cassirer and Its Significance in Relation to the History of Anthropological Thought," in P. A. Schilpp, ed., The Philosophy of Ernst Cassirer (Evanston, 1949), pp. 465–544.

—— "The Problem of Social and Cultural Evolution: a Reply to A. R. Radcliffe-Brown," *American Anthropologist*, XLIX (1947),524–27.

—— The Psychology and Ethics of Spinoza. New Haven, Conn., 1940.

—— Review of Ernst Cassirer, *The Myth of the State* (New Haven, 1946), *American Anthropologist*, XLIX (1947), 481–83.

—— Review of Paul Radin, *The Road of Life and Death: a Ritual Drama of* the American Indians (New York, 1945), *Journal of the History of Medicine*, II (1947), 406–7.

—— "Toward a Psychocultural Definition of the Concept of Personality," in S. Stansfeld Sargent and Marian W. Smith, eds., Culture and Personality, Viking Fund, New York, 1949, pp. 31–55.

Blumenbach, Johann Friedrich. "On the Natural Variety of Mankind," in E. W. Count, ed., This Is Race, pp. 25–39.

Blumenthal, Albert. "A New Definition of Culture," *American Anthropologist*, XLII (1940), 571–86.

Blumer, H. "The Problem of the Concept in Social Psychology," *American Journal of Sociology*, XLV (1939–40), 707–19.

Boas, Franz. Anthropology. New York, 1908.

—— "Anthropology," in *Encyclopaedia of the Social Sciences*, II, 73–110.

—— "Liberty among Primitive People," in Ruth Nanda Anshen, ed., Freedom; Its Meaning (London, 1942), pp. 50–55.

—— The Mind of Primitive Man. New York, 1911 and 1938.

—— "Mythology and Folklore," in Franz Boas, ed., General Anthropology (New York, 1938; Washington, D.C., War Department ed., 1944), pp. 609–26.

—— "Mythology and Folk-Tales of the North American Indians," in Franz Boas and others, Anthropology in North America (New York, 1915), pp. 306–49.

——"The Origin of Totemism," *American Anthropologist*, XVIII (1916), 319–26. Reprinted in Franz Boas, *Race, Language and Culture* (New York, 1948).

—— Race, Language and Culture. New York, 1948.

Boas, Franz and others. Anthropology in North America. New York, 1915.

Boas, Franz, ed. General Anthropology. New York, 1938; Washington, D.C., War Department ed., 1944.

Born, Max. Natural Philosophy of Cause and Chance. Oxford, 1949.

Bridges, Robert. The Testament of Beauty. New York, 1930.

Briffault, Robert. Rational Evolution (the Making of Humanity). New York, 1930.

Brill, Abraham A. Basic Principles of Psychoanalysis. Garden City, N.Y., 1949.

Bryson, Gladys. Man and Society; the Scottish Inquiry of the Eighteenth Century. Princeton, 1946.

Bryson, Lyman, Louis Finkelstein, and R. M. MacIver, eds. Learning and World Peace. Eighth Symposium, Conference on Science, Philosophy and Religion. New York, 1948.

Buckle, Henry Thomas. History of Civilization in England. 2 vols. London, 1857–61.

Buffon, Comte de. "A Natural History, General and Particular," in E. W. Count, ed., This Is Race, pp. 3–15.

Bury, J. B. The Idea of Progress. New York, 1932.

Calhoun, Donald W. "William Graham Sumner," *Social Forces,* XXIV (1945), 15–32.

Callender, Harold. "Explaining France's Views of Us," The New York *Times* Magazine, March 12, 1950.

Carlton, William G. "Ideology or Balance of Power?" *Yale Review,* XXXVI (1946–47), 590–602.

Carr, B. H. The Twenty Years' Crisis, 1919–39. London, 1942.

Cassirer, Ernst. An Essay on Man. New Haven, Conn., 1944.

—— Language and Myth, tr. by Susanne K. Langer. New York and London, 1946.

—— The Myth of the State. New Haven, 1946.

—— The Philosophy of the Enlightenment, tr. by F. C. A. Koellen and James Pettigrove. Princeton, 1951.

—— The Problem of Knowledge. New Haven, 1950.

Cassirer, Ernst, Paul O. Kristeller, and John Herman Randall, Jr., eds. The Renaissance Philosophy of Man. Chicago, 1948.

Casson, Stanley. The Discovery of Man. New York and London, 1939.

Chandler, Albert R. Rosenberg's Nazi Myth. Ithaca, N.Y., 1945.

Childe, V. Gordon. Man Makes Himself. London, 1941.

—— Social Evolution. London, 1951.

—— What Happened in History. New York, 1946.

Cobban, Alfred. The Crisis of Civilization. London, 1941.

Cohen, Felix S. "The Role of Science in Government," *Scientific Monthly,* LXV (August, 1947), 155–64.

Collingwood, R. G. The Idea of History. Oxford, 1946.

Comte, Auguste. The Positive Philosophy of Auguste Comte, tr. by H. Martineau. London, 1853.

Conant, James B. On Understanding Science. New Haven, 1947.

Cooley, Charles H. Human Nature and the Social Order. New York, 1902.

Count, Earl W., ed. This Is Race; an Anthology Selected from the International Literature on the Races of Man. New York, 1950.

Crossman, Richard, ed. The God That Failed. New York, 1949.

Dante. The Divine Comedy. Modern Library. New York, 1932.

Darlington, C. D., and K. Mather. The Elements of Genetics. New York, 1949.

Dawson, Christopher. Religion and Culture. London, 1948.

Degré, Gerard L. Society and Ideology. New York, 1943.

De Lys, Claudia. A Treasury of American Superstitions. New York, 1948.

Demos, R. Review of F. S. C. Northrop, *The Meeting of East and West* (New York, 1946), *Philosophy and Phenomenological Research,* VIII (1947–48), 276–80.

Dewey, John. German Philosophy and Politics. New York, 1915.

—— "Human Nature," in *Encyclopaedia of the Social Sciences,* VIII (New York, 1937), 531–37.

—— Human Nature and Conduct. New York, 1933.

Dixon, R. B. The Building of Cultures. New York, 1928.

Dixon, W. M. The Human Situation. New York, 1937.

Dollard, John. "Culture, Society, Impulse, and Socialization," *American Journal of Sociology*, XLV (1939–40), 50–63.

Du Bois, Cora. The People of Alor: a Social Psychological Study of an East Indian Island. Minneapolis, 1944.

Dunham, Barrows. Man against Myth. Boston, 1947.

Durkheim, Emile. The Elementary Forms of the Religious Life; tr. by J. W. Swain. Reprint ed. Glencoe, Ill., 1947.

—— "Le Dualisme de la nature humaine et ses conditions sociales," *Scientia*, XV (1914), 206–21.

Einstein, A. "Einstein on the Atomic Bomb as Told to Raymond Swing," *Atlantic Monthly*, CLXXVI (1945), 43–45.

Emergency Committee of Atomic Scientists, Statement, New York *Times*, June 30, 1947.

Engels, Friedrich. The Origin of the Family, Private Property and the State. New York, 1942.

Eubank, E. E. The Concepts of Sociology. New York, 1932.

Evans-Pritchard, E. E. Social Anthropology. Glencoe, Ill., 1951.

—— "Social Anthropology: Past and Present," *Man*, L (1950), 118–24.

Faris, Ellsworth. The Nature of Human Nature. New York, 1937.

Farrington, Benjamin. Greek Science. 2 vols. Harmondsworth, England, 1944, 1949. Penguin Books.

Feibleman, James. The Theory of Human Culture. New York, 1946.

Fejos, Paul. Ethnography of the Yagua. New York, 1943. Viking Fund Publications in Anthropology, No. 1.

Ferguson, Adam. An Essay on the History of Civil Society. 7th ed. Boston, 1809.

Fichte, Johann Gottlieb. The Vocation of Man; tr. by William Smith. Reprint ed. Chicago, 1925.

Firth, Raymond. "Contemporary British Social Anthropology," *American Anthropologist*, LIII (1951), 474–89.

—— Elements of Social Organization. London, 1951.

Ford, C. S. Review of E. A. Hoebel, *Man in the Primitive World* (New York, 1949), *American Anthropologist*, LII (1950), 245–46.

Forde, Daryll. "Anthropology, Science and History," *Man*, L (1950), 155–56.

Frank, Jerome. Fate and Freedom. New York, 1945.

Frank, Philipp. Einstein, His Life and Times. New York, 1947.

Frazer, J. G. Folklore in the Old Testament. Abridged ed. New York, 1923.

—— The Golden Bough. Abridged ed. New York, 1942.

—— Totemism and Exogamy. London, 1910.

Fromm, Erich. The Forgotten Language. New York, 1951.

Freud, Sigmund. Civilization and Its Discontents. New York, 1930.

—— The Future of an Illusion; tr. by W. D. Robson-Scott. New York, 1949.

—— "Totem and Taboo," in his The Basic Writings of Sigmund Freud; tr. by A. A. Brill (New York, 1938), pp. 807–930.

472 *Bibliography*

Gayley, G. M. The Classic Myths in English Literature and in Art. Boston, 1911.

Gesell, Arnold L., and Frances L. Ilg. Infant and Child in the Culture of To-day. New York and London, 1943.

Gibbon, Edward. The Decline and Fall of the Roman Empire. 2 vols. New York, n.d. Modern Library.

Gillin, John Lewis, and John Philip Gillin. An Introduction to Sociology. New York, 1943.

Gillin, John Philip. "Cultural Adjustment," *American Anthropologist,* XLVI (1944), 429–47.

—— The Ways of Men. New York, 1948.

Gilson, Etienne H. The Spirit of Mediaeval Philosophy; tr. by A. H. C. Downes. New York, 1940.

Gluckman, Max. An Analysis of the Sociological Theories of Bronislaw Malinowski. London and New York, 1949.

Goldenweiser, A. A. Anthropology. New York, 1937.

—— "The Autonomy of the Social," *American Anthropologist,* XIX (1917), 447–49.

—— "Cultural Anthropology," in H. E. Barnes, ed., The History and Prospects of the Social Sciences (New York, 1925), pp. 210–54.

—— Early Civilization. New York, 1922.

—— History, Psychology, and Culture. New York, 1933.

Gooch, G. P. History and Historians in the Nineteenth Century. New York, 1913.

Greenman, Emerson F. "Material Culture and the Organism," *American Anthropologist,* XLVII (1945), 211–31.

Haddon, A. C. Introduction to E. B. Tylor, *Anthropology,* London, 1930, pp. v–ix.

Haeberlin, H. K. "Anti-Professions," *American Anthropologist,* XVII (1915), 756–59.

Hallowell, A. Irving. "Personality Structure and the Evolution of Man," *American Anthropologist,* LII (1950), 159–73.

—— "The Rorschach Technique in the Study of Personality and Culture," *American Anthropologist,* XLVII (1945), 195–210.

Harris, Zellig S., Review of Selected Writings of Edward Sapir, *Language,* XXVII (1951), 288–333.

Herskovits, Melville J. Man and His Works. New York, 1948.

—— Review of E. Huntington, *Mainsprings of Civilization* (New York and London, 1945), *American Anthropologist,* XLVIII (1946), 455–57.

—— "Statement on Human Rights," *American Anthropologist,* XLIX (1947), 539–43.

Hobbes, Thomas. Leviathan. Reprint edition. London and New York, 1924. Everyman's Library.

Hoebel, E. A. Man in the Primitive World. New York, 1949.

Hofstadter, Richard. Social Darwinism in American Thought, 1860–1915. Philadelphia, 1945.

Hooper, Stanley R. The Crisis of Faith. New York, 1944.

Hooton, E. A. Man's Poor Relations. New York, 1942.

—— Why Men Behave Like Apes and Vice Versa; or Body and Behavior. Princeton, 1940.

Hume, David. Moral and Political Philosophy; ed. by H. D. Aiken. New York, 1948.

Hunt, J. McV., ed. Personality and the Behavior Disorders. 2 vols. New York, 1944.

Huntington, E. Climate and Civilization. New Haven, 1924.

—— Mainsprings of Civilization. New York and London, 1945.

Husserl, Edmund. Ideas: General Introduction to Pure Phenomenology. London and New York, 1931.

Hutton, Maurice. The Greek Point of View. London, 1925.

Huxley, Julian. Heredity, East and West. New York, 1949.

—— Man in the Modern World. New York, 1948. Mentor Books.

Jaeger, Werner W. Paideia; the Ideals of Greek Culture; tr. by Gilbert Highet. New York, 1939.

James, William. The Varieties of Religious Experience. New York, 1902. Modern Library.

—— "The Will to Believe," in William James, Selected Papers on Philosophy (London and New York, 1924), pp. 99–124.

Jenkins, I. "What Is a Normative Science?" *Journal of Philosophy*, XLV (1948), 309–32.

Johnson, F. E., ed. Foundations of Democracy. New York, 1947. Institute for Religious and Social Studies.

Jung, C. G., and C. Karenyi. Essays on a Science of Mythology; tr. by R. F. C. Hull. New York, 1948. Bollingen Series, Vol. XXII.

Kallen, Horace M. The Education of Free Men. New York, 1949.

Kant, Immanuel. Critique of Practical Reason and Other Writings in Moral Philosophy; tr. and ed. with an introd. by Lewis White Beck. Chicago, 1949.

—— Critique of Pure Reason; tr. by F. Max Müller. New York, 1927.

—— Fundamental Principles of the Metaphysics of Ethics; tr. by T. K. Abbott. London, 1923.

—— "Idea for a Universal History with Cosmopolitan Intent," in Carl J. Friedrich, ed., The Philosophy of Kant (New York, 1949) pp. 116–31. Modern Library.

—— "On the Distinctiveness of the Races in General," in E. W. Count, ed., This Is Race, pp. 16–24.

—— The Philosophy of Kant; ed. by Carl J. Friedrich. New York, 1949. Modern Library.

Kardiner, Abram. The Individual and His Society. New York, 1939.

Kardiner, Abram, and others. The Psychological Frontiers of Society. New York, 1945.

Keesing, F. M. "Applied Anthropology in Colonial Administration," in Ralph Linton, ed., The Science of Man in the World Crisis (New York, 1945), pp. 373–98.

—— The South Seas in the Modern World. New York, 1941.

Keller, A. G. Net Impressions. New Haven, 1942.

Kennan, George F. "The Sources of Soviet Conduct," under pseudonym X in *Foreign Affairs,* XXV (1946–47), 566–82.

Kennedy, John H. Jesuit and Savage in New France. New Haven, 1950.

Kennedy, Raymond. "The Colonial Crisis and the Future," in Ralph Linton, ed., The Science of Man in the World Crisis (New York, 1945), pp. 306–46.

Kierkegaard, Soren. Concluding Unscientific Postscript; tr. by D. F. Swenson. Princeton, 1944.

—— Either/Or. Princeton, 1944.

Klein, D. B. "Psychology's Progress and the Armchair Taboo," *Psychological Review,* XLIX (1942), 226–34.

Klineberg, Otto, "Racial Psychology," in Ralph Linton, ed., The Science of Man in the World Crisis (New York, 1945), pp. 63–77.

Kluckhohn, Clyde. Mirror for Man; the Relation of Anthropology to Modern Life. New York, 1949.

—— "Patterning as Exemplified in Navaho Culture," in Leslie Spier and others, eds., Language, Culture, and Personality; Essays in Memory of Edward Sapir (Menasha, Wis., 1941), pp. 109–30.

—— Review of A. L. Kroeber, *Configurations of Culture Growth* (Berkeley, 1944), *American Journal of Sociology,* LI (1946), 336–41.

Kluckhohn, Clyde, and O. H. Mowrer. "Culture and Personality; a Conceptual Scheme," *American Anthropologist,* XLVI (1944), 1–29.

—— "Dynamic Theory of Personality," in J. McV. Hunt, ed., Personality and the Behavior Disorders (New York, 1944), Vol. I, pp. 69–135.

Kluckhohn, Clyde, and Henry A. Murray, eds. Personality in Nature, Society, and Culture. New York, 1948.

Koestler, Arthur. The Yogi and the Commissar. New York, 1945.

Koppers, W. Primitive Man and His World Picture; tr. by Edith Raybould. London and New York, 1952.

Kroeber, A. L. Anthropology. New ed., revised. New York, 1948.

—— "Classificatory Systems of Relationship," *Journal of the Royal Anthropological Institute,* XXXIX (1909), 77–84.

—— "The Concept of Culture in Science," *The Journal of General Education,* III (1948–49), 182–96.

—— Configurations of Culture Growth. Berkeley, 1944.

—— "Eighteen Professions," *American Anthropologist,* XVII (1915), 283–88.

—— "History and Evolution," *Southwestern Journal of Anthropology,* II (1946), 1–15.

—— "History and Science in Anthropology," *American Anthropologist,* XXXVII (1935), 539–69.

—— "The Morals of Uncivilized People," *American Anthropologist,* XII (1910), 437–47.

—— The Nature of Culture. Chicago, 1952.

—— "On the Principle of Order in Civilization as Exemplified by Changes of Fashion," *American Anthropologist,* XXI (1919), 235–63.

—— "The Possibility of a Social Psychology," *American Journal of Sociology*, XXIII (1917–18), 633–50.

—— Review of F. S. C. Northrop, *The Meeting of East and West* (New York, 1946), *American Anthropologist*, XLIX (1947), 306–9.

—— "So-called Social Science," *Journal of Social Philosophy*, I (1935–36), 317–40.

—— "The Superorganic," *American Anthropologist*, XIX (1917), 162–213.

—— "Totem and Taboo in Retrospect," *American Journal of Sociology*, XLV (1939–40), 446–51.

—— "White's View of Culture," *American Anthropologist*, L (1948), 405–15.

Kroeber, A. L., ed. Anthropology Today: an Encyclopedic Inventory. Chicago, 1953.

Kroeber, A. L., and Clyde Kluckhohn. Culture: a Critical Review of Concepts and Definitions. Papers of the Peabody Museum of American Archaeology and Ethnology, Harvard University, XLVII, No. 1, Cambridge, Mass., 1952.

Kroeber, A. L., and Jane Richardson. "Three Centuries of Women's Dress Fashions; a Quantitative Analysis," University of California Publications in *Anthropological Records*, V (1940), 118–54.

Krogman, W. M. "The Concept of Race," in Ralph Linton, ed., The Science of Man in the World Crisis (New York, 1945), pp. 38–62.

Kuhn, Helmut. Review of Ernst Cassirer's *Essay on Man* (New Haven, 1944), *Journal of Philosophy*, XLII (1945), 497–504.

Lang, Andrew. The Making of Religion. London and New York, 1900.

Langer, Susanne K. Philosophy in a New Key. Pelican Books edition. New York, 1948.

La Piere, R. T., and P. R. Farnsworth. Social Psychology. 2d ed. New York, 1942.

Leacock, Stephen. Last Leaves. New York, 1946.

Lee, Dorothy D. Religious Perspectives in Anthropology. New Haven, 1950.

Lenin, V. I. State and Revolution. New York, 1932. Little Lenin Library, Vol. XIV.

—— What Is to Be Done? London, 1929. Little Lenin Library, Vol. IV.

Lévi-Strauss, Claude. "Histoire et ethnologie," *Revue de Métaphysique et de Morale*, LIV (1949), 363–91.

—— "Language and the Analysis of Social Laws," *American Anthropologist*, LIII (1951), 155–63.

—— Les Structures elémentaires de la parenté. Paris, 1949.

Lévy-Bruhl, Lucien. Ethics and Moral Science; tr. by Elizabeth Lee. London, 1905.

—— How Natives Think. London and New York, 1926.

—— La Mythologie primitive. Paris, 1935.

—— Les Carnets de; preface by Maurice Leenhardt. Paris, 1949. Bibliothèque de Philosophie Contemporaine.

—— The Philosophy of Auguste Comte; tr. by F. Harrison. London and New York, 1903.

—— Primitives and the Supernatural. London, 1936.

Lévy-Bruhl, Lucien. The "Soul" of the Primitive. London and New York, 1928.

Linton, Ralph. The Cultural Background of Personality. New York, 1945.

—— "Culture, Society, and the Individual," *Journal of Abnormal and Social Psychology*, XXXIII (1938), 425–36.

—— "The Scope and Aims of Anthropology," in Ralph Linton, ed., The Science of Man in the World Crisis (New York, 1945), pp. 3–18.

—— The Study of Man. New York, 1936.

Linton, Ralph, ed. The Science of Man in the World Crisis. New York, 1945.

Locke, John. An Essay concerning Human Understanding. 24th ed. London, 1824.

—— Two Treatises of Government. New York, 1947. Hafner Library of Classics, No. 2.

Lovejoy, Arthur O. Essays in the History of Ideas. Baltimore, 1948.

—— The Great Chain of Being. Reprint ed. Cambridge, Mass., 1948.

Lovejoy, Arthur O., and others, eds. A Documentary History of Primitivism and Related Ideas. Baltimore, 1935. Vol. I.

Lowie, Robert H. Culture and Ethnology. New York, 1917 and 1929.

—— "Evolution in Cultural Anthropology; a Reply to Leslie White," *American Anthropologist*, XLVIII (1946), 223–33.

—— The History of Ethnological Theory. New York, 1937.

—— Primitive Religion. New York, 1924; revised ed., 1948.

—— "Professor White and 'Anti-Evolutionist' Schools," *Southwestern Journal of Anthropology*, II (1946), 240–41.

—— "Psychology and Sociology," *American Journal of Sociology*, XXI (1915–16), 217–29.

Lucretius. Of the Nature of Things; tr. by William E. Leonard. London and New York, 1921. Everyman's Library.

Lundberg, George A. Foundations of Sociology. New York, 1939.

Lynd, R. S. Knowledge for What? Princeton, 1939.

McCormick, Anne O'Hare. "Empires Moving in Opposite Directions," New York *Times*, March 16, 1946.

McCulloch, Warren S. "A Heterarchy of Values Determined by the Topology of Nervous Sets," *Bulletin of Mathematical Biophysics*, VII (1945), 89–93.

McGill, V. J. "Northrop's *Meeting of East and West*" (New York, 1946), *Science and Society*, XI (1947), 249–59.

MacGregor, Gordon. Warriors without Weapons. Chicago, 1946.

MacIver, R. M. Society: a Textbook of Sociology. New York, 1937; revised ed. New York, 1949.

—— The Web of Government. New York, 1947.

Maine, Henry J. S. Ancient Law. London and New York, 1917. Everyman's Library.

Maitland, F. W. Selected Essays; ed. by H. D. Hazeltine and others. Cambridge, 1936.

Malinowski, Bronislaw. "Culture," in *Encyclopaedia of the Social Sciences*, IV, 621–45.

—— The Dynamics of Culture Change; an Inquiry into Race Relations in Africa; ed. by Phyllis M. Kaberry. New Haven, 1945.

—— The Foundations of Faith and Morals. London, 1946.

—— Freedom and Civilization. New York, 1944.

—— Magic, Science and Religion, and Other Essays; ed. by Robert Redfield. Boston and Glencoe, Ill., 1948.

—— "The Problem of Meaning in Primitive Languages," in C. K. Ogden and I. A. Richards, The Meaning of Meaning (New York and London, 1923), pp. 451–510.

—— A Scientific Theory of Culture and Other Essays. Chapel Hill, N.C., 1944.

—— "Social Anthropology," in *Encyclopaedia Britannica* (14th ed., 1940), XX, 862–70.

Mannheim, Karl. Diagnosis of Our Time. New York, 1944.

—— Ideology and Utopia. New York, 1936.

Marett, R. R. "Anthropology and Religion," in W. F. Ogburn and A. A. Goldenweiser, eds., The Social Sciences and Their Interrelation (New York, 1927), pp. 89–96.

—— Man in the Making. London, 1928.

—— Tylor. London, 1936.

Margenau, Henry. "Western Culture and Scientific Method," in Lyman Bryson and others, Conflicts of Power in Modern Culture (Seventh Symposium, Conference on Science, Philosophy and Religion. New York, 1947), pp. 13–28.

Maritain, Jacques. The Degrees of Knowledge. New York, 1938.

Markham, S. F. Climate and the Energy of Nations. London, 1944.

Masters, Dexter, and Katherine Way, eds. One World or None. New York, 1946.

Maugham, W. Somerset. Of Human Bondage. Garden City, New York.

May, M. A. "The Foundations of Personality," in P. S. Achilles, ed., Psychology at Work (New York and London, 1932), ch. iv.

Mead, George H. Mind, Self and Society; ed. by Charles W. Morris. Chicago, 1934.

Mead, Margaret. "The Concept of Culture and the Psychosomatic Approach," in D. G. Haring, ed., Personal Character and Cultural Milieu (Syracuse, N.Y., 1948), pp. 518–38.

—— "The Cultural Approach to Personality," in P. L. Harriman, ed., Encyclopedia of Psychology (New York, 1946), pp. 477–88.

—— Male and Female; a Study of the Sexes in a Changing World, 1949.

—— "On the Implications for Anthropology of the Gesell-Ilg Approach to Maturation," *American Anthropologist*, XLIX (1947), 69–77.

Mead, Margaret, ed. Co-operation and Competition among Primitive Peoples. New York, 1937.

Meggers, Betty J. "Recent Trends in American Ethnology," *American Anthropologist*, XLVIII (1946), 176–214.

Millar, M. F. X. "The Founding Fathers," in F. E. Johnson, ed., Foundations of Democracy (Institute for Religious and Social Studies, New York, 1947).

Montagu, M. F. Ashley. Man's Most Dangerous Myth; the Fallacy of Race. 2d ed. New York, 1945.

—— "Some Anthropological Terms; a Study in the Systematics of Confusion," *American Anthropologist,* XLVII (1945), 119–33.

Montesquieu, Charles de. The Spirit of the Laws; tr. by Thomas Nugent; introd. by Franz Neumann. 2 vols. New York, 1949.

Morgan, Lewis H. Ancient Society. New York, 1877; reprint, Chicago, n.d.

Müller, C. O. Introduction to a Scientific System of Mythology; tr. by John Leitch. London, 1844.

Mullahy, Patrick. Oedipus; Myth and Complex. New York, 1948.

Mumford, Lewis. The Condition of Man. New York, 1944.

Murdock, G. P. "British Social Anthropology," *American Anthropologist,* LIII (1951), 465–73.

—— "The Common Denominator of Cultures," in Ralph Linton, ed., The Science of Man in the World Crisis (New York, 1945), pp. 123–42.

—— "The Science of Human Learning, Society, Culture, and Personality," *Scientific Monthly,* LXIX (1949), 377–81.

—— Social Structure. New York, 1949.

Murphy, Gardner. Personality. New York, 1947.

Murray, Gilbert. Five Stages of Greek Religion. London, 1943. Thinker's Library.

Myrdal, Gunnar. An American Dilemma. 2 vols. New York, 1944.

Myres, John L. "The Influence of Anthropology on the Course of Political Science," in University of California *Publications in History,* Vol. IV, No. 1 (Berkeley, 1916–17).

Nadel, S. F. The Foundations of Social Anthropology. London, 1951.

Needham, Joseph, ed. Science, Religion and Reality. New York, 1928.

Niebuhr, Reinhold. Faith and History. New York, 1949.

Nietzsche, Friedrich. "The Birth of Tragedy," in F. Nietzsche, The Philosophy of Nietzsche (tr. by Clifton P. Fadiman, New York, 1927. Modern Library), pp. 947–1088.

—— "The Genealogy of Morals," in his The Philosophy of Nietzsche (New York, 1937, Modern Library), pp. 617–807.

Northrop, F. S. C. "Ethics and the Integration of Natural Knowledge," in The Nature of Concepts, Their Inter-relation and Role in Social Structure (Proceedings of the Stillwater Conference, Stillwater, Okla., June, 1950), pp. 116–39.

—— The Logic of the Sciences and the Humanities. New York, 1947.

—— The Meeting of East and West. New York, 1946.

—— "Philosophy and World Peace," in Lyman Bryson and others, eds., Approaches to World Peace (Fourth Symposium, Conference on Science, Philosophy and Religion, New York, 1944), pp. 642–91.

Northrop, F. S. C., ed. Ideological Differences and World Order. New Haven, 1949.

Northrup, John H. "The Quick and the Dead," in Serving through Science

Series (Radio Broadcast, published by U.S. Rubber Company, New York, 1946).

Ogburn, W. F., and M. F. Nimkoff. Sociology. Cambridge, Mass., 1940.

Oneal, James, and G. A. Werner. American Communism. New and rev. ed. New York, 1947.

Opler, Morris E. "Cultural and Organic Conceptions in Contemporary World History," *American Anthropologist,* XLVI (1944), 448–59.

—— "Themes as Dynamic Forces in Culture," *American Journal of Sociology,* LI (1945), 198–206.

Ortega y Gasset, José. Concord and Liberty and Other Essays. New York, 1946.

—— "History as a System," in Philosophy and History, Essays Presented to Ernst Cassirer (Oxford, 1936), pp. 283–322.

—— Mission of the University; introd. by Howard Lee Nostrand. Princeton, 1944.

Osgood, Cornelius. "Culture: Its Empirical and Non-empirical Character," *Southwestern Journal of Anthropology,* VII (1951), 202–14.

—— Ingalik Material Culture. New Haven, 1940.

Paine, Thomas. "The Crisis Papers," in Howard Fast, ed., The Selected Work of Tom Paine (New York, 1946; Modern Library), pp. 43–92.

Pareto, Vilfredo. The Mind and Society; ed. by Arthur Livingston. 4 vols. New York, 1935.

Penniman, T. K. A Hundred Years of Anthropology. New York, 1936.

Philo, Judaeus. On the Account of the World's Creation Given by Moses; tr. by F. H. Colson and G. H. Whitaker. London and New York, 1929. Loeb Classical Library, Vol. I.

Pico della Mirandola, Giovanni. "Oration on the Dignity of Man," in Ernst Cassirer, Paul O. Kristeller, and John H. Randall, Jr., eds., The Renaissance Philosophy of Man (Chicago, 1948), pp. 223–54.

Pitt-Rivers, George Henry Lane-Fox. The Clash of Culture and the Contact of Races. London, 1927.

Planck, Max. "The Meaning and Limits of Exact Science," *Science,* CX (1949), 319–27.

—— Scientific Autobiography and Other Papers. New York, 1949.

Plato. The Republic, in Plato, The Dialogues of Plato (tr. by B. Jowett, Oxford, 1871), Vol. II.

Radcliffe-Brown, A. R. "Evolution, Social or Cultural?" *American Anthropologist,* XLIX (1947), 78–83.

—— "Historical Note on British Social Anthropology," *American Anthropologist,* LIV (1952), 275–77.

—— "On the Concept of Function in Social Science." *American Anthropologist,* XXXVII (1935), 394–402.

—— Structure and Function in Primitive Society. London, 1952.

Radin, Paul. Primitive Man as a Philosopher. New York, 1927.

—— The Road of Life and Death; a Ritual Drama of the American Indians. New York, 1945.

Radin, Paul. "What Is Anthropology?" a Review of Clyde Kluckhohn, *Mirror for Man* (New York, 1949) and Clyde Kluckhohn and Henry A. Murray, eds., *Personality in Nature, Society, and Culture* (New York, 1948), *Kenyon Review*, XI (1949), 523–26.

Reavey, George. Soviet Literature To-Day. New Haven, 1947.

Redfield, Robert. The Folk Culture of Yucatan. Chicago, 1941.

Reed, S. W. The Making of Modern New Guinea. Philadelphia, 1943.

Reich, Wilhelm. The Mass Psychology of Fascism. 3d rev. and enl. ed., tr. by Theodore P. Wolfe. New York, 1946.

Reves, Emery. The Anatomy of Peace. New York, 1945.

Rice, P. B. "Children of Narcissus: Some Themes of French Speculation," *Kenyon Review*, XII (1950), 116–37.

Richardson, Jane, and A. L. Kroeber. "Three Centuries of Women's Dress Fashions; a Quantitative Analysis," University of California Publications in *Anthropological Records*, V (1940), 118–54.

Rickert, Heinrich. Kulturwissenschaft und Naturwissenschaft. Tübingen, 1926.

Rivers, W. H. R. Kinship and Social Organization. London, 1914.

—— Psychology and Ethnology. London, 1926.

Robinson, James Harvey. The Mind in the Making. New York, 1921.

Roheim, Geza. "Psychoanalysis and Anthropology," reprinted in D. G. Haring, ed., Personal Character and Cultural Milieu (Syracuse, N.Y., 1948), pp. 565–88.

—— Psychoanalysis and Anthropology; Culture, Personality and the Unconscious. New York, 1950.

—— The Origin and Function of Culture. New York, 1943. Nervous and Mental Diseases Monographs, No. 69.

Rouse, Irving. Prehistory in Haiti. New Haven, 1940.

Rousseau, Jean Jacques. "A Discourse on Political Economy," in J. J. Rousseau, The Social Contract, and Discourses (London and Toronto, 1913; reprint ed., 1923), pp. 249–87.

—— "A Discourse on the Origin of Inequality," in J. J. Rousseau, The Social Contract, and Discourses (London and Toronto, 1913; reprint ed., 1923), pp. 155–246.

—— The Social Contract, and Discourses. London and Toronto, 1913; reprint ed., 1923. Everyman's Library.

Russell, Bertrand. "The Science to Save Us from Science," New York *Times* Magazine, March 19, 1950.

Sallustius. "On the Gods and the World," in Gilbert Murray, Five Stages of Greek Religion (London, 1943), pp. 200 225.

Santayana, George. Interpretations of Poetry and Religion. New York, 1900.

Sapir, Edward. "Culture, Genuine and Spurious," *American Journal of Sociology*, XXIX (1924), 401–29.

—— "Do We Need a Superorganic?" *American Anthropologist*, XIX (1917), 441–47.

—— "The Emergence of the Concept of Personality in a Study of Cultures," *Journal of Social Psychology*, V (1934), 408–15.

—— Language. New York, 1921.

—— "Language, Race, and Culture," in V. F. Calverton, ed., The Making of Man (New York, 1931), pp. 142–54.

—— Selected Writings of Edward Sapir; ed. by David G. Mandelbaum. Berkeley, 1949.

—— "The Unconscious Patterning of Behavior in Society," in E. S. Dummer, ed., The Unconscious; a Symposium (New York, 1927), pp. 114–42; also reprinted in Selected Writings of Edward Sapir.

Sartre, Jean Paul. L'Existentialisme est un humanisme. Paris, 1946.

Saul, Leon J. Emotional Maturity. Philadelphia and London, 1948.

Sax, Karl. "Soviet Science and Political Philosophy," *Scientific Monthly*, LXV (July, 1947), 43–47.

Schlesinger, Arthur M., Jr. The Age of Jackson. Boston, 1945.

Schmidt, Wilhelm. The Culture Historical Method of Ethnology; tr. by S. A. Sieber. New York, 1939.

—— The Origin and Growth of Religion; tr. by H. J. Rose. London, 1931, 1935.

Schwarz, Richard. Adolf Bastian's Lehre vom Elementar und Völkergedanken. Leipzig, 1909. Dissertation.

Shapiro, H. L. "Society and Biological Man," in Ralph Linton, ed., The Science of Man in the World Crisis (New York, 1945), pp. 19–37.

Sheldon, William Herbert. The Varieties of Temperament. New York, 1944.

Sheldon, Wilmon Henry. Process and Polarity. New York, 1944.

Shih, Kuo-Heng. China Enters the Machine Age. Cambridge, Mass., 1944.

Sigerist, Henry E. Civilization and Disease. Ithaca, N.Y., 1944.

Singer, Charles. "Historical Relations of Religion and Science," in J. Needham, ed., Science, Religion and Reality (London and New York, 1925), pp. 85–148.

Singleton, Charles S. "Dante and Myth," *Journal of the History of Ideas*, X (1949), 482–502.

Sinnott, Edmund W. "Ten Million Scientists," *Science*, CXI (1950), 123–29.

Smith, Adam. An Inquiry into the Nature and Causes of the Wealth of Nations. 2 vols. London, Toronto and New York, 1910 and 1924. Everyman's Library.

Smith, G. Elliot. In the Beginning; the Origin of Civilization. 1st and 2d eds. London, 1932 and 1946. Thinker's Library, No. 29.

—— "Introduction: Dr. Rivers and the New Vision in Ethnology," in W. H. R. Rivers, Psychology and Ethnology (London, 1926), pp. ix–xxviii.

Smith, W. Robertson. The Religion of the Semites. London, 1894.

Smith, Walter Bedell. My Three Years in Moscow. New York, 1949.

Sorel, Georges. Reflections on Violence; tr. by T. E. Hulme and R. Roth. Glencoe, Ill., 1950.

Sorokin, Pitirim. Contemporary Sociological Theories. New York, 1928.

—— The Crisis of Our Age. New York, 1941.

—— Social and Cultural Dynamics. 4 vols. New York, 1937–41.

—— Society, Culture, and Personality. New York and London, 1947.

Spencer, Herbert. The Principles of Sociology. 3 vols. New York and London, 1910.

Spengler, Oswald. The Decline of the West. London, 1937.

Spinoza, Benedictus de. Ethics of Spinoza. New York, 1934. Everyman's Library.

—— Tractatus Theologico-Politicus; ed. by R. H. M. Elwes. London, 1906.

Stalin, Joseph. Foundations of Leninism. New York, 1937. Little Lenin Library, No. 18.

Stapleton, Laurence. Justice and World Society. Chapel Hill, N.C., 1944.

Steinberg, Milton. A Partisan Guide to the Jewish Problem. New York, 1946.

Steward, Julian H. "Cultural Causality and Law; a Trial Formulation of the Development of Early Civilizations," *American Anthropologist*, LI (1949), 1–27.

Stewart, J. A., tr. and ed. The Myths of Plato. London, 1905.

Sturtevant, Edgar H. An Introduction to Linguistic Science. New Haven, 1947.

Sumner, William Graham. Folkways. 3d ed. Boston, 1940.

Sumner, William Graham, and A. G. Keller. The Science of Society. New Haven, 1927.

Swanton, J. R. "Some Anthropological Misconceptions," *American Anthropologist*, XIX (1917), 459–70.

Tannous, Afif. "Extension Work among the Arab Fellahin," *Applied Anthropology*, III (1944), 1–12.

Taylor, A. E. Plato; the Man and His Work. New ed. New York, 1936.

Taylor, Walter W. A Study of Archeology. 1948. Published by the American Anthropological Association, Memoir No. 69.

Thompson, Laura, and Alice Joseph. The Hopi Way. Chicago, 1944. Indian Educational Research Series, No. 1.

Thompson, Stith. The Folktale. New York, 1946.

Timasheff, N. S. "Definitions in the Social Sciences," *American Journal of Sociology*, LIII (1947–48), 201–9.

Toynbee, Arnold J. A Study of History. New York, 1947.

Tozzer, A. M. Social Origins and Social Continuities. New York, 1926.

Trevelyan, G. M. An Autobiography and Other Essays. New York, 1949.

Turner, Ralph E. The Great Cultural Traditions. 2 vols. New York and London, 1941.

Tylor, E. B. Anthropology. 2 vols. London, 1930. The Thinker's Library.

—— Primitive Culture. 2 vols. 1st and 5th eds. London, 1871 and 1913.

—— Researches into the Early History of Mankind and the Development of Civilization. London, 1870.

Urban, W. M. The Intelligible World. London and New York, 1929.

Vaihinger, Hans. The Philosophy of "As If"; tr. by C. K. Ogden. New York, 1924.

Veblen, Thorstein. The Place of Science in Modern Civilization and Other Essays. New York, 1942.

Vico, Giovanni Battista. The New Science of Giambattista Vico; tr. from the 3d ed. by T. G. Bergin and M. H. Fisch. Ithaca, N.Y., 1948.

Vives, Juan Luis. "A Fable about Man," in Ernst Cassirer, Paul O. Kristeller, and John H. Randall, Jr., eds., The Renaissance Philosophy of Man (Chicago, 1948), pp. 387–93.

Voegelin, C. F. "Culture, Language, and the Human Organism," *Southwestern Journal of Anthropology*, VII (1951), 357–73.

Warden, Carl J. The Emergence of Human Culture. New York, 1936.

Wegrocki, Henry J. "A Critique of Cultural and Statistical Concepts of Abnormality," in Clyde Kluckhohn and Henry A. Murray, eds., Personality in Nature, Society, and Culture (New York, 1948), pp. 551–61.

Weizmann, Chaim. Trial and Error. New York, 1949.

White, L. A. "Culturological vs. Psychological Interpretations of Human Behavior," *American Sociological Review*, XII (1947), 686–98.

—— " 'Diffusion vs. Evolution': an Anti-evolutionist Fallacy." *American Anthropologist*, XLVII (1945), 339–56.

—— "Ethnological Theory," in Roy W. Sellars and others, eds., Philosophy for the Future (New York, 1949), pp. 357–84.

—— "Kroeber's 'Configurations of Culture Growth,' " *American Anthropologist*, XLVIII (1946), 78–93.

—— The Science of Culture; a Study of Man and Civilization. New York, 1949.

Whitehead, Alfred North. The Philosophy of Alfred North Whitehead; ed. by P. A. Schilpp. Evanston and Chicago, 1941.

Whorf, B. L., Four Articles on Metalinguistics. Washington, D.C., Dept. of State, 1950.

—— "Language, Mind, and Reality," *Etc.*, IX (1952), 167–88.

Willkie, Wendell L. One World. New York, 1943.

Wilson, Godfrey, and Monica Wilson. The Analysis of Social Change. Cambridge, England, 1945.

Wirth, Louis. "The Problem of Minority Groups," in Ralph Linton, ed., The Science of Man in the World Crisis (New York, 1945), pp. 347–72.

Wissler, Clark. An Introduction to Social Anthropology. New York, 1929.

—— Man and Culture. New York, 1923.

—— "Material Cultures of the North American Indians." *American Anthropologist*, XVI (1914), 447–503.

—— "Psychological and Historical Interpretations for Culture," *Science*, XLIII (1916), 193–201.

Wolfe, Bertram D. "Lenin as a Philosopher," *Partisan Review*, XIV (1947), 396–413.

Woodruff, Lorande L. "Biology," in L. L. Woodruff, ed., The Development of the Sciences, second series (New Haven, Conn., 1941).

Wundt, Wilhelm. Elements of Folk Psychology. New York, 1916.

Young, Kimball. Social Psychology. 2d ed. New York, 1945.

Zinsser, Hans. Rats, Lice and History. Boston, 1935.

Znaniecki, Florian. Cultural Reality. Chicago, 1919.

—— Cultural Sciences; Their Origin and Development. Urbana, Illinois, 1952.

# Index

# Index

Abiogenesis, 149

Absolute ideal: dangers of, 421; humanity as an, 407; Plato's, 461; pragmatism and, 428; Rousseau's, 461; in Soviet myth, 421; in theory and practice, 378

Absolute values, 425, 428

Abstraction: culture as, of the mind, 175, 371, 373; methodological, 106-113

Acculturation: crises of, 360-62; influence on cultural changes in society, 353; of native peoples, 361; world, 362

Ackerknecht, Erwin H., 134, 161, 352

Adam and Eve, myth of, 319, 320, 324

Adler, G., 320n

Aesthetics: concept of beauty, 413; culture as an aesthetic norm, 401-407; integration of culture, 371-74

Africanism, Herskovits' scale of intensity of, 279

Age of reason, 287

Agriculture, cultural stages in, 241

Agrofacts, 130, 174

Alexander, Samuel, 46

Allegory: Dante on, 313; Jung on, 320; myth and, 302, 304; Neo-Platonic and Stoic interpretation of, 305; Plato on, 304, 312; Vico on, 306

Allport, F. H., 29n

American culture: European civilization and, 222; Indians and, 406; moral orientation of, 411; state of nature in, 236; Tylor's evaluation of, 193-94; *see also* Western culture

American school of anthropology, 98-103

*Ancient Law* (Maine), 208-209

*Ancient Society* (Morgan), 209

Andaman Islanders, 290

Angels, 42

Angyal, A., 335n

Animal fable, 287

Animals: in Aristotle's *scala naturae*, 40; capability of acquiring culture, 127; mental functions of, 4; superorganic evolution and, 35

Animism: elimination of, 118; essence of, 110; myth and, 325; primitive, 124; Tylor's theory of, 162

Anthropoculture, 125, 142

Anthropology: beginnings of the science of, 44-45; Boas on, 216; British and American schools of, 98-103; definitions of, 102; foundations of, 118; humanistic approach to, 143; Maitland on, 262; Radin on, 183; relation to history of, 98; relation to sociology of, 85, 97, 118

*Anthropology* (Kroeber), 71, 95, 103, 176, 330

*Anthropology* (Tylor), 200

Anthropology, cultural: definition of culture and, 97; historical approach to, 248; as historical and normative science, 18; as natural science, 177-78

Anthropology, physical, 76

Anthropology, social: American anthropologists and, 101; British anthropologists and, 97; defined, 102; Evans-Pritchard on, 260-68; Firth's linkage of, with other sciences, 100; functionalism and, 366; relation to ethnology, 98

Apollonian culture, 405, 406

Apollonian mentality, 405, 407

Arabs, 354

Arendt, H., 139n

Aristotle: on creativity of human imagination, 439; law of nature conceived by, 12; myth interpretation of, 304, 305, 306; organisms classification by, 39; sciences classification by, 40; teleological approach to study of nature by, 409

Arnold, Matthew, 31

Art: Apollonian and Dionysian forms of, 405; development of, 218; as expression of cultural stages, 211; human